Economic Development in the An
Endowments and Institutions

This book brings together a number of previously published articles by Stanley L. Engerman and Kenneth L. Sokoloff. Its essays examine differences in the rates of economic growth in Latin America and mainland North America, specifically the United States and Canada. It demonstrates how relative differences in growth over time are related to differences in the institutions that developed in different economies. This variation is driven by differences in major institutions – suffrage, education, tax policy, land and immigration policy, and banking and financial organizations. These factors, in turn, are all related to differences in endowments, climate, and natural resources. Providing a comprehensive treatment of its topic, the essays have been revised to reflect new developments and research.

Stanley L. Engerman is John H. Munro Professor of Economics and Professor of History at the University of Rochester and visiting professor of Economics at Harvard University. He is the author of *Slavery, Emancipation, and Freedom: Comparative Perspectives* (2007); co-author of *Time on the Cross* (with Robert W. Fogel, 1974); co-author of *Naval Blockades in Peace and War* (with Lance Davis, 2007); and co-editor of *Finance, Intermediaries, and Economic Development* (with Philip T. Hoffman, Kenneth L. Sokoloff, and Jean-Laurent Rosenthal, Cambridge, 2003). He is a co-editor of the three-volume *Cambridge Economic History of the United States* (with Robert E. Gallman) and of the multi-volume *Cambridge World History of Slavery* (with Keith Bradley, Paul Cartledge, and David Eltis).

Kenneth L. Sokoloff (1952–2007) was a Professor in the Department of Economics at the University of California, Los Angeles. Among his many publications, he co-edited *Slavery in the Development of the Americas* and *Human Capital and Institutions: A Long-Run View* (both with David Eltis and Frank D. Lewis, Cambridge, 2004, 2009) and *Finance, Intermediaries, and Economic Development* (with Stanley L. Engerman, Philip T. Hoffman, and Jean-Laurent Rosenthal, Cambridge, 2003).

National Bureau of Economic Research (NBER) Series on Long-term Factors in Economic Development

Edited by *Claudia Goldin*

Claudia Goldin, *Understanding the Gender Gap: An Economic History of American Women* (Oxford University Press, 1990)

Roderick Floud, Kenneth Wachter, and Annabel Gregory, *Height, Health and History: Nutritional Status in the United Kingdom, 1750–1980* (Cambridge University Press, 1990)

Robert A. Margo, *Race and Schooling in the South, 1880–1950: An Economic History* (University of Chicago Press, 1990)

Samuel H. Preston and Michael R. Haines, *Fatal Years: Child Mortality in Late Nineteenth-Century America* (Princeton University Press, 1991)

Barry Eichengreen, *Golden Fetters: The Gold Standard and the Great Depression, 1919–1939* (Oxford University Press, 1992)

Ronald N. Johnson and Gary D. Libecap, *The Federal Civil Service System and the Problem of Bureaucracy: The Economics and Politics of Institutional Change* (University of Chicago Press, 1994)

Naomi R. Lamoreaux, *Insider Lending: Banks, Personal Connections, and Economic Development in Industrial New England, 1784–1912* (Cambridge University Press, 1994)

Lance E. Davis, Robert E. Gallman, and Karin Gleiter, *In Pursuit of Leviathan: Technology, Institutions, Productivity, and Profits in American Whaling, 1816–1906* (University of Chicago Press, 1997)

Dora L. Costa, *The Evolution of Retirement: An American Economic History, 1880–1990* (University of Chicago Press, 1998)

Joseph P. Ferrie, *Yankeys Now: Immigrants in the Antebellum U.S., 1840–1860* (Oxford University Press, 1999)

Robert A. Margo, *Wages and Labor Markets in the United States, 1820–1860* (University of Chicago Press, 2000)

Price V. Fishback and Shawn Everett Kantor, *A Prelude to the Welfare State: The Origins of Workers' Compensation* (University of Chicago Press, 2000)

Gerardo della Paolera and Alan M. Taylor, *Straining at the Anchor: The Argentine Currency Board and the Search for Macroeconomic Stability, 1880–1935* (University of Chicago Press, 2001)

Werner Troesken, *Water, Race, and Disease* (MIT Press, 2004)

B. Zorina Khan, *The Democratization of Invention: Patents and Copyrights in American Economic Development, 1790–1920* (Cambridge University Press, 2005)

Dora L. Costa and Matthew E. Kahn, *Heroes and Cowards: The Social Face of War* (Princeton University Press, 2008)

Roderick Floud, Robert W. Fogel, Bernard Harris, and Sok Chul Hong, *The Changing Body: Health, Nutrition, and Human Development in the Western World since 1700* (Cambridge University Press, 2011)

Relation of the Directors to the
Work and Publications of NBER

1. The object of the NBER is to ascertain and present to the economics profession, and to the public more generally, important economic facts and their interpretation in a scientific manner without policy recommendations. The Board of Directors is charged with the responsibility of ensuring that the work of the NBER is carried on in strict conformity with this object.

2. The President shall establish an internal review process to ensure that book manuscripts proposed for publication DO NOT contain policy recommendations. This shall apply both to the proceedings of conferences and to manuscripts by a single author or by one or more coauthors but shall not apply to authors of comments at NBER conferences who are not NBER affiliates.

3. No book manuscript reporting research shall be published by the NBER until the President has sent to each member of the Board a notice that a manuscript is recommended for publication and that in the President's opinion it is suitable for publication in accordance with the above principles of the NBER. Such notification will include a table of contents and an abstract or summary of the manuscript's content, a list of contributors if applicable, and a response form for use by Directors who desire a copy of the manuscript for review. Each manuscript shall contain a summary drawing attention to the nature and treatment of the problem studied and the main conclusions reached.

4. No volume shall be published until forty-five days have elapsed from the above notification of intention to publish it. During this period a copy shall be sent to any Director requesting it, and if any Director objects to publication on the grounds that the manuscript contains policy recommendations, the objection will be presented to the author(s) or editor(s). In case of dispute, all members of the Board shall be notified, and the President shall appoint an ad hoc committee of the Board to decide the matter; thirty days additional shall be granted for this purpose.

5. The President shall present annually to the Board a report describing the internal manuscript review process, any objections made by Directors before publication or by anyone after publication, any disputes about such matters, and how they were handled.

6. Publications of the NBER issued for informational purposes concerning the work of the Bureau, or issued to inform the public of the activities at the Bureau, including but not limited to the NBER Digest and Reporter, shall be consistent with the object stated in paragraph 1. They shall contain a specific disclaimer noting that they have not passed through the review procedures required in this resolution. The Executive Committee of the Board is charged with the review of all such publications from time to time.

7. NBER working papers and manuscripts distributed on the Bureau's Web site are not deemed to be publications for the purpose of this resolution, but they shall be consistent with the object stated in paragraph 1. Working papers shall contain a specific disclaimer noting that they have not passed through the review procedures required in this resolution. The NBER's Web site shall contain a similar disclaimer. The President shall establish an internal review process to ensure that the working papers and the Web site do not contain policy recommendations, and shall report annually to the Board on this process and any concerns raised in connection with it.

8. Unless otherwise determined by the Board or exempted by the terms of paragraphs 6 and 7, a copy of this resolution shall be printed in each NBER publication as described in paragraph 2 above.

Economic Development in the Americas since 1500

Endowments and Institutions

STANLEY L. ENGERMAN

Departments of Economics and History, University of Rochester

KENNETH L. SOKOLOFF

University of California, Los Angeles

*with contributions
by Stephen Haber
Elisa V. Mariscal
Eric M. Zolt*

NBER

CAMBRIDGE
UNIVERSITY PRESS

CAMBRIDGE UNIVERSITY PRESS
Cambridge, New York, Melbourne, Madrid, Cape Town,
Singapore, São Paulo, Delhi, Tokyo, Mexico City

Cambridge University Press
32 Avenue of the Americas, New York, NY 10013-2473, USA

www.cambridge.org
Information on this title: www.cambridge.org/9780521251372

First published 2012
Printed in the United States of America

A catalog record for this publication is available from the British Library.

Library of Congress Cataloging in Publication data
Engerman, Stanley L.
Economic development in the Americas since 1500 : endowments and institutions /
Stanley L. Engerman, Kenneth L. Sokoloff.
p.   cm. – (NBER series on long-term factors in economic development)
Includes bibliographical references and index.
ISBN 978-1-107-00955-4 (hardback) – ISBN 978-0-521-25137-2 (paperback)
1. America – Economic conditions.   2. Social institutions – America.
3. Political institutions – America.   I. Sokoloff, Kenneth Lee.   II. Title.
HC94.E64   2011
338.973–dc22   2011015745

ISBN 978-1-107-00955-4 Hardback
ISBN 978-0-521-25137-2 Paperback

To Dr. Louis Sokoloff and to Judy Engerman

Contents

Figures

Tables

Beginnings

Memoirs by Claudia Goldin and Stanley Engerman, Two of Ken Sokoloff's Friends and Teachers

Kenneth Sokoloff's academic career ended much too early. Ken did not like endings. He disliked them so much that it was difficult for him to finish papers and projects, end conversations, or leave a dinner table. It was impossible for him to say good-bye. He would welcome guests to his home but he would never say farewell. It was difficult for each of us to say good-bye to our friend. This volume honors his memory by finishing some of what he did not in his lifetime.

Memoir by Claudia Goldin

I first met Ken in 1975 when he was a second year graduate student at Harvard and I was an assistant professor teaching at Princeton. I had earned a semester of leave at Princeton after teaching a heavy load my first two years. Just as I was planning my research leave, the phone rang. It was Bob Fogel. "Claudia," he said, "I have a once-in-a-lifetime opportunity for you. You can teach my graduate course at Harvard." The rest of the conversation is a blur. I had learned, long before, that one does not say "no" to Bob Fogel.

I taught Bob's graduate economic history courses at Harvard in the Fall 1975 and Spring 1976, both required for the Ph.D. In some ways teaching at Harvard 1975 through 1976 was the dumbest thing I could have done with my leave; in many other ways it was one of the very smartest things I ever did. I got to know David Landes; I met many superb graduate students interested in economic history, all of whom thought Bob Fogel would be their teacher; and I met Ken Sokoloff.

Ken entered graduate school with deep interests in economic history, probably nurtured by his undergraduate institution, the University of Pennsylvania. He wrote his research paper for my course on early twentieth century immigration. When Bob Fogel returned, Ken turned his attention to other aspects of economic history, including productivity and manufacturing. Ken and I kept in close contact during the remainder of his graduate years. My work on women in the labor force was greatly informed by the manufacturing data Ken had compiled.

Ken wrote his dissertation on productivity change in manufacturing during the Early Republic. Although Ken never finished his planned volume, *In Pursuit of Private Comfort: Early American Industrialization, 1790 to 1860*, he did leave a large legacy on aspects of early industrialization that are contained in several papers. Among these papers is the long piece in the NBER-CRIW volume number 51, edited by Stanley Engerman and Robert Gallman, *Long-term Factors in American Economic Growth*. There is also a paper in *Explorations in Economic History* on the transition to the factory system from the artisanal shop. And there are two papers with me, one in the *Journal of Economic History* on "Women, Children, and Industrialization," and "The Relative Productivity Hypothesis," in the *Quarterly Journal of Economics*.

The work on early industrialization was primarily based on the manuscripts from three censuses of manufacturers (1820, 1850, and 1860) and the McLane Report of 1832, an incomparable document on manufacturing compiled from surveys by the Treasury Secretary. Ken also used primary documents given to him by Jeremy Atack as well as published census volumes.

The findings were novel, exciting, debate-provoking, and deeply historical. Ken's questions were several. How rapid was productivity change (labor and total factor) in manufacturing in the period of the Early Republic (1820 to 1860)? To what degree was manufacturing the "Engine of Growth"? How did productivity change vary across different industries? What accounted for productivity change?

The main findings of his work were that the pace of productivity growth was high, particularly relative to agriculture. The manufacturing "Engine of Growth," moreover, was ubiquitous and was not found only in the much-celebrated textile industry. Furthermore, productivity growth was not just associated with capital deepening, the increase in capital per unit of labor. And it was not just associated with increased sources of motive power. The striking finding was that productivity change was only slightly greater for the mechanized and capital intensive industries.

Productivity change of some magnitude could be uncovered in virtually every part of manufacturing, even industries that operated with small workshops. The increase in labor productivity was mainly accounted for by an increase in technological change, as measured by the residual, and an increase in the raw materials used per unit of labor. Very little was due to an increase in capital per worker.

These findings came as a shock to many economic historians and historians, such as David Landes, who had believed that productivity advance was mainly due to mechanization and an increase in capital intensity. But Ken's results would not have surprised Adam Smith, who knew that organizational change could have profound effects, even in the lowly pin factory.

Ken also demonstrated that small factories without capital were far more productive than artisanal shops. Size mattered, à la Smith. Another surprise was the predominance of women and young workers in America's early factories and that this type of labor composition was not isolated to textiles. Females, moreover, increased as a fraction of the workforce as firm size increased. The higher fraction of females as firms increased in size meant that there was an increased division of labor with larger firms. Smith would have noted, as did Ken, that greater division of labor was another productivity enhancing innovation.

Ken's work on early industrialization, manufacturing, and productivity morphed into a wide-ranging project on patents. The two lines of research are clearly related, but his work on patents took on a life of its own. It was yet another project that Ken could not bear to end by writing the definitive book. Thankfully, Naomi Lamoreaux, one of his co-authors on the patent project, will finish the volume.

Memoir by Stanley Engerman

I first met Ken when he was still a graduate student at Harvard. We had many discussions about his and my work, discussions that continued after he went to UCLA. I had read most of what he had written, and his work remained, as always, interesting and stimulating, but little thought was given to finding a project upon which to work as co-authors. My interests continued to be on the economics of slavery in the U.S. south, the Caribbean, and elsewhere, and Ken's remained the study of productivity and the economic growth of rich and poor countries.

Our initial attempt at joint authorship came when Steve Haber asked Ken to write a concluding essay to a conference volume on the backwardness of Latin America. After discussing the problem, it was decided that given our overlapping interests in economic growth, factor endowments, and income distribution there would be benefits from a cooperative effect. Our attention to the role of climate and factor endowments in shaping income distribution and institutions in colonial settlement served as a complement (or alternative) to arguments based exclusively on the European institutions that persisted in the settlements.

Although this argument attracted some favorable reactions, we felt that to solidify our points we needed to study, on a comparative basis, certain characteristics of the political economy such as suffrage, education, taxation, land policy, and, although it was left to Steve Haber to do, banking and finance. These new essays were published in a variety of places including journals, conference volumes, and book chapters. Ken's involvement with the World Bank led to publications of some of these pieces in World Bank outlets and related places. These publications did not always reach a large scholarly audience, but they did get more public attention than we had anticipated. The present volume includes all of the articles (or excerpts) written as part of this project, edited to avoid too much repetition and overlap.

Working with Ken was always an exhilarating experience, intellectually exciting and very pleasant personally. Ken knew a lot about many things, enjoyed the process of learning more, and was willing to discuss and debate all issues. Disagreements existed, of course, but with the give-and-take over time they were resolved to mutual agreement. Of course, not everything was perfect in our joint work, but it was always enjoyable.

This memoir began with the description of Ken's disinclination to end projects. My file drawers are filled with copies of many papers that Ken marked "Final Draft." The difference between successive drafts is often no more than four or five words. If I were better organized this might not have been as big a problem. Alas, no matter how much I tried, I often found in working on this volume that I was initially using an earlier version of a "Final Draft," and not the appropriate "Final Draft." Hopefully Ken's *final* "Final Draft" has made it into this volume.

Preface

This volume is based on a number of published essays dealing with a set of issues in economic history – the explanation for the dramatic change in the relative rankings of countries by income in different parts of the Americas. Mexico, the Caribbean, Central America, and South America, the first areas to be settled by the European colonizers in the Western Hemisphere down to the eighteenth century, had greater income and wealth than the two leading countries in mainland North America, the United States and Canada. The Latin American colonies were initially wealthier than those of North America, both at the time of the Native American settlement and in the first two centuries of European expansion, but they then fell dramatically behind the North American colonies after the eighteenth century. In explaining this transition, we focus on the role of important economic institutions, what determined them, and what impact they had on economic behavior and structures. Understanding institutions is essential to understanding the process of economic development, and it is important to see how they developed in different societies. The institutions that developed were no doubt influenced both by those present in the European metropolis as well as the natural and other conditions in the New World. Natural conditions in the Americas determined the crops that could be profitably grown and the means of their production, as well as political circumstances. The climates and soils of North and South America differed dramatically, leading to marked differences in crops produced, and these, we argue, had long-term impacts on the institutions of societies throughout the Americas.

In addition to the chapters presenting the general arguments, there are separate chapters on key institutions influencing economics and politics.

These chapters discuss suffrage, education, taxation, land and immigration policy, and banking and financial systems. In each case we argue that the institutions that emerged in North America were more favorable to economic growth and to political equality than those elsewhere in the Americas. We are concerned both with demonstrating the differences and explaining them. We have both worked in economic history, economics, and history long enough to know that not all scholars will be convinced by all or even some of our arguments; nevertheless, we believe that the evidence presented is sufficient to argue for the important contributions of endowments, resources, and climate in helping to explain economic and political differentials in the Americas, as well as elsewhere.

All of the basic essays in this volume (except for Chapter 8) were completed before the most untimely death of Kenneth Sokoloff. Stanley Engerman completed all the subsequent editing for consistency and to avoid duplication. With the exception of Chapters 6 and 8, all essays were jointly written, and we both accepted full responsibility for their contents. Working with Ken for all the years was a most exciting and enjoyable personal and intellectual experience, and I hope this book provides an appropriate remembrance of both his scholarship and his personal contributions.

Acknowledgments

Multiple Thanks to

Daron Acemoglu
David Dollar
David Eltis
Jeff Frieden
Claudia Goldin
Stephen Haber
Karla Hoff
Zorina Khan

Naomi Lamoreaux
Peter Lindert
Douglass North
James Robinson
Jean-Laurent Rosenthal
William Summerhill and
John Wallis.

Additional Thanks to

Alberto Alesina
George Alter
Jeremy Atack
Tim Begley
Richard Bird
Francois Bourguignon
Sam Bowles
Robin Burgess
Charles Calomaris
Ann Case
Gregory Clark
Roberto Cortés Conde
Janet Currie

Lance Davis
Angus Deaton
Seymour Drescher
William Easterly
Michael Edelstein
Sebastian Edwards
Yael Elad
Price Fishback
Gerald Friedman
David Galenson
Robert Gallman
Barbara Geddes
Aurora Gomez

Avner Greif
James Irwin
Estelle James
Lawrence Katz
Daniel Kaufmann
Sukkoo Kim
Elhart King
Margaret Levenstein
Margaret Levi
Ross Levine
Frank Lewis
Nora Lustig
John Majewski
Noel Maurer
Deirdre McCloskey
Cynthia Morris
Gerardo della Paolera
Mario Pastore

Rose Razaghian
Armando Razo
Elyce Rotella
Mary Shirley
John Skinner
Joel Slemrod
Kirk Stark
Pam Starr
Frederico Sturzenegger
Alan Taylor
Peter Temin
Mariano Tommasi
Dan Treisman
Miguel Urquiola
Jeffrey Williamson
Gavin Wright and
Eric Zolt.

We also wish to thank Frank Smith for encouragement and editorial assistance and Ken Karpinski, of Aptara, for project management.

Research Assistants

Jason Breen
Leah Brooks
Patricia Juarez

Ana Maria Loboguerrero
Elisa Mariscal
Luis Zegarra

Sources of Support

All Souls College, Oxford
Russell Sage Foundation
National Science Foundation
Academic Senate, UCLA
International Studies and
    Overseas Programs, UCLA
University of Rochester

University of Rochester,
    Department of Economics
National Bureau of Economic
    Research
Harvard University, Department
    of Economics
UCLA, Department
    of Economics

Seminar Presentations

Harvard University
University of Toronto
Oxford University
Royal Holloway
University of London
University of Texas
National Bureau of Economic
  Research
All UC Group
UC Berkeley

UCLA
UC Davis
Princeton University
Yale University
Washington University
Cliometrics Society
Duke University
Economic History Association
Stanford University
University of Rochester

Introduction

I

This book will be concerned with explaining the patterns of economic growth in the different parts of the New World settled by European nations, and how these patterns were influenced by differences in factor endowments and institutions. The initial economic development of most Latin American nations led to higher income levels for two centuries than those in North America, but then a dramatic shift occurred in relative economic levels leading to the economic dominance of the major nations of mainland North America, the United States and Canada, and the continued falling behind of the nations of Latin America. The roles of the economic and political forces and institutions in answering these questions are the main interests of our study. Our work on comparisons of development began over fifteen years ago with "How Latin American Fell Behind," a conference organized by Steve Haber.[1]

We focused on several factors long familiar to economists studying these questions and we examined the factors' evolution over time. Most striking at the start were the marked differences among the natural resources and endowments in the different geographic regions, including climate, waterways, rainfall, and topography, all of which had influenced the pattern of settlement by Native Americans even before the European

---

[1] The article "Factor Endowments, Institutions, and Differential Paths of Growth Among New World Economies: A View From Economic Historians of the United States" was presented at a conference at Stanford University in January 1992, and published in Stephen Haber (ed.) *How Latin America Fell Behind: Essays in the Economic Histories of Brazil and Mexico, 1800–1914* (Stanford: Stanford University Press, 1997).

arrival and subsequently influenced the pattern of European settlement. Another key factor was the nature of institutions – the rules of economic and political behavior – held by the Native Americans as well as those introduced by the varying European settlers, based initially on the institutions established in their own metropolitan nations. The distinction between New World endowments and European institutions had been noted by many earlier travelers and later by historians and had become important in explaining the range of adjustments in different areas of the Americas over time.

Our initial studies examined the settlement of the Americas, which tended to occur in areas of low population density with, therefore, a need to acquire a productive labor force, which was often acquired elsewhere. Other areas with similar land abundance include Australia, New Zealand, and South Africa, among the areas settled by Europeans, and the same was the case for eastern Russia (Siberia). While these areas did make certain institutional choices, there were other forms of colonial control which posed rather different problems. In most of Asia and parts of Africa, European settlement was in areas of high population density and thus entailed the settlement of very few whites relative to the native population, often on the order of less than one percent. Although these institutions differed dramatically from those of North America, they also reflected the importance of endowments and characteristics at the time of settlement and acquisition of control. These often presented some differences from the arrangements in the metropole. The choice to seek and accept immigrants was also a consideration, as decisions concerning racial and ethnic homogeneity or heterogeneity influenced the initial willingness to import either black slaves or white Europeans – or both of these groups. The issues relating to marked differences in population levels and colonies with high population density will require more attention in future work, but for the present we wished to concentrate mainly on the areas of low population density in the Americas – which seem to present the link between endowments and institutions most sharply – and where the process of obtaining independence differed in timing and nature.

What struck us regarding the Americas, based on the particulars of the British and French settlements, were the differences in economic, political, and other institutions in regions of distinct resource endowments. These differences, we argued, led to distinct patterns of income inequality and abilities to participate in the market sector. These institutions, often formed in response to conditions in the New World, produced patterns distinct from those in the European metropoles and the differences in inequality that they generated had a major impact on the future growth rates of different regions. Thus, we pointed out, there was a link of endowments and crops, and subsequent economic growth that, we believed, was an important explanation for differential patterns of economic development.

II

Our initial argument was based on the comparison of North and South America, admittedly only one part of the larger world and one part of the broader pattern of the overall process of colonization by European and other nations. Looking at the settlement patterns of the New World led to an interest in colonization elsewhere to see if similar patterns had emerged. We looked at settlements outside of the Americas in areas with low population densities that had a need to attract more labor, coerced or free, and at the major colonies in Asia and Africa that tended to be of high population density that did not need to attract large numbers of workers.

It appeared that low population density and a need to attract labor from elsewhere led to settlers creating different forms of institutions than did settlers in areas of high population density. Population density must be considered in relation to the basic endowments, since low-density areas, such as arctic areas, are not suitable for agriculture and have thus received few immigrants. Temperate-zone areas of low population density have been the major locations for successful settlement and economic growth, while neither tropic nor arctic areas, for different reasons related to climate and the technology of crop production, have been successful at development in the long run.

Among the significant factors that we considered were factor endowments: natural resources, indigenous population density, location in relation to waterways, and the area's topography. In a preindustrial age with primitive technology, these forces will have a great impact on the population. We paid particular attention to the importance of climate, as did notable predecessors such as Aristotle, Machiavelli, Montesquieu, and Hume. They noted many different aspects of climate, such as the disease environment, the effect of heat on labor intensity and input and the production and availability of consumer goods. Climate is also a limiting factor in determining what crops could be successfully produced. The difficulties associated with climate could be avoided by shifts in settlement location and improved knowledge of health measures influencing disease control, as well as by innovations in crop and livestock production and marketing methods. Different temperature and topographical requirements needed for producing sugar cane (in contrast to crops such as wheat and other grains) are central to understanding the settlement of the Americas. Clearly the crops that can be grown in arctic climates remain quite limited. Thus the desire to produce certain crops, such as sugar, in response to relative prices, will determine the areas of settlement, as would concerns about the effect of location on health and life expectation.

The choice of crop has an important impact on income distribution because of the requirements and constraints on the size of units of production and the nature of labor inputs. There might be a broad range of unit sizes over which production could occur, and the optimum scale for different crops can differ significantly. The efficient scale for some crops is larger than for others. Units of different sizes require different scales of production and sizes of labor force and also need different forms of labor controls. Cane-farming as developed in India, and then elsewhere in the world in the late-nineteenth century, was a feasible means of producing sugar, but apparently at a higher cost than the plantation production of sugar. If plantations were possible, as with the use of slave or indentured labor, this would be the preferred choice for landowners. Free workers avoided the intensity of plantation work as well as the tropical climate in which sugar was produced. Generally, also, the labor required for sugar production could be unskilled. Grains, however, could be grown in a (somewhat) more temperate climate, and the required scale of production in this pre-mechanical period was relatively small and could be accomplished on a family-size farm. Given the relative prices and availability of different forms of labor, particularly when slavery was legally and morally acceptable, there would be differences in the nature of labor used and the labor incentives and controls.

It is important to distinguish the size of the units of ownership and control from the size of the actual nature of the production process. This distinction is important when understanding the role of tenantry, wherein small units of production were consistent with large-scale ownership of land (which occurred, for example, in Argentina). It is also characteristic of serfdom, in which production on smallholdings with some coerced labor time existed with ownership of extensive land holdings, the peasants being suppressed by laws, taxes, or compulsion. These possibilities point to an important interaction between political power and economic forces, since in much of North America the initial attempts to establish manorial or seigniorial land systems in grain-growing areas were not sustainable and led to small yeoman holdings rather than tenant systems. If the availability of free land came with the appropriate political and cultural conditions, it could lead to a relatively equal income distribution, as Adam Smith (and later Frederick Jackson Turner) argued. This was characteristic of the American North, with free men able to capture the economic surplus, while free land, carrying different circumstances politically, might lead to slavery or serfdom. It is this political variation that also influenced the marked differences in various institutions.

Another aspect of natural resources at the time of settlement concerns the locations of mines that produced, among other metals, gold and silver, which for reasons of labor control and organization, the need for supervision, and the requirement to get workers to the units and to ensure the level of their output, tended to be produced on large units. Such large-scale organization characterized mining when done by Native Americans prior to the Spanish arrival, as well as when it was subsequently undertaken by the Spanish settlers. The labor used was primarily unskilled and did not directly benefit from extensive productivity improvement.

III

Economic development, particularly in a preindustrial age, reflects the interplay of endowments and institutions, while in technological development the role of endowments might be more limited although the effects of institutions remain. The range of institutions that have been previously discussed by scholars is quite extensive, including the nature of property rights, suffrage, the rule of law, and the existence of trust, whether formal or informal, to institutions based on the specific legislation regarding suffrage, education, banking laws, labor relations, and the appropriate use of specific means of production. Such a broad range of institutions, with so many possible variations in each, leads to some uncertainty in interpreting the relationship between institutions and the economy, since what is at issue is the nature of the mix of institutions and not just the presence or absence of any specific one. We chose to restrict our attention to a limited number of key institutions that would exist in most societies, and then contrasted their levels, rates of change, and variability over time. The principal institutions we discuss are suffrage, education, and land policy, because of their major impacts on the level of production and the distribution of incomes over time. Other institutions discussed in detail are tax systems and the financial systems (discussed by Steve Haber), and more briefly, patent regulations. We believe that each of these institutions can initiate significant differences between nations.

Governments are responsible for a wide variety of policies that influence individuals in society, including policies that can determine both the level and distribution of income. Some of these are explicitly economic, and others, while they are intended for more general purposes, will influence economic circumstances. Voting is significant in determining the choices made among different policies within a society. The greater the numbers of people voting, the more representative the policies should be and the wider the distribution of benefits of government policy across society.

Rules limiting voting within society have included a variety of constraints: gender, age, literacy, property ownership, income, tax payments, and citizenship; voting can be by secret ballot or by open ballot. The fewer the restrictions, the broader the base of voters, the larger the percentage of possible voters, and the greater the percentage of the population able to participate in the nation's social and economic life. The rights to suffrage can be self-reinforcing, because the greater the electorate at any moment of time, the easier it can be to extend the suffrage rights in the future. A key question is how the initial stages of voting with a highly restricted electorate can permit a widening of the franchise over time. Whether this widening of suffrage results from a changing balance in political power, an actual or potential uprising from nonvoters, a desire to attract migrants who might wish the right to vote, or reflected reasons of social cohesion are not clear, but, as we shall see, the broader the suffrage, the wider the benefits of government are likely to be distributed.

Another one of the more important governmental decisions is the nature and magnitude of education provided to individuals. Schooling tends to make individuals more productive and permits more income for themselves, as well as generating a higher level of national output. The education can be provided or financed by the government or paid for by private individuals. Individuals would wish to obtain education, and the opportunity to obtain education might encourage immigration, but limits on voting imposed by elites could lead to holding down the general level of education. Elites concerned with the effects of education could influence policy to have limited amounts of education for lower classes than would occur with a broadened suffrage. Thus there could be a positive relationship between voting and literacy. Reflecting these nonelite preferences, and the expected positive relation between suffrage and education, there should be an important contribution of broadened suffrage to increased education and economic improvement.

In primarily agricultural societies the key asset owned by individuals is land. In some cases land ownership was a requirement for voting, so the wider the distribution of land ownership the broader the suffrage. A wider distribution of land ownership will also mean a more equal distribution of income and wealth. There are several key influences on the size of landholdings and on the number of landowners, as opposed to laborers and tenants working on the land. The initial size of land-grants by the settling metropolis, the specifics of making land available to settlers, the laws controlling the nature of the labor supply, the optimum production size for specific crops and forms of agriculture, the willingness of landowners to obtain less than the maximum possible income from their landholdings, and, correspondingly, the willingness of small-scale planters to forego some income in their desire for independence, would each influence the nature of the outcome of land policy. Many of the initial land settlements were intended to be on manors or plantations, which were maintained only where there was large-scale production such as sugar or mining. In areas where the optimum scale for planters was smaller, as with the production of grains and mixed agriculture, manors gave way to ownership of smaller farms by landowners. Thus there was an adjustment in farm size based on the importance of the output of certain crops produced and this led to a distribution of ownership sizes in different parts of the Americas, with large units in much of Latin America and smaller ones in North America. Furthermore, in those areas that developed small landholdings and had available land to settle and a political desire to encourage settlement of this type, subsequent land policies did more to encourage higher settlement rates than was the case where elites intended to limit or slow-down movement. Thus, with a broad distribution of land ownership, the preferred land policy in much of North America was meant to encourage a continuation of small-scale settlement, while areas with landholders who controlled voting maintained a pattern of large holdings with limited sales to smaller units, maintaining the existing inequality, although the results might differ when based on the size of real wages in manufacturing and in agriculture.

The central government also plays a key role in establishing governmental expenditure and tax policy – at what level taxation and expenditures will take place, what the main forms of taxation will be and at what level they will be set, and what is the accepted mix of public versus private expenditures. The important aspects of the banking and financial system are heavily influenced by the government's policies. These will influence the number and size of banks, the ability to issue certain liabilities such as deposits and paper money, and also the alternative means of financing economic activity. The discussions below demonstrate the impact of endowments and institutions on the policies that exist and persist in different parts of the Americas.

IV

This book will be divided into three sections. Chapters 1 through 3 describe the overall patterns of economic development in the New World countries. Chapters 4 through 9 detail the role of colonization and institutions and discusses several of the major institutions – suffrage, education, taxation, banking and finances, and land policy. Chapters 10 and 11 detail the importance of institutions and several of the ongoing debates about their roles in influencing economic development.

I

Paths of Development: An Overview

I

Introduction

As Europeans established colonies in the New World of North and South America during the sixteenth, seventeenth, and eighteenth centuries, some knowledgeable observers regarded the North American mainland to be of relatively marginal economic interest, when compared with the extraordinary opportunities available in the Caribbean and Latin America. Early in the eighteenth century the French finance minister argued against settling Canada, arguing, in effect, that no area north of 40 degrees latitude ever produced wealth. Voltaire considered the conflict in North America between the French and the British during the Seven Years' War (1756–63) to be madness and characterized the two countries as "fighting over a few acres of snow." The victorious British were later to engage in a lively public debate over which territory should be taken from the French as reparations after the war of 1756–63 – the Caribbean island of Guadeloupe (1705 square km.) or Canada.[1] Several centuries later, however, the U.S. and Canadian economies ultimately proved far more successful than the other economies of the hemisphere. The puzzle, therefore, is how and why the areas that were favored by the forecasters of that era, and the destinations of the vast majority of migrants to the Americas through 1800, fell behind economically.

---

[1] W. J. Eccles, *France in America* (New York: Harper & Row, 1972); Carl Ludwig Lokke, *France and the Colonial Question* (New York: Columbia University Press, 1932). Despite the great difference in area, the population of Canada was only about five times larger than that of Guadeloupe.

TABLE 1.1. *Gross Domestic Product Per Capita in Selected New World Economies, 1700–1997*

	GDP per capita relative to the United States			
	1700	1800	1900	1997
Argentina	–	102	52	35
Barbados	150	–	–	51
Brazil	–	50	10	22
Chile	–	46	38	42
Cuba	167	112	–	–
Mexico	89	50	35	28
Peru	–	41	20	15
Canada	–	–	67	76
United States (GDP per capita in 1985D)	550	807	3,859	20,230

Sources and Notes: The relative GDP per capita figures for Latin American countries come primarily from Coatsworth (1998). Coatsworth relied extensively on Maddison (1994), and we draw our estimates for Canada and the United States in 1800 and 1900 from the same source (using linear interpolation to obtain the 1900 figures from 1890 and 1913 estimates). The GDP per capita estimates for Barbados in 1700 are from Eltis (1995). The 1997 figures are based on the estimates of GDP with purchasing power parity adjustments in World Bank (1999). Since there was no adjustment factor reported for Barbados in that year, we used that for Jamaica in our calculations. The 1700 figure for the United States was obtained from Gallman (2000), by projecting backward the same rate of growth that Gallman estimated between 1774 and 1800. Maddison (1991) has published alternative sets of estimates, which yield somewhat different growth paths (especially for Argentina) during the late nineteenth and early twentieth centuries, and he has a more positive assessment of Brazilian economic performance during the early nineteenth century than does Coatsworth, but the qualitative implications of the different estimates are essentially the same for our purposes.

Systematic estimates of per capita income over time have not yet been constructed for many economies, and those that exist are rough estimates. Table 1.1 and Figure 1.1 convey a sense of the current state of knowledge for a selected group of New World countries relative to the United States. The figures suggest that the economic leadership of the United States and Canada did not emerge until several centuries after the Europeans arrived and began establishing colonies. In 1700, there seems to have been virtual parity in per capita income between Mexico and the British colonies that were to become the United States, and the most prosperous economies of the New World were in the Caribbean.[2] Barbados and

---

[2] For general discussions of the diversity among British colonies in the New World, as well as its sources, see Jack P. Greene, *Pursuits of Happiness* (Chapel Hill: University of North Carolina Press, 1988).

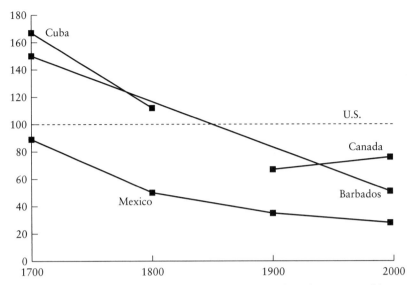

FIGURE 1.1. Gross Domestic Product Per Capita: Selected New World Economics, 1700–1997 USA=100

Cuba, for example, had per capita incomes that have been estimated as 50 and 67 percent higher, respectively, than that of (what was later to be) the United States. Although the latter economy may have begun to grow and pull ahead of most economies in Latin America by 1800, it still lagged behind those in the Caribbean, and Haiti was likely the richest society in the world on a per capita income basis in 1790, on the eve of its Revolution. It was not until industrialization got under way in North America over the nineteenth century that the major divergence between the United States and Canada and the rest of the hemisphere opened up. The magnitude of the gap has been essentially constant in proportional terms since 1900.

The differences in levels of per capita income among the New World economies established by Europeans have increased sharply over the last few centuries. From a situation in which differences in income levels may have been quite small – indeed where the per capita incomes in parts of Latin America exceeded those in the regions that were to compose the United States and Canada – the gap has grown so that the latter two nations have a per capita income much higher than that of Latin America overall. This is especially puzzling because the areas that were first settled, and the choices of the first Europeans to colonize parts of the Americas, were those that fell behind. Conversely, those that were established by

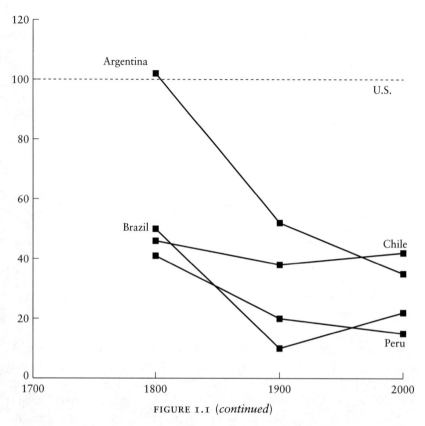

FIGURE 1.1 (*continued*)

Europeans who came late and had to settle for areas viewed less favorably in terms of prospects, have proved far more successful in economic terms over the long run. The explanations for these differentials in growth rates and income levels provided by economists and historians have run the gamut, from an emphasis on strictly economic factors to mainly cultural and religious factors. In recent years, the critical role of institutions has been argued by economists, but there has been relatively limited progress in analyzing where these institutions came from. This is unfortunate in that the sources of institutional change will affect not only the patterns of economic growth, but also the manner in which we interpret the role of institutions.[3]

[3] For general discussions of the role of institutions in worldwide economic growth, see Douglass C. North and Robert Paul Thomas, *The Rise of the Western World* (Cambridge: Cambridge University Press, 1973); Douglass C. North, *Structure and Change in Economic History* (New York: Norton, 1981); and E. L. Jones, *Growth Recurring: Economic Change in World History* (Oxford: Oxford University Press, 1988). See, more recently,

II

Institutions

Institutions matter for the process of economic change and they must form part of any explanation for changes. Yet, that being said, there are important questions as to where institutions come from, and whether or not institutions are exogenous or endogenous. The answers may, of course, vary across different types of institutions, depending on how they were introduced, and how they evolved over time. For example, the early institutions in the New World societies arose from conjunctions between several different sets of institutions, and involved conflicts as well as cooperation amongst settlers, between settlers and the Native Americans already in the area, and between the Europeans who had settled in the New World and the authorities back in Europe. The European settlers were able to draw initially upon their backgrounds in Europe, as well as on adaptations previously made by the Native Americans. Given the wide range of environments in which colonies were established, the geographic variations in Native American population densities, and forms of social organization, it should be possible to give attention both to the extent to which the Europeans borrowed from native institutions and attempted to incorporate them into their settlement patterns, as well as to the manner in which the different institutional backgrounds interacted more generally.

We wish to distinguish three types of institutional forms that have had a significant impact on the process of economic development. First, certain political and legal arrangements form the basic formal rules and laws within which individuals and firms operate. These arrangements reflect the political power relationships among the ruling elite and may vary over time with changes in the balance of power within the society. Second, within the economic sphere, there are voluntary and cooperative choices made that will influence the nature or organization of exchange. These choices are generally the result of interactions among individuals and firms, and will vary over time with changes in the progress of knowledge, technology, and resources as well as with shifts in the relative market power of different actors. Third, there is the significance of cultural and religious values and beliefs which influence economic behavior, through their impact upon the willingness to enter and follow the rules of the market and through affecting the nature of goods, services, and

Douglass C. North, John Joseph Wallis, and Barry R. Weingast, *Violence and Social Orders: A Conceptual Framework for Interpreting Recorded Human History* (Cambridge: Cambridge University Press, 2009).

non-pecuniary items desired. The importance of differences in all of these types of institutions over time and place is clear, and it is the sources of the different paths of institutional development that provide the subject of the research we have undertaken. Our study also highlights the significance of variation in the flexibility and speed of change of institutions, because these qualities have a fundamental bearing on the capacity for societies to overcome the difficulties imposed by unfavorable structures.

III

Growth Differentials

Our examination of the basis for differential paths of growth is inspired by the observation that both the British and also the French colonies in the New World, despite beginning with roughly the same legal and cultural background, as well as drawing immigrants from similar places and economic classes, evolved quite distinct societies and sets of economic institutions. Only a few colonies were able to realize sustained economic growth before the end of the nineteenth century. The majority that failed shared certain salient features of their factor endowments with Latin American New World societies, and we suggest that although these conditions allowed for average standards of living that were high for that time, they were less well-suited for the realization of sustained economic growth than were those prevailing in economies like the United States and Canada.

These differentials in paths of development have long been of central concern to scholars of Latin America and have recently attracted more attention from economic historians and economists more generally.[4] Although conventional economic factors have certainly not been ignored, the explanations offered for the contrasting records in growth have most often focused on institutions and highlighted the variation across

---

[4] Douglass C. North, "Institutions, Economic Growth and Freedom: An Historical Introduction," in *Freedom, Democracy and Economic Welfare*, ed. Michael A. Walker 3–25 (Vancouver: Fraser Institute, 1988): John H. Coatsworth, "Notes on the Comparative Economic History of Latin America and the United States," in *Development and Underdevelopment in America: Contrasts of Economic Growth in North and Latin America in Historical Perspective*, eds. Walter L. Bernecker and Hans Werner Tobler 10–30 (Berlin: Walter de Gruyter, 1993): John H. Coatsworth, "Economic and Institutional Trajectories in Nineteenth-Century Latin America," in *Latin America and the World Economy Since 1980*, eds. John H. Coatsworth and Alan M. Taylor: 33–54 (Cambridge, MA: Harvard University/David Rockefeller Center for Latin American Studies, 1998). Also see, Ch. 2.

societies in conditions relevant to growth such as the security of property rights, prevalence (or lack) of corruption, structures of the financial sector, investment in public infrastructure and social capital, and the inclination of individuals in the societies to work hard or to be entrepreneurial. But ascribing differences in development to differences in institutions raises the challenge of explaining where the differences in institutions come from. Those who have addressed this formidable problem have typically emphasized the importance of presumed exogenous (to the colonies) differences in religion or national heritage. Douglass North, for example, is one of many who have attributed the relative success of the United States and Canada to British institutions being more conducive to growth than those of Spain and other European colonizers. Others, like John Coatsworth, are skeptical of such generalizations, and suggest that they may obscure the insight that can be gained by examining the extreme diversity of experiences observed across the Americas, even across societies with the same national heritage.

Indeed, a striking implication of the estimates in Table 1.1 and Figure 1.1 are that the relationship between national heritage and economic performance is weaker than popularly thought. During the colonial period, the economies with the highest per capita incomes were those in the Caribbean, and it made little difference whether they were of Spanish, British, or French origin. The case for the superiority of British institutions is usually based on the records of the United States and Canada, but the majority of the New World societies established by the British – including Barbados, Jamaica, Belize, Guiana, and the lesser-known Puritan colony on Providence Island[5] – were like their other neighbors in not beginning to industrialize until much later, if at all. Having been part of the British Empire was far from a guarantee of economic growth.[6] Likewise, there was considerable diversity across the economies of Spanish America. This is most evident in the contrasts between the experiences of the nations of the southern cone and those with large populations of Native American descent, such as Mexico and Peru. It is the former class of countries, including Argentina, that of all the other economies of the New World most closely resemble the United States and Canada in experience over time.

[5] For a fascinating account of radical divergence even among the Puritan colonies in the New World, see Karen Ordahl Kupperman, *Providence Island, 1630–1641: The Other Puritan Colony* (Cambridge: Cambridge University Press, 1993), especially the discussions of the unusual patterns of land ownership and settlement.

[6] Greene, *Pursuits of Happiness;* Kupperman, *Providence Island.*

With the evidence of wide disparities even among economies of the same European heritage, scholars have begun to reexamine alternative sources of differences. Though not denying the significance of national heritage, nor of idiosyncratic conditions that are unique to individual countries, they have begun to explore the possibility that initial conditions, or factor endowments broadly conceived, could have had profound and enduring impacts on long-run paths of institutional and economic development in the New World. Economists have traditionally emphasized the pervasive influence of factor endowments, so the qualitative thrust of this approach will not be entirely novel.[7] What is new, however, is the specific focus on how the extremely different environments in which the Europeans established their colonies may have led to societies with very different degrees of inequality, and on how these differences might have persisted over time and affected the course of development through their impact on the institutions that evolved. In particular, while essentially all the economies established in the New World began with an abundance of land and natural resources relative to labor, and thus high living standards on average, other aspects of their factor endowments varied in ways that meant that the majority were characterized virtually from the outset by extreme inequality in wealth, human capital, and political power. From this perspective, the colonies that came to compose the United States and Canada stand out as somewhat deviant cases.

IV

Labor Migration
In the Americas, the fraction of migrants who were slaves increased continuously, from roughly 25 percent prior to 1580 to nearly 80 percent between 1700 and 1760 (see Table 1.2). As late as the period 1760 to 1820, over 80 percent of immigrants were still enslaved, and it was only after the 1820s that the balance shifted toward European migration. The prominence of slaves, as well as the increase over time in the proportion of migrants going to the colonies of Portugal, France, and the Netherlands, and the continued quantitative dominance in the destinations of migrants to British American colonies in the West Indies and

---

[7] Robert E. Baldwin, "Patterns of Development in Newly Settled Regions," *Manchester School of Economic and Social Studies* 24 (May 1956): 161–79; W. Arthur Lewis, "Economic Development with Unlimited Supplies of Labor," *Manchester School of Economic and Social Studies* 23 (May 1955): 139–91; Evsey D. Domar, "The Causes of Slavery or Serfdom: A Hypothesis," *Journal of Economic History* 30 (March 1970): 18–32.

TABLE 1.2. *European-Directed Transatlantic Migration by European Nation and Continent of Origin, 1492–1880*

	Africans leaving Africa on ships of each nation	Europeans leaving their nations for Americas	Africans arriving in American regions claimed by specific nations
(a) Before 1580			
Spain	10	139	45
Portugal	56	58	13
Britain	2	0	0
Total	68	197	58
(b) 1580–1640			
Spain	0	188	289
Portugal	594	110	181
France	0	4	2
Netherlands	10	2	8
Britain	3	87	4
Total	607	391	484
(c) 1640–1700			
Spain	0	158	141
Portugal	259	50	225
France	40	23	75
Netherlands	151	13	49
Britain	379	285	277
Total	829	529	767
(d) 1700–1760			
Spain	1	193	271
Portugal	958	300	768
France	458	27	414
Netherlands	223	5	123
Britain	1206	222	1013
Total	2846	747	2589
(e) 1760–1820			
Spain	186	n.a.	
Portugal	1507	n.a.	
Netherlands	140	n.a.	
Britain	1605	n.a.	
France	701	n.a.	
USA	186	n.a.	
Total	4325	773	
(f) 1820–1880			
Spain	612	n.a.	
Portugal	1510	n.a.	
Netherlands	0	n.a.	
Britain	0	n.a.	
France	158	n.a.	
USA	16	n.a.	
Total	2296	13702	

Source: Eltis (1999, 2002). There are no data estimates for Africans arriving after 1760.

on the southern mainland, reflects the increasing specialization by the New World over the colonial period in the production of sugar, coffee, and other staple crops for world markets. These colonies attracted heavy inflows of labor (especially slaves) because their soils and climates made them extraordinarily well-suited for growing these lucrative commodities, and because of the substantial economies of scale in producing such crops on large slave plantations.[8] Indeed, there are few examples of significant colonies which were not so specialized: only the Spanish settlements on the mainlands of North and South America (some of which had labor concentrations in silver or other mines) and the New England, Middle Atlantic, and Canadian settlements of Britain and France were different. It was not coincidental that these were also the colonies that relied least on slaves for their labor force.

The economies that specialized in the production of sugar and other highly valued crops associated with extensive use of slaves had the highest per capita (even including slaves in the denominator) incomes in the New World. Most, including Barbados, Cuba, St. Dominique, and Jamaica, were in the West Indies, but some (mainly Brazil) were in South America. They specialized in these crops early in their histories, and through the persistent working of technological advantages and international markets in slaves, their economies came to be dominated by large slave plantations populated by slaves of African descent.[9] The greater efficiency of the very large plantations, and the overwhelming fraction of the populations were black slaves, made the distributions of wealth and human capital extremely unequal. Even among the free population, there was greater inequality in such economies than in those on the North American mainland.[10]

---

[8] Robert William Fogel, *Without Consent or Contract* (New York: Norton, 1989).

[9] Richard S. Dunn, *Sugar and Slaves: The Rise of the Planter Class in the English West Indies, 1624–1713*, (Chapel Hill: University of North Carolina Press, 1972); Richard Sheridan, *Sugar and Slavery: An Economic History of the British West Indies, 1623–1775* (Baltimore: Johns Hopkins University Press, 1974); Manuel Moreno Fraginals, *The Sugarmill: The Socioeconomic Complex of Sugar in Cuba* (New York: Monthly Review Press, 1976); Stuart B. Schwartz, *Sugar Plantations in the Formation of Brazilian Society: Bahia, 1550–1835* (Cambridge: Cambridge University Press, 1985); Franklin W. Knight, *The Caribbean: The Genesis of a Fragmented Nationalism*, 2nd ed. (New York: Oxford University Press, 1990).

[10] David W. Galenson, "The Settlement and Growth of the Colonies: Population, Labor, and Economic Development," In *The Cambridge Economic History of the United States*, 3 vols., vol. 1, *The Colonial Period*, eds. Stanley L. Engerman and Robert E. Gallman: 135–207 (Cambridge: Cambridge University Press, 1996).

Although the basis for the predominance of an elite class in such colonies may have been the enormous advantages in sugar production available to those who were able to assemble a large company of slaves – as well as the extreme disparities in human capital between blacks and whites (both before and after emancipation) – the long-run success and stability of the members of this elite were also facilitated by their disproportionate political influence. Together with the legally codified inequality intrinsic to slavery, the greater inequality in wealth contributed to the evolution of institutions that protected the privileges of the elites and restricted opportunities for the broad mass of the population to fully participate in the commercial economy even after the abolition of slavery.

The importance of factor endowments is also evident in a second category of New World colonies that can be thought of as Spanish America, although it also included some islands in the Caribbean. Spain focused its attention on, and designed their New World policies around conditions in, colonies such as Mexico and Peru, whose factor endowments were characterized by rich mineral resources and the substantial numbers of natives surviving contact with the European colonizers. Building on preconquest social organizations whereby Indian elites extracted tribute from the general population, the Spanish authorities adopted the approach of distributing, among a privileged few, mineral resources and enormous grants of land, often including claims to a stream of income from the native labor residing in the vicinity. The resulting large-scale estates and mines, established early in the histories of these colonies, endured even where the principal production activities were lacking in economies of scale.

Although small-scale production was typical of grain agriculture during this era, their essentially nontradeable property rights to tribute from rather sedentary groups of natives (tied to locations by community property rights in land) gave large landholders the means and the motive to operate at a large scale. Although the processes are not well understood, it is evident that large-scale agriculture remained dominant in Spanish America, especially in districts with linkages to extensive markets, and that the distribution of wealth remained highly unequal over time. Elite families generally acted as local representatives of the Spanish government in the countryside during the colonial period and maintained their status long after independence. The persistence and stability of elites, as well as inequality in general, were also certainly aided by the restrictive immigration policies applied by Spain to its colonies, and by laws throughout Spanish America requiring that a *vecino* (citizen) might have the right to vote and other privileges even if they did not always need to own land. In the postindependence period there were constitutions which required literacy and a specified economic standing to be able to vote. For different reasons, therefore, Spanish America was like the colonies specializing in the production of crops like sugar, in that they generated an economic structure in which wealth, human capital, and political power were distributed very unequally, and in which the elites were drawn from a relatively small group that comprised those who were of European descent and racially distinct from the bulk of the population.[11]

As in the colonial sugar economies, the economic structures that evolved in this second class of colonies were greatly influenced by the factor endowments, viewed in broad terms. The fabulously valuable mineral resources and abundance of labor with low amounts of human capital were certainly major contributors to the extremely unequal distributions of wealth and income that came to prevail in these economies. Moreover, without the extensive supply of native labor, it is unlikely that Spain could have maintained its policies of tight restrictions on European migration to its colonies and generous awards of property and tribute to the earliest settlers. The colonists in Spanish America had faced formidable requirements for obtaining permission to go to the New World – a policy that limited the flow of migrants and helped to preserve the political and economic advantages enjoyed by those of European descent who had already made the move. In 1800, less than 20 percent of the population in Spanish colonies such as Mexico, Peru, and Chile was composed of whites; it would not be until the inflows from Europe late in the nineteenth century that Latin American countries such as Argentina and Chile would attain the predominantly European character they have today.[12]

The third class of colonies, seen primarily in New England and the middle–Atlantic states, was mostly based on white settlement that grew

---

[11] James Lockhart and Stuart B. Schwartz, *Early Latin America: A History of Colonial Spanish America and Brazil* (Cambridge: Cambridge University Press, 1983); François Chevalier, *Land and Society in Colonial Mexico: The Great Hacienda* (Berkeley: University of California Press, 1963); Eric Van Young, "Mexican Rural History Since Chevalier: The Historiography of the Colonial Hacienda," *Latin American Research Review* 18, No. 3, (1983): 5–62; James Lockhart, *Spanish Peru: 1532–1560. A Social History*, 2nd ed. (Madison: University of Wisconsin Press, 1994); Nils Jacobsen, *Mirages of Transition: The Peruvian Altiplano, 1780–1930* (Berkeley: University of California Press, 1993).

[12] Cuba and Brazil received many Europeans after the ending of slavery, as, at that time, did Uruguay. Chile did not receive a large amount of immigrants but its small population meant that this did change the black-white ratio.

grains on small-scale agricultural units. Those areas differed from the first two patterns in terms of racial mixture and crops that were produced.

V

The Role of Institutions in the Persistence of Inequality

There is strong evidence that various features of the factor endowments of the three categories of New World economies, including soils, climates, and the size or density of the native population, predisposed the economies toward paths of development associated with different degrees of inequality in wealth, human capital, and political power. Although these conditions might reasonably be treated as exogenous at the beginning of European colonization, it is clear that such an assumption becomes increasingly tenuous as one examines its trajectory over time. Particularly given that both Latin America and many of the economies of the first category, such as Haiti and Jamaica, are known today as generally the most unequal in the world, we suggest that the initial conditions had lingering effects, not only because certain fundamental characteristics of New World economies were difficult to change, but also because government policies and other institutions tended to reproduce them.[13] Specifically, in those societies that began with extreme inequality, elites were better able to establish a legal framework that insured them disproportionate shares of political power, and to use that greater influence to establish rules, laws, and other government policies that advantaged members of the elite relative to nonmembers contributing to persistence over time of the high degree of inequality.[14] In societies that began with greater equality or homogeneity among the population, however, efforts by elites to institutionalize an unequal distribution of political power were relatively unsuccessful, and the rules, laws, and other government policies that came to be adopted tended to provide more equal treatment and opportunities to members of the population.

Land policy provides an illustration of how institutions may have fostered persistence in the extent of inequality in New World economies over time. Since the governments of each colony or nation were regarded as the owners of the public lands, they set those policies which influenced the

[13] Klaus Deninger and Lyn Squire, "A New Data Set and Measure of Income Inequality," *World Bank Economic Review* 10 (September 1996): 565–91.

[14] J. Morgan Kousser, *The Shaping of Southern Politics: Suffrage Restrictions and the Establishment of the One-Party South, 1880–1910* (New Haven: Yale University Press, 1974).

pace of settlement as well as the distribution of wealth, by controlling its availability, setting prices, establishing minimum or maximum acreages, and designing tax systems.[15] We can point to the highly concentrated pattern of land ownership produced and perpetuated by land policies in most of Spanish America. In the United States, where there were never major obstacles to acquiring land, the terms of land acquisition became even easier over the course of nineteenth century. Similar changes were sought around the mid-nineteenth century in Argentina, Brazil, and Chile, discussed as a means to encourage immigration, but these steps were either not implemented or were less successful than in the United States and Canada in getting land to smallholders. The major crops produced in the expansion of the United States and Canada were grains, which permitted relatively small farms given the technology of the times and which may help to explain why such a policy of smallholding was implemented and ultimately effective. But as the example of Argentina indicates, small-scale production of wheat was possible even with ownership of land in large units, maintaining a greater degree of overall inequality in wealth and political power.

The contrast between the United States and Canada, with their practices of offering small units of land for disposal and maintaining open immigration, and the rest of the Americas, where land and labor policies led to large landholdings and great inequality, seems to extend across a wide spectrum of institutions and other government interventions. In the areas of law and administration pertaining to the establishment of corporations, the regulation of financial institutions, the granting of property rights in intellectual capital (patents), industrial policies, as well as the provision of access to minerals and other natural resources on government owned land, New World societies with greater inequality tended to adopt policies that were more selective in the offering of opportunities.[16] Of course, members of wealthy elites almost always enjoy privileged

[15] Paul W. Gates, *History of Public Land Law Development* (Washington, D.C.: Government Printing Office, 1968); Carl E. Solberg, *The Prairies and the Pampas: Agrarian Policy in Canada and Argentina, 1880–1913* (Stanford: Stanford University Press, 1987); Jeremy Adelman, *Frontier Development: Land, Labor, and Capital on Wheatlands of Argentina and Canada, 1890–1914* (Oxford: Oxford University Press, 1994); Emilia Viotti da Costa, *The Brazilian Empire: Myths and Histories* (Chicago: University of Chicago Press, 1985).

[16] See Ch. 3; Stephen H. Haber, "Industrial Concentration and the Capital Markets: A Comparative Study of Brazil, Mexico, and the United States, 1830–1930," *Journal of Economic History* 51 (September 1991): 559–80.

positions, but these societies were relatively extreme in the degree to which their institutions advantaged elites. Moreover, this contrast across New World societies with respect to the differences in the breadth of the respective populations having effective access to opportunities for economic and social advancement seems much more systematic than has been generally recognized.

Perhaps the most straightforward way of subjecting our hypothesis – that elites in societies which began with greater inequality evolved more power to influence the choice of legal and economic institutions – to an empirical test is to look at how broadly the franchise was extended and what fractions of respective populations actually voted in elections. Since most societies in the Americas were nominally democracies by the middle of the nineteenth century, this sort of information has a direct bearing on the extent to which elites – based largely on wealth, human capital, and gender – held disproportionate political power in their respective countries. Summary information about the differences across New World societies during the late nineteenth and early twentieth centuries in how the right to vote was restricted is reported in Table 1.3. The estimates reveal that although it was common in all countries to reserve the right to vote to adult males until the twentieth century, the United States and Canada were the clear leaders in doing away with restrictions based on wealth or literacy, and in attaining secrecy in balloting.

The contrast was not so evident at the outset. Despite the sentiments popularly attributed to the Founding Fathers, voting in the United States was largely a privilege reserved for white men with significant amounts of property, as it was elsewhere in the hemisphere, until early in the nineteenth century. Only four states had adopted universal white male suffrage before 1815, but after that year virtually all that entered the Union (with Mississippi, in 1817, as the sole exception) did so without wealth- or tax-based qualifications for the franchise. With the rapid growth of the then western states, where labor was scarce and the wealth distribution relatively equal, and with some lowering of requirements in those previously settled, the proportion of the population voting in presidential elections surged from about 3 percent in 1824 to 14 percent in 1840. In contrast, the original thirteen states revised their laws to broaden the franchise only gradually, generally after intense political struggles (five still retained some sort of economic-based qualification on the eve of the Civil War). Former President John Adams and Senator Daniel Webster were among those who argued strongly for retaining a property qualification

TABLE 1.3. *Laws Governing the Franchise and the Extent of Voting in Selected American Countries, 1840–1940*

		Lack of Secrecy In Balloting	Wealth Requirement	Literacy Requirement	Proportion of the Population Voting (%)
		1840–80			
Chile	1869	Y	Y	Y	1.6
Ecuador	1856	Y	Y	Y	0.1
Mexico	1840	Y	Y	Y	–
Peru	1875	Y	Y	Y	–
Uruguay	1880	Y	Y	Y	–
Venezuela	1880	Y	Y	Y	–
Canada	1867	Y	Y	N	7.7
	1878	N	Y	N	12.9
United States	1850[a]	N	N	N	12.9
	1880	N	N	N	18.3
		1881–1920			
Argentina	1896	Y	Y	Y	1.8[b]
	1916	N	N	N	9.0
Brazil	1914	Y	Y	Y	2.4
Chile	1920	Y	N	Y	4.4
Colombia	1918[c]	N	N	N	6.9
Costa Rica	1890	Y	Y	Y	–
	1912	Y	Y	Y	–
	1919	Y	N	N	10.6
Ecuador	1894	N	N	Y	3.3
Mexico	1920	N	N	N	8.6
Peru	1920	Y	Y	Y	–
Uruguay	1900	Y	Y	Y	–
	1920	N	N	N	13.8
Venezuela	1920	Y	Y	Y	–
Canada	1917	N	N	N	20.5
United States	1900	N	N	Y[d]	18.4
	1920	N	N	Y	25.1
		1921–40			
Argentina	1937	N	N	N	15.0
Bolivia	1951	–	Y	Y	4.1
Brazil	1930	Y	Y	Y	5.7
Colombia	1930	N	N	N	11.1

(*continued*)

		Lack of Secrecy In Balloting	Wealth Requirement	Literacy Requirement	Proportion of the Population Voting (%)
Chile	1931	Y	N	Y	6.5
Costa Rica	1940	N	N	N	17.6
Ecuador	1940	N	N	Y	3.3
Mexico	1940	N	N	N	11.8
Peru	1940	N	N	Y	–
Uruguay	1940	N	N	N	19.7
Venezuela	1940	N	Y	Y	–
Canada	1940	N	N	N	41.1
United States	1940	N	N	Y	37.8

Source: Engerman, Haber, and Sokoloff (2000).

Notes:

[a] Two states, still mantained wealth requirements in 1850, but both eliminated them by 1860.

[b] This figure is for the city of Buenos Aires, and likely overstates the proportion who voted at the national level.

[c] The information on restrictions refers to national laws. The 1863 Constitution empowered provincial state governments to regulate electoral affairs. Afterwards, elections became restricted (in terms of the franchise for adult males) and indirect in some states. It was not until 1948 that a national law established universal adult male suffrage throughout the country.

[d] Eighteen states, seven southern and eleven nonsouthern, introduced literacy requirements between 1890 and 1926. These restrictions were directed primarily at blacks and immigrants.

at the Massachusetts constitutional convention of 1820, and although their eloquence was not enough to save it, a tax requirement was adopted in its place.[17]

A movement for the extension of the suffrage, with similar patterns across provinces, followed with a lag of several decades in Canada, but meaningful extension of the franchise occurred much later in Latin America.[18]

[17] Kirk H. Porter, *A History of Suffrage in the United States* (Chicago: University of Chicago Press, 1918); Spencer D. Albright, *The American Ballot* (Washington, D.C.: American Council of Public Affairs, 1942).

[18] See Ch. 4; Laurens Ballard Perry, *Juarez and Díaz: Machine Politics in Mexico* (DeKalb: Northern Illinois University Press, 1978); Joseph L. Love, "Political Participation in Brazil, 1881–1969," *Luso-Brazilian Review* 7 (December 1970): 3–24; James Scobie, *Argentina: A City and a Nation*, 2nd ed. (New York: Oxford University Press, 1971).

Neither the timing of the general movements across the nations of the Americas toward universal white male suffrage, nor the record of adoption across states within the United States, seem to fit well with the idea that higher per capita income can provide a full accounting of the patterns through its effect of increasing a population's demand for democracy. National heritage alone is likewise unable to account for why Argentina, Uruguay, and Costa Rica (the latter of which had a lower population density and a greater percentage of whites in the population than elsewhere in Central America), were far ahead of their Latin American neighbors in extending the franchise, nor why other British colonies in the New World lagged behind Canada and the United States. (Barbados, for example, maintained a property qualification until 1950.) Explanations based on ideology also have a problem in having to grapple with the observation that at the same time that populations in the Americas, whether independent countries or states within the United States, extended the franchise among males by easing landholding or wealth restrictions, they generally added qualifications aimed at maintaining the exclusion of groups that were racially distinct from the elites. In the United States, until the Fourteenth Amendment to the Constitution, this meant adding explicit racial qualifications; in Latin America, literacy was made a requirement for citizenship, and thus for the right to vote. The issue is obviously complex and requires more investigation, but the patterns appear more consistent with the view that the extent of equality or population homogeneity was highly relevant to understanding how quickly societies extended the franchise and introduced other democratizing reforms in the conduct of elections.

Our conjecture is that these differences across societies in the distribution of political power may have contributed to persistence in the relative degrees of inequality through the effects on institutional development. The institution of public primary schools, which was the principal vehicle for high rates of literacy attainment and an important contributor to human capital formation, is interesting to examine in this regard.[19] Nearly all of the New World economies were sufficiently prosperous by the beginning of the nineteenth century to establish a widespread network of primary schools. However, although many countries (through their national governments) expressed support for such efforts, few actually made investments on a scale sufficient to serve the general population before the twentieth century. The exceptional societies in terms of leadership were the United States and Canada. Virtually from the time

[19] Richard A. Easterlin, "Why Isn't the Whole World Developed?" *Journal of Economic History* 41 (March 1981): 1–19.

of settlement, these North Americans seem generally to have been convinced of the value of mobilizing the resources to provide their children with a basic education. Especially in New England, schools were frequently organized and funded at the village or town level. It is likely that the United States already had about the most literate white population in the world by 1800, but the "common school movement" that got underway in the 1820s (following closely after the movement for the extension of the franchise) put the country on an accelerated path of investment in educational institutions. Between 1821 and 1871, nearly every state in the American West or North that had not already done so enacted a law strongly encouraging localities to establish "free schools" open to all children that would be supported by general taxes. Although the movement made slower progress in the South, which had greater inequality and population heterogeneity than the North, schooling had spread sufficiently by the middle of the nineteenth century that over 40 percent of the school-age population was enrolled, and more than 90 percent of white adults were literate, as shown in Table 1.4. Schools were also widespread in early nineteenth-century Canada, and even though it lagged the United States by several decades in establishing tax supported schools with universal access, its literacy rates were nearly as high (Cubberley 1920).

The rest of the hemisphere trailed far behind the United States and Canada in primary schooling and in attaining literacy. Despite enormous wealth, the British colonies (with the exception of Barbados) were very slow to organize schooling institutions that served broad segments of the population. Indeed, it was evidently not until the British Colonial Office took an interest in the promotion of schooling late in the nineteenth century that significant steps were taken in this direction. Similarly, even the most progressive Latin American countries – like Argentina, Uruguay and Costa Rica – were more than seventy-five years behind the United States and Canada. Major investments in primary schooling did not generally occur in any Latin American country until the national governments provided the funds; in contrast to the pattern in North America, local and state governments in Latin America were generally not willing or able to fund them on their own.[20] As a consequence, most of these societies did not achieve high levels of literacy until well into the twentieth century.

[20] See Ch. 5; Claudia Goldin and Lawrence F. Katz, "Human and Social Capital: The Rise of Secondary Schooling in America, 1910 to 1940," *Journal of Interdisciplinary History*, 29 (Spring 1999): 683–723; Claudia Goldin and Lawrence F. Katz, "Why the United States Led in Education: Lessons from Secondary School Expansion, 1910 to 1940," in *Human Capital and Institutions: A Long-Run View*, eds. David Eltis, Frank Lewis, and Kenneth L. Sokoloff: 143–178 (Cambridge: Cambridge University Press, 2009).

TABLE 1.4. *Literacy Rates in the Americas, 1850–1950*

	Year	Ages (in Years)	Rate (%)
Argentina	1869	6+	23.8
	1895	6+	45.6
	1900	10+	52.0
	1925	10+	73.0
Barbados	1946	10+	92.7
Bolivia	1900	10+	17.0
Brazil	1872	7+	15.8
	1890	7+	14.8
	1900	7+	25.6
	1920	10+	30.0
	1939	10+	57.0
British Honduras (Belize)	1911	10+	59.6
	1931	10+	71.8
Chile	1865	7+	18.0
	1875	7+	25.7
	1885	7+	30.3
	1900	10+	43.0
	1925	10+	66.0
	1945	10+	76.0
Colombia	1918	15+	32.0
	1938	15+	56.0
	1951	15+	62.0
Costa Rica	1892	7+	23.6
	1900	10+	33.0
	1925	10+	64.0
Cuba	1861	7+	23.8(38.5, 5.3)*
	1899	10+	40.5
	1925	10+	67.0
	1946	10+	80.0
Guatemala	1893	7+	11.3
	1925	10+	15.0
	1945	10+	20.0
Honduras	1887	7+	15.2
	1925	10+	29.0
Jamaica	1871	5+	16.3
	1891	5+	32.0
	1911	5+	47.2
	1943	5+	67.9
	1943	10+	76.1
Mexico	1900	10+	22.2
	1925	10+	36.0
	1946	10+	48.4

(continued)

	Year	Ages (in Years)	Rate (%)
Paraguay	1886	7+	19.3
	1900	10+	30.0
Peru	1925	10+	38.0
Puerto Rico	1860	7+	11.8(19.8,3.1)*
Uruguay	1900	10+	54.0
	1925	10+	70.0
Venezuela	1925	10+	34.0
Canada	1861	20+	82.5
English–majority counties	1861	20+	93.0
French–majority counties	1861	20+	81.2
United States			
No. Whites	1860	20+	96.9
So. Whites	1860	20+	91.5
All	1870	14+	80.0(88.5, 20.1)*
	1890	14+	86.7(92.3,43.2)*
	1910	14+	92.3(95.0, 69.5)*

Sources and Notes: *The figures for Whites and Non-Whites are reported respectively within parentheses. For the countries in South America, Central America, and the Caribbean, see Newland (1991, 1994); Helg (1987); Roberts (1957); Britton (1994); Jamaica, Department of Statistics, *West Indian Census 1946*, Kingston: Central Bureau of Statistics, 1950. For the United States, see Carter, et al. (2006), Volume II, Table Bc 793–797. For Canada, see Egnal (1996): 81.

VI

Conclusions

These early differences in the extent of inequality across New World economies may have been preserved by the types of economic institutions that evolved and by the effects of those institutions on how broadly access to economic opportunities was shared. This path of institutional development may in turn have affected growth. Where there was extreme inequality, and institutions advantaged elites and limited the access of much of the population to economic opportunities, members of elites were better able to maintain their elite status over time, but at the cost of society not realizing the full economic potential of disadvantaged groups. Although the examples we have discussed – land ownership, the extension of the franchise, and investment in public schools – do not prove the general point, they are suggestive of a pattern whereby institutions in New World societies with greater inequality advantaged members of the elite, along with many other types of government policies, including those concerned with access to public lands and natural resources, the establishment and use of financial institutions, and property rights in technological information. Overall, where there existed elites who were sharply differentiated from the rest of the population on the basis of wealth, human capital, and political influence, they seem to have used their standing to restrict competition. Although one could imagine that extreme inequality could take generations to dissipate in even a free and even-handed society, such biases in the paths of institutional development likely go far in explaining the persistence of inequality over the long run in Latin America and elsewhere in the New World.

2

Factor Endowments and Institutions
(with Stephen Haber)

I

Geographic patterns in economic performance across societies have been analyzed, but there has been a recent revival of interest among economists in the actual current differences that need to be explained. Confronted by systematic evidence of powerful empirical regularities, such as the per capita income of countries near the equator lagging far behind that of their neighbors at more moderate latitudes, researchers hope to gain insight into the processes of economic growth by exploring the sources of these disparities. One group focuses on the direct effects of conditions closely associated with geography, such as climate, disease environment, soil quality, or access to markets, while focusing on the availability and productivity of labor and other factors of production. Other scholars, however, highlight how such differentials in performance could be rooted in the indirect effects that geography and factor endowments have on paths of development through their influences on the ways institutions evolve.[1] Both perspectives have distinguished intellectual traditions, but

---

[1] See Robert E. Hall and Charles L. Jones, "Why Do Some Countries Produce So Much More Output Per Worker Than Others?" *Quarterly Journal of Economics* 114 (February 1999): 83–116; John Luke Gallup and Jeffrey D. Sachs, with Andrew Mellinger "Geography and Economic Development," in *Annual World Bank Conference on Development Economics* (Washington, D.C.: World Bank, 1999); Jared Diamond, *Guns, Germs, and Steel: The Fate of Human Societies* (New York: Norton, 1997); Daron Acemoglu, Simon Johnson, and James Robinson, "The Colonial Origins of Comparative Development: An Empirical Investigation," *American Economic Review* 91 (December 2001): 1369–1401; Daron Acemoglu, Simon Johnson, and James Robinson, "Reversal of Fortune: Geography and Institutions in the Making of the Modern World Income Distribution," *Quarterly Journal of Economics* 117 (November 2002): 1231–94.

the question of whether there might be systematic reasons as to why some societies are more likely than others to evolve institutions that are conducive to growth seems to have generated particular interest. This should not be surprising. Despite an emerging consensus that institutions are important for growth, knowledge of their origins and how institutions that are bad for growth might persist over time remains very limited.

Although it may be obvious that institutions matter for growth, our understanding of just how they matter depends, in part, on whether they are exogenous or endogenous and on the factors that shape or determine them. The study of how institutions evolve, and whether and how they are related to factor endowments or geography, is not straightforward. Not only does institutional change take place gradually over long periods of time, but the likelihood of different causal mechanisms being involved further complicates analysis. Geographic factors might be associated with institutions and economic performance, either because they directly shape the sorts of institutions that evolve and thus indirectly affect performance or because they have a direct effect on economic performance, which in turn affects the quality of institutions. One method of attacking this empirical problem is to use geographic or historical variables as instruments for contemporary measures of the quality of institutions, and to estimate the relationship across countries between current economic performance and the exogenous component of institutional quality. This approach has yielded some important new findings about the patterns of long-term development, but it leaves open many questions about the mechanisms that link the geographic or historical factors to contemporary circumstances and about the processes of institutional change more generally.[2]

Our program for studying the sources of institutions and their relation to long-term paths of economic development has been centered on exploring the record in detail in a specific context – the societies of the New World. The experience of a limited number of European countries coming to the Americas to establish colonies in quite dissimilar environments within a relatively short span of time, makes for an extremely interesting "natural experiment." Investigators should, in principle, be able to employ the historical record to identify the degree to which colonies adapted the institutions they brought from their home countries to the

---

[2] See Acemoglu, Johnson, and Robinson, "Reversal of Fortune;" William Easterly and Ross Levine, "Tropics, Germs, and Crops: The Role of Endowments in Economic Development," *Journal of Monetary Economics* 50 (January 2003): 3–39.

new environments, and whether such adaptations followed any systematic patterns. Differences in income levels across the economies of the Americas were quite small for the first quarter of a millennium after the Europeans arrived, and per capita incomes in at least parts of the Caribbean and South America exceeded those in the colonies that were to become the United States and Canada. Looking back from the vantage point of the early twenty-first century, it is puzzling that the areas first settled, and the choices of the first Europeans to colonize parts of the Americas, were those that fell behind. Conversely, it is not clear why the societies that were established by Europeans who came late and had to settle for areas considered less favorable have proved more economically successful over the long run.

The explanations for these differentials in growth rates of per capita income over the second 250 years after the Europeans arrived in the Americas have, as noted, run the gamut, from an emphasis on strictly economic factors to mainly cultural and religious factors. Those who highlight the role of institutions traditionally credit the success of the North American economies to the superiority of English institutional heritage or to the better fit of Protestant beliefs with New World market institutions. Thus far, however, systematic investigation of these conceptions has been relatively limited, however, as has the analysis of just how these or other characteristics actually influenced the progress of institutional change over the long term.[3]

II

As stated in Chapter I, our examination of the basis for differential paths of development was originally inspired by the observation that the various British colonies in the New World evolved quite distinct societies and sets of economic institutions, despite beginning with roughly the same legal and cultural background and drawing immigrants from similar places and economic classes. Only a few were able to realize sustained economic

[3] For example, see Douglass C. North, "Institutions, Economic Growth and Freedom: An Historical Introduction," in *Freedom, Democracy and Economic Welfare*, Michael A. Walker, ed. 3–25 (Vancouver: Fraser Institute, 1988): John H. Coatsworth, "Notes on the Comparative Economic History of Latin America and the United States," in *Development and Underdevelopment in America: Contrasts of Economic Growth in North and Latin America in Historical Perspective*, eds. Walter L. Bernecker and Hans Werner Tobler 10–30 (Berlin: Walter de Gruyter, 1993): for discussions of why the English institutional heritage advantaged North America in realizing economic growth.

growth before the end of the nineteenth century. The majority that failed shared certain salient features with neighboring societies of different national heritages.[4] Impressed with how the evidence seemed inconsistent with the notions that British heritage or Protestantism were key, we developed an alternative explanation for the success of the colonies that came to make up the United States and Canada. Our view highlights the fundamental importance of the extreme differences across the New World societies in the extent of inequality in the distributions of wealth, human capital, and political influence that were present from the early histories of the colonies and due primarily to their respective factor endowments (or initial conditions, more generally).[5]

Some colonies, such as those established in the Caribbean or Brazil, enjoyed climate and soil conditions that were extremely well suited for growing crops such as sugar, coffee, rice, tobacco, and cotton. These crops were highly valued on world markets and most efficiently produced on large slave plantations. Their populations came to be dominated by large numbers of slaves obtained through international slave markets, and they quickly generated vastly unequal distributions of wealth, human capital, and political power. Spanish America was characterized early by extreme inequality, in large degree because of its factor endowments. The extensive native populations in the regions colonized by the Spanish (namely, Mexico and Peru) and the Spanish practices of awarding claims on land (which were significantly influenced by preexisting Native American organizations in those areas), native labor, and rich mineral resources available to members of the elite were powerful factors leading to inequality.[6]

---

[4] For analysis of differences among British colonies in the New World, and the causes of these differences, see the writing of Jack P. Greene, particularly, *Pursuits of Happiness* (Chapel Hill: University of North Carolina Press, 1988).

[5] See William M. Denevan, ed., *The Native Population in the Americas in 1492* (Madison: University of Wisconsin Press, 1976), Ch. 9.

[6] The pattern of European organized settlement and population growth differed quite considerably from the patterns in the Native American period. It is estimated that just prior to the coming of Columbus, the distribution of the Native American population was roughly 35 percent in South America, 10 percent in the Caribbean, 47 percent in Mexico and Central America, and 8 percent in what would become the United States and Canada. Mexico alone had 37 percent of the aboriginal American population. The earliest colonizer, Spain, went to the regions most heavily populated and the wealthiest at that time: Mexico, Peru, and elsewhere in South America and the Caribbean. The Portuguese went to Brazil – less heavily populated, but closer to the metropolis. Only the less densely populated areas of the United States, Canada, and the Caribbean were still available when the later colonizers, such as the British and French, arrived. See Denevan, ed., *Native Population*, 289–92. Prior to the arrival of the Spanish, the societies of Mexico and Peru

In contrast, small, family-sized farms were the rule in the northern colonies of the North American mainland, where climatic conditions favored a regime of mixed farming centered on grains and livestock that exhibited quite limited economies of scale in production and used few slaves. There were, moreover, relatively few Native Americans on the East Coast where the English, French, and Dutch colonies on the mainland were situated. These regions do not appear to have been very attractive to Europeans during the first quarter of a millennium after they began to colonize the New World, since only a small fraction of the migrants to the New World opted to locate there. These circumstances, however, fostered relatively homogeneous populations with relatively equal distributions of human capital and wealth.

These initial differences in the degree of inequality – which can be attributed largely to factor endowments broadly conceived – had profound and enduring effects on the paths of development of the respective economies. Previous treatments of the impact of inequality on growth have typically focused on the impact of inequality on savings or investment rates. Our hypothesis, however, concerns the possibility that the extreme differences in the extent of inequality that arose early in the history of the New World economies may have contributed to systematic differences in the ways institutions evolved. The logic is that great equality or homogeneity among the population led, over time, to more democratic political institutions, to more investment in public goods and infrastructure, and to institutions that offered relatively broad access to economic opportunities. In contrast, where there was extreme inequality, as in most of the societies of the Americas, political institutions were less democratic, investments in public goods and infrastructure were more limited, and the institutions that evolved tended to provide highly unbalanced access to economic opportunities and thereby greatly advantaged the elite. This mechanism, through which the extent of inequality affects the way institutions evolve, not only helps to explain the long-term persistence of differences in inequality among the respective societies, but it may also play a role in accounting for the differences in the growth rates

were quite sophisticated economically and politically. Agricultural production was high, permitting urbanization and a strong military, and the control of both the native-born and captive labor served as the basis for productive agricultural and mining sectors. The conquering Spanish directly adopted Native American institutions to provide for a labor force in these sectors, but this attempt was limited because of the large demographic decline triggered by European settlement. Much in terms of Native American production methods and labor-supply control was later adopted by the Spanish.

of per capita income over the last two centuries. If the processes of early industrialization were based on broad participation in the commercial economy, as suggested by evidence from the three leaders in that process (England, the United States, and the Netherlands), then economies with institutions that provided narrow access might have been less capable of realizing the potential of the new technologies, markets, and other economic opportunities that developed over the nineteenth century.

III

In the years since we first formulated this argument, we have engaged in an effort to subject the hypothesis to a test of consistency with the evidence. We have assembled a record of how certain strategic economic institutions evolved over time across the societies of the Americas, and we have examined in more detail the history of just how particular institutions developed in specific cases. This chapter lays out the historical basis for our theory and summarizes briefly what we have learned to date about the patterns in institutional development across the economies of the Americas. In general, we find systematic patterns in the way these institutions evolved. Societies that began with relatively extreme inequality tended to generate institutions that were more restrictive in providing access to economic opportunities than did those that began with relative equality or homogeneity among the population. The specific mechanisms that yield this pattern are complex, however, and they involve forces other than simply the political power of the elite. Such exercises in comparative history are nevertheless useful if, in specifying patterns of economic and institutional development, they lead to a better understanding of the issues involved and directions for future research.

IV

Many of the economic historians who study the United States have a reliance on Europe as their reference point. They normally focus on factor endowments in accounting for the record of economic changes. The explanations of U.S. growth based on resource endowments has a distinguished eighteenth century intellectual background. This country's long history of high and relatively equally distributed incomes, as well as impressive rates of advance, has been attributed to an extraordinarily favorable resource endowment. This conventional framework, tracing back to Benjamin Franklin and Adam Smith, highlights how widespread knowledge of European technologies among a free citizenry, coupled with the relative abundance of land and other resources per capita, would be expected to, as they did, yield a relatively high marginal productivity of labor or wage. Thus, a relatively egalitarian society was created, with a high standard of living and excellent prospects for realizing sustained progress. Hence, treatments of the settlement of the New World that are organized about a comparison of the thirteen colonies with the economies the settlers left behind provide a welcome test of the evidence and of the theory.[7]

Puzzles arise, however, when scholars of the United States turn to the experiences of Latin American economies. These New World societies also began with – by European standards of the time – vast supplies of land and natural resources per person and were among the most prosperous and coveted of the colonies in the seventeenth and eighteenth centuries. Indeed, so promising were these other regions that Europeans of the time generally regarded the thirteen British colonies on the North American mainland and Canada to be of relatively marginal economic interest – an opinion evidently shared by Native Americans who had concentrated disproportionately in the areas the Spanish eventually developed.[8] Yet, with their similar factor endowments, both the United States and Canada ultimately proved to be far more successful than the other colonies in realizing sustained economic growth over time. This stark contrast in performance suggests that factor endowments alone cannot explain the diversity of outcomes. In so doing, however, it raises the question of what can.

Those seeking to account for the divergent paths of the United States and Latin America often made reference to differences in institutions, where the concept is interpreted broadly to encompass not only formal political and legal structures but culture as well.[9] Many specific contrasts

---

7 See, for example, the discussion of colonial economic growth in John J. McCusker and Russell R. Menard, *The Economy of British America, 1607–1789* (Chapel Hill: University of North Carolina Press, 1985).

8 See the regional breakdowns provided in Denevan, ed., *Native Population*, 289–92, and Footnote 6, above.

9 For various discussions of the roles of institutions in economic growth, see Douglass C. North and Robert Paul Thomas, *The Rise of the Western World* (Cambridge: Cambridge University Press, 1973), and Douglass C. North, *Structure and Change in Economic History* (New York: Norton, 1981). For a comparison of Argentina and Canada that discusses the roles of institutions and makes reference to factor endowments, see Jeremy Adelman, *Frontier Development: Land, Labor, and Capital on Wheatlands of Argentina and Canada, 1890–1914* (Oxford: Oxford University Press, 1994).

in institutions have been proposed as being potentially significant, including the degree of democracy, the extent of rent seeking, security in property rights, the inclination to work hard or be entrepreneurial, as well as the specifics of culture and religion. Where there is explicit discussion of sources of institutional differences, the norm has been to relate them to presumed exogenous differences among the British, Spanish, Portuguese, and various Native American heritages. Although the possible influences of factor endowments on the path of economic and institutional development have not been ignored, it is useful to further identify and explore systematic patterns. It is as if the deviance of the Latin American economies from the United States has in itself been viewed as evidence of the predominance of exogenous, idiosyncratic factors. In reality, of course, it is the United States that has proved to be the atypical case.

Here we explore the possibility that the role of factor endowments has been underestimated, and the argument of independence of institutional development from New World factor endowments has been exaggerated. Our analysis is inspired by the observation that despite beginning with roughly the same legal and cultural background, as well as drawing immigrants from similar places and economic classes, the British colonies in the New World evolved quite distinct societies and sets of economic institutions. Only a few were ultimately able to realize sustained economic growth. The majority that failed shared certain salient features of their factor endowments with Latin American societies, and we suggest that although these conditions allowed for average standards of living that were high for that time, they were less well suited for the realization of sustained economic growth than were those prevailing in such economies as the United States and Canada.[10]

In brief we argue that a hemispheric perspective across the range of European colonies in the New World indicates that there were many influences – including factor endowments and attitudes toward them reflected in policy – that had enduring impacts on the structure of respective colonial economies and ultimately on their long-term paths of institutional and economic development. All colonies began with an abundance of land and other resources relative to labor, at least after the initial depopulation, but other aspects of their factor endowments varied, which contributed to substantial differences among them in the distribution of landholdings,

---

[10] For a description of the diversity among British colonies in the New World, see Greene, *Pursuits of Happiness*. See also Karen Ordahl Kupperman, *Providence Island, 1630–1641: The Other Puritan Colony* (Cambridge: Cambridge University Press, 1993).

wealth, and political power. The substantial shares of the populations composed of slaves and the scale economies served to generate vastly unequal distributions of both wealth and political power. The Spanish colonies in Mexico and Peru were likewise characterized early in their histories by extreme inequality, at least partially, because of their factor endowments. In these cases, the extensive existing populations of indigenous peoples and the Spanish practices of awarding claims on land, native labor, and rich mineral resources to members of the elite encouraged the formation of highly concentrated landholdings and extreme inequality.[11]

The circumstances in the colonies of the North American mainland encouraged the development of more equal distributions of wealth, more democratic political institutions, more extensive domestic markets, and the pursuit of more growth-oriented policies than did those in the former. We suggest further that there are reasons for expecting regions with more equal circumstances and rights to be more likely to realize sustained economic growth and that the breadth of evidence provided by the experiences of New World colonies supports this view.

V

The "discovery" and exploration of the Americas by the Europeans were part of a grand long-term effort to exploit the economic opportunities in under-populated or under-defended territories around the world. European nations competed for claims and set about extracting material and other advantages through both the pursuit of transitory enterprises, like expeditions, and the establishment of long-term settlements. At the individual level, people, both elite and humble, invested their energy and other resources across a range of activities and projects that were rent-seeking as well as conventionally entrepreneurial. At both the levels of

---

[11] This paragraph is based on readings in numerous primary and secondary sources. For Latin America, particularly useful secondary works were James Lockhart and Stuart B. Schwartz, *Early Latin America: A History of Colonial Spanish America and Brazil* (Cambridge: Cambridge University Press, 1983); Lyle N. McAlister, *Spain and Portugal in the New World, 1492–1700* (Minneapolis: University of Minnesota Press, 1984); Charles Gibson, *Spain in America* (New York: Harper & Row, 1966); Mark A. Burkholder and Lyman L. Johnson *Colonial Latin America* 3rd. ed. (New York: Oxford University Press, 1998); and Leslie Bethell, ed., *The Cambridge History of Latin America*, 11 vols. (Cambridge: Cambridge University Press, 1984–2008). For the British colonies, see McCusker and Menard, *Economy of British America*; and Robert E. Gallman and John J. Wallis, eds., *American Economic Growth and Standards of Living Before the Civil War*, 311–40 (Chicago: University of Chicago Press, 1992). For more on primary sources, see Ch. 7.

national governments and private agents, formidable problems of organization were raised by what appeared to the Europeans as radically novel environments as well as by the difficulties of effecting the massive and historically unprecedented intercontinental flows of labor and capital. In surveying the histories of the New World colonies, enormous diversity in the specific types of ventures and/or institutions is evident. The explanatory factors include differences among colonies in the backgrounds of their European and African immigrants, in the backgrounds of the indigenous populations, in factor endowments narrowly defined (land, labor, climate, and other resources), as well as chance or idiosyncratic circumstances.

A central issue, common to all of the colonies, was labor supply which had obvious and substantial implications for the ability to take advantage of the abundant natural resources available in the New World. The seriousness of this constraint was a major reason why the Spanish – the first Europeans to enter – chose to focus their efforts on the areas in the Americas with the largest concentrations of native populations, Mexico and Peru. Another indication of the high marginal productivity of labor is the extensive and unprecedented flow of migrants from Europe and Africa to the New World. This process occurred despite the high costs of traversing the Atlantic, and this flow accelerated over time (see Table 1.2).

Common to all New World colonies was a high marginal product of labor, especially of European labor. One indication of this return to labor is the extensive and unprecedented flow of migrants who sailed the Atlantic from Europe and Africa to virtually all of the colonies despite the high cost of transportation.[12] Moreover, the fact that over 60 percent of these immigrants were Africans brought over involuntarily as slaves

---

[12] Table 1.2 is based on the estimates of David Eltis. For estimates through 1930, see David Eltis, "Free and Coerced Transatlantic Migrations: Some Comparisons," *American Historical Review* 88 (April 1983): 251–280. For recent discussions and descriptions of migration flows in the period studied, see, in particular, Ralph Davis, *The Rise of the Atlantic Economies* (Ithaca: Cornell University Press, 1973); Nicholas Sánchez-Albornoz, *The Population of Latin America: A History* (Berkeley: University of California Press, 1974); Philip D. Curtin, *The Atlantic Slave Trade: A Census* (Madison: University of Wisconsin Press, 1969); P. C. Emmer and Magnus Mörner, eds., *European Expansion and Migration: Essays on the Intercontinental Migration from Africa, Asia, and Europe"* (New York: Berg, 1992); Ida Altman and James Horn, eds., *"To Make America": European Emigration in the Early Modern Period* (Berkeley: University of California Press, 1991); and the essays by Woodrow Borah, Peter Boyd-Bowman, and Magnus Mörner in Fredi Chiappelli, ed., *First Images of America: The Impact of the New World on the Old* (Berkeley: University of California Press, 1976).

is a testament to the predominance of the economic motive of capturing the gains associated with a high productivity of labor. With their prices set in competitive international markets, slaves ultimately flowed to those locations where their productivity met the international standard. There were no serious national or cultural barriers to owning or using them; slaves were welcomed in the colonies of all the major European powers, with only Spanish and British settlements drawing less than two-thirds of their pre-1760 immigrants from Africa. In contrast, over 80 percent of all immigrants in the French and Dutch colonies through 1760 were slaves, and the figure was over 70 percent in the Portuguese colonies.

As the rate of movement to the New World accelerated over time, there were several salient changes in the composition and direction of the flow of immigrants. First, the fraction of migrants who were slaves grew continuously over the four subperiods specified in Table 1.2, from roughly 25 percent prior to 1580 to nearly 80 percent between 1700 and 1760. Second, there was a marked shift in relative numbers away from the Spanish colonies, whose share of white and slave migrants declined continuously from over seventy percent between 1500 and 1580 to about 14 percent between 1700 and 1760. This precipitous fall in the relative prominence of the Spanish colonies was only partially due to the extraordinary rise of British America. The rate of flow to Spanish America peaked between 1580 and 1640, during which 477,000 immigrants settled in the colonies of Spain, with 291,000 of those to Portugal, and 6,000 of those to France. Between 1700 and 1760, however, the numbers of new settlers in Spanish America were stagnant at 464,000, while the numbers moving to the possessions of Portugal and France had grown to 1,068,000 and 441,000, respectively. During the interval of just over a century, the flow of migrants increased to the colonies of all major nations except Spain. This steep relative decline in migration to Spanish America does not appear to have been due to an unsustainably high flow from Spain during the early phase of colonization. As implied by the population estimates for the home countries shown in Table 2.1, Spain was contributing a far smaller percentage of its citizens than Portugal, and a roughly similar percentage to Britain, through 1760.[13]

---

[13] The decline in Spain's population during the early seventeenth century is generally attributed to the war between Spain and the Netherlands as well as an increased prevalence of disease throughout the Mediterranean, including outbreaks of the plague and cholera. As seen in Table 2.1, population had still not recovered by 1700. Whether the decline heightened Spanish concern about depopulation, and was a factor in accounting for the restrictive immigration policies that were implemented, is an interesting issue

TABLE 2.1. *Populations of European Countries During the Era of Colonization*

Country	1600 (millions)	1700 (millions)	1800 (millions)	Per annum growth rate, 1600–1800
Britain	6.25	9.30	16.00	0.47
France	20.50	22.00	29.00	0.17
Netherlands	1.50	2.00	2.00	0.14
Portugal	2.00	2.00	2.75	0.16
Spain	8.50	8.00	11.50	0.15

Source: McEvedy and Jones (1978), 49, 57, 65, 101, 103.

A more important factor in accounting for the stagnation of the rate at which the Spanish colonies attracted Europeans was Spain's severe tightening of the restrictions on the numbers who could come, reflecting the demographic difficulties faced by the Spanish with a declining population. Whereas the other big players in the Americas – Britain and Portugal – were neutral toward or encouraging of immigration, Spain, with the support if not instigation of the *peninsulares* and *criollos* who were already there, progressively raised obstacles to those who might have otherwise ventured to the New World to seek their fortunes.

Another, and not unrelated, change suggested by these figures is the growing share of immigrants settling in colonies that specialized in the production of sugar, tobacco, coffee, and other staple crops for world markets. This increased share of immigrants going to areas specializing in export crops is evident from the increasing proportion of migrants going to the colonies of Portugal, France, and the Netherlands, as well as the continued quantitative dominance of the West Indies and the southern mainland as preferred destinations of migrants to British America (more than 90 percent; see Table 2.2). Although these colonies suffered from high mortality rates, they attracted the great majority of European migrants because survivors could earn exceptionally high incomes. Virtually all of these colonies were heavily oriented toward the production of sugar and other such valuable crops, given their well-suited soils and climates (sugar was the most important commodity in world trade at the time).[14]

deserving of more study. See Jan de Vries, *The Economy of Europe in an Age of Crisis, 1600–1750* (Cambridge: Cambridge University Press, 1976), 4–5.

[14] There is now substantial literature documenting the existence of very significant economies in the production of certain agricultural products on large slave plantations. The magnitude of these economies varied from crop to crop, but appear to have been

TABLE 2.2. *Patterns of Net Migration to and Wealthholding in Categories of British Colonies*

Net migration (000)	New England		Middle Atlantic		Southern		West Indies	
	No.	Pct.	No.	Pct.	No.	Pct.	No.	Pct.
Whites								
1630–80	28	11.0	4	1.6	81	31.9	141	55.5
1680–1730	− 4	− 1.8	45	19.9	111	49.1	74	32.7
1730–80	− 27	− 10.7	101	40.1	136	54.0	42	16.7
TOTAL	− 3	− 0.4	150	20.5	328	44.8	257	35.1
Blacks								
1650–80	0	–	0	–	5	3.7	130	96.3
1680–1730	2	0.47	5	0.9	64	12.0	461	86.7
1730–80	− 6	− 0.9	− 1	− 0.2	150	23.4	497	77.7
TOTAL	− 4	− 0.3	4	0.3	219	16.8	1,088	83.2
1630–80	28	7.2	4	1.0	86	22.1	271	69.7
1680–1730	− 2	− 0.3	50	6.6	175	23.1	535	70.6
1730–80	− 33	− 3.7	100	11.2	286	32.1	539	60.4
GRAND TOTAL, 1630–1780	− 7	− 0.3	154	7.6	547	26.8	1,345	66.0
Wealthholding, c. 1774 (in £)								
Total per capita	36.6		41.9		54.7		84.1	
Nonhuman per capita	36.4		40.2		36.4		43.0	
Total per free capita	38.2		45.8		92.7		1,200.0	
Nonhuman per free capita	38.0		44.1		61.6		754.3	

Source: Galenson (1996).

Notes: The estimates for wealthholding in the West Indies pertain to Jamaica.

most extensive in the cultivation of sugar, coffee, rice, and cotton; small, but present, in tobacco; and absent in grains. Overall, there are two types of compelling evidence in support of this generalization. The first consists of comparisons of total factor productivity by size of the producing unit, as has been done for the U.S. South prior to the Civil War. The second is the consistent pattern across economies of dramatic and persistent differences in the sizes and types of farms producing different crops or in the shares of output of those crops accounted for by different classes of farms. For example, virtually all sugar in the New World was produced by large slave plantations until after the wave of slave emancipations during the nineteenth century. In contrast, the great bulk of wheat and other grains were produced on small-scale farms. For further discussions on the subject and evidence, see Robert William Fogel, *Without Consent or Contract* (New York: Norton, 1989); Stanley L. Engerman, "Contract Labor, Sugar and Technology in the Nineteenth Century," *Journal of Economic History* 43 (September 1983): 635–59; and Noël Deerr, *The History of Sugar*, 2 vols. (London: Chapman and Hall, 1949–1950).

What stands out from the estimates presented in Table 2.3 is that those of European descent made up small percentages of the populations that comprised nearly all of the New World economies, even well into the nineteenth century. The populations of those colonies suitable for cultivating sugar, like Barbados and Brazil, came to be quickly dominated by people of African descent who had been imported, thus having a major impact on income distribution.[15] The Spanish colonies were predominantly populated by Indians or mestizos, largely because they had generally been established and built up in those places where there had been substantial populations of Native Americans beforehand and because of the restrictive immigration policies of Spain. As a result, less than 20 percent of the population in colonies like Mexico, Peru, and Chile were composed of whites as late as the turn of the nineteenth century. The Spanish Antilles, however, did have a relatively large white population, reflecting the limited number of Indians after depopulation and the long lag between the beginnings of the settlement and the sugar boom that developed in Cuba only after the start of nineteenth century, when slave imports and the size of producing units both increased.[16]

VI

It is sometimes suggested that the distinctiveness of the colonies of the North American mainland was largely due to the effects of the British institutional heritage. Consideration of the experiences of the French New World colonies, however, tends to highlight the importance of environment and factor endowments. French settlements resembled the British including two distinct types. In the Caribbean, the French sugar islands, particularly Saint Domingue, grew rapidly over the eighteenth century, to such an extent that they became more populous and productive than

---

[15] See, in particular, Richard S. Dunn, *Sugar and Slaves: The Rise of the Planter Class in the English West Indies, 1624–1713* (Chapel Hill: University of North Carolina Press, 1972) on the English colonies; Stuart B. Schwartz, *Sugar Plantations in the Formation of Brazilian Society: Bahia, 1550–1835* (Cambridge: Cambridge University Press, 1985) on Brazil.

[16] On the Caribbean in general, and for a discussion of the patterns of Cuban settlement, see Franklin W. Knight, *The Caribbean: The Genesis of a Fragmented Nationalism*, 2nd ed. (New York: Oxford University Press, 1990). For an ethnic breakdown of Caribbean populations in 1750, 1830, and 1880, see Stanley L. Engerman and B. W. Higman, "The Demographic Structure of the Caribbean Slave Societies in the Eighteenth and Nineteenth Centuries," in *General History of the Caribbean*, vol. 3: *The Plantation Economies*, ed. Franklin W. Knight: 45–104 (Paris: UNESCO, 1997).

TABLE 2.3. *Distribution and Composition of Population in New World Economies*

Economy	Year	White (%)	Black (%)	Native American Population (%)	Share of Region in New World Population
PANEL A					
Spanish America	1570	1.3	2.5	96.3	83.5
	1650	6.3	9.3	84.4	84.3
	1825	18.0	22.5	59.5	55.2
	1935	35.5	13.3	50.4	30.3
Brazil	1570	2.4	3.5	94.1	7.6
	1650	7.4	13.7	78.9	7.7
	1825	23.4	55.6	21.0	11.6
	1935	41.0	35.5	23.0	17.1
U.S. and Canada	1570	0.2	0.2	99.6	8.9
	1650	12.0	2.2	85.8	8.1
	1825	79.6	16.7	3.7	33.2
	1935	89.4	8.9	1.4	52.6
PANEL B					
1. Barbados	1690	25.0	75.0	–	
2. Barbados	1801	19.3	80.7	–	
3. Mexico	1793	18.0	10.0	72.0	
4. Peru	1795	12.6	7.3	80.1	
5. Venezuela	1800–09	25.0	62.0	13.0	
6. Cuba	1792	49.0	51.0	–	
7. Brazil	1798	31.1	61.2	7.8	
8. Chile	1790	8.3	6.7	85.0	
9. U.S. Nation	1860	84.9	14.0	1.1	
10. U.S. South	1860	61.7	37.7	0.7	
11. U.S. North	1860	96.2	2.6	1.3	
12. Canada	1881	97.0	0.5	2.5	
13. Argentina	1918	95.6	1.2	3.2	

Sources:
Panel A: The data for 1570, 1650, and 1825 are from Rosenblat 1954: 88 (1570); 58 (1650); 35–36 (1825). The data for 1935 are from Kuczynski 1936:109–10.
Panel B: (1–2) Watts 1987: 311; (3–6) Lockhart and Schwartz 1983: 342; (7) Merrick and Graham 1979: 29; (8) Mamalakis 1980: 7–9; (9–11) U.S. Census Bureau 1864: 598–99; (12) Leacy 1983: Series A154 – 184; (13) Tornquist & Co. 1919: 23.
Notes:
Panel A: The Antilles have been included with Spanish America in all years. The 1825 category *castas*, which included *mestizajes* and *mulattos* and represented 18.17 percent of the total population in Spanish America, was divided two-thirds Indian, and one-third black (except for the Antilles, where all were considered to be blacks). In 1935, there were a number of people counted as "others" (generally Asians), so the distributions may not total 100 percent.
Panel B: The Argentine figure for Indians is considerably lower than that for 1825 given in Kuczynski (67.9 percent), 106 and by Rosenblat (31.7 percent – possibly about one-third castas, most being mestizaje), but is above that of Kuczynski for 1935, which is under 1 percent of the total population. Lockhart and Schwartz (1983), 342, estimate, the share of Indians in the Buenos Aires population at the start of the nineteenth century was similar to that in Argentina at the start of the twentieth century.

the British islands.[17] Moreover, the French islands produced more of the principal products of sugar and coffee than their British neighbors, and several contemporaries argued for a greater efficiency of the French in sugar production.[18] The basic institutions of the French colonies in the Caribbean were similar to those of the British, with large slave plantations producing sugar, and in both cases they were required to trade with the metropolitan power. The end of French power in this area was not related to trade or production misfortunes, but rather to a successful uprising of the slave population in Haiti in 1791, leading to independence in 1804.[19] The second revolution in the Americas did, however, lead in a different direction than had the American Revolution against the British. For Haiti, the sugar economy never recovered, and for both political as well as economic reasons, imports from and exports to France declined dramatically. The independent United States, however, was one of Britain's leading trading partners.

France's second major colony in the New World was Canada, whose climate made it seem of less value than the northeastern regions of the British colonies – to say nothing of the colonies in the Caribbean. The French began settlement with an attempt to introduce a seignorial system for agricultural landholdings. This legally persisted until the nineteenth century, but it was not successfully enforced and gave way to a structure of small farms producing grains. There were some restrictions on immigration to French Canada by nationality and religion, and overall it received very few immigrants compared to the British mainland colonies. Limited population no doubt cost the French during the Seven Years War, which ended with the transfer of Canada to the British in 1763. After the military takeover, the British did little to change the basic social institutions, particularly regarding religion, education, and landholding. Slavery had never been strongly entrenched in Canada, and freedom was granted to the relatively few slaves there within a half-century.

---

[17] See, for example, David Eltis, "The Slave Economies of the Caribbean: Structure, Performance, Evolution and Significance," in UNESCO *General History of the Caribbean,* vol. 3: *The Plantation Economies,* ed. Franklin W. Knight: 105–137 (Paris: UNESCO, 1997).

[18] See, for example, Adam Smith, *Inquiry Into the Nature and Causes of the Wealth of Nations* (Oxford: Clarendon Press, 1976).

[19] See Laurent Dubois, *Avengers of the New World: The Story of the Haitian Revolution* (Cambridge, MA: Harvard University Press, 2004).

VII

The territories that were to become the United States and Canada had only small numbers of Native Americans prior to the arrival of the Europeans, so that the composition of their populations soon came to be essentially determined by the groups who immigrated and their respective rates of natural increase. Because their endowments were generally more hospitable to the cultivation of grains than of sugar, these colonies absorbed relatively more Europeans than African slaves, as compared to other areas of high immigration in the New World, and their populations were, accordingly, composed primarily of whites. Even with substantial numbers of slaves in the U.S. South, roughly 80 percent of the population in the United States and Canada was white in 1825, while the shares in Brazil and in the remainder of the New World economies overall were below 25 and 20 percent respectively. It would not be until later in the nineteenth century that the populations of Latin American countries like Argentina and Chile would attain the predominantly European character that they have today, both through inflows from Europe as well as increased death rates and low fertility among native Indians. This greater prevalence of white property owners in the United States and Canada may help to explain why there was less inequality and more potential for economic growth in these economies. Both the more equal distributions of human capital and other resources, as well as the relative abundance of the politically and economically powerful racial group, encouraged the evolution of legal and political institutions that were more conducive to active participation in a competitive market economy by broad segments of the population.

The estimates of the composition of the population suggest that colonists of European descent could enjoy relatively elite status and rely on slaves and Indians to provide the bulk of the manual labor in most of the New World. It should not be surprising, therefore, that the principal areas of exception, the northern United States and Canada, were at first less attractive to Europeans. Reasons other than economic for the European movement to the New World must have been of secondary importance in general. If they were not attracted primarily by the prospect of improvements in material welfare and rights to the ownership of land, it is not easy to comprehend why so many of them would have voluntarily made multiyear commitments to serve as indentured servants, braved the discomfort and substantial risks to their lives on their voyages, which were located in the adverse, disease-infested environments characteristic of the places best suited for growing sugar and tobacco. The implications of the magnitude of the intercontinental migration are made all the more compelling by the awareness that the relative, if not absolute, stagnation of flow to Spanish colonies was to a large degree affected by the tight control of the authorities over the number and composition of migrants.[20]

Although direct information on the productivity or incomes of individuals during the colonial period is fragmentary, the overall weight of the evidence seems clear. The patterns of migration, wage rates prevailing in free labor markets, anthropometric measurements,[21] as well as data on wealth-holdings, all suggest that incomes and labor productivity for Europeans throughout the New World must have been high by Old World standards. The estimates of wealth-holdings on the eve of the American Revolution for the English colonies, presented in Table 2.2, provide perhaps the most systematic, comparative record of economic performance across colonies. The qualitative result is robust no matter which of the four alternative definitions of wealth is employed. Jamaica, representative of the many colonies in the Caribbean specializing in sugar, generated as much nonhuman wealth per capita as any group of colonies on the North American mainland, and much more per free individual. The stark contrast between the per capita and per free individual figures reflects the larger shares of the population composed of slaves, the high

---

[20] In addition to note 12 above, see the discussions of Spanish migration in Ida Altman, *Emigrants and Society: Extremadura and America in the Sixteenth Century.* (Berkeley: University of California Press, 1989); Magnus Mörner, *Adventurers and Proletarians: The Story of Migrants in Latin America* (Pittsburgh: University of Pittsburgh Press, 1985); and Mary M. Kritz, "The British and Spanish Migration Systems in the Colonial Era: A Policy Framework," in *The Peopling of the Americas,* vol. 1, 263–81 (Vera Cruz: IUSSP, 1992): as well as several old classics: E. G. Bourne, *Spain in America, 1450–1580* (New York: Harper Brothers, 1904); Bernard Moses, *The Establishment of Spanish Rule in America* (New York: G. P. Putnam, 1898); and C. H. Haring, *The Spanish Empire in America* (New York: Oxford University Press, 1947). Spanish policies also reduced the numbers of slaves being imported, both through direct limitations as well as by decreasing demand by placing more restrictions than other New World economies on the use of slaves in its colonies (lessening their value to slaveholders). These policies may help to explain why Spanish colonies like Mexico, Cuba, and Puerto Rico were relatively slow to turn to production of sugar on large-scale plantations. See Fogel, *Without Consent,* 36–40 for a discussion of this issue.

[21] See the work of Kenneth Sokoloff and Georgia Villaflor, "The Early Achievement of Modern Stature in America," *Social Science History* 6 (Summer 1982): 453–481, and Kenneth Sokoloff "The Heights of Americas in Three Centuries: Some Economic and Demographic Implications," in *The Biological Standard of Living in Three Continents* John Komlos, ed., 133–150 (Boulder: Westview Press, 1995).

returns to ownership of slaves, and the much greater inequality in the sugar colonies. Among those on the mainland, the record of the southern colonies (from the Chesapeake and South) fell between that of Jamaica and those of their northern neighbors (New England and the Middle Atlantic) – with roughly equivalent performance on a per capita basis but offering much more wealth to the average free individual.

Systematic estimates of the records of relative per capita income over time have not yet been constructed for a number of the New World economies, but Table 1.1 and Figure 1.1 convey a sense of the current state of knowledge. The figures suggest that the advantage in per capita income enjoyed by the United States and Canada over Latin American economies materialized during the late eighteenth and nineteenth centuries, when the United States as well as Canada began to realize sustained economic growth well ahead of their neighbors in the hemisphere. Indeed, as John Coatsworth has suggested, there may have been virtual parity (given the roughness in estimates) in terms of per capita income (and perhaps also inequality) in 1700 between Mexico and the British colonies on the mainland (that were to become the United States). Moreover, product per capita (as well as, in Jamaica, capital per capita) appears to have been far greater in the sugar Caribbean, while David Eltis finds that in Barbados the level of per capita income was more than 50 percent higher.[22] If the current estimates are correct, then those of European descent in Mexico and Barbados (as well as possibly in Cuba) were much better off than their counterparts on the North American mainland, because they accounted for a much smaller share of the population and their incomes were far higher than those of the Native Americans or slaves. Estimates of per capita income for other Latin American economies do not extend as far back, but it does seem apparent that they must have been closer to U.S. levels during this era than they have been since. Moreover, by the same logic as proposed for Mexico, incomes generated by those of European descent must have been comparable or higher in South America and the Caribbean than in the northern parts of North America.

Although all of the major New World colonies may have provided high living standards for Europeans, it is clear that they evolved dissimilar economic structures and institutions early in their histories. This divergence has long been noted and explanations have often made in reference to

---

[22] See John H Coatsworth, "Notes on the Comparative Economic History of Latin America and the United States," and David Eltis, "The Total Product of Barbados, 1664–1701," *Journal of Economic History* 55 (June 1995): 321–38.

differences in the origins or backgrounds of the settlers. With the recent accumulation of evidence regarding wide disparities among colonies of the same European country, alternative sources of diversity deserve an examination.

Our analysis of the role of factor endowments has antecedents in the work of Evsey Domar and W. Arthur Lewis, who were concerned with the problems that factor endowments can pose for underdeveloped economies. These scholars explored diametrically opposed cases, with Domar focusing on labor scarcity and Lewis on labor surplus.[23] We interpret factor endowment more broadly, however, and argue that the United States and Canada were relatively unusual among New World colonies, because their factor endowments (including climates, soils, and the density of native populations) predisposed them toward paths with relatively equal distributions of wealth and income and corresponding institutions that favored the participation of a broad range of the population in commercial and public activity. The patterns of early industrialization in the United States suggest that such widespread involvement in commercial activity was important in realizing the onset of economic growth. In contrast, the factor endowments of the other New World colonies led to highly unequal distributions of wealth, income, human capital, and political power early in their histories, along with institutions that protected the elites. Together, these conditions inhibited the spread of commercial activity among the general population, lessening, in our view, the prospects for growth.

VIII

Similar paths of development were repeated among all of the Spanish colonies that retained substantial native populations.[24] During the initial phase of conquest and settlement, the Spanish authorities allocated

---

[23] Evsey D. Domar, "The Causes of Slavery or Serfdom: A Hypothesis," *Journal of Economic History* 30 (March 1970): 18–32. The problem of growth with "unlimited supplies of labor" occupied most of W. Arthur Lewis's work on economic development. Probably the first full presentation of this model can be seen in W. Arthur Lewis, "Economic Development with Unlimited Supplies of Labor," *Manchester School of Economic and Social Studies* 23 (May 1955): 139–91.

[24] Indeed, there are striking similarities even in colonies that did not retain substantial native populations. In formulating policies, the Spanish authorities seem to have focused on circumstances in major colonies like Mexico and Peru, but applied them systemwide. Hence, policies like restrictions on migration from Europe and grants of large blocks of land, mineral resources, and native labor to the early settlers were generally in effect throughout Spanish America. See Lockhart and Schwartz, *Early Latin America*; and

encomiendas, often involving vast areas with claims on labor and tributes from natives to relatively small numbers of individuals. The value of these grants was somewhat eroded over time by reassignment or expiration, new awards, and the precipitous decline of the native population over the sixteenth century that necessarily decreased the amount of tribute to be extracted. These *encomiendas* had powerful lingering effects, however, and ultimately gave way to large-scale *estancias* or *haciendas*, which obtained their labor services partially through obligations from natives but increasingly through local labor markets. Although the processes of transition from *encomienda* to *hacienda* are not well understood, it is evident that large-scale agriculture remained dominant, especially in districts with linkages to extensive markets. It is also clear that the distribution of wealth remained highly unequal, not only at given points in time but also over time, because elite families were able to maintain their status over generations. These same families, of course, generally acted as *corregidors* and other local representatives of the Spanish government in the countryside, wielding considerable local political authority.[25]

An important category of New World colonies is best typified by the colonies on the North American mainland – chiefly those that became the United States but some that became Canada, as well. With the exception of the southern states of the United States, these economies were neither endowed with substantial indigenous populations able to provide labor nor with climates or soils that gave them a comparative advantage in the production of crops characterized by major economies of scale or slave labor. For these reasons, their growth and development, especially in areas north of the Chesapeake, were based on the labor of those of European descent who had similar and relatively high levels of human capital. Correspondingly equal distributions of wealth were also encouraged by the limited advantages to large producers in the production of grains and hays

James Lockhart, *Spanish Peru: 1532–1560. A Social History*, 2nd ed. (Madison: University of Wisconsin Press, 1994).

[25] See the excellent and comprehensive overview of the *encomienda*, the evolution of large-scale estates, and their relation to preconquest forms of social organization in different parts of Spanish America that is provided by Lockhart and Schwartz, *Early Latin America*. As they emphasize, the paths of institutional development varied somewhat among the Spanish colonies, reflecting significant differences between Indian populations in "social capabilities" and other attributes. For example, the preconquest forms of social organization for Indians in highland areas were quite different from those of populations on the plains or in the jungle. For a fascinating discussion of the workings of the early *encomienda* system in Peru, including differences in the system among the colonies due to the different interests of early and late arrivals, and to the relevance of mineral resources, see Lockhart, *Spanish Peru*.

predominant in regions like the Middle Atlantic and New England. With abundant land and low capital requirements, the great majority of adult men were able to operate as independent proprietors. Conditions were somewhat different in the southern colonies, where crops like tobacco and rice did exhibit some scale economies, but even here, the size of the slave plantations, as well as the degree of inequality in these colonies, was quite modest by the standards of Brazil or the sugar islands.[26]

The first major export products from Spanish America were not agricultural products, but silver and gold mined primarily in Mexico, Peru, and what is now Bolivia. These mines had existed and were used by various groups of Native Americans prior to Spanish settlement. Throughout the world, mining had long relied on some variant of coerced labor, and the pattern in Spanish America was no different. The labor force consisted largely of Native Americans, who were nominally free but were coerced by various mechanisms to serve in the mines. Without this compulsion, mining output would, no doubt, have been quite limited, as labor in mines was exhausting and associated with high death rates. This was not of primary concern to the ruling elite, however. Indeed, the great value that Spanish policymakers placed on silver and gold meant that areas without mines, such as the colonies in the Caribbean and Argentina, were of secondary interest and were forced to deal with policies that had been framed to support the colonies with mines. This typically meant limitations on shipping and trade that held back development in these outlying areas.

To almost the same degree as in the colonial sugar economies, the economic structures that evolved in this group of colonies were greatly influenced by the factor endowments, viewed in broad terms. The valuable mineral resources and the abundance of low-human-capital labor certainly contributed to the extremely unequal distributions of wealth and income that generally came to prevail in these economies. Moreover, without the abundant supply of native labor, the generous awards of property and tribute to the earliest settlers would either not have been worth so much or not been possible, and it is highly unlikely that Spain would have introduced the tight restrictions on European migration to

---

[26] For a dissenting analysis regarding the Brazilian slave distributions based on early nineteenth-century data, see Schwartz, *Sugar Plantations*, chap. 16, which is based on Stuart B. Schwartz, "Patterns of Slaveholding in the Americas: New Evidence From Brazil," *American Historical Review* 87 (February 1982): 56–86. For another skeptical view, regarding the US, see James R. Irwin, "Exploring the Affinity of Wheat and Slavery in the Virginia Piedmont," *Explorations in Economic History* 25 (July 1988): 295–332.

its colonies that resulted in the small share of European descendants in the population. The early settlers in Spanish America had endorsed, and won, formidable requirements for obtaining permission to go to the New World – a policy that surely limited the flow of migrants and helped to preserve the political and economic advantages the early settlers enjoyed.[27]

IX

Efforts to implant a European-style organization of agriculture in North America, based on concentrated ownership of land combined with labor provided by tenant farmers or indentured servants (as when Pennsylvania and New York were established) invariably failed: The large landholdings unraveled because even men of comparatively ordinary means could set up independent farms when land was cheap and scale economies were absent. William Penn, for example, who was a central member of the elite, was not able to get what he wanted in such an environment despite his enormous wealth.

In the United States, the South thrived in terms of output per capita, free and slave, and it attracted the bulk of migrants to the British colonies on the mainland through the eighteenth century. It lagged behind the North, however, both before and after the Civil War, in evolving a set of political institutions that were conducive to broad participation in the commercial economy. The South was thus an intermediate case: It displayed many parallels with other New World economies that relied on slavery early in their histories, but it ultimately realized a record of development more like the northern United States or Canada, and it ultimately achieved a per capita income equal to that of the North.

Spain also had several colonies that might be considered to fall between categories. Most notable among them are Argentina, Costa Rica, and Uruguay. These regions are not suited for growing sugar as a major crop, and Argentina ultimately flourished as a grain producer.[28] Yet substantial

---

[27] Because of the differences in settlement patterns, the fights for control between *criollos* and *peninsulares* in Spanish America took a different form from the colonial-metropolitan conflicts of British America. For a discussion of a more traditional form of conflict between the colonies and the metropolis with respect to the empire's trade policy, see Geoffrey J. Walker, *Spanish Politics and Imperial Trade, 1700–1789* (Bloomington: Indiana University Press, 1979). For a discussion of early Peru, see Lockhart *Spanish Peru.*

[28] On the late and never really important Argentine sugar industry, see Donna J. Guy *Argentine Sugar Politics: Tucuman and the Generation of Eighty* (Tempe: Center for Latin American Studies, Arizona State University, 1980). On the Argentine economy in

inequality in the distributions of land, human capital, and political influence was clearly apparent in Argentina by the second half of the nineteenth century. Argentina remained sparsely populated at the time of independence, largely as a result of Spanish restrictions on immigration and trade. Spain had directed shipping to its colonies in South America through Mexico and Peru until the Bourbon reforms of the late eighteenth century. The initial development of inequality probably came with the massive grants of land made to favored families and military leaders during the first half of the nineteenth century. These large landholdings might have been expected to splinter over time in an environment of extreme labor scarcity but this tendency appears to have been at least partially offset by several factors: The public lands disposed of in these early allocations proved to be among the most valuable throughout the country in terms of both fertility and location. Scale economies in raising (or harvesting) the cattle that ran wild on the pampas made it infeasible to make productive use of smaller parcels of land. Argentina lacked a land policy that was oriented toward improving access to land, in contrast to Canada or the United States. Indeed, despite protracted political debate on the connection between land policy and immigration, Argentina continued to dispose of its public lands through large allotments to the military or private development companies until late in the nineteenth century.[29] Substantial inequality was thus in place here before the development of the economy was far along, although it was not nearly as extreme as it was in most of the other Spanish American societies, and the process by which it had evolved was more complicated.

Finally, another way of illustrating that the marked differences in the extent of inequality across New World economies emerged early and were due primarily to initial factor endowments (or initial conditions) is

general, see Carlos F. Diaz Alejandro, *Essays on the Economic History of the Argentine Republic* (New Haven: Yale University Press, 1970); and for a description of land and immigration policy in Argentina, see Donald Castro, *The Development and Politics of Argentine Immigration Policy, 1852–1914: To Govern is to Populate* (San Francisco: Mellen Research University Press, 1991); Adelman, *Frontier Development*; Jeremy Adelman, *Republic of Capital: Buenos Aires and the Legal Transformation of the Atlantic World* (Stanford: Stanford University Press, 1999); and Gerardo della Paolera and Alan M. Taylor eds. *A New Economic History of Argentina* (Cambridge: Cambridge University Press, 2003).

[29] For most of the period, the dominant political faction, with support based in Buenos Aires, opposed the implementation of policies that would have provided for broad access to land. See Castro, *Argentine Immigration Policy*, for extensive discussion of this issue and the linkages between the debates over immigration and land policies.

to specifically address the issue of whether national or religious heritage was the fundamental determinant of the respective path of institutional and economic development. Clearly, they did have impacts, but we note that the importance of adjustments that individuals and societies made in response to new or changing environments has not been sufficiently appreciated. Some often presume that institutions are inflexible, even across very different circumstances or over a long period of time. As already noted, the idea that the distinctiveness of the North American mainland colonies was largely due to the effects of the British institutional heritage seems inconsistent with the observation that there was extraordinary diversity in paths of development across the many other New World societies with a British or other European heritage, as was also true of the colonists of the different British colonies. Most did not fare quite so well, and Guiana, Belize, and Jamaica generally resemble their neighbors that began with similar factor endowments but with other national heritages. Perhaps the most striking example is the contrast between the two colonies established simultaneously by the Puritans early in the seventeenth century: Providence Island (off the coast of Nicaragua and now part of Colombia) and the more famous Massachusetts Bay Colony. Although the eventual overrunning of Providence Island makes for a rather short time series, Karen Kupperman's comparative study demonstrates that the paths of the two Puritan colonies diverged radically from the beginning.[30] We are all familiar with the intense work ethic of the Puritans who settled in the cold harsh New England environment, but the Puritans who located on Providence Island quickly determined that manual labor was for Native Americans, slaves, and indentured servants – not the Puritans.

Differences in colonial institutions reflected differences in endowments, including climate and crop potential as well as levels of domestic population at the time of settlement and the sources of imported labor supply. Adaptations to differences in climate and crop potential led to differences in economic and political structure. While expectations at the time of settlement may have been for a broad similarity in economic structures, adjusting to variations in the profitability of different crops and production methods led to quite different outcomes and patterns of institutions for the European settlers, and these had significant and prolonged impacts.

[30] Kupperman, *Providence Island*.

X

In our discussion of the categories of New World colonies, we raised the possibility that the relatively small fractions of their populations composed of whites, as well as their highly unequal distributions of wealth, contributed to the evolution of political, legal, and economic institutions that were less favorable toward full participation in the commercial economy by a broad spectrum of the population. The deviant case represented by the United States and Canada highlights this point. It seems unlikely to have been coincidental that colonies with more homogeneous populations – after the onset of settlement in terms of both human capital and other forms of wealth – evolved a set of institutions that were more oriented toward economic aspirations in terms of desire to achieve income and wealth within the bulk of the adult male population. These patterns may not be a permanent condition, since in recent years growth rates in parts of Latin America have finally come to exceed those of the United States and Canada for some uncertain reasons, but even so the time to convergence is quite long.

3

The Role of Institutions in Shaping Factor Endowments

I

Factor Endowments
We will argue that various features of factor endowments, including soils, climates, and the size or density of the native population, predisposed colonies in the three categories toward paths of development. These paths have been associated with different degrees of inequality in wealth and particularly human capital and different political power, as well as with different rates of economic growth. Although these conditions might reasonably be treated as exogenous at the beginning of European colonization, it is clear that such an assumption becomes increasingly tenuous as one moves later in time after settlement. Factor endowments may influence the directions in which institutions evolve, but these institutions in turn ultimately affect the evolution of the factor endowments. It is our contention, however, that the initial conditions had long, lingering effects, both because government policies and other institutions reproduced the factor endowments that gave rise to them and because certain fundamental characteristics of the New World economies and their factor endowments were difficult to change. Further, government policies and other institutions generally tended to reproduce the sorts of conditions that gave rise to them.

More specifically, in societies that began with extreme inequality, the elites were both inclined and able to establish a basic legal framework that ensured them a disproportionate share of political power and the ability to use that influence to establish rules, laws, and other government policies that gave them greater access to economic opportunities than the rest of the population, thereby contributing to the persistence of the high degree of inequality. In societies that began with greater equality in wealth and human capital or homogeneity among the population, the elites were either less able or less inclined to institutionalize rules, laws, and other government policies that grossly advantaged them, and thus the institutions that evolved tended to provide more equal treatment and opportunities, thereby contributing to the persistence of the relatively high degree of equality.

The nature of rules for land disposal and immigration, in those parts of the Americas where land and labor policies led to large landholdings and great inequality, seems to extend across a wide spectrum of institutions and other government interventions. In the areas of both law and administration pertaining to the establishment of corporations, the certification and regulation of financial institutions, the granting of property rights in intellectual capital (patents), the creation of industrial policies, and the provision of access to minerals and other natural resources on government-owned land, New World societies with greater inequality tended to adopt policies that were more selective in the offering of opportunities.

Responding to widespread sentiment that there should be few obstacles to private initiatives as well as to a broad opposition to privilege, the United States government set low fees and thresholds for the securing of property rights to the development of intellectual capital, land, and natural resources from virtually the beginning of the nation, and state governments had in effect routinized the process of forming financial institutions and corporations in general with general laws and modest capital requirements by the middle of the nineteenth century.[1] This pattern stands in rather stark contrast to those in the many New World

---

[1] Human capital appears to have been more broadly distributed in the United States, paralleling the greater equality in the distributions of wealth and political power. Higher rates of literacy and schooling may have contributed to the higher rates of innovation, technological diffusion, and entrepreneurship which are thought to have characterized the United States. See Richard A. Easterlin, "Why Isn't the Whole World Developed?" *Journal of Economic History* 41 (March 1981): 1–19; and Theodore W. Schultz, *Transforming Traditional Agriculture.* (Chicago: University of Chicago Press, 1964.) The patent system in the United States was more favorable to common people in several dimensions. First, the cost of obtaining a patent was much less, especially relative to the annual wage, than in any other country with a functioning patent system. Second, the granting of patents operated according to prescribed rules which were independent of the social class of the applicant for the patent, and these rules appear to have been adhered to. Third, the property rights in invention entailed in a patent appear to have been well enforced by the courts, making it much easier for a person of limited wealth to secure returns to his or her inventions. No other country had such favorable conditions for inventors from modest backgrounds. See also note 29.

societies, which had much greater inequality, such as Mexico and Brazil.[2] In these countries, the rights or abilities to organize corporations and financial institutions, and to develop intellectual capital, land, and natural resources, were generally restricted by costs and procedures to favor the wealthy and influential. Of course members of wealthy elites typically enjoy privileged positions, but it is our contention that the paths of institutional development in these societies were relatively extreme in the degree to which the elites were advantaged. Indeed, we argue that this contrast across New World societies with respect to the differences in inequality meant elites had relatively more power to influence the choice of legal and economic institutions in Latin America.

There was crucial legislation influencing the evolution of factor endowments, as well as the pace and pattern of economic development. Important policies were those relevant to land policy, policy regarding immigration, and the regulation of trading arrangements between colonies, the metropolis, and the outside world. During the era of colonization, most European countries followed some variant of mercantilism. Although the specifics of national policy could vary with economic and other circumstances, the aim of colonies was to benefit the metropolis. Significant changes occurred in the late eighteenth century for the British, with the successful revolution in the American colonies and the full acquisition of Canada and various Caribbean islands from the French. In the first quarter of the nineteenth century, most of the mainland North and South American colonies of Spain achieved their independence, as did Brazil from Portugal. These newly independent nations did not necessarily pursue the same sets of policies they had as colonies; at the very least, even if variants of mercantilism were still being pursued, they were now aimed at benefiting the former colonies and not the metropolis.

II

Immigration
The colonies settled by the Spanish had more Native Americans than did those settled by the British. Also important was the nature of the crops

---

[2] See Stephen H. Haber, *Industry and Underdevelopment: The Industrialization of Mexico 1890–1940* (Stanford: Stanford University Press, 1989); Stephen H. Haber, "Industrial Concentration and the Capital Markets: A Comparative Study of Brazil, Mexico, and the United States 1830–1930," *Journal of Economic History* 51 (September 1991): 559–80; and Edward Beatty, "Patents and Technological Change in Late Industrialization: The Case of Nineteenth Century Mexico in Comparative Perspective," *History of Technology* 24 (2002): 121–150.

produced and traded in international markets – a condition influenced by natural factors as well as by governmental regulations. Since all New World economies were able to obtain slaves from Africa, and the relative productivity of slaves versus free workers varied across regions with crops and other outputs produced, the composition of the population in different regions reflected the numbers of whites and Native Americans only in part.

Immigration policies were among the most crucial institutions for the evolution of factor endowments and the extent of inequality, and major differences arose across the New World economies early in the histories of European colonization. They were not, of course, the sole determinant of the composition of the population in the respective colonies. The areas settled by the Spanish, for example, had much larger numbers of Native Americans prior to the arrival of Europeans than did those areas settled by the British; the Spanish were attracted by this resource and introduced additional controls over Indians to better exploit and obtain labor from them. Because of the accepted white-Indian contacts the South American nations had relatively large *mestizo* populations (Table 2.3). Britain, a latecomer to the colonization of the New World, had to settle for territories with relatively few Native Americans.

In stark contract, Spanish immigration was tightly controlled, and it even declined somewhat over time. The authorities in Spain seem to have been motivated both by a desire to keep costs down and by the desires of those who had already migrated to maintain their levels of support and privileged positions.[3] A restrictive stance toward further immigration could not have been retained, however, if there had not already been a substantial supply of Indians to work the land and otherwise service the assets owned by the elites and the Spanish Crown; in this sense, at least, the policy must have been due to the factor endowment.[4] Overall,

---

[3] Large blocks of land and claims on Native American labor were often granted as incentives or rewards to the early waves of settlers, especially military men, missionaries, and others of some prominence. Although smaller holdings could be obtained through sales, extensive governmental land grants tended to result in large holdings and unequal distributions of wealth and political power. The initial land grants were often nontradable by the recipients, though transferable by the Spanish Crown. Later migrants to the colonies might thus have eroded the value of the property rights held by earlier cohorts. It is not difficult to comprehend why the already established population of European descent was less than enthusiastic about a liberal immigration policy during the colonial era.

[4] The fact that Spanish authorities did not actively encourage immigration to colonies without a substantial supply of readily available Indian labor, like Argentina, may seem contradictory to the idea that the factor endowment was the crucial determinant of policy.

the authorities exercised strict control over who could settle in the Americas, with preference shown to relatives of those already there and with permission denied to citizens of other European countries and to those not Catholic, in the purported interest of achieving a more homogeneous white society. Grants of permission to emigrate were initially restricted to single men, but they were ultimately extended to married men accompanied by their families; single white women were never allowed.

After the wave of independence movements early in the nineteenth century, most Latin American nations followed a relatively free immigration policy to attract new workers, mainly from Europe, with only a few restrictions on the racial or ethnic composition of the immigrants. Several countries advertised for migrants and introduced subsidies or other measures to induce more permanent arrivals. By that time, however, the United States had already begun to industrialize. Even with the marked easing of restrictions on immigration by Latin American countries, therefore, the dominant stream of European transatlantic migratory flows was directed to the United States, reflecting the higher per capita income and easier access to opportunities (as suggested by public policies toward land, suffrage, and schooling) available there and the lower costs of transportation from northern European countries (where most of the immigrants of this period came from). It was not until late in the century that the Latin American economies received substantial new inflows of labor from Europe.[5]

It seems likely, however, that Spanish policy toward immigration to places like Argentina was simply incidental, with the overall policy in regards to immigration to the New World based on the factor endowments and politics in the whole of Spanish America. Spanish policy was probably driven by conditions in Mexico and Peru, the most populous and valued colonies. Since these centers of Spanish America had an abundance of Indian labor, the local elites and the authorities in Spain were able to maintain restrictive policies.

[5] For the basic data on international migration during this period, see Walter Willcox, with Imre Frencz, *International Migrations* (2 vols.; New York: National Bureau of Economic Research, 1929, 1931). Despite the problems these American societies had in attracting Europeans and the continued importation of African slaves and contract labor into some areas, free white migration accounted for the bulk of new immigrants to the Americas in the nineteenth century overall. For estimates and discussion, see David Eltis, *Economic Growth and the Ending of the Transatlantic Slave Trade* (New York: Oxford University Press, 1987); Stanley L. Engerman, "Servants to Slaves to Servants: Contract Labour and European Expansion," in *Colonialism and Migration: Indentured Labor Before and After Slavery*, ed. P. C. Emmer 263–94 (Dordrecht: Martinus Nijhoff, 1986). For a recent survey of antebellum migration to the US, see Raymond L. Cohn, *Mass Migration under Sail: European Immigration to the Antebellum United States* (Cambridge: Cambridge University Press, 2009).

African slaves were imported into some areas until the 1860s, with especially large flows into Brazil and Cuba during the 1830s and 1840s – partially due to the ending of the British and U.S. slave trades in 1808 and the emancipation of British slaves in the 1830s.[6] In the aftermath of slavery (and in the case of Cuba, while slavery still existed), extensive contract labor movements from India, China, and elsewhere in Asia took place to various parts of the Caribbean.[7] There was also some movement of contract workers from China, Japan, and, for a few years, Polynesia, to Peru for sugar production. Peru's principal export crop at mid-century, guano, was a government monopoly, using the labor of slaves, contract workers, convicts, and military deserters for production.[8] In general, however, while slaves and indentured servants dominated the eighteenth century, it was free white migration that accounted for the bulk of new immigrants to most parts of the Americas in the nineteenth century. There was, even here, another important difference in the nature of the immigrants to the United States, Canada, and Latin America. The former two received migrants primarily from northwestern Europe, where economic growth was already under way and literacy was expanding. The major recipients in Latin America, such as Argentina and Brazil, drew mainly from areas that had lagged, such as Italy, Spain, and Portugal. Thus, even after restrictions on European migration were lifted, it is probable that those going to the United States and Canada had generally higher levels of human capital than those moving to Latin America.[9]

III

Land Policy

Another way in which institutions may have contributed to the changes in inequality over the long run is land policy. Virtually all the economies in the Americas had ample supplies of public lands well into the nineteenth century and beyond. The governments of each colony, province, or nation

---

[6] See Eltis, *Economic Growth.*

[7] For data and references on contract labor movements, see Engerman, "Servants to Slaves."

[8] See W. M. Mathew, "A Primitive Export Sector: Guano Production in Mid-Nineteenth-Century Peru," *Journal of Latin American Studies* 8 (May 1977): 35–57; Jimmy M. Skaggs, *The Great Guano Rush: Entrepreneurs and American Overseas Expansion* (New York: St. Martin's Press, 1994).

[9] For a comparison of the streams of Italian migrations to North and to South America, pointing to a different pattern for each, see Herbert S. Klein, "The Integration of Italian Immigrants into the United States and Argentina: A Comparative Analysis," *American Historical Review* 88 (April 1983): 306–29.

were regarded as the owners of land, so they were able to influence the distribution of wealth and the pace of settlement. Land policy was also used as an instrument to influence the size and location of the labor force.

The United States never experienced major problems in making land widely available over the course of the nineteenth century.[10] Attempts by Argentina and Brazil to encourage immigration were, however, less successful than in the United States and Canada, as was their aim to getting land to smallholders.[11] That the major crops produced in the expansion of the United States and Canada were grains, permitting relatively small farms given the technology of the times, may help explain why such a policy of smallholding was implemented and was effective.[12]

Argentina, in the second half of the nineteenth century, was somewhat unusual in not having a national land policy, that being left to individual state governments.[13] Unlike in the United States, however, where rivalry among the subfederal governments seemed to spur investment in transportation infrastructure and banks, accelerating the pace of economic growth, no such beneficial effects were manifest in Argentina. Thus, the nature of factor endowments (inclusive of soils, climates, the composition and relative sizes of populations, and existing distributions of land and political power), as well as the particular crops grown, did influence land policies, and the particular land policies pursued in different areas had significant impacts on future levels and distributions of income. The ruling political coalitions may have gotten what they sought, but that did not mean that the country would grow more rapidly.

[10] See Paul W. Gates, *History of Public Land Law Development* (Washington, D.C.: Government Printing Office, 1968) for a comprehensive overview of U.S. land policy.

[11] There are discussions of Canadian land policy in Carl E. Solberg, *The Prairies and the Pampas: Agrarian Policy in Canada and Argentina 1880–1913* (Stanford: Stanford University Press, 1987); Richard Pomfret, *The Economic Development of Canada* (Toronto: Methuen, 1981): 111–19; Jeremy Adelman, *Frontier Development: Land, Labor, and Capital on Wheatlands of Argentina and Canada, 1890–1914* (Oxford: Oxford University Press, 1994).

[12] On northern U.S. agriculture, see Jeremy Atack and Fred Bateman, *To Their Own Soil: Agriculture in the Antebellum North* (Ames: Iowa State University Press, 1987); Clarence H. Danhof, *Change in Agriculture: The Northern United States, 1820–1870* (Cambridge, MA: Harvard University Press, 1969).

[13] See Carl E. Solberg, *Immigration and Nationalism: Argentina and Chile, 1890–1914* (Austin: University of Texas Press, 1970); Solberg, *Prairies and the Pampas*. In addition to grains, livestock production also increased dramatically during the late nineteenth century on the basis of large landholdings. Indeed, scale economies in the raising of livestock may have helped maintain the large estates. For a description of Chile, see Andrea Ruiz Esquide, unpublished Columbia University dissertation, 2000.

It is rather difficult to design the counterfactual worlds necessary to demonstrate whether land policies in countries such as the United States, which generally encouraged rapid settlement, influenced economic growth relative to an alternative that would have meant slower settlement, permitting land to be sold only in larger, more expensive units. Arguments for a slower, more concentrated pattern of development were made by such contemporary observers as Henry Carey and Edward G. Wakefield, who claimed that the benefits of increased production due to economies of scale would be possible from higher population density and cheaper workers who would be available to labor in nascent industrial establishments if there were no "open frontier" into which potential labor could expand.[14] Whether this earlier application of the Nieboer-Domar hypothesis points to a higher national income or not, it does suggest a difference in economic structure, increasing manufacturing output relative to agriculture (or output in settled agricultural areas relative to frontier agriculture), as well as raising the returns to capital and land relative to those of labor. Greater access to land, on the other hand, promoted agriculture, led to higher rates of internal and external mobility, and was important in attaining a greater degree of equality among whites in the antebellum United States than existed elsewhere in the world at the time. Together with the high per capita income, this degree of equality, in turn, led to a broad participation in commercial activity, to a large middle-class market permitting mass production of standardized goods via "the American System of Manufactures," and to conditions conducive to a sustained increase in the commitment to inventive activity with a corresponding acceleration of technical change.[15] In this way, the early achievement of economic growth in the United States can be related to its unusual, even for the New World, resource endowment.

The basic classification of New World colonies indicates that the United States (particularly the northern states) and Canada, with their reliance on grain agriculture and relatively small landholdings, were

[14] The theme is developed by Henry Charles Carey in many of his works, such as Henry Charles Carey, *Principles of Political Economy* 4 pts in 3 vols. (Philadelphia: Carey, Lea and Blanchard, 1837–1840). The clearest statement by Wakefield is found in Edward Gibbon Wakefield, "A View of the Art of Colonization with Present Reference to the British Empire," *in Letters Between a Statesman and a Colonist* (London: J. W. Parker, 1849).

[15] For systematic information on the extent of U.S. income and wealth inequality, see Jeffrey G. Williamson and Peter N. Lindert, *American Inequality: A Macroeconomic History* (New York: Academic Press, 1980); Lee Soltow, "Inequalities in the Standards of Living in the United States," in *American Economic Growth and Standards of Living Before the Civil War*, eds. Robert E. Gallman and John Joseph Wallis (Chicago: Univerity of Chicago Press, 1992): 121–72.

unique both in their rates of long-term growth and degrees of equality. The influence of their factor endowments was reinforced by their policies of offering small units of land for disposal and maintaining open immigration by Europeans. Elsewhere there were large landholdings, greater inequality, and, ultimately, a later achievement, if any, of modern economic growth. In much of the Caribbean, this meant the importance of sugar plantations producing for world markets and with large number of slaves in their populations. In areas such as Mexico (where corn was the principal crop), Peru, and Argentina, land and labor policies led to large landholdings and great inequality, whether on the basis of large numbers of Native Americans (as in Mexico and Peru) or with immigrant renters (as in Argentina). The latter nations had relatively few Africans and only a small plantation sector, but their patterns of land distribution during the earlier stages of settlement meant that more substantial inequalities were generated than in the United States and Canada (see Table 3.1).

Lands were frequently given as grants to military men, missionaries, and other settlers, as well as made available, often through sales, to other individuals in what could be smaller holdings. More important were the governmental land grants (for example, those within the Spanish colonies), where holdings tended to be larger, and the more unequal the distributions of wealth and political power would become, relative to places where small holdings were made available. The size of holdings was often shaped by the nature of the crop to be produced and its technological requirements, but, as seen in the case of *encomienda* in Spanish America, the importance of renters in the late-nineteenth-century Argentina, and the rise of sharecropping in the postemancipation US South, the distribution of land ownership need not be the same as the size and distribution of operating farms. Nevertheless, the initial policy of land distribution did have a profound influence on the distribution of wealth and political power and thus on the future course of growth. Because the postsettlement policies for allocation of land were affected by the distribution of political power determined from the policies at the time of settlement, the long-term economic and political significance of these early policies is manifest.[16]

---

[16] Some of the colonies on the North American continent, such as Pennsylvania, began with proprietors – like William Penn – who were awarded very large grants of land. However, it was typically not long before these blocks began to be broken up and sold off in small plots at flexible terms. The desire to attract many immigrants appears to have been the major impetus, and "not many of the original proprietors intended to retain their holdings intact or to manage them as large estates." See Percy Wells Bidwell and John I. Falconer, *History of Agriculture in the Northern United States, 1620–1860* (Washington,

TABLE 3.1. *Landholding in Rural Regions of Mexico, the United States, Canada, and Argentina, c. 1900*

Country, year, and region	Proportion of household heads who own land[a]
Mexico, 1910	
North Pacific	5.6
North	3.4
Central	2.0
Gulf	2.1
South Pacific	1.5
Total rural Mexico	2.4
United States, 1900	
North Atlantic	79.2
South Atlantic	55.8
North Central	72.1
South Central	51.4
Western	83.4
Total United States	74.5
Canada, 1901	
British Columbia	87.1
Alberta	95.8
Saskatchewan	96.2
Manitoba	88.9
Ontario	80.2
Quebec	90.1
Maritime[b]	95.0
Total Canada	87.1
Argentina, 1895	
Chaco	27.8
Formosa	18.5
Missiones	26.7
La Pampa	9.7
Neuquén	12,3
Rio Negro	15.4
Chubut	35.2
Santa Cruz	20.2
Total for areas covered	18.8

Source: Engerman and Sokoloff (2002).

Notes:

a. Landownership is defined as follows: in Mexico, household heads who own land; in the United States, farms that are owner operated; in Canada, total occupiers of farmlands who are owners; and in Argentina, the ratio of landowners to the number of males between the ages of 18 and 50.

b. The Maritime region includes Nova Scotia, New Brunswick, and Prince Edward Island.

All the New World colonies were settled at a time of relatively low population densities in the productive sectors and thus confronted the problems of attracting sufficient labor while determining the rate at which (and by whom) new lands would be brought into production. In understanding the nature of policies regarding land, it is useful to point not only to the land's expanse (which will influence the ease of getting away from areas of high density), but also its soil type, surrounding climate, and disease environment, which will influence which crops can profitably be grown, as well as the desirability of settlement by different groups. Policies concerning transportation development influenced the accessibility to markets, and the willingness of the various governments to construct, operate, and subsidize such activities affected the pace of settlement and the relative production of different crops.

These considerations, determining which crops could be produced by settlers, given appropriate trade policies and the availability of labor, thus dictate the technology to be used in profitable production and the optimum scale of production. The optimum scale will, in turn, affect the nature of landholdings and the form of the allocation of land, while the preferences and desired working conditions of free workers will influence the type of labor that could be used in production. It is therefore expected that those British colonies in which sugar was the primary crop had a different racial composition of their labor force and distribution of wealth and political power than those in which grains were the principal crop. Given changing world market demands and shifting patterns of crop production, the long-run benefits of particular patterns of crop production would often be uncertain.

Land policy could also be used to influence the labor force, either by encouraging immigration or by increasing the pool of wage labor in older areas through limiting land availability in newer areas. In most cases, although there were initial attempts at a slow, orderly process of settlement, this became more difficult to control over time. In the United States, land acquisition became less costly during the nineteenth century. These changes essentially made land free in plots suitable for family farms to those who settled and worked the land for a specified period. The Homestead Act of 1862 in the United States was the culmination of this policy. Canada pursued similar policies, and the Dominion Lands

D.C.: Carnegie Institution, 1925): 60–61. For detailed discussion of the experience in Pennsylvania, see Wesley Frank Craven, *The Colonies in Transition, 1660–1713* (New York: Harper & Row, 1968); and Gary B. Nash, *Quakers and Politics: Pennsylvania, 1681–1726* (Boston: Northeastern University Press, 1993).

Act of 1872 closely resembled the Homestead Act of 1862. Argentina and Brazil instituted similar changes in the second half of the nineteenth century, in part to encourage immigration, but these attempts were much less successful at getting land to smallholders than were the programs in the United States and Canada.[17]

In Argentina, a number of factors explain the contrast in outcomes. First, the elites of Buenos Aires, whose interests favored keeping scarce labor in the province, if not the capital city, were much more effective at weakening or blocking programs than were their urban counterparts in North America: This outcome may have resulted from the relatively greater economic prominence and power of Buenos Aires within the national arena. Second, even those policies nominally intended to broaden access tended to involve large grants to land developers (with the logic that allocative efficiency could best be achieved through exchanges between private agents) or transfers to occupants who were already using the land (including those who were grazing livestock). Thus they generally conveyed public lands to private owners in much larger holdings than occurred in the United States and Canada. Third, the process by which large landholdings might have been divided may have operated more slowly in Argentina once the land was in private hands, the potential value of land in grazing may have set too high a floor on land prices for immigrants and other would-be farmers. Also important was the effect of the underdevelopment of mortgage and financial institutions more generally.[18]

---

[17] See Warren Dean, "Latifundia and Land Policy in Nineteenth Century Brazil," *Hispanic American Historical Review* 51 (November 1971): 602–25; Emilia Viotti da Costa, *The Brazilian Empire: Myths and Histories* (Chicago: University of Chicago Press, 1985), Ch. 4; Solberg, *Prairies and the Pampas*; Solberg's essay in D. C. M. Platt and Guido di Tella, eds. *Argentina, Australia, and Canada: Studies in Comparative Development, 1870–1965* (London: Macmillan, 1985): 53–75, and the excellent discussions in Adelman, *Frontier Development*.

[18] Because the major crops produced in the expansion of the United States and Canada were grains, the land could be profitably worked on relatively small farms, given the technology of the times. This may help explain why such a policy of smallholding was implemented and effective. See Atack and Bateman, *To Their Own Soil*; Danhof, *Change in Agriculture*. In Argentina, however, small-scale wheat production coincided with ownership of land in large units, thereby maintaining a greater degree of overall inequality in wealth and political power. See Solberg, *Immigration and Nationalism* and Solberg, *Prairies and the Pampas*. In addition to grains, livestock production on large landholdings, also increased dramatically in the late nineteenth century, and scale economies in the raising of livestock may have helped maintain the large estates. For an example of a Spanish American country that came to be characterized by small-scale agriculture and also followed a path of institutional development more like that in the

In Table 3.1, we present estimates of the fractions of household heads, or a near equivalent, that owned land in agricultural areas in the late nineteenth and early twentieth centuries for four countries. The proportion of landowners is far from an ideal measure of the extent of inequality, and it is sensitive to the mix of products produced in the respective areas. Nevertheless, the numbers do provide useful insight into the impact or effectiveness of the land policies pursued, and one can assemble a set of estimates that are comparable across a broad range of economies. There were enormous differences across the countries in the prevalence of land ownership among the adult male population in rural areas. On the eve of the Mexican Revolution, the figure from the 1910 census suggests that only 2.4 percent of household heads in rural Mexico owned land.[19] The basic qualitative result of extreme inequality is confirmed by the observation that the proportion of the population that was Native American varied across regions (as well as states) in the way one would expect since few Native Americans would have the right to own land.

In contrast, the proportion of adult males that owned land in rural areas was quite high in the United States, at just below 75 percent in 1900. Canada had an even higher proportion, with nearly 90 percent of household heads owning the agricultural lands they occupied in 1901. The rural regions of Argentina constituted a set of frontier provinces, where one would expect higher rates of ownership than in Buenos Aires. The numbers, however, suggest a much lower prevalence of land ownership in Argentina than in the two North American economies, but the shares for each of these economies were considerably higher than for Mexico.[20]

United States, see the discussion of Costa Rica in Ralph Lee Woodward, Jr., *Central America: A Nation Divided* (New York: Oxford University Press, 1976); Hector Perez-Brignoli, *A Brief History of Central America* (Berkeley: University of California Press, 1989).

[19] For further discussion of Mexico, see George McCuthchen McBride, *The Land Systems of Mexico* (New York: American Geographic Society, 1923); Frank Tannenbaum, *The Mexican Agrarian Revolution* (New York: Macmillan, 1929); Robert Holden, *Mexico and the Survey of Public Lands. The Management of Modernization, 1876–1911* (DeKalb: Northern Illinois University Press, 1994).

[20] Our preliminary work with the data from the 1914 census yields the same qualitative results. It is worth noting that the proportions of families that owned land are exaggerated by the 1895 census figure. A close examination of the manuscripts indicates that double counting, in which both the husband and wife were listed as landowners, was prevalent in many parts of Argentina.

IV

Voting

If the elite did indeed have relatively more political power, than the institutions would be more likely organized in a way that would advantage the elite over others. As a first step toward subjecting this notion to an empirical test, it is reasonable to look at how broadly the franchise was extended and also what fractions of respective populations actually voted in elections. Because most of the societies in the Americas were nominal democracies by the middle of the nineteenth century, this sort of information has a direct bearing on the extent to which elites based largely on wealth, human capital, and gender held disproportionate political power in their respective countries and how this disproportionality varied across the societies with their initial factor endowments.

Summary information about the differences across New World societies during the late-nineteenth and early-twentieth centuries in how the right to vote was restricted is reported in Table 1.3. The estimates reveal that it was common in all countries until the twentieth century to reserve the right to vote to adult males. The United States and Canada were the clear leaders in doing away with restrictions based on wealth and literacy, and had much higher fractions of their populations voting than anywhere else in the Americas. Not only did they attain the secret ballot and extend the franchise to even the poor and illiterate much earlier (although this control was admittedly re-introduced in the United States at the expense of blacks in the 1890s). In regard to the proportions of the population voting, the United States and Canada were at least a half-century ahead of even the most democratic countries of South America (Uruguay, Argentina, and Costa Rica) who were generally regarded as the least inegalitarian of Latin American societies and whose initial factor endowments were perhaps most like those of the United States and Canada.

The contrast was not so evident at the outset. In the United States, those who founded the nation initially believed voting was largely a privilege reserved for white men with significant amounts of property. As the movement to do away with political inequality gained strength, the rest of the country followed suit; virtually all new entrants to the Union extended voting rights to all white men (with explicit racial restrictions generally introduced in the same state constitutions that did away with economic requirements), and older states revised their laws in the wake of protracted political debates. The key states of New York and Massachusetts made the break with wealth restrictions in the 1820s, and the shift to full white adult male suffrage was largely complete by the late 1850s. The relatively more egalitarian populations of the western states were the clear leaders in the movement. The rapid extension of access to the franchise in these areas not coincidentally paralleled liberal policies toward public schools and access to land, as well as other policies that were expected to be attractive to potential migrants.[21]

Similar political movements with similar outcomes followed with a short lag in the various Canadian provinces, but the analogous developments did not occur in Latin America until the twentieth century. As a result, through 1940 the United States and Canada routinely had proportions voting that were 50 to 100 percent higher than their most progressive neighbors to the South, three times higher than Mexico, and five to ten times higher than countries such as Brazil, Bolivia, Ecuador, and even Chile. It is remarkable that as late as 1900, none of the countries in Latin America had the secret ballot or more than a miniscule fraction of the population casting votes.[22] The great majority of European nations, as well as the United States and Canada, achieved secrecy in balloting and universal adult male suffrage long before other countries in the western hemisphere, and the proportions of the populations voting in the former were always higher, often four to five times higher. Although many factors may have contributed to the low levels of participation in South America and the Caribbean, wealth and literacy requirements were serious binding constraints. Some societies, such as Barbados, maintained wealth-based suffrage restrictions until the mid-twentieth century, while most joined the United States and Canada in moving away from economic requirements in the nineteenth century. However, whereas the states in the United States frequently adopted explicit racial limitations, when they abandoned economic requirements, Latin American countries typically chose to screen by literacy.

---

[21] Below, this chapter.

[22] There is some controversy about whether Argentina had wealth and literacy requirements for suffrage. Whatever the case, the proportions of the population voting were very low in that country (1.8 percent in 1896) until the electoral reform law of 1912. Those who point to the absence of such electoral restrictions at the level of the national government suggest that the low voter participation was due to failure of immigrants to change their citizenship and vote, as well as to the lack of a secret ballot. Others believe that restrictions on the franchise had, in fact, been enacted and were enforced at the provincial level until 1912. For a discussion on the shifting patterns in Brazil, see Richard Graham, *Patronage and Politics in Nineteenth-Century Brazil* (Stanford: Stanford University Press, 1990).

That the attainments of universal male suffrage and the secret ballot in the United States and Canada were the products of a long series of hard-fought and incremental political battles over the early nineteenth century, is certainly consistent with our view. Alternative explanations, such as the importance of national heritage, are not very useful in identifying why Argentina, Uruguay, and Costa Rica pulled so far ahead of their Latin American neighbors, and why other British colonies in the New World lagged behind Canada. The second question is whether differences in the distribution of political power influenced the distribution of wealth and human capital. Inspired perhaps by the experience of blacks in the U.S. South during their period of effective disenfranchisement even as a free people between 1890 and the 1960s, we believe that it did. Our studies suggest that there are indeed powerful interactions between the different types of inequality.

By providing a broad international perspective, Table 1.3 highlights how slowly most of the New World societies, despite being nominal democracies, extended the franchise to the bulk of their respective populations. Although many factors may have contributed to the relatively low vote totals in Latin America, wealth and literacy requirements were serious binding constraints.

Two fundamental questions arise about the patterns of diffusion of universal male suffrage across New World economies. The first is the issue of whether differences in the degrees of inequality in wealth, human capital, and political influence were related to the likelihood of adopting such an institutional change. The cross-sectional patterns indicate that the expansion of male suffrage and of the secret ballot were against the desires of the elite, who were more likely to be opposed to liberalizing the franchise. Another important factor, however, was the desire to attract immigrants. It is striking that pioneers in extending suffrage, such as new states in the United States and of Argentina and Uruguay, did so during periods in which they hoped to attract immigrants, such that the rights to suffrage formed part of a package of policies thought to be potentially attractive to those contemplating relocation. When elites, such as land or other asset holders, desired common men to locate in the polity, they chose to extend access to privileges and opportunities even without threat of civil disorder; indeed, a polity (or one set of elites) may have found itself competing with another to attract the labor or whatever else was desired.[23]

---

[23] See Daron Acemoglu and James A. Robinson "Why Did the West Extend the Franchise? Democracy, Inequality and Growth in Historical Perspective," *Quarterly Journal of*

V

Education

A fundamental question is whether differences in the distribution of political power were fed back on the distribution of access to economic opportunities or on investment in public goods in ways that had implications for long-run paths of institutional and economic development. Schooling institutions, together with literacy attainment, are among the first areas we have examined. Increases in a society's levels of schooling and literacy have been related, theoretically as well as empirically, to many socioeconomic changes conducive to growth, including higher labor productivity, more rapid technological change, and higher rates of commercial and political participation. Moreover, in addition to promoting growth, they also have a major influence on the distribution of the benefits of growth.[24]

The New World is a very interesting context in which to study investment in schooling in that many societies were so prosperous that they clearly had the resources to support the establishment of a widespread network of primary schools. However, few made such investments on a scale sufficient to serve the general population before the twentieth century. The exceptional societies, in terms of leadership in investing in institutions of primary education, were the United States and Canada. Virtually from the time of settlement, these North Americans seem generally to have been convinced of the value of providing their children with a basic education, including the ability to read and write. Especially in New England, schools were frequently organized and funded at the village or town level. It is likely that among whites, the United States had the most literate population in the world by 1800, but the "common school movement," getting under way in the 1820s (following closely after the movement for the extension of the franchise), put the country on an even more accelerated path of investment in education institutions. Between 1821 and 1871, nearly every northern state that had not previously done so enacted a law strongly encouraging localities to establish "free schools" open to all children and supported by general taxes, although these were not always binding.[25] Although the movement made

---

Economics 115 (November 2000): 1167–99, who argue that the franchise was extended under threat.

[24] See Easterlin, "Whole World."

[25] See the discussion in Ellwood P. Cubberley, *The History of Education* (Boston: Houghton Mifflin, 1920). The competition for number one in the eighteenth century was Scotland. See John E. Craig, "The Expansion of Education," *Review of Research in Education* 9 (1981): 151–213; Kenneth Lockridge, *Literacy in Colonial New England: An Enquiry into the Social Context of Literacy in the Early Modern West* (New York: Norton,

slower progress in the South, schooling had spread sufficiently by the middle of the nineteenth century so that more than fourty percent of the school-age population (white and black) was enrolled, and nearly ninety percent of white adults were literate. Schools were also widespread in early-nineteenth-century Canada, and even though it lagged behind the United States by several decades in establishing tax-supported schools with universal access, its literacy rates were nearly as high.

The rest of the hemisphere trailed far behind the United States and Canada in primary schooling and in attaining literacy (see Table 1.4). Despite enormous wealth, the British colonies (with the exception of Barbados) were very slow to organize schooling institutions that served broad segments of the population. Indeed, it was evidently not until the British Colonial Office took an interest in the promotion of schooling, late in the nineteenth century, that significant steps were taken in this direction. Similarly, even the most progressive Latin American countries – like Argentina and Uruguay – were more than seventy-five years behind the United States and Canada.

The records of how institutions of suffrage and schooling developed over time across the Americas seem quite consistent with our hypothesis that the initial extent of inequality in society influenced how strategic economic institutions evolved over time. Where inequality was relatively low, the institutions were more likely to make opportunities more accessible to the general population; this served, in our view, both to preserve a relatively greater degree of equality in wealth, human capital, and political influence, as well as to promote growth by stimulating broad participation in commercial or otherwise growth-enhancing activities (such as human-capital accumulation). Where inequality was relatively high, institutions tended to evolve in such a way as to restrict access to opportunities, favoring elite groups and thus preserving relative inequality, but perhaps reducing the prospects for sustained economic growth. These dynamics of institutional change help account for the role of initial differences in the extent of inequality in having long-term effects through the tendency for them to persist over time.

These societies began to boost their investments in public schooling at roughly the same time that they intensified their efforts to attract

1974); and Lawrence Stone, "Literacy and Education in England, 1640–1900," *Past and Present* 42 (February 1981): 69–139. Since slaves were only 10 to 20 percent of the US population, even including them with zero literacy would not substantially effect these comparisons.

migrants from Europe, well before they implemented a general liberalization of the franchise. This association might be interpreted as providing
for the socialization of foreign immigrants, but it also suggests that the
elites may have been inclined to extend access to opportunities as part
of an effort to attract the scarce labor for which they were directly or
indirectly competing. The latter perspective is supported by the observation that major investments in primary schooling did not generally occur
in any Latin American country until the national governments provided
the funds; in contrast to the pattern in North America, local and state
governments in Latin America were not willing or able to take on this
responsibility on their own. Most of these societies did not achieve high
levels of literacy until well into the twentieth century. Fairly generous
support was made available in Latin America, however, for universities
and other institutions of higher learning that were more geared toward
children of the elite.

We will explore the question of what accounts for this pattern of differential investments in primary education in Chapter V. We find that
although differences in per capita income and in the support for and
timing of efforts to attract and assimilate immigrants from Europe play
important roles, detailed examination of specific cases and pooled multivariate regressions indicate that differences in the degree of inequality, or
population heterogeneity, have explanatory power as well.[26] Two mechanisms help explain why extreme levels of inequality depressed investments
in schooling. First, in settings where private schooling predominated or
where parents paid user fees for their children, greater wealth or income
inequality would generally reduce the fraction of the school-age population enrolled, holding per capita income constant. Second, greater
inequality likely exacerbated the collective-action problems associated
with the establishment and funding of universal public schools, either
because the distribution of benefits across the population was quite different from the incidence of taxes and other costs or simply because
population heterogeneity made it more difficult for communities to reach
consensus on public projects. Where the wealthy enjoyed disproportionate political power, they were able to procure schooling services for their
own children and to resist being taxed to underwrite or subsidize services to others. This, as well as the differences in income levels across

---

[26] See Ch. 5. This chapter establishes the correlation between schooling and literacy rates
with inequality in political power as reflected in the proportion of the population who
vote.

regions within countries, may account for the very substantial disparities in schooling and literacy between urban and rural areas in virtually all of the New World societies except the United States and Canada.

VI

Finance and Banks

Another example of how early differences in the degrees of inequality in the distributions of wealth, human capital, and political power may have affected the paths of institutional development is provided by the contrasting patterns of banking and capital formation in the North American mainland and Latin American economies. These differences in financial institutions emerged during the colonial period. Although no private banks were established in the British colonies on the mainland prior to the Revolution, loans among farmers and planters in commercial agriculture were commonplace by the early eighteenth century. The much higher prevalence of landholding facilitated the growth of this form of exchange among individuals to a much greater extent than in the Latin American colonies, where a relatively small fraction of the population had land to offer as collateral. A proportionately larger part of the North American population was also involved in credit and banking-like transactions.

After the American Revolution, a fundamental unique pattern of private banking was introduced to the United States based on particular political and economic conditions. The result of the separate chartering of colonies by the British led to a federal system, framed by the Constitution, with powers shared between the central government and various state governments. The central government was responsible for defining the monetary standard for the nation, but control over bank formation and banking structure was left to the respective state governments. The competition among states for advantages in economic growth in turn helped shape the laws and conditions governing the establishment and regulation of banks. Specific votes of state legislatures were generally required for the chartering of a bank through the early 1800s. This led to political conflicts and disagreements, as well as corruption, but the relative openness of the political system meant that many charters were issued and that banks were subject to considerable competition and turnover. As the franchise was extended over the first quarter of the nineteenth century to achieve virtual full white-male suffrage, the obstacles to bank formation were successively reduced, and the process of chartering became increasingly a matter of administrative routine.[27]

Although not explicitly provided for in the Constitution, two large, protocentral banks were created with a mixture of financial support from the federal government and private sources: namely, the First Bank of the United States (1791–1811) and the Second Bank of the United States (1816–1836). While larger than other banks, they coexisted with them, were subject to similar regulatory constraints as were private banks, and did not have monopoly positions. Nevertheless, both were ended by political attacks about their relative size and influence on the political and economic sphere, thus aiding the smaller state-level private banks. The opposition to the large national banks was strongest among the Jacksonian Democrats, and in those areas, such as the West, that were leaders in extending the franchise and in establishing universal primary schools. There was a general recognition that the more the chartering of banks was in the hands of states, including those of recent settlement, the broader the range of the population that would have access to financial institutions and the more reallocation of investment across regions became possible.

Thus, early in the nineteenth century, the banking system in the United States had already come to be characterized, particularly in the Northeast and the Midwest, by numerous, relatively small banks with extensive competition and great flexibility. This pattern was radically different from the systems that developed in the major Latin American nations. In countries such as Brazil and Mexico, for example, where wealth and political influence were distributed highly unequally, the chartering of banks was tightly controlled by the national governments, leading to highly concentrated financial sectors dominated by a few banks, often with either formal or informal links to the respective governments.[28] Financial

---

[27] Bray Hammond, *Banks and Politics in America, From the Revolution to the Civil War* (Princeton: Princeton University Press, 1957); Edwin J. Perkins, *American Public Finance and Financial Services, 1700–1815* (Columbus: Ohio State University Press, 1994). See also Howard Bodenhorn, *A History of Banking in Antebellum America: Financial Markets and Economic Development in an Era of Nation-Building* (Cambridge: Cambridge University Press, 1997).

[28] Haber, *Industrial Concentration*, 559–80, and Stephen H. Haber, "Financial Markets and Industrial Development: A Comparative Study of Governmental Regulation, Financial Innovation, and Industrial Structure in Brazil and Mexico, 1840–1930," in *How Latin America Fell Behind*, ed. Stephen Haber 146–78 (Stanford: Stanford University 1997). See also Ch. 8.

sectors were never so constrained in the United States or Canada. Even in the U.S. South, where state governments frequently held equity stakes and were involved in operating banks, free entry and competitiveness were generally maintained.

The banking systems of the United States and, to a lesser extent, Canada, were not just a reserve of the wealthy elite, as they were in much of Latin America. On the contrary, a broad spectrum of the population could take advantage of opportunities to obtain loans and invest savings in such institutions. Although we have as of yet only limited knowledge of the comparative record of rules regarding collateral for borrowing and the costs of bankruptcy in the case of default, the United States clearly offered greater flexibility than other countries in the region. The looser strictures on banks there, whatever the costs in terms of periodic bank panics, led to wider participation and more diffused use of bank-created and bank-acquired funds.

Banks were the first major financial institution in the United States, and they were soon followed, in New York and elsewhere, by securities exchanges bringing together investors operating under private rules. These institutions were initially confined mainly to transactions in government and social overhead securities, but they gradually moved into transactions in industrial securities. The growth and expansion of such exchanges and the use of such securities was greatly enhanced by the progression of laws providing for easier organization of limited liability, joint stock companies. Latin American nations, in contrast, were very slow to develop securities exchanges, and legislation providing for the organization of joint-stock companies was introduced late – and even then it was highly restrictive. In Mexico, for example, no body of mortgage credit laws was written until 1884, and the first general incorporation law was enacted in 1889. For most of the century, therefore, it was extremely difficult to enforce loan contracts and establish joint-stock companies. Consequently, impersonal sources of capital were not substantially developed in Latin American nations until the twentieth century, such that the individuals who wanted to pursue commercial activities generally had to rely on kinship networks to obtain capital. Because members of the elite were much more capable of tapping such sources, they were greatly advantaged in relative terms in such an institutional environment. The prospects for economic growth, however, were likely to have served both to preserve a relatively greater degree of equality in wealth, human capital, and political influence and to promote growth by stimulating broad participation in commercial or otherwise growth-enhancing activities (such as human capital accumulation). Where inequality was relatively high, however, institutions tended to evolve in such a way as to restrict access to opportunities, advantaging members of the elite and thus preserving relative inequality, but perhaps reducing the prospects for sustained economic growth. These dynamics of institutional change help account for the persistence of initial differences in the degree of inequality over time.

VII

Patents

Recent work with United States patent records has demonstrated that the growth of inventive activity was strongly and positively associated with the extension of markets as economic growth began to accelerate during the first half of the nineteenth century.[29] The independent effect of expanding markets was isolated by examining how the record of patenting across geographic areas (down to the county level) varied with proximity to navigable inland waterways, the cheapest form of transportation for all but short routes prior to the railroad. Not only was patenting higher in districts with such access to broad markets, but the construction of canals or other additions to the transportation infrastructure yielded immediate and larger jumps in patenting activity. Also indicative of the importance of contact with the market, and economic opportunity more generally, was the widening range of social classes represented among patentees in those geographic areas where patenting per capita rose. This pattern is evident in the first panel of Table 3.2, which shows that the proportion of urban patentees who were from elite occupations fell sharply as rates of patenting began to rise rapidly from 1805 on. Even in focusing on so-called "great inventors" credited with responsibility for significant technological discoveries, as does the second panel, one is impressed with how broad a range of the population was involved in inventive activity.

A broad spectrum of the population appears to have become engaged in looking for better ways of carrying out production, spurring the rate at which improved methods diffused as well as boosting rates of invention

---

[29] This discussion draws on Kenneth L. Sokoloff, "Inventive Activity in Early Industrial America: Evidence from Patent Records, 1790–1846," *Journal of Economic History* 48 (December 1988): 813–50; Kenneth L. Sokoloff and B. Zorina Khan, "The Democratization of Invention During Early Industrialization: Evidence From the United States, 1790–1846," *Journal of Economic History* 50 (June 1990): 363–78; B. Zorina Khan and Kenneth L. Sokoloff, "'Schemes of Practical Utility': Entrepreneurship and Innovation Among 'Great Inventors' in the United States, 1790–1865," *Journal of Economic History* 53 (June 1993): 289–307.

TABLE 3.2. *Characteristics of Inventors in the United States, 1790–1846*
(Distribution of Urban Patents by Patentee Occupation)

Characteristics	1790–1804		1805–1822		1823–1836		1837–1846	
	No.	(%)	No.	(%)	No.	(%)	No.	(%)
General commerce & professional (merchants, doctors, gentlemen)	13	50.0	60	38.7	59	24.6	43	18.6
Artisans working with renewable materials (carpenters, shoemakers)	4	15.4	32	20.7	58	24.2	41	17.8
Precision artisans (makers of watches, jewelry, instruments)	5	19.2	16	10.3	22	9.2	26	11.3
Machinists/toolmakers	1	3.9	17	11.0	34	14.2	40	17.3
Other producers/dealers of metal products (stove manufacturers, blacksmiths)	2	7.7	17	11.0	40	16.7	49	21.2
Other occupations or none listed	1	3.9	13	8.4	27	11.3	32	13.9

Backgrounds of Great Inventors, 1790–1846

	Number	Percentage
Educational background		
None to several years of schooling	76	47. 5
More than several years	22	13.8
Attended college	38	23.8
Unknown	24	15.0
Occupational class at first major invention		
Artisan	24	15.0
Farmer	8	5.0
Engineer/machinist/full-time inventor	53	33.1
Merchant/professional	36	22.5
Manufacturer	37	23.1
Other/missing	2	1.3

Sources: The estimates are drawn from Sokoloff and Khan (1990): 369; Khan and Sokoloff (1993): 293.

Notes: The top panel reports the number and share of patents filed by patentees of each occupational category during four sub-periods. The lower panel reports, for a group of inventors credited with responsibility for technologically significant inventions, the distributions across classes defined first by educational background and then by occupational class at the time of their first invention. Inventors whose extent of schooling is unknown seem likely to have had low levels of education.

and innovation. Moreover, the association between patenting and access to broad markets held for ordinary patents as well as for the presumably more important patents (on average) awarded to the "great inventors." Evidence that manufacturing firms in districts with higher patenting rates, holding other factors constant, had higher total factor productivity provides further support for the interpretation that invention and technical change were induced by the expansion of markets.[30]

VIII

Markets
There are several reasons for believing that the association of markets with economic growth during the first half of the nineteenth century is relevant to the question of whether the condition of greater overall equality was an important contributor to the earlier onset of industrialization in the United States more so than elsewhere in the New World. First, the coincidence of high per capita incomes with equality would be expected to attract relatively more resources to the production and elaboration of standardized manufacturers, because free whites of the middling sort would ultimately expend higher shares of their income on manufactures than would the poor (or than slaveholders would expend on their slaves).[31] Moreover, although the wealthy might devote large shares of income to manufactures, they generally consumed manufactures that

[30] Kenneth L. Sokoloff, "Invention, Innovation, and Manufacturing Productivity Growth in the Antebellum Northeast," in *American Economic Growth and Standards of Living Before the Civil War*, eds. Robert E. Gallman and John Joseph Wallis (Chicago: University of Chicago Press, 1992): 345–84.

An interesting contemporary argument for the importance of the patent system (brought to our attention by Claudia Goldin) was made by Mark Twain in *A Connecticut Yankee in King Arthur's Court*. The Connecticut Yankee comments that the first thing you want in a new country "was to start a patent office." He claimed that "a country without a patent office and good patent laws was just a crab, and couldn't travel any way but sideways or backwards."

On the role of patents in long-term British economic development, see Douglass C. North, and Robert Paul Thomas, *The Rise of the Western World: A New Economic History* (Cambridge: Cambridge University Press, 1973); and Max Weber, *General Economic History* (New York: Collier Books, 1961(1927)): 231–2.

[31] This idea is related to the well-established relationship between per capita income and the proportion of expenditures devoted to nonagricultural products. Slaves, however, were unable to choose their consumption bundles. We are relying on Viken Tchakerian, "Productivity, Extent of Markets, and Manufacturing in the Late Antebellum South and Midwest," *Journal of Economic History* 54 (September 1994): 497–527; Fred Bateman and Thomas Weiss, *A Deplorable Scarcity: The Failure of Industrialization in a Slave Economy* (Chapel Hill: University of North Carolina Press, 1981). These scholars

were nonstandard or customized. This is significant, both because markets were more likely to develop around goods or assets with uniform characteristics and because many of the most fundamental advances in technology during the nineteenth century were concerned with the production of standardized manufacturing production.

Second, greater equality in wealth, human capital, and political power likely promoted the evolution of broad, deep markets through the supply side as well. In some cases, the stimulus was associated with the existence of scale economies in activities, such as transportation or financial intermediation, with high fixed costs or capital intensity. Greater densities of potential users and beneficiaries raised the projected returns on investment in such projects and facilitated the mobilization of necessary political and financial backing. In the northeast region of the United States, for example, the great majority of banks and much of the transportation infrastructure in place during the initial phase of growth (roads and canals) were organized locally and relied on broad public participation and use.[32] Without the substantial numbers of small businesses (including farms) and households seeking better access to product and capital markets, there would have been less potential for realizing the substantial scale economies characteristic of transportation and financial intermediation – and much less investment in these crucial areas.[33]

find relatively little manufacturing output per capita in the South as compared to agricultural areas in the North, as well as a relative lack of firms producing standardized manufactures.

[32] For an excellent overview of these developments, see George Rogers Taylor, *The Transportation Revolution, 1815–1860* (New York: Rinehart, 1951); John Majewski, *A House Dividing: Economic Development in Pennsylvania and Virginia Before the Civil War* (Cambridge: Cambridge University Press, 2000).

[33] For discussions of the extensive scale economics in transportation and in financial intermediaries during this era, and of the importance of broad political support for investment in such enterprises, see Albert Fishlow, *American Railroads and the Transformation of the Antebellum Economy* (Cambridge, MA: Harvard University Press, 1965); Carter Goodrich, *Government Promotion of American Canals and Railroads* (New York: Columbia University Press, 1960); Lance E. Davis and Robert E. Gallman, "Capital Formation in the United States During the Nineteenth Century," in *The Cambridge Economic History of Europe*, vol. 7, *The Industrial Economies: Part 2, The United States, Japan, and Russia*, eds. Peter Mathias and M. M. Postan 1–69 (Cambridge: Cambridge University Press, 1978): Lance E. Davis and Robert E. Gallman "Savings, Investment, and Economic Growth: The United States in the Nineteenth Century," in *Capitalism in Context: Essays on Economic Development and Cultural Change in Honor of R. M. Hartwell*, eds. John A. James and Mark Thomas 202–229 (Chicago: University of Chicago Press, 1994): and Majewski, *House Dividing*).

Although further study is needed, the development of policies and institutions related to immigration, public lands, suffrage, schooling, and finance over time across the Americas seems consistent with our hypothesis that the initial extent of inequality in a society affected the evolution of strategic economic institutions. Where there was relative equality and population homogeneity, the institutions that evolved were more likely to make opportunities more accessible to the general population.

IX

Early Modern Growth as the Result of Broad-Based Participation and Incremental Improvements

It is important to distinguish two views of economic growth. In the first view, greater equality is less than favorable for the onset of growth, on the grounds that savings or investment rates are higher among the well-to-do.[34] Proponents of this view generally highlight the importance of mobilizing capital, in the belief that capital deepening and the introduction of new generations of technologies embodied in capital equipment are necessary for sustained growth. They are skeptical that labor-intensive sectors or small-scale enterprises can generate much in terms of technological progress.[35] A second perspective, in contrast, views economic growth as the cumulative impact of incremental advances made by individuals throughout the economy, rather than as a process driven by progress in a single industry or by the actions of a narrow elite. By highlighting how the extension of markets and economic opportunities elicits responses from broad segments of the population, it suggests a greater potential for the

---

[34] For a recent discussion of this long-debated idea that is grounded in the early development of the United States, see Davis and Gallman, "U.S. Economic Growth." For treatments that have a more contemporary, cross-country orientation that is not focused on the early stages of growth, see Alberto F. Alesina and Dani Rodrik, "Distributive Politics and Economic Growth," *Quarterly Journal of Economics* 109 (May 1994): 465–90; Torsten Persson and Guido Tabellini, "Is Inequality Harmful for Growth? Theory and Evidence," *American Economic Review* 84 (June 1994): 600–21.

[35] See W. W. Rostow, *The Stages of Economic Growth* (Cambridge: Cambridge University Press, 1960); W. Paul Strassman, "Economic Growth and Income Distribution," *Quarterly Journal of Economics* 70 (August 1956): 202–29. These points were at issue in the debates among development economists during the 1950s and 1960s concerning the relative importance of theorizing about balanced growth in contrast to an emphasis on so-called leading sectors. Robert Fogel's work on the railroads represents a basic criticism of the leading sector approach as applied to the United States by Rostow; see Robert William Fogel, *Railroads and Amercian Economic Growth*, (Baltimore: Johns Hopkins University Press, 1964).

realization of growth in economies combining high per capita incomes and relative equality in circumstances.[36]

Our vision of how initial conditions, especially the extent of inequality, had long-lasting effects on the path of development is obviously akin to the latter approach. In our view, the tendency of New World economies that began with extreme inequality to adopt institutions that served to advantage members of the elite and hamper social mobility made it more difficult for these economies to realize sustained growth.[37] Especially during the nineteenth century, incentives for ordinary people to participate in the commercial economy played a fundamental role in the process of early industrialization. Despite the complexity of the relation between equality and the onset of growth, and the likelihood that it varies with context, research on the experience in the United States supports the hypothesis that New World economies with broad access to economic opportunities and participation were better positioned to realize economic growth during the late eighteenth and nineteenth centuries. Evidence comes primarily from investigations into the sources and nature of productivity growth in the era when the United States pulled ahead. Studies of both agriculture and manufacturing find that productivity increased substantially during the first stages of industrialization, but these advances were based largely on changes in organization, methods, and design that were individually incremental but widely adopted and cumulatively important. Using the extension of navigable waterways as one of several indicators of the expansion of markets, we find that firms (and farms) in a wide range of early manufacturing industries responded to increasing opportunities and competition by raising total factor productivity at nearly modern rates from the 1820s on, despite small firm size and limited diffusion of mechanization and inanimate sources of power. This fundamental aspect of the record, dramatized by the result that the less capital-intensive industries registered rates of total factor productivity growth roughly equivalent to those of the more capital-intensive ones, suggests that the early-nineteenth-century sources of technological progress, on which the onset of growth was based, were not at all dependent on

---

[36] See, for example, Strassman, "Income Distribution;" Sokoloff, "Innovation and Manufacturing."

[37] Brazil and a number of other Latin American countries have had among the most unequal income distributions in the world. Although the United States, Canada, and Costa Rica are far from the most equal, they still rank very high on this scale in the Western Hemisphere. See Klaus Deininger and Lyn Squire, "A New Data Set and Measure of Income Inequality," *World Bank Economic Review* 10 (September 1996): 565–91.

capital deepening or the introduction of radically new and expensive capital equipment.[38]

Indicative of the importance of broad access to the market and to economic opportunity was, as discussed above, the wide range of social groups represented among both ordinary patentees and the so-called great inventors credited with responsibility for particularly significant technological discoveries.[39] Scholars of early industrialization in Great Britain and the Netherlands have reported similar patterns of broad participation in the commercial economy and in innovation.[40]

One might ask whether it is possible to legitimately draw inferences about the experiences of the New World economies in Latin America based on the experience of the United States. Our implicit assumption is that the fundamental nature of the process of early economic growth in the eighteenth and nineteenth centuries, prior to the widespread introduction of mechanization and other heavily capital-intensive technologies, could essentially be the same across all economies. A complex and heroic counterfactual is obviously involved, but there are reasons to be encouraged. The region of the United States that was most like the other categories of New World societies, namely, the South, had an economic structure that resembled those of its Latin American neighbors in the concentration on large-scale agriculture and the high degree of overall inequality – at the same time that its processes of economic growth were much like those under way in the northern United States. Two features of the South are critical for explaining why its economy performed better over the long run. First, its general unsuitability for sugar production

---

[38] See, for example, Winifred B. Rothenberg, "The Productivity Consequences of Market Integration: Agriculture in Massachusetts, 1771–1801," and Kenneth Sokoloff, "Invention, Innovation, and Manufacturing" both in *American Economic Growth*, eds. Gallman and Wallis, 311–40, 345–84. Sokoloff; "Was the Transition from the Artisinal Shop to the Nonmechanized Factory Associated with Gains in Efficiency?: Evidence from the U.S. Manufacturing Censuses of 1820 and 1850," *Explorations in Economic History* 21 (October 1984): 351–82. "Productivity Growth in Manufacturing During Early Industrialization: Evidence from the American Northeast, 1820 to 1860." In *Long-Term Factors in American Economic Growth*, eds. Stanley L. Engerman and Robert E. Gallman, 639–736 (Chicago: University of Chicago Press).

[39] See Kenneth L. Sokoloff, "Inventive Activity in Early Industrial America"; Sokoloff and Khan, "The Democratization of Invention"; Khan and Sokoloff, "Schemes of Practical Utility."

[40] See, for example, Jan de Vries, *The Dutch Rural Economy in the Golden Age, 1500–1700* (New Haven: Yale University Press, 1974); Robert C. Allen, *Enclosure and the Yeoman: The Agricultural Development of the South Midlands, 1450–1850* (Oxford: Clarendon Press, 1992); Maxine Berg, *The Age of Manufactures, 1700–1820: Industry, Innovation, and Work in Britain* 2nd ed. (London: Routledge, 1994).

meant that the scale of slave plantations and the share of the population composed of slaves were never as great in the South as in the Caribbean. Inequality in income, human capital, and political power was accordingly never as extreme. Second, many of the significant economic institutions in southern states were either determined at the national level or shaped by competition among states, and they therefore had many features in common with those of northern states. These circumstances helped the South evolve a more commercialized and competitive economy, with a broader range of its population participating fully, than did other New World economies with a legacy of slavery.

We have argued that economic institutions shape opportunities. Even in democracies, economic and political institutions can emerge and persist that foreclose to a broad section of the population opportunities to own land, to obtain schooling, to vote, and to borrow to obtain capital. We have presented evidence of one piece of the puzzle as to why the initially more prosperous and attractive areas of the New World fell behind, and why large sections of their populations remain in extreme poverty. Other parts of the puzzle remain to be explained. How powerful are the various institutions we described – in schooling or banking or land policy, for example – in accounting for or explaining the slower rates of growth among the New World societies that lagged? How can the processes of great inequality and institutions that entrap populations in poverty be short-circuited? We have implicitly suggested a counterfactual: if economies in Latin America and the Caribbean had had climates and soils less suited to activities characterized by slave-based scale economies, or had they had greater scarcity of labor, they would have developed along very different paths – paths with more rapid long-term economic growth, more equal distributions of income, and thus less poverty.

X

The Extent of Inequality and the Timing of Industrialization
We have argued above that despite the high living standards all New World colonies offered Europeans, fundamental differences in their factor endowments, which were perpetuated by government policies, may have predisposed them toward different long-term growth paths. Many of these economies developed extremely unequal distributions of wealth, human capital, and political power early in their histories as colonies and maintained them after independence. The United States and Canada stand out as rather exceptional in being characterized from the beginning by

TABLE 3.3. *Annual Growth Rates of Labor and Total Factor Productivity for Selected Manufacturing Industries in the American Northeast, 1820–60*

Industry	Labor productivity		Total factor productivity	
	Value added	Gross output	Value added	Gross output
Boots/shoes	2.0–2.1	2.2–2.5	1.4–2.0	1.3–1.6
Coaches/harnesses	2.0–2.4	1.7–2.2	1.7–1.9	1.3–1.3
Cotton textiles	2.2–3.3	2.5–3.5	2.3–2.9	1.4–1.7
Furniture/woodwork	2.9–3.0	2.9–3.0	2.7–2.8	2.0–2.1
Glass	2.5	1.8	2.2	1.6
Hats	2.4–2.5	2.7–3.1	2.1–2.5	1.4–1.6
Iron	1.5–1.7	1.7–2.0	1.4–1.4	1.1–1.1
Liquors	1.7–1.9	1.9–2.1	1.2–1.2	1.2
Flour/grist mills	0.6–0.7	1.3–1.3	0.2–0.3	1.0–1.0
Paper	4.3–5.5	5.3–6.2	3.9–4.5	2.3–2.6
Leather tanning	1.2–1.7	2.0–2.6	0.7–1.1	0.9–1.1
Tobacco	2.1–2.4	1.5–2.7	1.4–2.0	0.7–1.0
Wool textiles	2.7–2.8	3.6–3.7	2.4–2.5	1.8–1.9
Capital-intensive industries	[2.0]–2.7	[2.5]–2.9	[1.8]–2.2	[1.3]–1.4
Other industries	[2.3]–2.4	2.3–[2.6]	[1.9]–2.2	[1.4]–1.6
Weighted average total – all industries	[2.2]–2.5	[2.5]–2.7	[1.8]–2.2	[1.3]–1.5

Source: These estimates are drawn from Sokoloff (1986): 698, 706, 719, 722.

Notes: The ranges of estimates reflect the different figures derived from firm data and from industry-wide data. The estimates for the capital-intensive, other, and all industries were computed as weighted averages of the relevant industry-specific figures, The capital-intensive industries include cotton textiles, wool textiles, paper, flour/grist mills, iron, liquors, and leather tanning. The figures in brackets pertain to averages based on fewer than the full complement of industries in the respective class.

high material living standards among both elites and common people, as well as by relative equality in other dimensions. It may, we suggest, not be coincidental that the economies in this latter group began to industrialize much earlier and thus realized more growth over the long run.

Reported in Table 3.3 are estimates of manufacturing productivity growth between 1820 and 1860 computed from cross sections of firm data. They indicate that a wide range of manufacturing industries were able to raise productivity at nearly modern rates, despite the small firm sizes and limited diffusion of mechanization and inanimate sources of power characteristic of most industries until the 1850s. This fundamental aspect of the record, dramatized by the result that the less capital-intensive industries registered rates of total factor productivity growth roughly equivalent to those of the more capital-intensive, suggests that the sources of technological progress during the onset of growth extended across virtually all industries and were not dependent on radically new or specific capital equipment or capital deepening. The implication that increases in the amount of capital used per worker did not play a major role in accounting for technical change during early industrialization is further reinforced by the estimates that the dominant share of labor productivity growth is due instead to advances in total factor productivity.[41]

This pattern of relatively balanced productivity growth across a broad spectrum of industries is difficult to attribute to a fundamental break-through in technology or a general increase in the capital intensity of production. On the contrary, it appears instead to be more consistent with the hypothesis that firms and individuals throughout the economy were responding to a common environmental stimulus for improvements in technology – like the dramatic expansion of markets that characterized the period. Indeed, this view that broad advances in productivity were induced by the growth in the volume and geographic extent of commerce, originating in the extension of networks of low-cost transportation and increases in income, has received strong support from recent scholarship. Studies of agriculture have found that farms with easy access to major markets became more specialized, used their labor more intensively, and were more apt to adopt new crops and products. Studies of manufacturing have found that firms in proximity to broad markets maintained higher average levels of productivity and were generally distinguished by operating at a larger scale, with a more extensive division (and perhaps intensification) of labor, and with a more standardized product – but without markedly different ratios of capital to labor. The conclusion that growth was stimulated by market development is consistent with both the geographic patterns of productivity as well as the incremental nature of the changes made in technique. Although their cumulative impact could have been major, it is conceivable, if not entirely natural, to think of individually marginal improvements as outcomes of efforts to respond creatively to technological problems raised by competition and opportunities in the marketplace.

[41] For the results of such a decomposition of the sources of labor productivity growth, and discussion, see Sokoloff, "Productivity Growth in Manufacturing," Sokoloff, "Invention, Innovation and Manufacturing." The qualitative finding of the relative insignificance of capital deepening in most industries is evident, however, from the pattern in Table 3.3 showing that when output is measured in terms of value added, the rate of total factor productivity growth is nearly as rapid as the rate of labor productivity growth.

Greater equality in economic circumstances among the U.S. population not only encouraged investment in financial intermediaries and transportation directly through the structure of demand but also through a legal framework that was conducive to private enterprise in both law and administration. The right to charter corporations was reserved to state governments, and this authority was generously wielded in order to promote investments, first in transportation and financial institutions but ultimately in manufacturing as well. Responding to widespread sentiment that there should be few obstacles to private initiatives, as well as an opposition to privilege, many state governments had in effect routinized the process of forming a corporation with general laws of incorporation by the middle of the nineteenth century.[42] Another example of a legal system that encouraged private enterprise is provided by the relationship between equality and rates of invention. Not only is it likely that the greater equality in human capital accounted partially for the high rates of invention in the United States overall, but the more general concern with the opportunities for extracting the returns from invention contributed to a patent system that was probably the most favorable in the world to common people at the time.[43] This pattern stands in stark contrast to that in Mexico and Brazil, where patents were restricted by costs and procedures to the wealthy or influential and where the rights to organize corporations and financial institutions were granted sparingly, largely to protect the value of rights already held by powerful interests.[44] Differences in the degree of equality in circumstances between these economies and the United States seem likely to play an important role in explaining the divergence in experience. For a variety of reasons, therefore, a

---

[42] On the changing means of forming corporations in the United States, see George Heberton Evans, Jr., *Business Incorporation in the United States: 1800–1943* (New York: National Bureau of Economic Research, 1948). Also see Joseph Stancliffe Davis, *Essays in the Earlier History of American Corporations*, 2 vols. (Cambridge: Cambridge University Press, 1917); Shaw Livermore, "Unlimited Liability in Early American Corporations," *Journal of Political Economy* 43 (October 1935): 674–87.

[43] For international comparisons of patent systems, as well as a discussion of the concern with enforcement in the United States, see H. I. Dutton, *The Patent System and Inventive Activity During the Industrial Revolution, 1750–1852* (Manchester: Manchester University Press, 1984); B. Zorina Khan, "Property Rights and Patent Litigation in Early Nineteenth Century America," *Journal of Economic History* 55 (March 1995): 58–97; Fritz Machlup, *An Economic Review of the Patent System* (Washington, D.C.: Government Printing Office, 1958), Study of the Committee on the Judiciary, United States Senate.

[44] See Haber, *Industry and Underdevelopment*; Haber, "Industrial Concentration;" Beatty, "Evolution of Patent Systems."

large degree of inequality might be expected to hamper the evolution of markets and hence delay the realization of sustained economic growth.[45]

XI

The U.S. South: A Different Case?

The U.S. South thrived in terms of growth of output per capita, but both before and after the Civil War, the South lagged behind the North in the evolution of a set of political and economic institutions that were conducive to broad participation in the commercial economy and in the development of extensive capital and product markets.[46] The successes of the antebellum plantation meant that the southern population was more rural than the northern, with general production of manufactures as well as foodstuffs on the farm. Together with the greater inequality in income and human capital, this relative self-sufficiency of slave plantations reduced the extent of market development, both relative to the North and to what might otherwise have been in the South.[47] Moreover, the scale of labor requirements and the nature of differing seasonal patterns of production encouraged a greater degree of diversification on the part of southern slave plantations than was the case in small-scale northern agriculture, resulting in relatively few commercial cities and towns. Because manufacturing productivity was strongly associated with proximity to extensive markets, the limited extent of markets in the South likely contributed to that region's lower levels of manufacturing output

[45] As highly capital-intensive technologies became available, the need to involve broad segments of the population in the market economy in order to achieve sustained growth may have diminished. For a classic statement of a closely related idea, see Alexander Gerschenkron, *Economic Backwardness in Historical Perspective: A Book of Essays* (Cambridge, MA: Harvard University Press, 1962): Ch. 1. For a discussion of different stages in technology and in the sources of productivity growth, see Sokoloff, "Invention, Innovation and Manufacturing."

[46] Jack P. Greene, *Pursuits of Happiness* (Chapel Hill: University of North Carolina Press, 1988); Majewski, *House Dividing*; C. Vann Woodward, *Origins of the New South, 1877–1913* (Baton Rouge: Louisiana State University Press, 1971); J. Morgan Kousser, *The Shaping of Southern Politics: Suffrage Restrictions and the Establishment of the One-Party South, 1880–1910* (New Haven: Yale University Press, 1974).

[47] Ralph V. Anderson and Robert E. Gallman, "Slavery as Fixed Capital: Slave Labor and Southern Economic Development," *Journal of American History* 64 (June 1977): 24–46; William N. Parker, "Slavery and Southern Economic Development: A Hypothesis and Some Evidence," *Agricultural History* 44 (1970): 115–25; Fogel, *Without Consent or Contract*; Eugene D. Genovese, *The Political Economy of Slavery. Studies in the Economy and Society of the Slave South* (New York: Pantheon, 1965).

per capita as well as lower manufacturing productivity.[48] Inventive activity, at least as gauged by patenting, was also lower than in the North.

The Civil War and the emancipation of the slaves led to dramatic changes in southern agriculture, with the disappearance of the plantation as a producing unit.[49] While concentration of landholdings persisted, the dominant producing unit became the small farm, whether owner-operated or worked by tenants under various arrangements.[50] These tenants in the South, particularly blacks, generally had limited incomes and wealth relative to farmers in the North, and they faced major obstacles to their accumulation of both physical and human capital.[51] It was several decades before the South began to develop a more urbanized economy with a larger manufacturing base, and the region continued to trail the rest of the nation for nearly a century.

XII

Conclusion

Why have the United States and Canada been so much more successful than other New World economies since the era of European colonization? Many of the other New World societies enjoyed high levels of product per capita early in their histories. The divergence in paths can be traced back to the achievement of sustained economic growth by the United States and Canada during the eighteenth and early nineteenth centuries, while the others did not manage to attain this goal until late in the nineteenth or in the twentieth century, if ever. Although many explanations have been offered, in this chapter we have highlighted the relevance of substantial differences in the degree of inequality in wealth, human capital, and political power in accounting for the divergence in the records of growth. Moreover, we have suggested that the roots of these disparities in the extent of inequality lay in differences in the initial factor endowments of the respective colonies. Of particular significance for generating extreme

---

[48] Tchakerian, "Productivity, Extent of Markets."

[49] Fogel, *Without Consent*; Ralph Shlomowitz, "Transition From Slave to Freedom: Labor Arrangements in Southern Agriculture, 1865–1870," unpublished Ph.D. dissertation, University of Chicago, 1979; Nancy Lynn Virts, "Plantations, Land Tenure and Efficiency in the Postbellum South: The Effects of Emancipation on Southern Agriculture," unpublished Ph.D. dissertation, University of California, Los Angeles, 1985.

[50] Robert Higgs, *Competition and Coercion: Blacks in the American Economy, 1865–1914* (Cambridge: Cambridge University Press, 1977); Robert A. Margo, *Race and Schooling in the South, 1880–1950* (Chicago: University of Chicago Press, 1990).

[51] For a different view, see Fogel, *Without Consent*.

inequality were the suitability of some regions for the cultivation of sugar and other highly valued commodities, in which economies of production could be achieved through the use of slaves, as well as the presence in some colonies of large concentrations of Native Americans. Both of these conditions encouraged the evolution of societies where relatively small elites of European descent could hold highly disproportionate shares of the wealth, human capital, and political power – and establish economic and political dominance over the mass of the population. Conspicuously absent from the nearly all-inclusive list of New World colonies with these conditions were the British settlements in the northern part of the North American continent.

We have also called attention to the tendencies of governmental policies toward maintaining the basic importance of the initial factor endowment or the same general degree of inequality along their respective economy's path of development. The atypical immigration policies of Spanish America have been given special emphasis in this regard; while other European nations promoted and experienced mushrooming immigration to their New World colonies, Spain restricted the flows of Europeans, leading to a stagnant or declining number of migrants to its settlements during the late seventeenth and eighteenth centuries. It was not until late in the nineteenth century that former Spanish colonies like Argentina and Cuba began to recruit and attract Europeans in sufficiently large quantities to shift the composition of their populations and erode the rather elite status and positions of the small communities of old families of European descent. The New World economies that had long histories of importing slaves to exploit the advantages of their soils and climates for the production of crops like sugar also continued to be characterized by much inequality and to be dominated by small, white segments of their populations. Why extreme inequality persisted for centuries in these classes of New World economies is not entirely clear. Certainly large deficits in wealth, human capital, and political power, such as plagued Native Americans and slaves (and free blacks, after emancipation), are difficult to overcome, especially in preindustrial societies. Elites would be expected to (and did) use their political control to restrict competition they faced over resources, and large gaps in literacy, familiarity with technology or markets, and in other forms of human capital could take generations to close in even a free and seemingly evenhanded society. Indeed, these factors undoubtedly go far in explaining the persistence of inequality over the long run in the New World cases of concern here. The close correspondences between economic standing and race, however, may also have contributed to the maintenance of substantial inequality, either through natural, unconscious processes or by increasing the efficacy of direct action by elites to retain their privileged positions and holdings.

Our discussion of why the United States and Canada led other New World economies in the realization of sustained economic growth during the eighteenth and nineteenth centuries raises another old controversy. Past treatments of the relationship between economic growth and inequality have tended to focus either on the effect of equality on rates of capital accumulation or on the impact of growth on the extent of inequality. Our emphasis on the implications of greater equality for the evolution of markets, institutions conducive to widespread commercialization, and technological change, proposes a different direction for future research. This hypothesis is suggested by recent findings about the process of early industrialization in the United States and should be understood as pertaining to a particular era and range of inequality. It is based on the idea, consistent with the evidence examined to date, that preindustrial economies of the late eighteenth and early nineteenth centuries had a large potential for sustained productivity growth derived from an accumulation of innumerable incremental improvements discovered and implemented throughout an economy by small-scale producers with rather ordinary sets of skills. These advances in practice were induced in the United States by alterations in incentives and opportunities associated with the spread of markets, and were made possible by a broad acquaintance with basic technological knowledge as well as by broad access to full participation in the commercial economy.

Our conjecture – that other New World economies might have been able to realize growth in much the same way as the United States if not for their initial factor endowments and the governmental policies that upheld their influence – is obviously speculative and requires further study. Nevertheless, regardless of the outcome of such evaluations, the systematic patterns we have identified in the development of the New World economies should stand.

4

The Evolution of Suffrage Institutions

I

The conduct of elections, including the definition of who holds the right to vote, is one of the most crucial institutions in any society. Varying the rules or organization of how votes are cast and of who casts them can have a fundamental impact on the policy choices made by the elected representatives – who in some sense constitute the collective government of the electors. As governments generally have monopoly of power over certain important activities, there are often major implications for how a society's resources and wealth are distributed across the population, as well as for the pace of economic growth. Given what is at stake, it should not be surprising that throughout history many have fought and died over both the design of the rules and the outcomes of elections.

There has been a renewed appreciation by political scientists and economists of how democratic rules for electing government representatives might contribute to different paths of institutional and economic development, and a particular focus on the background to, and consequences of, decisions to extend the franchise. Where an economic elite wields highly disproportionate political power, or a political elite exploits its position for economic advantage, a broadening of political influence through an extension of the franchise could diminish its material standing.[1] It is not obvious, therefore, why a political elite would choose

---

[1] Alberto F. Alesina and Dani Rodrik, "Distributive Politics and Economic Growth," *Quarterly Journal of Economics* 109 (May 1994): 465–90; and Torsten Persson and Guido Tabellini, "Is Inequality Harmful for Growth? Theory and Evidence," *American Economic Review* 84 (June 1994): 600–21.

to concede more formal influence to other groups. Based on their examination of the experiences in selected Western Europe countries, Daron Acemoglu and James Robinson argued that the franchise was extended when there were threats to the basic social order from below. Elites agreed to share the right to vote in elections, and accepted the moderate loss of political power that stems from such institutional change, because their primary interest was in preserving social stability and the returns to their property. Many, however, have questioned this emphasis on suffrage reform arising solely out of potentially violent class conflict. For example, Alessandro Lizzeri and Nicola Persico contend that the suffrage was extended in nineteenth-century Britain without apparent danger of upheaval. They point out that segments of the elite can actually benefit directly from broadening access to the franchise if there is competition between political parties and if the policy preferences of a subset of the elite coincide in part with those of the disfranchised.[2]

The view that it might be in the interests of the politically powerful to freely choose to share their authority has a rich tradition in American history. Frederick Jackson Turner is the best-known proponent of the idea that the special characteristics of frontier society nourished the evolution of democratic institutions. By his argument, not only did the greater equality prevailing on the frontier inspire demands for broad access to opportunities, but also the scarcity of people meant that local and state governments were extremely concerned with attracting migrants. Because population inflows would lower the cost of labor, and boost land values and tax revenues, frontier societies were induced to adopt institutions congenial to newcomers. Among the conditions that appealed most to migrants were cheap land and full participation in the election of government representatives.[3]

Many scholars have posited a relation between the breadth of the franchise, or of the distribution of political influence more generally, and the choices governments make about public policies, such as how the tax

---

[2] See Alessandro Lizzeri and Nichola Persico, "Why Did the Elites Extend the Suffrage? Democracy and the Scope of Government with an Application to Britain's 'Age of Reform,'" *Quarterly Journal of Economics* 119 (May 2004): 707–65. See also Moshe Justman and Mark Gradstein, "The Industrial Revolution, Political Transition, and the Subsequent Decline in Inequality in 19th Century Britain," *Explorations in Economic History* 36 (April 1999): 109–27, for yet another view.

[3] Frederick Jackson Turner, *The Rise of the New West, 1819–1829* (New York: Harper & Brothers, 1906); Frederick Jackson Turner, *The Frontier in American History* (New York: H. Holt, 1920).

system is structured, what public services to provide, or how to define and enforce property rights.[4] Thus, in addition to reflecting economic and social circumstances, whether, when, and to whom society extends the suffrage may have implications for its long-run path of development. One possibility is that more democratic electorates might be prone to schemes of redistribution that discourage investment and harm the prospects for growth. Another, more favorable outlook, however, is that a broad distribution of political influence fosters higher investments in schooling, infrastructure, and other public goods and services conducive to long-run economic growth.[5]

We may all agree that suffrage institutions have an impact on development, but our understanding of the mechanism varies depending on how the institutions evolved at the times and places they did. In order to improve our knowledge of the origins of institutions, this chapter examines how the rules governing the extension of suffrage evolved in the Americas, across countries and over time. The substantial variation in the initial characteristics of these societies, and the shocks associated with European colonization of the New World, make for a wonderful "natural laboratory" to study the conditions that gave rise to more democratic political institutions.

Extreme variation across the New World existed in the evolution of social and economic institutions. Beginning in the sixteenth century and continuing through the eighteenth century, Europeans established colonies throughout the Americas as part of a worldwide effort to economically exploit underpopulated or underdefended territories. Nations and private agents set about extracting economic and other advantages

---

[4] Alexis de Tocqueville, *Democracy in America* ed. J. P. Mayer (Garden City: Doubleday, 1969), provides a classic discussion. Richard A. Musgrave, *Fiscal Systems* (New Haven: Yale University Press, 1969), discusses patterns of change in government expenditures after the extension of suffrage in many nations over the twentieth century. For other more recent examples of a vast literature, see Robert J. Barro, *Determinants of Economic Growth* (Cambridge, MA: MIT Press, 1997); and Roberto Perotti "Growth, Income Distribution and Democracy," *Journal of Economic Growth* 1 (June 1996): 149–87.

[5] Roland Bénabou, "Unequal Societies: Income Distribution and the Social Contract," *American Economic Review* 90 (March 2000): 96–129; and Gilles Saint-Paul and Thierry Verdier, "Education, Democracy, and Growth," *Journal of Development Economics*, 42 (December 1993): 399–407. The construction and maintenance of a rich cross-country dataset for the modern period has tended to focus attention on the experience of the late twentieth century, to the neglect of processes that play out over earlier and longer periods of time. See Robert Summers and Alan Heston, "The Penn World Table (Mark 5): An Expanded Set of International Comparisons, 1950–1988," *Quarterly Journal of Economics* 106 (May 1991): 327–68.

from unfamiliar types of environments, and there was great diversity in the characteristics of the societies and institutions that evolved. Common to all of the New World colonies was a high marginal product of labor and, for that era, high per capita income. Among the crucial dimensions in which colonies differed, however, was in the homogeneity of the population and in the extent of inequality in the distributions of income and human capital.[6]

We have argued that the substantial variation across these colonies in their initial degrees of inequality was largely attributable to factor endowments broadly conceived.[7] Extreme inequality arose in the colonies of the Caribbean and in Brazil, because their soils and climates gave them a comparative advantage in growing sugar and other lucrative crops produced at lowest cost on large slave plantations. With the consequent importation of enormous numbers of slaves, their populations came to be composed of a small elite of European descent with the dominant share of the population consisting of black slaves, or (later) nonwhite freedmen and their descendants. Extreme inequality in wealth and human capital came to characterize much of Spanish America as well. The inequality arose here from the large concentrations of Native Americans present before the Europeans arrived, and the Spanish practices of awarding claims on land, native labor, and rich mineral resources to members of the elite (although some societies, settled by the Spanish, such as Argentina, Uruguay, and Costa Rica, were less affected). In contrast, the societies of the northern part of North America developed with relative equality and population homogeneity, because there were relatively few Native Americans and the climates and soils favored a regime of family farms centered on grains and livestock instead of one of large slave plantations. Conditions varied across subregions, of course, and those encouraging greater equality were especially prevalent in the northern frontier areas beyond the initial band of settlements on the eastern rim of the continent.

---

[6] For excellent surveys of the early development of the colonies in the New World, see David W. Galenson, "The Settlement and Growth of the Colonies: Population, Labor, and Economic Development," in *The Cambridge Economic History of the United States*, 3 vols., vol. 1, *The Colonial Period* eds. Stanley L. Engerman and Robert E. Gallman: 135–207 (Cambridge: Cambridge University Press, 1996) and James Lockhart and Stuart B. Schwartz, *Early Latin America: A History of Colonial Spanish America and Brazil* (Cambridge: Cambridge University Press, 1983).

[7] See Ch. 1 and Ch. 2. Contemporary estimates indicating that Latin America has, as a region, the greatest degree of income inequality in the world today are suggestive that the extreme disparities of the colonial era have persisted to the present day. See Klaus Deininger and Lyn Squire, "A New Data Set and Measure of Income Inequality," *World Bank Economic Review* 10 (September 1996): 565–91.

We hypothesized, moreover, that the exceptional differences in the degree of inequality across the societies of the Americas, rooted in their respective factor endowments and evident during the colonial era, came to be reflected in the institutions that evolved. In our view, the more disproportionate their claims to resources and political influence, the more effective elites in any society were in shaping legal frameworks and state policies to advantage themselves relative to the rest of the population. In what follows, we show that the early patterns of the extension of the franchise, the proportions of the respective populations voting, and other aspects of the conduct of elections across the Americas are indeed consistent with our argument. Specifically, where there was greater inequality or heterogeneity, the proportion of the population that had the right to vote was generally lower, and the extensions of this right from elite groups to a broad population generally occurred later than it did in areas where a scarcity of labor encouraged measures to attract migrants or where there was relative homogeneity in the population. These relationships, which seem to have held both across the individual states of the United States as well as across the nations of the hemisphere, are all the more striking because most of the New World societies were at least nominal democracies by the middle of the nineteenth century, and had embraced the rhetoric of revolution and modernization during their respective movements for independence. Only a few, however, would extend to most of the population the right to vote and to political influence before the twentieth century.

II

Despite the sentiments popularly attributed to the Founding Fathers of the United States, the formal or conceptual differences across New World societies in who had the right to participate in community decisions were not large even late into the eighteenth century. The British colonies on the mainland, like those elsewhere in the hemisphere, reserved the privilege of voting to white adult men with significant holdings of real estate, although differences in the extent of inequality in landholding across colonies as well as in the specified thresholds meant that the same sort of legal limitation on the franchise implied very different proportions of the population eligible to vote.[8] This practice was rooted in a philosophy

[8] Kirk H. Porter, *A History of Suffrage in the United States* (Chicago: University of Chicago Press, 1918); and Chilton Williamson, *American Suffrage: From Property to Democracy 1760–1860* (Princeton: Princeton University Press, 1960).

tracing back to medieval Britain, in which the right to vote was reserved to "freeholders." The logic was that their stake in land gave them more of a long-term interest in the welfare of the community, and thus the right to be a decision-maker and voter, compared to mere freemen.[9] Communities were treated as akin to business corporations, with landowners analogous to shareholders who were entitled to vote.[10] Indeed, even nonresidents who owned property were frequently permitted to vote. Over time, as the colonies became more diverse socially and economically, the restrictions on the suffrage evolved to take account of the more complex society.

Two general considerations might be said to have framed the political debates that guided the changes in the qualifications for suffrage across the British mainland colonies. One focused on the individual and was concerned with what characteristics gave a person the "right to vote," for example, ownership of property, the payment of taxes, residency, or simply being an adult white male. The other general issue was what would be good for the community or the society. Would it be in the best interests of the society for nonresidents, non-property holders, women, illiterates, criminals, or non-church members to be allowed to vote? Overall, the dominant trend over the colonial period was the movement away from the idea that the right to vote should be based solely on the ownership of land. There was a growing appreciation, especially in urban settings, of how suffrage qualifications specified along this single dimension might exclude otherwise appropriate individuals, Over time, colonies began to introduce means of substituting other assets to meet property requirements, and this development ultimately led to the acceptance of economic qualifications based on the amount of tax payments. In no colony, however, was there a serious challenge to the notion that suffrage should be restricted to property owners.[11]

All thirteen colonies maintained some sort of property qualification for the franchise on the eve of the American Revolution. Georgia, North Carolina, Virginia, New Jersey, New Hampshire, New York, and Rhode Island had minimum real estate requirements, specified in terms of either acreage or value. The remaining six colonies allowed for more flexibility,

---

[9] See Williamson, *American Suffrage* for a discussion of precedents, as well as of the range of "freehold" requirements in the colonies. Long-term leases, extending beyond a lifetime, sometimes satisfied such qualifications.

[10] The notion that communities were like corporations was perhaps most appropriate in colonies.

[11] There were often different qualifications for local than for colony-wide elections, and Williamson, *American Suffrage* has suggested that one reason was to influence the pool of individuals who could serve as local officials.

with the property requirement allowing either landholding, ownership of some other property exceeding a specified minimum, or (in the case of South Carolina) payment of a certain amount of taxes. Given the issues at stake in the conflict between the thirteen colonies and Britain, it should not be surprising that the question of suffrage reform was central to many of the vigorous debates after the Revolution about the organization of state governments, which were sparked by the need for the now independent colonies to establish frameworks for governance. Although some states, such as Rhode Island, merely carried over the voting qualifications in place during the colonial era, eight of the thirteen made substantial changes through the constitutions they adopted during the Revolutionary era. Most moved in the direction of expanding the franchise somewhat, such as by providing for alternative ways of meeting standards for property holders or adopting differential requirements for elections to different posts (such as New York's having higher property requirements for the election of state senators and the governor than for the election of members of its assembly), but only Pennsylvania eliminated wealth qualifications (replacing them with a taxpaying requirement).[12]

The paucity of detailed information on the distribution of wealth poses severe challenges for anyone hoping to construct precise estimates of how these changes in the laws governing suffrage impacted the numbers of eligible voters, but many scholars seem to believe the de facto effects were modest.[13] Although the stringency with which the economic

---

[12] Economic-based qualifications for suffrage were not the only way wealthier classes were granted privileged status in regards to political standing. In 1787 all of the thirteen states except Pennsylvania had economic qualifications for holding office. In six of the twelve (Maryland, Massachusetts, New Hampshire, North Carolina, New Jersey, and South Carolina) the property requirements were considerably higher for serving as governor, senator, or as a representative than they were for voting. See Dudley O. McGovney, *The American Suffrage Medley* (Chicago: University of Chicago Press, 1949): Ch. 1; and Frank Hayden Miller, "Legal Qualifications for Office in America," in *Annual Report of the American Historical Association for the Year 1899* (Washington, D.C.: Government Printing Office, 1900): 89–153.

[13] Porter, *History of Suffrage*, Ch. 1 and Ch. 2. Williamson, *American Suffrage* appears to be more impressed with the conceptual import of the legal changes during the Revolutionary era than was Porter, but skeptical about their direct impact. McGovney, *American Suffrage Medley*, Ch. 1, suggests that roughly half of the adult white male population was eligible to vote in 1787. Charles S. Sydnor, *Gentleman Freeholders: Political Practices in Washington's Virginia* (Chapel Hill: University of North Carolina Press, 1952) has a similar estimate for Virginia. Although recognizing the trend toward easing property requirements, Alexander Keyssar, *The Right to Vote: The Contested History of Democracy in the United States* (New York: Basic Books, 2000), suggests that the proportion of the population eligible to vote may have decreased over the late eighteenth century because of the growing numbers of relatively poor urban workers.

requirements were enforced is unclear, opponents of wealth-based suffrage qualifications often argued that such restrictions were difficult to administer because the amount of wealth held by an individual could change quickly (especially in areas with rapid population growth), and that decisions about valuation involved some degree of arbitrariness. That there were protracted political struggles, waged both inside and outside of state constitutional conventions, over the fixing of the requirements for the suffrage and the procedures for registration suggest that the laws made a difference in who was able to vote. Nevertheless, in cases where the desire to vote was intense and the distinctions to be drawn between individuals were fine, if not minute, something less than rigorous application of the requirements might have seemed prudent to the authorities.

In general, the major institutional innovation of doing away with all suffrage qualifications related to property, or economic standing more generally, was led by new states entering the Union (see Table 4.1). Not a single state that entered the union after the thirteen colonies had a property requirement for the franchise, and although a few adopted tax-based qualifications, it was only in Louisiana that the restriction was a serious constraint and endured for very long. Most of the original thirteen states (all but Rhode Island, Virginia, and North Carolina) eliminated property qualifications by the middle of the 1820s, but tax-based requirements for suffrage (and for the holding of public office) lingered on in many of them into the middle of the nineteenth century and beyond. Of the states that formed the originally settled areas, the leaders in doing away with economic-based qualifications for the franchise were those that were sparsely settled and were on the fringe (Vermont, New Hampshire, and Georgia).

The spirit of the Revolution undoubtedly contributed to the movement for the extension of the franchise, but the rather systematic pattern of where the changes were made seems significant and deserves attention.[14]

---

[14] Although many observers during that era noted how the new states, and especially those in the West, were more democratic in their suffrage laws and in other respects, Frederick Jackson Turner, (*Rise* and *Frontier*) was perhaps the first major scholar to examine why they did so, and their effects on the old states: "The frontier States that came into the Union in the first quarter of a century of its existence came in with democratic suffrage provisions, and had reactive effects of the highest importance upon the older States whose peoples were being attracted there." See Turner, *Frontier*, p. 30. Williamson, *American Suffrage*, was skeptical of the notion the West was unique, however, and suggested that the prevalence of universal suffrage in the frontier states may have been due to the difficulty of establishing freehold rights in a newly settled area

TABLE 4.1. *Summary of Economic-based Qualifications for Suffrage*

	Qualifications in 1787 or Year of Entry	Year Economic Qualifications Ended, or Qualifications in 1860
Original Thirteen Colonies		
New Hampshire	tax	1792
Massachusetts	property	1821 (property), tax requirement in 1860
Rhode Island	property	1842 (property), tax requirement in 1860
Connecticut	property	1818 (property), 1845 (tax)
New York	property	1821 (property), 1826 (tax)
New Jersey	property	1807 (property), 1844 (tax)
Pennsylvania	tax	tax requirement in 1860
Delaware	property	1792 (property), tax requirement in 1860
Maryland	property	1802
Virginia	property	1850
North Carolina	property	1856 (property), tax requirement in 1860
South Carolina	tax	1810 (tax)
Georgia	property	1789 (property), 1798 (tax)
New States		
Vermont	none (1791)	
Kentucky	none (1792)	
Tennessee	none (1796)	
Ohio	tax (1803)	1851 (tax)
Louisiana	tax (1812)	1845 (tax)
Indiana	none (1816)	
Mississippi	tax (1817)	1832 (tax)
Illinois	none (1818)	
Maine	none (1819)	
Alabama	none (1819)	
Missouri	none (1820)	

Sources: Porter (1918); Williamson (1960); and Keyssar (2000).
Notes: Tax requirement in 1860 means that a tax-based qualification for suffrage was still in effect in that year.

where land titling was imperfect and recent. It is interesting, however, that this pattern of frontier states providing broader access to suffrage, and to property rights, was repeated later in these states more liberal treatment of women. See John R. Lott, Jr. and Lawrence W. Kenny, "Did Women's Suffrage Change the Size and Scope of Government?" *Journal of Political Economy* 10 (December 1999): 1163–98 and B. Zorina Khan, "Married Women's Property Laws and Female Commercial Activity," *Journal*

Why were frontier states more liberal in extending the franchise than the original states that had long been settled? One possible explanation is that the U.S. Constitution and Congress had laid out a process for new states to join the union and that process may have favored the adoption of state constitutions with universal white male suffrage.[15] Although this hypothesis certainly has some relevance, the initial policy laid out in the Northwest Ordinance of 1787 (reaffirmed in 1789 by the first Congress) specified a freehold requirement for suffrage that held for elections of territorial governments as well as of delegates to constitutional conventions. Such a law would not seem to bias new states toward universal white male suffrage. The freehold requirement held until 1811, when Congress – spurred by concerns of territories that relatively few of their residents could meet the freehold requirement – replaced it with a taxpaying requirement for all territorial residents (aliens as well as U.S. citizens). Thus, the pattern of frontier areas or new states choosing to extend the franchise more broadly than their neighboring states to the East does not appear to have been driven by the preferences of the U.S. Congress, but rather by conditions in those states.

Scarcity of labor is a condition characteristic of frontier areas, as well as newly settled regions with small native populations, that might have encouraged new states to place fewer restrictions on who had the right to vote. Nearly all of the residents of such territories or states, and certainly property holders and the elite more generally, would have had a strong interest in attracting more people to settle there. If the right to participate in the political process was desirable to potential migrants, the new states thus had an economic incentive to adopt liberal suffrage provisions as a lure.[16] That voter participation was higher in western states than in eastern, and that migrants wrote back to friends and relatives in Europe to proudly tell them about how they had cast votes, is

---

of Economic History 56 (June 1996): 356–88. See also Richard P. McCormick, "New Perspectives on Jacksonian Politics," *American Historical Review* 65 (January 1960): 288–301; and Richard P. McCormick, *The Second American Party System: Party Formation in the Jacksonian Era* (Chapel Hill: University of North Carolina Press, 1966), for discussion of the variation over states and time in the proportion of adult white males who voted.

[15] See the discussion in Keyssar, *Right*.

[16] The significance of this incentive is dramatically illustrated by the movement of states in the Midwest, such as Wisconsin, Michigan, Indiana, Kansas, and Minnesota, to ease residency requirements for aliens. After Wisconsin (which had the highest proportion of foreign born in its population of any state in 1850) moved first in 1848, Michigan and Indiana soon followed. See the discussion in Keyssar, *Right*, p. 33.

perhaps a testament that this right was highly valued.[17] Not all potential migrants would have attached such significance to being able to vote, but frontier states typically offered many other enticements as well (some inscribed in state or territorial laws and some grounded in federal policies, as in the case of the Northwest Ordinance) including cheap land, generous provision of public services, and laws conducive to broad access to economic opportunities.[18] In other words, the liberal constitutional provisions regarding suffrage were only one part of a major organized effort, involving many institutions, to attract migrants – a campaign that appears to have been systematically encouraged by the conditions prevalent in the frontier states.[19] Moreover, once some of these states moved to offer these attractions to potential migrants, other states likely felt pressure to

[17] McCormick, *Second American Party System*, 326, concludes that voting rates in the new states were "on the whole above the national average, except in 1832," even after most of the older states adopted universal white male suffrage. For an example of how immigrants valued easy access to suffrage and citizenship, see Walter B. Kamphoefner, Wolfgang Helbich, and Ulrike Sommer, eds., *News From the Land of Freedom: German Immigrants Write Home* (Ithaca: Cornell University Press, 1996): 166. "This time we have elected the famous General Grand [sic]. I also voted for him; may God grant him the wisdom & understanding & moderation & strength to govern this troubled country for the best. I can't help saying that I feel proud at the thought of being an American citizen ... It is a wonderful feeling to realize that you can replace a hateful government with another one."

[18] This was less true in the southern states, but the extension of suffrage to all adult white males had the additional benefit in such areas of strengthening solidarity among the white population. See Lance E. Davis and Douglass C. North, *Institutional Change and American Economic Growth* (Cambridge: Cambridge University Press, 1971), for discussion of the Northwest Ordinance; and Paul W. Gates, *History of Public Land Law Development* (Washington, D.C.: Government Printing Office, 1968), for discussion of land policies. Support for public schools and other publicly provided goods might be considered as other means of offering greater opportunities to potential migrants. Although many factors were involved, and the relationships were undoubtedly complex, the West had a rather good record overall. For evidence on regional patterns in the development of public schools, and in the regulation of entry into the financial sector, see Albert Fishlow, "The Common School Revival: Fact or Fancy?" in *Industrialization in Two Systems: Essays in Honor of Alexander Gerschenkron*, ed. Henry Rosovsky, 40–67 (New York: Wiley, 1946), and Hugh Rockoff, "The Free Banking Era: A Reexamination," *Journal of Money, Credit, and Banking* 6 (May 1974): 141–67. Of perhaps particular relevance here is Fishlow's account of how it was in the West that the public sector played an especially important role in promoting primary schooling during the antebellum period.

[19] In the words of Carl Wittke, *We Who Built America: The Saga of the Immigrant* (New York: Prentice Hall, 1939): 105–06:

In the middle of the last century, the Middle West needed population above everything else. To attract desirable immigrants was the overpowering ambition of practically every new state in this region. State after state began to enact legislation to encourage and stimulate migration to its borders artificially. The attractions offered

alter their laws to remain competitive. It need hardly be recounted that these early frontier states were indeed extremely successful at attracting migrants.

Elites in labor-scarce frontier areas should have been more strongly motivated to attract migrants and stimulate population growth than their counterparts in long-settled areas, but there may have been other mechanisms at work linking labor scarcity to broader suffrage institutions as well. For example, as one would expect in places with a relative abundance of land and scarcity of labor, frontier areas were characterized by greater equality or homogeneity among the population.[20] Either because of the political ideologies fostered by such homogeneity, the hazards of

by favorable legislation and the persuasiveness of the agents of state immigration commissions were important factors in explaining the immigrant tide into the Mississippi Valley. By its constitution of 1850, Michigan gave the franchise to all newcomers who had declared their intention to become naturalized and who had resided in the state for two and a half years. Its immigration agency, established in 1848 and not abolished until 1885, issued attractive pamphlets in German, and its first immigration commissioner was instructed to spend half his time in New York and half in Stuttgart, Germany. Wisconsin had a special commission as early as 1851 . . . The Wisconsin Constitutional Convention of 1846 gave the franchise to immigrants after a declaration of their intention to become naturalized and one year's residence in the state.

Billington saw similar processes at work in the South during the early decades of the century. See Ray Allen Billington, *Westward Expansion: A History of the American Frontier*, 2nd ed. (New York: Macmillan, 1960): 324.

The "Great Migration" into the Gulf Plains made statehood possible for both Mississippi and Alabama. Mississippi acted first, for its concentrated population was able to apply greater pressure, and in 1817 entered the Union; Alabama followed two years later. Both adopted constitutions reflecting the leveling influence of the frontier. Neither required property for voting; both granted the franchise to all male whites residing there one year. Each made the legislative supreme over the governor – whose veto of any act could be overridden by a simple majority vote – and vested in that elective body power to appoint most state officials including judges. Representation in the assemblies was apportioned on the basis of free white population, thus giving the planter no advantage over the small farmer in government matters. The liberalism of the constitutions served as an additional inducement to settlers.

Also see Benjamin Horace Hibbard, *A History of the Public Land Policies* (New York: Macmillan, 1924).

[20] For evidence of the relative equality of populations in frontier states, see Lee Soltow, *Men and Wealth in the United States, 1850–1870* (New Haven: Yale University Press, 1975); William H. Newell, "Inheritance on the Maturing Frontier. Butler County, Ohio, 1803–1865," and J. R. Kearl and Clayne Pope, "Choices, Rents, and Luck: Economic Mobility of Nineteenth-Century Utah Households," in *Long-Term Factors in American Economic Growth*, eds. Stanley L. Engerman and Gallman, 261–303 and 225–260 (Chicago: University of Chicago Press, 1986). Also see David W. Galenson and Clayne L. Pope, "Economic and Geographic Mobility on the Farming Frontier: Evidence From Appanoose County, Iowa, 1850–1870," *Journal of Economic History* 49

trying to define a meaningful and consequential threshold within a relatively continuous distribution, or because the amount of property owned
at a particular point in time was not very informative of an individual's
life course or commitment to his community in such settings, the greater
equality in the new states may have made it more difficult to sustain
a case for discriminating among otherwise rather similar individuals on
the basis of wealth or economic standing. Thus, while the relationship
may have been the result of a variety of different processes, the observation that the new states were the leaders in doing away with wealth
and other economic-based qualifications for the franchise is certainly
consistent with the hypothesis regarding the importance of equality in
accounting for the way institutions evolved.

The movement toward universal white adult male suffrage, or the
elimination of all economic-based qualifications for the vote, began when
Vermont and Kentucky joined the United States in 1791 and 1792, respectively. Perhaps inspired by its neighbor in 1792, New Hampshire – which
resembled a frontier area in many respects – swept away the taxpaying
qualification that it had previously adopted (in 1784) to replace a rather
high property requirement. Although making suffrage reform a live issue
of political debate, these states did not immediately attract a flood of
imitators, especially because both Pennsylvania and South Carolina had
in 1790 adopted new state constitutions which maintained, in slightly
weakened forms, qualifications that were primarily tax based.[21]

The suffrage issue was of course only one of many important issues that
divided the population, and the coalitions that formed to fight political
battles were somewhat different in each state. In general, however, the
struggles over economic-based restrictions on the franchise were more
intense, and extended over much longer periods, in the older states,
such as Massachusetts, New York, Rhode Island, and Virginia. The new
entrants to the union, in contrast, rarely adopted meaningful economic
requirements for suffrage during this era.[22] Louisiana, the only significant
deviation from the pattern among new states, joined the union in 1812

(September 1989): 635–55 for evidence on the returns accruing to early settlers from
immigration to frontier or labor-scarce areas.

[21] During the last decade of the eighteenth century, Tennessee joined the union with a
freehold requirement (but one that was waived for those who had been residents for
six months) for the suffrage, and Delaware and Georgia revised their laws to set the
payment of a state or country tax, or of any assessed taxes, as the test. See Porter,
History of Suffrage; Williamson, *American Suffrage*; McCormick, "New Perspectives";
and Keyssar, *Right*.

[22] After Tennessee, the next state to join the union was Ohio, in 1803, which required of
its voters that they had paid a county tax or else worked on the public highway.

with a landholding alternative to a relatively stringent tax qualification; anyone who had actually purchased land from the United States government had the right to vote, however, only as long as he was a white male who had resided in the county in question for a year.[23]

Louisiana notwithstanding, the innovations in suffrage laws over the first two decades of the United States signify a critical juncture. The use of wealth as a basis for distinguishing who should vote was clearly becoming less viable, and the ultimate fate of such qualifications was becoming clear.[24] This did not mean, however, that there was opposition to all restrictions on who could vote. White men might come to believe that differentiation on the basis of wealth was unfair, unreasonable, or inconsistent with basic rights, especially where wealth was relatively equally distributed and there was substantial social mobility among that relatively homogeneous population. But they remained comfortable supporting the exclusion of groups that were, in their view, obviously distinctive and unsuitable for participating in community decisions: blacks, women, children, Native Americans, the mentally incompetent, those with criminal records, and those (immigrants as well as native born) who had not long been resident in the county or state.[25] When there were wealth-based restrictions, there had been no real need for provisions that dealt specifically with these classes, but as states eliminated or weakened the

[23] It is notable that Louisiana failed to follow the examples of some southern states such as Georgia, Maryland, and South Carolina, which had formally or effectively done away with economic-based requirements and allowed white adult males to qualify for suffrage by length of residency in 1798, 1802, and 1810, respectively. The changes in these state constitutions to extend the suffrage were highly controversial, with the alignments in favor and in opposition not corresponding all that strongly with political party. Some other reforms dealing with the conduct of elections, such as the introduction of balloting (as opposed to voice votes) and the expansion of the number of polling places were also introduced at about the same time. In South Carolina, the movement for suffrage reform coincided with concern about the possibility of war with Britain and seems to have benefited somewhat from the view that those who bore arms in the militia should be able to vote. See Williamson, *American Suffrage*, Ch. 8.

[24] Mississippi, in 1817, was the last state to enter the union without universal adult white male suffrage, and from then on the maintenance of economic-based restrictions was largely a holding action. Many of the original thirteen states replaced wealth qualifications with tax-based requirements, but it is not clear how binding they were. Of course, the use of poll taxes expanded greatly in the late nineteenth and early twentieth centuries as a way of obstructing blacks and immigrants from voting.

[25] See the discussion in Keyssar, *Right*, Ch. 3. We make reference to the significance of "homogeneity" and "heterogeneity" throughout this volume, even though they are rather subjective concepts and difficult to measure. The terms are useful for us, and for social scientists generally, because they encompass variation along many dimensions of individual characteristics, including those we think were especially important for social and legal standing across the Americas during the period under study: race and ethnicity, gender, and economic status. We recognize, however, that the salience of any of these

economic-based qualifications, there was increasing emphasis on introducing or tightening qualifications that would keep undesirable groups out of the electorate.[26] At the same time that Delaware, Maryland, Connecticut, New Jersey, and Pennsylvania eased their economic qualifications, each altered its constitution to exclude blacks. On the eve of the Civil War, only New York (where a property requirement of $250 was applied to blacks alone) and five New England states (where those of African descent were exceptionally rare) had extended the franchise to blacks.[27]

Indiana, Illinois, and Missouri were brought into the nation between 1815 and 1820. None had any suffrage qualification related to wealth or to tax payments. There was little support within the relatively homogenous populations of the western states for drawing a line to distinguish the franchised from the disfranchised among white adult males; indeed, a modest proposal to require a tax payment was voted down resoundingly in the Missouri constitutional convention of 1820. After Ohio was admitted in 1803, no northern state admitted to the union came in with a property or taxpaying qualification (and no southern state, after Mississippi in 1817). Residency requirements, strictures on race, gender, and age, as well as disqualifications for infamous crimes were the only constraints on suffrage imposed in the more newly settled areas. Lines continued to be drawn, but the population was increasingly skeptical of basing them on purely pecuniary factors.[28]

---

characteristics may vary with context. Groups that seem obviously distinctive in one context, may not seem so different in another. See the insightful discussions of this and related issues in Lauren Benton, *Law and Colonial Cultures: Legal Regimes in World History, 1400–1900* (Cambridge: Cambridge University Press, 2002), especially Ch. 2.

[26] Indeed, it was typical for a package of reforms affecting the composition of the electorate to be adopted together with the requirements for length of residence and mental health strengthened to offset the effects of lower economic-based qualifications. It is notable that despite the fact that virtually all of the new states beyond the original thirteen entered the union with weak or no economic-based requirements for the franchise, Kentucky (only for a brief period) and Vermont were the only ones that allowed blacks to vote. The list of those that never allowed blacks to vote before the Fourteenth Amendment includes California, Colorado, Illinois, Indiana, Iowa, Kansas, Michigan, Minnesota, Missouri, Nebraska, Nevada, Ohio, Oregon, Utah, and Wisconsin, as well as all of the southern states.

[27] See the discussion in Porter, *History of Suffrage*, Chs. 2–4; and Kenneth M. Stampp, *America in 1857: A Nation on the Brink* (New York: Oxford University Press, 1990): 134. In some states, Indians who were living in tribes or who had not paid taxes were specifically excluded from voting.

[28] Maine, once part of Massachusetts, joined the United States in 1819, and its constitutional convention issued a public statement describing its stand on the question: "Pecuniary qualifications have been productive of little benefit; sometimes of injustice.

Property- or tax-based qualifications were most strongly entrenched in the original thirteen states, and dramatic political battles took place at a series of prominent state constitutional conventions held during the late 1810s and 1820s. For example, although the Committee on Elective Franchise to the New York State convention of 1821 had recommended the abolition of all property distinctions (requiring of voters only virtue and morality), opponents of universal suffrage put up a spirited defense. After lengthy discussion, and a strong vote against an explicit property qualification, a compromise plan that offered a wide set of alternatives was enacted: a voter must have paid a state or county tax, or have performed military service, or have worked on a public highway, or have lived three years in the state (instead of the ordinary one-year requirement); in 1826, these qualifications were dispensed with in favor of universal white adult male suffrage for residents.[29] Another heated debate took place at the Massachusetts convention of 1820, where John Adams and other notables warned of the consequences of extending the franchise. Although their eloquence was not sufficient to save a property qualification, the new constitution did include a requirement that either a county or state tax had been paid. At an equally turbulent convention in 1829, with James Madison, James Monroe, and John Marshall participating, the delegates revised the Virginia constitution but maintained a rather stringent property requirement. This lasted until 1850. In general, the changes in the laws governing suffrage were introduced without violence. Rhode Island is the one exception. There, protracted political conflict led in 1842 to civil strife quelled by federal troops, and the reform adopted in that year included maintaining the existing property requirement and a long residency requirement for those (mostly Irish) born outside of the United States.[30]

They are too often relaxed or strained to suit the purposes of the day. The convention has therefore extended the right of suffrage, so that no person is disqualified for want of property unless he be a pauper." See Porter, *History of Suffrage*, 50–51. Of the two southern states established during these years, Alabama made no reference to property in its suffrage laws, but Mississippi did adopt a requirement of either a tax payment or service in the state militia (one that was abandoned in 1832). Both devoted considerable attention to specifying which classes of the population could vote, and which – including various classes of criminals – could not.

[29] See the discussions in Porter, *History of Suffrage*; Williamson, *American Suffrage*; and Marchette Chute, *The First Liberty. A History of the Right to Vote in America, 1619–1850* (New York: Dutton, 1969). Most of the so-called founding fathers were believers in property requirements. Benjamin Franklin and Thomas Jefferson were in the minority.

[30] See Keyssar, *Right*, 71–76, for a discussion of the Dorr War in Rhode Island. He argues that the emergence of a significant working class population made the question of whether to do away with economic qualifications a much more problematic proposition for elites.

Vigorous political struggles were necessary to do away with property or tax-based qualifications in the majority of the original thirteen states. The restrictions were incrementally but continuously eroded – often to the point of a token tax payment of a dollar or two. Because of our limited knowledge about patterns of wealthholding and of tax payments, and because of shifts in the regional distribution of the population, it is difficult to construct precise estimates of how the eligible pool of voters changed over time. As shown in Table 4.2, however, comparisons of the number of votes cast with the adult white male population indicate that a very high rate of voter participation was realized rather early in the nineteenth century. These figures suggest that by 1820 more than half of adult white males were casting votes, except in those states that still retained property requirements or substantial tax requirements for the franchise – Virginia and Rhode Island (the two states that maintained property restrictions through 1840), and New York as well as Louisiana.[31] The clear implication is that the adoption of laws that extended suffrage contributed to the attainment of broad participation in elections. Some may consider the estimates puzzling in that the voting rates are higher in early nonpresidential elections than in the presidential elections, but that is probably a testament to citizens caring most about local issues during this era and presidential races not generally being contested seriously at the state level.[32] Overall, the remarkably high rates of voter participation,

[31] Ohio seems also to have had a low rate of voting before 1824, but not afterwards. It is not clear why. It did maintain a requirement that adult white males had to have paid a state or county tax, or had been compelled to labor on the "roads" in order to have the right to vote. However, that requirement was not repealed until 1851, long after the rate of voting had risen sharply to levels above the regional average.

[32] This view helps to explain why the right to vote may have been so important to populations in recently settled or rapidly growing areas. Residents would likely have strong interests in public projects, and naturally value the ability to directly influence local and state officials. The evidence of high rates of voting in local and state elections, despite the presumably high cost of going to the polls in that era, is consistent with the observations of de Tocqueville, *Democracy in America*, 243, who was much impressed with how involved Americans were in local political affairs and governance:

The greatest political movement which keeps American legislatures in a state of continual agitation, and which alone is noticed from the outside, is only an episode and a sort of extension of the universal movement, which begins in the lowest ranks of the people and thence spreads successively through all ranks of citizens. No one could work harder to be happy. It is hard to explain the place filled by political concerns in the life of an American. To take a hand in the government of society and to talk about it is his most important business and, so to say, the only pleasure he knows.

TABLE 4.2. *Percentages of Adult White Males Voting in Elections*

| | Highest Percentage of Adult White Males Before 1824 | | Presidential Elections | | | | | |
	Year	Percentage	1824	1828	1832	1836	1840	1844
Maine	1812	62.0	18.9	42.7	66.2	37.4	82.2	67.5
New Hampshire	1814	80.8	16.8	76.5	74.2	38.2	86.4	65.6
Vermont	1812	79.9	–	55.8	50.0	52.5	74.0	65.7
Massachusetts	1812	67.4	29.1	25.7	39.3	45.1	66.4	59.3
Rhode Island	1812	49.4	12.4	18.0	22.4	24.1	33.2	39.8
Connecticut	1819	54.5	14.9	27.1	45.9	52.3	75.7	76.1
New York	1810	41.5	–	70.4	72.1	60.2	77.7	73.6
New Jersey	1808	71.8	31.1	70.9	60.9	69.3	80.4	81.6
Pennsylvania	1808	71.5	19.6	56.6	52.7	53.1	77.4	75.5
Delaware	1804	81.9	–	–	67.0	69.4	82.8	85.0
Maryland	1820	69.0	53.7	76.2	55.6	67.5	84.6	80.3
Virginia	*1800*	*25.9*	*11.5*	*27.6*	*30.8*	*35.1*	*54.6*	*54.5*
North Carolina	–	–	42.2	56.8	31.7	52.9	83.1	79.1
Georgia	1812	62.3	–	35.9	33.0	64.9	88.9	94.0
Kentucky	1820	74.4	25.3	70.7	73.9	61.1	74.3	80.3
Tennessee	1817	80.0	26.8	49.8	28.8	55.2	89.6	89.6
Louisiana	*1812*	*34.2*	–	*36.3*	*24.4*	*19.2*	*39.4*	*44.7*
Alabama	1819	96.7	52.1	53.6	33.3	65.0	89.8	82.7
Mississippi	1823	79.8	41.6	56.6	32.8	62.8	88.2	89.7
Ohio	1822	46.5	34.8	75.8	73.8	75.5	84.5	83.6
Indiana	1822	52.4	37.5	68.3	61.8	70.1	86.0	84.9
Illinois	1822	55.8	24.2	51.9	45.6	43.7	85.9	76.3
Missouri	1820	71.9	20.1	54.3	40.8	35.6	74.0	74.7
National Average			26.5	56.3	54.9	55.2	78.0	74.9

Source: McCormick (1960).

Notes: The elections that were conducted under a property-based requirement for the franchise appear in italics. Although North Carolina had a property qualification in voting for certain state posts, there appears to have been none in the presidential elections. The Louisiana figures also appear in italics, because McCormick characterized its tax-based qualification as unusually stringent. The estimates of the highest proportions of adult males voting before 1824 were prepared by McCormick because of his desire to highlight how participation in the elections during the Jacksonian period was not exceptionally high. As McCormick recognized, it is potentially misleading to use the highest figure before 1824 as the basis for comparison, and the examination of the record over time is complicated by the changes that were made in the methods of electing governors and presidential electors, but he reports that the average voter participation before 1824 was obviously higher (than in the three Jackson elections) in Alabama, Connecticut, Massachusetts, Mississippi, New Hampshire, Pennsylvania, Rhode Island, Tennessee, and Vermont.

especially by modern standards, suggest that the bulk of the population was keen to exercise political influence. This evident enthusiasm for voting seems likely to have contributed to how suffrage institutions evolved, as it became ever more difficult for legislators or delegates to constitutional conventions to resist the pressure to broaden access.[33]

By 1840 only three states retained a property qualification, North Carolina (for some state-wide offices only), Rhode Island, and Virginia. In 1856 North Carolina was the last state to end the practice. Tax-paying qualifications were also gone in all but a few states by the Civil War, but they survived into the twentieth century in Pennsylvania and Rhode Island.[34] Poll taxes were revived during the 1890s and the first decade of the twentieth century, along with the introduction of literacy tests, as a number of southern states revised their constitutions or enacted new laws to sharply restrict voting by blacks.[35] This effort was successful, and the experience of blacks in the South – where they were flagrantly denied equal access to public services – dramatizes how important the right to vote can be.[36] Despite this episode, what stands out from the U.S. record is how rare such measures were as compared to virtually all of the other societies in the hemisphere (at least by the proportion of the population affected). But it must be remembered that qualifications based on race, gender, residency, as well as on criminal record and mental health, were too commonplace to support the notion that the relative absence of restrictions on the franchise was due to an ideology that everyone had an innate right to vote. On the contrary, the pattern by which such qualifications were introduced and stiffened as property and tax-based standards were relaxed or abandoned suggests that the requirements for the franchise were being set through a process that accepted the drawing

[33] For discussion of the long-term decline in voter participation during the late nineteenth century, see Mark Lawrence Kornbluh, *Why America Stopped Voting: The Decline of Participatory Democracy and the Emergence of Modern American Politics* (New York: New York University Press, 2000).

[34] Porter, *History of Suffrage*, Ch. 4.

[35] The institution of literacy tests was not confined to the South. During the 1850s Connecticut and Massachusetts instituted literacy tests directed primarily at immigrants. However, the major move toward introducing literacy tests occurred later, between 1889 and 1926, when sixteen states, seven southern and nine nonsouthern, did so. Blacks were the principal group target for exclusion in the South, Asians in the West, and immigrants from Europe in the Northeast.

[36] See J. Morgan Kousser, *The Shaping of Southern Politics: Suffrage Restrictions and the Establishment of the One-Party South, 1880–1910* (New Haven: Yale University Press, 1974).

of lines but would change or vary them depending on circumstances.[37] As regards the question of what circumstances favored universal white manhood suffrage, perhaps the most telling observation is that the western or frontier states, together with highly rural northern ones, were the first movers.

Of course much of the concern with the factors influencing the evolution of suffrage institutions arises from the belief that as the composition of the electorate changed, so did the types of policies adopted by the elected representatives. In principle, the movement away from economic qualifications for the franchise should have led to laws that were more favorable to the less wealthy, and indeed there is much evidence in support of this view. Historians of education in the United States, for example, typically highlight the fact that the common school movement was one of a number of campaigns for democratization in various social and economic policies that coincided with, or followed shortly after, widespread extension of the suffrage. Although there had previously been scattered successes in achieving the goal of universal access to a primary education, the movement is usually dated as beginning about 1820 and ending about 1870, by which time virtually every northern state had passed and implemented laws to aid townships or counties to establish tax-supported common schools that were "free" to all who wanted to attend. This fifty-year period was marked by intense political struggle in state after state, with especially strong support coming from urban dwellers, members of labor organizations, and residents of western states – groups that were most likely to have benefited from the establishment of the schools, as well as from the extension of the franchise. Opposition is said to have come primarily from the wealthier classes who bore disproportionately more of the increases in the taxes needed to fund the schools.[38] By 1860, however, universal primary schools were the norm through most of the United States, and are generally credited with responsibility for the country having the highest literacy rates in the world.[39] The movement for the establishment of public schools supported by local property

---

[37] It is relevant to note that after emancipation, the British colonies in the West Indies generally increased the levels of wealth required to be eligible to vote. The result was very low proportions of the population voting in elections.

[38] See Ellwood P. Cubberley, *The History of Education* (Boston: Houghton Mifflin, 1920); as well as the discussion in Lee Soltow and Edward Stevens, *The Rise of Literacy and the Common School in the United States* (Chicago: University of Chicago Press, 1981).

[39] See Table 1.4.

taxes closely and successfully followed the expansion of the suffrage, which strongly suggests that the latter did indeed make a difference for policy.

III

The weakening and ultimate removal of wealth-based restrictions on the franchise were clearly important in raising the fraction of the population voting in U.S. elections. The United States had the highest proportion of the population voting in the world by the middle of the nineteenth century, and together with its spread of more secrecy in balloting and other reforms in the conduct of elections, it had arguably the most equal distribution of political influence. None of the Latin American countries, which were characterized from the early colonial period by much greater inequality, would attain this rate of suffrage for another seventy-five years. Indeed, throughout the hemisphere, only Canada, where similar movements for the extension of the franchise with similar outcomes lagged those in the United States, was much of a rival in political participation. As is evident from Table 1.3, the United States had perhaps one-and-a-half times the rate of population voting as did Canada, and eight or more times the rate as elsewhere in the hemisphere. Given that most of these societies were at least nominal democracies, it is important to ask where this profound gap in political participation came from.

The chief issue is whether the contrasts in the proportions of the population voting were due to differences in the numbers eligible to vote under law, or to some other disparity in conditions. If attributable to differences in qualifications for the suffrage, what accounted for the differences in the laws? Even a cursory examination is sufficient to demonstrate that the requirements for voting were much more restrictive elsewhere in the Americas than in the United States or Canada. Qualifications based on wealth or income were very common throughout Latin America during the early 1800s, but over time the requirement of literacy came to be virtually universal in Latin America as well. These latter strictures, which were generally set forth as qualifications for being a citizen, effectively barred the great majority of wage-earners, whether urban or rural, and the great majority of Native Americans, from voting. In such a legal environment, and with extremely low literacy rates (perpetuated by very limited support for public schools) and with unequal distributions of land and wealth, it is not surprising that the proportions of the populations voting were no higher than 1 or 2 percent until late in the nineteenth century.

The independent Latin American nations maintained the same political institutions and policies in place during the colonial period, excluding non-property owners from legal standing to vote. Although the Spanish Crown had appointed the chief officials in its colonies, municipal councils (*cabildos*) were charged with responsibility for providing local public services and granted the authority to levy taxes to pay for them. These councils were primarily composed of appointments from the ranks of prominent citizens (*vecinos*) of the municipality or pueblo, but some members were selected by election. Participation in such elections (and frequently membership on the council as well as the holding of other offices) was generally restricted.[40] In restricting the right to vote to an elite propertied class, the regulation of suffrage in the Spanish colonies resembled that in the English colonies but was much more restrictive with respect to the proportion of the population that had voting rights.

As in the United States, however, the nature of the suffrage qualifications changed over time. Restrictions that had typically been specified in terms of land ownership during the colonial period were made more flexible. Qualifications were revised in early constitutions to encompass those who owned different types of property, satisfied an income threshold, or had a certain social standing or professional occupation. Scholars of Latin America have often attributed these sorts of changes in postindependence political institutions to the interests of the *criollo* elite – who were much broader in composition, if not distinct from, the major landowning families, and accordingly favored different sorts of requirements.[41] An alternative gauge of status that came to be extensively employed was the ability to read and write – a capacity that was quite rare in these societies, especially among Native Americans. In time the literacy test, which may have been an administratively easier and more effective screen than wealth to distinguish a socioeconomic elite, evolved to become the dominant standard.

Indeed, the introduction and emphasis on a literacy requirement was the major change that occurred after independence in the laws governing the franchise. This development is remarkable not only for spreading rapidly throughout Latin America, but also for it being rather novel, at

---

[40] See, for example, the discussions in Stanley J. Stein and Barbara H. Stein, *The Colonial Heritage of Latin America* (Oxford: Oxford University Press, 1970); Lockhart and Schwartz, *Early Latin America*; and Constantino Bayle, *Los Cabildos Seculares en la Américo Española* (Madrid: Sapientia, 1952). For a recent study on suffrage and politics in Latin America, see also, Paul W. Drake, *Between Tyranny and Anarchy: A History of Democracy in Latin America* (Stanford: Stanford University Press, 2009).

[41] Stein and Stein, *Colonial Heritage*, Ch. 6.

that time, in the New World. Whereas literacy qualifications were not much used in the United States until after amendments to its constitution had forbade restrictions based on race, virtually all Latin American countries included a literacy requirement for citizenship (encompassing the right to vote) in their first constitution or soon afterward. For example: Bolivia advanced a literacy restriction in its 1826 constitution, which was maintained beyond the 1945 constitution; Costa Rica had one in its first constitution as an independent state (1844) but eliminated it in 1913; Chile adopted a literacy requirement in 1833 and maintained one through 1970; Ecuador abandoned its property requirements for voters in its 1861 constitution, but replaced them with a literacy requirement (which endured until 1978); El Salvador had a literacy restriction in its first constitution as an independent state (1864), but seems to have eliminated it in 1945; Guatemala had a literacy restriction in its first full constitution (1879), and maintained it through its 1945 constitution (when illiterates were given the right to a public vote – illiterates with a profession had been given the right to vote in 1935), Mexico had a literacy qualification in its 1835 constitution, but did away with it in the 1857 constitution (which also nationalized church property and spurred a civil war); Peru had a literacy qualification in its 1826 constitution that was largely maintained through 1979 (there have been more than twenty constitutions, and a few of them prior to 1979 relaxed the qualification albeit briefly); and Uruguay had a literacy requirement from the 1830 constitution until the 1918 constitution. Brazil, despite a different national heritage, also had property-based restrictions after independence, but replaced them with a literacy qualification in 1891. This requirement endured until 1988. The only major Latin American countries that did not have literacy requirements at the national level were Argentina and Colombia. In both of these cases, however, states or provinces were allowed considerable latitude in regulating elections and voting, and it seems that some did impose literacy qualifications.[42]

---

[42] See the discussion of the evolution of constitutions in Russell H. Fitzgibbon, *The Constitutions of the Americas* (Chicago: University of Chicago Press, 1948). In addition to restrictions on who can vote, there are many other practices that tend to reduce voter participation or increase the relative influence of the well-to-do or more powerful in elections: lack of secrecy in voting; buying of votes (especially where secrecy is compromised); selective placement of voting places; intimidation of selected classes of the population; or fraud in the handling or counting of votes. These phenomena are of course present, at least to some degree, wherever votes are held. For example, see Spencer D. Albright, *The American Ballot* (Washington, D.C.: American Council of Public Affairs, 1942) for a discussion of how some of the problems concerned with the

To an even greater extent than in the United States, the requirements for suffrage appear to have made a difference in the rates of political participation across Latin America. This is apparent from Table 1.3. The countries with the most progressive suffrage laws and the highest proportions of the population voting (Argentina, Costa Rica, and Uruguay) are also the countries in the region with histories of relative equality, population homogeneity, and labor scarcity. That the literacy restrictions could have had such a great impact on participation in elections is evident from the exceptionally low literacy rates in Latin America.[43] Within countries, even the short-term responses to laws extending suffrage were significant in terms of increasing the proportions of the population voting. In Chile, for example, after the electoral law of 1874 relieved literate males of the requirement to show proof of wealth or income, the proportion of registered voters in the population more than tripled within a few years.[44] In Argentina, the 1912 reform that introduced the so-called "Australian ballot," with secrecy and standardized public ballots, as well as universal and compulsory suffrage for men over 18, led to a rapid and dramatic increase in political participation, as "voting increased threefold or fourfold in the parliamentary elections of 1912, 1913, and 1914, and rose still further in the presidential elections of 1916."[45] Indeed, the change in the law is generally credited with being responsible for a historic defeat of the long dominant National Autonomist Party (PAN) and the election of the

ballot were confronted in the United States over the nineteenth century. Many observers have suggested that such practices were more prevalent in, and may have long endured, in many Latin American countries, and that they help account for why voter participation was sometimes low even when formal restrictions on who held the franchise were not so binding. For example, the substantial increase in the proportion of the people who voted in Argentina after 1912 is normally credited more to the change in the law related to the conduct of elections (replacing a system of public voting in a limited number of voting places with a secret standardized ballot in an expanded set of voting places), than to the institution of a legal requirement that all adult male citizens vote.

[43] Indeed, there were severe limitations on the franchise and low rates of participation in elections nearly everywhere in the hemisphere, including the British, French, and Dutch colonies around the Caribbean basin and Central America, except for the United States and Canada, until the twentieth century. Given the extreme inequality in these other areas, the pattern is as expected.

[44] Samuel J. Valenzuela, "Building Aspects of Democracy Before Democracy: Electoral Practices in Nineteenth Century Chile," in *Elections Before Democracy: The History of Elections in Europe and Latin America*, ed. Eduardo Posada-Carbó 223–258 (New York: Macmillan, 1996).

[45] Ezequiel Gallo, "Argentina: Society and Politics 1880–1916," in *The Cambridge Economic History of Latin America: 1870–1930*, 11 volumes, ed. Leslie Bethell (Cambridge: Cambridge University Press, 1986): 5, 359–91.

presidential candidate of the principal opposition Radical Civic Union. Such evidence that the extent of the franchise mattered both quantitatively and qualitatively is consistent with the observation that intense political debates normally surrounded changes in the suffrage laws in all of these countries.

IV

The record of suffrage in the Americas highlights a series of fundamental questions about the evolution of political institutions.[46] What factors account for the systematic variation across the societies of the New World in the stringency of the restrictions on who was eligible to vote, and in the fraction of the population that voted? What factors accounted for the variation in form of the restrictions over place and time, and did they matter? What were the effects of these restrictions on the respective societies?

These important issues deserve further study. Nevertheless, a few observations seem warranted at this point. First, in regards to the existence and sources of systematic variation in the extent of suffrage, several patterns stand out. Most strikingly, states or countries with greater equality or homogeneity (incorporating both socioeconomic and ethnic/racial attributes) among the population tended to extend the franchise earlier and more broadly, contributing to the evolution, or persistence, of a more equal distribution of political influence. This characterization is suggested not only by the contrast between the countries that began as English colonies on the North American mainland and those that began as Spanish colonies in Central and South America, but also by the variation in experience across the states and societies with the same national heritage. It was, for example, the western or frontier states within the United States, where labor was relatively scarce and both human and

---

[46] In 1900 most European countries had markedly higher fractions of the total population voting in elections than did any of the nations in Latin America (with a few exceptions, including Austria, Finland, Italy, and Sweden), and with a few actually exceeding the figures for the United States and Canada (Belgium at 22 percent, France at 19.4 percent, Norway at 19.5 percent, and Switzerland at 22.3 percent). For a discussion of the extension of the franchise in Australia, see I. D. McNaughtan, "Colonial Liberalism, 1851–1891," in *Australia: A Social and Political History*, ed. Gordon Greenwood (New York: Praeger, 1955): 98–144. Australia made a relatively rapid transition to universal adult white male suffrage, but like virtually all of the societies established as colonies by the Europeans, it effectively denied the franchise to most racial minorities – such as Aborigines or Pacific Islanders – until the twentieth century.

nonhuman capital were relatively equally distributed, that took the lead in doing away with wealth or income-based qualifications for the franchise and establishing universal white manhood suffrage. Here, no threat of civil disorder from below was needed to convince elites that they could benefit by broadening access to the right to suffrage, as well as to other privileges.

Why the states in the United States at first moved from economic-based to race-based qualifications for suffrage, instead of the Latin American pattern of going from economic-based to literacy-based qualifications, is a fascinating and important question. Although eliminating economic-based qualifications (such as land, other forms of wealth, income, or taxes paid) extended the franchise to some groups, the adoption of the new sets of qualifications were clearly intended by those who played a role in designing the new laws to disfranchise other groups. It is not obvious that the elites in the North American states and societies were more ideologically committed to broad suffrage than their counterparts in South America. All nations acted to exclude a segment of the male population that was perceived to be very different. In the United States, this distinct class composed a smaller proportion of the population than did the distinct classes of most of the Latin American societies. The situation in the United States was perhaps also different from that of Latin America in that, until the adoption of the Fourteenth and Fifteenth Amendments, race could be legally and effectively specified as a qualification for suffrage. In Latin America, for whatever reason – perhaps cultural, perhaps due to the greater continuity in the racial distribution of the population – explicit use of race or ethnic background as a requirement for suffrage does not seem to have been feasible. The Latin American pattern (excluding Argentina) of employing literacy as a requirement for suffrage (and citizenship) not only served the purpose of excluding large fractions of the respective populations from voting, but may also have had the effect of discouraging elites, and the societies they dominated, from investing in the establishment of an extensive system of public schools, as discussed in Chapter V.

At least at the national level, the hypothesis that societies with greater equality or homogeneity tended to adopt suffrage institutions that provided broader suffrage or a more equal distribution of political influence seems to be consistent with the historical record in Latin America. Those countries that are thought to have long had more economically and ethnically homogenous populations, such as Argentina, Uruguay, and Costa Rica, were the first to implement suffrage institutions associated with greater access to and use of the franchise. Although this pattern is consistent with the hypothesis, the limited information available means that this is a weak test. More evidence needs to be retrieved. It would be especially interesting to identify the variation in suffrage institutions across the provinces and states of Argentina, Colombia, and other countries that – like the United States – allowed such jurisdictions to set the qualifications for voting.

Finally, there is the fundamental issue of whether the patterns in the evolving suffrage institutions were consequential for long-run patterns of economic development. In theory we would expect so, if different classes of voters had systematically different interests in the economic policies that were on the agenda, and if the governments of these nominal democracies were influenced by the opinions of the voters. The salient case of the losses suffered by blacks in the U.S. South when they were effectively disfranchised by the diffusion of literacy tests and poll taxes between 1890 and 1910, to cite a familiar and well-documented example,[47] seems highly relevant to the contexts considered here. Indeed, we argue, here and in Chapter 5, that the extreme inequality pervasive in most of Latin America since the colonial period explains much of the region's long history of exceedingly low levels of investment in public schooling and of literacy attainment.[48] The evolution of suffrage institutions might constitute a mechanism by which relative differences across societies in the extent of inequality persist over time, and influence paths of economic development.

---

[47] Powerful examples of how changes in the composition of the electorate can lead to changes in government policy are detailed in Kousser, *Suffrage Restrictions* and Lott and Kenny, "Women's Suffrage."

[48] For a treatment that focuses particularly on the evolution of educational institutions, see Ch. 5.

5

The Evolution of Schooling, 1800–1925
(with Elisa V. Mariscal)

I

As the importance of institutions in economic growth has come to be more fully appreciated in recent years, schools are widely acknowledged as among the most fundamental of such institutions. Levels of schooling and literacy have been related, theoretically as well as empirically, to labor productivity, technological change, and rates of commercial and political participation. In addition to promoting growth, educational institutions can have a powerful influence on the distribution of these benefits through providing avenues for individuals to realize upward mobility.[1] Substantial differences in the prevalence of schooling and literacy across countries may have been important contributors to disparities in their patterns of economic growth. Nevertheless, we lack a basic understanding of how these differences first emerged and evolved over time.

[1] For seminal discussions of the importance of schooling and literacy, see Theodore W. Schultz, *The Economic Value of Education* (New York: Columbia University Press, 1963) and Richard A. Easterlin, "Why Isn't the Whole World Developed?" *Journal of Economic History* 41 (March 1981): 1–19. For recent studies in a spirit similar to our own, in terms of trying to understand what accounts for the variation in the establishment of public schools and other public goods, see Claudia Goldin, "Egalitarianism and the Returns to Education During the Great Transformation of American Education," *Journal of Political Economy* 107 (December 1999): 565–94, Claudia Goldin and Lawrence F. Katz, *The Race Between Education and Technology* (Cambridge, MA: Harvard University Press, 2008); and Claudia Goldin and Lawrence F. Katz, "Human and Social Capital in the Rise of Secondary Schooling in America, 1910 to 1940," *Journal of Interdisciplinary History*, 29 (Spring 1999): 683–723; Alberto Alesina, Reza Baqir, and William Easterly, "Public Goods and Ethnic Divisions," *Quarterly Journal of Economics* 114 (November 1999): 1243–84; Sun Go and Peter Lindert, "The Uneven Rise of American Public Schools to 1850," *Journal of Economic History* 70 (March 2010): 1–26.

The New World is ideal for studying investment in schooling and literacy, because many of the societies arising out of European colonization were sufficiently prosperous by the early nineteenth century to support the broad establishment of institutions of primary education.[2] Only a relatively small number, however, made such investments on a scale sufficient to serve the general population before the twentieth century. Such contrasts in institutional development across the Americas have often been attributed to differences in wealth, national heritage, culture, or religion, but systematic comparative studies are rare.[3] Even those that have been conducted confine their focus to cross-sectional variations in the contemporary world and often neglect how the institutions developed over the long run.

One striking feature of the development of education institutions in the Americas is the major investment in primary education made by the United States and Canada early in their histories. From the time of initial settlement, residents in mainland North America above the Rio Grande seem have to provided their children with a basic education, including the ability to read and write, and they established schools to accomplish this goal. In colonial New England, schooling was generally organized at the village or town level, and funded through a variety of sources: charity, lotteries, sales of public lands, and license fees for dogs, taverns, marriages, traders in slaves, as well as the so-called "rate bill" – whereby all but designated paupers would be charged when they had children enrolled in school. Instruction by family members, neighbors, or private tutors often filled in where formal schools were not convenient or available. The United States had probably the most literate white population in the world by the beginning of the nineteenth century, but the "common school movement," put the country on a new path of investment in education. Between 1821 and 1871 nearly every northern state enacted a law strongly encouraging or requiring localities to establish "free schools," open to all children and supported by general taxes, although some localities had previously introduced the practice.[4] The movement made slower

---

[2] Literacy refers to the ability to read and/or write at an adequate level. This, of course, means that standards may vary over time and place.

[3] For a comparative approach to the study of the rise of social spending in OECD countries, see Peter H. Lindert, "The Rise of Social Spending," *Explorations in Economic History* 31 (January 1994): 1–37, and for a detailed study of Latin America education, see Maria Teresa Ramirez and Irene Salazar, "The Emergence of Education in the Republic of Colombia in the 19th Century: Where Did We Go Wrong?" (Unpublished, 2008. This was published in Spanish in 2010).

[4] See Goldin and Katz *Race* (2008): 139–146, particularly Table 4.

progress in the South, but schooling had spread sufficiently by the middle of the nineteenth century that more than 40 percent of the school-age population in the United States overall was enrolled, and nearly 90 percent of white adults were literate. In early nineteenth-century Canada schools were also widespread, and even though this northernmost English colony lagged behind the United States by several decades in establishing tax-supported primary schools with universal access, its literacy rates were nearly as high.

The other regions of the hemisphere trailed far behind the United States and Canada in education and literacy. Although municipal and state (or provincial) governments were virtually everywhere granted the authority to establish schools and to levy taxes to mobilize resources on their behalf, with either public few were effective at doing so, except in these two northern countries. Public schools, with either public provision or public financing, were thus exceedingly rare elsewhere in the Americas, and parents who sought primary education for their children had to rely largely on private classes until late in the nineteenth century, when some national governments began to promote the expansion of public education. For example, despite their wealth, the British colonies in the Caribbean basin were slow to organize schooling institutions that would serve broad segments of the population. It was not until after emancipation that the British Colonial Office took a direct interest in the promotion of schooling, that significant steps were taken in this direction, perhaps inspired by the movements to increase support for public schools in Britain itself. Even Argentina and Uruguay, the most progressive of the Latin American countries, were more than seventy-five years behind the United States and Canada in providing wide access to primary schooling and attaining high levels of literacy. Most of Latin America was unable to achieve these standards until well into the twentieth century, if then.

This relative backwardness in the organization of institutions of primary education could well have had a significant impact on the long-run development of these other nations of the Americas, and thus the question of what accounts for this pattern is especially intriguing. Differences in the resources available to invest in schooling, as reflected in per capita income, is perhaps the first possibility that comes to mind in explaining why the rest of the hemisphere lagged behind the United States and Canada; however, these countries do not appear to have been much advantaged in that dimension at the time they began to move ahead in the promotion of education. Religion is another potentially significant factor, and some have suggested that societies in which Catholics predominated may have been slow to invest in public schools, either because the Church valued education, at least for ordinary people, less than their Protestant counterparts, or because the Church stifled individual or community initiatives to organize private or public schools. Although plausible and consistent with the greater prominence of Catholicism in Latin America, this view has to contend with the relatively high levels of schooling and literacy in French Canada, as well as the modest levels among the British (and largely Protestant) colonies in the Caribbean basin.

A third possibility is that differences in ethnicity or national heritage played an important role in determining which societies made major investments in schooling early in the process of development and which did not. This sort of explanation encompasses arguments that Native Americans did not consider the establishment of schools an attractive use of resources because of the association of schooling with western ways of thinking, or that populations with English backgrounds had a greater appreciation for education than those of Spanish descent. Yet another possibility is that the long tradition of centralized structures of government in Latin American countries may have impeded the organization of schools on a widespread basis. For example, local or provincial governments may have been more constrained in carrying out such initiatives in Spanish America than elsewhere, even though they had similar legal authority.

Another hypothesis is that the long-standing greater degree of inequality in Latin American, as compared to the United States or Canada, played a role in explaining the differential record in establishing educational institutions. Several mechanisms could have led extreme levels of inequality to depress investments in schooling institutions. First, in a setting where private schooling predominated, or where parents paid school-user fees, greater wealth or income inequality would generally reduce the fraction of the school-age population enrolled. Second, greater inequality may also have exacerbated the collective action problems associated with the establishment and funding of universal public schools, because the distribution of benefits across the population would be quite different from the incidence of taxes and other costs, or because population heterogeneity made it more difficult for communities to reach consensus on public projects. Given that early public schooling systems were almost universally organized and managed at the local level, these problems may have been especially relevant. Where the wealthy enjoyed disproportionate political power, elites could procure schooling for their own children, and resist being taxed to underwrite or subsidize services to others.[5] Extreme inequality in wealth or income might also lead to low levels of schooling on a national basis if it were associated with substantial disparities across communities or geographic areas. As long as schools had to be supported by local resources, poor districts might not have been able to sustain an extensive system of primary education. Only the populations of wealthy districts, presumably small in number, would then have easy access to schooling.

Our original motivation for undertaking this comparative examination was an interest in whether and how the extreme differences across countries in the extent of inequality in wealth, human capital, and political power that emerged early in their histories might have influenced the evolution of education institutions, and thus their paths of development over time. Indeed, this concern with the impact and persistence of the extreme inequality characterizing much of the New World is largely responsible for the organization of this chapter. In the next two sections, we survey the record of schooling and literacy in the Americas, highlighting salient patterns and discussing the general consistency of the history with some of the explanations for divergence that have been suggested. In the fourth section we systematically examine the evidence, and find that, although investment in schooling is strongly and positively correlated with per capita income over time and across countries, much variation remains to be explained. Moreover, the extent of inequality in political power, as reflected in the proportion of the population who can vote, does seem to be associated with lower literacy and schooling rates. Although the comparison between the experiences of the United States and Canada with those of other countries in the hemisphere serves as our reference point, we are also concerned with the variation within the latter group. Argentina, Uruguay, Cuba, Costa Rica, Chile, and Barbados may have lagged behind the United States and Canada, but they made earlier and greater progress at educating their populations than did their neighbors. Other explanations for the variation across the Americas in levels of investment in education may ultimately prove as powerful as ones derived from differences in the degree of inequality, but this comparative examination should nevertheless help improve our understanding of the differential paths of development observed in the New World. Whatever

---

[5] Daron Acemoglu and James A. Robinson argue that the increase in the equality of political power associated with the extension of the franchise led to increased funding for public schools in a number of European countries.

tended to reduce or delay investments in schooling institutions fostered inequality in the distribution of human capital, and likely retarded long-run economic growth.

II

It was not long after the Europeans established permanent settlements on the northern part of the North American mainland that they began to organize schools. Foremost among them were primary schools for local children that communities administered and supported. Massachusetts is frequently celebrated as the leader, but other colonies in New England conceded little in their enthusiasm for basic and widespread education.[6] Indeed, all of the region's states had made some provision for public education by 1800, generally requiring towns in rural areas beyond a certain size to support a primary or grammar school. Despite resistance to the levying of school taxes slowing the responses to these government initiatives, New Englanders already enjoyed relatively broad access to primary education and had attained high rates of literacy through a combination of local public schools, private institutions, and home instruction. Elsewhere in the United States, schooling was not so widespread. Private schools generally predominated in the Middle Atlantic and the South. Until the early 1800s, few governments in these regions, aside from New York, went beyond requiring public schooling to be provided to the children of paupers. Access to schools was especially limited in the South, even among the white population.

A major breakthrough in the expansion of schooling occurred during the second quarter of the nineteenth century with a series of political battles, known as the "common school movement," for tax-supported, locally controlled "free" schools, that took place throughout the country. Such schools were to be open to all, supported primarily through local taxes (though often receiving some aid from state governments), and managed by local authorities (with state-appointed officers typically providing some oversight to the multitude of local school systems that operated within the respective states). The movement is usually dated as beginning about 1820 and ending about 1870, by which time virtually every northern state had passed and implemented laws to encourage townships or counties to establish common schools.

---

[6] The classic source on the early history of schooling is Ellwood P. Cubberley, *The History of Education* (Boston: Houghton Mifflin, 1920).

This fifty-year period was marked by intense political struggles in state after state, with especially strong support for free schools coming from urban dwellers, members of labor organizations, and residents of western states – reflecting the general drive for democratization that occurred during the Jacksonian era. Opposition is said to have come from religious and private-school interests as well as from the wealthier classes who might have expected to bear a disproportionate increase in taxes.[7] Entirely free schools emerged only gradually, however, as the progression of laws and township policies chipped away incrementally at the traditional use of permanent endowments, licensing fees, lotteries, and "rate bills" (tuition or user fees) to finance the schools, and replaced them with general taxes. Resistance to raising rates or levying new taxes was always a factor to be overcome, and state governments often tied inducements like financial aid for schools to decisions by districts to agree to tax themselves. Some northern states such as New Jersey continued to rely on a combination of taxes and "rate-bills" to fund their schools as late as 1871. Although some southern states passed legislation allowing for free schools as early as the 1830s, there was limited progress in establishing them until after the Civil War.[8]

Historians of education typically highlight the fact that the common school movement was one of a number of campaigns for democratization included in various social and economic policies that coincided with, or followed shortly after, widespread extension of suffrage.[9] As discussed in Chapter IV, until early in the nineteenth century and despite the sentiments popularly attributed to the Founding Fathers, voting in the United States was largely a privilege reserved for white men with significant amounts of property. By 1815, only four of the original thirteen states (and seven overall) had adopted universal white male suffrage, but as the movement to do away with political inequality gained strength, they were joined by the rest of the country as virtually all new entrants to the Union extended voting privileges to all white men, and older states revised their laws. The shift to full adult white-male suffrage was largely complete by the late 1840s.[10] Overall, the timing of the movements for extending

---

[7] See Cubberley, *History of Education*, as well as the discussion in Lee Soltow and Edward Stevens, *The Rise of Literacy and the Common School in the United States* (Chicago: University of Chicago Press, 1981).

[8] Cubberley, *History of Education*.

[9] Ibid.

[10] For discussions of the series of reforms involving both the extension of the franchise and the conduct of voting more generally, see Kirk H. Porter, *A History of Suffrage in the United States* (Chicago: University of Chicago Press, 1918); Spencer D. Albright, *The*

the suffrage as well as for common schools is consistent with the view that increasing equality in political influence helped promote increased investments in public schooling, and, correspondingly, greater access to primary education. That the southern states were generally the laggards in both broadening the electorate and starting common schools, while New England and the western states were leaders in both, likewise provides support for this view. Since doing away with property restrictions on the franchise enhanced the political voice of the groups that would benefit most from the establishment of tax-supported free schools, and the most important single source of tax revenue for local and state governments was property taxes, it should not be surprising that greater equality in political influence led to the institutional changes that contributed to greater equality in the distribution of human capital.

Although both the French and English areas of Canada had relatively few schools and low levels of literacy in 1800, as compared with their neighbor to the south, this northern-most country in the hemisphere was another leader in extending institutions of primary education to the general population. By the end of the nineteenth century, Canada ranked second in the world, behind only the United States, in literacy and the fraction of its school-aged population actually enrolled. Despite being influenced by political developments in both Britain and France, there was a pronounced impact on Canada arising from extensive economic contacts with the northeastern part of the United States. Whatever the source, Canadian concern with the establishment of a broad system of public schools began increasing at the beginning of the nineteenth century. The organization, management, and financing of education were carried out primarily at the district level, but some supervision and financial aid were provided by provincial governments. Canada's school systems first expanded in the second quarter of the nineteenth century and public support grew as well, as was happening in the United States. Tax-supported free primary schools, however, were not fully realized on a widespread basis until the third quarter of the nineteenth century.[11] Under the Union

American Ballot (Washington, D.C.: American Council of Public Affairs, 1942); Paul Kleppner, *Who Voted? The Dynamics of Electoral Turnout, 1870–1980* (New York: Praeger, 1982); and P. Flora, J. Alber, R. Eichenberg, J. Kohl, and F. Kraus, *State, Economy, and Society in Western Europe, 1815–1975*, 2 vols, vol. 1. *The Growth of Mass Democracies and Welfare States* (Chicago: St. James Press, 1983).

[11] Compulsory education legislation followed over the 1870s: Ontario (1870), British Columbia (1873), and Manitoba (1876), but Quebec did not pass such legislation until 1943. For detailed histories of schools in Canada, see Charles E. Phillips, *The Development of Education in Canada* (Toronto: W. J. Gage, 1957); and J. Donald Wilson, Robert M. Stamp, and Louis-Philippe Auder, eds. *Canadian Education: A History*

Act of 1841 and the British North America Act of 1867, allowance was made for separate secular and religious schools, both of which would be state-financed for those provinces that wanted them.[12] Although Canada was clearly behind the United States in both schooling and literacy for most of the nineteenth century, the country managed to virtually close the gap by 1895 in terms of the ratio of students in school to the population aged 5 to 19 (0.60 to 0.62 respectively). In both countries the progress of the movement for tax-supported public schools coincided generally in time with, or followed soon after, extensions of the franchise.[13]

Many elements seem to have contributed to the early spread of tax-supported primary schools in the United States and Canada. First, these societies may have been more inclined to invest in public education because of the religious views that were more prevalent in English colonies. Proponents of the idea that religious faith was an important, if not critical, factor typically cite the example of seventeenth-century New England, where the organization of primary schools was often rationalized as necessary for ensuring that all members of the population were able to read the Bible. Although the role of religion is undeniable, the force of the argument can be exaggerated. Not only did New England account for only a small share of the U.S. population at the end of the eighteenth century, but even their rates of adult illiteracy were substantial, if markedly lower than in other areas of the country. That all regions of the United States and Canada compared favorably in literacy to England, Europe more generally, and to the British colonies in the Caribbean, would seem to cast doubt on the notion that their high rates of primary schooling were due solely to either English heritage or religion. It is worth noting how the supporters of public schooling during the common school movement stressed the economic and civic rather than religious importance of education. Schooling would help equip men for self-governance and participation in a democracy, and provide an avenue for self-improvement and upward mobility.[14]

(Scarborough, Ontario: Prentice-Hall, 1970). For a useful study of economic growth in nineteenth-century Canada, see Frank D. Lewis and M. C. Urquhart, "Growth of the Standard of Living in a Pioneer Economy: Upper Canada, 1821 to 1851," *William and Mary Quarterly* 56 (January 1999): 151–81.

[12] Most important here was Quebec, which maintained, in addition to a secular school system, separate Catholic and Protestant schools.

[13] For a discussion of the process involved in the extension of the franchise, and its effects in Western Europe, see Danon Acemoglu and James A. Robinson "Why Did the West Extend the Franchise? Democracy, Inequality, and Growth Historical Perspective: *Quarterly Journal of Economics* 115 (November 2000), 1167–99.

[14] Common schools served girls (despite their lacking the vote) as well as boys, and estimates of literacy from the late 1700s through the 1850s suggest that although the expansion

Another potential explanation for why the United States and Canada were well ahead of their hemispheric neighbors in making commitments to public schooling is that they could better afford the cost. The United States, and to a lesser extent Canada, was beginning to industrialize and pull ahead of most of its neighbors in the New World in terms of per capita income by the time they embraced the common school movement during the mid-nineteenth century, although the high wage effects of industrialization may have meant a shift for children from schooling to employment. Certainly their levels of material resources were a contributing factor. However, although they were no doubt aided by their prosperity, it is important to remember that the United States and Canada had begun to distinguish themselves in their propensity to invest in schooling long before they enjoyed a marked advantage in per capita income. Moreover, a number of New World economies continued to surpass or at least rival their northern neighbors in this gauge of economic performance well into the nineteenth century, and it is clear that the great majority commanded sufficient resources to establish institutions offering broad access to primary education throughout the period.[15]

A related idea is that the greater support for public education institutions in the United States and Canada was due not to differences in their capacity to pay as gauged by per capita income, but rather to differences in their ability or willingness to mobilize tax revenue for that purpose. This way of framing the problem highlights issues of government or administrative structure as well as of political economy. Although the societies of the Americas evolved diverse governmental structures, it is striking that during the early nineteenth century virtually all of them (in their laws or constitutions) explicitly gave local or provincial governments responsibility for operating public schools and granted them authority to levy taxes. That all throughout the Americas local and provincial governments apparently had the power to levy taxes to support public schools leads to the question of why some were so much more inclined

---

of common schools benefited all, they helped females close a gender gap. See Soltow and Stevens, *Rise of Literacy* for more discussion of the temporal and regional patterns of literacy in the United States, and how well they conform to various hypotheses about why that country and Canada should be so distinctive. See also Carl F. Kaestle, *Pillars of the Republic: Common Schools and American Society* (New York: Hill and Wang, 1983) for a discussion of the ethnic and religious debates in northern schooling in the antebellum United States.

[15] See Kaestle, *Pillars of the Republic*, Ch. 3.

to take effective advantage of this capacity. We have been especially concerned with the possibility that such differences across countries, if not jurisdictions, may have had something to do with differences in income inequality or ethnic homogeneity.[16] The logic is based on the observation that the well-to-do can always obtain schooling for their children through the private market, but that public investment in schooling systems, or broad access to schooling, generally involves some transfers between those who bear a disproportionate share of the costs and those who realize a disproportionate share of the benefits. In the nineteenth-century United States, for example, it was typical for local governments – the main providers of public school funds – to raise the overwhelming share of their revenue through property taxes. As a result, where there was relative equality or population homogeneity, as in the United States and Canada (compared to elsewhere in the Americas), one would expect a relatively even sharing of costs and benefits and less severe collective-action problems, thus resulting in a greater likelihood of a community taxing itself to finance universal primary schools. However, where inequality was more extreme, and especially where the wealthier segments of the population had disproportionate political influence, one would expect a lower propensity of communities to tax themselves to support investment in public goods. Support for this notion of the significance of political equality comes from the coincidence in time between the beginnings of the common school movement of the 1820s and 1830s in the United States and the broadening of the franchise during that same era, and from similar associations between suffrage reform and the passage of measures to support public schools in Canada, England, and elsewhere in Europe.[17]

Whatever the reasons for it, the United States and Canada benefited from their greater investments in public schooling, as evidenced by how

---

[16] For a discussion of this idea in another context, see Goldin and Katz, *Race*. For a detailed account of how inequality, and especially political inequality, played a role in restricting the access of blacks to schooling and other public goods in the postbellum South, see J. Morgan Kousser, *The Shaping of Southern Politics: Suffrage Restrictions and the Establishment of the One-Party South, 1880–1910* (New Haven: Yale University Press, 1974); Robert Higgs, *Competition and Coercion: Blacks in the American Economy, 1865–1914* (Cambridge: Cambridge University Press, 1977), and Robert Margo. *Race and Schooling in the South, 1880–1950. An Economic History* (Chicago: University of Chicago Press, 1990).

[17] Also consistent with this view is the cross-sectional correspondence across states between leadership in broadening the franchise and leadership in the establishment of universal common schools. For discussions of the connection between extensions of suffrage and public schooling in many countries and contexts, see Cubberley, *History of Education*.

far ahead they were of their neighbors in the Americas in attaining literacy throughout the 1800s and well into the 1900s (see Table 1.4). By 1870, more than 80 percent of the population aged 10 or older in both the United States and Canada were literate, more than triple the proportions in Argentina, Chile, Costa Rica, and Cuba, and four times the proportions in Brazil and Mexico. These stark contrasts were partly due to high literacy in the United States and Canada, but much of the explanation seems to be in the poor performance of the other societies in the Americas. Even during the era of European colonization – when their levels of per capita income were comparable – these societies clearly trailed the colonies that were to become the United States and Canada, in developing institutions of primary education and in literacy. Moreover, even those that were more successful at realizing economic growth in the late-nineteenth and early-twentieth centuries, such as Argentina, were much slower to establish systems of public schooling that reached broad segments of their population. Even the non-white population in the United States had literacy rates comparable to, or higher than, those for the entire population in Argentina in 1870, 1890, and 1910.

Overall, the United States and Canada were the only societies in the Americas to attain high levels of literacy by the middle of the nineteenth century. In contrast, not until late in the 1800s were two other sets of New World societies able to raise literacy rates much above the relatively modest level of 30 percent. The first of these groups was a number of British colonies in the Caribbean basin, where investments in public schools date back to the British emancipation of slaves in 1834, when grants were made to each colony for the education of blacks. These grants ended in 1845, after which each colony was responsible for its own educational policies and expenditures. Only Barbados seems to have maintained, if not increased, this early support for primary schools, with costs being covered by a mixture of local taxes, charity, school fees, and private aid generally provided to both religious as well as secular schools. The British Colonial Office continued to support the expansion of public schooling, however, and their advocacy may have been responsible for the general upturn in school enrollments and literacy that got under way throughout the British Caribbean during the last several decades of the century.[18] Barbados appears to have been the major success story, with estimated

---

[18] Compulsory schooling laws did begin to be introduced, first in British Guiana in 1876, with Saint Lucia and the Leeward Islands following in 1889 and 1890, respectively, but they were rather ineffectively enforced.

literacy rates placing it among the more developed nations of the world. In other colonies, like Belize and Jamaica, however, improvements were steady but slower, with the most striking increases in literacy occurring after 1891.[19]

The other group of New World societies that began to realize substantial increases in literacy and major extensions of public schooling during the late 1800s was a subset of former Spanish colonies. Argentina and Uruguay were the clear leaders among them (although still far behind the United States and Canada), with more than half their populations (10 years and older) literate by 1900. Chile and Cuba trailed somewhat behind, with roughly 40 percent literacy, and Costa Rica was further behind still, at 33 percent. These five countries, which varied considerably in many important respects, had attained literacy rates greater than 66 percent by 1925. In contrast, a broad range of other Latin American countries, including Mexico, Brazil, Venezuela, Peru, Colombia, Bolivia, Guatemala, and Honduras, were not able to move much beyond 30 percent literacy until after 1925.

III

Although virtually all New World economies enjoyed high levels of per capita income by the standards of the period, the United States and Canada had pulled far ahead of their Latin American neighbors in the establishment of schools and literacy attainment by the beginning of the nineteenth century. This sharp contrast with the North is perhaps the most salient feature of Latin America's overall record in the development of education institutions, but it should not be allowed to obscure the important differences across countries within the region (see Tables 1.4, 5.1, and 5.2). There was little public provision of primary education anywhere in Latin America until late in the nineteenth century, but literacy rose quickly in those countries that took the lead in promoting schooling. By 1900, Argentina, Chile, Cuba, and Uruguay had literacy rates exceeding 40 percent, followed by Costa Rica with 33 percent. These figures are quite low relative to those of the United States and Canada, but much higher than those of the two largest Latin American nations, Mexico and Brazil, which had rates of only 22 and 26 percent respectively. Moreover,

---

[19] Rates of literacy for blacks were generally lower in most of the British colonies in the Caribbean than in the United States, but were comparable to or above those of most countries in South and Central America.

TABLE 5.1. *Students as a Percentage of the Population in Selected Latin American Countries*

Countries	Population (c. 1895)	Students (c. 1895)	Students as a percentage of total population (%) (c. 1895)
Costa Rica	243,205	21,829	8.98
Uruguay	800,000	67,878	8.48
Argentina	4,086,492	268,401	6.57
Paraguay	329,645	18,944	5.75
Mexico	11,395,712	543,977	4.77
Guatemala	1,460,017	65,322	4.47
Venezuela	2,323,527	100,026	4.30
Nicaragua	282,845	11,914	4.21
Ecuador	1,271,861	52,830	4.15
El Salvador	777,895	29,427	3.78
Chile	3,267,441	95,456	2.92
Peru	2,700,945	53,276	1.97
Colombia	3,878,600	73,200	1.89
Brazil	14,002,335	207,973	1.49
Bolivia	2,300,000	24,244	1.05

Source: Oficina Nacional de Estadística, República de Costa Rica *Resúmenes Estadísticos: Años 1883–1910, Demografía.* (1912). This is a Costa Rican document, with no sources and discussion provided. San José Impr. National.

Note: Neither the level of schooling, the length of the school year, nor the mix of private vs. public schools is provided. The document does provide, however, unusual information that is somewhat consistent with other data, although not perfectly correlated with literacy.

countries like Bolivia, Guatemala, and Honduras fell even further behind, with literacy rates ranging from 11 to 17 percent. Since all these countries had similar government structures (federations), and national heritages (Spanish or Portuguese), the issue of the sources of these large differences seems both intriguing and relevant to understanding the conditions that were conducive to early investment in primary schools.

The local governments established under Spanish colonial rule reflected the corporate quality of Latin American society, characterized by a hierarchical structure where only *vecinos* (neighbors) were considered citizens.[20] Such sharp distinctions in social class endured after independence, and *vecinos* continued to dominate the political order

[20] See the discussion of *vecinos, vecindad* privileges, and the structure of the *cabildo* (government of any settlement that included both the executive and judicial branches) in Constantino Bayle, *Los Cabildos Seculares en la Américo Española.* (Madrid: Sapientia,

TABLE 5.2. *Literacy Rates in Selected Cities*

Place	Year	Male	Female	Total	Country literacy rate
Boston, MA	1850	–	–	91.1	95.1(*)
New York City, NY	1850	–	–	93.6	93.9(*)
Philadelphia, PA	1850	–	–	93.2	93.1(*)
Santiago, Chile	1854	52.4	43.3	47.1	13.3
Buenos Aires	1855	56.0	48.0	52.0	23.8 (1869)
San Juan, Puerto Rico	1860	52.3	43.0	47.9	11.8
San Juan, PR (W)	1860	67.4	79.4	71.8	19.8
San Juan, PR (C)	1860	22.5	15.4	18.2	3.1
Havana, Cuba	1861	45.9	34.1	41.3	23.8
Havana (W)	1861	58.4	55.6	57.5	38.5
Havana (C)	1861	8.2	6.7	7.4	5.3
San Jose, Costa Rica	1864	57.0	23.0	40.2	23.6 (1892)
Buenos Aires	1869	55.0	47.0	52.2	23.8
Kingston, Jamaica	1871	–	–	40.4	16.3
Kingston, Jamaica	1891	–	–	59.2	32.0
Santiago, Chile	1875	37.0	33.3	34.4	25.7
São Paulo, Brazil	1882	–	–	42.0	15.3 (c. 1882)
Buenos Aires	1895	75.0	64.0	71.8	45.6

Sources: Newland (1991); Bethell (1984, vols. 4 and 5; 1986); Roberts (1957, 78) U.S. Bureau of the Census, *Seventh Census of the United States: 1850* (1853).
Notes:
[1] (*) Literacy level is for the state, not the country, i.e. Massachusetts, New York, Pennsylvania. Also, literacy rates correspond to population over the age of 20.
[2] W = white, C = colored population.

throughout the nineteenth century by way of political systems based on indirect elections and restrictions on voting that included some combination of income and wealth, as well as literacy requirements. With extreme inequality in the distributions of income and political power, it is perhaps not surprising that in Latin American local governments often failed to organize schools that were tax-supported and open to all. In Latin America, national governments often had to directly intervene in promoting education institutions before substantial progress was to be made. This

1952). See also Horst Pietschmann, *Las reformas borbónicas y el sistema del intendencias en Nueva España: En Estudio political administrativo* (Mexico: Fondo de Cultura Económica, 1996). For schooling patterns in the early settlement of Spanish America, see C. H. Haring, *The Spanish Empire in America* (New York: Oxford University Press, 1947). For a useful bibliography for the history of education in Latin America, see *Sociedad y Educación; Ensayos Sobre Historia de la Educación en América Latina* (Bogotá: Universidad Pedagogica National, Colciencias, 1995).

pattern stands in stark contrast with the experience in the United States and Canada, where local and state governments were the pioneers in establishing such schools.[21]

The greater importance of national government policy in Latin America and some of the conditions that influenced the timing for national government involvement are illustrated by the experiences that we will discuss in the following selected cases: Argentina, Chile, Colombia, Costa Rica, Cuba, Guatemala, Mexico, and Peru. Several patterns stand out. First, across countries, or across regions within countries, the polities that had greater equality or population homogeneity generally led in establishing broad access to primary schooling and in attaining higher literacy. Urban areas are an example of such polities, and were more able or inclined to make such investments. Second, within a country, the timing of the major expansions of public schools seems to have been more closely associated with economic booms or with campaigns to attract immigrants from outside the polity than with political turmoil or civil strife (Cuba stands out as an exception). Third, although it was not uncommon for some isolated cities or provinces to undertake significant investment in public schooling, the country as a whole would make substantial progress only when national governments chose, or were able, to get involved in promoting this goal. In Latin America, federalism, with its greater potential for competition between states or provinces in the provision of public services to attract migrants, was not enough to ensure higher investments in education.

In the United States, the system of federalism led to a highly productive competition among states in providing transportation improvement and education. This rivalry may have led to some overall over-expenditures but they clearly led to a higher level of economically-valuable expenditures than one might have otherwise expected. While in the United States federalism and state rivalry furthered the growth process, this was not an inevitable result of intra-national rivalry and federalism. There were four Latin American countries that had long-standing federalism in the nineteenth century – Argentina, Brazil, Mexico, and Venezuela – none

---

[21] Those skeptical of the contrast being so stark might question how well groups such as Native Americans and blacks were served by schools in the United States or Canada. However, as is indicated in Table 1.4, the literacy rates for United States blacks in the late nineteenth and early twentieth centuries were as high, if not higher, than those for the entire population of Argentina. Since the immigrants to Argentina were significantly more literate than the native born, this implies that blacks born and schooled in the United States had higher literacy than those whites born and schooled in Argentina.

of which experienced the same success as did the United States. Whether this was due to a failure to permit the competitive geographic division of labor as in the United States or to a failure to perform adequately at the sub-national level is not certain, but Latin American federalism did not spur educational increases.

Argentina

Though initially constrained by the 1853 constitution assigning provincial governments the responsibility for primary schooling, during the 1860s the national government began to play an active role in promoting mass education. These efforts were led by President Domingo Sarmiento and others who saw the United States and Canada as models for development.[22] Their conviction that the provincial governments were not expanding access to schools seems borne out by the low rates of literacy in the country especially among the native born and those living outside of Buenos Aires (see Tables 5.3 and 5.4). The first major intervention came in 1881, with the granting of authority for schools in the federal district of Buenos Aires and national territories to the National Council of Education.[23] Educational policy outside these federal districts continued to be made by local and provincial authorities, but the national government assumed the right to intervene where elementary school systems proved to be inadequate or resources for education were scarce. This opening to federal involvement was soon followed by an 1884 law calling for free primary schools, compulsory attendance for all children between the ages of 6 and 14, limits on the distance that a student would have to travel to attend, and the establishment of one school for every 1,500 inhabitants. These standards were not uniformly adhered to, however, and in 1904 the Lainez Law undercut local authority further by giving the federal government the power to establish primary schools anywhere in the country in order to raise school standards. This extension of the

[22] Our brief overview of the development of schooling in Argentina draws on Marta Maltoni, *Educación y Reformas Constitucionales, 1819–1987* (Buenos Aires: Libería "El Atenco" Editorial, 1988); Vincenzo Misuriello, *Politica de la Immigración en la Argentina: 1853–1970* (Tucumán: Universidad National de Tucumán, 1993); Alberto B. Martínez, *República Argentina Censo General de Educación: Levantado el 23 de Mayo de 1909*, vols. 1–3 (Buenos Aires: Oficina Meterológica Argentina, 1910); and Zulma Recchini de Lattes and Alfredo E. Lattes, *Migraciones en la Argentina: Estudio de la Migraciones Internas e Internacionales Basado en Datos Censales, 1869–1960* (Buenos Aires: Instituto Torcuato di Tella, 1969).

[23] It is notable that when the responsibility for the Federal District was transferred to the national government, the municipal government of Buenos Aires was explicitly required to increase its expenditures on education.

TABLE 5.3. *Provincial Government Expenditures on Primary Education in Argentina, on a Per Capita Basis*

Provinces	Per capita annual expenditures (nominal pesos)	
	1874	1896
Buenos Aires	0.30	1.16
LITTORAL: EAST	0.37	0.56
Santa Fé	0.47	0.67
Entre Rios	0.12	0.50
Corrientes	0.56	0.48
CENTRAL	0.11	0.29
Córdoba	0.09	0.29
San Luis	0.29	0.42
Santiago del Estero	0.06	0.24
ANDINA: WEST	0.38	0.60
Mendoza	0.71	0.72
San Juán	0.55	0.78
La Rioja	0.10	0.34
Catamarca	0.14	0.48
NORTEÑA	0.36	0.46
Tucumán	0.50	0.49
Salta	0.18	0.38
Jujuy	0.07	0.38
TOTAL	0.28	0.68

Source: Carlos Vedoya (1973), 89.
Note: 1896 data were converted into pesos fuertes ($1 peso = $0.35 peso fuerte), to make figures comparable. Per capita figures were obtained by dividing provincial budgets for education for the years 1874, 1896 by census figures for the population for 1869 and 1895.

powers of the central government led to a sharp rise in federal funds over the next few decades.

These efforts to expand primary schooling in time produced impressive advances in educational attainment; the literacy rate rose from 23.8 percent in 1869 to over 60 percent in 1914. Progress was far from even across geographic areas, however. The more prosperous regions, large cities such as Buenos Aires, and areas with greater numbers of foreign born had higher school-attendance rates and much higher literacy, a pattern that was typical of New World societies other than the United States and Canada (see Table 5.4).

TABLE 5.4. *Literacy Rates for Argentina by Province and Country of Birth for the Years 1895, 1909, and 1914*

	Foreign Born			Natives		
Province	1895 (All ages)	1909* (6–14)	1914 (All ages)	1895 (All ages)	1909* (6–14)	1914 (All ages)
Capital Region	68%	71%	74%	53%	78%	65%
Martin García Island	n.a.	100	71	n.a.	61	72
LITTORAL: EAST						
Buenos Aires	60	57	64	37	60	50
Santa Fé	60	52	63	30	59	46
Entre Ríos	57	52	64	27	50	42
Corrientes	41	52	55	18	45	33
CENTRAL						
Córdoba	58	51	67	27	51	43
San Luis	70	58	74	27	49	46
Santiago del Estero	71	52	63	11	33	26
ANDINA: WEST						
Mendoza	53	45	54	31	49	42
San Juán	56	52	51	32	54	42
La Rioja	65	48	63	22	39	39
Catamarca	68	59	69	21	40	39
NORTEÑA						
Tucumán	64	56	56	19	50	38
Salta	41	55	53	18	64	36
Jujuy	25	42	24	17	43	30
TERRITORIES						
North						
Misiones	20	38	38	17	45	34
Formosa	31	44	39	20	50	33
Chaco	51	52	56	15	50	35
Los Andes	n.a.	8	47	n.a.	28	26
Center						
La Pampa	61	44	67	18	41	34
West						
Neuquén	23	47	42	8	39	22
South						
Rio Negro	44	46	54	20	43	28
Chubut	77	63	67	28	56	36
Santa Cruz	73	n.a.	77	26	n.a.	45
Tierra del Fuego	84	67	78	39	61	54
TOTAL	55	57	59	25	56	40

Sources: For years 1895 and 1914, *Resúmen de la República de Argentina*, The numbers represent the literate foreign or native population divided by the total foreign or native population. For the year 1909, see Alberto Martinez (1910) *Censo General de Educación* (1909). The numbers represents the literate foreign or native population divided by the foreign (native) population between the ages of 6 and 14.

Notes:

[1] The 1909 figure for the total is a weighted average.

[2] Los Andes existed transitorily between the years 1900 and 1943. Its surface was then divided between the provinces of Catamarca and Jujuy. We therefore classify it among the northern territories.

Part of this gap between the urban and the rural was undoubtedly due to the amount of resources invested in schooling. Federal funds were largely restricted to the capital city and other federal territories, while poor provinces were less able to raise the funds to establish and operate a high quality primary school system. Between 1875 and 1896, virtually all regions in Argentina substantially boosted their per capita expenditures on primary schooling. Nevertheless, the province of Buenos Aires, which included the capital city as well as the most productive farmlands in the country, pulled far ahead as it increased per capita spending by nearly 300 percent, a significant increase compared to the national average which rose by roughly 140 percent (see Table 5.3).

Table 5.4 presents literacy rates by province and country of birth, respectively, and allow for a closer examination of the relationships between literacy, expenditures on primary schools, and geographic location. Among the features that stand out are first, a general cross-sectional correspondence between increases in the literacy rates of the native born, and growing expenditures on primary schooling, at least through 1896, which is the last year for which we have information on provincial governments' expenditures before federal aid became more substantial and widely disbursed. Thereafter a trend toward regional convergence followed. Table 5.3 shows that the more prosperous regions and large cities had higher per capita expenditures; the notable outlier being Buenos Aires, consistent with our view. It is notable that the rich agricultural provinces of the Littoral and Andina regions were clearly ahead of the provinces of the Central and Norteña regions in support of primary schooling. From Table 5.4 we can see that the figures on the literacy of the native born indicate dramatic improvement within a few decades around the turn of the twentieth century, paralleling the major increase in public support for primary schooling. Finally, the foreign born, mainly from Spain and Italy, had much higher literacy rates than did the native born, although the disparity declined over the late-nineteenth and early-twentieth centuries as public schooling in Argentina expanded.[24] Although the foreign born in Buenos Aires were more literate than those elsewhere in Argentina, regional variation in literacy was much less among the foreign born than among natives.

---

[24] It is interesting to note that the differential between the foreign and native-born appears to have been due exclusively to the sharp contrasts in literacy among the respective groups of adults. This is yet another indication that literacy rates were rising rapidly over cohorts born in Argentina during this period.

Overall, the late-nineteenth and early-twentieth century surge in investment in public schooling is consistent with the idea that such expenditures were at least partially driven by income; the Argentine economy boomed during these decades, and its economic growth made more resources available and, at the same time, raised both the private and social rates of return to education. The increasing prosperity of Argentina also encouraged many policymakers, such as Sarmiento, to conceive of the United States and Canada as offering the country realistic models for development. Immigration, which grew rapidly over these decades, also seems to have had a positive impact on literacy. Not only were the foreign born relatively more literate than the native population and more demanding of public services such as schools, but the Argentine government was concerned with attracting these more discriminating European immigrants. The provision of public primary education served both as a means of encouraging immigration and of helping immigrants assimilate.[25]

It is hard to think of the expansion of the public schools in Argentina as part of a general movement for democratization. Major electoral reforms did not precede the first big push at establishing more and better-funded public schools as they did in the United States and Europe. The 1853 Constitution had not included restrictions on the right to vote based on income, wealth, or literacy, though a venue for political expression by the poor and illiterate was constrained by the absence of a secret ballot and the limited number of polling places that characterized elections until the Sáenz Peña Law of 1912.[26] Partly due to a puzzling lack of desire by the foreign born to apply for citizenship and obtain the right to vote, the fraction of the population who voted remained very low until the reforms of 1912.[27] Although the impetus of the late-nineteenth century movement to expand public schools was not related to any wave of democratization,

[25] Evidence that suggests that the conscious socializing element that education had for the national government is a 1920 law that established that the primary educational system should create state schools without ethnic or religious discrimination.

[26] For an excellent discussion of who held the right to vote, the conduct of elections, and who actually voted, see Paula Alonso, "Politics and Elections in Buenos Aires, 1890–1898: The Performance of the Radical Party," *Journal of Latin American Studies* 25 (October 1993): 464–87; Paula Alonso, "Voting in Buenos Aires Before 1912," in *Elections Before Democracy: The History of Elections in Europe and Latin America*, ed. Eduardo Posada-Carbó: 181–200 (New York: Macmillan, 1996). Among her findings are that in Buenos Aires, both the proportion of the population who voted and the relative probability of illiterate individuals voting were extremely low.

[27] As evident in Series C 181–194 in United States Bureau of the Census, *Historical Statistics of the United States: Colonial Times to 1970* (Washington, D.C.: Government Printing Office, 1975), the rate of naturalization was also low in the United States at the turn of

the extent of economic and political equality in Argentina may help us understand why the country was one of the leaders in extending access to schooling in Latin America, but lagged the United States and Canada. Compared to other Latin American nations in the late nineteenth century, Argentina (and Uruguay) had relatively scarce labor and a homogenous population – conditions that in principle made it easier for Argentina to work out collective action problems associated with financing public primary schools. Indeed the possibility of attracting immigrants through investments in public schools provided incentives for political and economic elites to support such policies. On the other hand, the country was in other dimensions much less equal than its peers in the northern hemisphere, and thus would be expected to have lagged in public school investment.

Chile

Schooling institutions in early-nineteenth century Chile resembled those in most of the other former Spanish colonies in the Americas that had recently gained independence. Despite expressions of support for education in the Constitution of 1833, schools of any sort – public or private – were few in number and served a very small fraction of the population. Most of the limited funding for public institutions came from municipal governments, and what came from the national government was predominantly directed to the University of Chile, which was founded in 1842, and to other schools above the primary level. Literacy rates were quite low, especially among the native born in Chile. For example, in 1854 the rate of literacy was 13.3 percent for the country as a whole, but 46.3 percent for the foreign born.[28]

Expanding primary schooling began to receive higher priority around mid-century. Between 1845 and 1860, the share of the national budget's allocation to education rose from 11 percent to 31 percent.[29] As in

the twentieth century (between 60 and 70 percent for males over age 21). However, the rate in the United States appears to have been much higher than in Argentina.

[28] Carlos Newland, "La Educación Elemental en Hispanoamérica: Desde la Independencia hasta la Centralización de los Sistemas Educativos Nacionales," *Hispanic American Historical Review* 71 (May 1991): 335–64.

[29] Even then, only about two-thirds of primary and secondary students were enrolled in public schools. See Gertrude M. Yeager, "Elite Education in Nineteenth-Century Chile," *Hispanic American Historical Review* 71 (February 1991): 73–105. See also Luis A. Brahm, Patricio Cariola, S. J. Patricio, and Juan José Silva, *Educación Particular en Chile: Antecedents y Dilemas.* (Santiago: Centro de Investigacion y Doecncia Economica, 1971).

Argentina, however, the real surge in public school expenditures appears to have begun with an economic boom, related to exports of nitrates and other mineral products, which took place during the second half of the nineteenth century and coincided with a wave of immigration. In 1860, a law was enacted committing the state to free primary schooling. At the same time, it was acknowledged that municipal governments might be unable to provide adequate funds, and so an enhanced role for the national government was recognized in establishing, financing, and operating schools. Although the rhetoric may have been inclusive, the growth in national government expenditures on schooling seems to have been associated with greater regional disparities in schooling and literacy. Literacy among the entire population rose from about 30 percent in 1885 to over 40 percent in 1907, but even in 1907, the literate were heavily concentrated either in large cities or in provinces that benefited from revenues derived from the export of nitrates. Among the first group were the cities of Santiago and Valparaíso with literacy rates of 50.6 and 53.6 percent respectively; in the second group were the provinces of Tacna, Tarapaca, and Antofagasta with rates of 47.7, 57.0, and 56.6, respectively.

Striking about the Chilean experience was its ability to attain relatively high levels of education and literacy when compared with the rest of Latin America, despite a substantial share of its population being of Native American descent. For example, in 1925, Chile's literacy rate of 66 percent was similar to Cuba's 67 percent, and rivaled Argentina's and Uruguay's, which stood at 73 and 70 percent respectively. By Latin American standards, Chile's accomplishment in supporting education may seem a bit puzzling. While systematic estimates of income or wealth equality are not available for the period, laws governing who could vote, the fraction of the population that did vote in elections, and evidence of the low literacy rate among the native born are consistent with the judgment of historians of Chile that there was rather marked political and economic inequality.[30] Such inequality would normally be expected to hamper the

---

[30] The 1833 constitution established income and property requirements that could easily be met by artisans, salaried workers, miners, petty merchants, and public employees. It deliberately lowered even those thresholds in 1840 to enfranchise 60,000 national guard troops. There was, however, a binding literacy requirement, although veterans of the wars of independence were exempted from both the literacy and income tests. In 1874, the income and wealth tests were dropped, as was the literacy requirement in 1878, but the latter was restored in 1885. Overall, political power may not have been as unequally distributed in Chile as in most of Latin America, but perhaps more unequally distributed than in Argentina, Costa Rica, and Uruguay.

development of a public school system and, in so doing, keep literacy rates low. That expectation is realized but only to the extent that Chile did not do well by the standards of its more prosperous neighbors in North America, countries with greater political and income equality and more homogeneous populations.

The real issue though is why Chile had one of the best records of Latin American societies in promoting primary education and attaining high rates of literacy. There are several factors that may have played a role. First, Chile – like Argentina – was competing with other countries to attract immigrants from Europe who were better educated and valued schooling more than the native born. Under such circumstances, it should not be surprising that the national government would have supported public schools, especially in the larger cities and mining centers where foreign immigrants were most likely to settle. A second factor is that by the second half of the nineteenth century, Chile had among the most urban populations in Latin America. Many observers attribute this development to the growth of the mining sector, and the stimulus it provided to the expansion of urban industries. Given that private and social returns to schooling and literacy are generally higher in urban than in rural jobs, greater urbanization should have encouraged more investment in education. Finally, the boom in nitrates and other mineral products generated revenue that could be invested in the public school system.

As was true of other Latin American countries, economic booms, whether at the regional or national level, often triggered a resource-based increase in public schools funding. In contrast, governments that had to rely more on direct taxes levied on voters seem to have faced greater resistance to public investment in education. Whatever the precise role of these explanatory factors, in Chile, as elsewhere in Latin America, the initial shift toward a policy of promoting schooling institutions appears not to have been induced by a wave of democratization.

Colombia and Peru
These two often-compared Andean nations both have large Native American populations and great topographic diversity. Nonetheless, they are generally regarded as having followed divergent paths of political development, and it is perhaps surprising then to find that in 1925 their average literacy rates were quite similar at the national level, and both experienced similar variation in literacy rates within each country.

Both countries explicitly recognized the importance of schooling and education in their early constitutions and laws. By the 1820s, the government of Francisco de Paula Santander began to promote the establishment of primary schools in Colombia.[31] The government used the Lancasterian system of mutual instruction to overcome the scarcity of qualified teachers. Through the 1830s, Santander's program was remarkably successful in increasing the number of schools and students, but national support for schools slackened by the end of his presidency. The federal government renewed a role in supporting schools by the late 1860s, when it enacted a tax on property to finance public education. It also assumed responsibility for creating a school to train teachers, as well as developing public libraries. The financing and operation of schools was left largely to state or municipal governments.

Few polities appear to have had the resources and political will to make major investments in public schooling. One exception is the state of Antioquia, which stands out most in promoting education. Distinguished at first by a relatively sparse population, the increased production of gold and the introduction of coffee during the mid-nineteenth century substantially increased its income and led to policies directly aimed at attracting migrants from other parts of the country. Throughout this period, the state and municipal governments in Antioquia were mostly controlled by Conservative governments who wished to encourage this internal migration, and their support of public schools as well as the liberal land policies they pursued were certainly consistent with this goal.[32] The neighboring "frontier" states of Caldas and Valle Del Cauca were similar in many ways to Antioquia and they too remained far ahead of the country in literacy and schooling enrollment rates into the twentieth century. Both their prosperity and their relative equality were associated with a scarcity of labor, high rates of land ownership, and the prevalence of small and

---

[31] See Aline Helg, *La Educación en Colombia, 1918–1957: Una Historia Social Económica y Política* (Bogatá: Fondo Editorial (CEREC), 1987).

[32] For a discussion of land policies, see Marco Palacios, *Coffee in Colombia, 1850–1970: An Economic, Social and Political History* (Cambridge: Cambridge University Press, 1980); and Catherine LeGrand, *Frontier Expansion and Peasant Protest in Colombia, 1850–1936* (Albuquerque: University of New Mexico Press, 1986). For evidence of the rapid expansion of schooling in Antioquia, see Departmento Administrativo Nacional de Estradistica, *Panorama Estadístico de Antioquia, Siglos XIX y XX* (Bogatá: D. E. Republica de Colombia, Departmento Administrativo Nacional de Estadística, 1981): 120–21.

medium-sized farms, which contributed to their relatively strong educational outcomes. The only, and intriguing, exception to this pattern is San Andres y Providencia, which had the highest literacy rate in Colombia in 1918. This small, isolated island in the Caribbean had originally been colonized by the Puritans in the early seventeenth century, but was taken over by the Spanish soon after.

Thus, in Colombia, even with a decentralized and federalist approach to education, only a small number of states had made substantial investments in public schooling by the early twentieth century. Most other states lagged far behind, with the result that around 1920 the national literacy rate of 32 percent was roughly half that of Argentina, Uruguay, or Chile. In 1925, Peru had a literacy rate of 38 percent, and, as was the case of Colombia, it exhibited extreme inter-regional variation in schooling and literacy. In 1876, when the national literacy rate was 18.9 percent, literacy rates in the major cities of Lima, Ica, and Callao were between 44 and 68 percent. Such inequality persisted into the twentieth century.[33]

The high literacy of the more urbanized coastal cities and provinces was likely due to the fact that the national government played a minor role promoting public schools throughout the nineteenth century. Although the right to an education was generally recognized in the various Peruvian constitutions, actual efforts to promote public schooling were sporadic, ineffective, and largely confined to establishing advisory bodies or commissions. Since there was not a sustained commitment of funds, the financial burden fell almost exclusively on municipal governments. The resources and organizational capacity to meet those challenges were centered in cities, not in the highlands and the jungle provinces, where the Native Americans were predominant. Of course, the higher rates of schooling and literacy in the large cities related also to the fact that many more urban residents had the means to obtain private schooling for their children. Still, in 1876, roughly 60 percent of the 215 primary schools in Lima were public schools.[34] It was not until the twentieth century

---

[33] This pattern mirrors that in 1940, when the national rate was 40.4 percent, and the figures for Lima, Ica, and Callao were 82.1, 72.1, and 91.2 percent, respectively.

[34] For the figures on Lima, provincial rates of literacy, and more detailed information on the history of schooling in Peru, see Jorge Basadre, *Historia de la Republica del Peru*, 6th ed., 17 vols. (Lima: Editorial Universitaria, 1968); Jorge Rosales and Hernan Fernández, *Educacion, una Mirada Hacia Dentro: Analfabetismo, Repitencia y Deserción* (Lima: Instituto de Pedagogía Popular, 1990); Alida Diaz, *El Censo del 1876 en el Perú* (Lima: Seminario de Historia Rural Andina, 1974); and Rolland Paulston, *Society, Schools and Progress in Peru* (Oxford: Oxford University Press, 1971).

during the presidencies of Jose Pardo and Augusto Leguia that the national government began to contribute significant and ongoing resources to the support of public schools, and to devote attention to racial and regional disparities.

Costa Rica and Guatemala

Costa Rica has long been recognized as the Latin American society with perhaps the least inequality, its distinctiveness a result of factor endowments: a high land to labor ratio and a relatively homogenous population. Early in its history, a small indigenous population, the lack of precious minerals, and its mountainous terrain led to an economy dominated by small farmers.[35] In this respect, Costa Rica was perhaps more like the United States and Canada than any Latin American economy.

Costa Rica was also like the United States and Canada in the important role played by local governments in education. After independence, the country maintained *ayuntamientos* (city councils), which had been originally set up by Spain's Cádiz Constitution between 1812 and 1814, as a basic governmental structure with many powers and responsibilities that included the provision and control of schooling.[36] Indeed, the central role of the municipalities in running the schools was bolstered during the 1820s as the national government instituted a series of measures that helped municipal governments raise revenue for education.[37]

[35] See, for example, John A. Booth, "Costa Rica: The Roots of Democratic Stability," in *Democracy in Developing Countries*, 4 vols., eds. Larry Diamond, Juan J. Linz and Seymour Martin Lipset, 387–422 (Boulder: L. Rienner, 1988); and Ralph Lee Woodward, Jr., *Central America: A Nation Divided* (New York: Oxford University Press, 1976).

[36] See Luis Fernando Sibaja Chasán, "Ayuntamientos y Estado en los Primero Años de Vida Independinete de Costa Rica (1821–1835)," in *Actas del III Congreso de Academias Iberoamericanas de la Historia: El Municipio en Iberoamerica (Cabildos e Instituciones Locales)*, 2 vols, (Montevideo: Instituto Histórico y Geográfico del Uruguay, 1955) for a discussion of the responsibilities and powers granted to the councils. During the conflicts for control of the newly independent states in Central America that went on between Guatemala and León (in Nicaragua), these councils assumed many of the functions that are now typical of a national state, such as defense, and until 1823 they decided to rotate the seat of government every three months between the four principal cities: Cartago, San José, Alajuela, and Heredia. It is therefore not surprising that after the newly independent nation of Costa Rica was established, the government chose to honor the authority of the *ayuntamientos*.

[37] Astrid Fischel, *Concenso y Represión: Una Interpretacion Socio-politica de la Educación Costarricense* (San José: Editorial Costa Rica, 1987). Local taxes included taxes on butchering cattle (the largest source of revenue), fines (including those charged for not attending school), money from the commutation of a sentence, taxes for the sale of tobacco and liquor, donations and contributions, vacant inheritances, and taxes on heads of family.

The 1869 Constitution made primary education obligatory for both sexes and tuition-free, and explicitly left municipalities in charge of the schools and all other expenses associated with operating them. At the same time, the federal government extended its rights to inspect and oversee the schools, and the Treasury assumed the responsibility for paying teachers' salaries.[38] Perhaps the key changes, not wholly unlike those introduced in parts of the United States, came in 1885 and 1886, with two laws, the Fundamental Law of Public Instruction and the General Law of Common Education, that set the basis for reform "from the bottom up": while ultimate control was reserved for the national executive, primary education was to be administered by local authorities, and all citizens of a district were required to pay for public schools' infrastructure.[39]

The increase in national government funds assigned to primary education in the 1885 and 1886 laws reflected an interest in and support of public schooling in Costa Rica unlike that of any other Latin American country (see Figure 5.1). Costa Ricans attributed particular significance to primary education, which was seen as the basis for a democracy, and were quite unusual in the degree to which they made it a priority. During the 1881 economic crisis, when the price of coffee fell and a fiscal crisis ensued, subsidies from the federal government to the school system were suspended for secondary and higher education (including normal schools), but not for primary education.[40] The priority given to primary schools stands in stark contrast with other Latin American nations. In Chile in 1875, for example, while substantial resources were assigned for education, primary schools received roughly equivalent amounts as secondary and higher education institutions, in spite of the fact that many more students attended primary school. This unequal per capita spending

[38] Primary schools were a high priority, and the assistance of the Treasury appears to have been motivated by a recognition of the severe fiscal problems faced by local governments.

[39] This duty became an obligation when the resources collected were insufficient. In addition, the laws increased the federal budget allocated to education, and the national government began buying school supplies in bulk and selling them to the local boards of education at a discount. In August 1888, Congress approved a federal loan for education of 300,000 pesos at 9 percent interest. Although the districts that benefited most from this loan were those that had enough revenue to cover the interest payments, localities with lower revenues were entitled under the law to receive government aid if they could not raise sufficient funds by taxing their own constituents. One important reason for the success of these reforms was that the Minister of Public Instruction, Mauro Fernández, was also the Minister of Finance at this time; which made the coordination of the educational reforms and the reforms concerning local public finances easier to implement.

[40] Fischel, *Concenso y Represión.*

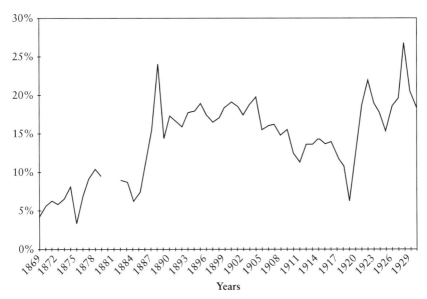

FIGURE 5.1. *Ratio of Federal Expenditures on Education to Total Ordinary Expenses, Costa Rica 1869–1930.*

in the different levels of education can also be seen in 1900 Mexico, as government spending for every secondary and higher education student was estimated to be 105 pesos and 126 pesos respectively, while per capita funding for primary students was only 0.20 pesos.

Guatemala, a close neighbor of Costa Rica, makes for an interesting contrast. Despite its proximity and similar reliance on coffee exports, Guatemala, if not the rest of Central America generally, has always been distinguished from Costa Rica by a relative abundance of labor (due largely to an initial and continuing dense population of Native Americans), and a much larger scale of agricultural production. That Guatemala was characterized early by extreme inequality and low per capita income partially helps account for an abysmal record at investing in primary education. For the first half century after independence, the operation of schools was overwhelmingly left to the Church. By 1867, a report to the Guatemalan Congress noted that government spending (at any level) on education was minuscule, and that the ratio of students enrolled to total population was among the lowest in Latin America, at just 0.6 percent. Although government funding of schools increased during the 1870s when coffee exports boomed and the Liberal governments displaced the Conservatives in power, enrollments were not enough to have a big impact on literacy. In 1925, the literacy rate for those aged 10 and over was about 15 percent, far below Costa Rica's 64 percent level. During the twentieth century, Guatemala continued to lag its hemispheric neighbors. In 1950, it, along with Nicaragua, Honduras, and Bolivia, ranked near the bottom in both school enrollment rates and literacy for the continents as a whole.

Cuba

Despite enjoying one of the highest levels of per capita income in all the Americas, well into the nineteenth century, Cuba was much slower than the United States and Canada in extending its system of public schooling and achieving high rates of literacy. During the eighteenth and early-nineteenth centuries, public authorities paid more attention to higher education than to primary schooling, as they did in other parts of Latin America. Primary schooling was almost exclusively private and obtained through religious congregations, payment of fees, or the rather isolated efforts of various private organizations. But during the 1830s, interest in public education began to grow, and in 1842 the first Law on Public Instruction was enacted. Public schools were to be supported by municipal governments and managed locally, but a central colony-wide office for inspection and coordination as well as a school to train teachers were set up. These actions spurred the formation of both primary and secondary public schools. Still, by 1860, just 60 percent of the country's 464 schools were public. Overall literacy was as high in Cuba as anywhere in Latin America, but at 23.8 percent, it was much less than in the United States or Canada.[41]

The War of 1868, which Cubans fought unsuccessfully to obtain their independence from Spain, was a catalyst for change. Within a few years of regaining control, Spain embarked on a series of reforms, including a royal decree and a second Law of Public Instruction that authorized a major expansion of public school system education at both the primary and secondary levels. Municipalities were obliged to cover the costs of primary and secondary public schools, which were free to all children from low-income families. The change in policy did yield some results:

---

[41] See the extensive discussion of the early development of schooling in Cuban Economic Research Project, *A Study on Cuba: The Colonial and Republican Periods* (Coral Gables: University of Miami Press, 1965): Ch. 2. The estimate of the rate of literacy in 1899 presented there (44.6 percent) is slightly higher than the estimate we have reported in Table 1.4, apparently because it includes those who attended school but did not report an ability to read.

TABLE 5.5. Combined State and Municipal Revenue and Primary School Expenditures (in Pesos Per Capita) in Mexico During the *Porfiriato*

State	Combined State and Municipal Revenue		Percent Increase in Per Capita Revenue	Expenditures in Primary Education		Percent Increase in Primary School Expenditures
	1888	1907	1888–1907	1874	1907	1874–1907
North West						
Baja California*						
Baja California Sur*						
Nayarit*						
Sinaloa	4.44	4.65	4.73	0.31	0.60	93.55
Sonora	3.67	6.56	78.75	0.38	0.98	157.89
North						
Chihuahua	2.96	6.98	135.81	0.02	0.98	4800
Coahuila	3.47	6.66	91.93	0.25	1.12	348
Durango	1.15	2.47	114.78	0.10	0.53	430
Zacatecas	2.62	2.87	9.54	0.08	0.52	550
North East						
Nuevo León	1.40	3.31	136.43	0.36	0.68	88.89
Tamaulipas	1.34	5.66	322.39	0.07	0.77	1000
Central West						
Aguascalientes	1.40	4.24	202.86	0.11	0.38	245.45
Guanajuato	1.74	2.01	15.52	0.24	0.19	−20.83
Jalisco	1.09	2.53	132.11	0.05	0.34	580
Querétaro	1.49	2.45	64.43	0.09	0.18	100
San Luis Potosi	2.63	2.53	−3.80	0.17	0.28	64.71
Gulf						
Tabasco	3.26	5.35	64.11	0.25	0.52	108
Veracruz	4.82	4.05	−15.98	0.19	0.46	142.11
Central South						
Distrito Federal*						
Hidalgo	2.10	2.80	33.33	0.18	0.39	116.67
México	1.24	2.93	136.29	0.24	0.31	29.17
Morelos	3.20	4.04	26.25	0.27	0.51	88.89
Puebla	2.15	3.64	69.30	0.20	0.30	50
Tlaxcala	1.12	2.09	86.61	0.16	0.35	118.75
South						
Chiapas	0.66	2.43	268.18	0.03	0.23	666.67
Colima	2.25	4.45	97.78	0.21	0.61	190.48
Guerrero	1.58	1.25	−20.89	0.22	0.18	−18.18
Michoacán	1.16	1.56	34.48	0.07	0.12	71.43
Oaxaca	0.77	1.59	106.49	0.09	0.24	166.67

continued

TABLE 5.5 (*continued*)

State	Combined State and Municipal Revenue		Percent Increase in Per Capita Revenue	Expenditures in Primary Education		Percent Increase in Primary School Expenditures
	1888	1907	1888–1907	1874	1907	1874–1907
South East						
Campeche	3.16	7.24	129.11	0.18	1.00	455.56
Quintana Roo*						
Yucatan	2.35	11.51	389.79	0.17	0.80	370.59
TOTAL	38.17	68.69		3.12	7.39	
AVERAGE	2.01	3.62	95.58	0.16	0.39	185.58

Source: Vaughan (1982).
Notes:
[1] The federal government alone funded the Federal District and the states marked with an asterisk.
[2] The federal government spent $1.37 per inhabitant on education in 1878, and $6.92 in 1910.
[3] The regional division for Mexico is based on Angel Bassols's (UNAM, Department of Economics) economic classification of states, based on the physical characteristics of the region.

between 1861 and 1899, many new schools were opened, enrollments increased, and the literacy rate rose to 40.5 percent. In addition, the gap between blacks and whites narrowed considerably. On the other hand, the gains were less than in other parts of Latin America, such as Argentina, Uruguay, and Chile, which had advanced even more rapidly and, by 1900, had higher rates of literacy than Cuba. Once independence was achieved, the United States began to provide extensive assistance to build up the educational institutions of the new nation. By 1925, Cuba was again near the forefront of Latin American countries in literacy, and roughly maintained that position through 1950. Argentina and Uruguay were the only nations to consistently surpass Cuba in this dimension.

Mexico

In Mexico, schooling was regarded as important from the very beginning of Spanish rule, as the Catholic Church used schools to convert the indigenous population. By the end of the eighteenth century the Bourbon dynasty set up a system to encourage the expansion of schooling by giving *cabildos* (town councils) control over all matters relating to primary education. The 1812 Cádiz Constitution established a General Directorate to oversee all educational matters in the colonies, and instructed the colonial government to build primary schools where children would be taught to "read, write and count, and catechism." After independence, the 1824 Constitution sought to preserve local authority in issues related to schooling, and recognized the right of the new federal entities to organize their education according to their specific needs.[42]

In principle, local governments had the right to control schools, but the climate of uncertainty created by 10 years of civil war, following Iturbide's rule in the 1820s, together with almost 50 years of persistent deadlock between conservative and liberal governments, complicated the task of expanding the public school system. Progress was slow, and it was not until the late 1860s that laws of public instruction incorporating a legal outline were enacted.

Significant investment in public schools began under the presidency of Porfirio Díaz.[43] In contrast to the Costa Rican experience, Mexico moved to centralize education, as a reorganization took place at the national level.[44] The laws of 1867 and 1869 suppressed religious education, and set out conditions relating to the number of schools, study plans, and calendars that were meant to apply throughout the country. However, because of Mexico's federal structure the laws were implemented only in the Federal District (DF), or capital city, and the federal territories (Baja California, Quintana Roo, and Tepic). Conflicts soon arose over the perceived erosion of state and municipal authority in educational

---

[42] Antonio Amnino, "The Ballot, Land and Sovereignty: Cadiz and the Origins of Mexican Local Government, 1812–1820," in *Elections Before Democracy: The History of Elections in Europe and Latin America*, ed. Eduardo Pardo-Carbó, 61–86 (New York: Macmillan, 1996). Even though most of the articles in the Cádiz Constitution were not implemented as law, due to the wars of independence (1810–21), it began a process of decentralization by creating more *cabildos*. These town councils were used as a political instrument aimed at weakening insurgency, but in fact they gave the town greater local autonomy and reinforced insurgency from the periphery to the center. Schooling was obviously an important issue, and attracted frequent comment. It was declared "necessary for all citizens" in the provisional constitution of 1814, and in addition to the 1824 constitution, the 1833 constitution declared schooling obligatory for men and women, children, and adults. Also see Fernando Solana, Raúl Cardiel Reyes and Raúl Bolaños, coordinators, *Historia de la Educación Pública en* Mexico: (Mexico: Fondo de Culture Económica, 1982).

[43] The period of the Porfiriato started in 1876 when Porfirio Díaz assumed the presidency for the first time; it ended in 1910 with the Mexican Revolution.

[44] This brief overview of the experience in Mexico draws on Miguel Angel Escobar Alvarez, *La Instrucción pública*, and Alicia Hernández Chávez, "Las tensiones internas del federalismo mexicanol," in *Hacia un Nuevo federalismo?* ed Alicia Hernández Chavez, (Mexico: Fondo de Culture Económica, 1996); Alberto J. Pani, et al. *Una Encuesta Sobre Educacion Popular* (Mexico: Departmento de Aprovisionamientos Generales, 1918); and Carlos Rivera Borbón, *El Gasto del Gobierno Federal Mexicano a Través de la Secretaria de Educación Pública* (Mexico: Secretariá de Educación Públicas Dirección General de Administración, 1970).

matters, with Congress supporting more local control and opposing the executive. From 1896 onward, the Díaz government had to implement all legislation relating to education by presidential decree. This strategy of bypassing Congress continued long after the Porfiriato.[45]

With the 1888 Federal Law of Primary Instruction, the federal government began the process of establishing a network of tuition-free primary schools. At least partially motivated by the desire to maintain some authority in education policy, many state governments soon passed similar laws supporting municipal schools, which had received little or no support. By the 1920s schools were run by a system of parallel bureaucracies – one associated with the state government and the other with the federal.[46] Thus, it was the federal government that initiated the expansion of the public school system, although both federal and state governments gradually took over the responsibility for education.[47]

During the Porfiriato, when the federal government began pursuing an active educational policy, the gap between the expenditures of the federal government and those of the states widened. By 1910, 6.92 pesos per person were being spent in the DF and federal territories, and just 0.36 pesos per person were spent by the state governments (see Table 5.5). The difference reflected the federal government's area of authority in educational matters, as well as the limited support of public schools by most states. However, the generally more prosperous states of northern Mexico were an exception. Coahuila, Sonora, Nuevo León, Tamaulipas, and Chihuahua had among the highest educational expenditures and literacy rates in the country. In some of these areas public schools with

---

[45] A key example was what happened with the Law of Public Instruction of 1888, which created a unified federally directed primary school system. The result was a de facto congressional veto, which was essentially overturned when the Minister of Public Instruction called two national education congresses and got them to agree on a uniform national system. See Mary Kay Vaughan, *The State, Education, and Social Class in Mexico, 1880–1928* (DeKalb: Northern Illinois University Press, 1982).

[46] The 1920s also marked the creation of the Ministry of Education (1921) and the launching of the first national campaigns to implant literacy nationwide (called cultural missions) by the two most prominent secretaries of education in Mexican history: José Vasconcelos (1921–24) and Moises Sáez (1928). These campaigns coincided with the largest increase in the federal budget for education at that time, 15 percent of the total federal budget for the year 1923, which then fell to its pre-Revolutionary level of 7–9 percent by 1930.

[47] Vaughan, *Social Class in Mexico*. State expenditures on schooling went from 10.52 percent in 1878 to 23.08 percent in 1910, becoming the largest item in states' budgets. Combined expenditures on education for both the federal and state governments during the Porfiriato increased at an impressive pace: from $26,767,224 in 1878 to $126,177,950 in 1910 – a rise of more than 370 percent.

broad access were established early in the nineteenth century, not unlike what happened in the United States and Canada.

The cities and towns of northern Mexico had relatively homogeneous populations of largely European descent, who had isolated or exterminated the indigenous groups of the region. The result tended toward communities with relative equality in income and created and reinforced the power of local governments. The city of Chihuahua, for example, founded in 1709, opened its first primary public school in 1786 when its population was 18,288, and in 1797, efforts were begun to develop a system of public schools in every large town in the state of Chihuahua. By 1808 there were public primary schools in five different localities.[48] The centralization of political power that took place in the late nineteenth century, and the center's control of resources, left many localities and states without the funds to set their own priorities. It is likely that some of the more progressive states, like those in the north, may have actually had their school systems deteriorate because of a redistribution of resources across states, or toward the center, by federal taxation.

Although Mexico is a rather extreme case of the centralized administration of education, it resembles Argentina and Chile – if not quite Costa Rica and Colombia – in the leadership role played by the national government in primary schooling. This approach, which was characteristic of Latin America, raises the question of why national governments were more important than state or local governments, in those societies in the Americas where public schooling came late.[49] One possible answer is that in localities with greater inequality or population heterogeneity, elites, who would have borne a greater than proportionate share of the costs and received a less than proportionate share of the benefits, used their disproportionate political influence to limit the mobilization and disbursement of funds for public schools. In such cases, the federal government needed to step in to solve the collective action problem or compel a redistribution of resources. Another possibility is that the national government was best positioned to appreciate the positive externalities associated with the expansion of public schooling, whether through increased immigration or the effects of having a better educated citizenry.

---

[48] Luis Alboites, *Breve Historia de Chihuahua* (Mexico: Fondo de Cultura Económica, 1944). See also Moises T. De la Peña, *Chihuahua Económico. Tomos I, II, III* (Mexico: Tall, Gráf de A. Morales S., 1948) and Miguel Ahumada, *Memoria de la Administración Pública del Estado de Chihuahua* (Chihuahua: Impresa del Gobierno en Palacio, 1896).

[49] Another interesting question is how schooling systems managed and funded by national governments differ from those managed and funded by local governments.

Summary

The experience of these eight countries illustrates that the pattern common to the northern part of North America, where early on localities or states mobilized resources to establish widely accessible primary schools, was rare in Latin America. Moreover, those relatively few areas where there was early public support, such as large cities, or certain regions (parts of northern Mexico, the highlands of Colombia, and Costa Rica), either had large middle classes, or were regions that resembled the United States and Canada in being labor scarce and having relatively homogeneous populations.[50] Our findings seem consistent with the idea that the degree of population homogeneity and equality in economic and political circumstances may be the key to understanding differences in educational investment. From this perspective, it is not surprising that the highly stratified societies of Latin America lagged far behind the United States and Canada in establishing schooling institutions and attaining high rates of literacy.

We have emphasized two closely related reasons why population homogeneity might favor successful completion of collective action projects like the establishment of universal schools. First, citizens with similar values, endowments, and behavior should find it easier to agree on whether and how to carry out such an enterprise. Second, unequal distribution of benefits and costs of a project will increase the probability that a group might attempt to block the project, particularly where this group enjoys disproportionate political power. This type of situation is seen throughout Latin America in the restrictions on the conduct of elections – who had the right to vote and whether ballots were secret or public. Income (or wealth) and literacy requirements for suffrage were common, but it was mainly the latter, combined with low literacy, that limited the population who could participate politically as citizens. Thus, the inequality in the distributions of income, political power, and human capital that arose out of the conditions of colonial settlements tended to persist over time – perpetuated at first by the institutions of imperial

---

[50] Northern Mexico and Costa Rica are both, along with Argentina and Uruguay, noted for having relatively small proportions of Native Americans in their populations as compared to other parts of Latin America. To say that the population of northern Mexico was homogenous may not be strictly accurate. Although precise figures are not available, it seems likely that there were many Native Americans living in isolated areas. The towns and more densely settled districts, however, had relatively homogenous populations of European descent.

Spain and then by those that evolved (or failed to evolve) in the newly formed states after independence.

IV

Our argument that the extent of inequality affected the social spending decision to invest on public education seems reasonable and consistent with the evidence on the Americas, but one would like to subject the proposition to more systematic tests. There are, however, several hurdles to overcome. First, estimates of income and wealth inequality in the nineteenth century are available for only a few countries. Second, identifying the line of causation is difficult because schooling, especially public schooling, affects the degree of inequality in each of the various dimensions we focus on: wealth/income, human capital, and political power. In this case, discerning what is exogenous and what is endogenous is not transparent.

The equality of political power illustrates this problem. Throughout the nineteenth century, citizenship and the right to vote were both linked to literacy in most of the Americas. Nearly all Latin American countries maintained, with minor exceptions, both literacy and wealth requirements for the franchise up to the early twentieth century (see Table 1.3). In addition, Latin American countries conditioned citizenship to literacy. In Venezuela citizens had to have the capacity to read and write; Cuba and Puerto Rico, which followed the Cádiz Constitution of 1812, required their citizens to be literate by the year 1830; Peru went back and forth, first stating in its 1823 Constitution that literacy should be a binding condition for citizenship by the year 1840, while a new constitution in 1826 made it a binding condition immediately; in Mexico, although each state decided on the date when literacy would become a binding requirement for citizenship, most states set the dates between 1836 and 1850.[51] As evident from both Tables 1.4 and 5.6, the proportions of the

---

[51] Dorothy Tanck de Estrada, "Las Cortes de Cadiz y el Desarrollo de la Educacion en Mexico," *Historia Mexicana* 29 (July–September 1979): 3–34. The literacy requirements may have been especially binding because schools typically taught individuals to write after they had learned to read, and many of the definitions of citizenship in newly independent Latin American countries made reading and writing separate requirements; an individual had to both read and to write in order to obtain full citizenship rights. The literacy restrictions seem generally to have been enforced, albeit with some exceptions. In Chile, a voting registry was created from the very beginning and political parties sought to enroll most of their support in this registry, one logical choice of supporters for the ruling parties was the National Guard. In order to enfranchise the National Guard,

population voting in Latin American elections varied markedly across countries and were generally low, especially in those countries with low literacy rates. The result was that in countries with low literacy rates the obstacles to mobilizing support for public schools were all the more formidable because those who had the right to vote were most likely those who would have paid most of the taxes for operating new schools, while reaping fewer of the benefits. Thus inequality in human capital and political power were self-reinforcing.

A test of the hypothesis that inequality in political power delayed the establishment of a broad-based system of public schooling is to compare schooling levels with the extent of the franchise. Summary information about the policies governing who had the right to vote in the Americas is reported in Table 5.6. Until the early twentieth century, the right to vote was generally restricted to adult males, but the United States and Canada were the clear leaders in doing away with limits based on wealth and literacy, and a much higher fraction of their populations voted than anywhere else in the New World. In terms of voting rights, the United States and Canada were about a half-century ahead of even the most democratic countries of Latin America, namely Uruguay, Argentina, and Costa Rica. By 1940 the proportion voting in the United States and Canada was three times higher than in Mexico, up to ten times higher than in countries such as Brazil and Bolivia, and 50 to 100 percent higher than in the most progressive countries of Latin America.

This empirical association between education and voting rights is consistent with our hypothesis, but there might be alternative interpretations for this finding. The low proportions voting in countries with low literacy may be a consequence of the fact that such societies tended to have literacy requirements. But this begs the questions of why it was that countries with low literacy rates were more likely to maintain the literacy requirements, or why countries that dropped such restrictions were more likely to establish public schools. The empirical association, it might be argued, was largely due to the legacy of British institutions; but there are reasons to be skeptical of this view as well. Not only does it fail to explain the variation in schooling within Latin America, it also ignores the fact that

the government had to lower income restrictions and lower literacy requirements (a person was required to read and write their name), and by doing so it enfranchised most of the population. See J. Samuel Valenzuela, "Building Aspects of Democracy Before Democracy: Electoral Practices in Nineteenth Century Chile," in *Elections Before Democracy: The History of Elections in Europe and Latin America* ed. Eduardo Posada-Carbó: 223–258 (New York: Macmillan, 1996).

TABLE 5.6. *International Comparisons of Laws Relating to Suffrage and the Extent of Voting*

	Year When Secret Ballot Attained	Year When Women Gained the Vote	Year of Universal Equal Suffrage	Proportion of Population Voting (%)
Austria	1907	1919	1907	7.9
Belgium	1877	1948	1919	22.0
Denmark	1901	1918	1918	16.5
Finland	1907	1907	1907	4.6
France	1831	1945	1848	28.4
Germany	1848	1919	1872	22.4
Italy	1861	1946	1919	6.8
Netherlands	1849	1922	1918	12.0
Norway	1885	1909	1921	19.5
Sweden	1866	1921	1921	7.1
Switzerland	1872	1971	1848	22.3
United Kingdom	1872	1918	1948	16.2
Canada	1874	1917	1898[a]	17.9
United States	1849[b]	1920	1870[c]	18.4
Argentina	1912	1947	–	1.8[d]
Bolivia	–	–	1956	–
Brazil	1932	1932	1988	3.0
Chile	1833	1949	1970	4.2
Costa Rica	1925	1949	1913	–
Ecuador	1861	1929	1978	3.3
El Salvador	1950	1939	1950	–
Guatemala	1946[e]	1946	1965	–
Peru	1931	1955	1979	–
Uruguay	1918	1932	1918	–
Venezuela	1946	1945	1946[f]	–

Sources: See Source notes to Tables 1.3 and 5.7.

Notes:

[a] By 1898, all but two Canadian provinces had instituted universal equal suffrage for males.

[b] By the end of the 1840s, all states except for Illinois and Virginia had adopted the secret ballot.

[c] Eighteen states, seven southern and eleven nonsouthern, introduced literacy requirements between 1890 and 1926. These restrictions were directed primarily at blacks and immigrants.

[d] This figure is for the city of Buenos Aires, and likely overestimates the national figure.

[e] Illiterate males did not obtain the secret ballot until 1956; females did not obtain it until 1965.

[f] The 1858 Constitution declared universal male suffrage, but this provision was dropped in later constitutions. All restrictions on universal adult suffrage were ended in 1946, with the exception of different age restrictions for literate persons and illiterates.

few of the many British colonies in the Americas came close to matching the records of the United States and Canada.

The extension of suffrage in the United States and Canada, and its relationship to the establishment of tax-supported primary schools, help establish a path of causation. Although not excluding the possibility of other factors influencing social decisions to expand public schooling, they show that at least in some of the countries in the Americas a change in the extent of political inequality acted as a salient stimulus for investment in education. The achievement of universal white male suffrage in the United States was the product of a long series of hard-fought political battles over the first decades of the nineteenth century, not due to a commitment on the part of those who drafted the Constitution. Historians of education have judged it no coincidence that this movement triumphed in the 1820s in the United States at the same time that the movement for "common schools" got started. Other prominent occurrences of extension of suffrage being implemented just before major expansions of schooling include the passage in England of the landmark Elementary Education law of 1870 (and a series of further laws through 1891 expanding access to primary schools) not long after the Second Reform Act of 1867.[52]

By providing an even broader international perspective, Table 5.6 highlights how slow most of the New World societies, despite being nominal democracies, were to extend the franchise. The great majority of European nations, as well as the United States and Canada, introduced secrecy in balloting and universal adult male suffrage long before the countries in Latin America and the Caribbean, and the proportions of the population voting in the former were always higher, often four to five times those in the latter. Although many factors may have contributed to the relatively low vote percentages in Latin America and the Caribbean, political decisions to maintain wealth and literacy requirements appear to have been of central importance.

In order to examine the empirical association between the extent of suffrage (a proxy for the degree of equality in political power) and investment in schooling institutions more directly, we bring together information on student enrollment with the fraction of the population who cast votes for a wide range of countries in the Americas and Europe (see Table 5.7). Several features are immediately apparent. First, the United States and Canada stand out early as having the highest proportions of children attending school in the world, 62 and 60 percent respectively

---

[52] Cubberley, *History of Education*, 641–44.

TABLE 5.7 *Ratio of Students in School to Total Ages 5–19, and the Proportion of the Population Voting for Selected Countries, 1895–1945*

	c. 1895	c. 1920	c. 1945
Argentina			
Schooling ratios[a]	0.21	0.41	0.51
Suffrage[b]	1.8%	10.9%	15.0%
Bolivia			
Schooling ratios	0.14	–	0.18
Suffrage	–	–	–
Brazil			
Schooling ratios	0.08	0.10	0.18
Suffrage	2.2%	4.0%	5.7%
Chile			
Schooling ratios	0.16	0.34	0.43
Suffrage	4.2%	4.4%	9.4%
Colombia			
Schooling ratios	–	0.18	0.18
Suffrage	–	6.9%	11.1%
Costa Rica			
Schooling ratios	0.25	0.22	0.29
Suffrage	–	10.6%	17.6%
Cuba			
Schooling ratios	–	0.31	0.31
Suffrage	–	–	–
Mexico			
Schooling ratios	0.13	0.17	0.22
Suffrage	5.4%	8.6%	11.8%
Peru			
Schooling ratios	–	–	0.31
Suffrage	–	–	–
Uruguay			
Schooling ratios	0.13	0.34	–
Suffrage	–	13.8%	–
Canada			
Schooling ratios	0.60	0.65	0.64
Suffrage	17.9%	20.5%	41.1%
United States			
Schooling ratios	0.62	0.68	0.76
Suffrage	18.4%	25.1%	37.8%

(continued)

TABLE 5.7 (*continued*)

	c. 1895	c. 1920	c. 1945
Austria			
Schooling ratios	0.45	0.52	0.58
Suffrage	7.9%	46.1%	46.9%
Belgium			
Schooling ratios	0.42	0.46	0.53
Suffrage	20.1%	26.3%	28.9%
Denmark			
Schooling ratios	0.49	0.49	0.50
Suffrage	9.9%	30.3%	50.8%
Finland			
Schooling ratios	0.12	0.29	0.53
Suffrage	4.6%	27.3%	44.3%
France			
Schooling ratios	0.56	0.43	0.60
Suffrage	19.4%	21.0%	49.3%
Germany			
Schooling ratios	0.54	0.53	0.55
Suffrage	14.6%	45.6%	48.8%
Ireland			
Schooling ratios	0.32	0.54	0.53
Suffrage	–	21.9%	41.1%
Italy			
Schooling ratios	0.27	0.36	0.47
Suffrage	4.1%	16.2%	52.5%
Netherlands			
Schooling ratios	0.44	0.45	0.56
Suffrage	5.1%	20.5%	49.5%
Norway			
Schooling ratios	0.48	0.50	0.52
Suffrage	7.9%	32.1%	47.5%
Portugal			
Schooling ratios	0.14	0.17	0.26
Suffrage	–	–	–
Spain			
Schooling ratios	–	0.27	0.34
Suffrage	–	–	–
Sweden			
Schooling ratios	0.50	0.42	0.45
Suffrage	2.8%	11.2%	46.4%

(*continued*)

	c. 1895	c. 1920	c. 1945
Switzerland			
Schooling ratios	0.53	0.54	0.49
Suffrage	11.8%	19.2%	20.5%
United Kingdom			
Schooling ratios	0.45	0.51	0.66
Suffrage	9.8%	30.4%	49.9%

Sources: For the schooling data: Mitchell, (1993) and (1992).
For the data on suffrage: Flora et al. (1983, vol. 1); and Nohlan, ed.
Enciclopedia Electoral Latinamericana y del Caribe (1993)
Notes:
[a] Schooling ratios were calculated by dividing the total number of students (regardless of age) by the population between the ages 5–19. When groups of the population were different from this range (5–19 years old) we assumed that there was the same number of people in each age group, and weighed the population figures so as to make them comparable. Bolivia is an example of this.
[b] Suffrage is used here to represent the proportion of the population that votes in each country.

in 1895. The only other nations that came close were France, Germany, and Switzerland (the only three countries in Europe that attained universal equal male suffrage in the nineteenth century) with 56, 54, and 53 percent respectively. Notably, Britain lagged behind its neighbors despite having higher per capita income. The United States and Canada were also distinguished at 1895 as having, with the exception of Belgium, the highest fractions of their populations voting.

The Latin American countries generally lagged their North American neighbors and Europe both in schooling participation and the extension of the franchise. In South and Central America, Argentina had the highest proportion attending school in 1895, but at 0.21 this was barely a third of the levels prevailing in the United States and Canada. Given the especially small proportion of the Argentinean population voting in 1895, 1.8 percent, it seems inaccurate to attribute the country's relatively high schooling ratio to factors related to the franchise. At the same time, it might be noted that Argentina was the one Latin American nation to have done away with both wealth and literacy restrictions. Also, the greater preference of immigrants for education may have played a role.[53] By

---

[53] Although even qualified immigrants were reluctant (mysteriously so to the many scholars who have studied the phenomenon) to change their citizenship to obtain the right to vote, their children would be doing so within a generation.

1920, both Argentina and Uruguay had introduced the secret ballot and made other reforms, and both the schooling ratios and the proportions of voting soared. By 1920, they had the highest proportions voting as well as the highest schooling ratios – with the exception of Chile nosing out Uruguay for second place in Latin America.

Between 1895 and 1945, nearly all the European countries, as well as the United States and Canada, further extended the franchise, both through broadening male suffrage and giving women the right to vote. The United States, Canada, France, Germany, and Belgium, which already had achieved high schooling participation and had high voting percentages by 1895, achieved only modest increases in their schooling ratios through 1945, even though a greater percentage of their population was now voting. Those that began in 1895 with rather low schooling ratios and proportions voting, such as Finland, Ireland, Italy, and the Netherlands, experienced both a great expansion of suffrage as well as substantial increases in the fraction of the school-aged population in school. Portugal and Spain, were monarchies, and had no significant voting rights, had the lowest schooling ratios in Europe throughout the entire period. Only three of the Scandinavian countries, Sweden, Norway, and Denmark, deviated significantly from the general pattern. Despite restrictions on the franchise and low proportions voting, they had high schooling ratios in 1895.

Schooling ratios and the proportions voting rose over time throughout Latin America, but they remained consistently low by international standards. By 1945 Argentina, Uruguay, and Chile did, however, approach the schooling ratios in some European democracies, notably Italy, Sweden, and Switzerland.[54] From a broad international perspective, the empirical association between the extent of the franchise and schooling participation is clear, but it holds as well, though in a weaker form, within Latin America.

These comparative statistics are informative, but a multivariate analysis with controls for variation across countries and over time in per capita income would improve our understanding of the systematic patterns in the data. Such a regression (See Table 5.8), based on a pooled cross-section from the data for 1895, 1920, and 1945) has the ratio of students in school to the school-age population as the dependent variable. The schooling ratio is positively and significantly related to per capita

---

[54] The other exception to this generalization are the European monarchies (Portugal and Spain), who fell comfortably within the Latin American distribution in schooling ratios.

TABLE 5.8. *Schooling and Suffrage, 1895–1945*

	Coefficient	*t*-statistic
Constant	−1.09	−6.02
Suffrage	0.496	5.37
Year 1920	−0.087	−2.97
Year 1945	−0.132	−3.77
Log (per capita income)	0.189	7.92
Number of Observations	56	
Adjusted R²	0.72	

Sources and Notes: Data on per capita income from Maddison (1995). The schooling ratio is the dependent variable.

income. Although one cannot feasibly distinguish between alternative paths of causation from these regressions alone, the results indicate that inequality in political power, as reflected in the proportion of the population who voted, was significantly related to the fraction of the population who took up schooling. The coefficient on the variable representing the proportion of the population voting is positive and large. It is, moreover, of an analytically important magnitude as well as statistically significant. Overall, it is quite impressive that suffrage is significantly related to the schooling ratio, even after controlling for year and per capita income. One implication is that the regional differences in schooling can be "accounted for" by differences in per capita income and our measure of inequality in political influence.

V

In earlier studies we highlighted the potential relevance of differences across societies in the degree of inequality in wealth, human capital, and political power in accounting for differential paths of development in the Americas, and argued that the roots of these disparities lay in differences in the initial factor endowments of the respective colonies. We argued that the extent of inequality exerted significant influence on the way in which economic institutions evolved over time. Where inequality was relatively low, the institutions that tended to develop extended opportunity to the general population, promoting growth by stimulating broad participation in commercial activities, increasing productivity, and preserving relative equality in the society at large. Where inequality was relatively high, institutions favored the elite groups, maintained inequality, and reduced the prospects for sustained economic growth.

In this chapter we have examined the development of primary schools and the increase in literacy in the Americas. Not only were the United States and Canada well ahead of their neighbors in establishing institutions of public primary education open to all, but even among the other countries in the New World, those societies that were more equal organized public schools earlier, and attained higher levels of literacy. The cross-sectional patterns are not the only features of the record that are consistent with the proposition that equality and education are related. In both the United States and Canada, political decisions to expand public schools closely followed the extension of suffrage. Moreover, in many Latin American societies the goal of increasing schooling rates was often frustrated by collective action problems at the local or state/provincial levels, especially where there was great inequality and populations were heterogeneous. That progress typically required the intervention of national governments lends support to our view.

Although our account focuses on the importance of inequality in explaining how education institutions such as universal primary schooling and high literacy rates evolved in the Americas, other factors, both systematic and idiosyncratic, also played significant roles. Foremost among them was income, or the availability of resources to invest in schooling institutions. Although many of the societies in the Americas were sufficiently prosperous during the nineteenth century to bear the costs of providing the broad population with a primary education, few did. Those that did tended to be more equal and homogeneous, but they also had higher per capita incomes. Moreover, economic booms often triggered public authorities to increase investments in schooling. Another contribution to the expansion of public education was immigration. In Argentina, Chile, and the highlands of Colombia, the desire to attract immigrants encouraged investments in public schooling and raised literacy. Immigrants to Latin America tended to place a higher value on education and were generally more literate than the native born. Another issue of importance in Latin America was the relationship between the national government and local and state authorities. In contrast to the experience in the United States and Canada, national governments were almost always the central force behind the establishment of public schools in Latin America countries. They were better positioned to overcome the collective action problems that made it difficult for local and even provincial governments to raise sufficient revenue on their own. But even when the national governments provided resources to promote public schooling, they had to resolve difficulties in coordination that arose from the demarcation of legal authority. Both the form and the severity of these problems varied across countries, and influenced the timing and effectiveness of national government intervention in education policy.[55]

Overall, the evidence is consistent with the hypothesis that the extent of inequality and population heterogeneity had a major impact on the evolution of educational institutions in the New World. The relative inequality characteristic of Latin America, in contrast with the United States and Canada, helps explain why universal schooling and high literacy came much later and may also explain why extreme inequality in Latin America has persisted to the present day. Our hypothesis remains speculative and clearly requires further study, but we hope that this attempt to examine how the paths of various New World economies diverged will stimulate more work on the interplay between factor endowments, inequality, education, and economic growth – in this context and in general.

---

[55] Perhaps another factor in accounting for the variation across economies is what might be called the British colony effect. Although it seems unlikely that the early investments in public schooling by the United States and Canada can be attributed to their British heritage, the rapid increase in schooling throughout the British colonies in the Caribbean basin in the late-nineteenth century may well have been related to the activities of the British Colonial Office during that period. As is indicated in Table 5.7, schooling ratios in the United States and Canada were generally much higher (on the order of 30 percent through 1920) than in Britain. For a recent discussion of twentieth-century education in Latin America, see Ewout Frankema" The Expansion of Mass Education – Twentieth-Century Latin America: A Global Comparative Perspective *Journal of Iberian and Latin American Economic History* 27 (Winter 2009): 359–396.

6

Inequality and the Evolution of Taxation
(Sokoloff with Eric M. Zolt)

I

As discussed in Chapters I through III, the importance of institutions in the processes of economic growth and development is now well recognized.[1] Unfortunately, the study of how institutions evolve is not straightforward. Not only does institutional change take place gradually over long periods of time, but the likelihood of different causal mechanisms being involved further complicates analysis.[2] Tax systems are among the oldest and most fundamental of institutions. Taxes are necessary to raise revenue for governments so they may fund their operations and finance investments in public goods and services that are conducive to general welfare and economic growth. How governments raise revenue can have profound effects on society. The technical efficiency of the tax system is important. Taxes alter the decisions of private agents, as taxpayers strive to reduce their tax liabilities.[3] Taxes also impose enforcement costs on governments and compliance costs on taxpayers. The structure of taxes, as well as of other forms of government regulation, may also influence the organization of economic activities, such as whether firms operate in the

---

[1] See, for example, Douglass C. North, *Structure and Change in Economic History* (New York: Norton, 1981).

[2] See B. Zorina Khan and Kenneth L. Sokoloff, "Intellectual Property Institutions in the United States: Early Development," *Journal of Economic Perspectives* 5 (Summer 2001): 233–46.

[3] Such adjustments can often lead economies to operate below their productive capacity, as taxpayers allocate their resources to those activities that yield the highest net returns after taxes, opposed to those that would make the most productive use of resources.

formal or informal sector or whether firms enter into formal or informal employment arrangements with workers.

The tax system determines how much of the costs of publicly provided goods and services are borne by different segments of the population. The incidence of taxes affects both the distribution of disposable income across the population as well as the constellation of political support for various public projects. Individuals are more willing to support government programs if they expect that the benefits they, or their peer groups, would realize from the higher level of expenditures will roughly match or exceed the corresponding increase in their tax liabilities.[4]

Although the lines of causation are not always clear, how societies choose to raise tax revenue is related to the relative degrees of authority of local, state, and national governments. Control over public expenditures generally follows the power to tax. As the political and administrative feasibility of levying certain taxes may be sensitive to economy-specific circumstances, those circumstances may also influence the structure of government as well as the extent and direction of government activities. For example, to the extent that local governments are more dependent on property taxes than are other levels of government, societies that lack the public authority or administrative capacity to effectively implement such taxes might be expected to have relatively small local governments and low levels of public investments and expenditure programs (for example, spending on schools or local roads) whose benefits accrue primarily to local residents.

Striking contrasts exist today between the tax systems of developed and developing countries.[5] Tax systems in developed countries today derive most of their revenue from individual income taxes, corporate

---

[4] Recent studies of quite distinct settings have yielded remarkably consistent findings regarding less government provision of public services in ethnically or otherwise heterogeneous polities. The mechanisms that account for this pattern remain unclear, but may have to do with more diverse populations being hampered by higher costs of reaching a consensus (resolving the collective action problem) or with there being greater economic and political inequality across social groups in such contexts. For examples of this literature, see Alberto Alesina, Reza Baqir, and William Easterly, "Public Goods and Ethnic Divisions," *Quarterly Journal of Economics* 114 (November 1999): 1243–84; and Latika Chaudhary, "Determinants of Primary Schooling in British India," *Journal of Economic History* 69 (March 2009): 269–302. For a discussion of the mechanisms by which the option of the rich to substitute private goods for public goods can inhibit reform or provision of government services, see Albert O. Hirschman, *Exit, Voice, and Loyalty: Response to Decline in Firms, Organizations, and States* (Cambridge, MA: Harvard University Press, 1970).

[5] See Vito Tanzi, "Quantitative Characteristics of the Tax Systems in Developing Countries," in *The Theory of Taxation for Developing Countries*, eds. David Newberry and

income taxes, and broad-based consumption taxes. Such tax systems are commonly regarded as more progressive in incidence than those of developing countries whose tax revenues come largely from taxes on consumption, in the form of value-added or turnover taxes, excise taxes, and taxes on foreign trade. As a percentage of gross domestic product, aggregate tax revenues in developing countries are only about half the tax revenues of developed countries. Developing countries are also more likely to impose and collect taxes at the national level rather than extend substantial taxing authority to state and local governments.

Why tax systems vary is a difficult question. Scholars have noted that both the level of taxation and the relative use of different tax instruments tend to be systematically related across economies to factors such as per capita income, the share of wages as a percentage of national income, the share of national income generated by large establishments, the share of agriculture in total production, and the level of imports and exports.[6] Many observers have suggested that these patterns arise primarily from technical or resource issues in the design of tax structures. Proponents of this view highlight how, for example, it is less feasible to adminis- ter an individual income tax in countries with a large informal sector than it would be in countries where most individuals have stable full- time employment relationships with large firms.[7] They contend that the major reason for the striking differences between the tax systems of the developed and less developed nations is that rich countries have more choices in deciding the level of taxation and the tax mix (the relative use of different tax instruments).[8] Although not inconsistent with this common wisdom, other scholars have emphasized how political factors can influence the design and administration of tax systems.[9] Groups with

Nicholas Stern, 205–241 (New York: Oxford University Press, 1987); and Robin Burgess and Nicholas Stern, "Taxation and Development," *Journal of Economic Literature* 31 (June 1993): 762–830.

[6] See, for example, Alan A. Tait, M. Gratz, and Barry J. Eichengreen, "International Com- parisons of Taxation for Selected Developing Countries, 1972–1976," *IMF Staff Papers* 26 (March 1979), 123–156.

[7] See Richard Goode, *Government Finance in Developing Countries* (Washington, D.C.: Brookings Institution, 1984); and Richard A. Musgrave and Peggy B. Musgrave, *Public Finance in Theory and Practice*, 4th ed. (New York: McGraw-Hill, 1984): 790–96.

[8] See Vito Tanzi and Howell H. Zee, "Tax Policy for Emerging Markets: Developing Coun- tries," *IMF Working Paper no. 00–35* (March 2000), (Washington, D.C.: International Monetary Fund): 1–35.

[9] For a pioneering discussion of the influence of politics on the design of tax systems in Central America, see Michael H. Best, "Political Power and Tax Revenues in Central America," *Journal of Development Economics* 3 (March 1976): 49–82. More generally, see Thomas J. Reese, *The Politics of Taxation* (Westport: Greenwood, 1980).

great influence are able to tilt or shape the structures of taxation, if not of public finance more generally, in their favor.

We turn to history to gain a better perspective on how and why tax systems vary. Our focus is on the societies of the Americas over the nineteenth and twentieth centuries. Our interest in the experiences in North and Latin America has two principal sources. First, despite the region having the most extreme inequality in the world, the tax structures of Latin America are generally recognized as among the most regressive, even by developing country standards.[10] Moreover, Latin American countries typically (though there are exceptions) have low levels of taxation and collect relatively modest tax revenues at the provincial or local level. Improving our knowledge of when and how these rather distinctive patterns in taxation and public finance emerged may help us to better understand both the long-term development of the region as well as the processes of institutional formation and change more generally.

Second, as has come to be appreciated by social scientists, the colonization and development of the Americas constitute a "natural experiment" of sorts that students of economic and social development can exploit. Beginning more than 500 years ago, a small number of European countries established colonies in diverse environments in many hemispheres. The different circumstances meant that largely exogenous differences existed across these societies, not only in national heritage, but also in the extent of inequality. Relatively high per capita incomes (by the standards of the time) prevailed throughout the Americas, at least through the late eighteenth century, and many of these colonies had gained their independence from their European colonizers by the early nineteenth century. The record of what sorts of institutions these new, prosperous, and nominally democratic nations established, and how they evolved over time, provides scholars with a useful laboratory to study the sources of systematic patterns in the evolution of tax systems.

When tax scholars explore the relationship between inequality and taxation, they tend to focus on how tax systems may alter the after-tax distribution of income or wealth, either directly through government takings or transfers, or indirectly through their influence on the decisions of

---

[10] For estimates of income inequality in Latin America and extensive treatment of these issues, see David De Ferranti, Guillermo Perry, Francisco Ferreira, and Michael Walton, *Inequality in Latin America: Breaking with History?* (Washington, D.C.: World Bank, 2004). Also see the discussion of the regressivity of tax systems in Latin America in Richard M. Bird, "Taxation in Latin America: Reflections on Sustainability and the Balance Between Equity and Efficiency," (Toronto: Unpublished Working Paper, 2003).

individuals (or households) about labor supply, savings, or investments.[11] Here we take a different approach, by examining whether exogenous differences in the extent of inequality might have influenced the design and implementation of tax systems. We highlight how even when the income levels across the societies of the Americas were relatively similar, the tax structures in the United States and Canada looked very different from those in Latin America. Moreover, we raise the question of whether these differences in taxes, and in related spending patterns, might have played a role in accounting for quite divergent paths of long-run development. Our claim that inequality plays an important independent role in influencing the structure of taxation is also supported by comparisons across regions of the United States.

Previous chapters have shown how initial and rather extreme differences in the extent of inequality seem to have contributed to systematic differences in the ways that strategic economic institutions evolved across the Americas.[12] This explored how a number of mediating mechanisms (paths of institutional development) through which high initial inequality may have led to poor economic outcomes through its impact on the evolution of fundamental policies influencing access to suffrage, schooling, and land. The purpose of this chapter is to examine whether the ways tax policy evolved were affected by the extreme differences in inequality that were present across the economies of the Americas soon after colonization began. We argue that they were, and we proceed as follows. Part II examines the tax systems in Latin America and North America in the nineteenth century. Part III discusses how these tax structures evolved over the twentieth century. In Part IV we offer some tentative conclusions about what the legacy of extreme inequality in Latin America meant for the long-run pattern of tax design and expenditure policy in that region.

Several salient patterns emerge. The United States and Canada (similar to Britain, France, Germany, and even Spain) were much more inclined to tax wealth and income during their early stages of growth, and into the twentieth century, than were their neighbors to the south.[13] Although the United States and Canadian federal governments were similar to those of

---

[11] For example, see Joel Slemrod and Jon M. Bakija, "Growing Inequality and Decreased Tax Progressivity," in *Inequality and Tax Policy*, eds. Kevin A. Hassett and R. Glenn Hubbard, 129–146 (Washington, D.C.: American Enterprise Institute, 2001).

[12] Above, Chs. 2 and 3.

[13] For example, land and other assessed taxes generally accounted for between 15 and 40 percent of revenue to the British government over the period 1690 to 1790. See John Brewer, *The Sinews of Power: War, Money, and the English State, 1688–1783* (Cambridge, MA: Harvard University Press, 1990): 98.

their counterparts in Latin America in relying primarily on the taxation of foreign trade (overwhelmingly tariffs) and excise taxes, the greater success or inclination of state (or provincial) and local governments in North America to tax wealth (primarily in the form of property or estate taxes) and income (primarily in the form of business taxes), as well as the much larger relative sizes of these subnational governments in North America, accounted for a radical divergence in the overall structure of taxation. Tapping these progressive (at least as conventionally understood) sources of government revenue, state and local governments in the United States and Canada, even before independence, began directing substantial resources toward public schools, improvements in infrastructure involving transportation and health, and other social programs.[14] In contrast, the societies of Latin America, which had come to be characterized soon after initial settlement by rather extreme inequality in wealth, human capital, and political influence, tended to adopt tax structures that were significantly less progressive in incidence and manifested greater reluctance or inability to impose local taxes to fund local public investments and services. These patterns have persisted well into the twentieth century indeed, up to the present day.

II

The colonial tax structures established by the Europeans in the Americas were generally alike in obtaining much of their revenue from trade or closely related activities. Great Britain levied relatively light tax burdens on the residents of its colonies. Revenues came from regulation of trade and from the taxes this imposed on the importation into Britain of New World produced commodities, including sugar and tobacco. Given that the probable demand for these goods was highly inelastic, British consumers likely bore most of the burden of these duties. When Britain attempted to increase tax revenues to offset more of the costs of defending its colonies on the North American mainland through excise taxes, import duties, and higher fees, the change in policy was fiercely and famously resisted.[15]

---

[14] For a discussion of the evolution of suffrage institutions, see note 13, Ch. 4. It is worth emphasizing that most of the countries discussed here were independent of their colonial masters and were nominal democracies by the middle of the nineteenth century.

[15] See Brewer, *Sinews of Power*. For excellent discussions of how Britain and Spain collected revenue from its colonies, and of how local authorities in their colonies raised revenue, see Lawrence Gipson, *The British Empire Before the American Revolution* (Caldwell:

Spain and Portugal, in contrast, were much more intent on, and effective at, raising revenue directly from their colonies. This may have been at least partially attributable to the enormous wealth their colonies possessed. The Spanish Crown levied a vast range of taxes, with revenue derived from impositions on a variety of activities, commodities, commercial and administrative transactions, and from tribute exacted from Native Americans varying across colonies and districts with the composition of the economy and of the population. In general, however, most of the revenues seem to have come from taxes on the sales of various commodities (the *alcabala*), custom duties, mining (especially silver and gold production), and from various state monopolies in tobacco, salt, and other commodities.[16]

In Brazil, the sugar industry was the primary source of revenue to Portugal during the colony's early history, but direct taxes on sugar production hampered the competitiveness of Brazilian producers as sugar cultivation spread across the West Indies.[17] By the end of the sixteenth century, Portugal introduced new taxes on imports into Brazil, as well as sales taxes on goods exported by Brazil to Portugal. The diversification of taxes, and the eventual boom in gold production (another activity ripe for taxation) contributed to a relative, if gradual, decline in the burden on the sugar industry. Taxation of trade, or of production of commodities intended for export, however, was to remain a central feature of the tax system.

Although the various taxes levied by the British Crown on the residents of their colonies were relatively light, the local and provincial governments set up by the colonists themselves seem to have raised more revenues from their populations (at least those segments that were not

Caxton Printers, 1936); Edwin J. Perkins, *The Economy of Colonial America* (New York: Columbia University Press, 1980); Edwin J. Perkins, *American Public Finance and Financial Services, 1700–1815* (Columbus: Ohio State University Press, 1994); and J. H. Elliott, *Empires of the Atlantic World: Britain and Spain in America: 1493–1830* (New Haven: Yale University Press, 2006).

[16] For example, in Mexico during the late 1780s about a quarter of the colonial government's revenue came from the *alcabala*, nearly 45 percent from state monopolies, and roughly 20 percent from taxes on gold, silver, and other mining activities. See Barbara Tenenbaum, *The Politics of Penury: Debt and Taxes in Mexico, 1821–1856* (Albuquerque: University of New Mexico Press, 1986). The relative importance of taxes on mining seems to have declined, and the relative importance of the tobacco and other monopolies increased over time. See also Mark A. Burkholder and Lyman L. Johnson, *Colonial Latin America*, 3rd ed. (New York: Oxford University Press, 1998).

[17] Even municipal or local governments at times assessed taxes on sugar production.

Native Americans) than did their counterparts in Latin America. This pattern both reflected and contributed to a more decentralized structure of British America. These taxes allowed local or colonial governments greater autonomy in how they operated. The New England colonies exhibited a preference for property or faculty taxes (based on estimated earnings potential) at both the colonial and local government levels rather early in their histories, and indeed in 1634 the General Court of Massachusetts held that "in all rates and publique charges," every man should be taxed "according to his estate." The expenses of the provincial governments were quite modest, generally consisting of the bare necessities of civil government, but local authorities used their revenues to support investments in quasi-public or public goods and services such as public schools and roads. In contrast, the southern colonies, perhaps influenced by the interests of large landowners (as well as the inelastic demand for some of their prominent exports, such as tobacco), tended to rely more on taxing imports and exports. The Middle Atlantic colonies' tax institutions fell somewhere in between, but already by the time of the Revolution both the Middle Atlantic colonies and the New England colonies made extensive use of property taxes.[18]

The reliance on trade taxes as the principal source of tax revenue continued (at least at the national government level) throughout the hemisphere after the wave of independence movements in the late eighteenth and early nineteenth centuries. In the United States, a 1789 law establishing the tariff was one of the first laws enacted by the federal government. Although the federal government had other sources of revenues, such as excise taxes, proceeds from sales of public lands, a duty on receipts for legacies, and even taxes (generally of brief duration and occurring during wartime) on dwelling houses, land, and slaves, tariffs provided by far the dominant share of national government revenue (typically well above 80 percent) up through the Civil War. These revenues amounted to roughly 1 to 2 percent of GNP, excluding spurts during wartime, and were almost exclusively spent in covering the costs of defense, paying off the debt, and general government expenses. Only a small fraction, about 5 percent of federal government expenditures, went to support capital investments

---

[18] See Perkins, *Economy of Colonial America*, and for an exceptionally fine treatment of how the tax structures of the colony, commonwealth, and state of Massachusetts evolved from colonial times through the early twentieth century (and the source of the quote in the text), see Charles J. Bullock, "Historical Sketch of the Finances and Financial Policy of Massachusetts," *Publications of the American Economic Association* 3rd series, (May 1907): 2.

such as public buildings, roads and canals, and improvements to rivers and harbors. As was recognized, and has often been noted, the U.S. government was extremely conscientious about maintaining its reputation in financial markets, and was loath to finance much of its expenditures through borrowing or issuance of paper money. In Canada, tariffs were the major source of revenue for the national government after the confederation formed in 1867, generally accounting for between 60 and 70 percent of dominion revenue (and over 80 percent of dominion tax revenue) into the twentieth century.[19]

In Latin America the overall patterns of national government taxation, if not of the extent of reliance on debt, were remarkably similar to that in the United States and Canada over the nineteenth century. Although wars and other shocks occasionally generated transitory impositions of, or increases in, *direct contributions* (direct levies, applied to land or a proxy for income), customs duties and excise taxes (on commodities such as liquors) normally accounted for the bulk of revenues. Indeed, there were only two notable differences in how Latin American central governments financed themselves. First, unlike in the United States and Canada, state monopolies (a holdover from the colonial period) and levies on the production of certain staples and minerals intended for export (such as coffee, sugar, guano, gold, silver, nitrates, and copper) were at times significant generators of revenue.[20] The other salient divergence was the greater inclination of Latin American countries to incur debt or issue paper money to finance operating deficits.[21] Notwithstanding these differences, Latin American central governments were like the North American

[19] Together with excise taxes (levied primarily on liquors and tobacco), the revenue from tariffs generally accounted for between 75 and 85 percent of dominion revenue. In 1870, the tariffs on sugar and molasses, spirits and wine, tea, cottons, and woolens were the largest contributors, jointly accounting for 65.8 percent of all tariff revenue. See J. Harvey Perry, *Taxes, Tariffs, & Subsidies: A History of Canadian Fiscal Development* (Toronto: University of Toronto Press, 1955): table 3. Customs revenue had been the major source of provincial revenue before the Confederation, but the terms of the unification agreement stripped the provinces of the right to levy such taxes.

[20] Most countries did collect some government revenue from duties on exports, but their abilities to rely on such taxes were constrained by international competition and the power of exporters. It was generally only in cases where exporters had market power and could pass on some significant portion of taxes to the consumers (such as coffee in Brazil, guano in Peru, or nitrates in Chile) that duties on exports accounted for substantial shares of national government revenue.

[21] Not only were Latin American countries more willing to borrow, but they also seem to have been less committed to maintaining confidence in their service of the debt. Their poor record at debt service constrained their ability to tap external credit, and thus Latin

central governments in raising most of their revenue from tariffs and from taxes levied on commodities generally thought to be income inelastic. In Mexico, for example, port taxes, income from the tobacco monopoly, and excise taxes yielded 75 to 85 percent of national government revenue over the latter half of the nineteenth century. Taxes on property and on businesses existed, but these typically accounted for less than 10 percent of revenue. In Brazil, between 1823 and 1888, more than 50 percent of total national revenue consistently came from tariffs on imports, with excise taxes and assessments on exports contributing roughly 14 and 25 percent of total revenue, respectively. In Chile, taxes assessed at ports and revenue raised by state monopolies consistently accounted for just under 80 percent of national government revenue throughout the second half of the nineteenth century and well into the twentieth century. Colombia provides yet another example. Already by the 1830s, soon after independence, customs duties and income from state monopolies on commodities such as tobacco and salt brought in 60 percent of national revenues. By the 1840s, their cumulative share rose to nearly 80 percent.

Wars and other threats to the social order (such as the War of 1812, the U.S. Civil War, the war between Mexico and the United States, and various internal uprisings) did sometimes stimulate the imposition of direct taxes that extended the reach of national governments in progressive directions (that is, the income tax in the United States during the Civil War, and the property tax in Mexico during its war with the United States), but the general pattern throughout the hemisphere was reliance by national governments on taxes that targeted commodities or trade rather than income or wealth.[22] As is evident in Table 6.1, and discussed

American countries were typically quite reliant on internal sources. This may have had unfortunate effects on the development of banks and other financial institutions.

[22] A close examination of the variation over time in the amounts of tax revenue raised, and the manner by which national governments in Latin America financed their operations, suggests that there was often a reluctance as with other countries, to increase taxes during periods of war. Rather, the approach seemed to be either inflating the money supply or borrowing from foreign lenders or domestic banks. This pattern stands in contrast to the behavior of the U.S. government during wartime, but it is interesting to note the resemblance to how the Confederacy financed its operations during the U.S. Civil War. In an intriguing article, which explores the voting patterns among members of the Confederate Congress, Rose Razaghian finds that it was those that came from the states and districts with large slave plantations (and likely the greatest inequality) that were (until the very late stages of the war) most opposed to taxing income – and thus most inclined toward financing the Confederacy through inflationary monetary policy, loans, and excise taxes. See Rose Razaghian, "Financing the Civil War: The Confederacy's Financial Strategy," *Yale ICF Working Paper no. 04-45* (New Haven: Yale University, 2005).

TABLE 6.1. *The Shares of National Government Revenue Accounted for by Tariffs, Excise Taxes, and Taxes on Income and Wealth*

Country/ Year	Customs (%)	Income and wealth taxes (%)	Country/ Year	Customs (%)	Income and wealth taxes (%)
Argentina			Mexico[b]		
1872	94.0		1870	92.3	3.6
1895	71.2	3.2	1890	79.7	4.7
1920	58.4	2.9	1910	86.0	11.1
1940	24.7	17.9	1929	29.8	10.6
Brazil[a]			1940	29.5	17.0
1870	71.4		Peru[d]		
1888	69.1		1871	95.6	
1900	65.5		1899	59.1	3.6
1920	56.8		1920	51.9	6.0
1940	50.3	10.2	1940	26.5	18.4
Chile			Uruguay		
1895	73.8	0.6	1895	66.7	
1920	70.2	6.0	1910	60.0	
1940	41.1	23.7	1929	32.2	18.6
Colombia			1940	40.0	14.0
1872	69.5		Canada		
1928	56.0	5.3	1870	63.2	
1940	36.7	30.4	1905	57.5	
Costa Rica[c]			1920	37.3	10.5
1871	91.4		1940	15.0	28.4
1885	81.3		United States		
1910	86.8		1820	83.3	
1918	64.4	18,3	1860	94.6	
1930	78.1	7.2	1870	47.5	9.3
El Salvador[a]			1900	41.1	
1897	84.0		1927	17.0	64.8
1910	75.0		1940	5.8	43.0
Guatemala[a]					
1872	76.0				

Sources: The general source for these estimates is Mitchell (1993), but the estimates reported by Mitchell were interpreted with, and complemented by, the greater detail obtained for a number of individual countries in other sources. For Argentina, Oficina de Estadistica Nacional (1875). For Brazil, Carreira (1889) For Chile, Molina (1898). For Colombia, Melo-Gonzalez (1989); Park (1985); and López Garavito (1992). For Costa Rica, Soley Guell (1975); Ministerio Economia y Hacienda (1953); and Román Trigo (1995). For Mexico, Marichal, Miño Grijalva, and Riguzz (1994). For Peru, Direacián de Estadistical (1928 and 1940); and Tantalean Arbulu (1983).

Notes:

[a] The revenue included under customs includes sales and excise taxes as well as customs.

[b] The estimates of customs revenue for 1870 through 1910 include the amounts collected from indirect taxes (almost exclusively levies on imports and exports), as well as revenue from stamps (the major component), ports, the post office, lotteries, railroads, and coinage. The income and wealth figures for those years encompass indirect taxes, most of which are taxes on property held in districts under the federal government authority. The share in total revenue accounted for by indirect taxes trends from 72.7 percent in 1870 to 50.8 percent in 1890 to 44.4 percent in 1910.

[c] The revenues reported under customs revenue include tariffs on imports, a tax on coffee exports, sale or excise taxes (mostly composed of a levy on tobacco consumption until 1908), and revenue obtained from the state monopoly on liquors.

[d] The customs revenue for Peru includes the revenue from the export of guano.

TABLE 6.2. *Distribution of Tax Revenues Across Levels of Government During the Nineteenth Century: Brazil, Colombia, Mexico, Canada, and the United States*

Country/Year	National government (%)	Provincial governments (%)	Municipalities or other local governments (%)
Brazil[a]			
1826	30.8	69.2	0.0
1856	79.5	17.1	3.3
1860	78.2	18.2	3.5
1885/86	76.3	18.5	5.2
Colombia[b]			
1839	88.4	2.9	8.7
1842	91.8	1.6	6.7
1850	85.4	8.7	5.8
1870	46.6	30.8	22.6
1894	60.0	32.0	8.0
1898	66.7	28.6	4.8
Mexico			
1882	69.1	19.5	11.5
1890	74.7	16.3	9.0
1900	67.3	19.8	12.9
1908	70.6	17.1	12.3
Canada[c]			
1933	42.5	17.9	39.6
1950	68.7	18.7	12.6
United States[d]			
1855	25.5	17.4	57.1
1875	39.6	16.4	44.0
1895	36.0	14.0	50.0
1913	29.1	13.2	57.6
1927	35.5	18.0	46.5
1950	68.3	17.3	14.4

Notes:

[a] For Brazil, see Carreira (1889). The substantial change in the distribution of tax revenues between 1826 and 1856 reflects the growth in the relative power of the national government, relative to the provinces, after independence. There were explicit divisions of authority across the levels of government in regards to what could be taxed, but those divisions changed somewhat over time. In 1834, the national government was given the authority to raise revenue by collecting taxes on imports, exports, slaves, and the production of gold, sugar, cotton, and various other products, as well as through port fees, stamp requirements, and the sale of official posts and titles. The division of authority changed over time, with perhaps the principal impact being the shift of taxes on slaves to provinces, with the right to tax immobile property going to the national government.

(*continued*)

TABLE 6.2 *(continued)*

Notes continued:

[b] For Colombia, see Melo-Gonzalez (1989). As seen in the table, in the 1830s and 1840s, the national government collected a major part of the fiscal revenues. The situation changed drastically after the reform of 1850, which intended to decentralize fiscal revenues and spending. The states would be in charge of the elaboration of their own budgets. In the case of revenues, the national government would keep mainly the revenues from customs, salt monopoly, stamped paper, income from the mint, and the postal and telegraph services, while the states would collect the revenues from taxes on the gross value of the production of gold and certain agricultural commodities. These taxes were phased out during mid-century, however, and the states created new taxes then, such as a direct tax, in order to raise more revenues. Not only taxation was decentralized: spending was also reallocated. The states were put in charge of the spending on public instruction, police, prisons, justice administration, roads, and public works. Between 1863 and 1886 the decentralization process became more significant. The Constitution of 1863 established the federal system in the Estados Unidos de Colombia (United States of Colombia), which was confirmed by nine sovereign states: Antioquia, Bolivar, Boyaca, Cauca, Cundinamarca, Magdalena, Panáma, Santander, and Tolima. The decentralization of revenues had a significant impact while in 1850 the revenues collected by states represented 8.7 percent of total revenues, in 1870 they represented 30 percent. In the case of the municipalities, their revenues also increased in importance from 6 percent to 23 percent between 1850 and 1870. It is important to notice that Antioquia and Cundinamarca, the two states that realized the most growth over the period in both income and state tax revenue, had been characterized by relative labor scarcity and likely had greater equality.

[c] For Canada, see Perry (1955): appendix C, table 1.

[d] For the United States, the figures for 1855, 1875, and 1895, were computed as a weighted average of regional estimates of per capita revenue raised for different levels of government. The federal figures include revenue raised through land sales. See Davis and Legler (1966). For the estimates for 1913, 1927, 1950, see U.S. Bureau of the Census (2001).

in more detail in Section III, it was only in the twentieth century that national governments in the United States, Canada, and Latin American countries introduced permanent peacetime taxes on income and wealth (including estates and gifts).[23]

Stark contrasts existed across the societies of the Americas, however, in the size and revenue sources of state, provincial, and local governments. Local governments were far more prominent in the United States and Canada than in Latin America (see Table 6.2), and this feature is of fundamental importance because of the radically different tax instruments used by state and local governments as compared to those of the national governments. A predisposition of the North American populations to organize and support local governments was evident as early

---

[23] These new assessments, together with payroll taxes, came to be the dominant source of revenue – especially in the United States and Canada – during the 1930s and 1940s, and coincided with a sharp increase in the size of the central governments.

TABLE 6.3. *Sources and Percentages of Tax Revenue for U.S. Local Governments, 1890–1950*

Taxes	1890	1902	1913	1927	1940	1950
Income					0.4	0.9
Sales and excise			0.2	0.6	2.8	5.9
Property	92.5	88.6	91.0	96.8	91.3	86.2
Payroll			0.2	0.6	1.5	2.3
Other	7.5	11.4	8.6	2.1	3.9	4.7
Total	100.0	100.0	100.0	100.0	100.0	100.0

Notes: For the 1890 estimates, see Copeland (1961). Copeland also provides extensive discussion, as well as estimates that conform with those presented in Ratner (1980), table 1. We employ Ratner for the estimates after 1890, as this source covers the years up to 1950. The estimates represent the share of local government tax revenues accounted for by the respective taxes. Transfers of resources to local governments accounted for less than 10 percent of total resources available for local government expenditures through 1913 (and most of those transfers were grants for schools or roads), rose to a bit less than 15 percent by 1932, but jumped to more than 25 percent by the early 1940s.

as the seventeenth century, despite the absence during that era of distinctively high per capita incomes (as compared to other societies in the Americas). Likewise distinctive was the tendency of these governments to raise the vast majority of revenues through property taxes.

Local governments certainly grew very rapidly in the United States during the early decades of the nineteenth century as the common school movement progressed; there were substantial investments in building roads and other infrastructure demanded by an early industrializing economy. Indeed local governments were the largest component of the overall government sector throughout the nineteenth century (with a share of total government revenue of 57.1 percent in 1855, for example), with only a few brief exceptions intervals during and after major wars. Their heavy reliance on the property tax (see Table 6.3) suggests that a rather progressive tax structure prevailed among local governments, and given the relative prominence of this level of government, among the overall government sector as well.

For example, between 1861 and 1905, property taxes accounted for between 76 and 87 percent of all the tax revenue collected by the state and local governments in Massachusetts.[24] The contours of public finance, in

---

[24] These figures, computed from data reported in Bullock, "Historical Sketch," are all the more striking, because the state of Massachusetts depended much more on taxing corporations than did most other states. Moreover, the implication of the figures in Bullock, 127, 135 is that property taxes accounted for more than 90 percent of the tax

TABLE 6.4. *Sources and Percentages of Revenue for Canada's Municipal Governments, 1913–1950*

Revenue	1913	1933	1950
Income taxes		1.4	
Sales and excise taxes			4.3
Property/Wealth taxes	82.2	78.6	69.6
Other taxes	6.0	6.1	9.2
Nontax revenues	11.8	13.9	14.3
Subsidies from other governments			2.6
Total	100.0	100.0	100.0

Source: Statistics Canada (1983), Series H 52–74.

regards to both the prominence of local governments and the importance of property taxes appear to have been much the same in Canada. Our earliest estimate is that property taxes accounted for over 82 percent of local government revenue in 1913 (see Table 6.4), but less comprehensive information suggests that the share of tax revenue accounted for by levies on property may have been even greater during the nineteenth century, especially in Ontario.[25]

State governments in the United States and provincial governments in Canada generally represented relatively small parts of their respective aggregate government sectors during the late nineteenth and early twentieth centuries, at least as measured by share of tax revenues. In neither

revenue raised by local governments in that state between 1880 and 1900, if not before as well. We do not yet have evidence from many states on the shares of revenue to local governments coming from different taxes earlier in the nineteenth century, but scattered information is consistent with the implication of the estimate for 1902 in Table 6.3, that local governments obtained well over 90 percent of revenue from property taxes. See John Joseph Wallis, "A History of the Property Tax in America," in *Property Taxation and Local Government Finance: Essays in Honor of C. Lowell Harriss*, ed. Wallace E. Oates, 123–147 (Cambridge, MA: Lincoln Institute of Land Policy, 2001) for further discussion of how the relative importance of the property tax as a source of state revenue varied over the nineteenth century.

[25] See Perry, *Taxes, Tariffs, & Subsidies*, especially chapters 2, 5, and 12. Perry finds that property taxes played an important role in the development of municipal or local governments. The taxes were extensively used in Upper Canada during the early nineteenth century. Indeed, Perry suggests that almost everywhere in Canada where significant municipal government developed the property tax was the dominant source of revenue. Property taxes were less important in Quebec than Ontario, because French Canada was able to obtain substantial revenue from customs fees and statutory road levies. Property taxes were also low in the Maritime Provinces (especially Nova Scotia) because of the limited development of local government in that region. Perry attributes the limited development of local government there to the heterogeneity of the population.

country did state or provincial governments account for more than 20 percent of aggregate government tax revenues before the 1920s. They differed, however, in how they obtained revenues to finance their expenditures. Even after the confederation of Canadian provinces in 1867, provincial governments in Canada raised most of their revenues from either subsidies or transfers from the Dominion (whose revenues came primarily from tariffs or excise duties) or from assessments levied on mining, cutting timber, and other exploitation of natural resources. It was only after the scale of provincial programs increased, inspired by rapid population and economic growth on the eve of the twentieth century, that provincial governments enacted new levies, such as taxes on corporations, property, and succession duties, to increase their revenues. These measures did not raise substantial amounts, however, and as late as the first decade of the twentieth century, they generally yielded less than a quarter of provincial revenue.

The state governments in the United States made much more use of direct taxes than their counterparts in Canada, and relied heavily on property taxes both early and late in the nineteenth century.[26] The property tax was likely the largest single source of state government revenue in the United States at the beginning of the nineteenth century, but the onset of industrialization opened up or improved alternative means of states raising funds. By the 1820s and 1830s, state governments began to reduce or even eliminate property taxes, as more and more revenues rolled in from other sources, including fees assessed for issuing corporate charters, taxes on corporate capital (especially banks and insurance companies), and returns on investments they had made to stoke development in various banks, transportation companies, and other infrastructure. When the economic contractions of the late 1830s and early 1840s sharply curtailed these sources of revenue, however, many state governments found themselves on the brink of, or well into, bankruptcy. These fiscal challenges compelled state governments to revive their property taxes and/or design other relatively stable revenue sources, which were particularly crucial if they hoped to issue debt for the financing of additional investments in infrastructure. Although states were creative in devising a wide variety of alternative methods of raising revenue, property taxes were restored to being the most important tax revenue source for state governments by

---

[26] Another direct tax sometimes levied by state governments in the United States was the poll tax, but the significance of poll taxes as a revenue source diminished greatly over the nineteenth century.

TABLE 6.5. *Sources and Percentages of Tax Revenue for U.S. State Governments, 1890–1950*

Tax revenue	1890	1902	1913	1927	1940	1950
Individual income				4.0	4.7	7.4
Corporate income				5.3	3.5	6.0
Sales and excise	a	17.9	19.9	42.8	51.0	55.6
Property	70.0	52.6	46.5	21.2	5.9	3.1
Payroll				7.9	24.5	18.8
Death and gift		29.5	33.6	18.9	10.3	9.1
Other	30.0					
Total	100.0	100.0	100.0	100.0	100.0	100.0

Notes: See the note to table 6.3. The estimates represent the share of state government tax revenues accounted for by the respective taxes. Nontax revenues appear to have been substantial, however, accounting perhaps for as much as 40 percent of revenue in 1913.
a The sales and gross receipts taxes for 1890 are included in the Other category.

the end of the nineteenth century (roughly 70 percent of tax revenue in 1890; see Table 6.5).

Given the very large size of the local governments in the United States and Canada, and their heavy reliance on property and wealth taxes into the twentieth century, it should perhaps not be surprising that these same taxes loom large when one considers the total tax revenue collected by governments at all levels. For the United States, in both 1902 and 1913 (see Table 6.6), property, gift, and estate taxes accounted for between 60 and 70 percent of the revenue to the overall government sector. Although our estimates for Canada do not extend that far back (see Table 6.7), it

TABLE 6.6. *Sources and Percentages of Tax Revenue in the United States for all Levels of Government, 1902–1950*

Tax revenue	1902	1913	1927	1940	1950
Individual income			9.8	8.1	29.3
Corporate income		1.5	13.9	8.7	19.6
Sales and excise	19.8	16.1	13.2	28.5	23.6
Customs duties	17.7	13.6	6.0	2.3	0.7
Property	51.4	58.6	48.8	30.3	13.0
Payroll		0.1	2.4	13.3	9.7
Death and gift	11.1	10.1	5.8	8.9	4.2
Total	100.0	100.0	100.0	100.0	100.0

Source: Ratner (1980), table 1.
Note: The estimates represent the share of total government tax revenue (national, state, and local considered together) accounted for by the respective taxes.

TABLE 6.7. *Sources and Percentages of Revenue in Canada for all Levels of Government, 1933–1950*

Revenue	1933	1950
Income taxes	12.4	44.5
Sales and excise taxes	26.2	32.0
Customs duties	13.5	7.9
Property and Wealth taxes	39.2	10.8
Other taxes	8.7	4.8
Total	100.0	100.0

Source: Statistics Canada (1983), Series H 52–74.

is clear that there, too – largely due to the prominence of local or municipal governments – taxes on property and wealth were very important sources of revenue for the government sector overall (nearly 40 percent as late as 1933). Even if the respective levels of government in Latin America relied on the same tax instruments as did their counterparts to the north, the fact that local governments were so much smaller implies that property and wealth holders would contribute a relatively modest proportion of government revenue overall. Local municipal authorities accounted for only about 10 percent of total government tax revenue in Brazil, Colombia, and Mexico throughout the nineteenth century (and in Chile, between 10 and 20 percent during the second decade of the twentieth century, despite the absence of state or provincial governments). The contrast with the United States and Canada is dramatic. In the United States, local governments generated 57.1 percent of total government tax revenue in 1855, and the figure remained near 50 percent for the rest of the century. Even as late as the 1930s, the share of local government revenue was near 40 percent in both the United States and Canada.

From the exceedingly modest investments in public schooling characteristic of Latin America into the twentieth century (and reflected in the low literacy rates that prevailed throughout the region until national governments became more aggressive in promoting public schooling) the qualitative pattern evident in the figures for Brazil, Colombia, and Mexico seems to be representative. Municipal governments in Latin American countries never grew very large, especially in rural areas and where Native Americans composed larger proportions of the population. The basis for our claim that during the nineteenth century the overall tax structures in the United States and Canada were much more progressive (in the sense of placing more of the burden on wealthy elites) than in Latin America, however, does not rest solely on the relative sizes of the different levels of

TABLE 6.8. *Sources and Percentages of Revenue to Chile's Municipal Governments*

Year	Taxes on income	Taxes/Fees on professions and industries	Taxes on alcoholic beverages	Taxes on slaughtering	Taxes on mines	Taxes on carriages	Other
1913	39.0	7.1	6.0	4.0	2.1	3.0	38.8
1915	50.0	6.7	4.1	3.3	2.5	2.5	30.9
1920	38.7	15.7	2.7	2.1	2.3	2.4	36.1

Source: Chile, Central Bureau of Statistics (1921).

government. The evidence on the relative use of tax instruments suggest that local governments in Latin America relied much less on the property tax than did their counterparts in the United States and Canada. Early in the twentieth century, local governments in Chile and Colombia (see Tables 6.8 and 6.9) raised less than half of their revenue from property and income taxes (less than 25 percent in Cundinamarca, Colombia), while these taxes were dominant in the accounts of Canada (78 percent) and the United States (over 90 percent). When one considers these local governments in Latin America, as compared to even U.S. state governments (which, as reported in Table 6.5, were raising more than 80 percent of their revenue from property, death, and gift taxes as late as 1913), the disinclination of Latin American governments to tax property holders and their unwillingness to do so stands out in especially stark terms.

The underdevelopment of local government in Latin America, where both economic and political inequality was extreme and elites might have been expected to resist the levying of property and wealth taxes to fund

TABLE 6.9. *Sources and Percentages of Revenue to Colombia's Municipal Governments in the Department of Cundinamarca, 1918*

Revenue	Total for all municipalities in Cundinamarca	City of Bogotá alone
Property tax	22.5	14.2
Almotacen and plaza (tax on market)	11.7	15.0
Taxes on slaughtering	5.7	4.0
Bullfighting and other legal games	1.7	1.0
Rental income	1.2	0.1
Fines	2.7	1.6
Other sources	54.5	64.1
Total	100.0	100.0

Source: República de Colombia (1919).

TABLE 6.10. *Local and State Taxes as Shares of Income by Region in the*
United States, 1860 and 1880

Year/Region	Percent state taxes	Percent local taxes	Per capita income in US dollars (1860)
1860			
Northeast	0.91	3.65	181
North Central	1.25	6.22	89
South Atlantic	2.21	3.07	81
East South Central	1.12	1.79	89
West South Central	0.68	2.20	184
National Average	1.22	2.58	128
1880			
Northeast	0.93	4.08	244
North Central	0.84	4.40	170
South Atlantic	2.04	3.33	84
East South Central	1.23	1.97	95
West South Central	0.97	4.31	112
National Average	0.90	3.97	173

Source: Estimate of state and local revenues are from Davis and Legler (1966) and per capita income estimates are from Fogel and Engerman (1974).

Note: We do not include estimates for the national government as a share of income, because the receipt is based on point of collection, and thus implies higher taxes in regions with ports or substantial land sales. However, our estimates of the national figures for the total tax revenue relative to income are 6.67 and 8.96 percent in 1860 and 1880, respectively. Some of the later settled regions are excluded here because of incomplete information.

broad provision of public services, raises the issue of whether the two conditions are causally related to each other. A theoretical argument can certainly be made that elites might have had an interest in resisting the growth of public services, especially those provided to segments of the population that were perceived as quite unlike their own. This notion receives some support from the observation that during the nineteenth century local governments in the United States were relatively larger (as judged both by the local government share of regional income as well as relative to the income share of state income) in regions with less inequality such as the Midwest, or even the Northeast (see Table 6.10).

Not only were local governments much smaller in Latin American countries generally, but the state or provincial governments in that region made less use of property taxes, and relied more on taxes that placed a lighter tax burden on the elite. As reflected in Tables 6.11 and 6.12, which present the sources of revenue (in percentage terms) for all of the state or provincial governments in Argentina and Colombia, and a sampling of them for Brazil and Mexico at various points during the second half of the

TABLE 6.11. *Sources and Percentages of Revenue to State and Provincial Governments in Argentina and Colombia, c. 1870*

Argentina, 1872	
Revenue of the provincial governments	
Direct contribution (taxes)	13.2
Constitution-mandated share of tariff revenue	15.2
Other subvention from national treasury	9.7
Sales of land	30.5
Alcabala (sales tax)	0.2
Rent of land	0.2
Inheritances	0.1
Stamped paper, tolls, tax on fruit, and other miscellaneous	30.9
Colombia, 1870	
Revenue of the state governments	
Direct taxes on industry and capital	11.7
Tax on real estate	7.1
Tax on slaughtered livestock	18.3
Tax on liquors	15.1
Tax on foreign merchandise	12.9
Excise taxes on cacao, tobacco, and anise	7.0
Stamps	5.7
Miscellaneous/Other	22.1

Source: For Argentina, Oficina de Estadística Nacional (1875). For Colombia, López Garavito (1992).

nineteenth century, taxes on land or property (the so-called *direct contributions*) accounted for markedly lower proportions of state government revenue in Latin America than did such taxes in the United States. In these four countries (the first three of which are among the most decentralized in Latin America), taxes on different types of property or on businesses rarely accounted for more than 10 to 15 percent (and generally less) of state or provincial revenue, as compared to 70 percent in the United States in 1890. Instead, state or provincial governments in Latin America relied on excise taxes (such as on liquors, tobacco, flour, slaughtered livestock, and foreign merchandise), tolls on roads and other modes of transportation, fines and various fees for government services, levies on products intended largely for export (such as coffee in Brazil), and a variety of other sources. Although patterns of incidence are not always transparent, the methods of raising revenue to fund the operations of state and provincial governments in Latin America would generally be expected to impose a proportionally lighter burden on the wealthy classes.

TABLE 6.12. *Sources and Percentages of Revenue to Selected State and Provincial Governments in Brazil and Mexico, c. 1870–1910*

Brazil	1871–1872		1910
São Paulo			
Taxes on exports			40.7
Transit fees/taxes	79.1		3.6
Taxes/Fees on inheritances and property transfers	7.9		15.9
Taxes on property	1.2		2.0
Taxes on capital of producers			5.7
Taxes on slaves and slave trade	5.8		
Taxes on water and sewers			8.4
Judiciary, state stamps, lotteries, fines, fees, and other miscellaneous	6.0		24.7
Minas Geraes	1876	1892	1905
Taxes on exports	5.7	64.4	59.0
Taxes on coffee, gold, salt, and diamonds	22.3	0.8	1.5
Transit fees/taxes	16.4	0.9	1.0
Taxes/Fees on inheritances and property transfers	7.9	14.1	8.7
Transfer and registration of slaves	17.4		
Taxes on property	2.8		6.1
Taxes on private consumption		7.6	2.3
Taxes on industries and profits			8.0
Judiciary, state stamps, and other fees	1.0	8.2	4.9
Official posts and titles	7.4		2.8
Lotteries, water, sewers, and other miscellaneous	19.1	4.0	5.7
Mexico	1870		
Yucatan			
Income from public lands and sea salt fields	27.5		
Taxes on liquors	14.6		
Sales tax on livestock and flour	20.6		
Taxes on imports	3.5		
Transfer fees and fines	19.1		
Other miscellaneous fees and taxes	14.6		

Sources: For Brazil, in 1876 and 1892, Torres (1961), and for 1905, Barbosa (1966). For Mexico, Levy (2003).

Notes: The relatively high figure for the miscellaneous/other category in Minas Gereas in 1876 is due to 9.9 percent of the revenue coming from "direitos de 6% sobre outros generos." The high transit tax revenue in São Paulo in 1871 is due primarily to the Taxas das Barreiras, which was a state road tax, whereby stations on state roads collected tolls for carts, wagons, coaches, and animals on the hoof.

In Brazil, for example, the allocation of taxing authority between the provinces and the national government changed several times over the nineteenth century. Under the 1840 constitution, the main provincial taxes were taxes on sugar and coffee production, but revenues were also obtained from taxes or fees on legacies and inheritance, on transference of properties, on the sale of *novhos e velhos direitos* (official posts and titles), on the slave trade, and revenues were obtained especially from drivers in toll fees for traveling along provincial roads. Taxes on property generated only a tiny share of total revenue. Until relatively late in the nineteenth century, the fees charged for traveling on provincial roads (*estradas provinciais*) and small internal rivers (*rios internos*) – fees that were called by different names, such as itinerary fees, fees on departure, or fees on traveling – were among the most important sources of provincial revenues. For example, in the province of São Paulo in the period 1871–72, the rights to departure raised 56 percent of the total revenues of the province, while the taxation on the slave trade and the tax on legacies accounted for 6 percent and 8 percent, respectively. In the province of Minas Gerais, in 1876, the main sources of provincial revenue were taxes on coffee (20 percent of the total revenues of the province), itinerary fees (16 percent), and taxes on transfer, registration, and trade of slaves (15 percent).

Direct taxes did not become important until late in the nineteenth century, but even then the reliance in Brazil on property and other taxes progressive in character was modest compared to the United States. The Brazilian Constitution of 1891 established a republic, and the provinces then became designated states with expanded rights to collect taxes on exports (rights previously reserved for the national government), as well as taxes on property, on transference of property, and on industries and profits. This change transformed the tributary structure of the most prosperous states, such as Minas Gerais, whose economies were largely directed at foreign trade. In Minas Gerais, levies on exports had raised only 5 percent of the total revenues of the province in 1889, but with the expanded power to tax, this share jumped to 64 percent in 1892. Similarly, in 1910 the tax on exports raised 40 percent of the total revenues of São Paulo, whereas in 1871 it had yielded no revenue for the province.[27]

The states also increased the shares of revenue they derived from taxes on property, legacies, and others transferences of property, and on

[27] See, on Brazil, André C. Martinez Fitscher and Aldo Musacchio, "Endowments, Fiscal Federalism, and the Cost of Capital for States: Evidence from Brazil, 1891–1930," *Financial History Review*, 17 (April 2010): 13–50.

industrial profits. In Minas Gerais, the tax on property (known as the *imposto predial* or territorial tax) accounted for 2.8 percent of the total revenues of the province in 1876, but its share rose to 6.1 percent in 1905. There were no taxes on industries and profits prior to the establishment of the republic, but they accounted for 8 percent of revenue in 1905. Taxes and fees on inheritance and transfers of property generated 8.7 percent of total revenues. Such taxes were of similar importance in São Paulo. In 1910, the state of São Paulo raised 2 percent of state revenue from property taxes, 5.7 percent of revenue from a tax on the capital of producers, and 15.9 percent of revenues from taxes or fees on inheritances, legacies, and transfers of property. Thus, in Minas Gerais and São Paulo, perhaps the two major states of Brazil, these progressive taxes accounted for 22.8 and 23.6 percent of state revenue, respectively. As is evident in Table 6.5, the corresponding figure for state governments in the United States in 1902 was 82.1 percent. This contrast is dramatic and telling.

If it is indeed true that less reliance on taxation of property or wealth is indicative of elites bearing a lighter tax burden, then the evidence does sustain the idea that the tax institutions that characterized Latin America during the nineteenth century were especially favorable to their interests. Not only were the local authorities (which were more likely to tax wealth than those at other levels of government) extremely stunted in regards to the scale of their activities and demands for revenue, but both the local and state governments in Latin America made much less use of property, wealth, or other taxes than did their counterparts in the North. Of course, the mix of tax instruments was applied to raise revenue, but we should not assess the burdens of taxation by the amount of revenue raised. It might be argued, for example, that the United States and Canada were generally more disposed toward government involvement, and thus had a greater need to levy taxes.

One response to this sort of explanation of the comparatively small size of local governments in Latin America is to point out that any bias against governments in Latin America was obviously not neutral across levels of government. The evidence is clear that the local governments in Latin America were stunted relative to national governments, a pattern we find particularly interesting because local governments in virtually all contexts seem to rely more on taxing wealth and property than other levels of government. We explore the issue further in Table 6.13, where estimates of the amount of national government taxes collected per capita in 1870, as well as the shares of these taxes to national income, are presented for a range of countries around the world. Perhaps not surprisingly,

TABLE 6.13. *National Government Tax Revenue Per Capita, c. 1870*

	Taxes per capita in USD (1870)	Index of tax revenue relative to national income (100 = US)
Americas		
Argentina	9.4	155
Bolivia	1.2	
Brazil	6.7	195
Chile	6.7	
Colombia	1.1	
Costa Rica	9.0	
Ecuador	1.3	
El Salvador	2.2	
Guatemala	1.7	
Honduras	0.9	
Mexico	3.1	94
Nicaragua	2.9	
Peru	14.0	
Venezuela	5.1	
United States	114	100
Europe		
Belgium	7.1	58
Denmark	9.3	104
England	13.0	86
France	12.3	143
Germany	5.6	63
Greece	4.8	
Holland	14.0	114
Portugal	4.5	
Sweden and Norway	3.7	51
Switzerland	2.0	20

Notes: The information on taxes per capita is from López Garavito (1992, 202–203). The values of the index of tax revenue relative to national income were computed as the respective ratios of the estimates of taxes per capita to the estimates of per capita income for 1870 contained in Maddison (1995). The index values are expressed relative to the U.S. value, which was normalized to a standard of 100.

given its higher per capita income, the U.S. national government collected substantial taxes on a per capita basis. The only country in the Americas that collected more taxes was Peru, which realized extensive revenue over a period of several decades from exports of guano – a natural resource that was all too soon depleted.[28] Judged as a share of national income,

[28] For a brief account of the rise and fall of this remarkably lucrative industry, see W. M. Matthew, "A Primitive Export Sector: Guano Production in Mid-Nineteenth-Century Peru," *Journal of Latin American Studies* 8 (May 1977): 35–57.

however, the amount of revenue going to the national government was not at all high in the United States. On the contrary, Argentina and Brazil (and undoubtedly Peru) raised far more revenue for their respective central governments relative to their national incomes than did the United States, and Mexico collected nearly as much.

Admittedly, if one considers the much larger share of total government revenue that goes to local and state governments in the United States than in Latin America, it is evident that the revenue going to the government sector in the aggregate is far higher as a share of national income in the United States than in any other country in the hemisphere with the exception of Brazil (and Peru, during the bonanza from guano), where the ratio of total taxes to income (in the 7 to 8 percent range) seems roughly similar. Nevertheless, the substantive point remains. It is not the case that the Latin American countries were lightly taxed, but rather that their property and wealth taxes, and the levels of government that were more reliant on these sources of revenue during the nineteenth and early twentieth centuries especially, were of minor significance by the standards of their neighbors in North America in the structure and financing of government.

The striking contrast we have highlighted is consistent with our conjecture that the extreme inequality in Latin America encouraged a distinctly different path of evolution of tax institutions and/or government structures among these societies over the nineteenth century. One alternative hypothesis for this pattern, however, is that the reluctance or inability to tax property and wealth in Latin America was due to conditions characteristic of less-developed economies that made it difficult to administer such levies. There may indeed be some merit to this type of explanation, but we would emphasize how the colonies in the northern part of North America, such as those in New England and the Middle Atlantic, made effective use of these sorts of instruments for raising tax revenue in support of local and state governments as early as the seventeenth century. It seems unlikely that these latter polities could be considered more developed than many of the nineteenth century Latin America nations. Other possible rationales are that the Latin American societies may have had less demand for the sorts of public goods and services that were provided by local governments, or that they simply chose to satisfy that demand through national government programs. These interesting theories deserve further study, but it is worth noting that Latin American societies were characterized by low rates of investment in public schools (and the low literacy rates that accompanied them) well into the twentieth century (if not the present day), even after accounting for their levels of per capita income.[29] Moreover, even if a radically different demand for public services, such as schools, does explain the patterns in the size of local governments and in government revenue sources, might this be considered yet another mechanism by which extreme inequality impacts on the institutions of taxation?

III

Throughout the Americas, the size of the government sector grew substantially over the twentieth century, and major changes in the tax structures were introduced to fund the increase in government expenditures. But in some respects, much has remained the same. As compared to the United States and Canada, Latin American governments continue to be highly centralized and generally rely on consumption taxes instead of taxes on wealth, income (especially those of individuals), or other levies that place a serious burden on elites. Indeed, most observers judge the progressivity of Latin American tax (and expenditure) programs to be remarkably modest, especially in light of the extreme inequality prevailing in that region of the world.[30]

At the beginning of the twentieth century, the U.S. federal, state, and local governments together accounted for only about 7 percent of GDP. Even by 1930, they had grown to no more than 10 percent. During the Depression and World War II, however, the size of the government sector exploded, to roughly 25 to 30 percent of the economy, with the federal government coming to assume the dominant role it plays today.[31] In Canada, similar developments took place.[32] Most of the major tax

---

[29] Ch. 5, as well as De Ferranti, et al., *Inequality*.

[30] This discussion relies on several excellent cross-country studies of tax systems in Latin America as well as *Government Finance Statistics* from the International Monetary Fund. See Richard M. Bird, "Tax Reform in Latin America: A Review of Some Recent Experiences," *Latin American Research Review* 27 No. (1) (1992): 7–36; Parthasarthi Shome, "Taxation in Latin America: Structural Trends and Impact of Administration," *IMF Working Paper no. 99–19* (Washington, D.C.: International Monetary Fund, 1999); Tanzi and Zee, "Tax Policies for Emerging Markets;" Janet Stotsky and Asegedech WoldeMariam, "Central American Tax Reform: Trends and Possibilities," *IMF Working Paper no. 02–227* (Washington, D.C.: Internal Monetary Fund, 2002); and International Monetary Fund, *Government Finance Statistics Year Book* (Washington, D.C.: International Monetary Fund, 2001, 2004).

[31] See C. Eugene Steuerle, *Contemporary US Tax Policy* (Washington, D.C.: Urban Institute Press, 2004); and Slemrod and Bakija, *Taxing Ourselves*. See also Steven R. Weisman, *The Great Tax Wars* (New York: Simon & Schuster, 2002).

[32] See Karin Treff and David B. Perry, *Finances of the Nation 2003* (Toronto: Canadian Tax Foundation, 2004), at ttp://www.ctf.ca/FN2003/finances2003.asp

changes at the U.S. and Canadian federal levels were related to the need
to finance the higher level of expenditures associated with the conduct
of World Wars I and II, but in both countries the expanded revenues
were tapped in the aftermath of those conflicts to support the peacetime
growth of the national governments. In the United States, facilitated by
the passage of the constitutional amendment in 1913 that cleared away
legal obstacles to a federal individual income tax (which followed the
passage of a corporate income tax in 1909), the relative tax and spending
shares among the federal, state, and local governments began to shift.
The fiscal landscape changed further with the adoption of social security
taxes in 1937.

Over the course of the twentieth century, the individual income tax
in the United States replaced the property tax as the primary tax on
individuals.[33] The federal government first adopted an income tax during
the 1860s, similar to the British approach for raising funds to finance the
Crimean War. After the Civil War, the income tax was subject to political
attacks and was eliminated, restored, and then struck down on constitutional grounds. Following the passage of the Sixteenth Amendment
in 1913, however, the Underwood-Simmons Tariff Act reestablished the
income tax in a less progressive and less ambitious form than the Civil
War version or the 1894 legislation.[34] The scope of the individual income
tax was changed greatly by the revenue demands associated with the
world wars. For example, in the United States, the number of individual
income taxpayers grew from 3.9 million in 1939 to 42.6 million in 1945,
and tax revenues increased from $2.2 billion in 1939 to $35.1 billion in
1945. This increase in federal tax revenue from the income tax changed
the balance in the relative size of the federal government. Only during
World War II did federal tax revenues begin to exceed state and local tax
revenues.

As discussed previously, national or central governments were, except
during periods of wartime, quite small throughout the Americas during
the nineteenth century. This was certainly true of the U.S. federal government, whose peacetime activities were largely confined to defense, general

[33] It is interesting that when Congress required additional revenue during the War of 1812,
the solution was a supplemental property tax collected through a direct assessment of the
states. By the time of the Civil War, funding the revenue needs of war financing through
property taxation had less political appeal. See W. Elliot Brownlee, *Federal Taxation
in America: A Short History* (Washington, D.C.: Woodrow Wilson Center Press, 1996)
and Weisman, *Tax Wars* for more discussion.

[34] For more discussion of the history of the income tax, see Brownlee, *Federal Taxation*,
and Weisman, *Tax Wars*.

administration, and foreign affairs and oversight of foreign trade, with only extremely modest contributions going to infrastructure. State and local government assumed nearly all of the responsibility for the provision of schooling and publicly provided transportation, such as roads. Much of this division of activities evolved naturally, as local governments took on the tasks that communities wanted accomplished and were willing to pay for. State governments succeeded the provincial governments of colonial times, and were keen to undertake programs that would stimulate economic activity or otherwise improve welfare within their polities, whether supporting transportation projects beyond the scope of towns, such as railroads, or contributing supplemental funds to encourage the expansion of public education. It might well be argued that the state and local governments were dominant in the provision of these sorts of public services, because these levels of government were more responsive to micro level concerns, or that the population was more willing to pay taxes for projects that were clearly visible and likely to benefit those bearing the cost. Part of the relatively small size of the federal government during this era, however, may have been attributable to constitutional restrictions imposed on the federal government's taxing authority. The framers severely limited the power of the federal government to impose and collect direct taxes and they required any duties, imposts, or excises to be uniform throughout the United States.[35] Both measures were adopted to prevent regional interests from using the federal government to shift a disproportionate tax burden to other groups. While the constitutional limitation on direct taxes became better known as a barrier to adopting a federal income tax,[36] the limitation was primarily adopted by the Founding Fathers to prevent federal government property taxes.[37]

---

[35] Article 1, Section 8 of the Consitution provided Congress with the general authority to lay and collect taxes, duties, imposts, and excises, subject to the limitation that such taxes be uniform throughout the United States. Article 1, Section 9 limited the ability of the federal government to impose direct taxes by requiring "No capitation or other direct tax shall be laid, unless in proportion to the census." See, generally, Brownlee, *Federal Taxation*, 11–20.

[36] In *Pollock v. Farmers' Loan & Trust Co.* (157 US 429, aff'd on rehearing 158 US 601) (1895), the Supreme Court held the income tax of the Wilson-Gorman Tariff unconstitutional because it violated the prohibition on unapportioned direct taxes in Article 1, Section 9. The Sixteenth Amendment, adopted in 1913, allowed Congress the power to impose income taxes without apportionment among the States and without regard to any census of enumeration.

[37] Representatives from slave states were concerned that a federal property tax would treat slaves as property; farm states' representatives were concerned that the tax might be based on the size rather than the value of landholdings, and representatives of urban

TABLE 6.14. *Shares and Percentages of Tax Revenue for the Aggregate Government Sector in the United States, 1902–2000*

Year	Federal tax revenues (excluding Social Security)	State tax revenues	Local tax revenues	Social Security revenues
1902	37.4	11.4	51.3	
1912	29.2	13.3	57.6	
1922	45.6	12.8	41.5	
1932	22.7	23.7	53.6	
1940	33.9	23.0	31.2	11.9
1950	63.4	14.3	14.4	7.9
1960	60.3	14.1	14.1	11.S
1970	52.5	17.2	14.0	16.3
1980	47.9	18.7	11.8	21.6
1990	41.8	19.8	13.3	251
2000	45.6	19.2	11.9	23.3

Sources: U.S. Bureau of the Census (1975); U.S. Census Bureau (1983, 1992, 2003); and Steurle (2004), page 260.

As is evident from Table 6.14, as the federal government has grown since the 1940s, the relative shares of tax revenue for the federal, state, and local governments have changed dramatically. Even though their tax revenues increased from roughly 6.1 percent of GDP early in the twentieth century to a post–WWII high of 9.7 percent of GDP in 1972, the relative size of local governments plunged over the first half of the century (from over 50 to below 15 percent), and has drifted down a bit more since, particularly as constitutional and statutory limitations on the use of property taxes began to bite.[38]

The composition of tax revenues for state and local governments in the United States has changed as well. Although property taxes continue to be the major source of tax revenues for local governments, state governments

---

commercial areas were concerned that the property tax would be based on assessed value. Brownlee, *Federal Taxation*, 14–15.

[38] See Steuerle, *Contemporary U.S. Tax Policy*, 37, for changes in the size of local governments relative to the economy. A series of changes in state constitutions and statutes during the late 1970s and 1980s restricted the use of property taxes. In 1978, California voters passed Proposition 13, which imposed a maximum property tax rate of 1 percent. As of 2002, forty-four states had some type of restriction on the ability of local government to impose property taxes. These limitations take different forms: thirty-three states impose property tax rate limitations, twenty-seven states impose limitations on property tax revenues, and six states impose limits on increases in assessed property values. See David Brunori, *Local Tax Policy: A Federalist Perspective* (Washington, D.C.: Urban Institute Press, 2003): 61–62.

rely far less on them than before. Some of the impetus for this latter shift was the growing dissatisfaction with the property tax that began to surface during the late nineteenth century.[39] Spurred both by these concerns and perhaps by the reintroduction of the federal income tax as well, most states abolished general state-level property taxes during the first half of the twentieth century and replaced them with state-level income taxes, excise taxes (including levies on automobiles and gasoline to help pay for roads), and sales taxes.[40] Taxes on real property were left to local governments. Property taxes contributed over half the revenues of state governments at the beginning of the century, but by the 1940s they accounted for less than 6 percent. Today, property taxes account for 28.6 percent of total state and local revenue, general sales taxes account for 24.7 percent, selective sales taxes account for 10.8 percent, individual income taxes account for 24.3 percent, corporate income taxes account for 4.1 percent, and other taxes account for 7.6 percent.

The regional variation in the relative size of local governments and the use of tax instruments noted earlier for the nineteenth century persisted through the late twentieth century. Not only did the Midwest and the Northeast continue to have relatively larger local governments, and rely more on property taxes as a share of total state and local government revenue than did the South and the West, but a marked association across

[39] The property tax worked well (or was politically palatable) when the bulk of personal wealth consisted of real property, and there was confidence in the ability of the electorate to monitor the expenditures of local (or state) governments, and a sense that tax revenues funded public goods and services that enhanced property values. As the variety of assets available to individuals increased, however, criticisms that property taxes were both inequitable and inefficient because of either design or enforcement issues led to different forms of wealth being taxed at different rates. State governments responded by nominally increasing the legal scope of their property taxes to cover all types of property, such as cash, bonds, stocks, and mortgages, but in reality the burden fell primarily on owners of real estate. Among the prominent critics of the property tax were Richard T. Ely and Edwin R. A. Seligman. See Richard T. Ely, *Taxation of American States and Cities* (New York: Thomas Y. Crowell, 1888); and Edwin R. A. Seligman, *Essays in Taxation* (New York: Macmillan, 1895). Seligman contended that the property tax was defective in five ways: (a) lack of uniformity or inequality in assessment; (b) lack of universality in its failure to effectively tax personal property; (c) incentives to dishonesty in reporting and classifying property; (d) potential for regressivity; and (e) potential for double taxation (see Seligman, *Essays in Taxation*, 19–32). Seligman suggested that in the early 1900s the property tax in New York fell 95 percent on real estate property and only 5 percent on personal property, despite the relative increase in the proportion of wealth held in intangible personal property.

[40] See the discussion in Robin Einhorn, *American Taxation, American Slavery* (Chicago: University of Chicago Press, 2006).

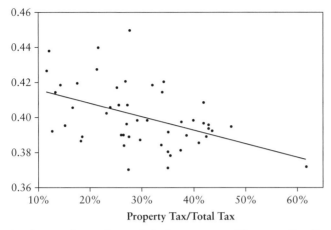

FIGURE 6.1. Income Inequality and the Importance of Property Tax Revenue: A Plot of the Gini Coefficients by the Share Of Property Taxes in Total State and Local Government Revenue Across all States, 1980.

states between the extent of income inequality and the importance of property taxes for financing government goods and services was evident until late in the twentieth century (for example, see Figure 6.1 for the pattern in 1980).

In Canada, the government sector began to grow rapidly following confederation in 1867. Not only did the British North America Act provide for a centralized federal government with general taxing authority, but provincial governments came under more pressure to raise revenues to support the increasing demand for public services that accompanied the population and economic booms of the late nineteenth and early twentieth centuries. Tariffs and revenues obtained from public lands and resource taxes were at first the major sources of funds for the national and provincial governments, but this began to change after Canada introduced its first federal income tax, in 1917, to fund the costs of Canada's participation in World War I. Overall, the record of the evolution of tax institutions in Canada over the twentieth century resembled that in the United States, perhaps most notably in the prominence of the income tax (both at the federal and provincial levels). The Canadian pattern was also much like that of the United States in the relative importance of the local governments declining markedly over time (from nearly 40 percent of the overall government sector as late as the 1920s to less than 10 percent today) and the property tax remaining the dominant source of revenue for local governments (with property tax receipts accounting for roughly 70 percent of revenue in 1950).[41]

IV

Latin American countries experienced major economic and political changes over the late-nineteenth and twentieth centuries. Of greatest significance was a sharp and broad (extending across much of Latin America) acceleration in economic growth that began during the 1870s and 1880s and was spurred, in large part, by exogenous factors such as the expansion of international trade around the world and higher prices for commodities in which the region had a comparative advantage. Although this boom was fueled by improvements in the technology and organization of international transport and trade, as well as increases in demand for raw materials and foodstuffs by rapidly-industrializing Europe, another major stimulus to expanded production of tradable goods came from the real depreciation of the silver-backed currencies (common throughout Latin America) that occurred during the late-nineteenth and early twentieth centuries, as the price of silver declined relative to gold. Where this latter development occurred, the surge in commodity output extended beyond agricultural produce (coffee, sugar, animal products, and so on) and natural resources (such as oil, copper, and other minerals) to manufacturing production (which helped to nurture the development of a powerful constituency for higher tariffs). Although there were interruptions in the ascent of their economies, and the records and rates of progress varied somewhat across countries, Latin America as a whole has grown at nearly the same rate as the United States since 1870, after a period of relative stagnation for roughly the previous century.[42]

---

[41] Substantial variation exists among the provinces as to the percentage of total local government revenue from property and related taxes. In New Brunswick, Ontario, and Saskatchewan, property tax revenues are about half of total revenues while in Newfoundland and Labrador, Prince Edward Island, and the Northwest Territories property taxes are only about 20 percent of total local government revenues. See Treff and Perry, *Finances of the Nation.*

[42] For an overview of industrial development in Latin America over the late nineteenth and twentieth centuries, see Stephen H. Haber, "Development Strategy or Endogenous Process: The Industrialization of Latin America," Stanford Center for International Development Working Paper. For general histories of economic, political, and social changes in Latin America during the era, see Donghi Tulio Halperin, *The Contemporary History of Latin America* (Durham: Duke University Press, 1993); Rosemary Thorp, *Progress, Poverty and Exclusion: An Economic History of Latin America in the 20th Century* (Baltimore: Johns Hopkins University Press, 1998), and Victor Bulmer-Thomas,

The initial phase of relatively sustained economic growth in Latin America was powered largely by the production of goods for foreign markets. The growth in trade that this pursuit of international comparative advantage led to meant increased revenues from tariffs (some of which had been raised to protect local industry) and increased revenues from export taxes (or other means of procuring revenues from the exploitation of natural resources) that supported an expansion of central governments.[43] In the more progressive and prosperous countries, such as Argentina, Chile, Costa Rica, and Uruguay, this era of trade-based growth yielded a sharp increase in national government support for public services such as schools (which local governments had conspicuously failed to support). In other generally less democratic regimes such as Mexico and Peru, where military officers were not infrequently prominent in political affairs, the increases in revenue were often diverted to enhancing domestic security or the armed forces.[44] Central governments in Latin America did grow during the economic expansion of the late-nineteenth and early-twentieth centuries, but in general (with some exceptions such as Argentina and Brazil) their sizes remained modest by the standards of the United States or Canada. This is so, especially considering the relatively large local and state or provincial governments in those countries, as gauged relative to GDP, until the second half of the twentieth century. Unlike the experience of their neighbors to the north, it was not until the 1950s that most central governments in Latin America began to realize substantial growth relative to their respective economies (see Table 6.15). At first, the additional tax revenues were obtained by the introduction and raising of income taxes on individuals and corporations. The major increases in tax revenues that came during the 1960s, 1970s, and 1980s, however, were generated largely by greater collections from turnover taxes and the value-added tax (VAT). In a few countries (most notably

---

The Economic History of Latin America Since Independence, 2nd ed. (New York: Cambridge University Press, 2003).

[43] For example, Brazil, Chile, Ecuador, Mexico, Panama, and Venezuela generally had substantial nontax revenues, from either state-owned resources, or to support government operations, mostly from mining, oil production, or in the case of Panama, income from the Canal.

[44] Such contrasts call attention to the slow pace of democratization in Latin America and its implication for tax structures and government policies overall. As highlighted in Table 1.3, even the more progressive countries did not achieve rates of participation in elections comparable to those in the United States and Canada until the second half of the twentieth century.

TABLE 6.15. *National Government Tax Revenue as a Share of GDP (in Percentages)*

Country	1900	1910	1920	1930	1940	1950	1960	1970	1980	1990	2000
Argentina	10	7	5	7	8	10	10	8	13	10	14
Bolivia	n.a.	n.a.	n.a.	n.a.	n.a.	n.a.	5	10	5	14	18
Brazil	10	11	9	8	10	7	7	10	10	24	23
Chile	n.a.	n.a.	n.a.	n.a.	9	11	17	16	32	21	24
Colombia	n.a.	n.a.	n.a.	n.a.	4	7	8	10	12	13	14
Costa Rica	n.a.	n.a.	n.a.	n.a.	n.a.	10	12	14	18	23	21
Mexico	5	4	n.a.	6	7	9	8	9	16	16	15
Peru	n.a.	n.a.	n.a.	n.a.	n.a.	11	16	16	17	13	16
Uruguay	n.a.	n.a.	n.a.	n.a.	n.a.	n.a.	n.a.	n.a.	22	24	28
Venezuela	n.a.	n.a.	8	9	12	18	27	19	26	24	20

Sources: University of Oxford Latin American Centre (2006); United Nations Online Network in Public Administration and Finance (UNPAN, 2006).
Note: n.a. = not available.

Venezuela), expansions of the public sector were financed by taxes on the production of petroleum or other natural resources.[45]

Given the widespread recognition that the relative size of the government sector typically increases with per capita income, it is perhaps not surprising that tax burdens in Latin American countries were lower throughout the twentieth century than tax burdens in the United States and Canada. What is more striking is that tax burdens are typically lighter in Latin American countries than in other comparable developing countries.[46] For example, using estimates from the 1997 IMF *Government Finance Statistics*, we can compare the aggregate tax burdens for Latin American countries to those of other economies with similar levels of per capita income. Low-income developing countries (GDP per capita less than $1,000) are reported as having a tax revenue/GDP ratio of 12.1 percent, medium income developing countries (GDP per capita between $1,000 and $5,000) a ratio of 17.1 percent, and high-income

[45] For example, in Venezuela during the late 1950s, taxes on petroleum accounted for two-thirds of total tax revenue. See Raynard M. Sommerfeld, *Tax Reform and the Alliance for Progress* (Austin: University of Texas Press, 1966): 57.

[46] Economic theory provides relatively little guidance as to optimal levels of taxation, but at least until some level of taxation there is a positive correlation between per capita GDP and tax levels, see Robin Burgess and Nicholas Stern, *Taxation and Development*, 762–830. For the poorer developing countries, Burgess and Stern find a stronger correlation between increasing GDP and levels of taxation than in either richer developing countries or in developed countries. See Inter-American Development Bank, *Latin America After a Decade of Reforms, Economic and Social Progress* (Baltimore: Johns Hopkins University Press, 1997): Table C-10.

developing countries (GDP per capita between $5,000 and $20,000) a tax revenue/GDP ratio of 25.6 percent.[47] With the exceptions of Uruguay, Nicaragua, and Panama (which derives revenue from the Canal), the aggregate tax burdens in Latin American countries are lower than the average tax burdens for their respective income classes in developing countries.

Looking at aggregate tax burdens tells only part of the story. In order to better appreciate how the structure of taxes evolved in Latin America over the twentieth century and the factors that contributed to those changes, it is necessary to examine the relative use of different tax instruments. What stands out from this record is that despite the substantial increase in tax revenues raised over the twentieth century, the pattern of Latin American tax institutions that generally avoid taxes commonly understood as progressive has persisted. As we have discussed above, during the first decades of the twentieth century, Latin American countries continued to rely heavily on customs revenue, with tariffs set both to raise central government revenue as well as to protect influential economic interests (including local industry and workers) from foreign competition.[48] In 1930, for example, taxes on international trade (primarily tariffs but some taxes on exports) accounted for 44 percent of central government revenue in Brazil, 48 percent in Argentina, 54 percent in Chile, 55 percent in Colombia, 41 percent in Mexico, and 51 percent in Venezuela. The importance of these taxes on international trade decreased dramatically over the second half of the century, however, and nowhere today do they account for more than 15 percent. For a short interval during the 1950s, 1960s, and 1970s, income taxes (which fell much more heavily on corporations than on individuals) replaced tariffs as the major source of revenue, but in recent decades there has been a return to the longstanding practice of relying on commodity taxes. Perhaps encouraged by international movements toward greater openness, taxes on domestic goods and

---

[47] These statistics are roughly comparable to estimates available from other studies. For example, Tanzi and Zee, "Tax Policies for Emerging Markets", estimated that the tax-revenue-to-GDP ratio for all developing countries was 18.2 percent, and for OECD countries the ratio was 37.9 percent for the period 1995–97. Using a larger sample of countries, William F. Fox and Tami Gurley, "An Exploration of Tax Patterns Around the World," *Tax Notes International* 37 (2005): 794–95, found that low-income countries (per capita GDP of less than $1,000) raised tax revenue amounting to 15.8 percent of GDP, medium-income countries (per capita GDP of between US $1,000–17,000) raised about 20.0 percent, and high income countries (per capita GDP greater than US $17,000) raised 27.2 percent. These estimates do not include social insurance payments.

[48] Haber, "Development Strategy"; Bulmer-Thomas, *Economic History*.

services (particularly the VAT) have assumed the dominant role in raising revenue.[49]

Table 6.16 provides a representative snapshot of the current sources of tax revenue to the central governments in Latin America and in the United States and Canada. Most salient is the much greater importance of indirect taxation in Latin America (and the corresponding much greater importance of income taxation in the two northern countries). Even aside from the obvious centrality of the VAT,[50] it is striking that nearly everywhere in Latin America more revenue (and often far more) is raised from both trade taxes as well as excise taxes than from individual income taxes.[51]

It is to be expected that low-income countries employ different types of taxes than do high-income countries, but Latin American societies stand out relative to other economies at similar levels of development. Table 6.17 presents a summary of the relative use of different tax instruments

---

[49] Our characterizations of the change over time in the relative use of tax instruments are based on the data and estimates presented in Bulmer-Thomas, *Economic History*, Table 6.6; International Monetary Fund, *Finance Statistics Yearbook*; Richard Musgrave and Malcolm Gillis, *Fiscal Reform for Colombia Final Report and Staff Papers of the Colombian Commission on Tax Reform* (Cambridge, MA: Harvard University International Tax Program, 1971): 271–73, tables 3–5; Sommerfeld, *Tax Reform*, 56, table 5); Wayne Thirsk, ed., *Tax Reform in Developing Countries* (Washington, D.C.: World Bank, 1967): 289, table 7.1; and Thorp, *Progress, Poverty, and Exclusion*: 346, tables 7.1–2.

[50] The introduction and diffusion of the VAT over the second half of the twentieth century changed the tax landscape throughout the world (with the notable exception of the United States). See Liam P. Ebrill, Michael Keen, Jean-Paul Bodin, and Victoria Summers, *The Modern VAT* (Washington, D.C.: International Monetary Fund, 2001) for a review of this development. Latin American countries were among the leaders in replacing an inefficient collection of turnover taxes with VATs. From a political economy perspective the relative success of the VATs came along at a very good time. It allowed many Latin American countries to increase tax revenues (and reduce tariffs) without substantial reliance on income taxes. See Michael Keen and Jenny E. Ligthart, "Coordinating Tariff Reduction and Domestic Tax Reform," (Washington, D.C.: International Monetary Fund, 1999), *IMF Working Paper no. 99–93*. Brazil was the first Latin American country to adopt the VAT (1967), followed by Ecuador (1970), Uruguay (1970), Bolivia (1973), Argentina (1975), Colombia (1975), Honduras (1976), Peru (1976), Panama (1977), Guatemala (1983), Mexico (1980), and the Dominican Republic (1983).

[51] Janet Stotsky and Asegedech WoldeMariam, "Central American Tax Reform," table 7. Today, revenues from excise taxes account for over 20 percent of total tax revenues in Bolivia, the Dominican Republic, and Nicaragua, but less than 5 percent in Colombia and Mexico. For most other countries in Latin America, revenues from excise taxes account for about 10 to 15 percent of total tax revenues. In contrast, revenues from excise taxes represent only 3 to 4 percent of the total tax revenues in the United States and Canada. In the early 1980s, only in Chile, Colombia, and Mexico did individual income tax revenues exceed excise tax revenues.

TABLE 6.16. *Sources and Percentages of Tax Revenue for Current National Governments in the Americas*

| Country | Income tax | | | Property | Domestic tax on goods and services | | Taxes on international trade and transportation | Social security | Other taxes |
	Total	Corporate	Individual		Total	Excises			
United States	59	10	50	1	3	3	1	35	0
Canada	58	12	43	0	18	4	1	23	0
Argentina	19	13	6	4	45	15	6	27	0
Bolivia	9	9	0	10	58	22	7	13	3
Brazil	24			0	26	9	3	41	5
Chile	23			0	57	12	7	8	5
Colombia	41	39	2	3	46	4	10		0
Costa Rica	15	13	1	1	45	11	6	33	0
Dominican Republic	21	9	12	1	35	31	38	4	1
Mexico	38			0	30	3	4	24	3
Nicaragua	14			0	59	24	9	18	0
Panama	27			2	16	8	15	35	4
Paraguay	19	19	0	0	59	16	18	0	4
Peru	23	13	10	0	56	13	10	8	4
Uruguay	16	9	7	6	42	12	4	30	3
Venezuela	30	29	2	8	44	8	12	6	1

Sources: International Monetary Fund (2006).

Notes: The figures represent averages for tax years 1998–2003. Certain country data for 1998–2003 were incomplete and only the years in parentheses are included for Brazil (1998), Colombia (1998–2000), Mexico (1998–2000), and Panama (2001). Paraguay makes use of budgeted data only. Social security and other taxes were removed for Colombia to better reflect consistent categories over time. Additionally, breakdowns of income taxes between individual and corporate taxes were frequently not available for Latin American countries. In some cases, rounding causes the sum of component shares to appear to exceed or fall below aggregate shares.

by countries at different per capita income levels. First, consider general taxes on domestic goods and services as well as excise taxes. As discussed previously, Latin American countries rely on these taxes for about 57 percent of their total tax revenue.[52] Moreover, they generally rely more on these revenue sources than do their counterparts in the respective ranges of per capita income. For example, while most Latin American countries would be considered richer developing countries (with per capita incomes between $5,000 and $20,000), the average collected from excise

---

[52] The statistics in Table 6.16 are in line with the estimates of Tanzi and Zee, "Tax Policies for Emerging Markets". They confirm that most countries rely on general consumption taxes, such as the VAT, excise taxes, and trade taxes to fund a substantial portion of government operations. In OECD countries, general consumption tax revenues for 1995–97 account for 11.4 percent of GDP. By comparison, in developing countries, general consumption tax revenues for the same time period account for 10.5 percent of GDP.

TABLE 6.17. *Percentage Relative Use of Different Tax Instruments by National Governments, by Per Capita Income Level: World Averages (1990–1995, GDP Estimates, USD)*

	150–500	500–5,000	5,000–20,000	20,000	All
Tax revenue as percent of total government revenue	84	87	87	87	87
Total tax revenue					
Individual and corporate tax	23	21	35	33	26
Corporate tax	11	11	13	8	10
Individual income tax	12	10	22	25	16
Taxes on property	3	1	2	3	2
Domestic taxes on goods and services	43	45	34	32	39
Excises	17	13	12	9	12
Taxes on international trade and transportation	21	10	9	1	9
Import duties	20	10	9	1	9
Social security	11	23	20	30	24

Source: International Monetary Fund (2004), for years 1998 through 2002.

and domestic taxes for that class is 46 percent.[53] Perhaps the most distinguishing feature of this perspective on Latin American tax systems, however, is again in their neglect of income taxes, especially individual income taxes. On average, Latin American countries raise about 25 percent of total tax revenues from income taxes, with about 19 percent from corporate tax revenues and about 6 percent from individual income tax revenues. In contrast, the richer developing countries on average raise about 36 percent of tax revenues from income taxes (13 percent from corporate and 22 percent from individual income tax revenues).[54] Given

[53] A few Latin American countries, such as Bolivia and Paraguay, belong in the middle-income group (with per capita income between $500 and $5000), but their reliance on domestic taxes on goods and services as well as excises (58 and 59 percent, respectively), is roughly equal to the average for this category (58 percent).

[54] It may also be useful to compare the relative use of tax instruments by Latin American countries to choices made by governments in developing countries in other parts of the world. Perhaps the most interesting comparisons are between developing countries in Africa and in Latin America. As compared to Latin America, African countries rely more on income taxes (28 percent to 14 percent from corporate and 14 percent from individual income tax revenues) and taxes on international trade (31 percent), and less on domestic taxes on goods and services (22 percent), excise taxes (11 percent), and social security taxes (5 percent). Again, what is striking is the relative use of individual income taxes. Whereas African countries raise 14 percent of total tax revenues from individual income taxes, Latin American countries raise only about 6 percent. For the period between

that the individual income tax is often viewed today as the most progressive major tax instrument, its minor role in Latin America might seem a continuation of a long tradition of gentle treatment of the elite by the tax institutions of that region.

As we emphasized earlier, perhaps the most distinctive and fundamentally important feature of Latin American governmental and tax structures during the nineteenth century was the high degree of centralization. Local governments in Latin America were quite small by the standards of North American countries. In recent decades there has been an increased awareness in Latin America of the possible implications of stunted local governments, especially in the provision of public services. This has led to a wave of policies across the region that are aimed at transferring more resources from the central government to local (if not also provincial) governments. Table 6.18 presents estimates for five Latin American countries of the distribution of tax revenues and expenditures across levels of government, before and after the first generation of decentralization that began in the early 1980s.[55] Substantial variation in the size of local and provincial governments is evident, with Argentina, Brazil, and Colombia having the largest subnational governments (especially Brazil, which has relatively large provincial governments), Venezuela, Mexico, and Bolivia somewhere in the middle, and all other countries having even smaller national governments.[56] Largely because of the enormous increase in the size of the federal governments in the United States and Canada, as well as the large transfers from the central to the provincial governments in Brazil

1996 and 2002, developing countries in Asia raised, on average, about 37 percent of total tax revenue from income taxes (16 percent from individual income taxes and 21 percent from corporate income taxes), 45 percent from general consumption and excise taxes, and 14 percent from trade taxes, International Monetary Fund, *Finance Statistics Yearbook*, online version.

[55] See Eduardo Wiesner, *Fiscal Federalism in Latin America: From Entitlements to Markets* (Washington, D.C.: Inter-American Development Bank, 2003): 10, describing the first generation of decentralization as characterized by: (a) implementation of constitutional reforms that provided for automatic and largely unconditional transfers from central government to subnational governments; (b) introduction of targeted fiscal transfers through formulas to specific sectors and to low-income groups; (c) an alleged process of devolving resources together with devolving responsibilities; (d) delegation of some limited taxing and spending authority; and (e) a general lack of any independent evaluation of results. The second generation of decentralization policies began in the late 1990s and provided for tighter macroeconomic budget constraints, stronger intergovernmental regulatory frameworks, and more intensive use of incentives at the sectoral level. See Wiesner, *Fiscal Federalism*, 12.

[56] Eliza Wills, Christopher da C. B. Garman and Stephen Haggard, "The Politics of Decentralization in Latin America," *Latin American Research Review* 34 No. (1) (1999): 7–56 review the movements toward decentralization in Argentina, Brazil, Colombia, Mexico, and Venezuela, examining the influence that central government has over local finances.

TABLE 6.18. *Shares of Total Government Tax Revenues and Expenditures by Level of Government in Selected Latin American Countries: Before and After Programs to Decentralize*

	Share of total government tax revenue collected by level of government (%)		Share of total government expenditure by level of government (%)	
	Before decentralization	With decentralization	Before decentralization	With decentralization
Argentina[a]				
Central	79.3	80.0	63.5	51.9
Provincial	13.7	15.4	31.0	39.5
Local	7.0	4.6	5.4	8.6
Brazil[b]				
Central	59.8	47.1	50.2	36.5
State	36.9	49.4	36.2	40.7
Local	3.8	3.6	13.6	22.8
Colombia[c]				
Central	82.2	81.6	72.8	67.0
Departmental	12.2	11.1	16.7	15.7
Local	5.6	7.3	10.5	17.3
Mexico[d]				
Central	90.7	82.7	90.2	87.8
State	8.3	13.4	8.8	9.5
Local	1.0	3.9	1.0	2.8
Venezuela[e]				
Central	95.8	96.9	76.0	77.7
State	0.1	0.1	14.9	15.7
Local	4.0	3.1	9.1	6.5

Sources: For Argentina and Colombia, López Murphy (1995), 22, 25, 33. For Brazil, Shah (1990), 15. For Venezuela, World Bank (1992), 5. For Mexico, Rodriguez (1987), 271; and INEGI (1994).
Notes:
[a] Figures before decentralization as of 1983, under decentralization as of 1992.
[b] Figures before decentralization as of 1974, under decentralization as of 1988.
[c] Figures before decentralization as of 1980, under decentralization as of 1991.
[d] Figures before decentralization as of 1982, under decentralization as of 1992.
[e] Figures before decentralization as of 1980, under decentralization as of 1989.

and Argentina, the contrast between the rich countries in the North and their neighbors in Latin America is not nearly as stark in this dimension

They examine the relative discretion the federal government has in determining the amount of transferred funds, the ability of central governments to impose conditions on the use of funds, and the ability of local governments to borrow funds. They find that the degree of decentralization reflects the relative political power of presidents, legislators, and subnational governments, and that the structure of political parties in the respective countries influences the level of autonomy of lower levels of government.

as it was in the past. Nevertheless, subnational governments remain quite modest throughout Latin America, and the nineteenth century pattern endures, especially when gauged by tax revenues.

V

In this chapter we explored how the extreme inequality that came to characterize nearly all Latin American countries during their colonial periods may have influenced how their tax institutions evolved. We seek to understand why the tax structures of Latin American countries are so distinctive today, even relative to other developing countries with roughly similar per capita incomes, and why their national governments have historically been so dominant and their local governments stunted. One traditional explanation for the types of tax regimes adopted by Latin American countries highlights technical or resource constraints. Developing countries have a much more limited administrative capacity to collect income and other complex taxes involving the monitoring of individuals than developed countries. The existence of large, informal service and agricultural sectors further complicates the task of tax design and enforcement. Thus, it is not surprising that Latin American and other developing countries focus more on revenue sources such as taxes on trade, taxes imposed on foreign corporations, and general consumption and excise taxes.

That being said, our examination suggests that the government and tax structures of the Latin American societies had already diverged from those in the United States and Canada by the middle of the nineteenth century, if not before – not long after attaining independence and before there were large differences in per capita income. Although the causal mechanisms remain to be explored, we emphasize the striking parallels between how the institutions of taxation evolved across the hemisphere and how other fundamental social and economic institutions evolved (such as those involving suffrage, education, and ownership of land). In Latin America, where a substantial gap existed and persisted in the economic circumstances and political influence between elites and the bulk of the population, these institutions tended to develop along paths that greatly advantaged those elites. Control over voting rules assured elites of greatly disproportionate political representation. Very modest commitments to public investments, such as schooling, kept taxes low and competition in the labor markets for elites limited. Land policies kept land ownership in the hands of a relative few. Where government services were provided, funds were raised primarily through means other than direct taxation of income, wealth, or property.

This path of institutional development was radically different from those followed by the relatively homogenous Canada and United States. Although there may be other explanations for these patterns, the evidence seems consistent with the hypothesis that differences in the extent of inequality across these societies contributed to the different political decisions they made regarding the nature and size of different levels of government and the relative use of different tax instruments (if not the types and scale of government expenditure programs). As we have shown, there were no major differences during the nineteenth century in how national governments chose to raise their revenue. The United States, Canada, and Latin American countries all relied overwhelmingly on customs duties, other levies on foreign trade, and excise taxes. However, the United States and Canada were quite unlike their Latin American counterparts in financing local governments whose programs (generally public schools, roads, water and sanitation projects, other public health measures, and so on) were so extensive that they rivaled or exceeded their respective central government in resources consumed and services rendered. The funding for these substantial local governments came overwhelmingly from taxes on property, wealth, and income. State and local governments were successful in raising revenue through such instruments primarily because the large share of nineteenth century wealth was held in land, but it is telling that Latin American societies did not experience the same growth of local governments. Given that the record in Canada and the United States, where local governments funded primarily by property taxes trace back to the seventeenth and eighteenth centuries, it appears difficult to argue that the Latin American policies were dictated by technical or resource constraints on their ability to administer such taxes.

Latin American countries continue to have the highest rates of income inequality in the world. They still have relatively low aggregate tax burdens and generally rely on taxes on consumption, rather than on taxes on individual income, wealth, or property. Likewise, the central governments are still more dominant, relative to state and local authorities, than they are in the United States, Canada, and other regions of the world. It is not clear whether the persistence in the character of tax institutions and government structures can be attributed to the same factors and processes that operated during the nineteenth century. Much has changed in Latin America over the twentieth century. The progress in broadening the distribution of political influence (democratization), for example, would lead one to expect that the relative influence of elites on the design of institutions should be diminished and the demand for certain types of government programs should be increased. Even with political changes, however, it is difficult to design progressive tax structures in societies marked by great inequality. In addition, in recent years, the range of options available to government tax authorities has narrowed as economies have become more open and capital more mobile. While changes in Latin America over the last 10 to 15 years have increased expenditures on social programs and, often, increased the resources available to local governments to fund these programs, the changes in taxation have been less dramatic. Perhaps future political and economic developments will change the patterns of taxation in Latin America. In looking at the current structures, however, the evidence suggests that the long history of extreme inequality in Latin America is central to understanding the distinctive set of tax institutions that have evolved in Latin America.[57]

---

[57] For discussions of earlier tax policy, see, on colonial North America, Alvin Rabushka, *Taxation in Colonial America*. (Princeton: Princeton University Press, 2008), and on early Spanish America, see Herbert S. Klein, *The American Finances of the Spanish Empire: Royal Income and Expenditure in Colonial Mexico, Peru, and Bolivia, 1680–1809* (Albuquerque: University of New Mexico Press, 1998) and for later dates, see Carlos Marichal, *A Century of Dept Crises in Latin America. From Independence to the Great Depression 1820–1930* (Princeton: Princeton University Press, 1989).

7

Land and Immigration Policies

I

Once upon a time, more than five hundred years ago, Europeans began a grand, long-term campaign to extract material and other advantages from underpopulated or underdefended territories by establishing permanent settlements around the world.[1] There had been extensive migration within Europe, both eastward and westward, including settlements of areas within Europe conquered by both Europeans and non-Europeans.[2] In the eighteenth and nineteenth centuries there was also a large movement of contracted labor from east and central Europe to Russia and to Siberia.[3] The radically novel and diverse environments they encountered

---

[1] For a recent description of the world economy since year 1000, see Ronald Findlay and Kevin H. O'Rourke, *Power and Plenty: Trade, War, and the World Economy in the Second Millennium* (Princeton: Princeton University Press, 2007).

[2] See the studies in Leslie Page Moch, *Moving Europeans: Migration in Western Europe Since 1650* (Bloomington: Indiana University Press, 1992); P. C. Emmer and Magnus Mörner, eds., *European Expansion and Migration: Essays on the Intercontinental Migration From Africa, Asia, and Europe* (New York: Berg, 1992); Nicholas Canny, ed. *Europeans on the Move: Studies in European Migration, 1500–1800* (Oxford: Clarendon Press, 1994), particularly the essay by Phillips; and Ida Altman and James Horn, eds., *"To Make America": European Emigration in the Early Modern Period* (Berkeley: University of California Press, 1991). There had earlier been movements into Europe by the Mongols and the Ottomans, among others.

[3] For the earlier period, see Robert Bartlett, *The Making of Europe: Conquest, Colonization and Cultural Change, 950–1300* (Princeton: Princeton University Press, 1993); and for the later years see Roger P. Bartlett, *Human Capital: The Settlement of Foreigners in Russia, 1762–1804* (Cambridge: Cambridge University Press, 1979). Peter Lindert, has noted that the eastward movement of peasants in Russia led to a tying down of workers and was not due to their enticement by the availability of small farms. See also Peter H.

offered great economic opportunities, but also posed formidable problems of organization. Such circumstances made adaptation and innovation essential, and enormous variety in the economic structures and institutions that evolved over time is evident across colonies, even among those of the same European nation.[4] Inspired by the goal of improving understanding of the role of institutions in the processes of economic growth and development, many scholars have recently come to appreciate how the history of European colonization provides a rich supply of "natural experiment" evidence that can be analyzed to determine whether there were systematic patterns in how institutions or economies evolved with respect to initial conditions, and what causal mechanisms may be involved.[5]

The European movements into Africa and Asia, beginning at about the same time as did the colonization of the Americas, were to areas of high population density that provided more than ample native labor forces and left little need for extensive inflows of settlers or migrants from elsewhere. Few Europeans were to make the trek to these colonies, and their numbers, relative to the aboriginal populations, accordingly remained quite small (see Table 7.1 for the population composition of colonies late in the nineteenth century). There was also extensive movements by the British after 1788 to Australia and then to New Zealand, both of which had population and settlement patterns somewhat similar to the Americas, and at the end of the nineteenth century, by Britain and other European nations to Africa and to Oceania.

In the Americas, however, the Europeans confronted very different sorts of environments than in Asia and Africa. Although conditions varied across space, overall low population density (and therefore labor scarcity) was the rule, and thus the economic problems of the colonizers centered on how to exploit the abundant land and other natural resources without initially having much labor on-hand to do the productive work. Two fundamental and closely related issues were central to this challenge. First, how would ownership or use rights in land be allocated among the interested parties, such as the state or the corporate entity behind any particular colony, as well as to individual settlers, Native Americans, and

---

Lindert, "The Rise of Social Spending," *Explorations in Economic History* 31 (January 1994): 1–37.

4 For discussion of institutional changes and their effects, see note 3, Ch. 2. There had been nine European nations involved in the settlement of the Americas, many of whom were also involved with settlements in Asia and Africa.

5 See, for example, the various listed writings of Daron Acemoglu, Simon Johnson, and James A. Robinson on colonial and related issues.

TABLE 7.1. *The Composition of Populations in European Colonial Domains*

		Non-Whites	Whites	Ratio of Whites to Others
BRITAIN	1850			
Europe		15	347,691	23.179.4
Asia		97,356,000	62,162	0.001
Australasia		155,000	131,800	0.850
Africa		242,800	67,868	0.280
North America		120,000	1,410,400	11.753
South America		99,571	3,958	0.040
West Indies		639,708	71,350	0.112
TOTAL		98,613,094	2,095,229	0.021
FRANCE	1926			
Africa (all)		32,883,000	1,331,400	0.040
Americas (all)		492,500	48,500	0.098
Asia		20,415,000	23,500	0.001
Oceania		71,600	16,400	0.229
TOTAL		53,862,100	1,419,800	0.026
GERMANY	1913			
Africa		12,084,436	22,405	0.002
Pacific-Oceania		961,000	6,454	0.007
ITALY	1931			
Africa		2,380,560	69,441	0.029
PORTUGAL	1935			
Africa		7,619,258	85,024	0.011
BELGIUM	1900			
Africa		30,000,000	1,958	0.00007
NETHERLANDS				
East Indies	1900	36,000,000	75,927	0.002
West Indies	1835	85,571	6,310	.074

Sources: For Britain Martin, (1967); for France, Southworth (1931), 26; for Germany, Townsend (1930), 265–266; for Belgium *Statesman's Yearbook* (1904), 505; for Italy, Clark (1936), 35; for Portugal Kuczynski (1936), 95; for Netherlands West Indies, *Statesman's Yearbook* (1904), 932, and for Netherlands West Indies, Kuczynski (1836), 106.

Note: Given the periodic demographic and political changes, the racial compositions of the Spanish colonies, mainly in the Americas and the Philippines, as well as in Africa, varied considerably over time. For estimates for 1570 and 1650 see Table 2.3. In 1890, prior to the losses in the Spanish-American War, the colonies of Cuba, Puerto Rico, and the Philippines were about 85 percent non-white, with the largest proportion non-white being in the Philippines. See *Statesman's Yearbook* (1894).

the church? Land disposal policy not only affected the rate at which this critical resource was opened to investment and to the generation of output, but it also influenced the supply and location of labor, by means such as making it easier for individuals to realize the returns to the land they worked (and might invest in) and subsidies via land granted to potential immigrants (international as well as intra-national). In some cases, land policies involved making unoccupied or unemployed land available; however, not infrequently, ownership or use rights were transferred or seized from previous users – such as Natives or squatters – to be used by other parties. Land policy had a major impact on the pace of regional development, but it was influenced by the degree of centralization of authority, and questions as to whether the national government would have exclusive jurisdiction over land policy, or whether states, provinces, or other subnational districts should be permitted separate land policies.

Another critical issue that faced the colonial authorities was how to secure or attract enough labor to realize the potential fruits of the abundant land and natural resources. The colonies in the Americas were hardly unique in their attention to the adequacy of labor supply.[6] Indeed, population had been a longstanding concern of many elites and statesmen, especially those of a mercantilist bent, in many societies around the globe.[7] Some were concerned with underpopulation and introduced restrictions on emigration, although some national policymakers, as in England believed that there was overpopulation and resulting Malthusian difficulties within parts of Europe and this encouraged outmigration.[8] The

---

[6] For discussions of settlement issues in British North America see David W. Galenson, "The Settlement and Growth of the Colonies: Population, Labor, and Economic Development," in *The Cambridge Economic History of the United States*, 3 vols., vol. 1, *The Colonial Period*, eds. Stanley L. Engerman and Robert E. Gallman, 135–207 (Cambridge: Cambridge University Press, 1996); Abbot Emerson Smith, *Colonists in Bondage: White Servitude and Convict Labor in America, 1607–1776* (Chapel Hill: University of North Carolina Press, 1947; and Marilyn C. Baseler, *"Asylum for Mankind:" America 1607–1800*, (Ithaca: Cornell University Press, 1998). For a description of the related problem in the Spanish colonies, see J. H. Elliott, *Empires of the Atlantic World: Britain and Spain in America, 1492–1830* (New Haven: Yale University Press, 2006). The French situation is described in Philip P. Bouchard, *France and the American Tropics to 1700* (Baltimore: Johns Hopkins University Press, 2008); and James Prichard, *In Search of Empire: The French in the Americas, 1670–1730* (Cambridge: Cambridge University Press, 2004).

[7] See Eli F. Heckscher, *Mercantilism*, 2 vols. (London: G. Allen and Unwin, 1935).

[8] For England the major problem was seen to be overpopulation, leading to an encouragement of emigration. Elsewhere, as seen in the attempts to restrict out-migration, the problem was quite the opposite. For an examination of emigration restrictions, see Stanley L. Engerman, "Changing Laws and Regulations and Their Impact on Migration," in

situation in the New World was quite different, however, because of the extreme scarcity of labor that the European colonizers found in the New World, either on contact, or soon afterward as the diseases they brought with them wrought depopulation of the Native Americans, estimated to by some to be a decline of more than 80 percent of the population.[9] Prior to the great decline which occurred after 1492, it was possible that the population of the Americas exceeded the total population of the twelve major Western European nations.[10] The recognition that labor was essential to extract income from colonies was one major reason (the wealth of the areas settled was another) why the Spanish, the first Europeans to organize colonies in the Americas, chose to focus their efforts on the more densely populated and richer areas we know today as Mexico and Peru. There, the Spanish adapted some of the hierarchical institutions utilized by the Aztecs and Incas, and introduced their own systems (such as *encomienda*) involving grants to Spanish settlers of claims to labor or tribute from Native Americans, to obtain much of the desired labor supplies.

Colonies established later, after a period of about one century, whether British, French, Portuguese, Dutch, Swedish, or Danish, had to manage without much in the way of a native labor force, and they therefore had to tap outside sources. Unconstrained by law or morality (no colony or country in the New World, for example, maintained more than a temporary prohibition on slavery or on the slave trade before 1777), those with climates and soils well suited for crops such as sugar or cacao obtained the dominant share of their labor forces from the African market in slaves.[11] Although their heavy reliance on slaves may have been encouraged somewhat by proximity to Africa, by far the factor most responsible seems to have been the development of the gang and other systems of organizing

Coerced and Free Migration: Global Perspectives, ed. David Eltis, 75–93 (Stanford: Stanford University Press, 2002). For a general discussion of European population at this time, see Jan de Vries, *The Economy of Europe in an Age of Crisis 1600–1750* (Cambridge: Cambridge University Press, 1976).

[9] See the summary essay by Ubelaker in William M. Denevan, ed. *The Native Population in the Americas in 1492* (Madison: University of Wisconsin Press, 1976).

[10] For European population c. 1500, see Angus Maddison, *The World Economy: Historical Statistics* (Paris: OECD, 2003). The population of these twelve Western European countries is estimated at 48,000,000. For a survey of estimates made of the Native populations of the America, prior to European arrival, see Nicholas Sánchez-Albornoz, *The Population of Latin America: A History* (Berkeley: University of California Press, 1974). No firm conclusion is presented within a range of 13.3 million to 112 million.

[11] In 1777 the state of Vermont became the first locale to end slavery, but this did require a period of apprenticeships and freed, at most, 19 slaves. Most later slave emancipations did not lead to an immediate freeing, but required a period of apprenticeship of some 15 to 30 years for those considered to be born free.

slave labor that gave large slave plantations a substantial efficiency advantage in producing those highly profitable commodities.[12] Colonies with the appropriate natural endowments soon came to specialize in these crops, and their demand for labor kept slave prices above what employers in areas more fit for grain or mixed agriculture could afford.[13] The result was that the relatively few colonies in the Americas that lacked either a large native population or the conditions conducive to growing sugar and other slave-intensive staples, had to exert themselves to mobilize labor forces drawn from Europe and of European descent.

The British colonies on the North American mainland above the Rio Grande exemplified this pattern. Having been established in locales with only sparse numbers of Native Americans, especially after the Indians suffered from the introduction of diseases from Europe, and receiving only modest inflows of slaves until well into the eighteenth century (especially the states north of the Mason-Dixon line), the thirteen colonies (or their ruling authorities) realized that they would have to increase their populations if they were to be successful. They quickly set about devising institutions and policies that would attract migrants from Europe. The basic foundation of their campaign was the institution of indentured servitude, which meant an exchange of the cost of transport for several years of labor, permitting those with inadequate funds to migrate. After a protracted process of passing and implementing laws aimed at improving the enforcement of both sides of the indenture contract (and improving terms to secure an edge over competitors), this was enormously effective and it accounted for possibly about 75 percent of arrivals from Europe to the thirteen colonies.[14] Other inducements, which were offered in some form for extended periods by all of these colonies, included easy and low-cost access to owning land and some forms of tax exemption.

[12] Slavery was not an institutional innovation of the American settlers, as slavery had long existed in many places. Nor was the plantation production of sugar by slave labor, as this had been important in the Mediterranean after the Crusades. See J. H. Galloway, *The Sugar Cane Industry: An Historical Geography From its Origins to 1914* (Cambridge: Cambridge University Press, 1989).

[13] The development of slavery and sugar production in the British and French West Indies did take some 25–50 years, the initial period being based primarily on free white or indentured labor producing tobacco. For the French case see Bouchard, *France and the American Tropics* and for the British, John C. Appleby, "English Settlement in the Lesser Antilles During War and Peace, 1603–1660," in *The Lesser Antilles in the Age of European Expansion*, eds. Robert L. Paquette and Stanley L. Engerman (Gainesville: University of Florida Press, 1996): 86–104.

[14] See, among others, Smith, *Colonists in Bondage* Galenson, "Settlement and Growth," and Farley Grubb, "The Incidence of Servitude in Trans-Atlantic Migration, 1771–1804," *Explorations in Economic History* 22 (July 1985): 316–339. For a discussion of French indentured labor, see Bouchard, *France and the American Tropics*.

The active pursuit of European migrants by the British colonies on the mainland contrasts sharply with the policies of Spanish America.[15] Although the first waves of settlers in Spain's colonies, particularly those from the military or from elite backgrounds, were rewarded with grants of land, claims on Native Americans, relief from taxes, and other incentives, the Crown began early in the sixteenth century to regulate and restrict the flow of European migrants to its colonies in the Americas.[16] The stringency of the limits did vary somewhat over time, due to the population changes and movements, such as the migration of expelled moriscos in the early seventeenth century. There were occasionally interventions designed to effect specific movements of population from Europe as well as of slaves to specific colonies, including Mexico and Peru, judged especially worthy or needy of support, but overall there is no doubt that Spanish policies limited, rather than encouraged, the migration of Europeans to the New World.[17] A salient illustration is the conspicuous failure of the Spanish Crown to approve proposals for indentured labor trading transportation in return for future labor services. The starkly divergent approaches of the Spanish and British mainland colonies toward migration may appear puzzling, especially as their agricultural sectors were similar in consisting largely of grain and animal products, but the fundamental explanation for this difference is that the most important Spanish colonies (that is, Mexico, Peru, and Colombia) were relatively abundant in labor as compared to their British mainland counterparts. The population density in 1700 in the three leading Spanish colonies was several times greater than for the British mainland colonies.[18] Their relatively substantial Native American and *mestizo* populations kept returns to unskilled labor low, and reduced the incentives for Spaniards who might have contemplated migration to the New World as well as reduced the desire of elites in the colonies to lobby the Crown to change its policies. The other important factor behind the maintenance of the strict limitations on immigration,

---

[15] See Elliott, *Empires of the Atlantic World*; C. H. Haring, *The Spanish Empire in* America (New York: Oxford University Press, 1947); and Altman and Horn, eds., *"To Make America."*

[16] Elliott, *Empires of the Atlantic World*.

[17] Sánchez-Albornoz, *Population of Latin America*; Altman and Horn, eds., *"To Make America."* In the seventeenth century, Spain also suffered from a population decline. See J. H. Parry, *The Spanish Seaborne Empire* (New York: Knopf, 1966).

[18] See estimates in Colin McEvedy and Richard Jones, *Atlas of World Population History* (New York: Penguin, 1978); Maddison, *The World Economy*; and Susan B. Carter, et al., eds., *Historical Statistics of the United States: Earliest Times to the Present, Millennial Edition* 5 vols. (Cambridge: Cambridge University Press, 2006).

in our view, was the greater centralization or concentration of political authority. Not only did the imposed controls apply to immigration to all of the Spanish colonies in the Americas, but centering the government structures for Spanish America in Mexico City and Lima meant that outlying areas with different conditions and demands for labor (such as Argentina) were largely deprived of autonomy or even influence in policy.

These contrasts in land and labor policies that had emerged early in the colonial period essentially endured into the nineteenth century, by which time most of the societies in the Americas were independent nations and nominal or actual democracies.[19] Despite periodic spells of political tension (if not conflict) about immigration, generally coinciding with macroeconomic contractions (or focused on specific ethnic groups), the United States (and Canada) continued to pursue policies that were generally extremely favorable to immigration. Although state, provincial, and local governments on or inside the western frontier at the time may have been the most aggressive in courting migrants, the importance of the consistently liberal stances of the U.S. and Canadian governments in making public land available in small plots at low cost to all who sought to settle should not be underestimated. The usefulness of offering easy access to land in attracting migrants was universally understood, and indeed helps to explain that in an era of labor scarcity, cities and long-settled areas in the East concerned about their labor supplies accounted for the major opposition to the federal governments disposing of land out West on generous terms.

Despite most societies having achieved independence, and other radical changes in their political environment, there was much continuity in Latin America. Most notably perhaps, the region remained largely dependent on the population born there – whether of European, Native American, or mixed descent. Immigration from abroad was not much more than a trickle, except for the experiences of Argentina, Uruguay, Brazil, and several of the smaller nations, but even these countries, immigration only began late in the nineteenth century.[20] Responsibility for this failure to attract immigrants cannot be laid solely on the policies of the nations of

---

[19] See Leslie B. Rout, *African Experience in Spanish America: 1502 to the Present Day* (Cambridge: Cambridge University Press, 1976), for the dates of Latin American independence.

[20] See Walter Willcox, with Imre Frencz, *International Migration*, 2 vols. (New York: National Bureau of Economic Research, 1929, 1931); and Maurice R. Davie, *World Immigration: With Special Reference to the United States* (New York: Macmillan, 1936).

Latin America. With the improving levels of material welfare and economic opportunity that the United States could offer as it industrialized it was now an increasingly tough competitor for immigrants from Europe, and it was the major recipient of migrants from Europe.[21] That being said, however, it is striking that although there were many appeals for programs to entice more immigrants, inspired in part by the evident success of the United States, most of the programs purporting to achieve that goal were either framed very narrowly or flawed in design. Even when public lands were to be made available for purchase, the terms or other details of the laws tended to keep prices high or greatly advantage the wealthy and privileged in access. This evident lack of concern by authorities regarding the incentives offered to migrants was similar to the poor record throughout Latin America (though better in Argentina, Uruguay, and Chile, which were relatively labor-scarce for the region), in providing for public schooling, as well as to the policies that a number of countries, such as Mexico and Colombia, implemented late in the nineteenth century (when land values had risen) that transferred the rights to land traditionally held and worked by Native Americans as community property to large landowners.

In this chapter we lay out the basis for our view that the record of the evolution of land and immigration institutions in the Americas since colonization provides broad support to the idea that the initial factor endowments were of fundamental importance. We highlight, in particular, the significance of labor scarcity or abundance and the more limited weight given to political factors. Where labor was scarce, even political and economic elites who may have had disproportionate power in shaping institutions were willing to extend privileges, including low-cost access to land, to ordinary people as a means of attracting or mobilizing them. Not only was the influence of labor scarcity direct and immediate, but it may also have had long-lasting effects in fostering greater economic and political equality and the different outcomes that might flow from such conditions. Where labor was relatively abundant, however, elites had less reason to share privileges as a means of attracting more labor, and likely were less constrained in their ability to shape institutions to advantage themselves. In Section II, we develop our argument with a brief sketch

[21] See Maddison, *The World Economy*, on the greatly widening gap between the per capita income of the United States and of Latin America during the nineteenth century. The increasing relative backwardness in Latin America seemingly occurs after independence from Spain, and amidst a series of civil and international wars. The changing political structure (or lack of same) requires more attention.

TABLE 7.2. *The Estimated Distribution of the Aboriginal American Population, c. 1492*

North America (the U.S., Canada, Alaska, and Greenland)	4,400,000
Mexico	21,400,000
Central America	5,650,000
Caribbean	5,850,000
Central Andes	11,500,000
Lowland South America	8,500,000

Source: Denevan, ed., (1976): 291.

of the history of land and immigration institutions during the colonial period. In Section III, we discuss how these institutions evolved during the nineteenth century, and devote some attention to detailing how variation across countries within Latin America and across the United States is generally consistent with our hypothesis. Section IV deals with several other British colonies and discusses the key similarities in patterns in different parts of the world, and Section V concludes.

II

A central issue for all of the colonies was labor supply. The importance of the limitation of this constraint was a major reason why the Spanish, the first Europeans to arrive, focused their efforts on the areas in the Americas with the largest and richest concentrations of native populations (see Table 7.2). Another indication of the relative labor scarcity that prevailed in the New World was the extensive flow of migrants from Europe and Africa (see Table 1.2) that crossed the Atlantic despite high costs of transportation.[22] That over 60 percent of migrants between 1500 and 1760, increasing from roughly 25 percent prior to 1580 and rising to nearly 80 percent between 1700 and 1760, were Africans brought over involuntarily as slaves is a testament to the high productivity of labor in the Americas. Given competitive international markets, slaves

---

[22] Table 1.2 is based upon the estimates of David Eltis, including; David Eltis, "Free and Coerced Migrations From the Old World to the New," in *Coerced and Free Migration, Global Perspectives*, ed. David Eltis, 33–74 (Stanford: Stanford University Press, 2002). For estimates through 1830, see David Eltis, "Free and Coerced Transatlantic Migrations: Some Comparisons," *American Historical Review* 99 (April 1983): 251–80. Perhaps the most striking of Eltis's findings concerning settlement patterns is that down to 1830 about three times as many enslaved Africans as free Europeans arrived in the New World.

flowed to those locations where their productivity was greatest, and their productivity tended to be greatest in areas with climates and soils well suited for the cultivation of sugar and a few other staple crops. Slavery was legal and welcomed in all of the colonies of the major European powers. The Spanish and British settlements each received between one-half and two-thirds of their pre-1760 immigrants from Africa; in contrast, the colonies of other nations were more dependent on slave labor, over 90 percent of all immigrants to the French and Dutch colonies were slaves, and the figure was over 75 percent for the Portuguese.

The areas in the Caribbean, the northern coast of South America, and Brazil had a comparative advantage in sugar, cacao, and a few other staple crops, and they relatively soon specialized in producing these commodities on large plantations, obtaining the majority of their labor force from the slave trade. These colonies had relatively little need for large numbers of European immigrants. For different reasons, the same was true for Spanish America. European immigrants (and *creoles*) were initially required to defeat the Native Americans, establish control over and then defend territory, and to provide the basic political and economic structures, but the majority of the overall labor force was provided by the Native Americans.

With Spain the pioneer in establishing substantial settlements, over 70 percent of the migrants to the Americas between 1500 and 1580 landed in Spanish colonies. That share plunged over time, to about 14 percent between 1700 and 1760. Part of this precipitous fall was due to the rise of the colonies of other European nations, but a more important factor was Spain's severe tightening of the restrictions on who was allowed to migrate to its colonies.[23] Unlike the other major European colonizers, Spain, with the support, if not instigation, of the *peninsulares* and *criollos* already there, progressively raised more formidable obstacles to those who might have otherwise ventured to the New World to seek their fortunes. The authorities in Spain seem to have been motivated both by a desire to keep costs down by limiting the number of population centers to defend, as well as the desires of those who had arrived early or their descendants, who fought to maintain their privileged positions.[24] Early in the sixteenth

---

[23] Spain's relative decline, however, was at a time during which there remained absolute increases in the number of migrants.

[24] Large blocks of land and claims on Native American labor were often granted as incentives or rewards to the early waves of settlers, especially military men, missionaries, and others of some prominence. Although smaller holdings could be obtained through sales, generally the more important were governmental land grants and the larger tended to be the holdings, the more unequal the distributions of wealth and political power

century, they began to impose strict controls as reflected in requirements for licenses over who could settle in the Americas, with preference shown for relatives of those already there, and permission denied to citizens of European countries other than Spain as well as to non-Catholics. Licenses to emigrate were initially restricted to single men, but were ultimately extended to married men accompanied by their families; single white women were never allowed, influenced in part on the availability of Native American and *mestizo* women.[25] It seems highly unlikely that such a restrictive stance toward immigration would have been retained if there had not already been a substantial supply of Indians and *mestizos* to work the land and otherwise produce with the assets owned by the elites and the Spanish Crown. In this sense, at least, the preferred policy must have been ultimately due to the factor endowments.[26] Another mechanism through which the relatively ample local supply of labor provided by the Native Americans and *mestizos* could have reduced immigration was through keeping the returns to unskilled labor low, and in so doing reducing the desire of Spanish unskilled labor to migrate.

What stands out from the estimates presented in Table 2.3 is how small the percentages of populations composed of those of European descent were in Spanish America and the in the economies that focused on sugar production into the nineteenth century. The populations of those colonies suitable for cultivating sugar, such as Jamaica, Barbados, and Brazil, came to be dominated by those of African descent imported to work on the large slave plantations.[27] The populations of the Spanish colonies were

would become. The initial land grants were often non-tradable by the recipients, and yet transferable by the Spanish Crown. Hence, later migrants to colonies might indeed have eroded the value of property rights held by earlier cohorts. It is not difficult to comprehend why the already established population of European descent was less than enthusiastic about a liberal immigration policy during the colonial era. On Spanish settlement of the Americas, see Elliott, *Empires of the Atlantic World*; and Charles Gibson, *Spain in America* (New York: Harper & Row, 1966).

[25] See Bernard Moses, *The Establishment of Spanish Role in America* (New York, G. P. Putnam, 1898), Elliott, *Empires of the Atlantic World*; and Parry, *Spanish Seaborne Empire*.

[26] At first it seems somewhat puzzling, or contradictory to the idea that the factor endowment was the crucial determinant of policy, that Spanish authorities did not actively encourage immigration to colonies without a substantial supply of readily available Indian labor, like Argentina. Spanish policy toward immigration to places like Argentina, however, was simply incidental, with the overall policy as regards immigration to the New World based on the factor endowments and politics in all of Spanish America together. Hence, Spanish policy was probably driven by conditions in Mexico and Peru. Since these centers of Spanish America had an abundance of Indian labor, the local elites and the authorities in Spain were able to maintain restrictive policies.

[27] See, in particular, Richard S. Dunn, *Sugar and Slaves: The Rise of the Planter Class in the English West Indies, 1624–1713* (Chapel Hill: University of North Carolina Press, 1972)

composed predominantly of Indians and *mestizos*, largely because these colonies had been established and built up in places where there had been substantial populations of Native Americans beforehand, and because flows of Europeans were constrained by the restrictive immigration policies of Spain. If not for these policies, it is probable that the societies in the southern cone of South America, such as Argentina and Chile, might well have attracted many more immigrants from Europe during the colonial period. As a result, less than 20 percent of the population in Spanish America was composed of whites as late as the beginning of the nineteenth century.[28]

It was the northern part of North America, the temperate-zone colonies that became the United States and Canada, that were distinctive in their reliance on attracting immigrants from Europe, a reliance forced later to some extent on the southern temperate zone colonies of Argentina, Chile, and Uruguay. The northern temperate areas had only very small numbers of Native Americans on the eastern rim of the continent, where the most substantial European settlements were located, and thus the composition of their populations soon came to be essentially determined by the groups who immigrated and their respective rates of natural increase. This was of particular significance in New England, where net migration was negative over the colonial period, but the rate of natural increase was very high. Although significant numbers of slaves were employed in the southern colonies, on the whole, the factor endowments in the thirteen colonies and Canada were far more hospitable to the cultivation of grains, tobacco, and animal products than sugar (or other crops that were grown on large slave plantations during this era). The colonies in this area accordingly absorbed far more Europeans than they did African slaves, and they stood

on the English colonies, and Stuart B. Schwartz, *Sugar Plantations in the Formation of Brazilian Society: Bahia, 1550–1835* (Cambridge: Cambridge University Press, 1985) on Brazil. In the early period of settlement in Brazil, slaves were also used in mining.

[28] The immigration policies were especially restrictive toward single European women, and this too likely contributed over the long run to the small proportion of the population that was white. The Spanish Antilles did have a relatively large white population, reflecting the limited number of Indians after depopulation, and the long lag between the beginnings of the settlement and the sugar boom that developed there only after the start of the nineteenth century. On the Caribbean in general, as well as a discussion of the patterns of Cuban settlement, see Franklin W. Knight, *The Caribbean: The Genesis of a Fragmented Nationalism*, 2nd ed (New York: Oxford University Press, 1990). For an ethnic breakdown of Caribbean populations in 1750, 1830, and 1880, see Stanley L. Engerman and B. W. Higman, "The Demographic Structure of the Caribbean Slave Societies in the Eighteenth and Nineteenth Centuries," in *UNESCO General History of the Caribbean*, vol. 3 ed. Franklin W. Knight, 45–104 (Paris: UNESCO, 1997).

out in the hemisphere with whites accounting for roughly 85 percent of the population and labor force.

Perhaps because it was the one region in the New World that was dependent on attracting large numbers of voluntary migrants from Europe during the colonial period, the colonies in the northern part of North America distinguished themselves soon after their establishment as having institutions supportive of immigration and attractive to immigrants. The willingness of the thirteen colonies to accept convict labor is an aspect of their history that Americans prefer to deemphasize, but a both better-known and important example of white immigration was indentured servitude, a contractual means of extending credit (primarily the cost of transportation across the Atlantic) whereby the servant promised to work for the recruitment agent (or the agent to which he assigned or sold the contract) in a specified colony and for a specified period of time. This system was first introduced to North America by the Virginia Company, designed explicitly to attract potential migrants from Britain, but the innovation, which was related in legal basis to contracts as servants of husbandry (if not apprentices as well) soon spread to carry migrants from a variety of countries in Europe to British colonies.[29] Over the entire colonial period, upwards of 75 percent of European migrants to British America came as indentured servants. Although some may regard the extensive use of indentured servitude in the British colonies as due primarily to a distinctive British heritage, this characterization seems unwarranted. Contractual forms similar to apprenticeships and servants of husbandry and migration of convicts existed in a number of European countries, including Spain, Portugal, France, and earlier in Northern Italy and Sicily. In Spain, however, the Crown chose not to implement a proposal to provide transport to its colonies in return for obligated labor services on arrival.[30] The evidence appears consistent with the view that the urgency of the demand for workers from Europe contributed to the institutional innovation and its diffusion among Europeans.

[29] On convict labor in America, see A. Roger Ekirch, *Bound for America: The Transportation of British Convicts to the Colonies, 1718–1775* (New York: Oxford University Press, 1987). See also David W. Galenson, *White Servitude in Colonial America: An Economic Analysis* (Cambridge: Cambridge University Press, 1981); James R. Perry, *The Formation of a Society on Virginia's Eastern Shore, 1615–1655* (Chapel Hill: University of North Carolina Press, 1990).

[30] See, for example, Robert L. Reynolds, "The Mediterranean Frontier, 1000–1400," in *The Frontier in Perspective*, eds. Walker D. Wyman and Clifton B. Kroeber (Madison: University of Wisconsin Press, 1957): 21–34; Timothy J. Coates, *Convicts and Orphans: Forced and State-Sponsored Colonizers in the Portuguese Empire, 1550–1755* (Stanford: Stanford University Press, 2001); Bouchard, *France and the American Tropics*; Altman and Horn, eds., *"To Make America."*

Another way in which the colonies in the northern part of North America strove to attract immigrants was through making ownership of plots of land rather accessible. Of course, with the enormous abundance of land relative to labor, land was relatively cheap, especially compared to the wage rates, and easy to obtain (by European standards) through the market. But the experience in the colonies on the North American mainland sometimes went well beyond that, with provincial authorities making deliberate use of land grants to attract migrants. In the British colonies, the distribution of land was left to the individual colonies, once the land was transferred from the Crown to proprietors or the government of the crown colonies. Over time, some quite different, but persistent, regional patterns emerged. The New England colonies made grants, generally of small plots, to individuals, but land grants were not directly used to attract indentured servants (as they were elsewhere), perhaps because of the relatively small number of immigrants who came or were needed to come to the region.[31]

It was in the southern colonies where staple crops such as tobacco and rice were grown and the demand for European and other field laborers may have been especially high, that land grants were most targeted at attracting indentured servants and other migrants. During the seventeenth century, Virginia introduced the headright system (grants of land to settlers, or to those who enticed others to settle) to stimulate in-migration, with the only requirement being a three-year period of settlement. Indentured servant laborers who came to Virginia were generally to be granted fifty acres when their term had expired. Variants of the headright system were adopted in Maryland and the Carolinas. The Middle Atlantic colonies of New Jersey and Pennsylvania also employed variants of the headright system, but, in both, the grants of land were subsidized, rather than free. Late in the eighteenth century, after independence, a number of what were now state governments extended their liberal land policies to include preemption for squatters.[32]

It is perhaps worth highlighting how different the attention to, and prevalence of, land ownership was in the northern part of North America

[31] Percy Wells Bidwell and John I. Falconer, *History of Agriculture in the Northern United States, 1620–1860* (Washington, D.C.: Carnegie Institution, 1925); Marshall Harris, *Origin of the Land Tenure System in the United States* (Ames: Iowa State College Press, 1953); and, on the Dutch case, Clarence White Rife, "Land Tenure in New Netherlands," in *Essays in Colonial History Presented to Charles McLean Andrews by his Students* (New Haven: Yale University Press, 1931): 41–73.

[32] Lewis Cecil Gray, *History of Agriculture in the Southern United States to 1860*, 2 vols. (Washington, D.C.: Carnegie Institution, 1933); Paul W. Gates, *History of Public Land Law Development* (Washington, D.C.: Government Printing Office, 1968).

as compared to Europe. Tenancy, and farm labor, were clearly much more common in Britain and France than in their American colonies on the mainland, with these arrangements and other means of allocating land achieved over a very long history and in environments with rather different land to labor ratios.[33] The attempts to bring variants of the British manorial system to, for example, Maryland and Pennsylvania, and the French seigneurial system (in Canada), were, however, not successful, given the land availability, crops to be grown, and their optimal scale of production. Thus, in the French and British mainland colonies, there was adaptation in land policy to allow for smaller units worked by owner-occupiers and for more flexibility in production.[34] These adaptations meant that the distribution and allocation of land were more similar across these colonies than they were compared with those in the metropolis in Europe. Because of the long tradition of property requirements for voting, the wider distribution of land was significant not just for economic purposes, but it also meant a broader base for voting.[35] Thus, not only could voting influence land policy, land policy could also influence voting.

There was, of course, no such liberality regarding land policy in Spanish America. Without any significant interest in attracting more immigration to its colonies, but with concern for maintaining control and a stream of revenue from the labor of the native labor force, the initial policy in nearly all of the colonies with substantial populations was the *encomienda* system, which consisted of Crown-awarded claims to

---

[33] On England, see Robert C. Allen, *Enclosure and the Yeoman: The Agricultural Development of the South Midlands, 1450–1850* (Oxford: Clarendon Press, 1992) and for an examination of France contrasted with England, see Colin Haywood, "The Role of the Peasantry in French Industrialization, 1815–1880," *Economic History Review* 34 (August 1981): 359–76. See also Curtis P. Nettels, *The Roots of American Civilization: A History of American Colonial Life*, 2nd ed. (New York: Appleton-Century-Crofts, 1963); Viola Florence Barnes, "Land Tenure in English Colonial Charters of the Seventeenth Century," in *Essays in Colonial History Presented to Charles McLean Andrews by his Students* (New Haven: Yale University Press, 1931): 4–40; Wesley Frank Craven, *The Southern Colonies in the Seventeenth Century, 1607–1689* (Baton Rouge: Louisiana State University Press, 1970); Robert K. Ackerman, *South Carolina Colonial Land Policies* (Columbia: University of South Carolina Press, 1977); and Beverley W. Bond, Jr., *The Quit-Rent System in the American Colonies* (New Haven: Yale University Press, 1919).

[34] On the seigniorial system in French Canada, see Marcel Trudel, *The Seigneural Regime* (Ottawa: Canadian Historical Association, 1971), and the literature cited there.

[35] See Alexander Keyssar, *The Right to Vote: The Contested History of Democracy in the United States* (New York: Basic Books, 2000); and Jerrold G. Rusk, *A Statistical History of the American Electorate* (Washington, D.C.: CQ Press, 2001). See also Ch. 4.

tribute (in goods, service, time, and cash) from a specified body of natives working on the land where they had previously resided. Relatively small numbers of these often enormous grants – never many more than 500 in the first half of the sixteenth century – were awarded in any single colony. Cortes was assigned 115,000 natives in Mexico, and Pizarro 20,000 in Peru. In Peru, for example, only 5 percent of the Spanish population in the mid-sixteenth century held *encomiendas*.[36] These *encomanderos* and their families became, in effect, the aristocracy of Spanish America. When pressure from depopulation and movement toward a cash economy, as well as Church concern about treatment of Native Americans, began to alter the *encomienda* system, they were well positioned to assemble large private holdings of much of the best located and most fertile land. The high concentration of land holding that developed over time in Spanish America paralleled the extreme inequality that prevailed in wealth, human capital, political influence, and other dimensions.

III

As the United States became a sovereign nation and most of Spanish America gained independence from Spain over the late eighteenth and early nineteenth centuries, there were many important changes across the Americas in institutions and in the economic environment of great relevance to immigration and land policy. First, if not foremost, the structures of government institutions were radically altered. Although Canada remained a colony with limited autonomy until the 1860s, and Brazil was, after 1822, an independent monarchy, most of the major societies were both independent and at least nominally democratic and if not free of slavery, held severe restrictions on slave imports.[37] The new national governments, and their ability to design policies targeted to the interests

---

[36] Mark A. Burkholder and Lyman L. Johnson, *Colonial Latin America*, 3rd ed. (New York: Oxford University Press, 1998). For discussions of the *economienda*, see, among other sources, Lesley Byrd Simpson, *The Encomienda in New Spain: The Beginning of Spanish Mexico* (Berkeley: University of California Press, 1982) and Robert Himmerich y Valencia, *The Encomenderos of New Spain, 1521–1555* (Austin: University of Texas Press, 1991); and on the mita system, see Jeffrey A. Cole, *The Potosí Mita, 1573–1700: Compulsory Indian Labor in the Andes* (Stanford: Stanford University Press, 1985). See also T. R. Ford, *Man and Land in Peru* (Gainesville: University of Florida Press, 1910).

[37] On Latin American slavery, see Rout, *African Experience;* and Herbert S. Klein, *African Slavery in Latin America and the Caribbean* (New York: Oxford University Press, 1986), and on the Spanish-American independence movement, see John Lynch, *The Spanish-American Revolutions, 1808–1826*, 2nd ed. (New York: Norton, 1986).

(as felt and expressed by various domestic groups) of their own individual countries, and to implement them, were crucial and novel elements. Among those interests of course, was the means of settling unoccupied territories within the national boundaries, if not expanding those boundaries, which led to costly wars in the nineteenth century.[38] This interest in new settlements gave impetus to liberal immigration as well as intra-country migration and land policies, particularly in countries where labor was especially scarce.

Also of great consequence for the formulation of immigration and land policy was the onset of industrialization in the United States and Western Europe and the acceleration of technological change. Economic growth and the decrease in the cost of trans-oceanic transportation increased the propensity of Europeans to migrate to the New World (without having to indenture themselves), but also increased the relative desirability of the United States as their destination, as compared to other countries in the hemisphere.[39] These advances also spurred the growth of international trade, and increased the returns to the exploitation of the abundant land and natural resources in the New World. In so doing, they contributed to an increase in the value of land, a development that not only likely influenced the behavior of immigrants in countries where land was accessible, but also that of elites in countries where they exercised disproportionate political power.

Although there were frequent changes in the precise details, overall there was remarkable continuity in the basic orientation of U.S. policies in favor of immigration and relatively easy access to land in small plots. At the national level, there were periodic calls for restrictions of immigration, but except for ending the international slave trade in 1808, those measures imposed in the name of public health, and those (after 1880) on Japanese and Chinese immigration, serious obstacles were not introduced until the 1920s.[40] State policies differed substantially, however.

---

[38] Gates, *History of Public Land.* On Latin America wars in the nineteenth century and data on wars with Indians in the United States, see Michael Clodfelter, *Warfare and Armed Conflicts: A Statistical Reference to Casualty and Other Figures, 1618–1991,* 2 vols. (Jefferson, N.C.: McFarland, 1992). For a survey of Indian-White relations in the United States and their impact on land changes, see Wilcomb E. Washburn, *The Indian in America* (New York: Harper and Row, 1975).

[39] See the data in Willcox, *International Migration;* and Davie, *World Immigration.*

[40] See Edward P. Hutchinson, *Legislative History of American Immigration Policy, 1789–1965* (Philadelphia: University of Pennsylvania Press, 1981); Erna Risch, "Encouragement of Immigration as Revealed in Colonial Legislation," *Virginia Magazine of History and Biography* 45 (January 1932): 1–10; and Henry W. Farnam, D.C., *Chapters in the*

Over the nineteenth century, those states new to the Union often sent abroad delegations or placed advertisements to attract immigrants to their environs, and highlighted liberal qualifications for residence and participation in local elections and commitments to public schools and other infrastructure of particular interest to potential migrants.[41] Later in the nineteenth century, however, concentrations of immigrants in industrial cities led some states (mostly in the northeast) to raise difficulties by introducing literacy tests for voting. Again, there seems a relation between labor scarcity and public policies toward immigrants.[42]

With the establishment of the United States, many of the original states gave up their claims to land in the West, and ceded principal authority in public land policy to the federal government. This may well have proved fortuitous for the maintenance of liberal land policies – which generally evolved over time through new legislations (see Table 7.3) to make the terms for individuals seeking to acquire and settle on land progressively easier.[43] These changes were the basis of debate among the representatives of the different regions in Congress and elsewhere, often intertwined with other aspects of political disagreement. This reflected the broad range of issues that the controversies over land dealt with. For example, because of the government's budget constraint, there was a tradeoff between revenues from land sales and revenues from the protective tariffs favored by northeastern manufacturers. Given that land policy could influence the distribution of population across regions (and thus wage rates), commodity prices, land value, and the location and structure of output, political disagreement should not have been surprising. What is most striking, perhaps, is that despite such political disagreements, a commitment to broad and easy access to those seeking to settle on public lands was generally sustained and deepened.[44]

History of Social Legislation in the United States to 1860 (Washington, D.C.: Carnegie Institution, 1938). See also Engerman, "Changing Laws and Regulations."

[41] See discussions in, among other sources, Benjamin Horace Hibbard, *A History of the Public Land Policies* (New York: Macmillan, 1924); Roy M. Robbins, *Our Landed Heritage: The Public Domain, 1776–1936* (Princeton: Princeton University Press, 1942); and George M. Stephenson, *The Political History of the Public Lands From 1840 to 1862: From Pre-emption to Homestead* (Boston: R. G. Badger, 1917).

[42] See sources cited in note 35.

[43] See Jeremy Atack, Fred Bateman and William N. Parker, "Northern Agriculture and the Westward Movement," in *Cambridge Economic History of the United States* 3 vols., vol. 2, *The Long Nineteenth Century* eds. Stanley L. Engerman and Robert E. Gallman, 285–328 (Cambridge: Cambridge University Press, 2000) and Gates, *Public Land Law.*

[44] See, among other sources, Raynor G. Wellington, *The Political and Sectional Influence of the Public Lands, 1828–1842* (Cambridge, MA: Riverside Press, 1914); and Daniel

TABLE 7.3. *Significant Public Land Laws in the United States, 1785–1916*

Year	Law	Minimum Price per Acreage	Minimum Acreage	Maximum Acreage	Conditions and Terms
1785	Land Ordinance of 1785	$1	640	none	cash
1787	Northwest Ordinance of 1787	$1	640	none	$\frac{1}{2}$ cash, balance in 3 months
1796	Land Act of 1796	$2	640	none	$\frac{1}{2}$ in 30 days, balance in 1 year
1800	Harrison Land Act	$2	320	none	$\frac{1}{4}$ in 30 days, balance in 3 years at 6%
1804	Land Act of 1804	$2	160	none	$1.64 per acre for cash; credit terms as per Harrison Land Act of 1800
1812	General Land Office Established				
1820	Land Act of 1820	$1.25	80	none	cash only
1830	Preemption Act of 1830	$1.25		160	permits squatters to purchase
1832	Land Act of 1832	$1.25	40	none	cash only
1841	General Preemption Act of 1841 $1.25	$1.25	40	160	preemption – cash only
1854	Graduation Act	$0,125	40	none	price progressively reduced on unsold lands to 12.5 cents per acre after 30 years
1862	Homestead Act	free	40	160	$10 registration fee; 5 years continuous residence on land for full title
1873	Timber Culture Act	free	160	160	cultivation of trees on $\frac{1}{4}$ of lot for title; amended in 1878 to 1/16th of lot

(continued)

TABLE 7.3 *(continued)*

Year	Law	Minimum Price per Acreage	Minimum Acreage	Maximum Acreage	Conditions and Terms
1877	Desert Land Act	$1.25		640	irrigation within 3 years; $0.25 per acre on entry, balance due upon compliance
1878	Timber and Stone Act	$2.50	40	160	stipulation that timber and stone for personal use only and not for speculation or other parties
1909	Enlarged Homestead Act	free		320	five years residence with continuous cultivation
1912	Three-Year Homestead Act	free		160	seven months residence a year for 3 years
1916	Stock Raising Homestead Act	free		640	on land only suitable for grazing

Source: Atack, Bateman, and Parker (2000).

What may have begun as a intended set policy, however, shifted numerous times over the antebellum period and later, generally in more liberal directions (see Table 7.3).[45] From 1796 to 1820, the government provided credit to purchasers, but this ended following the panic of 1819 and numerous defaults, but the growth of the banking system did minimize its impact. Other dimensions, however, went into a liberalized direction. The pace at which land was surveyed and made available increased. The Preemption Act of 1841, following a decade of more individualized legislation in which title was not specified beforehand, permitted settlers (squatters) to purchase settled lands before they would be auctioned, allowing them to keep the value of improvements made before title was legalized. The minimum size of purchases fell from 640 acres in 1796 to 40 acres as of 1832, before postbellum adjustments were made due

Feller, *The Public Lands in Jacksonian Politics* (Madison: University of Wisconsin Press, 1984).
[45] Gates, *Public Land Law.*

to requirements for larger holdings, for desert lands, timber culture, and related matters. With the minimum price per acre cut from $2 in 1796 to $1.25 after 1820, the minimum purchase price for a plot fell from $1,280 in 1796 to $50 in 1832. Other policies that made land more available followed. The Graduation Act of 1854 established that land not yet sold could be sold at a price below $1.25, with the price prorated based on the length of time before sale (30 cents per acre after thirty years). Additionally, in 1862, the Homestead Act (which was extended or liberalized several times more before 1920) provided 160 acres for each family head who either resided on land for five years or who paid $1.25 per acre after 6 months' residence. That the westward movement accelerated over the nineteenth century, and that more individuals from lower income groups were able to acquire land was to no small degree attributable to the liberal land policies.

The government's choice between a high price and a low price land policy had a number of implications. Low prices or free land would make it easy for more people to acquire land, attracting more people to the West, either initially as landowners, or else as tenants with the hopes of becoming landowners in the future. Low prices would mean, in general, low revenues, leading to more reliance on alternative sources of income such as tariffs, which the Northeast preferred. The encouragement to westward movement of workers would reduce the available labor supply and raise wage rates in the areas of outflow (which manufacturing interest in the Northeast would not like). The maintenance of liberal land policies was certainly not predestined in a complex political environment, but ultimately the highly democratic political institutions and the well founded belief that such policies would enhance returns to labor, plus the gains from immigration, may have been decisive.

That not everyone accepted the case for a liberal land policy, and that even in a country with labor scarcity it might not be advocated or adopted, is illustrated by the arguments for a high land price and or slow settlement policy offered by two renowned economists: the American Henry Charles Carey and the Englishman Edward Gibbon Wakefield.[46]

---

[46] See Henry Charles Carey, *Principles of Political Economy*, 4 pts. in 3 vols. (Philadelphia: Carey, Lea and Blanchard, 1837–40), and the discussion in Joseph Dorfman, *The Economic Mind in American Civilization* 5 vols. (New York: Viking Press, 1947). For Wakefield's arguments see Edward Gibbon Wakefield, *Letter from Sydney: The Principal Town of Australia, Together with the Outline of a System of Colonization* (London: J. Cross, 1829) and Edward Gibbon Wakefield, "A View of the Art of Colonization with Present Reference to the British Empire," in *Letters Between a Statesman and a*

Carey argued for high land prices to slow the pace of settlement, to benefit from the positive externalities he attributed to higher population density by maintaining people in urban and previously settled areas. A more influential set of policies, both in theory and in its effect upon policymakers, came from Wakefield. Wakefield was interested in British settlement of Australia and New Zealand, and thought that their growth and development would be aided by ensuring a labor force in older areas, while slowing down the pace of settlement by owners of land in the newer areas. This policy entailed a high price ("sufficient price") to limit the movement of labor from the older areas, with the use of funds collected tied to the payment to help subsidize new immigrants. Thus, Wakefield's proposals would have served to attract immigrants and yet create concentrations of labor with geographically limited settlement. Such a policy was in fact introduced in parts of both Australia and New Zealand, but, given the adaptability of institutions in response to the desires of smallholders, the land size requirements were reduced, and Wakefield's policies did not become a permanent fixture in either place.[47]

Another, and more long-lived, example of where Wakefield's ideas were embraced was in Brazil. In that country, after the grants policy (which also had provision for purchase of land at relatively low prices) of the colonial government had been abolished at independence in 1822, squatting became the dominant means by which individuals of all classes carved land to cultivate or settle on from virgin territory. These arrangements were generally not recognized under the law, and came to be viewed as a significant obstacle to the growth of coffee production and development in general. Coffee plantations needed well defined and secure rights to their land, but also required labor. The land law of 1850, the original draft of which was proposed in 1842, dealt with these issues in the ways prescribed by Wakefield.[48] Public lands were to be offered at high prices,

---

Colonist (London: J. W. Parker, 1849). Carey was familiar with Wakefield's writings. Wakefield had argued that the Spanish had failed in the Americas because of the absence of sufficient concentration of land. See Peter Burroughs, "Wakefield and the Ripon Land Regulations of 1831," *Historical Studies* 11 (April 1965): 452–66. While Carey apparently had little direct impact on land policy, Wakefield's ideas was implemented in several cases, although of limited success.

47 On Australia see Stephen H. Roberts, *History of Australian Land Settlement, 1788–1920* (Melbourne: Macmillan, 1968 [1924]); and J. M. Powell and M. Williams, *Australian Space, Australian Time; Geographic Perspectives* (Melbourne: Oxford University Press, 1975); and for New Zealand, see W. R. Jourdain, *Land Legislation and Settlement in New Zealand* (Wellington: W. A. G. Skinner, 1925); and J. D. N. McDonald, "New Zealand Land Legislation," *Historical Studies* 5 (November 1952): 195–209.

48 See Emilia Viotti de Costa, *The Brazilian Empire: Myths and Histories* (Chicago: University of Chicago Press, 1985).

with requirements that all plots purchased be surveyed at the expense of the purchaser. Although early drafts of the law provided for a land tax, which together with revenue from land sales and fees for surveying, was intended to pay for the subsidies to immigrants from abroad, the tax was dropped in the final legislation. The impact of the law was to seriously limit access to public lands for ordinary people, including immigrants, and aided elites due both to their differential capability of obtaining land and by lowering labor costs. Whether or not the land law of 1850 was a more effective stimulus to immigration than a policy of easy access to land would have been is unclear, but its particulars suggest that its passage and maintenance over time may have been at least partially due to the extreme political and economic inequality that prevailed in Brazil. Here, as in many other countries in Latin America, elites were more capable of shaping policies and institutions to serve their interests than in societies with more democracy and greater equality. The role of political power differences is crucial to understanding decisions made, but, it is argued, the nature of political power is itself influenced by the basic resource endowments.

As we have stressed, virtually all the economies in the Americas had ample supplies of public lands during the nineteenth century, especially when one acknowledges that land traditionally occupied and worked by Native Americans as community property was often viewed as public land – and as such completely unencumbered when depopulation or migration shifted long-time occupants away. Since the respective governments of each colony, province, or nation were regarded as the owners of this resource, they were able to influence the distribution of wealth, as well as the pace of settlement for effective production, by implementing policies to control the availability of land, set land prices, establish minimum or maximum acreages, provide credit for such purposes, and design tax systems on land. Because agriculture was the dominant sector throughout the Americas during the nineteenth century, questions of how best to employ this public resource for the national interest, and how to make the land available for private use, were widely recognized as highly important and often became the subject of protracted political debates and struggles. Land policy was also used as a policy instrument to influence the size of the labor force, both by encouraging immigration through making land readily available and by influencing the regional distribution of labor (or the supply of wage labor) through limiting access and setting land prices.

The United States never experienced major obstacles in this regard, and, as noted, the terms of land acquisition became easier over the course of the nineteenth century.[49] The Homestead Act of 1862, which essentially made land free in plots suitable for family farms to all those who settled and worked the land for a specified period, was perhaps the culmination of this policy of promoting broad access to land. Canada pursued similar policies: the Dominion Lands Act of 1872 closely resembled the Homestead Act in both spirit and substance.[50] Argentina and Brazil (as discussed) and also Chile, each instituted similar changes as a means to encourage immigration, but while these efforts had some benefits they were less successful than the programs in the United States and Canada.[51] Thus in Argentina where a comprehensive land law was passed in 1876, and followed by an extremely restrictive – applying only to Patagonia – Homestead Act in 1884, a number of factors seem to explain the difference in outcomes. The elites of Buenos Aires, where the city and province accounted for 40 percent of Argentina's population at the end of the nineteenth century, had interests that favored keeping scarce labor in the province, if not the capital city, were, because of the larger share of the urban population, much more effective at weakening programs than were their North American urban counterparts. Although the debates over the land laws made frequent reference to the examples provided by the country's North American neighbors, the Argentine laws generally conveyed public lands to private owners in much larger and concentrated

[49] See Gates, *Public Land Law* for a comprehensive overview of United States land policy. See also Atack, et al., "Northern Agriculture."

[50] Discussions of Canadian land policy include Chester Martin, *Dominion Land Policy*, (Toronto: McClelland and Stewart, 1973 [1938]); Carl E. Solberg, *The Prairies and the Pampas: Agrarian Policy in Canada and Argentina, 1880–1913* (Stanford: Stanford University Press, 1987); Jeremy Adelman, *Frontier Development: Land, Labor, and Capital on Wheatlands of Argentina and Canada, 1890–1914* (Oxford: Oxford University Press, 1994); and Richard Pomfret, *The Economic Development of Canada*, (Toronto: Methuen, 1981).

[51] On Argentina, see Adelman, *Frontier Development*; Samuel Amaral, *The Rise of Capitalism on the Pampas: The Estancias of Buenos Aires, 1785–1870* (Cambridge: Cambridge University Press, 1998); and Solberg, *Prairies and the Pampas*, and on Chile, see Solberg, "Discriminatory Frontier Land Policy." In addition to Viotti da Costa, *The Brazilian Empire* on Brazilian land policy see also Warren Dean, "Latifundia and Land Policy in Nineteenth Century Brazil," *Hispanic American Historical Review* 51 (November 1971): 602–25; the excellent discussion in Adelman, *Frontier Development*, as well as B. J. Barickman, *A Bahian Counterpoint: Sugar, Tobacco, Casava, and Slavery in the Recôncava, 1780–1860* (Stanford: Stanford University Press, 1998); Schwartz, *Sugar Plantations*; William R. Summerhill, *Order Against Progress: Government, Foreign Investment, and Railroads in Brazil, 1854–1913* (Stanford: Stanford University Press, 2003); and Lee J. Alston, Gary D. Libecap, and Bernardo Mueller, *Titles, Conflict and Land Use: The Development of Property Rights as Land Reform on the Brazilian Amazon Frontier* (Ann Arbor: University of Michigan Press, 1999).

holdings than did the policies in the United States and Canada. The processes by which large landholdings might have broken up in the absence of scale economies may have operated very slowly in Argentina: and once the land was in private hands, the potential value of land in raising or harvesting livestock may have been set too high. Such constraints were exacerbated by the underdevelopment of mortgage and financial institutions more generally.[52] Since these nations maintained policies similar to those by the Spanish regarding education and other matters, they did not greatly benefit from growth after independence.

Indeed, as the growing volume and diversity of international trade during the mid- and late-nineteenth century increased the value of land, there seems to have been a wave of policy changes throughout Latin America that not only eschewed the evidently successful U.S. example of liberal land policies, but also worked to increase the concentration of ownership. At the end of the nineteenth century in Brazil, the abolition of slavery brought about an increased demand for European labor from Spain, Portugal, and Italy to produce coffee for export, now on smaller units than the plantations.[53] This demand for labor led to the provision of subsidies of transportation, cash, or land to attract migrants from southern Europe. Another pattern, but with limited subsidized labor from Spain and Italy, developed in Argentina and in Chile, where slavery had ended much earlier and plantation crops had not developed to the extent that they had in Brazil.

In Table 3.1 we presented estimates for four countries of the fractions of household heads, (or of a near equivalent measure) that owned land in agricultural areas in the late nineteenth and early twentieth centuries. The figures indicate enormous differences across the countries in the prevalence of land ownership among the adult male population in rural areas. On the eve of the Mexican Revolution, the figures from the 1910 census

---

[52] It is generally thought that the introduction of livestock to Argentina, when the Spanish first arrived in the sixteenth century, was the basis for widespread herds of feral cattle that were present during the nineteenth century and would virtually be harvested. Such production of animal products (hides and beef) was associated with scale economies and did not require much in the way of labor. These conditions may have increased the economic viability of large estates where labor was scarce and land was abundant. In contrast, because the major crops produced in the expansion of the northern United States and Canada were grains, whose production was relatively labor intensive and characterized by quite limited scale economies, the policy of encouraging smalholding was effective. See Adelman, *Frontier Development*.

[53] On the post-slave adjustment in Brazil, see Peter L. Eisenberg, *The Sugar Industry in Pernambuco: Modernization Without Change, 1840–1910* (Berkeley: University of California Press, 1974).

suggest that only 2.4 percent of household heads in rural Mexico owned land. The number is astoundingly low. The dramatic land policy measures in Mexico at the end of the nineteenth century may have succeeded in privatizing most of the public lands, but they left the vast majority of the rural population without any land ownership at all. The evidence obviously conforms well with the idea that in societies that began with extreme inequality, such as Mexico, institutions evolved so as to greatly advantage the elite in access to economic opportunities, and they thus contributed to the persistence of that extreme inequality.[54]

In contrast, the proportion of adult males owning land in rural areas was quite high in the United States, at just below 75 percent in 1900. The prevalence of land ownership was markedly lower in the South, where blacks were disproportionately concentrated, with the share for whites being high. The overall picture for the United States is one of a series of liberal land policies, leading up to the Homestead Act of 1862, providing broad access to this fundamental type of economic opportunity. Canada had an even better record, with nearly 90 percent of household heads owning the agricultural lands they occupied in 1901. The estimates of landholding in these two countries support the notion that land policies made a difference, especially when compared to Argentina. The rural regions of Argentina constitute a set of frontier provinces, where one would expect higher rates of ownership than in Buenos Aires. The numbers, however, suggest a much lower prevalence of land ownership than in the two northernmost North American economies.[55] Nevertheless, all of these countries were far more effective than Mexico in making land ownership available to the general population. The contrast between the United States and Canada, with their practices of offering easy access to small units of land, and the rest of the Americas, as seen in the contrast with Argentina and Mexico, is consistent with the hypothesis that the initial extent of inequality influenced the way in which institutions evolved

---

[54] For discussions of Mexican land policy, see George McCutchen McBride, *The Land Systems of Mexico* (New York: America Geographic Society, 1923); Frank Tannenbaum, *The Mexican Agrarian Revolution* (New York: Macmillan, 1929); and Robert Holden, *Mexico and the Survey of Public Lands. The Management of Modernization, 1876–1911* (DeKalb: Northern Illinois University Press, 1994).

[55] Our work with the data from the 1914 Argentina census yields the same qualitative results. It is worth noting that the proportions of families that owned land are exaggerated by the 1895 census figures. A close examination of the manuscripts indicates that double counting, in which both the husband and wife were listed as landowners, was prevalent in many parts of Argentina.

and in so doing helped foster persistence in the degree of inequality over time.[56]

IV

Some brief descriptions of land policies elsewhere in the British Empire will demonstrate the similarity of patterns of change with those in the Americas. Australia apparently had a relatively significant population of aborigines when British settlement began in 1788, a population number

---

[56] We have omitted here discussion of other Latin American countries for which we have some information on land policy and its changes. For example, on Colombia see Charles W. Berquist, *Coffee and Conflict in Columbia, 1886–1910* (Durham: Duke University Press, 1998); David Bushnell, *The Making of Modern Colombia: A Nation in Spite of Itself* (Berkeley: University of California Press, 1993); William Paul McGreevey, *An Economic History of Colombia, 1845–1930* (New York: Cambridge University Press, 1971); and Marco Palacious, *Coffee in Colombia, 1850–1970: An Economic, Social and Political History* (New York: Cambridge University Press, 1980). On Peru see Keith A. Davies, *Landowners in Colonial Peru* (Austin: University of Texas Press, 1984); and Nils Jacobson, *Mirages of Transition: The Peruvian Altiplano, 1780–1930* (Berkeley: University of California Press, 1993). On Costa Rica see Lowell Gudmundson, *Costa Rica Before Coffee: Society and Economy on the Eve of the Export Boom* (Baton Rouge: Louisiana State University Press, 1986). On Bolivia see Herbert S. Klein, *Haciendas and Ayllus: Rural Society in the Bolivian Andes in the Eighteenth and Nineteenth Centuries* (Stanford: Stanford University Press, 1993). On El Salvador see Hector Lindo-Fuentes, *Weak Foundations: The Economy of El Salvador in the Nineteenth Century* (Berkeley: University of California Press, 1990). On Guatemala see David McCreery, *Rural Guatemala, 1760–1940* (Stanford: Stanford University Press, 1994): 49–84, 197–200; on the Dominican Republic see Frank Moya Pons, *The Dominican Republic: A National History* (New Rochelle: Hispaniola Books, 1995). On Central America see Hector Perez-Brignol, *A Brief History of Central America* (Berkeley: University of California Press, 1989); William Rosberry, Lowell Gudmundson, and Mario Samper Kutschbach, eds., *Coffee, Society, and Power in Latin America* (Baltimore: Johns Hopkins University Press, 1995). On Ecuador see Ronn F. Pineo, *Social and Economic Reform in Ecuador: Life and Work in Guayaquol* (Gainesville: University of Florida Press, 1996). On Venezuela see Doug Yarrington, *A Coffee Frontier: Land, Society, and Politics in Duaca, Venezuela, 1830–1936* (Pittsburgh: University of Pittsburgh Press, 1997). There is more generally useful material in volumes covering all of Latin America. See the various volumes edited by Bethell in Leslie Bethell, ed., *The Cambridge History of Latin America*, 11 vols. (Cambridge: Cambridge University Press, 1984–2008); Victor Bulmer-Thomas, John H. Coatsworth, and Roberto Cortés Conde (eds.), *The Cambridge Economic History of Latin America*, vol. 1, *The Colonial Era and the Short Nineteenth Century* (Cambridge: Cambridge University Press, 2006); William P. Glade, *The Latin American Economies: A Study of Their Institutional Evolution* (New York: American Book, 1969); and James Lockhart and Stuart B. Schwartz, *Early Latin America: A History of Colonial Spanish America and Brazil* (Cambridge: Cambridge University Press, 1983).

not achieved by Europeans until the 1850s, and after the decline with the English arrival, the aboriginal population has still not reached the earlier total today.[57] As in the Americas, the arrival of European diseases led to a dramatic decline in the native population. The British settlement initially began with large numbers of convicts, and while there were attempts to negotiate land purchases with the aborigines, they did not work out and were soon followed by military actions to enable Europeans to acquire land. Each Australian state initially had its own land policy, but these tended to become more similar over time. While Wakefield had proposed his land policy be applied to all Australia, it was only in South Australia and Western Australia that Wakefield's policy was introduced early in settlement, and in both states it ended within several decades.[58] Initially, New South Wales, the most populous of the states, provided large grants to individuals or companies, but over time squatters, whose holdings tended to be small, were able to get permanent titles to their land. Later it was policy to permit individuals to select between 40 and 320 acres by paying one-quarter of the purchase price, the balance to be paid in three years, usually at a minimal price per acre.[59] There are several ways in which Australia resembled the United States, with a high ratio of land to population, leading to the increased ease with which whites acquired land ownership over time. There was also a high percentage of ownership of relatively small farms, although the greater importance of sheep farming in Australia created a demand for larger units to permit pastoral agriculture. And, as in the United States, the original natives were pushed from the path of settlement and often relocated on reserves. Another similarity was the development of a sugar industry in the more tropical areas of both countries. This was based at first on some form of coerced labor, slaves in Louisiana before 1860 and indentured Pacific Islanders in Queensland,

---

[57] Wray Vamplew, ed., *Australians: Historical Statistics* (Broadway: Fairfax, Syme & Weldon, 1987). For a considerably higher estimate of the aboriginal population at the time of contact, see N. Butlin, *Our Original Aggression: Aboriginal Populations of Southeastern Australia, 1788–1850* (Sydney: G. Allen and Urwin, 1983).

[58] In addition to the sources cited in note 47, see also J. M. Powell, *The Public Lands of Australia Felix: Settlement and Land Appraisal in Victoria 1834–91 with Special Reference to the Western Plains* (Melbourne: Oxford University Press, 1970); A. G. L. Shaw, *Convicts and the Colonies: A Study of Penal Transportation From Great Britain and Ireland to Australian and Other Parts of the British Empire* (London: Faber and Faber, 1966); W. A. Sinclair, *The Process of Economic Development in Australia* (Melbourne: Cheshire, 1976); and T. A. Coghlan, *Labour and Industry in Australia*, 4 vols. (Melbourne: Macmillan, 1969 [1918]).

[59] See Powell, *Public Lands*.

by the 1870s.[60] As elsewhere, these sugar-producing plantations in both nations were considerably larger that was the typical grain farm.

New Zealand, settled from Australia in the 1840s, also had a native population – the Maoris – who did not suffer as severe a demographic decline after the Europeans arrived as did the natives in Australia (and the Americas).[61] Nevertheless, with the large immigration of whites, the Maoris represented less than 10 percent of the New Zealand population within several decades of white settlement. The Maoris reached better accommodation with the British, including selling land to whites, than did the Australian aborigines, but New Zealand remained a nation with a high ratio of land to population.

Land distribution in New Zealand was determined at the state level until 1876, and land was often used as a subsidy to immigrants. Homestead provisions required a set time of residence to acquire title to land, and the governments provided credit arrangements, facilitating sales of land. After several decades it was a general policy to aim at establishing smaller units of up to 320 acres. The earlier settlement pattern was influenced by the policies proposed by Wakefield, including use of land revenues to subsidize immigration, and the selling of large units at high prices, but, as elsewhere, this policy was modified over time to permit sales of cheap land to immigrants.[62] Thus in New Zealand, as in Australia, the general pattern over time was a liberalization of Wakefield's land policy, to make land more easily accessible to smaller landholders.

Another interesting example of British colonialism, in the adjacent areas of East Africa, demonstrates the variation in British colonial policy. The settlements of Kenya and Uganda at the end of the nineteenth century generated important differences in local institutions.[63] Both areas were

[60] On the United States, see Gray, *History of Agriculture*; and J. Carlyle Sitterson, *Sugar Country: The Cane Sugar Industry in the South, 1753–1950* (Lexington: University of Kentucky Press, 1953). For Australia, see Ross Fitzgerald, *A History of Queensland From the Dreaming to 1915* (St. Lucia: University of Queensland Press, 1982); Ralph Shlomowitz et al., *Mortality and Migration in the Modern World* (Aldershot: Variorum, 1996); and Adrian Graves, *Cane and Labour: The Political Economy of the Queensland Sugar Industry, 1862–1906* (Edinburgh: Edinburgh University Press, 1993).

[61] Gordon McLauchlan, ed., *Bateman New Zealand Encyclopedia* (Auckland: David Bateman, 1984).

[62] In addition to the sources cited in note 47, see J. B. Condliffe, *New Zealand in the Making: A Survey of Economic and Social Development* (Chicago: University of Chicago Press, 1930); G. R. Hawke, *The Making of New Zealand: An Economic History* (Cambridge: Cambridge University Press, 1985); and Keith Sinclair, *A History of New Zealand* (Harmondsworth: Penguin Books, 1959).

[63] This paragraph draws upon the following books: Roland Oliver and others, eds., *History of East Africa*, vol. 2 (Oxford: Clarendon Press, 1965); Van Zwanberg and

populated almost entirely by black Africans. In Kenya, land was made available to white settlers in units of from 160 to 640 acres, with five acres allotted to Africans and Asians for one year, with no ownership rights. By 1840 Europeans were about 1 percent of the population, and owned 18 percent of the land, that which was regarded as the best land. Uganda, larger in area but with a similar African and European population mix, developed a rather different set of institutions for land distribution. There were few European settlers and landholders since, at the time of establishing the Protectorate in 1894, much of the land was given to local chiefs to be held under freehold. Unlike Kenya, with European-owned production of plantation crops, such as coffee, for export using African labor, Uganda produced mainly cotton on small-scale peasant farms. In part these differences between Kenya and Uganda have been attributed to differences in climate and soil type, leading to the quite distinct set of institutions and political controls.

An earlier British African settlement with large amounts of land available, South Africa, finally conquered from the Dutch in 1814, had a somewhat different pattern.[64] Slave labor was imported from elsewhere, mainly the Indian Ocean region, but important controls were imposed on the local natives, coerced into labor for whites by a combination of dispossession and limits on land purchases. Slavery ended in 1834, by the British Emancipation Act. Whites represented a higher percentage of the population than in East Africa, about 33 percent in the Cape Colony in 1836, and lower for the overall colony, but as in Kenya, whites took

A. King, *An Economic History of Kenya and Uganda, 1800–1970* (London: Macmillan, 1975); Mwangi Wa-Githumo, *Land and Nationalism: The Impact of Land Expropriation and Land Grievances Upon the Rise and Development of Nationalist Movements in Kenya, 1885–1939* (Washington, D.C.: University Press of America, 1981); and William R. Ochieng', *A History of Kenya* (London: Macmillan, 1985). We have greatly benefited from the research of Tricia Redeker Hepner on these African colonies.

[64] See Charles H. Feinstein, *An Economic History of South Africa: Conquest, Discrimination and Development* (Cambridge: Cambridge University Press, 2005); Richard Elphick and Hermann Gilmore, *The Shaping of South African Society, 1965–1840*, 2nd ed. (Middletown: Wesleyan University Press, 1989); Monica Wilson and Leonard Thompson, eds., *The Oxford History of South Africa*, 2 vols. (New York: Oxford University Press, 1969); Leslie Clement Duly, *British Land Policy at the Cape: A Study of Administrative Policies in the Empire* (Durham: Duke University Press, 1968); Robert Ross, *Beyond the Pale: Essays on the History of Colonial South Africa* (Hanover: Wesleyan University Press, 1993); and Ellen Hellman, ed., *Handbook on Race Relations in South Africa* (Cape Town: Oxford University Press, 1949).

measures to own the land to produce for export.[65] By 1780, landholding was generally regarded as reserved for whites, with coerced labor left for slaves and "free" resident Africans. Later, by 1913, legislation placed the native population on reserves, which accounted for 7 percent of the land, where they remained laborers for white planters and miners.[66]

V

This chapter treats the colonization of the Americas as a "natural experiment" that can be exploited to learn more about where institutions come from. Its focus has been on the long-term evolution of immigration and land and labor policies or institutions, commonly recognized as important for paths of economic development. Much work remains to be done, but our results seem consistent with the notion that the colonies were powerfully influenced by their factor endowments in how they chose to formulate their policies regarding immigration and land. During the colonial period, Spanish America benefited from being centered on regions with rather large populations of Native Americans, and was accordingly much less dependent on immigration, both voluntary and involuntary, than other areas. Indeed, Spain maintained very severe restrictions on who and how many could come. Brazil and the islands in the Caribbean, specializing in sugar and a few other tropical crops well suited for production on large slave plantations, relied heavily on importing slaves to deal with their labor scarcity problem. It was only the northern part of North America that had to obtain the bulk of its labor force through voluntary migration from Europe. Rather than coincidental, or due to their British national heritage, the innovation of the institution of indentured servitude and the liberal offering of land grants to migrants seems to have been policy instruments designed to solve the problem of labor scarcity and allow the colonies to take better advantage of their abundance of land and other resources.

After the independence movements swept across the Americas, there was a mixture of both continuity and change in the strategic land and immigration institutions. The United States, followed by Canada,

[65] Robert Montgomery Martin, *History of the Colonies of the British Empire* (London: Dawsons, 1967 [1834]); Feinstein, *An Economic History* provides an estimate of about 10 percent European in all of South Africa, c. 1850. The first census, 1904, gave a figure of 21.6 percent white.

[66] Feinstein, *An Economic History*.

continued to actively pursue immigrants from abroad. There was no longer a need or ability to acquire indentured servants, but both countries employed very liberal land policies to attract migrants. Again, it is striking that the regions most supportive of liberal land policies, and other policies that migrants were sensitive to, were the areas in the west of the United States and Canada which were most labor scarce. Of course, these boundaries evolved over time with settlement. The evidence for the endogeneity of these policies appears formidable. In contrast, the new nations of Spanish heritage (or Portuguese, in the case of Brazil), who were now free to formulate policies to suit their own interests, began to actively seek immigrants. Like their neighbors to the north (the United States and Canada), countries such as Brazil and Argentina were seemingly labor-scarce and abundant in available land for agricultural and other purposes from early in settlement.

It is curious, however, that the programs they adopted were far less generous in offering land to immigrants, or local residents than was the United States. This parsimony may be related to the general increase throughout Latin America in the value of land suitable for the production of agricultural exports, as was the movement in many other nations with large Native American populations regarding policies that, in effect, shifted control of land from Indians to elites. It may also be related to the extreme political and economic inequality that prevailed throughout Latin America, and that we have elsewhere attributed in large part to factor endowments broadly conceived.

8

Politics and Banking Systems
by Stephen Haber

One topic that earlier work did not fully explore, however, was banking and finance. This essay is to fill that lacuna. Specifically, it examines how differences in the distribution of human capital gave rise to vast differences across countries in terms of political power, how those differences in political power affected the policies governing banks, and how those policies, in turn, shaped the size and competitive structure of banking systems.

The comparative development of banking systems is an important topic for studying the effects of differences in factor endowments. In the first place, there is a large body of empirical research that demonstrates that the size and structure of the financial system exerts an independent, causal effect on the structure and growth of the real economy.[1] In the second place, banking systems are notoriously sensitive to the specific features

---

[1] Robert G. King and Ross Levine, "Finance and Growth: Schumpeter Might Be Right," *Quarterly Journal of Economics* 108 (August 1993a): 717–37; Robert G. King and Ross Levine, "Finance Entrepreneurship, and Growth." *Journal of Monetary Economics*, 32 (December 1993b): 513–42; Ross Levine and Sarah Zervos, "Stock Markets, Banks, and Economic Growth," *American Economic Review* 88 (June 1998): 537–58; Raghuram Rajan and Luigi Zingales, "Financial Dependence and Growth," *American Economic Review* 88 (June 1998): 559–86; Jeffrey Wurgler, "Financial Markets and the Allocation of Capital." *Journal of Financial Economics* 58 (June 2000): 187–214; Thorsten Beck, Ross Levine, and Norman Loayza, "Finance and the Sources of Growth," *Journal of Financial Economics*, 58 (Issues 1–2, 2000): 261–300; Thorsten Beck and Ross Levine, "Industry Growth and Capital Allocation: Does Having a Market-or-Bank System Matter?" *Journal of Financial Economics*, 64 (May 2002): 147–180; Sandra E. Black and Philip E. Strahan, "The Division of Spoils: Rent-Sharing and Discrimination in a Regulated Industry," *American Economic Review* 91 (September 2001): 814–31; Sandra E. Black and Philip E. Strahan, "Entrepreneurship and Bank Credit Availability." *Journal of Finance* 57 (December 2002): 2807–33; Raymond Fisman and Inessa Love,

of government regulation. The business of banking is the business of writing and trading contracts, and the value of those contracts – whether they are between bankers and debtors, between bankers and minority shareholders, or between bankers and depositors – depends on the degree to which the parties in control of the government choose to enforce them.

In the third place, bankers are in a position to influence the content of the regulations governing their industry in ways that would be difficult in other sectors. Governments need to borrow; and unless there is a vibrant secondary market for government debt, they typically borrow from banks. Thus, the parties in control of the government are not disinterested arbiters of property rights in banking: they simultaneously regulate the banks and borrow from them.

Unless there is some powerful countervailing force, the parties in control of the government have strong incentives to trade policies that generate rents for bankers for access to debt financing for the state. Making matters worse, the highly technical nature of bank regulation makes it relatively easy for the parties in control of the government to portray rent-generating policies as being in the public interest: usury laws can be presented as consumer protection; legal ceilings on deposit interest rates can be portrayed as encouraging bank stability; arcane procedures to obtain a bank charter can be portrayed as protecting the public from fly-by-night operators.

Making matters worse still, the public at large cannot easily coordinate against the distributional coalition formed by bankers and politicians. The problem is that the public at large has multiple, conflicting interests when it comes to the banking system. Some citizens are bank debtors. Others are bank creditors, by virtue of being depositors or note-holders. Still other citizens are minority shareholders in the banks. Many citizens may even believe that they have no stake at all in the distributional game that is being played, because they are neither bank creditors, debtors, nor minority shareholders. This group often finds out, however, that when a financial crisis occurs they have a very large stake indeed: as taxpayers they may bear the cost of bailing out some or all of the other groups.

The implication is clear: the property rights system that structures banking is not a passive response to some efficiency criterion, demanded

"Financial Development and Growth in the Short- and Long-Run," NBER Working Paper, no. 10236 (2004); "Does Local Financial Development Matter?" *Quarterly Journal of Economics* 119 (August 2004): 929–96; Nicola Cetorelli and Philip E. Strahan, "Finance as a Barrier to Entry: Bank Competition and Industry Structure in U.S. Local Markets," *Journal of Finance* 61 (February 2006): 437–61.

in an anonymous "market" for institutions; rather it is the product of political deals. The basis of those deals are bargains that are struck over which laws are passed, which judges are appointed, which groups of people have which licenses to contract with whom, for what, and on what terms. The result is sets of coalitions that, in ways both blatant and subtle, influence the regulation of entry, the standards of accounting and disclosure, the ease with which contracts can be enforced, and the flow of credit and its terms. These relationships are exceptionally complex – they involve sets of explicit trades and implicit alliances – but at root they are about the creation and distribution of economic rents and the maintenance of political power.

These deals are not neutral with respect to economic growth. Some deals will result in small and concentrated banking systems that allocate credit narrowly. Indeed, they may extend loans to a circle that extends no farther than the bank directors and their families. Other deals will result in large and competitive banking systems that allocate credit broadly, thereby providing credit access to firms and entrepreneurs who can use it most productively.

Which deal a society hits upon depends on the viability of the coalition that supports it. Some deals are unviable because no coalition can be formed. Imagine, for example, that the parties in control of the government have an extremely short planning horizon and no limits on their discretion: there is virtually no offer that can be made to investors to deploy their capital in a bank, because expropriation is a dead certainty as soon as the bank opens its doors. Some are unviable because they leave politically crucial actors out of the coalition. Imagine, for example, a coalition that includes the parties in control of the government, bankers, and minority shareholders to create and share rents by limiting entry. The deal that they have struck is only viable so long as debtors (or potential debtors, who have been rationed out of credit markets) are unable to vote for public officials who promise to ease regulatory barriers to bank entry in order to promote the expansion of credit. That is to say, this distributional coalition is stable only if the political power of nonelite groups is limited by political institutions such as restrictions on suffrage, indirect election of legislators, malapportionment, or requirements for legislative supermajorities.

None of this is to say that the demand for credit does not exert an influence on the size and structure of banking systems. Obviously, societies in which income is narrowly distributed (because human capital is unequally distributed) will generate less demand for finance than societies with more equitable distributions of income: in the former society, the rich can mobilize capital through informal networks, while everyone else is so poor that they have nothing to put up as collateral.

It is to say, however, that the distribution of human capital does not just work on credit markets through the demand side. The supply of financial intermediation is affected as well. Where human capital is narrowly distributed, elites craft political institutions that amplify their power and produce laws and regulations that limit competition in banking. The result is narrow financial development: bank charters are granted sparingly, and the banks that exist serve as the treasury arms of mercantile or industrial conglomerates. Why, after all, should bankers extend credit to entrepreneurs who will challenge the dominance of the firms they control in the nonfinancial sector? Even if bankers do not have direct nonfinancial interests themselves, why should they extend credit to entrepreneurs who will erode the rents of their established borrowers when doing so would reduce the probability of repayment?

It is also to say that where human capital is more broadly distributed, elites attempt to strike deals that limit competition in banking – but those deals are not viable. Potential debtors are able to undermine these deals by using their ability to demand increased access to credit through the political system, most particularly by voting for legislators who promise to oppose rent-seeking by bankers.

In order to explore these hypotheses the focus is on the histories of three New World societies – Brazil, Mexico, and the United States. Brazil had a warm, wet climate and fertile soils – conditions that were ideal for growing sugar. Brazil lacked, however, an indigenous population that could be drafted to work on sugar plantations. As a result, Brazil became the most fully developed slave society in the Americas. Even after Brazilian sugar lost its competitive position in the world market, plantation slavery thrived on the country's growing coffee *fazendas*. Not surprisingly, more African slaves were transported to Brazil than to any other New World destination, the Brazilian slave trade did not end until the British Navy put a stop to it in the 1850s, and Brazil was the last country in the Americas to emancipate its slaves (in 1888). In short, if there was an unequal society whose roots were located in plantation slavery, Brazil was it. One would therefore not expect Brazil's elites to have crafted banking regulations that encouraged competitive credit markets. As we shall explore below, they quite deliberately used their lock on the political system to block the spread of banking institutions – except for the ones under their control.

Colonial Mexico lacked Brazil's soils and climate, but it did have immense silver wealth and a large indigenous population that could be mobilized to work for the Spanish colonists through a draft rotary labor system that antedated the conquest by centuries – the *coatequitl*. That labor institution was itself an outcome of a pre-colonial, landlord-peasant social structure, in which a vast peasantry worked the domains of a native nobility. It was an easy matter for the Spaniards to transform the *coatequitl* into a labor institution recognized in Spanish law, the *encomienda*. It was also an easy matter for the Spaniards to acquire the lands that had been held by the native nobility – by marriage, by purchase, or by coercion – in order to create immense estates. Finally, it was an easy matter for the first émigrés to get the Spanish Crown to put binding limits on emigration from Spain, so as to minimize competition for native labor, which became increasingly scarce as European diseases took their toll. This is not to say that colonial Mexico lacked small farms. Indeed, they existed in such multitude that no one has tried to count them. It is to say, however, that at independence Mexico was a strikingly unequal society: a small Europeanized elite sat on top of a population of illiterate, innumerate, and politically unsophisticated Native Americans and *mestizos*. The political system represented the interests of that Europeanized elite. We would not expect, therefore, that the laws governing banking would encourage the creation of financial institutions designed to provide credit to Mexico's millions of small farmers.

The United States had none of the attractions of Brazil or Mexico. What it did have was land that was suitable for growing grains and an indigenous population whose low density and fractured political organization allowed it to be easily pushed out of the way. The labor force, created by white immigrants from Europe, resulted in a colonial society that was vastly more equal, and that equality was reflected in America's political institutions at independence.

This is not to suggest that America's elites did not try to blunt the political power of ordinary citizens. That was the whole point of creating a bicameral legislature, and selecting the upper house by indirect election. It was also the motivation behind the creation of the institution of the presidency – an indirectly-elected, temporary monarch who could veto any populist legislation that got past the indirectly elected Senate. The President and the Senate then appointed the Supreme Court, crucially without any input from the directly elected lower house of congress. Institutions at the state level had a similar anti-populist design, but added another twist: states decided the laws regarding suffrage, and all of them initially imposed restrictions based on wealth or social standing.

This is also not to suggest that America's elites did not use their political power in order to generate rents for themselves by constraining access to finance. As we shall discuss in detail, the initial organization of U.S.

banking was predicated on explicit deals between bankers and politicians, both at the state and national level, to create and share rents.

It is to suggest, however, that the underlying distribution of human capital in the United States was inconsistent with an elite-dominated political economy. Elites in the United States were forced to bargain with citizens. One reflection of this was the political annihilation of the Federalist Party. A second reflection was the ascendance of the Jacksonians, America's first genuinely populist political movement. A third reflection was that the laws that blocked access to finance by limiting the number of banks began to be undermined as early as the 1810s. America's bankers did not, of course, passively accept the idea that they should allow all of their rents to be dissipated by competition. They found ways to join coalitions – ironically, with anti-bank populists – that afforded them local monopolies and quasi-monopolies. The history of U.S. banking is, in fact, the story of how these monopolies were progressively made smaller and their rents dissipated – until they were finally undermined entirely in the 1990s.

The resulting competitive structure of the Mexican, Brazilian, and American banking systems could not have been more different. The banking systems of Brazil and Mexico were composed of, at most, a few dozen banks – and until very recently these primarily lent to enterprises controlled by their own board members. The U.S. banking system was composed of tens of thousands of banks, most of which were legally enjoined from opening branches until the 1970s. In Brazil and Mexico, until well into the twentieth century a single privately-owned bank was vested with sets of lucrative privileges, in exchange for which it served as the financial agent of the government. America's political and financial elites also set up a super-bank on this model – but it was undermined by the combination of populism and federalism. In fact, this experiment was carried out two times in American history – and it always produced the same result: the super-bank was driven out of existence.

The United States

Governments need banks in order to finance their survival, and banks need governments to grant them the privileges that make them attractive investments. America's first chartered bank, the Bank of North America (BNA), was not an exception to this general pattern. In order to finance the war for independence, in 1781 the Congress of the Confederation granted a charter to a group of shareholders to create a commercial bank that would also serve as the government's fiscal agent, the BNA. Right from the beginning, however, the idea of a privately-owned, national bank that had a special relationship with the central government ran into trouble. The fundamental problem was that the BNA competed with local banks that operated without charters (meaning that their shareholders had unlimited liability). The wedge that local banks were able to drive between the BNA and its charter was that the Articles of Confederation were ambiguous as to whether the central government actually had the authority to charter a bank. The BNA therefore had to be rechartered by the state of Pennsylvania. No sooner was this charter granted, however, that, at the behest of local unchartered banks, the BNA came under attack in the Pennsylvania State Legislature, which revoked the bank's charter in 1785. The legislature restored the charter two years later, following an agreement by the BNA to accept a series of restrictions on its activities that effectively meant that it could not serve as the banker to the central government.[2]

The Articles of Confederation were soon replaced by the Constitution of 1789, but the basic problem of state finance remained. The new central government lost little time in chartering a bank to replace the BNA – the Bank of the United States (BUS), founded in 1791. The BUS was a commercial bank, owned and operated by wealthy Federalist financiers, fully capable of taking deposits and making loans to private parties. The federal government subscribed twenty percent of the BUS' capital, without paying for those shares: instead, it received a loan from the bank and then repaid the loan out of the stream of dividends it received as a shareholder in the bank. In exchange, the BUS received a set of valuable privileges that were afforded no other bank: the right to limited liability for its shareholders; the right to hold federal government specie balances; the right to charge the federal government interest on loans from the bank (notes issued by the bank to cover federal expenses); and the right to open branches throughout the country. In short, the BUS was the product of a deal: the bankers financed the state, and the state gave the bankers a lucrative concession.

Had America's political institutions granted the federal government the sole right to charter banks, the BUS might have completely dominated the financial system. The federal organization of the U.S. government prevented that from happening, however. Under the Constitution, the states

[2] Howard Bodenhorn, *State Banking in Early America: A New Economic History* (New York: Oxford University Press, 2003): 128.

lost both the right to tax imports and exports and the right to issue paper money – both of those powers were vested with the federal government, in exchange for which the federal government assumed the considerable debts that the states had amassed under the Articles of Confederation. Having been denied their traditional sources of finance, the states began to search for alternative sources of revenue. Ironically, the Tenth Amendment to the Constitution provided one: any power not explicitly delegated to the federal government, or explicitly denied to the states, resided with the states. The Constitution said that states did not have the right to issue paper money – but it said nothing about the right of states to charter banks of issue, whose banknotes would circulate as currency.

States, therefore, had strong fiscal incentives to sell bank charters – and strong incentives to do whatever was necessary to maximize the value of those charters. States obviously received no charter fees from banks incorporated in other states: they therefore prohibited interstate branching.[3] States could earn income both by selling the charter and by owning stock in the bank: they therefore were almost universally major owners of bank shares, and they typically paid for those shares with a loan from the bank, which they then repaid out of the dividend stream. States received a larger stream of dividends when the banks earned monopoly rents: they therefore constrained the number of banks within their own borders. States might extract additional income from banks by threatening them with new entrants to the banking market: they therefore accepted "bonuses" from incumbent banks to deny the charter applications of potential competitors.[4] Not surprisingly, circa 1810–30, bank dividends and bank taxes often accounted for one-third of total state revenues.[5]

Banking in the Early Republican United States was therefore characterized by segmented monopolies. The four largest cities in the United States in 1800 – Boston, Philadelphia, New York, and Baltimore – had only two banks apiece. Smaller markets typically had only one bank, if they had a bank at all. As Table 8.1 shows, in 1800 there were only 28

[3] Randall S. Kroszner and Philip E. Strahan, "What Drives Deregulation? Economics and Politics of the Relaxation of Bank Branching Restrictions," *Quarterly Journal of Economics* 114 (November 1999): 1437–67.

[4] Bodenhorn, *State Banking in Early America*, 17, 244.

[5] Richard Sylla, John B. Legler, and John Wallis, "Banks and State Public Finance in the New Republic: The United States, 1790–1860," *Journal of Economic History* 47 (June 1987): 391–403; John Wallis, Richard Sylla, and John B. Legler, "The Interaction of Taxation and Regulation in Nineteenth Century U.S. Banking," in *The Regulated Economy: A Historical Approach to Political Economy*, eds. Claudia Goldin and Gary D. Libecap: 122–144 (Chicago: University of Chicago Press, 1994).

TABLE 8.1. *State-chartered Banks in the United States, 1790–1835*

	New England		South		U.S. Total	
Year	Number of Banks	Authorized Capital (Millions, USD)	Number of Banks	Authorized Capital (Millions, USD)	Number of Banks	Authorized Capital (Millions, USD)
1790	1	0.8			3	3.1
1795	11	4.1			20	13.5
1800	17	5.5			28	17.4
1805	45	13.2	6	3.5	71	38.9
1810	52	15.5	13	9.1	102	56.2
1815	71	24.5	22	17.2	212	115.2
1820	97	28.3	25	28.6	327	159.7
1825	159	42.2	32	33.3	330	156.1
1830	186	48.8	35	37.3	381	170.4
1835	285	71.5	63	111.6	584	308.3

Source: Sylla (2007).

banks (with a total capital of only $17.4 million) in the entire country. These banks, it should be pointed out, did not lend to all comers: they discriminated on the basis of profession, social standing, and political party affiliation.[6]

The system of a single national bank and segmented state monopolies was not stable given American political institutions. One crucial source of friction was the different incentives faced by the states and the central government. Bankers with state charters, and hence state legislatures, had opposed the BUS from the time of its initial chartering in 1791. The reason for their opposition was straightforward: branches of the BUS undermined local banking monopolies. State bankers therefore had incentives to form a coalition with the Jeffersonians, who were ideologically opposed to chartered corporations and "aristocratic" bankers, to eliminate the BUS. They initially tried to tax the bank notes of the BUS in order to give their own, state-chartered banks a competitive advantage. When that failed, they successfully lobbied state representatives not to renew the BUS charter, which expired in 1811.[7] The War of 1812 demonstrated, however, the importance of a bank that could serve as the

[6] Wallis, Sylla, and Legler, "The Interaction of Taxation," 135–39; Bodenhorn, *State Banking in Early America*, 142; John Majewski, "Jeffersonian Political Economy and Pennsylvania's Financial Revolution From Below, 1800–1820" (UCSB: Mimeo, 2004).

[7] Carl Lane, "For a 'Positive Profit': The Federal Investment in the First Bank of United States, 1792–1802," *William and Mary Quarterly* 54 (July 1997): 601–12; James Wettereau, "The Branches of the First Bank of the United States," *Journal of Economic*

financial agent of the federal government, and thus a new charter (for a Second Bank of the United States) was granted in 1816. The Second Bank of the United States was founded on the same principals as the first bank, and it faced opposition from the same state-banker–populist coalition. The populist presidency of Andrew Jackson therefore resulted in its demise: Jackson vetoed the renewal of the bank's charter in 1832, forcing it to close in 1836.[8]

A second source of friction was the interaction of federalism, an expanding frontier, and a broad suffrage. States had incentives to compete against one another for business enterprises and population – and this pushed their legislatures to undertake steps that ultimately undermined the monopoly banks they had earlier erected. State legislatures had incentives to construct canals that would funnel commerce from the expanding interior of the country through their states. They tended not, however, to have sufficient tax revenues to fund those public works projects. One response by states was to issue bonds (which caused a rash of state debt defaults), but another response was to charge a "charter bonus" on new bank charters. Such charter bonuses created, of course, an incentive for state legislatures to renege on the monopoly deals that they had already made with the incumbent banks.[9] State legislatures had a somewhat similar incentive to ratchet downwards restrictions on the right to vote. New states, eager to attract population, eliminated or reduced voting restrictions, forcing the original thirteen states to match their more permissive voting laws, or risk losing population. By the mid-1820s, property qualifications had been dropped or dramatically reduced in virtually all of the

History 2 (December 1942): 66–100; Richard Sylla, "Experimental Federalism: The Economics of American Government, 1789-1914," in *The Cambridge Economic History of the United States*, 3 vols, vol. 2 *The Long Nineteenth Century*, eds. Stanley L. Engerman and Robert E. Gallman (Cambridge: Cambridge University Press, 2000) 483–542; Hugh Rockoff, "Banking and Finance, 1789–1914," in *The Cambridge Economic History of the United States*, 3 vols, vol. 2 *The Long Nineteenth Century*, eds. Stanley L. Engerman and Robert E. Gallman, 643–684 (Cambridge: Cambridge University Press, 2000).

[8] Bray Hammond, "Jackson, Biddle, and the Bank of the United States," *Journal of Economic History* 7 (March 1947): 1–23; Peter Temin, "The Economic Consequences of the Bank War," *Journal of Political Economy*, 76 (March –April, 1968), 257–274; Stanley L. Engerman, "A Note on the Economic Consequences of the Second Bank of the United States," *Journal of Political Economy*, 78 (July/August, 1970): 725–728; Rockoff, "Banking and Finance."

[9] Arthur Grinath III, John Joseph Wallis, and Richard E. Sylla, "Debt, Default, and Revenue Structure: The American State Debt Crisis in the Early 1840s," (National Bureau of Economic Research: Historical Working Paper 0097, 1997); Sylla, "Experimental Federalism," Bodenhorn, *State Banking in Early America*, 86, 148, 152, 228–34.

original states.[10] The extension of the suffrage, in turn, allowed citizens to bring pressure to bear on legislatures, voting in legislators who were willing to remove constraints on the chartering of banks.

Political competition within and among states undermined the incentives of state legislatures to constrain the numbers of charters they granted. Massachusetts began to increase the number of charters it granted as early as 1812, abandoning its strategy of holding bank stock as a source of state finance and instead levying taxes on bank capital. Pennsylvania followed Massachusetts's lead with the Omnibus Banking Act of 1814. The act, passed over the objections of the state's governor, ended the cozy Philadelphia-based oligopoly that, until then, had dominated the state's banking industry. Rhode Island also followed Massachusetts' lead: in 1826 it sold its bank shares, increased the numbers of charters it granted and began to tax bank capital as a replacement for the income it had earned from dividends. It soon became, on a per capita basis, America's most heavily banked state.

These reforms did not allow all comers to charter banks or permit banks to open branches at will. Pennsylvania's Omnibus Banking Act of 1814, for example, divided the state into 27 banking districts and then allocated charters to 41 banks, with each district receiving at least one bank charter. A crucial aspect of the law was that banks were constrained from lending more than 20 percent of their capital to borrowers outside their districts, thereby limiting the amount of competition within any particular banking district. Additional restrictions placed on the banks favored local economic incumbents: 20 percent of banks' capital had to be lent to farmers, mechanics, and manufacturers; interest rates were capped by statute; bank indebtedness was capped by statute; and no more than 20 percent of capital could be invested in corporate or government securities. The rents earned by these local banking monopolies were then shared with the state government. Banks had to pay a 6 percent tax on dividends, and banks were required by law to pay dividends or risk the revocation of their charter. In addition, the banks had to make loans to the state government, at the government's discretion, at an interest rate that could not exceed 5 percent.[11] In short, Pennsylvania's Omnibus Banking Act was a compromise between potential debtors, who sought increased access to credit, incumbent bankers, who sought rents by limiting

---

[10] Ch. 4; Alexander Keyssar, *The Right to Vote: The Contested History of Democracy in the United States* (New York: Basic Books, 2000).

[11] Bodenhorn, *State Banking in Early America*, 142–143.

competition, and the state government, which needed a source of income and a mechanism to fund a public debt. The core feature of the deal was that banking monopolies would be allowed to persist: only they would be made smaller.

This process of reform allowed the U.S. banking system to grow at a rapid pace. As Table 8.1 shows, in 1820 there were 327 banks in operation with $160 million in capital – roughly three times as many banks and four times as much bank capital as in 1810. By 1835, there were 584 banks, with $308 million in capital – a nearly two-fold increase in just fifteen years. At this point, larger cities often had a dozen or more banks, while small towns had as many as two or three.[12]

As the number of banks increased they were forced to search out new classes of borrowers. The result was that banks, particularly in the Middle Atlantic States, lent funds to an increasingly wide variety of merchants, artisans, and farmers.[13] Even in New England, where insider lending dominated, the large number of banks and the ease of new bank formation made access to credit less of a binding constraint on the growth of nonfinancial firms.[14]

By the late 1830s the de facto policies of Northeast states to grant virtually all requests for bank charters became institutionalized in a series of laws known as free banking. Under free banking, bank charters no longer had to be approved by state legislatures. Rather, individuals could open banks provided that they registered with the state comptroller and deposited state or federal bonds with the comptroller as a guarantee of their note issues. Readers may wonder how such a system of free entry could have been compatible with the fiscal needs of state governments. The answer lies in the fact that under free banking all bank notes had to be 100 percent backed by high-grade securities that were deposited with the state comptroller of the currency. Free banks were forced, in essence, to grant a loan to the state government in exchange for the right to operate.

The first state to make the switch to de jure free banking was New York, in 1838 – and the reason for the switch was unambiguous: citizens who had been closed out of credit markets voted in a party that promised

---

[12] Ibid.
[13] Ta-Chen Wang, "Courts, Banks, and Credit Market in Early American Development," unpublished Ph.D. dissertation, Stanford University, 2006.
[14] Naomi Lamoreaux, *Insider Lending: Banks, Personal Connections, and Economic Development in Industrial New England* (Cambridge: Cambridge University Press, 1994).

to break an oligopoly. From the 1810s to the late 1830s, bank chartering in New York was controlled by the Albany Regency – a political machine run by Martin Van Buren. Bank charters were only granted to friends of the Regency, in exchange for which the legislators received various bribes, such as the ability to subscribe to initial public offerings of bank stock at par, even though the stock traded for a substantial premium.[15] The Regency's hold on bank chartering came to an end when the state's voting laws were amended in 1826, allowing universal manhood suffrage. Within a decade, the Regency lost its control of the state legislature, and in 1837 the now dominant Whig Party enacted America's first free banking law. By 1841, New Yorkers had established 43 free banks, with a total capital of $10.7 million. By 1849, the number of free banks mushroomed to 111, with $16.8 million in paid capital. By 1859 there were 274 free banks with paid in capital of $100.6 million.[16] Other states soon followed New York's lead – with the liberalization of banking laws correlating with the liberalization of suffrage laws.[17] By the early 1860s, 21 states adopted some variant of the New York law, and as they did so, they encouraged bank entry and increased competition.[18]

Free banking did not mean that the supply constraints on the credit market were completely eliminated. The free banking laws of most states

[15] Bodenhorn, *State Banking in Early America*, 134, 186–88; Bodenhorn, "Bank Chartering and Political Corruption in Antebellum New York: Free Banking as Reform," in *Corruption and Reform: Lessons from America's Economic History*, eds. Edward Glaeser and Claudia Goldin, 231–257 (Chicago: University of Chicago Press, 2006), Frank Otto Gatell, "Sober Second Thoughts on Van Buren, the Albany Regency, and the Wall Street Conspiracy," *Journal of American History* 53 (June 1966), 19–40: 26; David Moss and Sarah Brennan, "Regulation and Reaction: The Other Side of Free Banking in Antebellum New York," (Harvard Business School: Working Paper 04–038).

[16] Bodenhorn, *State Banking in Early America*, 186–92; Wallis, Sylla, and Legler, "The Interaction of Taxation," 122–144; Moss and Brennan, "Regulation and Reaction".

[17] Efrain Benmelech and Tobias J. Moskowitz, "The Political Economy of Financial Regulation: Evidence from U.S. State Usury Laws in the 19th Century" *Journal of Finance* 65 (June) 1029–1073.

[18] Howard Bodenhorn, "Entry, Rivalry, and Free Banking in Antebellum America," *Review of Economics and Statistics* 72 (November 1990): 682–86; Howard Bodenhorn, "The Business Cycle and Entry into Early American Banking," *Review of Economics and Statistics* 75 (August 1993): 531–35; Andrew Economopoulos and Heather O'Neill, "Bank Entry During the Antebellum Period," *Journal of Money, Credit and Banking* 27 (November 1995): 1071–85; Kenneth Ng, "Free Banking Laws and Barriers to Entry in Banking, 1838–1860," *Journal of Economic History* 48 (December 1988): 877–889; Hugh Rockoff, "The Free Banking Era: A Reexamination." *Journal of Money, Credit, and Banking* 6 (May 1974): 141–67; Hugh Rockoff, "New Evidence on Free Banking in the United States," *American Economic Review*, 75 (September 1985): 886–889.

precluded the chartering of branch banks. Thus, with the exception of Southern states, where free banking did not catch on, the banking systems of virtually all states were composed of unit (single branch) banks. This unusual organization of the banking system was the outcome of an unlikely political coalition: populists opposed to aristocratic bankers allied with bankers who wanted to create local monopolies. In short, free banking was not a complete rethinking of the earlier system of segmented monopolies: it simply expanded the number, and reduced the size, of those monopolies. The results were twofold: Some of the rents that had been earned by bankers were dissipated; and borrowers who had earlier been closed out of credit markets now had access to finance, though it came from a bank that had a great deal of local market power.

Readers may wonder why, if banks could not open branches in underserved markets, farmers, merchants, and manufacturers in those markets did not simply obtain credit from banks in larger towns? The answer is that, until the computer revolution, obtaining information about the quality of potential borrowers was very costly. Bankers assessed the creditworthiness of borrowers on the basis of personal relationships: sets of repeated interactions that allowed the banker to assess what was going on inside an informationally opaque enterprise or household. As a result, until the 1990s most small business loans were made by banks that were less than fifty-one miles away.[19]

From the point of view of the federal government, allowing the states to charter banks had a major drawback: It did not provide the federal government with a source of finance. This problem came to the fore during the Civil War, when the financial needs of the federal government skyrocketed. The federal government therefore passed laws in 1863, 1864, and 1865 that were designed to eliminate the state chartered banks and replace them with a system of national banks that would finance the government's war effort. Federally chartered banks had to invest one-third of their capital in federal government bonds, which were then held as reserves by the comptroller of the currency against note issues. That is, banks had to make a loan to the federal government in exchange for the right to issue notes. Consistent with the goal of maximizing credit to the federal government, the National Banking Act made the granting of a charter an administrative procedure: as long as minimum capital

---

[19] Mitchell A. Peterson and Raghuram G. Rajan, "Does Distance Still Matter? The Information Revolution in Small Business Lending," *Journal of Finance* 57 (December 2002): 2533–70.

and reserve requirements were met, the charter was granted. It was free banking on a national scale.[20]

The federal government could neither abrogate the right of states to charter banks, nor could it prevent state-chartered banks from issuing banknotes. It could, however, impose a 10 percent tax on banknotes, and then exempt federally chartered banks from the tax, thereby giving state banks strong incentives to obtain new, federal charters. In the short run, the response of private banks was as the federal government expected: as Table 8.2 shows, the number of state chartered banks declined from 1,579 in 1860 to 349 by 1865. Federal banks grew dramatically: from zero in 1860 to 1,294 in 1865. They then continued growing, reaching 7,518 by 1914, controlling $11.5 billion in assets in that year.

In the long run, however, the political institutions of the United States frustrated the federal government's goal of a single, federally chartered banking system. The federal government had effectively nationalized the right to issue bank notes by creating a 10 percent tax on the notes of state chartered banks in 1865. The law did not, however, say anything about checks drawn on accounts in state-chartered banks. State banks therefore aggressively pursued deposit banking, and checks drawn on those accounts became an increasingly common means of exchange in business transactions.[21] The result was that state chartered banks actually outgrew federally chartered banks during the period from 1865 to 1914. As Table 8.2 shows, in 1865 state banks accounted for only 21 percent of all banks and 17 percent of total bank assets. By 1890 there were more state banks than national banks, and state banks controlled the majority of assets. Circa 1914, 73 percent of all banks were state banks, and state banks controlled 58 percent of assets.

The result was a banking system with a most peculiar competitive structure: In 1914 there were 27,864 banks in the United States, 95 percent of which had no branches! The banks that did have branches tended to be small: The average number of branches operated by these banks was less than five.[22] The reason for the preponderance of "unit banks" was that most states had laws that prevented branch banking, even

[20] Richard Sylla, *The American Capital Market, 1846–1914: A Study of the Effects of Public Policy on Economic Development* (New York: Arno Press, 1975).

[21] Moss and Brennan, "Regulation and Reaction"; Sylla, *The American Capital Market*, 62–73; Lance E. Davis and Robert E. Gallman, *Evolving Financial Markets and International Capital Flows: Britain, the Americas, and Australia, 1865–1914* (Cambridge: Cambridge University Press, 2001): 272.

[22] Charles W. Calomiris and Eugene N. White, "The Origins of Federal Deposit Insurance," in *The Regulated Economy: A Historical Approach to Political Economy*, eds. Claudia

TABLE 8.2. *Number of U.S. Commercial Banks, 1860–1932*

Year	State Chartered Banks		National Banks		Total Banks		National Banks as Percent of Total	
	Number	Assets (Millions USD)	Number	Assets (Millions USD)	Number	Assets (Millions USD)	Number	Assets (Millions USD)
1860	1,579	423			1,579	423		
1865	349	231	1,294	1,127	1,643	1,358	79%	83%
1870	325	215	1,612	1,566	1,937	1,781	83%	88%
1875	1,260	1,291	2,076	1,913	3,336	3,204	62%	60%
1880	1,279	1,364	2,076	2,036	3,355	3,400	62%	60%
1885	1,661	2,005	2,689	2,422	4,350	4,427	62%	55%
1890	4,717	3,296	3,484	3,062	8,201	6,358	42%	48%
1895	6,103	4,139	3,715	3,471	9,818	7,610	38%	46%
1900	9,322	6,444	3,731	4,944	13,053	11,388	29%	43%
1905	13,103	10,186	5,664	7,325	18,767	17,511	30%	42%
1910	18,013	13,030	7,138	9,892	25,151	22,922	28%	43%
1914	20,346	15,872	7,518	11,477	27,864	27,349	27%	42%

Sources: Lamoreaux (1991), 540; Davis and Gallman (2000), 268; Calomiris and White (1994), 151; U.S. Federal Reserve System (1943), 24.

by nationally chartered banks. Those states that did not explicitly forbid branch banking had no provision in their laws for branches. In fact, unit bankers formed numerous local and state organizations to lobby against the relaxation of branch banking restrictions. They even succeeded in getting the American Bankers Association to adopt resolutions in 1916 and 1924 opposing branch banking in any form.[23] Urban banks could, of course, form a holding company and then open a free-standing unit bank in a rural market, thereby getting around the law – but only partially. That free-standing unit bank had to be just that: free-standing. It could not share back-office operations with the urban bank, and thus had to forego the opportunity to take advantage of scale economies in administration. The high overhead costs implied by this business model constituted a barrier to entry.[24]

Why did rural consumers go along with this arrangement? Why didn't they form a coalition with the urban bankers who wanted to open branches in their underserved markets? Calomiris summarizes a long line of research on this question. One reason is that unit bankers formed a coalition with agrarian populists, who viewed big-city business enterprises – as well as their plutocrat owners – as a threat to their way of life. One reflection of this coalition was the fact that William Jennings Bryan, the presidential candidate for both the Populist and Democratic Parties in 1896, was a strong anti-branch banking advocate. A second reason is that one particular subgroup of farmers – those in prosperous farming districts, who used unit banks to fund their operations and acquisitions – calculated that they had something to gain from unit banking. A local banker who was not part of a branch network had to lend to them, or lend to no one. From their point of view, unit banking provided "loan insurance." The higher interest rate they paid the unit banker for the loan was simply the premium for the insurance policy.

The creation of the Federal Reserve System (Fed) in 1913 did nothing to undermine this peculiar market structure. In fact, by providing liquidity to member banks, the Fed had the opposite effect: It allowed weak banks to weather crises by taking advantage of the Fed's discount window,

Goldin and Gary D. Libecap, 145–188 (Chicago: University of Chicago Press, 1994), Davis and Gallman, *Evolving Financial Markets*, 272.

[23] Burton A. Abrams and Russell F. Settle, "Pressure-group Influence and Institutional Change: Branch-Banking Legislation During the Great Depression," *Public Choice* 77 (December 1993): 687–705.

[24] Charles W. Calomiris, "The Political Lessons of Depression-Era Banking Reform," *Oxford Review of Economic Policy* 26 (Autumn 2010) 540–560.

when they would have otherwise gone out of business. As Calomiris[25] has pointed out, this was not an unintended consequence: the creation of the Fed required the accommodation of numerous constituencies, including unit bankers in rural markets.

Subsequent reforms – most particularly the creation of the Federal Deposit Insurance Corporation as part of the Glass-Steagall Act of 1933 – also propped up unit banks and their monopoly rents. In fact, the evidence is overwhelming that federal deposit insurance was not a necessary step in saving the banking system during the Great Depression, but was the product of lobbying by unit bankers who wanted to stifle the growth of branch banking in order to protect their rents. The facts are as follows: deposit insurance went into effect *after* the banking system had been intervened with and stabilized by government; President Roosevelt, as well as his Secretary of the Treasury and his Comptroller of the Currency, *opposed* deposit insurance; Carter Glass and the Senate Banking Committee, who drafted the initial legislation, also were *opposed* to deposit insurance, and only allowed it to be added to the Glass-Steagall Act at the eleventh hour, in order to get the support of the populist Chairman of the House Banking Committee, Representative Henry Steagall, and the American Banker's Association lobbied Roosevelt to *veto* the bill after it was logrolled through Congress.[26]

In order to understand why federal deposit insurance saved unit banks – and the monopoly rents they earned – it is necessary to understand that a system of unit banks with state-run deposit insurance, and a system of banks with branch networks, are substitutes for each other: a geographically diverse branch network is essentially a form of bank self-insurance. As Economides, Hubbard, and Palia have demonstrated,[27] in a mixed system, in which there are unit banks and branch banks, the unit banks will not survive unless there is deposit insurance: depositors will move their funds to the inherently more stable banks with branch networks. The only way that the unit banks can head off a depositor stampede to the branch banks is to signal that they are more stable by maintaining a larger buffer of equity capital. This is only a stop-gap

---

[25] Ibid.

[26] Calomiris and White, "The Origins of Federal Deposit Insurance," 145–188; Nicholas R. Economides, Glenn Hubbard, and Darius Palia, "The Political Economy of Branching Restrictions and Deposit Insurance: A Model of Monopolistic Competition Among Small and Large Banks," *Journal of Law and Economics* 39 (October 1996): 667–704; Calomiris, "Political Lessons."

[27] Economides, Hubbard, and Palia, "Political Economy of Branching," 667–704.

measure, however, because the need to maintain higher equity ratios will make the unit banks less profitable than the branching banks – unless the unit banks take more risks with their loan portfolios. Taking that step will, however, make the unit banks less stable, and thus they will be back to where they started: at a competitive disadvantage vis a vis the banks with branch networks. For precisely this reason, in a mixed system, unit banks will favor a state-run deposit insurance: depositors do not choose among banks based on their stability when the government guarantees their deposits. For the same reason, banks with branch networks will be opposed to state-run deposit insurance: it undermines their competitive advantage vis a vis unit banks.

Both approaches to creating a stable banking system – unit banks with deposit insurance, and branch banking without deposit insurance – had been tried prior to the Glass-Steagall Act. In fact, unit bankers had tried – on 150 separate occasions since the 1880s – to create federal deposit insurance. While they had failed miserably at the federal level, they had been somewhat more successful at the state level: in the years between 1908 and 1917, eight states enacted deposit insurance for their state-chartered banks. In all eight cases, however, the deposit insurance systems failed during the agricultural crises of the 1920s. The evidence indicates, in fact, that deposit insurance encouraged banks in these states to take excessive risks.[28] At the same time that these states were experimenting with deposit insurance, other states, trying to contend with large numbers of bank failures, were experimenting with branch banking. By 1930, eight states, primarily in the West and South, permitted unrestricted, state-wide branching. An additional thirteen states permitted branching, but restricted the geographic extent of branch networks in order to protect unit bankers in rural areas from competition: nine states restricted branches to the boundaries of the city where the banks' headquarters were located: two restricted branches to the boundaries of the county where the banks' headquarters were located; and two more restricted branches to counties that bordered the county where banks' headquarters were located.[29]

The wave of bank failures in the 1920s became a torrent during in the Great Depression, and it threatened to completely undermine political support for unit banking. Between 1930 and 1933 more than 9,100

---

[28] Calomiris and White, "Origins of Federal Deposit Insurance, 11; Economides, Hubbard, and Palia, "Political Economy"; Calomiris, "Political Lessons."

[29] Abrams and Settle, "Pressure-group Influence."

banks (38 percent of all banks) suspended operations. Depositors came to view unit banks (correctly) as more prone to failure. Moreover, the collapse of so many unit banks left thousands of agricultural communities, and even some suburbs of major cities, without any banks at all.[30] State legislatures, under pressure from their constituents, began to relax legal restrictions on branch banking. Thirteen of the twenty-seven states that had earlier prohibited branch banking of any kind rewrote their laws; seven of them went so far as to allow unrestricted state-wide branching. In addition, nine of the thirteen states that had limited branching to the boundaries of the city or county where the bank was headquartered relaxed those restrictions; some went so far as to allow unrestricted, state-wide branching.[31] The days of unit banks appeared to be numbered.

Deposit insurance reversed the trend toward branch banking. Once the federal government guaranteed deposits, legislatures did not face pressure from voters to allow branch banking: only four states relaxed their branching laws between 1939 and 1979. In fact, in the early 1970s, only twelve states allowed unrestricted intrastate branching; and no state allowed interstate branching.[32] The only incentive that depositors might have had to shift their funds out of unit banks and into branch banks were differences in deposit interest rates across the two bank types. That incentive had, however, also been undermined by Glass-Steagall: deposit interest rates were now regulated. In fact, interest payments on demand deposits were legally prohibited.[33]

These restrictions on both intrastate and interstate branch banking were finally undermined by two forces. The first force was technological: beginning in the 1970s the computer revolution drove down the cost of information storage and retrieval, allowing bankers to assess a borrower's credit-worthiness without having to rely on "soft information" that could only be obtained locally, and allowing consumers, via automatic teller machines, to access their accounts anywhere they wanted. In 1985, the U.S. Supreme Court ruled that an ATM was not a bank branch, thereby eviscerating state laws that set limits on banks with branch networks. The

---

[30] Ibid.

[31] Ibid.

[32] Black and Strahan, "The Division of Spoils"; Donald P. Morgan, Bertrand Rime, and Philip E. Strahan, "Bank Integration and State Business Cycles," *Quarterly Journal of Economics* 119 (November 2004): 1555–84. Some states did allow out-of-state bank holding companies to purchase banks within their borders, but they could not share back-office operations with an out of state bank. Thus, in 1975, only 10 percent of the bank assets in the typical state were owned by a multi-state bank holding company.

[33] Economides, Hubbard, and Palia, "Political Economy"; Calomiris, "Political Lessons."

second force was political: public sentiment shifted against local banks as a result of the bank and thrift failures (and their accompanying bailouts) in the 1980s. Just as had occurred in the Great Depression, a financial crisis exposed the inherent instability of financial institutions that could not spread risk across multiple markets and that could not respond to difficulties by shifting resources across branches of an interconnected network.[34] From 1979 to 1990, fifteen states relaxed their branching restrictions.[35]

A major blow to the state laws that prohibited interstate branching came in 1982, when Congress, in response to the Savings and Loan crisis, amended the Bank Holding Company Act of 1956 to allow failed banks to be acquired by any bank holding company, regardless of state laws. This induced many states to enter into regional or national reciprocal arrangements whereby their banks could be merged (not just purchased by a holding company) with banks from another state. Between 1984 and 1988, 38 states joined one of these reciprocal arrangements.[36] Banks operating national branching networks accounted for only 10 percent of the U.S. banking system in the early 1980s. By the mid-1990s, they accounted for more than 70 percent.[37] The final blow to the unit banks came in 1994, when Congress codified the process that had been taking place at the state level by passing the Riegle-Neal Interstate Banking and Branching Efficiency Act. Banks could now branch both within states and across state lines – a full two centuries after the chartering of the Bank of the United States.

Mexico

The experience of the United States, in which constraints on the supply of credit were gradually undermined by debtors whose interests were represented through the political system, could not be more different from that of Mexico. From independence until 2000, Mexico was anything but democratic: There were short-lived periods of republican government, in which the suffrage was constrained; periods of long-lived dictatorship; and periods of anarchy that punctuated the intervals between republicanism and dictatorship. The result was that Mexican citizens could not undermine the arrangements that created a narrow financial system. The

---

[34] Kroszner and Strahan, "What Drives Deregulation?"
[35] Calomiris, "Political Lessons."
[36] Kroszner and Strahan, "What Drives Deregulation?"
[37] Calomiris, "Political Lessons."

choice was between a highly concentrated banking system that extended credit narrowly, or no banking system at all.

Colonial Mexico was extremely wealthy, but that wealth was distributed unequally between a small elite of Spanish descent and a large mass of illiterate and politically disenfranchised Indians and *mestizos*. The weakness of the latter group is underlined by the process of Mexican independence. An independence movement that championed their rights, and that directly threatened the Spanish elite – the Hidalgo Rebellion of 1810 – was soundly defeated by the colonial elite, which quickly made common cause with the Spanish Viceroy and his army. When Mexico achieved independence eleven years later, it was as a reaction to a successful liberal revolution in Spain that threatened the colonial status quo. As a result, Mexico's independence did not produce a republic, but a constitutional monarch, who quickly proclaimed himself emperor and closed congress.

Emperor Iturbide lasted only eight months in power, but even after he was removed, political power remained concentrated among a narrow elite. One subgroup of this elite, the conservatives, sought to maintain all of the political and economic institutions of the colony, including the centralization of political power and exemptions from trial in civil courts for the army and clergy. A second subgroup, the liberals, wanted a federal republic in which states would be granted considerable autonomy and in which the political economy of the country would be guided by laissez faire principles. Both sides agreed on one issue: suffrage would be restricted and Europeanized elites should run the country.[38] Not surprisingly, as Chapter 4 shows, the right to vote in nineteenth century Mexico was constrained by both literacy and wealth requirements. These were binding constraints, because there were no public schools and most of the population eked out a living as subsistence farmers and day laborers.

While the conservatives and liberals agreed on the disenfranchisement of the mass of the population they could not agree on much else. They therefore engaged in a series of coups, counter-coups, and civil wars from independence to 1876. In the fifty-five years after independence Mexico had seventy-five presidents. For every constitutional president there were four interim, provisional, or temporary presidents. One military figure, Antonio López de Santa Ana, occupied the presidential chair on eleven different occasions. All sides in these conflicts preyed on the property

---

[38] Michael Costeloe, *The Central Republic in Mexico, 1835–1846: Hombres de Bien in the Age of Santa Anna* (Cambridge: Cambridge University Press, 2002).

rights of their opponents. Every government that came to power also inherited a depleted treasury and no ready source of income. To meet their need for a source of public finance, Mexico's nineteenth-century governments borrowed from the country's wealthy merchant-financiers. When governments changed, or when governments faced sufficient threat, they reneged on those debts.[39]

Given this environment, the country's financial incumbents – the wealthy merchant-financiers – had very weak incentives to obtain bank charters: Deploying their capital in a visible manner would only create a target for expropriation via forced loans. The severity of this problem is made evident by one of the Mexican government's most desperate moves. Precisely because there was so little bank credit, in 1830 the country's manufacturers pressured the government into founding a government-owned industrial development bank – the Banco de Avío. In 1842, desperate for cash, the government ransacked its vaults, which is to say that it expropriated its own bank.[40] Not surprisingly, Mexico had no private, chartered banks at all until 1863. To the degree that there was any financial intermediation, it was through the private banking houses of the merchant-financiers – but these lacked the advantages of a chartered bank: the ability to mobilize capital by selling equity to outside investors who would be protected by limited liability, primacy as a creditor in the event of borrower bankruptcy, and the ability to issue banknotes that had the status of legal tender. These private banking houses were thus necessarily limited in scale. When Mexico did finally charter its first bank in 1863 it was to a foreign entity (the British Bank of London, Mexico, and South America) and the charter was granted by the puppet government of a foreign power, the Emperor Maximilian, who had been installed by the French.

In the last decades of the nineteenth century, a political-military leader, Porfirio Díaz, finally brought political stability to Mexico – but he did so by creating a dictatorship that endured from 1877 to 1911. The Díaz dictatorship was characterized by three phenomena: the centralization of political power; heightened inequality; and rapid economic growth centered in large-scale enterprises owned by politically-connected elites.

---

[39] Barbara A. Tenenbaum, *The Politics of Penury: Debt and Taxes in Mexico, 1821–1856* (Albuquerque: University of New Mexico Press, 1986); David W. Walker, *Business, Kinship, and Politics: The Martínez del Río Family in Mexico, 1824–1867* (Austin: University of Texas Press, 1986).

[40] Robert Potash, *The Mexican Government and Industrial Development in the Early Republic: The Banco de Avio* (Amherst: University of Massachusetts Press, 1983).

Mexico nominally remained a federal republic, but Díaz quickly undermined whatever bite the institutions of federalism and suffrage had. He gradually appointed men loyal to him as governors – typically choosing individuals who were from outside the state and had few local ties, and thus owed their political survival to Díaz.[41] He then had the governors and other local officials he had appointed rig the elections for the Federal Congress and Senate, even sending them a list of the desired outcomes before the election took place, and by 1888 the Federal Congress and Senate were little more than rubber stamps for Díaz's decrees.

Centralized political power then became a vehicle to transfer wealth upwards, in order to create incentives for investment in an economy that had been moribund since independence. One area where this phenomena has been intensively studied is agriculture, where a host of studies all point in the same direction: State governors and other members of the local political elite allied with a subset of the large landowners in the state to dispossess small farmers and Indian villages. In some cases – Chihuahua being the most notorious – governors ran their states as family business enterprises, using their power to expropriate everything worth owning. Though the data on land tenure for this period are rough, the evidence indicates that by 1910, 95 percent of rural heads of families had no land of their own. Attempts by small farmers to resist the onslaught of the planters were dealt with by state-administered brutality.[42]

In order to make this political and economic system viable, Díaz needed a source of public finance. At the time that he took power, he lacked sufficient tax revenues to finance a government capable of unifying the country and putting an end to internecine warfare. Díaz could not easily borrow his way out of this situation because Mexico had a long history of defaulting on its debts to its international and domestic creditors. Simply promising not to behave like his predecessors was not an option: Mexico's political institutions did not impose binding limits on Díaz's authority,

---

[41] Stephen Haber, Armando Razo, and Noel Maurer, *The Politics of Property Rights: Political Instability, Credible Commitments, and Economic Growth in Mexico, 1876–1929* (Cambridge: Cambridge University Press, 2003): Ch. 3.

[42] John Womack, *Zapata and the Mexican Revolution* (New York: Knopf, 1969); Mark Wasserman, *Capitalists, Caciques, and Revolution: Elite and Foreign Enterprise in Chihuahua, Mexico, 1854–1911* (Chapel Hill: University of North Carolina Press, 1984); Dana Markiewicz, *The Mexican Revolution and the Limits of Agrarian Reform, 1915–1946* (Boulder, CO: Lynne Rienner Publishers, 1993); Robert H. Holden, *Mexico and the Survey of Public Lands: The Management of Modernization, 1876–1911* (DeKalb: Northern Illinois University Press, 1994); Friedrich Katz, *The Life and Times of Pancho Villa* (Stanford: Stanford University Press, 1998).

and thus no promise he made was credible because there was no obvious sanction for breaking it. In fact, Díaz himself had reneged on debts to some of the banks that had been founded in Mexico City during the early years of his rule.[43]

The solution that Díaz and Mexico's financiers hit upon was one that had been used by European governments since the late seventeenth century: create a semi-official super bank whose investors would be compensated for the risk of expropriation by extremely high rates of return. They did this by engineering the merger of the two largest banks in Mexico City in order to establish the Banco Nacional de México (Banamex). The deal was simple: Banamex got a charter from the government that gave it a set of extremely lucrative privileges; and, in return, Banamex extended a credit line to the government. These privileges included the right to issue banknotes up to three times the amount of its reserves, to act as the treasury's fiscal agent, to tax farm customs receipts, and to run the mint. In addition, the government established a 5 percent tax on all banknotes, and then exempted Banamex notes from the tax. Díaz simultaneously got congress to pass a commercial code that removed the authority of state governments to issue bank charters. Any bank that wanted to compete with Banamex had to obtain a charter from Díaz's Secretary of the Treasury.[44]

Mexico's already extant banks, some of which were owned by powerful provincial politicians, realized that the commercial code and Banamex' special privileges put them at a serious disadvantage. They therefore obtained an injunction against the 1884 Commercial Code, citing the 1857 Constitution's anti-monopoly clause. The ensuing legal and political battle ground on for thirteen years, until Secretary of Finance José Yves Limantour finally hammered out a compromise in 1897. Under this agreement, Banamex shared some of its special privileges with the Banco de Londres y México (the Spanish name of the British Bank of London, Mexico, and South America that had been chartered by Maximilian in

---

[43] Carlos Marichal, "The Construction of Credibility: Financial Market Reform and the Renegotiation of Mexico's External Debt in the 1880's," *The Mexican Economy, 1870–1930: Essays on the Economic History of Institutions, Revolution, and Growth* eds. Jeffrey L. Bortz and Stephen H. Haber, 93–119 (Stanford, CA: Stanford University Press, 2002); Noel Maurer and Andrei Gomberg, "When the State is Untrustworthy: Public Finance and Private Banking in Porfirian Mexico," *Journal of Economic History* 64 (December 2004): 1087–1107.

[44] Noel Maurer, *The Power and the Money: The Mexican Financial System, 1876–1932* (Stanford: Stanford University Press, 2002); Haber, Razo, Maurer, *The Politics of Property Rights*, Ch. 4; Maurer and Gomberg, "When the State is Untrustworthy."

1863), state governors chose which business group in the state would receive a bank charter from the federal government, and that state bank would effectively be granted a local monopoly. Legal barriers to entry into banking could not be eroded by competition between states, or between states and the federal government, because states did not have the right to charter banks.[45]

Mexico's 1897 banking law was deliberately crafted to limit the number of banks that could compete in any market. First, the law specified that bank charters (and additions to capital) had to be approved by the Secretary of the Treasury *and* the Federal Congress, which, was a rubber stamp for the dictator. Second, the law created high minimum capital requirements – more than twice the amount for a national bank in the United States.[46] Third, the law established a 2 percent annual tax on paid-in capital. The first bank granted a charter in each state, however, was granted an exemption from the tax. Fourth, banks with territorial charters were not allowed to branch outside of their concession territories, preventing banks chartered in one state from challenging the monopoly of a bank in an adjoining state. In short, the only threat to the monopoly of a state bank could come from a branch of Banamex or the Banco de Londres y México.[47]

These segmented monopolies made incentive compatible with the interests of Mexico's political elite, who received seats on the boards of the major banks, and thus were entitled to director's fees and stock distributions. The board of directors of Banamex, for example, was populated by members of Díaz's coterie, including the President of Congress, the Under-Secretary of the Treasury, the Senator for the Federal District, the President's Chief of Staff, and the brother of the Secretary of the Treasury. Banks with limited territorial concessions were similarly populated with powerful politicians, the only difference being that state governors, rather than cabinet ministers, sat on their boards.[48]

Why would minority shareholders have purchased stock in these banks? If the insiders were in a coalition with Díaz, what would keep them from expropriating the minority shareholders through tunneling

[45] Maurer, *The Power and the Money*, Ch. 5.
[46] Stephen Haber, "Industrial Concentration and the Capital Markets: A Comparative Study of Brazil, Mexico, and the United States, 1830–1930," *Journal of Economic History* 51 (September 1991): 559–80.
[47] Maurer, *The Power and the Money*, 2002.
[48] Haber, Razo, and Maurer, *The Politics of Property Rights*, Ch. 4; Amando Razo, *Social Foundations of Limited Dictatorship: Networks and Private Protection During Mexico's Early Industrialization* (Stanford: Stanford University Press, 2008).

and fraud? The answer is twofold. First, there were institutions that strongly militated against this. Bank directors had strong incentives to monitor one another, because the banks were very highly capitalized – equity ratios were on the order of 25 percent – and the directors owned a substantial share of the capital. In addition, there were independent directors appointed by minority shareholders – and those independent directors tended to be directors of other banks. There was therefore a high degree of cross-monitoring. Second, the minority shareholders were compensated for the risk of tunneling and fraud by receiving a rate of return on their investment that exceeded the rate of return that they could earn otherwise. An investor who purchased a portfolio of Mexican bank stocks in 1901 and held it to 1910 would have earned a return that was more than double the return he would have received by investing in the Dow Jones Industrials.[49]

The resulting banking system had one major advantage and one major disadvantage. The advantage was that, for the first time in Mexican history, there was a stable banking system. As Table 8.3 shows, this banking system was, by the standards of typical LDC banking systems today, quite sizable: in 1910, bank assets were 32 percent of GDP – about the same ratio as Mexico had in 2000. Moreover, this banking system provided the government with a source of public finance, which meant that the Díaz government did not have to prey upon property rights in order to maintain its fragile hold on power. Instead, it gave Díaz the financial breathing room he needed to slowly recraft the tax codes governing mining, petroleum, and interstate commerce, gradually increasing government tax revenues to the point that he ran balanced budgets.[50] It also allowed Díaz, with the help of Banamex's directors, to renegotiate Mexico's foreign debt – which had been in default for several decades. State governors obtained a similar advantage: the banks within their borders were a steady source of loans to the state government.[51]

[49] Noel Maurer and Stephen Haber, "Related Lending and Economic Performance: Evidence From Mexico," *Journal of Economic History* 67 (September 2007): 551–581.

[50] Marcello Carmagnani, et al. (eds.) *Federalismos Latinamercanos: México, Brasil, Argentina* (México: Fondo de Cultura Económica, 1993); Haber, Razo, and Maurer, *The Politics of Property Rights*, Chs. 3, 6, 7.

[51] Marichal, "*The Construction of Credibility*; Maurer, *The Power and the Money*; Gustavo Aguilar, "El sistema bancario en Sinaloa (1889–1926): Su influencia en el crecimento economico," in *La Banca Regional en Mexico, 1870–1930*, eds. Mario Cerutti and Carlos Marichal, 47–100 (Mexico: Fondo de Cultura Economica, 2003); Mario Cerutti, "Empresario y banca en el norte de Mexico, 1879–1910: La fundacion del Banco Refaccionario de la Laguna," in *La Banca Regional en Mexico, 1870–1930*,

TABLE 8.3. *The Mexican Banking Industry, 1897–1913*

Year	Number of Banks[1]	Total Assets (Millions of Nominal Pesos)	Assets as Percent of GDP	Average Equity Ratio[2]	Deposits as Percent of Assets	Bank of Issue Assets as Percent of Total Assets
1897	10	147	12%	32%	2%	93%
1898	16	175	15%	32%	3%	94%
1899	18	211	18%	31%	2%	90%
1900	20	259	20%	31%	5%	90%
1901	24	264	15%	35%	4%	87%
1902	25	317	19%	31%	5%	88%
1903	31	380	20%	31%	4%	86%
1904	32	435	24%	30%	3%	88%
1905	32	535	24%	28%	6%	87%
1906	32	629	28%	32%	9%	88%
1907	34	724	31%	30%	9%	83%
1908	34	757	31%	31%	9%	81%
1909	32	917	35%	26%	16%	80%
1910	32	1,005	32%	24%	16%	80%
1911	33	1,119		22%	13%	81%
1912	34	1,086		23%	15%	78%
1913	28	1,105		21%	15%	77%

Notes:
[1] Includes banks of issue, mortgage banks, and investment banks (bancos refaccionarios). The 1913 figure does not include six banks that did not report because of the revolution.
[2] Weighted by assets.
Source: Calculated from Secretaria de Hacienda y Crédito Público, *Anuario de Estadistica Fiscal, 1912–1913.*

The disadvantage was that Mexico's concentrated banking system gave rise to concentration in downstream industries. In 1911, there were only thirty-four incorporated banks in the entire country, and half of all assets

eds. Mario Cerutti and Carlos Marichal (Mexico: Fondo de Cultura Económica, 2003), 168–215; Gamboa Ojeda, 2003; Leonor Ludlow, "El Banco Mercantil de Veracruz, 1898-1906," in *La Banca Regional en Mexico, 1870-1930*, eds. Mario Cerutti and Carlos Marichal (Mexico: Fondo de Cultura Económica, 2003), 134–167; Jaime Olveda, "Bancos y banquenos en Guadalajara," in *La Banca Regional en Mexico, 1870-1930*, eds., Mario Cerutti and Carlos Marichal (Mexico: Fondo de Cultura Económica, 2003); Maria Guadalupe Rodríguez, "La banca porfiriana en Durango," in *Durango (1840-1915): Banca, transportes, tierra e industria*, ed. Maria Guadalupe Rodríguez et al. 7–34 (Durango Universidad Juárez del Estado de Durango, 1995); Maria Eugenia Romero Ibarra, "El Banco del Estado de Mexico 1897-1914," in *La Banca Regional en Mexico, 1870-1930*, ed. Mario Cerutti and Carlos Marichal: 216–57 (Mexico: Fondo de Cultura Económica, 2003).

TABLE 8.4. *Industrial Concentration in Cotton Textiles in Mexico, Brazil, India, and the United States*

	Four Firm Ratio				Herfindahl Index		
Year (Circa)	Mexico	Brazil	India	U.S.	Mexico	Brazil	India
1888	18%	37%		8%	0.022	0.058	
1893	29%				0.038		
1895	33%	35%			0.042	0.059	
1896	30%				0.041		
1900	30%		19%	7%	0.038	0.028	0.018
1904	33%	21%			0.042		
1909	38%				0.045		
1912	30%		19%	8%	0.039		0.018
1913	31%	14%			0.041	0.014	

Source: Maurer and Haber (2007).

were held in just two banks: Banamex and Banco de Londres y México.[52] The vast majority of markets had, at most, three banks: a branch of Banamex, a branch of the Banco de Londres y México, and a branch of the bank that held that state's territorial concession. Given the lack of competition, what incentives did bank directors have to invest in institutions that would allow them to enforce arm's-length loans? Why not just lend to their own manufacturing and mining enterprises, treating the banks, in effect, as the treasury arms of those enterprises? Mexico's bankers answered these questions the way one would expect: even under a set of conservative assumptions, Maurer and Haber (2007) show that the majority of lending was to enterprises owned by a bank's own directors. The logical implication of a small number of banks and insider lending was that there was a reduced number of firms in finance-dependent, downstream industries. The phenomena is shown in the structure of Mexico's cotton textile industry, as compared to the cotton textile industries of the United States, Brazil, and India. (See Table 8.4). Not only did Mexico have higher concentration indices than Brazil, India, and the United States, but concentration actually increased as the industry grew in size. This is not the result that one would anticipate from an industry characterized by constant returns to scale technology – but it is what one would expect when the largest firms in the industry shared directors with the largest banks in the country.

---

[52] Secretaria de Hacienda, Mexico, *Amario de Estadistica Fiscal, 1911–12* (Mexico City, Imprenta del Gobierno, 1912): 236, 255.

The coalition that supported Díaz's dictatorship fell apart after three decades. The same set of institutions that underpinned growth in banking – an alliance between economic and political elites that came at the expense of everyone else – also existed in other sectors of the economy. Indeed, restrictions on bank charters were a fundamental weapon in the arsenal of tactics employed by the country's largest industrialists to constrain competition in manufacturing.[53] As was the case in banking, the resulting growth in those sectors tended to heighten inequality, and produced, in time, organized resistance to the dictatorship. This resistance took up arms in 1910, removing Díaz from power in 1911, and opening up a decade-long period of coups, rebellions, and civil wars.

The lack of political stability meant that it was not possible for Mexico's bankers to forge a coalition with the parties in control of the government. Mexico's revolutionary governments, regardless of their stated ideologies, preyed upon the banks. By 1916 the banking system had become a shell, stripped of its liquid assets.[54] The outcome can be seen clearly in Table 8. 5: circa 1921, the total assets of Mexico's banks were only 5 percent of GDP, as compared to 32 percent in 1910.

The lack of a functioning banking system jeopardized the survival of Mexico's postrevolutionary governments. In fact, calling them governments implies a good deal more stability and institutionalization than actually existed. The Mexican political system in the 1920s was really little more than a fragile coalition of revolutionary warlords allied to corrupt labor leaders, and headed by two political-military strongmen, Alvaro Obregón and Plutarco Elias Calles. This regime faced several threats to its survival, including two attempted military coups, a rebellion led by the Secretary of the Treasury, a church-state civil war, and the assassination of Obregón in 1928. The regime tried to obtain the revenues it needed to fight these movements by increasing taxation on mining and petroleum, and failed at both.[55] This meant that it had strong incentives to create a banking system from which it could borrow. At the same time, the private sector – most importantly the country's manufacturers – clamored for the creation of a banking system that it could use to finance its operations. Given the fact that the regime was trying to hold together a fragile coalition, keeping the private sector aligned with Obregón and Calles was as important as finding a source of public finance.

[53] Haber, Razo, and Maurer, *The Politics of Property Rights*, Ch. 5.
[54] Maurer, *The Power and the Money*; Haber, Razo, and Maurer, *The Politics of Property Rights*, Ch. 4.
[55] Haber, Razo, and Maurer, *The Politics of Property Rights*, Chs. 6 and 7.

TABLE 8.5. *The Mexican Banking Industry: Assets as a Percent of GDP, 1897–1929*

Year	Assets as Percent of GDP
1897	12%
1898	15%
1899	18%
1900	20%
1901	15%
1902	19%
1903	20%
1904	24%
1905	24%
1906	28%
1907	31%
1908	31%
1909	35%
1910	32%
1921	5%
1922	3%
1923	3%
1924	4%
1925	4%
1926	8%
1927	10%
1928	10%
1929	12%

Sources: Haber, Razo, and Maurer (2003), Ch. 4; Maurer and Haber (2007).

The problem was that bankers did not view the Obregón-Calles regime as a credible partner: There was nothing to keep the regime from raiding bank assets. The government therefore had to repeat the same process that had taken place under Díaz in 1884: work with the bankers to craft a series of institutions designed to raise the rate of return on capital high enough to compensate them for the risk of expropriation. These institutional arrangements were laid down in 1925 at a convention that the Calles government organized with the country's private bankers, which essentially allowed the banking laws to be written by the bankers themselves. Not surprisingly, the law they created severely limited competition by keeping foreign banks out of retail banking and by giving the National Banking Commission, on which they had strong representation, the right to regulate the number of charters granted to new banks. The law also created a government-owned commercial bank, the Banco de México, which lent most of its funds to private bankers and powerful politicians.[56]

The Obregón-Calles regime morphed into an institutionalized, party-based dictatorship in the 1930s. This party, initially organized and led by Calles in 1929, went through various reorganizations, ultimately naming itself the Partido Revolucionario Institucional (PRI). The most important fact about this party, however, was not its name, but its complete monopoly of political power: the PRI financed its campaigns out of the federal treasury, decided which parties could run against it, monitored the elections, counted the votes, and certified the results. Not surprisingly, it "won" every gubernatorial and senatorial election from the late 1920s to the 1980s, and every presidential election until 2000. To maintain a façade of democracy, it crafted a complex set of electoral rules that allowed other parties, some of which were actually subsidized by the government, to win seats in the federal Chamber of Deputies (Mexico's lower house of congress) – but the PRI dominated this chamber by an overwhelming majority until the 1990s. The PRI used its electoral dominance to maintain control over Mexico's regulatory and legal systems: PRI leaders named state and federal judges and the directors of government-owned firms as well as making appointments in the federal bureaucracy. It was, in the words of the Peruvian novelist Mario Vargas Llosa, "a perfect dictatorship."

As soon as this dictatorship started to take shape in the 1930s the government began to claw back some of the policy-making authority that the Obregón-Calles regime had delegated to private bankers. In 1932, the government converted the Banco de México into a central bank. A further reform in 1936 required commercial banks to maintain cash reserves in the Banco de México, which is to say that banks had to lend part of their deposit base to the government. That same law also transferred many bank supervisory functions from the banker-influenced National Banking Commission to the Banco de México. In a further set of reforms enacted in 1941, the government forced commercial banks to divest their investment banking operations into separate corporations.[57]

[56] Maurer, *The Power and the Money*, 2002; Haber, Razo, and Maurer, *The Politics of Property Rights*, Ch. 4.

[57] Gustavo Del Ángel-Mobarak, "La banca mexicana antes de 1892," in *Cuando el estado se hizo banquero: consecuencias de la nacionalización bancaria en México*, eds. Gustavo del Ángel-Mobarak, Carlos Bazdresch Parada, and Francisco Suárez Dávila (Mexico City: Fondo de Cultura Económica, 2002, 2005).

Mexico's bankers did not roll over and play dead when the PRI began to reshape banking policies to its own ends. They responded by crafting an uneasy alliance of convenience with the leadership of the PRI. The deal was simple: the party created a favorable environment for Mexico's banker-industrialists; the banker-industrialists provided stable employment for millions of unionized workers; the unionized workers enthusiastically supported the party.[58]

The favorable environment for Mexico's banker industrialists basically came down to this: The government provided trade protection for their factories and limits on competition for their banks by controlling the number of charters. As a legal matter, Mexico possessed three different types of banks: commercial banks, which handled most retail banking operations and made short-term loans to business enterprises; investment banks (*financieras*), which made long-term loans to businesses and often held equity positions in those firms; and government-run development banks (the first of which had been founded in the 1930s), which made long-term loans to business enterprises, collateralized by shares in those firms. Regardless of who owned them, however, all three types of banks worked together to finance Mexico's largest industrial and commercial enterprises. Indeed, Mexico's industrial conglomerates typically owned both a commercial bank and an investment bank, and the portfolios of these banks tended to be composed of shares held in the enterprises that were part of the conglomerates.[59] These commercial and investment banks were, in essence, the treasury divisions of the conglomerates, much in the same way that the banks in Porfirian Mexico served as the treasury divisions of major manufacturing and mining groups. As a result, in 1974 the Mexican government gave up the legal fiction that commercial and investment banks were independent of one another, allowing them to merge into enterprises that were called multi-banks. The important thing to recognize about this private banking system is that it was quite small: As Table 8.6 shows, credit from commercial banks never exceeded 6 percent of GDP, and credit from *financieras* never exceeded 13 percent.

The policy justification for government-owned development banks was that they existed to compensate for an inadequate private banking system. The facts suggest, however, that development banks served as a mechanism to subsidize the private banks and the industrial conglomerates that were associated with them. One of the functions of the development banks

---

[58] Stephen Haber, Herbert S. Klein, Noel Maurer, and Kevin J. Middlebook, *Mexico Since 1980* (Cambridge: Cambridge University Press, 2008): Ch. 2.

[59] Del Ángel-Mobarak, "La banca mexicana".

TABLE 8.6. *Mexico, Sources of Credit, 1940–1978*

Year	Commercial Banks Percentage of GDP	Other Private Banks Percentage of GDP	Government Banks Percentage of GDP	System Total Percentage of GDP
1940	4%	1%	3%	8%
1941	5%	1%	4%	10%
1942	6%	1%	4%	11%
1943	6%	2%	4%	12%
1944	5%	2%	4%	10%
1945	5%	2%	4%	12%
1946	4%	2%	4%	11%
1947	4%	3%	5%	12%
1948	5%	3%	6%	13%
1949	5%	2%	6%	13%
1950	5%	2%	6%	14%
1951	5%	2%	7%	14%
1952	5%	2%	6%	14%
1953	5%	2%	8%	16%
1954	5%	2%	9%	16%
1955	5%	2%	7%	14%
1956	5%	3%	6%	14%
1957	5%	3%	6%	14%
1958	5%	3%	7%	14%
1959	5%	4%	8%	17%
1960	5%	4%	10%	19%
1961	5%	5%	12%	21%
1962	5%	5%	13%	23%
1963	5%	5%	13%	23%
1964	5%	6%	12%	23%
1965	6%	7%	11%	23%
1966	5%	8%	11%	24%
1967	6%	9%	12%	26%
1968	6%	10%	11%	27%
1969	6%	11%	12%	29%
1970	6%	13%	12%	31%
1971	6%	13%	13%	32%
1972	6%	13%	12%	31%
1973	5%	12%	12%	29%
1974	5%	10%	12%	27%
1975	5%	10%	12%	27%
1976	5%	9%	16%	30%
1977	5%	8%	17%	30%
1978	7%	7%	15%	28%

Source: Del Ángel-Mobarak (2005) 45.

was to serve as second-tier lenders, repurchasing loans made by commercial banks through special programs designed to channel credit to sectors the government deemed economically important.[60] These directed-credit programs represented a government guarantee to private banks because all of the default risk was born by the development bank, while the private bank earned income from originating and servicing the loan. Moreover, most of the firms that received these loans were large manufacturers and commercial enterprises, often with unionized workforces, that had the political clout to be designated as a strategic industry. This meant that industrial and commercial conglomerates could fund risky enterprises through the development banks rather than from the private banks that were under their control. It was not private bank depositors and shareholders who bore the risk; rather, it was the taxpayers who subsidized the development banks.

Development banks also made direct loans to private manufacturers, further subsidizing large industrial firms as well as the private banks that owned them. The largest and oldest development bank in Mexico, Nacional Financiera (NAFIN), obtained its capital by selling government-backed bonds and then made long-term loans to manufacturers that were collateralized by blocks of shares issued by those firms. NAFIN was supposed to provide credit to small and mid-sized manufacturing companies, which were often unable to obtain financing from commercial and investment banks. As a practical matter, however, NAFIN allocated most of its credit to the very same industrial conglomerates that received financing from private banks. The political pressure to lend to large firms, whose owners were politically well connected and which often had large, unionized, and electorally significant workforces, simply outweighed whatever original mandate NAFIN may have had.[61] Worse, because of the political importance of their workforces, the government came to use NAFIN as a mechanism to bail out manufacturers that were not economically viable. Even worse, the policy of bailouts encouraged moral hazard: Knowing that they would be bailed out, manufacturers undertook activities of doubtful profitability.[62]

This alliance of convenience between Mexico's bankers and the PRI dictatorship was always fragile. It was based on the fact that the bankers

---

[60] Ibid.
[61] Enrique Cárdenas, "The Process of Accelerated Industrialization in Mexico, 1929–82," in *Industrialization and State in Latin America: The Postwar Years*, vol. 3 of *An Economic History of Twentieth-Century Latin America*, eds. Enrique Cárdenas, Antonio Ocampo, and Rosemary Thorp., 176–204 (London: Palgrave, 2000).
[62] Cárdenas, "Accelerated Industrialization," 195.

and the manufacturers were one-in-the-same, that the PRI needed to reward organized labor for its political support; and that those organized workers were employed by the same industrial conglomerates that were owned by powerful bankers.[63] The implication is that if the political calculus of the PRI leadership changed, there was little that the bankers could do to protect themselves against expropriation.

The change in calculus occurred in the 1970s, as government expenditures began to outstrip revenues by a wide margin – and it resulted in a stepwise expropriation of the banks. In the 1960s, the Mexican government began to run modest budget deficits, and by the 1970s these modest deficits had ballooned to an average of 7 percent of GDP. These deficits were financed through two mechanisms: foreign borrowing and financial repression via increasing legal reserve ratios. As Table 8.7 makes clear, reserve ratios climbed from just 15 percent of deposits in 1959 to 43.5 percent by 1979. The central bank paid interest on these reserves, but that interest rate was below the rate of inflation. In other words, the government financed its deficits by expropriating nearly half of the deposits in the private banking system.[64] The banks responded by paying negative real interest rates, which caused the deposit base to contract and private credit to shrink.

By the summer of 1982 the government's strategy had become unsustainable: Mexico was entering into a hyper-inflation, much of the private banking system was no longer profitable because its deposit base had disappeared, and the foreign debt had reached unsustainable levels. The government therefore suspended payment on its international debts, converted dollar denominated bank accounts to pesos at the official rate of exchange (roughly half the black-market rate), blamed the bankers for the collapse of the exchange rate, and then expropriated the banks.

During the 1980s, Mexico's banks were essentially run as vehicles to finance government budget deficits. The government-owned banks took in deposits (which as of 1986 were insured by a government-run deposit insurance agency) and then invested the proceeds in government treasury bonds. Some credit was also directed to politically-crucial producer and consumer groups. These decisions were made more on the basis of political calculus than of their economic rationality. Indeed, in the late 1980s the ratio of nonperforming to total loans began to climb markedly, as

---

[63] Haber, Klein, Maurer, and Middlebrook, *Mexico Since 1980*, Ch. 2.
[64] Del Ángel-Mobarak "La banca mexicana," 285.

TABLE 8.7. *Mexico, Deposits, Loans, and Reserve Ratios, 1948–1982*

Year	Banking System Deposits as a Percentage of GDP	Total Bank Claims on Private Sector as a Percentage of GDP	Reserve Ratio (Deposits Divided by Reserves)
1948	15.75%	14.98%	26.09%
1949	16.82%	16.33%	24.42%
1950	16.18%	16.11%	34.61%
1951	17.49%	15.60%	25.00%
1952	17.17%	15.16%	23.14%
1953	19.27%	17.13%	21.71%
1954	19.83%	18.95%	17.56%
1955	18.68%	16.18%	18.30%
1956	17.76%	16.29%	17.52%
1957	17.72%	16.03%	15.35%
1958	18.06%	16.49%	15.27%
1959	19.70%	19.16%	14.89%
1960	21.85%	21.55%	11.78%
1961	24.15%	23.80%	10.48%
1962	25.73%	26.00%	10.84%
1963	28.14%	26.45%	11.75%
1964	29.81%	27.41%	10.35%
1965	30.21%	25.92%	9.31%
1966	31.92%	26.80%	10.45%
1967	35.63%	29.42%	10.02%
1968	37.59%	30.37%	11.34%
1969	40.22%	33.02%	11.28%
1970	39.66%	32.91%	10.36%
1971	41.58%	34.14%	11.14%
1972	41.35%	33.70%	21.69%
1973	39.52%	31.50%	24.04%
1974	36.52%	28.71%	29.54%
1975	38.29%	29.13%	32.75%
1976	42.00%	32.25%	13.96%
1977	25.39%	17.46%	48.26%
1978	27.26%	19.32%	43.45%
1979	28.19%	19.90%	43.54%
1980	26.99%	19.30%	44.81%
1981	29.74%	19.44%	43.53%
1982	29.77%	15.35%	57.56%

Source: Del Ángel-Mobarak (2005).

private loans were made to firms and individuals that had low probabilities of repayment.[65]

In 1991 the government of Carlos Salinas de Gortari (1988–94) sought to privatize this moribund banking system (along with a broad range of other state-run enterprises). The purpose of this privatization program was both fiscal and political. Salinas needed to balance the federal budget in order to stamp out runaway inflation, and at the same time he needed to find revenue sources to fund social programs that would help the PRI hold onto its six-decade-long political monopoly. The auction of state-owned firms solved both problems: their sales would reduce the drain that these (perennially unprofitable) firms put on the budget; and they would produce a one-time windfall that could be deployed in order to win the 1994 presidential election through politically-targeted spending on social welfare programs.

Salinas faced a variant of the problem that Díaz and Calles had faced before him: no promise his government made was credible, because there was no obvious sanction for breaking a promise. Salinas's problem was further compounded by the fact that he was not just trying to create a private banking system, he was trying to sell one that his party had expropriated just nine years before. Complicating the task even more was the fact that Salinas needed to obtain the highest price possible for the banks.

Aligning the incentives of the government and the bankers was not, therefore an easy process. The deal that was ultimately hit upon was a set of agreements that minimized the amount of capital that bankers and shareholders had at risk, thereby raising the rate of return on equity. The mechanism to do this, unfortunately, was that bankers and shareholders were able to borrow the funds to purchase the banks, sometimes from the same banks that they were buying, with the collateral being the bank shares.[66] The fact that neither the insiders nor the minority shareholders had much capital at risk meant that Mexico's depositors were seriously exposed. Not surprisingly, they pressured the government into

---

[65] Jeffrey W. Gunther, Robert S. Moore, and Genie D. Short, "Mexican Banks and the 1944 Peso Crisis: The Importance of Initial Conditions," *North American Journal of Economics and Finance*, 7 Issue 1 (1996): 125–33.

[66] Haluk Unal and Miguel Navarro (1999) "The Technical Process of Bank Privatization in Mexico." *Journal of Financial Services Research* (16 September 1999): 61–83; Michael W. Mackey. "Report of Michael W. Mackey on the Comprehensive Evaluation of the Operations and Function of the Fund for the Protection of Bank Saving "FOBAPROA" and the Quality of Supervision of the FOBAPROA Program 1995–1998 (n.p. 1999), 55, 61, 141, 216.

providing them with deposit insurance far beyond the statutory limits.[67] Precisely because there was unlimited deposit insurance, bank depositors did not police banks by withdrawing funds from banks with risky loan portfolios.[68]

The bottom line was that neither bankers, stockholders, nor the depositors had enough invested in the game to make them effective monitors. As a result, Mexico's banks went on a wild lending spree that produced a growing burden of nonperforming loans.[69] Within three years, the banks were insolvent. The government responded with a bailout of the banking system – the net effect of which was to expropriate taxpayers for the benefit of shareholders, depositors, and debtors. In fact, Mexico's bankers appear to have anticipated the bailout: they made large loans to themselves at low rates of interest, and then defaulted on the loans.[70]

The fact that the bailout involved an implicit transfer from taxpayers to depositors, debtors, and stockholders, who included some of Mexico's wealthiest men, produced a political firestorm in Mexico. It was one of the key reasons why the PRI finally lost control of the lower house of Congress in 1997 and the presidency in 2000.[71] That is, the collapse of the banking system produced a political reaction that finally ended the PRI's seven-decade monopoly on power.

The collapse of the PRI created, for the first time in Mexican history, a multi-party democracy with mass suffrage. It is still too early to make any statements about the effect of democratization on the availability of credit, but there are three salient features of Mexico's post-1997 banking system. First, as of 1997, foreign banks were allowed to purchase controlling interests in Mexican banks for the first time since 1884. Foreign banks now control three-quarters of bank assets in Mexico. Second, a series of reforms to accounting and lending standards, in conjunction with foreign ownership, has reduced the incentives for banks to lend to related parties. Third, demands for increased access to credit have caused successive Mexican governments to be somewhat more liberal in the granting of bank charters, as well as inducing the government to create second-tier

---

[67] Mackey, "Report": 44, 55.
[68] Martinez Peria, Maria Soledad, and Sergio J. Schmukler. "Do Depositors Punish Banks for Bad Behavior? Market Discipline, Deposit Insurance, and Banking Crises," *Journal of Finance* 56 (June 2001): 1029–51.
[69] Haber, "Mexico's Experiments with Banks."
[70] La Porta et al., "Related Lending," *Quarterly Journal of Economics* 18 (February 2003): 231–68.
[71] Beatriz Magaloni, *Voting for Autocracy: Hegemonic Party Survival and its Demise in Mexico* (New York: Cambridge University Press, 2006).

lenders designed to increase mortgage credit.[72] In point of fact, in 2006 the Mexican government allowed the giant retailer Wal-Mart to enter the retail banking market – something that, ironically, proved politically impossible to accomplish in the United States.

Brazil

Unlike Mexico, Brazil has had no de jure expropriations of its banking system since its creation as a sovereign country. That does not mean, however, that Brazil developed a banking system that allocated credit broadly. In fact, Brazil is a prime example of a country in which the parties in control of the government and bankers forged coalitions to limit competition and constrain access to credit. They were able to do so precisely because throughout the nineteenth and early twentieth centuries there were limits on suffrage and political institutions that amplified the power of elites.

These arrangements came under threat only once, when the monarchy that governed Brazil after independence was overthrown in 1889 and the new republican government that replaced it allowed virtually unlimited access to bank charters. Nevertheless, within a few years of the creation of the republic, the old set of arrangements was re-created and Brazil went back to a system in which the government limited the number of banks, and, in exchange, the banks extended credit to the government. Why voters allowed this to happen is an obvious question, which has an equally obvious answer: restrictions on the suffrage meant that less than five percent of the population had the right of suffrage. For most of the twentieth century, the Brazilian banking system consisted of a small number of banks that were the treasury departments of major industrial conglomerates and an equally small number of state-owned banks that existed to finance the budget deficits of states. The country's largest commercial bank was also the government's fiscal agent. These features of the Brazilian banking system were, in point of fact, the motivation for a broad literature on the role of "grupos" (bank-based industrial conglomerates) in developing countries.[73]

---

[72] Haber, "Mexico's Experiments with Banks," Stephen Haber, "Why Banks Don't Lend: The Mexican Financial System," in *No Growth Without Equity? Inequality, Interests, and Competition in Mexico*, eds. Santiago Levy and Michael Walton, (Washington, D.C.: World Bank/Palgrave Macmillan, 2009), 283–320.

[73] For example, Nathaniel Leff, "Industrial Organization and Entrepreneurship in the Developing Countries: The Economic Groups," *Economic Development and Cultural Change* 26 (July 1978): 661–75.

Brazil's first bank, the Banco do Brasil was created in 1808 by King Dom João VI of Portugal when he was transported to Brazil by the British Navy following the invasion of Portugal by Napoleon. Until then financial intermediation was handled by the merchant-financiers who dominated the import-export trade. Dom João needed revenue sources to administer his empire, but Brazil lacked an administrative structure to collect sufficient taxes. He therefore adopted a solution that by now should be familiar to readers: He granted a charter for a monopoly bank of issue. Much like Porfirio Díaz, Dom João could not make a credible commitment to the group of insiders (and by extension the minority shareholders) who would fund this bank. His absolute power meant that he could borrow from the bank, and then repudiate the loans. He therefore had to coax the investors in the Banco do Brasil into deploying their capital by granting the bank lucrative privileges. These included a monopoly on the issuance of paper money, a monopoly on the export of luxury goods, a monopoly on the handling of government financial operations, the right to have debts to the bank treated as having the same legal standing as debts owed to the royal treasury, and the right to collect new taxes imposed by the king – and to then hold those taxes as interest free deposits for a period of ten years.[74]

Even these privileges were insufficient. Investors remained so wary that the Banco do Brasil was unable to achieve its original capitalization goals until 1817, nine years after it was chartered. Their wariness was well founded: most of the bank's business consisted of printing bank notes that were then used to buy bonds issued by the imperial government. As the amount of banknotes increased, so too did inflation. In effect, the bank was the government's agent in creating an inflation tax, and that inflation tax hit everybody, including the bank's shareholders, who likely did not receive an inflation-adjusted rate of return adequate to compensate them for the opportunity cost of their capital. As Table 8.8 shows, the nominal rate of return on owner's equity in the Banco do Brasil from 1810 to 1820 averaged 10 percent per year, which, as near as it can be known, probably did not exceed the rate of inflation by a wide margin. Not surprisingly, as Table 8.8 shows, the shareholders of the bank paid out virtually all of the available returns to themselves as dividends. Worse still, in 1820, Dom João reneged on the arrangement by which the bank could hold the proceeds from the new taxes that he had created. The following year, he returned to Portugal, and took with

---

[74] Carlos Manuel Peláez, "The Establishment of Banking Institutions in a Backward Economy: Brazil, 1800–1851," *Business History Review* 49 (Winter 1975): 446–72.

TABLE 8.8. *Accounts of the First Banco do Brasil, 1809–1829* *

	Subscribed Capital (1)	Reserve Fund (100) (2)	Annual Taxes Transferred to Bank as Deposits (100)	Owner's Equity[1]	Estimated Earnings[2]	Return on Equity (100)	Dividends as Percentage of Earnings
1809	116	0	0	116	0	0%	77%
1810	120	0.3	0	120	1.3	1%	85%
1811	122	1	0	123	4.7	4%	83%
1812	172	2	0	174	6	3%	83%
1813	397	5.6	63	403	21.6	5%	84%
1814	502	14	58	516	51.4	10%	83%
1815	581	29	62	610	89	15%	83%
1816	690	53	88	743	144	19%	84%
1817	1189	83	65	1,272	183	14%	84%
1818	1719	122	75	1,841	241	13%	84%
1819	2037	163	73	2,200	249	11%	84%
1820	2215	207	16	2,422	271	11%	84%
1821	2235	275	0	2,510	421	17%	84%
1822	2248	329	0	2,577	336	13%	84%
1823	2357	404	0	2,761	467	17%	84%
1824	2662	482	0	3,144	502	16%	84%
1825	3600	570	0	4,170	539	13%	84%
1826	2600	692	0	3,292	762	23%	84%
1827	3600	819	0	4,419	796	18%	84%
1828	3600	954	0	4,554	851	19%	84%
1829	3600	1083	0	4,683	815	17%	84%

Notes:
*All Units in Thousands of Contos de Reis.
[1] Subscribed Capital plus reserve fund.
[2] Dividends plus change in reserves from previous year.
Source: Calculated from data in Peláez (1975), tables 3 and 4.

him all of the metals that he and his court had deposited in the bank, exchanging them for whatever banknotes they had in their possession. The Banco do Brasil then continued to function through the rest of the 1820s, and was used by Dom João's son, the Emperor Dom Pedro I, much in the same way as it had been used previously – to finance government budget deficits through note issues.[75]

In 1822 Dom Pedro, at the urging of local elites and with the consent of his father, declared Brazil independent. Independence did not do much to change the status quo ante for the great mass of slaves, free blacks, and native-born Brazilians of humble social origin. It did, however, allow Brazil's financial elites to constrain the emperor, forcing him into a coalition. The elites who drafted the Constitution of 1824 gave parliament, and not the emperor, the ultimate responsibility to tax, spend, and borrow. They also specified an elected lower house of parliament,

[75] Peláez, "The Establishment of Banking Institutions."

and restricted the vote on the basis of wealth so that the lower house represented their interests. As Summerhill has pointed out, this had two consequences: The emperor could not default on loans that he had contracted from the incumbent financial elite; and the financial elite could use its influence in parliament to make sure that competing economic groups could not obtain bank charters. From the closing of the Banco do Brasil by parliament in 1829 to the mid-1850s, parliament permitted only seven new banks to be formed – all of which had limited provincial charters that created local banking monopolies.

This set of arrangements worked well for the incumbent bankers, but it came at a cost to the emperor: After 1829 the imperial government did not have a bank that it could use to finance budget deficits. Finding a solution was difficult because creating a national bank large enough to finance the government required aligning the incentives of all the incumbent bankers – some of whom were able to use their influence in parliament to undo whatever deals the emperor struck. Thus, parliament authorized a second Banco do Brasil in 1853, but then removed its right to issue bank notes just four years later.[76]

A compromise was only reached in the 1860s when a coalition was formed between the bankers and the imperial government. An 1860 law specified that corporate charters, including those for banks, not only needed the approval of parliament and the emperor's cabinet, they also required approval from the Emperor's Council of State, whose members enjoyed life tenure. In 1863, the Second Banco do Brasil merged with two other Rio de Janeiro banks, the Banco Comercial e Agrícola and the Banco Rural e Hipotecario, which transferred to the Banco do Brasil their rights of note issue, thereby creating something that the emperor had been seeking for a decade: a note issuing bank that acted as the government's fiscal agent.[77] The government got its bank, and the economic elite got their banks, but no one else could get a bank charter – and no one from outside the small group of "barons" who sat on a bank board was eligible for a loan.[78]

Some sense of how restricted the banking industry in Brazil was can be gleaned from Table 8.9, which contains estimates of the size of the

---

[76] Anne G. Hanley, *Native Capital: Financial Institutions and Economic Development in Sao Paulo, Brazil, 1850–1920* (Stanford: Stanford University Press, 2005); William Summerhill, *Inglorious Revolution: Political Institutions, Sovereign Debt, and Financial Underdevelopment in Imperial Brazil* (New Haven: Yale University Press, forthcoming).

[77] Carlos Manuel Peláez and Wilson Suzigan, *História Monetariá do Brasil: Analise da Politica, Comportamento e Instituicoes Monetarias*, 2nd edition (Brasilia: Editora Universidade de Brasilia, 1976): 103.

[78] Peláez and Suzigan, *Historia Monetaria do Brasil*, 82–87.

TABLE 8.9. *Size Estimates of the Brazilian Banking System, 1875–1935*

Year	Entering Banks	Exiting Banks	Operating Banks	Estimated Total Paid-in Capital (Millions, 1900 Milreis)
1875	0	0	12	234
1880	0	0	12	197
1882	10	0	22	296
1888	4	1	27	358
1889	55	2	81	1,447
1890	38	20	112	2,048
1891	52	26	133	1,413
1892	11	18	127	922
1893	2	9	116	576
1894	1	2	110	486
1895	1	5	106	537
1896	2	4	0	487
1897	2	2	104	455
1898	0	9	102	384
1899	3	10	96	400
1900	0	2	86	311
1901	0	4	84	385
1902	2	11	81	445
1903	0	4	70	422
1904	0	4	67	380
1905	0	2	63	413
1906	1	0	62	356
1907	0	6	62	363
1908	0	4	55	326
1909	2	5	50	336
1910	2	6	51	341
1911	0	3	45	327
1912	4	0	46	393
1913	2	2	48	438
1914	2	0	48	563
1925	3	1	49	346
1926	1	5	50	323
1927	3	2	47	382
1929	2	1	47	369
1930	0	2	46	406
1931	1	0	45	486
1934	0	11	45	397
1935	1	5	36	237

Source: Estimated from data in *Jornal do Comercio*, various issues.

Brazilian banking sector based on information retrieved from the Rio de Janeiro stock exchange. In 1875 there were only twelve banks in the entire country. The number of banks then increased at a snail's pace throughout the rest of the imperial period: At the end of the first semester of 1888 there were only twenty-seven. Moreover, their combined capitalization had only increased by 53 percent over the thirteen-year period since 1875. Of this capital, 22 percent was concentrated in one bank, the third Banco do Brasil. Let us put this into comparative perspective. In 1888, bank assets per capita in Brazil totaled $2.40 USD. In Mexico in 1897, they were nearly three times this level, at $6.74. In the United States, in 1890, they were $85.00.

The coalition between the political elites who ran the government and the incumbent financial elite came under threat when the monarchy was overthrown and a federal republic was created in 1889. Space constraints prevent us from exploring how and why the coalition that had supported the emperor fell apart, but one crucial piece of the story was the abolition of slavery in 1888. Abolition drove a wedge between Brazil's planter class and the imperial government. In an effort to placate the planters by making credit more easily available, the imperial government awarded concessions to twelve banks of issue and provided seventeen banks with interest-free loans. The easy credit policies of 1888 were not enough, however, to stem the tide of Brazil's Repúblican movement. In November of 1889 Dom Pedro II was overthrown in a military coup and a federal republic was created.

The creation of a federal republic undermined for a time the arrangements that had supported a small and concentrated banking industry. The 1891 Constitution gave each of Brazil's twenty states considerable sovereignty, ending the central government's monopoly on the chartering of banks. This put the federal republic's first finance minister, Rui Barbosa, under considerable pressure: If he did not grant additional charters to new banks in order to satisfy the demand for credit from Brazil's growing regional economic elites – most particularly planters and manufacturers – those elites would get their own state governments to do so. As a result, Rui Barbosa quickly pushed through a series of financial reforms, one of whose features was that the federal government allocated bank charters to virtually all comers through a general incorporation law, and another of whose features was that banks could engage in whatever kind of financial transactions they wished. The results of these reforms were dramatic. Recall that in 1888 there were only twenty-seven banks in the entire country. In 1891, as Table 8.9 indicates, there were 133.

Moreover, their total real capitalization (in 1900 milreis) was four times that of the 1888 banks.

Brazil's bankers, and the central government, soon found themselves in a difficult position. The government had allocated the right to issue banknotes to a large number of banks, each of which aggressively printed and lent currency. Much of that currency, in fact, was used to purchase shares in hundreds of newly created joint stock companies. Brazil's bank insiders were, in effect, gambling with the funds of the minority stockholders and depositors. The central government did not clamp down on these activities because it was using the bond markets and the banks to fund its own budget shortfalls. The 1891 constitution denied it access to a crucial source of tax income, revenues from export taxes, which were now collected directly by states. It did not take long for this state of affairs to run its predictable course: In addition to borrowing domestically, the central government also borrowed abroad in gold-denominated loans. The result was a currency mismatch: a hard-currency denominated foreign debt, a domestic-currency denominated source of income (taxes paid in Brazilian milreis), and an inflation that drove down the international value of the domestic currency. The central government had three options: spend less, raise taxes, or curtail the growth of the money supply. It chose options two and three. In 1896 the government decided once again to restrict the right to issue currency to a single bank – the Banco da República, which was a private commercial bank that had a special charter that made it the agent of the treasury. Two years later, the government increased taxes and restructured its foreign debt. These moves, coupled with the already shaky financial situation of many of the banks produced by their speculation in the stock market, resulted in a massive contraction of the banking sector. In 1891, as Table 8.9 shows, there were 133 banks operating in Brazil. Ten years later there were 84, and their combined capital was only one-quarter that of the 1891 banks. The numbers kept falling, so that by the end of 1905 there were only 63 banks in operation with a total capital only one quarter that of 1891. Moreover, one-third of this capital was concentrated in the single bank that served as the government's financial agent, the Banco da República. In effect, the bankers and the parties in control of the central government had jointly expropriated depositors and minority shareholders.

The contraction of the banking sector brought about yet another round of reform – one which re-created the coalition between financial incumbents and political elites. Debtors and potential debtors lost out in this reform – and they did so because they had weak levers with which to structure the incentives of political elites. In the first place, less than 5 percent of the population had the right to vote. In the second place, power was concentrated in a strong presidency: Congress was more a consultative forum than a legislative body.[79] In the third place, the president was indirectly elected: He was chosen by Congress, thereby allowing the political elites of the two largest states, Minas Gerais and Sao Paulo, to form a coalition and trade the presidency between them.

The government nationalized the insolvent Banco da República, converting debts owed by the bank to the treasury into equity, and created a new bank, the Fourth Banco do Brasil. Like the Banco da República, the Fourth Banco do Brasil was a commercial bank fully capable of taking deposits and making private loans. It differed from the Banco da República, however, in that the central government was a major stockholder, owning almost one-third of its shares, and the President of the Republic had the right to name the president of the bank, along with one of its four directors.[80] In addition, the Fourth Banco do Brasil was not permitted to make loans with terms greater than six months and was not allowed to purchase stock in other companies. These restrictions were designed to guarantee that the bank would retain high levels of liquidity so that it could purchase treasury notes and bills, as well as to act as a lender of last resort in times of economic crisis.[81]

For the better part of the next six decades, the Brazilian banking system was dominated by the Fourth Banco do Brasil, which acted both as a commercial bank and as the treasury's financial agent. The charter that created the bank included a number of lucrative privileges, including the right to hold federal balances, issue banknotes, and have a monopoly on interstate branching. These privileges appear to have constituted a barrier to entry: the Banco do Brasil earned a rate of return on equity more than twice that of its competitors.[82] As a result, to the degree that there were competing banks in Brazil they were few in number. As Table 8.9 shows, as late as 1930, when the First Republic was overthrown in a coup, Brazil had fewer banks than it had in 1899.

---

[79] Gail Triner, *Banking and Economic Development: Brazil, 1889–1930* (New York: Palgrave, 2000), 18.

[80] Steven Topik, "State Enterprise in a Liberal Regime: The Banco do Brasil, 1905–1930," *Journal of Interamerican Studies and World Affairs* 22 (November 1980): 401–22.

[81] Steven Topik, *The Political Economy of the Brazilian State, 1889–1930* (Austin: University of Texas Press, 1987): 39.

[82] Aaron Berg and Stephen Haber, "Always Turkeys: Brazil's State-Owned Banks in Historical Perspective" (Mimeo: Stanford University, 2009).

In short, the political economy of Brazilian banking was not dramatically different from that of Mexico: regardless of which particular political elite was in power, that elite forged a coalition with incumbent financiers, and the arrangements they created provided bankers with oligopoly rents and the central government with a bank to fund its budget deficits. In the years following World War I, state governments began to copy the model of the Banco do Brasil, establishing joint state-private banks whose purpose was to finance their budget deficits. That is, the banks took deposits from private individuals, and then invested the proceeds in the bonds of state governments.

The disadvantages of this system were two. First, it allocated credit very narrowly: to state governments, the federal government, and large business enterprises whose owners were tied to the banks.[83] Second, it created a soft budget constraint for the state governments. They could sell debt to the state bank to the point that it became illiquid or insolvent, and then demand a bank rescue from the federal government. Federal governments, of whatever ideological stripe or regime type, went along with this system because it kept local political elites in whatever coalition had been formed. This was, in short, a recipe for continual state budget deficits, banking crises, and federal bailouts, which ultimately were paid for by taxpayers. This system persisted until the 1990s, when Brazil's newly created democratic government privatized the state-owned banks.[84]

Conclusions and Implications

The histories of these three cases are broadly consistent with the view that the size and structure of banking systems are the product of political deals, and are not the outcome of an endogenous process by which the demand for credit automatically produces a supply of banks. In all three cases, elites attempted to create distributional coalitions that would generate rents for bankers and a source of finance for the state. In Mexico and Brazil, those deals basically held until quite recently – and have only come under serious questioning since their recent experiments with democratization. In the United States, the ability of debtors and potential

---

[83] Morris Bornstein, "Banking Policy and Economic Development: A Brazilian Case Study," *Journal of Finance* 9 (September 1954): 312–313.

[84] Thorsten Beck, Juan Miguel Crivelli and William Summerhill, "State Bank Transformation in Brazil – Choices and Consequences," *Journal of Banking & Finance* 29 (August–September 2005): 2223–57.

debtors to influence legislation through candidate and party competition for office forced the deals between bankers and the parties in control of the government to change in the direction of increased competition and increased access to finance. That process was not, however, automatic or seamless: It proceeded in fits and starts as both political entrepreneurs and bankers adapted to changing circumstances by forming coalitions with reformers.

Several other patterns emerge as well. First, autocracies and representative democracies produce different banking systems because the problem of government expropriation looms more clearly in the former than in the latter. Second, representative institutions alone – such as Brazil's parliament in the nineteenth century – are necessary but not sufficient conditions to generate a broad allocation of credit. Financial incumbents can either capture the representative institutions or form coalitions with their members; thus effective suffrage is necessary in order to align the incentives of political elites with debtors. Third, the laws regarding the suffrage, as Chapter 4 shows, emerged over time. They were the outcome of an endogenous process that was strongly influenced by the distribution of human capital. Briefly put, the electoral system that emerged in the early nineteenth century United States was unthinkable in either Brazil or Mexico at a similar point in their histories.

Are these results generalizable? Obviously, more detailed case studies beyond the three presented here are necessary before any firm conclusions should be drawn, but the available evidence from large studies is broadly consistent with the patterns we find in Mexico, Brazil, and the United States. Barth, Caprio, and Levine analyzed a cross section of sixty-five countries in 2003 and found that democratic political institutions are associated with greater ease in obtaining a bank charter and fewer restrictions on the operation of banks.[85] They also found that the tight regulatory restrictions on banks created by autocratic political institutions were associated with lower credit market development and less bank stability, as well as with more corruption in lending. Bordo and Rousseau analyzed a panel of seventeen countries over a period from 1880 to 1997, and produced similar results: There was a strong, independent effect of proportional representation, frequent elections, female suffrage, and political stability on the size of the financial sector.[86] Quintyn

---

[85] Ibid.
[86] Michael Bordo and Peter Rousseau, "Legal-Political Factors and the Historical Evolution of the Finance-Growth Link," *European Review of Economic History* 10 (December 2006): 421–444.

and Verdier analyzed more than 200 episodes of "financial acceleration" around the world since 1960, and found that the likelihood of an acceleration leading to sustained financial development increased when the underlying political system was democratic.[87] Taken together, the case studies offered here, and the available statistical studies point in the same direction.

[87] Marc Quintyn and Geneviéve Verdier, "Mother Can I Trust the Government? Sustained Financial Deepening – A Political Institutions View," (IMF: Working Paper, 2010).

9

Five Hundred Years of European Colonization

The study, if not the practice, of colonialism is again in fashion. Over the last few years, colonialism has enjoyed a revival in interest among both scholars and the general public. The European record has been the subject of most intense study, but an appreciation of diversity is evident in the attention devoted to the colonization practices of the Mongols, the Chinese, the Russians, the Ottomans, the Incas, and the Aztecs. One reason for this reexamination may be sentimentality for a simpler ordered world, as a number of these new accounts cast colonial empires in a more favorable light than has generally been customary. Deepak Lal, for example, argues that those nations that established empires merit praise, as their creations normally brought about lower levels of conflict and costs of carrying out long-distance trade, as well as promoted greater prosperity in the affected societies.[1] Niall Ferguson highlights progressive sides to Britain's oversight of its colonies, such as the introduction of efficient civil services and rule of law, as well as the abolition of slavery.[2] The image of kinder and gentler imperial powers also has some foundation in the work of Lance Davis and Robert Huttenback, who in their meticulous and detailed estimates found that Britain was not nearly so aggressive or successful in extracting returns from its colonies as it could have been,

[1] Deepak Lal, *In Praise of Empires: Globalization and Order* (New York: Palgrave Macmillan, 2004).
[2] Niall Ferguson, *Empire: The Rise and the Demise of the British World Order and the Lessons for Global Power* (New York: Basic Books, 2003).

and indeed that its Empire generated little in the way of returns for the home country overall.[3]

Quite a different motivation, however, has been behind the recent proliferation of studies by economists of the European effort to colonize most of the rest of the world.[4] Inspired by the goal of improving understanding of the processes and institutions of economic growth, these scholars have been attracted by the "natural experiment" generated by a small number of European countries establishing many colonies across a wide range of environments. The logic is that the historical record of these different societies can be analyzed to determine whether there were systematic patterns in how their institutions or economies evolved with respect to initial conditions. For example, have colonies with a British heritage, or those in a particular sort of physical environment, realized more economic progress over time than have their counterparts? In other words, the history of European colonization provides scholars with a rich supply of evidence that can be used to study economic performance and the evolution of institutions over the long run. Because some of the characteristics of the colonies were in place at or near the time of settlement, and thus can reasonably be treated as exogenous, many economists have been hopeful that the data generated by their later development can be used to get at causal relationships or mechanisms.

Inequality is one of the key variables that emerge from these studies as of great consequence to long-run paths of development. Moreover, not only does extreme inequality seem to have had a profound influence on societies so afflicted, but the dynamics of European settlement generated many colonies with that condition. Several researchers have arrived at similar conclusions, but perhaps the most direct examination of the impact of inequality has been the work done on the economies of the Americas.

---

[3] Lance E. Davis and Robert A. Huttenback, *Mammon and the Pursuit of Empire: The Political Economy of British Imperialism, 1860–1912* (Cambridge: Cambridge University Press, 1986).

[4] For examples of what has become a substantial literature, see, in particular, Daron Acemoglu, Simon Johnson, and James A. Robinson, "The Colonial Origins of Comparative Development: An Empirical Investigation," *American Economic Review* 91 (December 2001): 1369–1401; Acemoglu, Johnson, and Robinson, "Reversal of Fortune: Geography and Institutions in the Making of the Modern World Income Distribution," *Quarterly Journal of Economics* 117 (November 2002): 1231–94; and William Easterly and Ross Levine, "Tropics, Germs, and Crops: The Role of Endowments in Economic Development," *Journal of Monetary Economics* 50 (January 2003): 3–39.

Our investigation begins with a question. Why was it that, for at least 250 years after the Europeans arrived to colonize the so-called New World, most observers regarded the English, French, Dutch, and Spanish settlements on the northern part of the North American continent as relative backwaters with limited economic prospects, and that the flows of resources to the Americas mirrored that view? The simple answer is that per capita incomes, especially for those of European descent, were higher in at least parts of the Caribbean and South America than they were in the colonies that were to become the United States and Canada well into the late eighteenth and early nineteenth centuries. Looking back from the vantage point of the early twenty-first century, however, it is clear that the real puzzle is why the colonies that were the choices of the first Europeans to settle in the Americas, were those that fell behind – and conversely, why the societies populated by those who came later and had to settle for areas considered less favorable have proved more successful economically over the long run. Another issue suggested by this experience is why it was not until 250 years after settlement began in the Americas and Asia, a period after many of the nations of the Americas had gained their independence, that there was a second burst of colonial expansion into much of Africa, the Pacific islands, and parts of Asia.

Impressed with how the evidence seemed inconsistent with the notions that British heritage or Protestantism was the sole key factor, we instead offered an alternative explanation of the divergent paths of development among the societies of the Americas.[5] We highlighted how the great majority of European colonies in the New World came to be characterized early in their histories, primarily because of their factor endowments, by extreme inequality in the distributions of wealth, human capital, and political influence. We argued, moreover, that these initial differences in inequality were of major import, because societies that began with great inequality tended, as compared to the small number – including those that came to make up the United States and Canada – that began with relative equality and homogeneity of the population, to evolve institutions that

---

[5] For example, see Douglass C. North, "Institutions, Economic Growth and Freedom: An Historical Introduction," in *Freedom, Democracy and Economic Welfare*, ed. Michael A. Walker, 3–25 (Vancouver: Fraser Institute, 1988) and John H. Coatsworth, "Notes on the Comparative Economic History of Latin America and the United States," in *Development and Underdevelopment in America: Contrasts of Economic Growth in North and Latin America in Historical Perspective*, eds. Walter L. Bernecker and Hans Werner Tobler, 10–30 (Berlin: Walter de Gruyter, 1993) for discussions of why the English institutional heritage helped Canada and the United States in realizing economic growth.

contributed to the persistence of substantial inequality and generally poor records of development over the long run.[6]

Although the great diversity of settlement patterns and economic structures across the Americas provide a particularly well suited context for the study of the impact of inequality on institutional and economic development, the patterns in that part of the world may well have important implications for the experience of societies established as European colonies elsewhere. With the exceptions of Australia and New Zealand, European settlements in other parts of the world were not based upon large numbers of European settlers who became the key productive laborers, but upon small numbers who remained on the perimeter of the country and exercised control through military power or political arrangements with the local rulers. For example, the Portuguese, Dutch, British, and French sailed around the Cape of Good Hope at roughly the same time as they went to the Americas, to acquire territories and control of large native populations in Asia. The numbers of European settlers were few and they were generally involved in either political administration or in operating very large agricultural units. And the Portuguese had a one-century lead over the British, the French, and the Dutch in colonizing Asia. These settler populations were rarely directly employed in producing commodities for sale in European markets, and their primary concern was more with control of production than with the direct production of economic surpluses. As for Africa, the early European settlements on the coast, mainly trading forts, were not able to exercise control over the native population because of disease factors as well as African military force. Even when Europeans were able to move inland during the nineteenth century, after the introduction of quinine, European domination was achieved with relatively few settlers, either through arrangements with local powers or via conflict and military prowess.[7] The last to be settled of the European colonies were the Pacific Ocean islands, including Fiji and Hawaii. There, too, and particularly where sugar could be grown, Europeans accounted for only small proportions of the population. In virtually all of these colonies, suffrage was restricted and expenditures on education and other public services tended to be miniscule, reflecting

---

[6] Above, Ch. 3. It is notable that the Latin American and Caribbean region continues to have the highest level of inequality in the world. See Klaus Deininger and Lyn Squire, "A New Data Set and Measure of Income Inequality," *World Bank Economic Review* 10 (September 1996): 565–91.

[7] The main exception to this generalization is South Africa, but even here those of European descent accounted for about 20 percent of the population.

(and contributing to) the magnitude of the inequality that existed between those of European descent and others.

Almost everywhere Europeans settled during their grand epoch of expansion across the globe, they did so with far higher levels of wealth, human capital (including literacy and familiarity with technology and markets), and political influence or power than most of the residents native to the area enjoyed. Thus, where the Europeans encountered large native populations who survived contact with western diseases (as in Indonesia and India), their advantages in human capital and other assets generally meant that Europeans did extremely well relative to the bulk of the natives, and that there was great inequality. Where they moved into fairly empty or depopulated territories, however (as in Australia, New Zealand, Canada, or the United States), relative equality tended to prevail.[8] The more heavily populated colonies, or those in tropical areas that could quickly increase population by drawing on imported slave labor, often had quite different comparative advantages than Europe (due to different climates and natural resources, and also to large native populations). As free populations were primarily motivated by the prospects of economic returns, these areas generally attracted the greater number of Europeans until the eighteenth century, when the greater opportunities associated with commercial grain agriculture and industrialization shifted attention to mainland North America. Overall, the phenomenon of European colonization generating many societies with extremely high degrees of inequality, and rather few with low inequality, seems unlikely to have been confined to the Americas.

II

In Chapter 1 of his *Imperialism*, John Hobson reproduced an interesting table first presented by Henry C. Morris in his *The History of Colonization*, constructed from data presented in the *Statesman's Yearbook*

---

[8] In those cases where the endowments were well suited to large-scale labor-intensive production of staples, slaves and contract labor were often brought in to provide a labor force. The importation of slaves to the Caribbean basin to grow sugar is the outstanding example of this, but the extensive use of contract labor from South Asia to augment the labor force, especially where land was relatively abundant, after the emancipation of slaves provides another. See Stanley L. Engerman, "Economic Adjustments to Emancipation in the United States and the British West Indies," *Journal of Interdisciplinary History* 12 (Autumn 1982): 191–220; Stanley L. Engerman, "Contract Labor, Sugar and Technology in the Nineteenth Century," *Journal of Economic History* 43 (September 1983): 635–59; Stanley L. Engerman, "Servants to Slaves to Servants: Contract Labour and European Expansion," in *Colonialism and Migration: Indentured Labor Before and After Slavery*, ed. P.C. Emmer, 263–294 (Dordrecht: Martinus Nijhoff, 1986)

TABLE 9.1. *Regional Distribution of Britain's Colonial Domain Over the Nineteenth Century*

	1815		1860		1880		1890–91		1899	
	(000)	(%)	(000)	(%)	(000)	(%)	(000)	(%)	(000)	(%)
EUROPE										
Pop	340	0.3	387	0.3	175	0.1	191	0.1	204	0.1
Land	–	–	1	0.0	0	0.0	0	0.0	0	0.0
ASIA										
Pop	124,200	98.3	137,279	94.6	256,149	95.6	288,436	94.7	291,587	94.4
Area	–	–	876	34.5	963	12.5	1,827	20.1	1,827	19.6
AFRICA										
Pop	244	0.2	836	0.6	2,718	1.0	4,963	1.6	4,932	1.6
Area	–	–	130	5.1	278	3.6	342	3.8	368	3.9
AMERICAS										
Pop	1,600	1.3	4,227	2.9	6,016	2.2	6,708	2.2	7,260	2.3
Area	–	–	954	37.5	3,359	43.7	3,769	41.4	3,953	42.4
AUSTRALASIA										
Pop	25	0.0	2,401	1.6	2,877	1.1	4,417	1.4	5,009	1.6
Area	–	–	580	22.8	3,084	40.1	3,175	34.8	3,176	34.1
TOTAL BRITISH DOMAIN										
Pop	126,408		145,129		267,935		304,716		308,992	
Area	–		2,541		7,685		9,113		9,324	
BRITISH DOMAIN AS PERCENTAGE OF ALL COLONIES, 1900										
Pop	66.2%									
Land	52.1									

Notes and Sources: The land area is measured in square miles. Morris (1900 II), 88, 318. These estimates of the colonial domain of Britain do not include some areas that many might consider to have been colonies. A prominent example is Ireland, which is not included because the Union Act of 1801 formed a kingdom of Great Britain and Ireland into the United Kingdom. In 1891, Ireland had a population of 4,704,750, and a land area of 32,531 square miles.

of 1900. That *Yearbook* presents 1899 data on area, population, and related matters for each independent country and their colonies, protectorates, and dependencies.[9] Among the figures Morris computed are the actual number of separate colonies that existed at that time, and the numbers belonging to each colonizing nation. The total number of colonies listed was 136, with Britain having 50 and France 33 (61 percent for the two together of the overall figure). In 1890, the domains of these two main colonial powers accounted for nearly 70 percent of the more than 22 million square miles and over 77 percent of the more than 500 million people living under colonial dominion (see Tables 9.1, 9.2, 9.3, and 9.4). Britain alone had 37 percent of the colonies, controlling more than half of the land area and over 66 percent of the population. Hobson

[9] See John A. Hobson, *Imperialism: A Study* (Ann Arbor: University of Michigan Press, 1965 [1902]).

TABLE 9.2. *Colonial Domains of Britain, c. 1899*

	Area in Sq. Miles (000)	Population (000)	Date of Acquisition
INDIA			
British India	1,068.3	221,173	1601–1856
Feudatory States	731.9	66,050	–
Total INDIA	1,800.2	287,223	
EUROPE			
Gibraltar	–	24	1704
Malta and Gozo	0.1	180	1800
OTHER ASIA			
Aden and Perim	0.1	42	1839
Ceylon	25.3	3,449	1795
Hong Kong	0.4	354	1842
Labuan	–	6	1846
Straits Settlement	1.5	512	1819
AFRICA			
Ascension	–	–	1815
Basutoland	10.3	250	1868–1883
Cape Colony	276.8	1,788	1806
Mauritius	0.7	338	1810
Natal and Zululand	35.0	902	1824
St. Helena	–	5	1651
WEST AFRICA			
Gambia	–	14	1631
Gold Coast	40.0	1,474	1661
Lagos	0.9	86	1787
Sierra Leone	4.0	75	1789
AMERICAS			
Bermudas	–	16	1609
Canada	3,653.9	5,186	1763
Falklands/So. Georgia Isl.	7.5	2	1833
British Guiana	109.0	286	1803
British Honduras	7.6	35	1670
Newfoundland/Labrador	162.2	202	1497
WEST INDIES			
Bahamas	4.5	53	1629
Jamaica/Turks Islands	4.4	733	1655
Barbados	0.1	190	1605
Leeward Islands	0.7	128	1600s
Windward Islands	0.8	155	1600s
Trinidad and Tobago	1.9	274	1763–1797
AUSTRALASIA			
Fiji	7.7	122	1874
New Guinea	90.5	350	1884
New South Wales	310.7	1,357	1788
New Zealand	104.5	796	1840
Queensland	668.5	499	1859
South Australia	903.7	363	1836
Tasmania	29.4	171	1803
Victoria	87.9	1,177	1850
Western Australia	975.9	168	1829
Total British Colonies	7,523.8	21,769	
GRAND TOTAL BRITISH COLONIES AND INDIA	9,324.0	308,992	

Notes and Sources: Morris (1900 II), 88–89.

TABLE 9.3. *Regional Distribution of France's Colonial Domain Over the Nineteenth Century*

	1815 (000)	1815 (%)	1860 (000)	1860 (%)	1880 (000)	1880 (%)	1890-91 (000)	1890-91 (%)	1899 (000)	1899 (%)
ASIA										
Pop	179	35.9	222	6.6	3,334	44.3	18,000	51.1	22,679	40.2
Area	–	1.1	–	0.1	69	9.2	201	8.4	363	9.7
AFRICA										
Pop	95	19.0	2,800	83.0	3,702	49.2	16,800	47.7	33,257	59.0
Area	1	6.0	186	76.9	625	83.3	2,129	89.2	3,320	88.7
AMERICAS										
Pop	225	45.1	300	8.9	391	5.2	373	1.1	384	0.7
Area	16	92.9	48	19.8	48	6.4	48	2.0	48	1.3
OCEANIA										
Pop	–	–	50	1.5	94	1.2	72	0.2	82	0.1
Area	–	–	8	3.3	9	1.2	9	0.4	9	0.2
TOTAL FRENCH DOMAIN										
Pop	499		3,372		7,521		35,245		56,402	
Area	17		242		750		2,387		3,741	

FRENCH DOMAIN AS PERCENTAGE OF ALL COLONIES, c. 1900

Pop	10.8%
Land	16.8

Notes and Sources: The land area is measured in square miles. Morris (1900), I, 419; II, 318.

TABLE 9.4. *Colonial Domains of France, c. 1899*

	Area in Square Miles (000)	Population (000)	Date of Acquisition
ASIA			
India	0.2	279	1679
Annarn	88.8	5,000	1884
Cambodia	40.5	1,500	1862
Cochin-China	23.1	2,400	1861
Tonquin (with Laos)	210.4	13,500	1884–93
AFRICA			
Algeria	184.5	4,430	1830
Algerian Sahara	123.5	50	–
Tunis	50.8	1,500	1881
Sahara Region	1,684.0	2,500	–
Senegal	120.0	2,000	1637
Sudan	300.0	2,500	1880
Ivory Coast	100.0	2,500	1843
Dahomey	50.0	1,000	1893
Congo and Gabon	425.0	12,000	1884
French Guinea	48.0	1,000	1843
Obok and Somali Coast	5.0	22	1864
Réunion	1.0	173	1649
Comoro Isles	0.6	53	1886
Mayotte	0.1	11	1843
Nossi-Bé	0.1	10	1841
Seinte Marie	0.1	8	1643
Madagascar	227.8	3,500	1896
AMERICAS			
Guiana	46.9	22	1626
Guadeloupe and Dependencies	0.7	167	1634
Martinique	0.4	188	1635
St. Pierre and Miquelon	0.1	6	1635
OCEANIA			
New Caledonia/Dependencies	7.7	53	1854
Other French Establishments	1.5	29	1841–1881
Total All French Colonies	3,740.8	56,402	

Sources: Morris (1900 I), 420–1.

pointed out that thirty-eight of the British colonies were annexed after 1870. By his reckoning, one-third of the land area of the British Empire, with one-quarter of its population, was acquired between 1870 and 1900. By 1900, the land area of the Empire had nearly quadrupled since 1860, and the population had more than doubled. France, whose extensive colonial holdings had been markedly depleted though military defeats in the late eighteenth and early nineteenth centuries, expanded its domain even more rapidly during the this period as the European nations made major moves into Africa and Southeast Asia; the land area and population encompassed by its colonies rose between 1860 and 1900 by 15.5 and 16.7 times respectively.

Britain and France were far from the only European countries engaged in colonial enterprise. Indeed, the scale of the colonization efforts carried out by the European countries is striking not only for the numbers of individual colonies and the vast land areas and populations involved, but also for the wide range of colonizers. The European colonizers included Austria-Hungary, Belgium, Denmark, France, Germany, Italy, the Netherlands, Portugal, Russia, Spain, and Turkey, as well as Britain (see Table 9.5 for an incomplete listing), and of these, only Belgium held just one colony. Only four had mother countries larger in area than their colonies,[10] and four mother countries had populations less than the population of the colonies.[11] Most of them had colonial domains that extended across two or more continents. The United States would join this group in 1898, with the possessions it gained during the Spanish-American War.[12] Especially when one considers that many of the colonies the Europeans (particularly the British, French, and Spanish) had established and long maintained in the Americas were independent by the late nineteenth century, one cannot fail to be impressed with how much of the globe – both in land area and population – had direct experience of being a colony.[13]

The large numbers of both colonies and colonizing countries, and the wide range of geographic locations and other characteristics, provide an excellent basis for a detailed examination of various contributions to the success (or lack) of colonial enterprise. What are also extremely valuable are the mixed associations between the identity of the colonizing country and the environmental variables, as well as the major differences across colonies in the date of acquisition. That European colonization of different parts of the world tended to occur in waves (and that many colonies experienced changes in the identity of the colonizer) provides the contemporary investigator with rich information that allows for study of

[10] Austria-Hungary, Russia, Turkey, and the United States.
[11] Britain, France, the Netherlands, and Portugal.
[12] China also merits inclusion in a list of colonizers of that era, and Morris includes China in his compilation.
[13] This assessment is reinforced by the observation that much of Europe was at some earlier point colonized by societies from Asia or the southern Mediterranean.

TABLE 9.5. *Colonial Domains of Selected Other European Powers, c. 1890*

	Area in Square Miles (000)	Population (000)
DENMARK		
Europe		
Faröe Islands	0.5	11.2
Greenland (coasts)	46.7	9.8
Iceland	39.8	72.4
West Indies		
St. John and St. Thomas	–	15.4
Santa Cruz (St. Croix)	0.1	18.4
Total DENMARK	87.1	127.2
% of All European Colonies, c. 1890	0.6%	0.0%
GERMANY		
Africa		
Cameraons	130.0	500.0
Damaraland/Luderitzland	342.0	250.0
German East Africa	344.8	1,755.0
Togoland	16.0	500.0
Pacific		
Bismarck Archipelago	18.2	188.0
Kaiser Wilhelm's Land	70.3	109.0
(New Guinea)		
Marshall Archipelago	–	10.0
Solomon Islands	8.5	80.0
Total GERMANY	929.8	3,392.0
% of All European Colonies, c. 1890	6.0%	0.9%
ITALY		
Africa		
Eritrea	56.1	659.0
Abyssinia	189.0	4,500.0
Somali Coast	70.0	210.0
Total ITALY	315.1	5,369.0
% of All European Colonies, c. 1890	2.0%	1.3%
NETHERLANDS		
East Indies		
Borneo	203.7	1,073.5
Celebes	72.0	2,000.0
Java (with Madura)	50.8	21,974.2
Moluccas	42.4	353.0
Sumatra	170.7	2,750.0
New Guinea	150.8	200.0
Other Islands	29.0	235.0
West Indies		
All Islands*	0.4	45.1
Suriname	46.1	74.1
Total NETHERLANDS	765.9	28,704.9
% of All European Colonies, c. 1890	4.9%	7.2%
PORTUGAL		
Africa		
Portuguese Guinea	11.6	150.0

(continued)

TABLE 9.5 *(continued)*

	Area in Square Miles (000)	Population (000) in
Angola	603.0	3,600.0
Madeira	0.3	132.0
Cape Verde Islands	1.5	111.0
Mozambique	293.0	1,500.0
Principe/St. Thomas' Island	0.4	21.0
Asia		
Goa, Daman, etc.	1.6	481.5
Macao	–	66.0
Timor, etc.	6.3	300.0
Total PORTUGAL	917.7	6,361.5
% of All European Colonies, c. 1890	5.9%	1.6%
SPAIN		
Africa		
Canaries	2:8	288.0
Gulf of Guinea	0.9	50.0
N. W Saharan Seaboard and Span. Morocco	243.0	106.0
Asia		
Philippine Islands	114.3	5,561.2
Other Islands**	2.0	119.7
West Indies		
Cuba (and Pinos)	43.2	1,521.7
Puerto Rico	3.6	784.7
Total SPAIN	409.8	8,431.3
% of All European Colonies, c. 1890	2.6%	2.1%

Sources and Notes: Gibbins, (1891) Appendix B. Not all European countries with colonies are included here. An outstanding example is Belgium, and its Belgian Congo colony in particular. After 1883, the Congo was owned, essentially by King Leopold II, and it was not until 1908 that there was a legal connection with Belgium (the Congo, now Zaire, gained its independence in 1960). In 1900, its white population of European descent was below 2,000 of its total population which was estimated at between 15 and 30 million. Its land area covered 900,000 square miles. See Hochschild (1998) and *Statesman's Yearbook* (1900). The table does not specify the colonies of Russia (including Finland), Turkey (including Egypt, the Egyptian Sudan, Bulgaria, Crete, and Samos), and Austria-Hungary (Cabelon on the Coromandel Coast and Banquibazar in Bengal, both through the Ostend Company), nor is it inclusive of quite all of the colonies of the European countries explicitly included (such as Ireland for Britain, or Libya for Italy). In 1899, the Congo and these latter colonies together had a land area of at least 3,279,494 square miles and a population of 59,221,660. If we include the Spanish colonies that were taken over by the United States in 1898, we estimate (somewhat conservatively in our view) that 18,008,094 square miles of land were encompassed in European colonies circa 1890, and that roughly 432,306,000 people resided in these areas. We use these latter figures as the basis for the calculations of the proportions of the total land area and population in European colonies reported here.

* Includes Buen Ayre, Curaçao, Aruba, Saba, St. Eustatius, and St. Martin.
** Includes Caroline, Pelew, Marianne, and Sulu Islands.

whether characteristics that are conducive to success in one era may have different effects in another. Of course the role of changes over time is a crucial and complex question. Did the era in which a colony was established affect its institutions or overall performance? Was there, for example, significant evolution in the world's legal or moral standards – such as the acceptability or its lack of slavery or indentured servitude – that influenced the foundation of institutions? For Hobson, while the "year 1870 has been taken as indicative of the beginning of a conscious policy of Imperialism, it will be evident that the movement did not attain its full impetus until the middle of the eighties."[14] We might expect, however, that earlier settlements – including those in the Americas that had already gained their independence after centuries under colonial rule – were in areas judged to have more favorable natural resources, factor endowments, or conditions more generally attractive or promising than those settled later. Another issue in determining whether the time of settlement made a difference to the performance of some African and Asian colonies is that these territories may have had long been politically independent and thus had longer periods to develop institutions on their own that may have had a long-term impact.

There are of course other questions about how to evaluate the performance of colonies. Should the focus be on the success of a colony over the period when a society was ruled by the colonizing country or on the record of the society over the longer term – including both the period after independence as well as the conditions prior to colonization? Should, moreover, success be gauged by the level of GNP per capita (or some other measure of material output or welfare), the income of the elites, the income of the native population, or perhaps by the relative improvement in levels since the time of colonization (as opposed to the absolute level)?

Colonies, as institutions, are a blend of the roles of the colonial power and of the resource and endowment base of the colonized areas. The process of colonization entails a change in political control of the land areas and the resources therein, with the settlers and/or colonizing nations acquiring the political authority to design and legislate institutions. The specific forms of the economic and political institutions that evolve will be influenced by the attributes of the controlling elite and of others (including the native population) already resident, as well as by the impacts of resources, demographic endowments, and other (including market) environmental conditions. The aims of settling nations are generally economic in character, for the individual settlers or for the entire nation, although at times they may be subsidiary to other goals, such as religious motives, the attainment of prestige, the strategic benefits of location, or the attempt

[14] Hobson, *Imperialism*, 19.

to triumph in international rivalry. That the circumstances prevailing in the world at the time of settlement will likely have a profound influence on the nature of the institutions in a colony seems obvious. As already alluded to, the legality and technical feasibility of different types of institutional arrangements change over time. For example, European nations abolished systems of slavery and serfdom over the course of the nineteenth century, and indentured labor was outlawed at the start of the twentieth century. Thus, settlements established at different times faced rather different institutional options for mobilizing labor from outside.

One of the critical factors in influencing institutions and the process of economic growth is the nature of the population endowment at the time of settlement, and the overall ratio of land (and resources more generally) to labor. The population density at the time of settlement, and the willingness of the resident population to supply labor (that is, to work the land for others), determined whether the desired level of labor input (as reflected in the productivity of labor relative to some subsistence standard) can be obtained from the existing population or whether labor needed to be attracted from elsewhere. The institutions in colonies with high population density should accordingly differ from those of colonies with lower population densities. Many colonial settlements were in areas with higher population density relative to labor requirements, and these entailed limited European migration and populations. For example, much of Latin America, particularly the areas settled by the Spanish, had large Native American and *mestizo* populations, even after the heavy mortality after European arrival, and there was limited need for immigration by Europeans or by African slaves.[15] Other areas where immigration from outside was quite limited include the overwhelming majority of colonies in Africa (except for South Africa) and those in Asia (particularly India and Indonesia), where the populations contained very few Europeans relative to the native populations.[16]

Some colonies with low ratios of labor to land (such as Australia) reflected relatively small native populations that had long characterized

[15] Indeed, early in the colonial period, the Spanish authorities adopted rather stringent restrictions on immigration. For more discussion, see above, Chs. 3 and 7. Coercive measures were sometimes employed, however, to get the worker to work where settlers wanted them to, although these measures often resembled those that had been used by Native American societies before European arrival.

[16] Although some of these areas did not produce many commodities for export, others appear to have been quite dependent on production for export markets. Indeed, in several of the latter cases – including Barbados and India – there was overpopulation, and low returns to labor, leading to encouragement of emigration.

the territories, but their labor mechanisms were based also upon the nature of their soils, climate, and comparative advantage in the world economy. Most prominently, colonies in the Caribbean and the U.S. South, producers of export crops and settled beginning in the seventeenth and eighteenth centuries, mobilized slave labor from Africa to meet the bulk of their labor needs, since there were limited Native American populations and substantial economies to producing the key crops cultivated on large plantations with slave labor. The populations of the so-called "sugar islands" in the Caribbean, especially, were generally about 80 to 90 percent black slave after the early years of settlement. A major change in institutions came with the ending of the slave trade and slavery by European powers, and such areas – not only in the Caribbean, but also in other sugar-growing areas of labor shortage such as Fiji and Natal – generally came to rely on indentured labor coming from poorer parts of the world, particularly India, while that for Queensland depended on Pacific Islanders for their labor supply. Presumably, if slavery had continued to be permitted, it would have been the predominant means of obtaining labor in these colonies.

A second type of area where labor was in short supply relative to land, but which had more temperate climates and less need for plantation labor producing exports, were key areas of British settlement, including the thirteen colonies that became the United States. This developed out of military conquest (versus the Native Americans, the Dutch, and the French) and purchase (from the French and Spanish): Canada (based on conquest in the Seven Years War), Australia, New Zealand, and (with a smaller ratio of whites than the others) South Africa (conquered from the Dutch; see Table 7.1), These areas sought primarily white labor, as they were unable to pay the high prices for slaves that prevailed in world markets because of the demand from the tropical colonies. The white labor these colonies attracted, generally from the metropole, could be of several forms, whether free or convict.

There are several institutional variants of free labor institutions, with quite different means of controls and cost allocations. The most straightforward, of course, is where the free migrants made their travel arrangements and were able to pay directly for the cost of their transportation. Many "free labor" migrants, and especially those from Asia or from Europe prior to the nineteenth century, were not so fortunate. People in this latter group sometimes depended on subsidies that were offered by potential employers (or intermediaries in labor markets) to attract labor to work on a specific crop or in a particular location. They chose to

become indentured servants, whereby they gave up control for a specified period of years of where and when to labor in exchange for having
transport costs paid for. In the case of indentured servants who traveled
from Europe to the Americas prior to the nineteenth century, almost all
workers became free after working off their commitments. Convict labor
from England was used to settle the thirteen colonies and, later, Australia.
Although convict workers would ultimately be freed, this institution of
labor entailed the individual worker giving up of his or her rights for a
period of years to serve punishment. Convict labor was also employed,
to some degree, in settling Portuguese and French colonies.

The relative scarcity of labor, as well as the numbers of those of European descent as compared to the numbers of natives and workers brought
in as slaves or under contract arrangements from Asia, varied enormously
across colonies (see Table 7.2). Whereas whites were the great majority
in the colonies established in mainland North America, Australia, and in
New Zealand and accounted for substantial shares of the population in
a few others such as the Cape of Good Hope, they generally constituted
only a miniscule proportion in those colonies that either had large aboriginal populations before the Europeans arrived or climates, soils, and
other resources conducive to the production of sugar and certain other
commodities that could be produced at low cost by attracting slave or
contract labor. Hence, regardless of the identity of the colonizing country,
whites numbered less than 1 percent of the population in the colonies in
Asia and (with the exception of South Africa) Sub-Saharan Africa, and
typically much less than 20 percent in the colonies of North Africa, the
West Indies, and Pacific/Oceania. Favored by generally higher (and more
appropriate to colonial societies) levels of human capital, wealth, and
legal privileges/rights, whites typically enjoyed far higher incomes and
political influence than did non-whites. There is reason to believe, therefore, that the circumstances that systematically contributed to the extreme
variation in the ethnic composition of the colonial populations, were
related to the extent of economic and political inequality that emerged
early in the histories of the respective societies, and that such conditions
(including differences in the extent of inequality) often persisted over
time.[17]

The stark contrasts in the degree of initial inequality that seem apparent
among the European colonies around the world allow scholars to study

[17] For a more extensive elaboration on this idea, focusing on the colonies established in
the Americas, see above Chs. 2 and 3.

whether and how inequality affects the processes and path of development. Whereas previous treatments of the impact of inequality on growth have often been concerned with how savings or investment rates might be affected, recent scholars who have sought to use the "natural experiment" provided by colonization focus on the hypothesis that extreme differences across colonies in the extent of inequality gave rise to systematic differences in the ways institutions evolved and, in turn, on paths of development.[18] The argument is that greater equality and/or homogeneity among the population led, over time, to more democratic political institutions, more investment in public goods and infrastructure, and to institutions that offered relatively broad access to property rights and economic opportunities.[19] In contrast, where there was extreme inequality, political institutions were less democratic, investments in public goods and infrastructure were far more limited, and the institutions that evolved tended to provide highly unbalanced (favoring elites) access to property rights and economic opportunities. The resulting differences in access to opportunities may be important in accounting for the disparate records of long-term growth, because where processes of early industrialization have been sustained (such as in Britain and the United States during the nineteenth century, and even East Asia in the twentieth century), they have generally involved broad participation in the commercial economy. Economies that only provided narrow access to opportunities might have been, and are, less capable of realizing sustained economic growth.[20]

There are a variety of mechanisms through which the extent of inequality in a society might affect the character of institutions that develop. The avenue that typically receives the most attention works through political

---

[18] For examples of the approach that highlight variation in savings rates with relative income or with rates of taxation, see in particular, Alberto F. Alesina and Dani Rodrik, "Distributive Politics and Economic Growth," *Quarterly Journal of Economics* (May 1994): 465–90 and Torsten Persson and Guido Tabellini, "Is Inequality Harmful for Growth? Theory and Evidence," *American Economic Review* 84 (June 1994): 600–21. For those investigating the impact of inequality on institutions more broadly, see above Ch. 3; Acemoglu, Johnson, and Robinson, "Colonial Origins," Acemoglu, Johnson, and Robinson, "Reversal of Fortune," and Easterly and Levine, "Tropics, Germs and Crops."

[19] There are, of course, some classic expositions of these and similar ideas. See, for example Alexis de Tocqueville, J. P. Mayer, ed, *Democracy in America* (Garden City: Doubleday 1969); and Frederick Jackson Turner, *The Rise of the New West, 1819–1829* (New York: Harper & Brothers, 1947).

[20] This point was made by Max Weber, in his *General Economic History* (1966 [1927]), 230, who states that "the decisive impetus toward capitalism could come from only one source, namely a mass market demand," entailing a "democratization of the demand."

inequality. When political power or influence is concentrated among a small segment of the population, that group is able to shape policies or institutions to its advantage. We expect members of such elites to act in their interest, for example, by inducing the government to make investments and provide services they favor while being assessed for a less than proportionate share of the costs, or to define and enforce property and other sorts of rights in ways that treat them in a preferential manner. Some activity of this sort is present in all societies, as the distribution of political influence is never entirely equal, and those with more resources generally fare better in the competition over influencing the government. But the extent and ultimate impact of such activity can vary even across nominal democracies, especially when the right to vote depends on literacy or wealth (or other attributes), or where ballots are not secret The absence of democracy, or a situation when one class of the population has the capability to impose its will by force if need be, is an extreme case of how political inequality can lead to institutions that favor a narrow range of the population.

The importance of political inequality (or military might) often figures prominently in discussions of how institutions are established in colonies. The presumption that those with a monopoly of force or a dominant share of the votes get their way does not seem an unreasonable presumption. Nevertheless, it is worth reflecting on the relevance of the well accepted modern adage of the Rolling Stones, *you can't always get what you want*. No matter how much inequality there is in political influence or in any other dimension, there are frequently constraints that inconveniently narrow the range of feasible possibilities for the fortunate individual or class. The initial objects of the colonies established in the Americas, and indeed elsewhere in the world, were generally the same – to generate economic returns for the respective European country and its individuals. Although the goals may have been similar, the diverse environments in which the colonies were located led to a variety of economic structures and institutions as the colonizers sought to take best advantage of the different opportunities and challenges they faced in the respective places. Miscalculations of the effects of various institutional designs, with resulting unintended consequences, were, of course, not uncommon. The colonists came with similar backgrounds and institutional heritages, but heterogeneity developed as they applied and adapted the technologies and institutional heritages they brought with them to conditions quite unlike those in the Old World. Moreover, the extent to which the metropolis, or any political authority, could effectively specify the institutions prevailing in any colony varied with the local circumstances.

Cases suggest that political inequality alone was not sufficient for elites to obtain institutions that greatly advantaged them with respect to government policies or access to property rights and other kinds of economic opportunities. In some environments, even when political or military power was highly concentrated in their hands, elites might have voluntarily, and without threat of violent upheaval, found it in their interest to provide better conditions and treatment to the humble. Although there are a variety of factors that might lead to such an evidently anomalous outcome, and ways of characterizing them, the relative scarcity of labor seems in the context of the European colonies to be a crucial one. Where labor was relatively scarce, as compared to land and other resources, political inequality was not accompanied by economic inequality. In such circumstances, the lack of economic inequality (or relative equality) circumscribed how far political elites could go in designing institutions to advantage their members. In a situation where there was relative political equality, however, economic inequality – as reflected in the relative scarcity of a key factor – might lead to institutions that greatly advantaged that scarce factor. Hence, economic inequality can sometimes, in the sorts of conditions that are not uncommon in colonies of less-developed countries (with an abundance of unskilled labor but a scarcity of capital and skilled labor), exert more of an influence on the way institutions evolve than political inequality per se.

III

There has long been debate over the impact of the European establishment of colonies around the world that took place over centuries, beginning in the 1400s. Much of the controversy has been concerned with issues such as how the long-term performance of the colonized areas and the colonizing economies were affected by the exchange of resources and terms of trade between them and the imbalance of military power. As we have argued, however, one of the most fundamental consequences of European colonization may have been in altering the composition of the populations in the societies colonized. Because the efforts of the Europeans generally meant implanting communities who were greatly advantaged over natives in terms of human capital and legal status, and because the trajectories of institutional development were sensitive to the incidence of extreme inequality that often followed, their activity had long, lingering effects. Although more study is needed to identify all of the mechanisms at work, it seems clear that colonies in the Americas with extreme inequality, as compared to those with relative equality, were systematically more likely to evolve institutions that restricted access to economic opportunities and to generate lower rates of public investment in schools and other infrastructure considered conducive to growth. These patterns of institutional development, which tend to yield persistence over time, may help to explain why a great many former European colonies that began with extreme inequality have suffered poor economic outcomes.

10

Institutional and Non-Institutional Explanations of Economic Development

I

Economists' concern with economic history comes not only from a desire to achieve a better understanding of the past, but also from a belief that such knowledge can serve as a guide for policymakers striving to improve the economic and social conditions of currently less-developed nations. Many scholars have set about making contributions to knowledge through detailed investigations of the processes of growth in individual countries. Others have sought to discern what factors were crucial through comparative studies, focusing on issues such as why nations differed with regard to the timing of the onset of growth or how and why their records of achieved rates of growth varied over long periods of time.

Recently considerable attention has been given to the question of why European nations and some of their overseas offshoots expanded more rapidly than did the economies of Asia, Africa, and Latin America after the eighteenth century – either generating new gaps in levels of income and rates of growth, or else greatly widening whatever differentials may have previously existed (see Table 10.1).[1] Previously the principal focus

[1] Among a vast literature, see Douglass C. North and Robert Paul Thomas, *The Rise of the Western World* (Cambridge: Cambridge University Press, 1973); Douglass C. North, *Structure and Change in Economic History* (New York: Norton, 1981); Nathan Rosenberg and L. E. Birdzell, Jr., *How the West Grew Rich: The Economic Transformation of the Industrial World* (New York: Basic Books, 1986); E. L. Jones, *The European Miracle: Environments, Economics, and Geopolitics in the History of Europe and Asia* (Cambridge: Cambridge University Press, 1981); David S. Landes, *The Wealth and Poverty of Nations: Why Some Are So Rich and Others So Poor* (New York: Norton, 1998); Kenneth Pomeranz, *The Great Divergence: China, Europe, and the Making of the Modern World*

TABLE 10.1. *Levels of Per Capita GDP and Interregional Differences,*
1500–1998 (in 1990 U.S. Dollars)

	1500	1820	1870	1913	1950	1973	1998
Western Europe	774	1232	1974	3473	4594	11534	17921
Western Offshoots	400	1201	2431	5257	9288	16172	26146
Japan	500	669	737	1387	1926	11439	20413
Asia (excl. Japan)	572	575	543	640	635	1231	2936
Latin America	416	665	698	1511	2554	4531	5795
Eastern Europe	483	667	917	1501	2601	5729	4354
Africa	400	418	444	585	852	1365	1368
World	565	667	867	1510	2114	4104	5709
Interregional Spreads	2:1	3:1	5:1	9:1	15:1	13:1	19:1

Source: Maddison (2001).

of historians examining the basis for differences in long-term economic performance had been on what led Great Britain to accomplish an Industrial Revolution sometime after the middle of the eighteenth century, ahead of its European rivals (see Table 10.2).[2] Given the greater similarity of economic, political, and social structures among the European nations than those between Europe and the rest of the world, the factors highlighted in the discussions of the development of the Industrial Revolution are rather different from those generally featured in the broader geographic comparisons. In both cases, however, what the economists and economic historians are seeking to explain is why some nations in today's world remain poor, relatively and absolutely, and what conditions can be changed in order to achieve success in spurring growth and improving the welfare of the respective populations. It is this problem that the recent study of institutions has sought to help resolve and this possibly represents its most significant contribution.

Economy (Princeton: Princeton University Press, 2000); Daron Acemoglu, Simon Johnson, and James A. Robinson, "The Colonial Origins of Comparative Development: An Empirical Investigation," *American Economic Review* 91 (December 2001): 1369–1401; Daron Acemoglu, Simon Johnson, and James A. Robinson, "Reversal of Fortune: Geography and Institutions in the Making of the Modern World Income Distribution," *Quarterly Journal of Economics* 117 (November 2002): 1231–94; William Easterly and Ross Levine, "Tropics, Germs, and Crops: The Role of Endowments in Economic Development," *Journal of Monetary Economics* 50 (January 2003): 3–39. For even earlier discussions, see Max Weber, *The Protestant Ethic and the Spirit of Capitalism* (New York: Scribner's, 1992 [1904–1905]); Max Weber, *General Economic History* (New York: Collier Books, 1966 [1927]); Werner Sombart, *The Jews and Modern Capitalism* (New York: Burt Franklin, 1969 [1913]).
[2] See, for example, R. M. Hartwell, *The Industrial Revolution and Economic Growth* (London: Methuen, 1971).

TABLE 10.2. *Per Capita GDP in Western Europe, 1500–1998*
(in 1990 U.S. Dollars)

	1500	1600	1700	1820	1870	1913	1998
Austria	707	837	993	1218	1863	3465	18905
Belgium	875	976	1144	1319	2697	4220	19442
Denmark	738	875	1039	1274	2003	3912	22123
Finland	453	538	638	781	1140	2111	18324
France	727	841	986	1230	1876	3485	19558
Germany	676	777	894	1058	1821	364S	17799
Italy	1100	1100	1100	1117	1499	2564	17759
Netherlands	754	1368	2110	1821	2753	4049	20224
Norway	640	760	900	1104	1432	2501	23660
Portugal	632	773	854	963	997	1244	12929
Spain	698	900	900	1063	1376	2255	14227
Sweden	695	824	977	1198	1664	3096	18685
Switzerland	742	880	1044	1280	2202	4266	21367
United Kingdom	714	974	1250	1707	3191	4921	18714
Total Western Europe	774	894	1024	1232	1974	3473	17921
World	565	593	615	667	867	1510	5709

Source: Maddison (2001).

It is not necessary here to attempt to catalogue the full set of explanations that have been given for differences in economic development, since many books and articles, published and forthcoming, have already done that. For present purposes, however, we highlight a transition over the last few decades from a concentration on the role of narrowly defined economic factors to a focus on the significance of social structures, institutions, and culture in providing the conditions conducive to economic development.[3]

Arguments based on conditions such as favorable natural resources (including accessible coal and iron, in the case of Britain), high rates of capital formation, and extensive markets or other circumstances that encourage a faster pace of technological change, which had long been central to our understanding of why some economies enjoyed better performance, have been supplemented (or replaced) by arguments concerned

---

[3] Earlier twentieth-century scholars, such as Max Weber, in *The Protestant Ethic*, and his, *General Economic History*, emphasized the role of culture, but the focus turned to real economic factors by the second half of the century. For a more extensive discussion of how thinking changed over time, see H. W. Arndt, *The Rise and Fall of Economic Growth: A Study in Contemporary Thought* (Chicago: University of Chicago Press, 1978) and H. W. Arndt, *Economic Development: The History of an Idea* (Chicago: University of Chicago Press, 1987).

with how differences across societies in political and cultural institutions arose, and how they influenced the process of growth.[4] Although we cannot conceive of processes of economic growth that do not involve institutional change, in this chapter we outline some reasons why one should be cautious about grounding a theory of growth exclusively on particular institutions. We emphasize how very different institutional structures have often been found to be reasonable substitutes for each other, both in dissimilar as well as similar contexts. The historical record, therefore, does not seem to support the notion that any one particular institution, narrowly defined, is indispensable for growth. Moreover, we discuss how the evidence that there are systematic patterns to the ways institutions evolve effects the idea that exogenous change in institutions is what powers growth. Institutions matter, but our thinking of how they matter recognizes that they are profoundly influenced by the political and economic environment, and that if any aspect of institutions is crucial for growth, it may be that institutions will change over time as circumstances change.

II

A basic categorization of explanations for economic growth would include economic, cultural, political, and institutional factors. The import of economic factors was much discussed in the ancient world, and the numerous economic factors that have been considered since that time include the following: natural resources; the opportunity to trade at low cost with other regions or nations, which provides markets that encourage

---

[4] On the role of coal, see Kindleberger and the comment by Parker in the same volume, Charles P. Kindleberger "International Trade and Investment and Resource Use in Economic Growth" and William N. Parker, "Comment," in *National Resources and Economic Growth*, ed. Joseph J. Spengler, 151–190 (Washington, D.C.: Resources for the Future, 1961). Although attention to the significance of coal had waned, it has recently revived with the works of E.A. Wrigley, *Continuity, Chance, and Change* (Cambridge: Cambridge University Press, 1988), and Pomeranz, *The Great Divergence*. For discussion of the relative importance of changes in savings rates, or in investment opportunities, see M. M. Postan, "Recent Trends in the Accumulation of Capital," *Economic History Review* 6 (October 1935): 1–12. For discussions of how the pace of technological change was responsive to economic factors, such as the extent of, or access to, markets, see David S. Landes, *The Unbound Prometheus: Technological Change and Industrial Development in Western Europe from 1750 to the Present*. (London: Cambridge University Press, 1969) and Kenneth L. Sokoloff, "Inventive Activity in Early Industrial America: Evidence From Patent Records, 1790–1846," *Journal of Economic History* 48 (December 1988): 813–50.

specialization in producing goods in which the economy has a comparative advantage (and perhaps stimulating more rapid technical progress) as well as serve as a source of imports that a nation may be incapable of producing; climate, which can influence productivity through a variety of mechanisms; colonial empire, which might be associated with especially high private or social returns to investment; and the role of population change. Some contend, for example, that rapid population growth has sometimes proved beneficial, fostering lower labor costs or the advantages of scale effects that come from higher total demand; others argue for the benefits of relatively slow growth in population, on the grounds that lower population density encourages higher per capita incomes and higher rates of capital formation. These, and other so-called economic explanations, say little explicitly about noneconomic factors and institutions, although this does not mean that the latter are not implicit in the analysis.

Discussions of the role of noneconomic factors (encompassing cultural, political, and institutional) in accounting for differences across societies in economic development can also be traced back many centuries. Several of the classic theories for the rise of European capitalism and some of the modern themes, are based on conditions – such as the spread of particular religious beliefs, be it the Protestantism pointed to by Max Weber, the Judaism highlighted by Werner Sombart, or shifts in the orientation of dominant religions – and are points that clearly fall outside of what most would consider economic.[5] Other arguments stress the contributions of the advance of scientific and rational thought, the impact of changing tastes for consumer goods, and the effects on choices between work and leisure on the supply and intensity of labor during industrialization.[6] Changes in legal systems, in degrees of trust and the extent of social capital, and in the nature of political organization and the extent of

[5] See the discussion of nonconformists in Britain in Weber, *The Protestant Ethic;* David C. McClelland, *The Achieving Society* (Princeton: Van Nostrand, 1961); and Robert William Fogel, *The Fourth Great Awakening and The Future of Egalitarianism* (Chicago: University of Chicago Press, 2000); see also Sombart, *Jews and Modern Capitalism.*

[6] See Sir James Steuart *An Inquiry Into the Principles of Political Economy* 2 vols. (London: A. Miller and T. Cadell, 1767); Elizabeth Gilboy, "Demand as a Factor in the Industrial Revolution," in *Facts and Factors in Economic History: Articles by Former Students of Edwin Francis Gay,* 620–639 (Cambridge, MA: Harvard University Press, 1932); John U. Nef, *Cultural Foundations of Industrial Civilization* (Cambridge: Cambridge University Press, 1958); Jan deVries, "The Industrial Revolution and the Industrious Revolution," *Journal of Economic History* 54 (June 1994): 249–70; and Margaret C. Jacob, *Scientific Culture and the Making of the Industrial West* (New York: Oxford University Press, 1997).

democracy, have more recently been advocated as critical factors used to explain differences in economic performance.[7] Nevertheless, the nature of the interaction between economic and so-called "noneconomic" factors may be complex. The contrast in views between Weber and of R. H. Tawney on the relationship between religious changes and the rise of capitalism in Britain, and in northern Europe more generally, corresponds to similar debates over the sources of change in many other purportedly noneconomic conditions relevant to economic growth.[8] Moreover, the implications of the very slow diffusion of cultural change (and of institutional change more generally) and economic growth around the world represent a puzzle for those who believe that introducing exogenous changes in these facets should have significant, favorable effects and constitute a viable instrument of economic policy within a relatively short time-frame.[9]

Quite a wide range of noneconomic conditions relevant for growth have featured in the debates over why Britain was the first industrial nation. Many can be subsumed in the blanket category of culture, where cultural factors are understood to include: religion, particularly the impact of nonconformists in the development of technology and entrepreneurship; the scientific spirit and the expansion of knowledge, including a willingness to search out new methods and technologies; and the emergence of an educational system that permitted a wide diffusion of information and skills among the population. Culture has also been defined to include family and kinship patterns; tastes and preferences regarding work versus leisure; time preferences determining the levels of savings and consumption, and the development of a widespread desire to financially profit-maximize or pursue material gain more generally. Proponents of the view that cultural change was responsible for economic change generally point to their coincidence in eighteenth-century Britain, and presume that culture consists of behaviors and values that

---

[7] See the views presented by Harold J. Berman, *Law and Revolution: The Formation of the Western Legal Tradition* (Cambridge, MA: Harvard University Press, 1983); Robert D. Putnam, ed., *Democracies in Flux: The Evolution of Social Capital in Contemporary Society* (Oxford: Oxford University Press, 2002); and Patrick K. O'Brien, "The Political Economy of British Taxation, 1660–1815," *Economic History Review* 41 (February 1998): 1–32.

[8] Whereas Weber is well-known for his theory of how the content of Protestant thought may have encouraged believers to behave in ways we associate with capitalism, Tawney highlighted how economic change supported change in religious beliefs. See Weber, *The Protestant Ethic*; and R. H. Tawney, *Religion and the Rise of Capitalism* (New York: Harcourt Brace, 1926).

[9] For a recent restatement of how the immutability of culture can explain continued backwardness, see Landes, *Wealth and Poverty of Nations*.

are determined independently of economic factors. This may, however, be an artificial distinction, because the economic effects of cultural factors, if not the cultural beliefs themselves, are often greatly influenced by the relative costs of different patterns of behavior and the amounts of income that people are willing to forgo to obtain chosen ends.[10]

Much recent work on the significance of institutions for understanding why Britain industrialized first gives relatively little attention to the role of culture per se. In emphasizing property rights and the British legal framework, it breaks sharply from the earlier stream of work on institutions by economists who emphasized culture in treating the evolution of economies, as part of a critique of classical economic theory.[11]

Current thinking about institutions instead follows the pioneering approach of Douglass North in grounding the analysis of the causes and consequences of institutions and institutional change on economic and political theory.[12] This perspective defines institutions as encompassing the specific organizations or rules that constrain and influence human behavior. A key aspect of these rules is that they structure human actions by providing incentives that shape economic and political organization. Formal rules, plus the informal constraints that develop, influence the costs of production and of transactions within society. Among the institutions that are most important for economic performance are those involving the definition of property rights, both between the government and private parties and between individuals within a society. The link between appropriate institutions and economic growth is that well-adapted institutions reduce the costs of production and distribution, allowing private agents more scope to benefit from specialization,

---

[10] For the linkage between morality and economics, see the discussion of Quakers and slavery in Adam Smith, *Inquiry into the Nature and Causes of the Wealth of Nations* (Oxford: Clarendon Press, 1976 [1776]); also see Robert William Fogel, *Without Consent or Contract* (New York: Norton, 1989).

[11] See the discussion of institutions, and the approaches of the British and Germans, in William Cunningham, *The Growth of English Industry and Commerce*, 2nd ed., 2 vols., (Cambridge: Cambridge University Press, 1890–1892 [1882]).

[12] See North, *Structure and Change*; Douglass C. North, "Institutions, Economic Growth and Freedom: An Historical Introduction," in *Freedom, Democracy and Economic Welfare*, ed. Michael A. Walker, 3–25 (Vancouver: Fraser Institute, 1988); Douglass C. North, *Institutions, Institutional Change and Economic Performance* (Cambridge: Cambridge University Press, 1990); North and Thomas, *Rise of the Western World*; Douglass C. North and Barry Weingast, "Constitutions and Commitment: The Evolution of Institutions Governing Public Choice in Seventeenth-Century England," *Journal of Economic History* 49 (December 1989): 803–32; and Lance E. Davis and Douglass C. North, *Institutional Change and American Economic Growth* (Cambridge: Cambridge University Press, 1971).

investment, and trade. Institutions are not the only constraints that society or private actors confront, since there are others due to the state of technological knowledge, demographic forces, nature (including climate and topography), as well as other features of the environment that may also have implications for the patterns of economic activity.[13]

Institutions play several related roles in the economy. They influence the beliefs and behaviors of individuals and groups, and thus the preferences and priorities expressed through both private and public decisions. Another important role of institutions is providing for efficient property rights, trust, and effective incentives, and thus facilitating transactions and interactions among individuals and firms. North and others claim that it was sound property rights and incentive schemes made possible by distinctive institutions that were key to Britain industrializing first.[14] No economic development is possible without secure property rights. The specification of formal rights is only one part of society's problem, however. The nature of the enforcement of institutional provisions, both as to legitimacy and effectiveness, is critical to the success of the institutions that exist. Legislative decisions and judicial rulings will influence outcomes, whether or not they seem consistent with the circumstances under which the respective constitutions were originally adopted. Enforcement is sometimes bilateral, between individuals, with no government role to ensure compliance, but in other cases enforcement requires government participation and action.

---

[13] For a classic treatment of how factor endowments can help to shape culture and institutions, see Alexis de Tocqueville J. P. Mayer, ed, *Democracy in America* (Garden City: Doubleday, 1969). For interesting discussions of the influences of factor endowments and political forces, see Robert Brenner, "Agrarian Class Structure and Economic Development in Pre-Industrial Europe," in *The Brenner Debate: Agrarian Class Structure and Economic Development in Pre-Industrial Europe*, eds. T. H. Aston and C. H. E. Philpin, 10–63 (Cambridge: Cambridge University Press, 1985); North, *Structure and Change*; North, *Institutions, Institutional Change;* and Douglass C. North, William Summerhill, and Barry Weingast, "Order, Disorder, and Economic Change: Latin America Versus North America," in *Governing for Prosperity*, eds. Bruce Bueno de Mesquita and Hilton L. Root (New Haven: Yale University Press, 2000).

[14] A major concern of the property rights literature is with private agents being secure from expropriation by the state. See North, *Structure and Change*; North and Weingast, "Constitutions and Commitment;" Stephen Knack and Philip Keefer, "Does Social Capital Have an Economic Payoff," *Quarterly Journal of Economics* 112 (November 1997): 1251–88; Daron Acemoglu and James A. Robinson, "Why Did the West Extend the Franchise? Democracy, Inequality and Growth in Historical Perspective," *Quarterly Journal of Economics* 115 (November 2000): 1167–99; and Stephen H. Haber, Amando Razo, and Noel Maurer, *The Politics of Property Rights* (Cambridge: Cambridge University Press, 2003).

Although those who stress the importance of the institutional framework have somewhat different concerns than those who highlight the significance of culture, these two perspectives share an emphasis on the extent to which "noneconomic" variables evolve independently of the processes of economic growth. Indeed, proponents of both views point out that the appreciation of this pattern, as well as of the impacts of those variables on the economy, constitute a salient intellectual advance over the earlier (circa 1950s through 1970s) literature on economic development, which focused primarily on economic variables. That generation of economists certainly accepted the importance of institutions, culture, or political stability, but presumed either that the appropriate institutions and beliefs existed already, or else that they would evolve in constructive directions relatively easily when the economic factors that could generate economic growth were in place. Since economic forces obviously do not operate in a vacuum, it may have been difficult to conceive of a noninstitutional interpretation of economic growth.

Even as a purely logical construct, a wholly noninstitutional (or anti-institutional) explanation of economic growth seems implausible (as would an explanation that takes no account of economic factors), but as discussed below, debate on the relative importance of institutional and noninstitutional forces has continued.[15] The essential questions, thus, seem to us to be empirical. How much of the variation in economic performance over country and time can be attributed to differences in institutions, with purely economic factors constant or exogenous with respect to institutions, and how much is due to differences in the economic variables, with institutions constant or endogenous? What are the processes that govern the ways specific institutions evolve, and under what circumstances can the introduction of exogenous institutional changes be considered the basis of all economic policies?

III

Although in principle these questions can be framed as empirical issues, it is far from easy to clearly distinguish between the relative power of the institutional and noninstitutional explanations of economic differences. Few would claim that there is a general answer, and indeed most individual cases seem to allow some role for each type of explanation. There

---

[15] Even Weber's discussion of the role of Calvinism points out that the relation "was true only when some possibility of capitalistic development in the areas in question was present." See Weber, *The Protestant Ethic*, 190.

has been considerable interest in recent years, however, in a manner of posing the problem that might appear to make the empirical work more tractable: Are the key elements in determining institutions exogenous or endogenous? This distinction has been with us for a long time, as in the debates over the superiority of British institutions, but has also figured prominently in the study of how the various economies established as colonies by Europeans (or others) developed over time. Even in the absence of a substantial indigenous population in the area of settlement, the presence of one group in the colony, arriving from the metropolis, and another remaining in the metropolis, means that there were probably different circumstances for institutional development. In principle, therefore, a researcher could evaluate just how much of an impact the different circumstances had on the ways the institutions evolved. That many of the European countries established multiple colonies, in very different environments, further enhances the quality of the information arising from the "natural experiment." If the institutions in the colonies were, or remained, the same as those of the metropolitan nation (or perhaps the same as those of the indigenous societies that pre-dated the arrival of the Europeans), they might be regarded as exogenous. In such a case, the institutions could be reasonably interpreted as evolving independently of the conditions in the respective colonial economies, and systematic patterns of subsequent differences in economic performance across the economies could, after controlling for the purely economic factors, be attributed to institutions. If, however, the institutions in the colonies diverged in ways that could be explained as adaptations to the different environment, natural or human, then it would support the view that institutions were endogenous with respect to circumstances. Because institutions are human-fashioned structures that reflect the efforts of populations trying to make the best of the opportunities and problems they face, some scholars would be surprised if they were not at least in part endogenous. Indeed, many scholars feel that the institutions that emerged across the colonies established by the Europeans do seem to have varied systematically with aspects of the environment such as climate, land type, and natural resources. Some would go even further and suggest that the direction of institutional change is often endogenous to the growth process, as changes in technology and in incomes generate changes in tastes, changes in the returns to organizing production and transactions in various ways, and changes in patterns of behavior more generally.

To acknowledge that there is some endogeneity to institutions does not imply that institutions are unimportant, or that they have only a limited impact on economic performance. Endogenous institutions, once in place, can prove as crucial as if they were exogenous, and they might persist for as long or even longer. The key difference between those who contend that institutions are exogenous and those who argue they are endogenous is not with their impact and influence, but instead with where institutions come from and with the extent to which they are – or might be expected to be – revised over time.

It is widely recognized that it is sometimes useful to fix some types of institutions over time. Credible commitment to property rights is perhaps the classic example of the value of certainty about policy action.[16] More generally, however, allowing some flexibility in institutions, such that they can be altered to make it easier for private or public agents to take advantage of the new opportunities that arise as technology or the environment changes, would normally be expected to foster good economic performance and more rapid growth. Among the many such innovations in institutions that could be cited to illustrate the utility of institutions changing as conditions change are those that created the modern patent system; those that extended suffrage to a broad range of the population; those providing for public tax-supported provision of education that were free to those who chose to attend; those responsible for the organization of corporations where shareholders are protected because they have limited liability; legislation defining terms for financial markets and institutions; and those responsible for the establishment of central or quasi-central banks such as the Federal Reserve System or the Bank of England.

Determining the optimum degree of flexibility in, and the designing of mechanisms well suited to respond constructively to ever-changing circumstances with institutional change, are complex issues. While some see the role of constitutional provisions as a means of ensuring stability in the decision-making process and institutions, most constitutions do have provisions for amendments, and allow some degree of legislative and governmental flexibility in setting the legal structure. Allowance for modifications to the laws need not harm the potential for growth, nor even yield instability, particularly given that the voting and other costs of implementing changes are typically high.[17]

---

[16] North and Weingast, "Constitutions and Commitment."

[17] In some cases of change there may be required compensation to be paid to those whose condition is weakened, requiring increased taxation of other members of the population. Nearly all serf and slavery systems that ended during the nineteenth century did so with

Perhaps the most important elements of institutional structures are those that ensure an ability to adapt to different conditions and to adjust to new circumstances as seems necessary, rather than those that entail the retention and maintenance of any specific set of policies.[18] The capability for adaptation, based in part on the population's education and their political liberties, may ultimately be more significant for economic growth than the continuation of any particular set of beliefs, rules, or behavior. Among the characteristics of a society that might be expected to enhance institutional flexibility are a population's level of education, their political liberties, the degree of decentralization in political or economic structures, and the extent of competition within and across polities. This was likely significant in the case of European expansion, where there was geographic movement to different environments, with different types of climates, soil types, natural resources, and economic problems. Even if there were some specific cultural carryovers from Europe to the Americas, and these did play a role early in the settlement process, it is not clear that these factors were immutable or remained unchanged for long periods. The confrontation with a new environment that offered rich opportunities, but in unfamiliar contexts, led to some adaptations, adjustments, and innovations in institutions in the interests of economic improvement.

Another issue that is central to understanding how institutions matter for growth concerns the likelihood that no one particular narrowly specified institution is required, as there are often alternative institutional forms or structures that are reasonable substitutes for each other and may achieve similar economic performance. Those who hold the view that non-optimal institutions may still be consistent with high rates of economic growth, though perhaps not the highest rate that might have seemed possible, often point to the stark contrasts across industrialized countries in the importance of banks relative to securities markets in financial intermediation, in the reliance on common or civil law, in how bankruptcy laws balance the rights of creditors and debtors, in systems and levels of taxation, and in the division of power between the executive, the legislature, and political party structures. These and many other examples, historical and contemporary, suggest the usefulness of institutions generally in helping societies take advantage of the opportunities the environment offers them, but support the idea that no single

---

compensation paid to property holders, not laborers. Often compensation was paid by the laborers, but there was no compensation of losers when the slave trade was ended.

[18] See the discussions in Bernard Elbaum and William Lazonick, eds., *The Decline of the British Economy* (Oxford: Oxford University Press, 1986).

institutional solution is crucial. In this way, the role of institutions might be considered analogous to the role of technology, in that the processes of change are important but no single method of accomplishing a goal is indispensable.[19]

A perhaps more serious issue is that among the feasible set of institutional solutions to a general problem, different approaches may have different implications for various segments of the population. Depending upon the manner in which institutions evolve or are designed in a society, they may develop to favor the interests of more powerful groups at the expense of others, or even of the population at large. For example, elites might prefer policies that raise their share of national income, even if they reduce long-run rates of growth. The nature of the political power structure in society is critical in determining which institutions are adopted. The suffrage, or the distribution of political influence more generally, may be rather broad and inclusive, with a relatively large share of the population able to vote.[20] Or, alternatively, the franchise may be limited, by requirements of literacy, wealth, nationality, age, and gender, with only a small minority of the population able to vote and to directly influence policy. When the suffrage is restricted, many members of society have only very limited political influence and no direct voice in establishing the institutional framework. Even a very small segment of the population, but one with highly disproportionate political power, would be able to establish institutions, legal codes, and property rights regimes that serve their own interests, and be able to exclude other members of society from benefits.[21] Thus, there could be a well-defined and enforced set of property rights, but one coincident with a large component of the population being outsiders to decisionmaking in society.[22]

---

[19] Thus, as suggested by Davis and North, evaluating institutional change may be subject to the same type of benefit-cost analysis as are other economic factors. See Davis and North, *Institutional Change*.

[20] See the discussions of the evolution of restrictions on suffrage in Alexander Keyssar, *The Right to Vote: The Contested History of Democracy in the United States* (New York: Basic Books, 2000); and above, Ch. 4.

[21] Of course, other conditions matter as well. Where there is extreme economic inequality, for example, an elite might be able to leverage its wealth into disproportionate political influence through informal channels. Another example of context mattering is where labor is scarce, such as on a frontier. The desire of an elite, even one with a monopoly on political voice, to attract migrants might lead to policies that benefit groups that have no formal representation. For a discussion of how this might have operated on the U.S. frontier, see above, Ch. 7.

[22] In most cases, we would expect that groups with no formal political influence would have circumscribed access to scarce resources. This limited access might be due to the

Slave societies in the Americas often had well-defined institutions and property rights, and were capable of rapid economic growth, but part of their population had no rights and no means to obtain any rights. These slave societies provide a powerful example, albeit an extreme one, of how the determination of the size and nature of the elite groups, by political, economic, and/or military means, is critical to the establishment of institutions. Being excluded from voting does not necessarily mean a failure to benefit from economic change, nor does it mean that there will not be subsequent improvements in the rights to suffrage, but the limited nature of the decision-making group still raises important issues for our understanding of the distribution of rewards from economic activity. More generally, the observation that societies vary in how much influence different segments of the population can exert in shaping institutions implies that there may be systematic patterns in how flexible they are in adapting (or innovating) their institutions to enhance the ability of their populations to take advantage of new opportunities created by changes in the environment.

IV

It is no doubt easier to isolate the effect of institutions if we believe that they are exogenously determined by the forces of past history or by forces outside of the current economy. Among the factors that have sometimes been suggested as playing this role are: externally generated changes in mentalité due to change in religious belief or secular attitudes; the outcome of a military conflict, either due to externally generated changes in the power structure or of internal revolutionary actions that altered the balance of political power; the nonmilitary introduction of new foreign influence and contacts, reflecting, in part, improvements in transportation and communication; and the settling of new areas by people from a

laws explicitly favoring the dominant groups, even if the property rights allowed the "outsiders" were enforceable. A de facto limited access might, however, arise if the outside group lacked the financial or other resources necessary to take advantage of an opportunity. Thus, even though all citizens might be entitled to bring civil suits to enforce contracts, the poor may find themselves less able to act on this right. The case of married women is an interesting one to consider in this regard, as in the United States (and many other countries) the law allowed them only very limited rights as to owning property or entering into contracts as compared to those allowed men or single women, until the second half of the nineteenth century. See B. Zorina Khan, "Married Women's Property Laws and Female Commercial Activity," *Journal of Economic History* 56 (June 1996): 356–88.

distant metropolis, whose institutions could be regarded as exogenous to the new area of settlement. In this context we consider noninstitutional explanations to be not an absence of institutions, but the presence of institutions regarded as endogenous to the socio-economic process, even when the circumstances giving rise to the institutions are themselves exogenous to the economy (as, for example, climate and natural resources). In evaluating whether institutions are endogenous, there are several approaches that could be taken. One concerns the impact of resources and natural and human endowments upon institutions. A number of scholars have recently argued that there were systematic patterns in the types of institutions that evolved as settlers in European colonies adjusted to conditions that differed from those of the metropolis in terms of disease environments and economic opportunities.[23] Subjecting this notion to empirical testing is complicated by the enormous range of institutions that attention could be directed at, some of which reflect metropolitan carryovers and others of which developed very differently in the colonies than they did in the metropolis. Metropolitan institutions did not necessarily disappear in the process of settlement, but many were modified depending on the conditions of the particular settlement. Thus English New World colonies may have employed English law, and French colonies continued French legal institutions, but English and French temperate zone colonies differed in many important regards from their Caribbean colonies. French and English Caribbean colonies had greater similarities than they did with either their mainland counterparts or the metropolis. Additionally, while the initial controls over free white labor may have been much the same in all of the colonies, only some English colonies and only some French colonies came to rely on free, rather than slave, labor.[24] Climate and resources were the most powerful determinants of the geographic incidence of slave labor, irrespective of the metropolitan institutional structure. Slavery was legal in all the British colonies until the Revolutionary War, and differences in legal circumstances did not account for the major differences in its prevalence across areas, such as that between New England and the British West Indies.[25]

---

[23] See Acemoglu, Johnson, and Robinson, "Colonial Origins," Acemoglu, Johnson, and Robinson, "Reversal of Fortune," Easterly and Levine, "Tropics, Germs, and Crops."

[24] For an interesting analysis of adjustments to the laws governing slavery, see Robert J. Cottrol, "The Long Lingering Shadow: Law, Liberalism, and Cultures of Racial Hierarchy and Identity in the Americas," *Tulane Law Review* 76 (November 2002): 11–79.

[25] For a discussion of the fascinating case of how the Georgia colony, established with a prohibition on slavery, came to have it lifted, see Betty Wood, *Slavery in Colonial Georgia, 1730–1775* (Athens: University of Georgia Press, 1984).

Another approach to the question of whether institutions are endogenous to the process of economic change is to consider whether economic growth influences people's attitudes and the nature of the economy's institutions. Does the economy itself contain the seeds of its own limitations, whether due to its failure or its successes? Karl Marx is certainly the most prominent of historical economists who have posited a sequence of self-generated endogenous changes in society, from feudalism to capitalism to socialism, with each of the first two stages being successful at first but then failing due to internal contradictions. Joseph Schumpeter claimed that the declining belief in the value of capitalism, which developed with economic growth, weakened capitalism's survival power, and he expected the "march into socialism" to occur based upon the economy's success. Mancur Olson argued that as economies develop over time, vested interests operating in their own self-interest emerge and cause a reduction in the future growth through their success at rent seeking. Other explanations of how self-generated changes in the economy and economic structures occur include the growth of large industrial firms and the development of bureaucracies in business and government, both of which can force institutional changes.

Scholars interested in how institutions evolve have recently devoted much attention to the contrasts between colonial and metropolitan influences on institutions in newly settled areas. A long-standing disagreement, tracing back centuries, regarding the thirteen colonies that became the United States, has been the cause of North-South differences in economic and demographic structures, including the explanation of the differences in the relative importance of slavery. Did those settling in different parts of the mainland arrive with different cultural patterns from Britain – differences that persisted after settlement – or did the various colonists from Britain arrive with similar cultural beliefs, but then adjusted their institutions, once they were established in the New World and confronted with a different set of conditions?[26] The evidence to date seems to favor the

---

[26] See, for example, Jack P. Greene, *Pursuits of Happiness* (Chapel Hill: University of North Carolina Press, 1988); Jack P. Greene, *The Intellectual Construction of America: Exceptionalism and Identity from 1492 to 1800* (Chapel Hill: University of North Carolina Press, 1993); Jack P. Greene, "Transatlantic Colonization and the Redefinition of Empire in the Early Modern Era: The British-America Experience," in *Negotiated Empires: Centers and Peripheries in the Americas, 1500–1820*, eds. Christine Daniels and Michael V. Kennedy, 267–282 (New York: Routledge, 2002); and David Hackett Fischer, *Albion's Seed: Four British Folkways in America* (New York: Oxford University Press, 1989).

latter view. Not only has recent work demonstrated that even the Puritans were deeply influenced by the environment in selecting institutions for their two New World colonies, but studies of those Englishmen who came to populate the various settlements in the Americas emphasize how they were drawn from roughly the same social classes.[27] In the words of Edward Channing:

> "Historical writers have been altogether too prone to draw a hard and fast line of demarcation between the settlers of the Southern colonies and those who founded colonies north of the fortieth parallel...It is sometimes said that the Northern colonist came to the New World for conscience sake and the Southern planters sought wealth alone; but no such generalization can truthfully be made. Moreover, it is oftentimes the custom to point out some mysterious differences between the Virginian and the New Englander, which can be expressed by the words 'cavalier' and 'Puritan'...No such characterization is possible."[28]

This perspective receives strong support from the record of slavery in the Americas. The basis for the success (to the owners) of slave labor in one area, and its failure in another, depended less on the initial attitudes of most settlers than upon the influence of climate and soil resources on the nature of those crops which could be grown and the technology and scales of efficient crop production. Wherever the soils and climates were suitable for growing sugar, the most valuable commodity in world trade during the seventeenth and eighteenth centuries and a crop that could be produced at lowest cost on large slave plantations (under the gang labor system, which allowed owners to achieve very high labor intensity), slavery became the dominant institution of labor (and those of African descent a dominant share of the population). Elsewhere, where soils and climates favored agricultural products, such as grains and hays, where the gang labor system and slave labor offered no particular advantages so landowners had to rely more on free (often their own) labor where the productivity of slaves would not warrant the high prices for slaves that prevailed on world markets. The populations of these settlements, based on free labor, accordingly came to be much more homogeneous in wealth, human capital, ethnicity, and other dimensions. Thus, the factor endowments in the various colonies had a major impact on determining which labor institutions were dominant, the distribution of rewards

---

[27] Karen Ordahl Kupperman, *Providence Island, 1630–1641: The Other Puritan Colony* (Cambridge: Cambridge University Press, 1993).

[28] Edward Channing, *A History of the United States*, vol. 1 (New York: Macmillan, 1926): 145–46.

between laborers and landowners, and the nature of political participation and decisionmaking. Because slavery was legal in all of the European colonies in the Americas, it is evident that not only did these natural forces lead to differences in institutions, but they also led to different outcomes from similar institutions. Although the Old World background was surely important, it is difficult to explain the extreme differences among the various areas within each colonial empire without reference to the effects of the New World circumstances.

The early history of the New World colonies established by the European nations permits one to examine some of the implications of focusing on exogenous factors in institutional development, as opposed to viewing institutions as largely endogenous. The locations of settlements were themselves subject to some choice, based on the demographic and economic characteristics of different locations. Moreover, the pattern of initial settlement was modified over time, as settlers learned more about prospects in different areas. In the settlement of the Caribbean by the British and the French, for example, the adjustments in terms of crops and labor institutions that took place over the first half-century of settlement were rather different from those that were to emerge in subsequent years. The problems that arise from selection by the colonizing powers notwithstanding, the "natural experiment" arising from the variety of settling metropolises – including Spain, Portugal, Britain, France, and Holland – and the extreme diversity of environments found among the colonies makes for a wonderful laboratory in which to study the relationships between factor endowments, institutions, and economic growth. This work, of course, does not amount to a comparison of institutional and non-institutional factors in economic growth, since everyone agrees on the importance of institutions. Rather the work has sought to determine whether institutions can be understood as exogenous to the circumstances or economic system, or whether the environment or circumstances more broadly exert a powerful influence on how institutions emerge and evolve over time. Put simply, where do institutions come from?

A key economic question is the explanation for the post-1900 differences in levels of per capita income between the countries of mainland North America and those of Latin America (Table 1.1 and Figure 1.1), differences that were much smaller during the colonial period. A closely related issue is why Latin America is the region of the world today with the most extreme inequality in income. Since the nations of South and Central America had been settled mainly by the Spanish (the Portuguese settled Brazil), and the United States and Canada mainly by the British (with pre-1763 Canada by the French and pre-1664 New York by the Dutch, among the relatively less-dominant settling nations), a traditional explanation holds that the different cultures, religions, and institutions of Britain and Spain could alone explain the divergent paths of economic development.

Since there were sharp contrasts between the home countries of Britain and Spain in terms of economic and political structures, it is argued that the transfer of Old World institutions established the behavior of the economies and societies of the colonies in the New World, as differences in property rights determination and enforcement, legal frameworks more generally, economic goals, and religious beliefs were carried over, with little or no modification, into the new areas of settlement. The institutions that failed to generate sustained economic growth on the Iberian peninsula likewise failed to do so in the New World, whereas the institutions that had evolved over centuries in Britain worked on both sides of the Atlantic. The logic is that either the beliefs of political elites of the metropolis were carried over into the colonies, providing the political and legal framework for the successful carryover of institutions, or else that the elites in the New World, though different from those of the metropolis, were able to use the same institutional structures to achieve similar ends by similar means.[29]

An alternative explanation focuses on the economic and geographic circumstances in the area of settlement, and their influence on the determination of institutions in the new areas. As with the previous argument, there is a long literature on the role of climate and resources in influencing institutions and economic development. While a most detailed examination was provided by Montesquieu in the 1740s, a similar argument was made considerably earlier by Plato.[30] The links include the nature of the effects of climate upon the willingness to work, the desire to emigrate or immigrate, the role played by slavery in society, and related economic concerns. Whether seen as the basic cause of the specific set of institutions,

---

[29] It may be, however, that the distance between colony and homeland weakens the ability of the metropolis to control the settlers, weakening the nature of any transfer of political structure. See Greene, *Pursuits of Happiness;* and Greene, *Transatlantic Colonization.* For the argument that the institutional heritage that British colonies drew on was more conducive to long-run growth than that of the Spanish colonies, see North, *Structure and Change.* It is useful to see how the initial settlers in the Chesapeake adapted to growing insight into disease environments.

[30] See Baron de Charles de Secondat Montesquieu, *The Spirit of Law* (New York: Hafner, 1949 [1748]; and Plato, *The Laws,* trans. T. J. Saunders (Harmondsworth: Penguin Books, 1980), book 5, section 9).

or as a reason to modify some pre-existing set of exogenous institutions, settlement societies can be argued to have been significantly influenced by factors other than some unchanged metropolitan institutions. Indeed most settlements made dramatic changes in their institutions after they were first established, in the search for ways to enhance their profitability and survivability. The impact of climate and resources can also help to explain why the different areas settled by the same metropolitan power had rather different economic structures and performances (as, for example, New England and the British West Indies), and why geographically contiguous and resource-similar areas settled by different metropolitan powers (as the British and French in the West Indies, as well as the Spanish, Danish, and Dutch there) came to resemble each other in many important ways. Indeed, recent scholarship has found some evidence of the systematic effects of initial factor endowments on the types of institutions (including institutions involving suffrage and the conduct of elections, schooling, finance, the disposition of public lands, property rights, and intellectual property) that evolved in different colonies (and on long-term economic performance in these colonies), both in the Americas and elsewhere, and highlighted limitations on the explanatory power of simply national heritage.[31]

A specific example of how institutions can be altered to fit changing circumstances, and of how the distribution of power (both political and economic) as well as the environment influence outcomes, is provided by the adjustments in the societies of the Americas to the abolition of slavery.[32] This most dramatic institutional change of the nineteenth century was, almost everywhere, imposed on a resistant slaveholding class

---

[31] There is some question of what the comparison of institutions would indicate if some different dates were used for the evaluation. Spain arrived in America earlier than the British, went to areas with greater wealth and resources, and it took about another hundred years before the British arrived and were forced to go to areas that they regarded as clearly less promising for economic growth. For a comparison based on the year 1700 we would find the Spanish position seemingly more favorable than that of the British, reflecting the early economic advantages of the areas of Spanish settlement. As pointed out by John TePaske, the Spanish had three successful centuries in the Americas, and the British only two. See John Jay TePaske, "The Vital Peripheries of Colonial South America," in *Negotiated Empires: Centers and Peripheries in the Americas, 1500–1820*, eds. Christine Daniels and Michael V. Kennedy, 29–42 (New York: Routledge, 2002). Also see Acemoglu, Johnson and Robinson, "Reversal of Fortune;" Easterly and Levine "Tropics, Germs and Crops;" ibid.

[32] The recent literature on the role of institutions in economic growth has raised important questions as to the extent to which political power is independent of economic power, and to the relative importance of political inequality and economic inequality for how institutions evolve. A full discussion of these issues is beyond the scope of this book,

in the aftermath of armed conflict or by a government elected by a population dominated by nonslaveholders (including European parliaments). All New World societies ended slavery between 1777 and 1888, and the nature of the abolitions were similar with most providing some form of compensation, in cash, bonds, or labor time to the slaveowners, with generally nothing going to the former slaves.[33] Nevertheless there were some striking differences in the range of post-emancipation responses. In the British West Indies, for example, slavery was abolished by 1834 and all colonial governments had the same basic goal of inducing labor to work on plantations and imposed legislation to try to accomplish this end. Different environments led to different outcomes, however, as evident in the corresponding variation of output changes with the ratio of land to labor (see Table 10.3).[34]

Areas of high population density such as Barbados maintained plantation systems and high sugar output, while those with low population density, with abundant frontier land, initially saw the end of the plantation system and a decline in sugar output. In those cases where the islands had become relatively unproductive before the end of slavery, sugar output continued to decline and the plantation system was never re-introduced. In those areas, however, which had been growing rapidly before emancipation (such as in Trinidad and British Guiana), and where land was

---

but we would argue that although they are clearly related, and there is certainly an association across societies (or over time) between political power and economic power, the correlation is far from perfect and it is not all that uncommon for them to diverge. Their relative weight in the processes of institutional development likely varies with context. Moreover, some institutions may be more sensitive to political inequality, while others depend more on the extent of economic inequality. For example, the distribution of political influence would generally be expected to have a greater impact on public institutions, such as laws, and the distribution of wealth matters relatively more for the kinds of private institutions, such as financial organizations, that evolve.

[33] The United States, in 1865, was the one major nation to free its slaves without any form of compensation provided to slaveowners in the form of cash, apprenticeship, or a "law of the free womb," which required the free-born offspring of slaves to labor for the mother's master into their late teens to twenties. Even Haiti agreed to pay compensation to the French after 1825, as a condition for the right to engage in trade with France.

[34] See Stanley L. Engerman, "Economic Adjustments to Emancipation in the United States and the British West Indies," *Journal of Interdisciplinary History*, 12 (Autumn 1982): 191–220; Stanley L. Engerman, "The Land and Labour Problem at the Time of the Legal Emancipation of the West Indian Slaves," in *West Indies Accounts: Essays in the History of the British Caribbean and the Atlantic Economy in Honor of Richard Sheridan*, ed. Roderick A. MacDonald, 297–318 (Barbados, The Press of University of West Indies Press, 1996). For a classic treatment of the relationship between the land to labor ratio and institutions, see Evsey D. Domar," The Causes of Slavery or Serfdom: A Hypothesis," *Journal of Economic History* 30 (March 1970), 18–32.

TABLE 10.3. *Land/Labor Ratios and Changes in Sugar Production in the British Slave Colonies Prior to and After Emancipation and Contract Labor Immigration*

	Land/Labor Ratio[1]	Percent Change in Annual Sugar Prod. 1824–33 to 1839–46	Ratio of Sugar Production in 1887–96 to 1839–46	Contract Labor Immigration 1834–1918 (Gross Inflow)
Antigua	3.1	+8.7	1.5	2,600
Barbados	1.7	+5.5	3.5	–
St. Kitts[2]	2.9	+3.8	2.7	2,900
Nevis	5.0	−43.1	2	2
Trinidad	47.7	+21.7[3]	3.0	157,700
British Guiana	832.4	−43.0	3.4	301,000
Mauritius	8.0	+54.3	3.1	451,800
Dominica	16.3	−6.4	0.7	6,000
St. Lucia	15.5	−21.8	1.7	5,200
Montserrat	4.6	−43.7	2.5	–
St. Vincent	5.7	−47.5	0.7	5,600
Tobago	8.8	−47.5	4	4
Jamaica	12.2	−51.2	0.6	53,900
Grenada	6.3	−55.9	0.0	6,200

Notes:
[1] Square miles per thousand total population, just prior to abolition.
[2] Nevis data merged with St. Kitts after 1882.
[3] Trinidad output did decline slightly after abolition, and it was not until 1845 that the 1834-level of output was regained.
[4] Tobago data merged with Trinidad after 1891. The 1877–86 level of sugar production in Tobago was about one-third less than it was in 1824–33.
Source: Engerman (1996).

highly productive, plantation systems returned in several decades, but were now based on indentured labor drawn mainly from India, and not on ex-slaves. Thus the elite's ability to achieve their desired end, extracting the returns to the land they owned, was influenced by various other conditions, including resource endowments. Their efforts to achieve their goals, subject to the dissimilar constraints they faced, led to differences in institutional development.

Another example of how the evolution of institutions across New World societies reflected adjustments to different or changed circumstances is provided by the history of how broadly the franchise was extended over time and what fractions of respective populations actually voted in elections. Since most of the societies in the Americas had achieved independence from their colonial masters, and were at least nominal democracies, by the middle of the nineteenth century, suffrage institutions had a direct bearing on the extent to which elites based largely on wealth, human capital, and gender held disproportionate political power in their respective countries, and on their ability to shape government policies. The ability and inclination of the elites to maintain disproportionate political influence through the formal rules associated with the electoral process varied with a variety of circumstances. Among these circumstances was the extent of inequality in wealth, human capital, and political influence that existed at the time of independence, generally when there were conventions held to draw up constitutions for the new nations. One simple or straight-forward explanation of this pattern is that the greater the disparity in resources (which, we have argued, was due to factor endowments during initial colonization), the greater was the ability of an elite to frame the rules in such a way as to preserve their relative political power.[35]

Among the other factors that appear to have had significant effects on the way institutions evolved was the relative scarcity of labor. Although elites may generally be reluctant to share their access to political influence and economic opportunity with other segments of the population, they were more likely to do so in settings where they would benefit from attracting or retaining a scarce resource – labor.

The evidence on the evolution of suffrage institutions in the New World is quite consistent with this view. Summary information on how the right to vote was restricted across New World societies in the nineteenth and early twentieth centuries is reported in Table 1.3. The estimates reveal that the United States and Canada were the clear leaders in doing away with restrictions based on wealth and literacy and introducing the secret ballot, and much higher fractions of the populations voted in these countries than anywhere else in the Americas. These societies were distinguished for their relative equality, population homogeneity, and scarcity of labor, and it is notable that others of British heritage, such as Barbados, generally retained stringent restrictions on the franchise well into the twentieth century. Moreover, it is striking that the leaders in extending the suffrage in South and Central America, such as Uruguay, Argentina, and Costa Rica, are generally regarded as having been historically the most

---

[35] For discussions of why factor endowments are the principal source of the differences in inequality, see above, Chs. 2 and 3.

egalitarian of Latin American societies, and having initial factor endowments most closely resembling those of the United States and Canada.

What accounts for this pattern of diffusion of universal male suffrage across New World societies? One obvious explanation is that differences in the degrees of inequality in wealth, human capital, and political influence were related to the likelihood of adopting such an institutional change. The cross-sectional patterns, as well as the histories indicating that the attainment of universal male suffrage and of the secret ballot was often the product of a long series of hard fought political battles, with the elites more likely to be opposed to liberalizing the franchise, are certainly consistent with this view.[36]

Another important factor, however, was the desire to attract immigrants. It is striking that pioneers in extending suffrage, such as new states (those after the original thirteen) in the United States, Argentina, and Uruguay, did so during periods in which they hoped to attract migrants, such that the rights to suffrage formed part of a package of policies thought to be potentially attractive to those contemplating relocation. When elites – such as large holders of land or other assets – desire common men to locate in the polity, they thus may choose to extend access to privileges and opportunities without threat of civil disorder; indeed, a polity (or one set of elites) may find itself competing with another to attract the labor or whatever else is desired.[37]

How broadly a society chooses to extend the franchise is a fundamental political arrangement. Many scholars, have noted that differences across polities in suffrage institutions, as well as changes over time, can often be related to decisions about government policies, such as what to do about public lands, what types of schooling and other public services and investments to support (and how to raise the revenue for them), and how to regulate financial institutions. As important as it is, however, the breadth of the franchise, or even the rate of participation in elections, is far from the only feature of political systems that matters. Many authoritarian governments stage elections, and voting is often as irrelevant in

---

[36] The achievements of a broadening of the formal requirements for suffrage, as well as of the more administrative procedures governing the conduct of elections, tend to overstate the reduction in the extent of political inequality. Economic elites always enjoy disproportionate informal political influence, and there is likely more scope for them to bypass formal procedures and channels in contexts where there is extreme inequality. Hence, it may not be so surprising that the outcomes did not improve more than they did after the extension of the suffrage in many of the Latin American societies.

[37] For a fuller discussion of the issues involved in the evolution of suffrage institutions in the New World, see above, Ch. 4 and also Acemoglu and Robinson "Why Did the West Extend," for treatment of the somewhat different pattern in Europe.

these contexts as it had been in the Soviet Union. Hence, although we have highlighted the uneven evolution of suffrage institutions across the Americas, we do not find it at all surprising that the attainment of something approximating universal adult suffrage throughout the hemisphere has thus far failed to dramatically reduce the disparities in the structure of institutions or in economic performance across countries. Not only is much more involved in determining political outcomes, but there are many factors other than the distribution of political influence that shape the development of institutions.

This brief excursion into specific historical examples of the evolution of key institutions illustrates several key points. The first obvious implication is that important changes in institutions, such as the adaptations to the plantation system after the abolition of slavery in the British West Indies and the expansion of the fraction of the population eligible to vote, do occur, and in different directions in different countries and contexts. A second observation is that there does appear to be a substantial systematic component to the variation in how these institutions evolved, with some explanatory power coming from circumstances that were not based only on exogenous or previously existing institutions.

V

There are always institutions present, and we cannot conceive of a framework for making sense of the processes of economic development that does not include a role for them. There is, moreover, no doubt that for any given society some institutions may limit the extent to which it realizes its potential economic output, while possible alternatives might do better. That being said, however, it is unclear how firmly theories of economic growth can be grounded on specific institutions. Economists do not yet have a very good understanding of where institutions come from, or why some societies have institutions that seem conducive to growth, while others are burdened by institutions less favorable for economic performance. Until they do, it will be quite difficult to specify the precise role of institutions in processes of growth.

As we have sought to highlight in this chapter, what little we presently know about the evolution of institutions suggests caution against making strong claims about their relationship to growth. First, it is clear that very different institutional structures often seem to be reasonable substitutes in being conducive to growth, both in dissimilar as well as in similar contexts. Narrow definitions of institutional prerequisites for growth do not, accordingly, seem appropriate. Second, the case for attributing growth to institutions may seem weaker if institutions are endogenous rather than exogenous, and the evidence that there are systematic patterns to the ways institutions evolve makes the latter view problematic. The recent studies of the "natural experiment" in institutional development provided by the European colonization of the Americas (and of many other parts of the globe), for example, imply that the broad environment (reflecting factor endowments, social arrangements, or technology) had powerful effects on the sorts of institutions that evolved in different colonies. Institutions obviously matter for growth, but the way we understand how they matter will be somewhat different if the agents and other forces shaping institutions are responsive to the conditions they face than if institutions develop independently of (or could be imposed in any) context.

The recognitions that the institutional structure appropriate for one environment may not be appropriate for another, and that the history of institutions in high-performing societies is often one of change over time in response to changing circumstances, suggest a different perspective on the relation between institutions and growth. Although we all understand that there are favorable aspects to governments making credible commitments to various obligations or arrangements they enter into, such as enforcement of property rights, it is also clear that in theory one would want institutions to vary over time and place with the environment, technology, and values. One might, therefore, think of societies with institutions conducive for growth as being those that have exhibited greater institutional flexibility – where by institutional flexibility we mean the ease with which institutional adaptations that respond constructively to changes in circumstances are innovated and/or diffused. Societies with good institutions would, therefore, have institutions well adapted for economic performance in their specific settings because they had implemented a series of institutional modifications or innovations (public and private) that cumulatively generated improvements in welfare. Societies with bad institutions will include those with institutional inflexibility, whose institutions did not respond constructively to take advantage of the opportunities created by the environment and state of knowledge. Such a framework would encourage scholars interested in the relation between institutions and growth to devote more attention to the factors influencing the rate and direction of institutional change and relatively less attention to the quest for a set of institutional structures that would be universally effective at all times at promoting growth.

Epilogue: Institutions in Political
and Economic Development

I

In recent years, economists and political scientists have again become concerned with the study of the origins, and impacts, of institutions. This has led to both more complete explanations of long-standing questions and a broadening of the types of issues examined. The most important reason for the resurgence of research on institutions has been the perceived failure of earlier explanations to provide satisfactory explanations of important economic and political phenomena, such as rates of economic growth, the distribution of income, and the changing political structures within society.

Within the study of economic growth, the belief developed that an exclusive reliance on so-called economic factors failed to explain why some countries had developed economically and others had remained poor, relatively and/or absolutely; why some nations that had developed early fell behind areas that developed later;[1] and how gaps between nations have greatly widened over time, whatever magnitudes of differentials existed in earlier times. These intellectual failures meant, in regard to contemporary policy, a limited ability to determine what conditions need to be changed to spur growth. Thus, a broader range of determinants of economic change have come to be considered, and these broadened

---

[1] This has long been a source of debate, given the changes (in the very long run) in patterns of economic leadership by broad continental areas as well as among particular nations within these areas. Obviously, in broad perspective, being first has never been a guarantee of long-term domination. Given these differences across time and space, it is not clear that the same explanation for economic development will hold in all cases, and it may be that arguments valid for the contemporary era may not be applicable to earlier times.

factors came to be applied to other economic issues, such as the nature of the firm and the operation of markets. In political science, the main questions involved formalization of the analysis of the rise, stability, and persistence of various political structures, such as dictatorship and democracy. The causes and consequences of democracy have been central issues in the study of the role of institutions within political science. Given the economists' interest in examining the impact of democracy on economic growth, there is some overlap in the studies of the two disciplines. As Thelen (1999) points out, one strand of the political science literature on institutions relies on methodological individualism and rational choice, and this strand of research has come to resemble that of economists. Another strand, that of historical institutionalism, is more concerned with the study of the historical emergence of institutions, and this fits in less well with the approach of economic theory.

II

The "old institutionalism" of the 1920s and 1930s – exemplified by the work of, among others, John R. Commons, Wesley Mitchell, Thorstein Veblen, and Richard Ely, and discussed by Dorfman (1949, 1959)[2] and Samuels (1987)[3] – was primarily concerned with describing the organization of the economy and the manner in which the structure of power influenced the control of the economic system. The basis of legal rights and constraints in the market sphere were critical issues in this early-twentieth-century institutionalism. In the nineteenth century, institutions had been examined by the historical schools in Germany and Great Britain. Much that traditional economic theory considered exogenous was argued to be endogenously determined within the society's system of behavior and beliefs. Consumer tastes were not exogenous, the legal codes reflected primarily the society's power structure, and market equilibria did not always have desirable social characteristics. The market itself was not regarded as an independent force but was merely another institution to be examined and whose existence was to be explained. These institutional studies also focused on the basis of the formation of the private and public organizations that influenced the economy. Institutionalism, at this time,

---

[2] See Joseph Dorfman, *The Economic Mind in American Civilization*, 5 vols. (New York: Viking Press, 1946–1959).

[3] See W. Samuels, "Institutional Economics," in *The New Palgrave: A Dictionary of Economics*, vol. 2, eds. J. Eatwell, M. Milgate, and P. Newman, 864–66 (London: Macmillan, 1987).

presented a critique of standard economic theory, providing a substitute analytical method, not a supplement.

The "new institutionalism" – exemplified by the more recent pioneering works of Douglass North, Ronald Coase, Oliver Williamson, and others – reflects a similar concern with the role of nonmarket arrangements in influencing economic behavior.[4] The key institutions of influence on the economy reflect informal arrangements either among individuals or between individuals and governmental units (or rather the individuals who compose the ruling elite and the individuals ruled by them).[5] The questions studied – which include the determination of how economies are organized and how the decisions that influence economic outcomes are made – resemble those of the old institutionalism, with their focus on the importance of nonmarket factors in market outcomes, the role of institutions in economic growth, and the factors that enable the existence of democracy and changes in government structure.

The main distinction between the old and new schools has been the use of formal economic and political science methods by the new institutionalists. Their analysis is based on the acceptance of economic theoretical models, particularly the formal methods of rational choice theory and game theory, to examine the nature of the impact of institutions on the political system and the manner by which individuals derive formal and informal rules to regulate behavior. The old institutionalists had regarded economic theory as an inappropriate way to understand the economy. The new institutionalism thus fits much better into mainstream economics than did the old, and there is now much more overlap in interest and approach between traditional economists and political scientists regarding institutions than before.

III

In recent years, economists have become concerned with explaining the past in order to design policy for future economic growth. As discussed

---

[4] Several useful collections of essays deal with these arrangements, including C. Ménard and M. M. Shirley, eds., *Handbook of New Institutional Economics* (Berlin: Springer, 2005); C. Ménard, *Institutions, Contracts, and Organizations: Perspectives from New Institutional Economics* (Cheltenham: Edward Elgar, 2000); and C. Ménard, *The Foundations of the New Institutional Economics* (Cheltenham: Edward Elgar, 2004).

[5] A. Greif, *Institutions and the Path to the Modern Economy: Lessons from Medieval Trade* (Cambridge: Cambridge University Press, 2006); and Daron Acemoglu and James A. Robinson, *Economic Origins of Dictatorship and Democracy* (Cambridge: Cambridge University Press, 2006) discuss each of these variants.

in Chapter 10, there has been a shift in the key variables of interest. In regard to the study of modern economic growth, a transition has occurred over the past few decades from a concentration on the role of narrowly defined economic factors to a focus on the significance of various social structures and culture in providing the conditions conducive to economic development.

Institutional structures that appear very different have often been found to be reasonable substitutes for each other. In the antebellum United States, for example, the North and South both grew relatively rapidly with their sharply contrasting institutions of labor. The historical record, therefore, does not seem to support the notion that any one particular institution, narrowly defined, is indispensable for growth.[6] Institutions matter, but they are influenced by the political and economic environment, and it may be that if any aspect of institutions is crucial for growth it is that institutions must change as circumstances change.

It has become fashionable to distinguish between economic and noneconomic factors. Discussions of noneconomic factors in accounting for differences across societies in economic development have a long history. Theories about the rise of European capitalism and the onset of modern economic growth are based on conditions that fall outside of the conventional definitions of economic forces. One such condition is the spread of particular religious beliefs, such as Protestantism or Judaism,[7] and changes in the orientation of Islamic empires.[8] Important also are the development of scientific and rational thoughts and the effects of choices between work and leisure and the degree of the intensity of labor.[9] The willingness of a society to exercise force, internally and

---

[6] Recently the rapid growth rate of the Chinese economy has raised questions about the frequent contentions that economic growth promotes democracy (and vice versa), and that political freedom is a necessary precondition for economic success. Chinese economic expansion without traditional freedoms seems, at present, an important counterexample to the familiar argument, although this may change over time.

[7] See Max Weber, *The Protestant Ethic and the Spirit of Capitalism* (New York: Scribner's, 1992 [1904–1905]): 40–5; on Judaism see Werner Sombart, *The Jews and Modern Capitalism* (New York: Burt Franklin, 1969 [1913]).

[8] After centuries of arguments that Confucianism retarded Chinese economic growth, it has recently been proclaimed a religion promoting rapid development. Although the *mentalités* of Catholicism may have served to hinder growth, as argued by Weber in *The Protestant Ethic*, the political changes within Europe due to the expansion of the Catholic church may have enhanced conditions for trade, migration, and capital flows, and thus served to generate economic expansion.

[9] See, for example, J. Mokyr, *The Gifts of Athena: Historical Origins of the Knowledge Economy* (Princeton: Princeton University Press, 2002); and Jan de Vries, "The Industrial

externally, will have a significant impact on its economic development, as wars and conflict sometimes help to cause (or perhaps retard) economic change. Although changes in many types of institutions are generally treated as exogenous to the economy, the distinction between "economic" and "noneconomic" factors can be somewhat artificial, as the nature and impact of cultural forces cannot be determined independent of economic forces (and, of course, vice versa).

Recent work attempting to explain why Britain industrialized first, and to understand differences in economic performance more generally, often gives more attention to institutions than to culture. The discussion of the importance of appropriate institutions, following the insights of Douglass North, defines institutions as encompassing the specific organizations or rules that constrain and influence human behavior.[10] The key connection between appropriate institutions and economic growth is that institutions can reduce the costs of production and distribution, permitting individuals to benefit from specialization and trade. Institutions, as human-imposed constraints, are not the only constraints that societies and private sectors confront. Other constraints are imposed by the state of technological knowledge, demographic forces, nature (including climate and topography), and various other features of the environment that have an influence on the patterns of economic activity. It is argued, by North and others, that it was the appropriate property rights and incentive schemes made possible by Britain's unique institutions that enabled it to industrialize first.[11]

The nature of the enforcement of institutional provisions is also critical to the success of whatever institutions exist. Enforcement must be effective and accepted as legitimate. Similarly, the nature of society's legislative decisions and judicial rulings will also influence politics and economics. Enforcement is sometimes between individuals, with no government role

---

Revolution and the Industrious Revolution," *Journal of Economic History* 54 (June 1994): 249–70.

[10] Douglass C. North and Robert Paul Thomas, *The Rise of the Western World* (Cambridge: Cambridge University Press, 1973); Douglass C. North and Barry Weingast, "Constitutions and Commitment: The Evolution of Institutions Governing Public Choice in Seventeenth-Century England," *Journal of Economic History* 49 (December 1989): 803–32; and Douglass C. North, *Institutions, Institutional Change and Economic Performance* (Cambridge: Cambridge University Press, 1990). For an interesting discussion regarding the choice of institutions in the United States, see Lance E. Davis and Douglass C. North, *Institutional Change and American Economic Growth* (Cambridge: Cambridge University Press, 1971).

[11] North and Weingast, "Constitutions and Commitment," 803–32.

to ensure compliance, but in other cases enforcement requires government action.

IV

It is often hard to distinguish between, or gauge the relative importance of, the institutional and noninstitutional explanations of economic changes. It is doubtful that anyone would claim there is a general answer covering all cases, and indeed most, if not all, individual cases seem to allow some role for each type of explanation. As discussed in Chapter 10, there are numerous possible causes of changes in institutions.

There has also been considerable recent interest in trying to make the empirical work relating institutions and economic growth more tractable. We asked, in Chapter 10, what are the major elements in determining whether the key institutions are exogenous or endogenous? This has long been debated by US colonial historians, who argue whether settlers' attitudes were based on their British background or on the conditions they faced after arrival in America.[12] This distinction has a long history, as have the debates over the superiority of British institutions, and has, more recently, figured prominently in the study of how the various economies established as colonies by Europeans (and others) developed.[13]

In evaluating whether institutions are endogenous, there are several approaches that could be taken. One concerns the impact of resources and natural and human endowments on institutions. A number of scholars have recently argued that systematic patterns in the types of institutions evolved as settlers in European colonies adjusted to conditions that differed from those of the metropolis in terms of crop potentials, disease environments, and economic opportunities. Subjecting this notion to empirical testing is complicated by the enormous range of institutions that could be tested, some of which reflect metropolitan carryovers, others of which developed very differently in the colonies than they did in the metropolis. Metropolitan institutions did not necessarily disappear in the process of settlement, but many were modified over time, and differences in economic performance across economies could be attributed

---

[12] Above, Ch. 10.
[13] Above, Ch. 3. Daron Acemoglu and James A. Robinson, "Economic Backwardness in Political Perspective" *American Political Science Review* 100 (February 2006): 115–31.

to adaptations to the new environment by endogenously determined institutions.[14]

V

It is generally argued that it is useful to society to have some institutions fixed and unchanged over time. Credible commitment to acknowledge private property rights, whether in the interests of the elite or the majority of the population, is the major example of the value of certainty about policy action. Nevertheless some flexibility in institutions, such that they can be changed to allow private or public agents to take fuller advantage of new opportunities that arise as technology or the environment changes, would also be expected to foster improved economic performance. Although some see a constitution as a means for ensuring stability in the decision-making process, many constitutions include provisions for amendment. There may be more cases where nations and economies suffered from inflexible institutions than from excessive flexibility, although this may vary with the rapidity of change.[15]

The argument for the necessity of fixed and determinable institutions is that they may promote higher income growth, either directly or (via greater social stability) indirectly. Certainty of behavior and a fixed set of rules should reduce risk and thus lead to more favorable outcomes. A frequent expectation is that a more stable and (presumably) more democratic set of institutions will provide "all good things," including higher growth and more equity, but this need not always be the case.

VI

The role of specific, and unchanging, institutions in influencing growth may often be problematic as imposing rigidity within a world of change.

---

[14] See J. A. Schumpeter, *Capitalism, Socialism, and Democracy* (New York: Harper, 1950), 42–43, 131–42, 156–63, 415–25 on the internal dynamics of the changes of capitalism. The most familiar model of endogenous internal change remains that of Karl Marx. Theories of the stages of economic development present a similar argument, as do the descriptions of evolving institutions by cultural anthropologists. See B. F. Hoselitz, J. J. Spengler, J. M. Letiche, E. McKinley, J. Buttrick and H. J. Bruton, *Theories of Economic Growth* (Glencoe: Free Press, 1960); M. J. Herskovits, *Man and His Works: The Science of Cultural Anthropology* (New York: Knopf, 1948); North and Weingast, "Constitutions and Commitment," 903–32.

[15] See Mancur Olson, *The Rise and Decline of Nations: Economic Growth, Stagflation, and Economic Rigidities* (New Haven: Yale University Press, 1982) on the causes and impacts of institutional rigidity.

Not only must the specific institution have favorable effects, but whether it contributes (and how much) to the social good will also depend on the overall set of institutions. For example, Weber argues that the Protestant ethic leads to capitalism and growth, but only in societies in which conditions permitting growth already exist.[16] It may be that one bad institution could prevent growth and that one good institution is insufficient to have the expected positive effects. Even if a particular institution is consistent with economic growth, it may not be the optimal institution for growth, since its presence along with different institutions might have facilitated higher economic growth. Unchanging institutions may dictate a fixed set of actions for long periods, beyond the time when any positive payoff is obtained.[17]

Belief in defined commitments did not characterize all aspects of early modern British society. Thus, in the debate in the 1790s about ending the British slave trade Edmund Burke argued that the government could always change policy, and this could be done without any new votes, since change was always understood to be a governmental prerogative. At about the same time, William Pitt argued that the government could always change policy without paying compensation to those hurt by the changes, since otherwise no government would be able to accomplish any changes. At this time, moreover, the British government did introduce legislation to not only end the slave trade (and a quarter century later, slavery), but also to limit hours of work for women and children in certain industries, to levy an income tax, and to expand the franchise.[18]

---

[16] Weber, *The Protestant Ethic*, 42–43, 190, points to the association of Calvinism with capitalist business sense, but then notes that "this, of course, was true only when some possibility of capitalistic development in the area in question was present. Max Weber, *General Economic History* (New York: Collier Books, 1966 [1927]), presents several other important arguments about economic and political change that are worth more attention. He discusses the need for "a mass market demand" (230) and the impact of warfare in democratizing society because of the rulers' need "to secure the co-operation of the nonaristocratic masses" (240).

[17] It is argued (for example, by North and Weingast, "Constitutions and Commitment") that early nineteenth-century British economic growth was spurred by a certain set of institutions, but presumably when these did not change in the second half of the nineteenth century, they were instrumental in the relative British decline. See Bernard Elbaum and William Lazonick, eds., *The Decline of the British Economy* (Oxford: Oxford University Press, 1986), particularly the editors' introduction, and P. Clarke and C. Trebilcock, eds., *Understanding Decline: Perceptions and Realities of British Economic Performance* (Cambridge: Cambridge University Press, 1997), particularly the essay by Barry Supple.

[18] On labor standards, see Stanley L. Engerman, "The History and Political Economy of International Labor Standards," in *International Labor Standards: History, Theory and*

In addition, the Peterloo Massacre led to the death of several protestors, and the Napoleonic Wars had extended the government's intervention in the economy, increasing taxation and the public debt. Perhaps these changes were not of great magnitude, nor did they have a decisive negative impact since economic growth did accelerate at this time – but they show that the government did not keep all its commitments and it did violate the terms of its trust. By introducing controls on business, it demonstrated a willingness to alter the form of its commitment to property rights. These changes were not as dramatic as those in other nations, but clearly the British did not maintain a fixed set of government policies and legal provisions, nor did the governments of any European or American nations in the nineteenth century (or before or after that time).

The capability for adaptation, may be more crucial for economic growth and political stability than the continuation of any particular set of beliefs, rules, or behavior. Adaptation was important in the case of European expansion, which introduced new climates, soil types, natural resources, and economic and political problems. The confrontation with a new environment that offered rich opportunities, but in an unfamiliar context, led to adjustments and innovations in institutions in the interest of economic improvement.[19]

Policy Options, eds. K. Basu, H. Horn, L. Romin, and J. Shapiro (Malden: Blackwell, 2003), 9–83. On changes in the franchise, see H. J. Hanham, *The Reformed Electoral System in Great Britain, 1832–1914* (London: Historical Association, 1968); Acemoglu and Robinson, *Economic Origins;* Daron Acemoglu and James A. Robinson, "Institutions as a Fundamental Cause of Long-run Growth," in *Handbook of Economic Growth* 2 vol., vol. 1, eds. P. Aghion and S. N. Durlauf, 385–472 (Amsterdam: Elsevier, 2005), and Alessandro Lizzeri and Nichola Persico, "Why Did the Elites Extend the Suffrage? Democracy and the Scope of Government with an Application to Britain's 'Age of Reform,'" *Quarterly Journal of Economics* 119 (May 2004): 707–65. Also important were frequent changes in tariff rates and variations in tax rates and government expenditure policy. See M. Daunton, *Trusting Leviathan: The Politics of Taxation in Britain, 1799–1914* (Cambridge: Cambridge University Press, 2001). For descriptions of the debates at this time on economic policy changes advocated by politicians and economists, see S. Checkland, *British Public Policy, 1776–1939: An Economic, Social, and Political Perspective* (Cambridge: Cambridge University Press, 1983); B. Gordon, *Economic Doctrine and Tory Liberalism, 1824–1830* (London: Macmillan, 1974); and F. W. Fetter, *The Economist in Parliament, 1780–1868* (Durham: Duke University Press, 1980). See also, D. H. Porter, *The Abolition of the Slave Trade in England, 1784–1807* (Hamden: Archon Books, 1970): 41–9; W. Cobbett, *Parliamentary History of England, From the Norman Conquest in 1066 to the year 1803* (London: T. C. Hansard, 1806–1820), 28: 96–97; 29: 1145–46.

[19] This argument is familiar from the challenge-and-response thesis of A. J. Toynbee, *A Study of History*, vol. 1 (New York: Oxford University Press, 1946), 60–145. It has attracted attention among US economic historians. The Habakkuk thesis relates high

As mentioned in Chapter 10, various institutional forms or structures are reasonable substitutes for each other. The differential between the benefits of the "best" and the "second best" institutional arrangements may be quite small. In this regard, the role of institutions might be considered similar to the role of technology, in that the contributions to change can be important but no single method of accomplishing a particular goal seems indispensable.[20]

The nature of the political power structure is critical in determining which institutions are adopted. Suffrage may be rather broad, with a relatively large share of the population permitted to vote; or alternatively, it may be limited, for example, by requirements of literacy, wealth, nationality, age, and gender, so that only a small minority of the population has the right to vote. A small segment of the population, if it had highly disproportionate political power, would be able to determine the specific institutions that exist, and to limit the benefits of the majority.[21]

---

rates of successful invention and innovation to labor scarcity in the economy. (Habakkuk attributes an earlier version of the argument to George Washington.) The more general issues are whether growth is greater if societies have things easy or difficult, and what the benefits of adversity are. Toynbee points out that any successful response had probably been preceded by numerous failures in dealing with the same challenge, Toynbee, *Study of History*, vol. 1 (New York, Oxford University Press, 1946). 141. For a related argument about the need for adaptability, see Plato's claim that "we must take care to lay down laws that do not fly in the face of such influences, noting the roles of wind, heat, water, and soil quality" (see Plato, *The Laws*, (Harmondsworth: Penguin Books, 1970): 219.

[20] For some examples based on legal and financial institutions, see R. W. Goldsmith, *Financial Structure and Development* (New Haven: Yale University Press, 1969); E. L. Glaeser and A. Shleifer, "Legal Origins," *Quarterly Journal of Economics* 117 (November 2002): 1193–229; T. Beck, A. Demirgöe-Kunt, and R. Levine, "Legal Theories of Financial Development," *Oxford Review of Economic Policy* 17, (Winter 2001): 483–50; and Naomi R. Lamoreaux and Jean-Laurent Rosenthal, "Legal Regime and Contractual Flexibility: A Comparison of Business's Organizational Choices in France and the United States During the Era of Industrialization," *American Law and Economics Review* 7 (Spring 2005): 28–61. See also Robert William Fogel, *Railroads and American Economic Growth: Essays in Econometric History* (Baltimore: Johns Hopkins University Press, 1964) for the classic statement of this point regarding the impact of one technological change.

[21] Property rights without opportunities for social mobility can limit growth, if that is in the interests of the elite. For much of Europe, the first decades of the twentieth century saw broadened suffrage and also an increase in the share of government expenditures in the national budget. See Richard A. Musgrave, *Fiscal Systems* (New Haven: Yale University Press, 1969); P. Flora, J. Alber, R. Eichenberg, J. Kohl, and F. Kraus, et al., *State, Economy, and Society in Western Europe, 1815–1975*, 2 vols., vol. 1 (Chicago: University of Chicago Press, 1983); Vito Tanzi and Howell Zee, "Tax Policy for Emerging Markets: Developing Countries," IMF Working Paper 00/35 (Washington, D.C.:

VII

The ability to impose franchise restrictions represents a major source of power within society.[22] To limit voting to the powerful elite should reduce the benefits presently going to the lower classes, as well as reduce their future gains. The power to influence elections and governmental policy has obvious effects on economic life.

Because most societies in the Americas had achieved independence from their colonial masters, and were at least nominal democracies, by the middle of the nineteenth century, suffrage institutions had a direct bearing on the extent to which elites (defined largely by wealth, human capital, and gender) held disproportionate power to shape government policies in their respective countries. The ability and inclination of the elites to maintain disproportionate political influence through the formal rules associated with the electoral process varied with a number of circumstances. Among these were the extent of inequality in wealth, human capital, and political influence that existed at the time of independence, when conventions were generally held to draw up constitutions for the new nations. Presumably, there was much less disparity in resources in the United States and Canada than in South America and the Caribbean. This led to a much higher rate of enfranchisement in North America than elsewhere. Thus, as late as 1900, few of the countries in Latin America had the secret ballot, and in most, the share of the adult male population casting votes was quite small. Most European nations, as well as the United States and Canada, achieved secrecy in balloting and universal adult male suffrage long before Latin American countries. Although many factors may have contributed to the low levels of political participation in South America and the Caribbean, wealth and literacy requirements, responding to the nature of factor endowments, presented binding constraints.[23]

International Monetary Fund, March 2000); T. S. Aidt, J. Dutta, and E. Loukoianova, "Democracy Comes to Europe: Franchise Extension and Fiscal Outcomes, 1830–1938," *European Economic Review* 50 (February 2006): 249–83.

[22] Above, Ch. 4.

[23] The changes in suffrage were not always due to threats of revolution. Although it is difficult to define effective threats (unless they succeed), areas that seemed less likely to have revolutions did have more democratic political regimes, whereas those in Latin America that seemed to have higher revolutionary prospects did not increase suffrage until much later. The impact of social discontent short of revolution remains important to consider.

On U.S. land policy and its effect on suffrage, see Benjamin Horace Hibbard, *A History of the Public Land Policies* (New York: Macmillan, 1924); Raynor G. Wellington, *The Political and Sectional Influence of the Public Lands, 1818–1842* (Cambridge, MA:

VIII

Two particularly important books on institutions were published in 2006. Although they deal with different aspects of institutions, both Greif and Acemoglu and Robinson greatly advance the discussion.[24] Both studies draw heavily on theory and historical examples, and both should prove to be influential for a long time. Both of these clearly argued works have opened up broader debates.

The main novelty of Greif's discussion of institutions is its primary concern with the endogenous generation of institutions, particularly the informal arrangements among individuals. The historical study deals with a small geographic area for a limited time period, but Greif wishes to generalize the analysis rather broadly. He deals little with the nature of the state, political rules, and legal institutions, which are the concern of Acemoglu and Robinson; indeed, a central contention of Greif relates to the generation of agreed-on institutions in the absence of a central authority. According to Greif, the key characteristics of institutions are those that are exogenous to each individual and "reflect intentional or unintentional human actions."[25] Institutions are nonphysical and rationally motivated, reflect shared cultural and religious beliefs, and are based on the interactions of individuals or coalitions of individuals.[26]

To Greif, the key sets of rules studied are those dealing with individual transactions. They might be written or unwritten, formally spelled out or informally known, but, in any case, they come to be accepted by the relevant members of society. Governments can provide the enforcement that increases the certainty of the rules being adhered to, but the government need not be a party to transactions. Greif describes in detail various means of enforcement.[27] An important point is that even without a direct governmental role, individuals will be able to form trading coalitions to enforce behavior. A major issue for Greif is whether the importance of recurring transactions among individuals or groups would lead to a different set of institutions than would infrequent transactions

Riverside Press, 1914); Roy M. Robbins, *Our Landed Heritage: The Public Domain, 1776–1936* (Princeton: Princeton University Press, 1942); Paul W. Gates, *History of the Public Land Law Development* (Washington, D.C.: Government Printing Office, 1968); above, Chapters 4 and 7.

[24] See Greif, *Institutions*, and Acemoglu and Robinson, *Economic Origins*.
[25] Greif, *Institutions*, 33.
[26] Ibid., 21, 30, 33.
[27] Ibid., Ch. 3 and 4, and the 441–43.

with few repeat contacts among trading units.[28] The influence of repeat dealings leads to a need for informal agreements to enforce the outcome of future negotiations. Even without government and formal laws, the behavior of rational people, motivated by observing the consequences of their actions, will be consistent with some form of codified rules governing transactions. The importance of trust, in permitting agreements without government imposition is reflected in the many private commercial dealings between individuals within nations and across international borders.

For Acemoglu and Robinson, the major concern is not bilateral individual agreements but the role of government and its impositions on private individuals. They provide an analytical framework with which to examine a rather broad question – the terms of establishing a democratic government and understanding how it changes with demographic and other factors. The preferred political system for most citizens is democracy, although in many cases constraints (via legislative rules and the court system) inhibit the effect of democratic outcomes. The government sets voting requirements and participation. A major interest for Acemoglu and Robinson is how or why democracy exists and what causes transitions in political power. Several different scenarios for changes are presented, including various degrees of repression the currently empowered regime might be willing to implement. The trade-off between coercion and more peaceful forms of transition remains an option for those ruling society, and the terms of the trade-off may be expected to vary over time, with military technology and social ideology.[29] Primary causes of transitions, within the Acemoglu and Robinson framework, are (a) revolution or the threat of revolution, (b) a shift in norms or ideology to a more egalitarian set of beliefs, (c) new ethical and moral codes about the role of individuals in society, (d) a split within the elite leading to some willingness to dilute their power in the interest of achieving specific goals, and (e) a bargain to obtain particular goals that can be accomplished with a changing franchise. They contend that "coups are more

---

[28] Ibid., 418–20 for a discussion of repeated games. The behavior of individuals is expected to vary with the number of transactions anticipated in the future. If none are anticipated, then opportunism should be expected. Fraudulent behavior might be expected to be relatively more likely the day before an individual leaves the country.

[29] See A. Drazen, W. Easterly, E. Spolaore, and E. Glaeser, "Four reviews of 'Economic Origins of Dictatorship and Democracy,'" *Economic Journal* 117 (February 2007): F162–83 for a description of the advances made by the authors and some pitfalls in their application. See also Acemoglu and Robinson, *Economic Origins*, 29.

likely in societies when there is greater inequality between the elites and the citizens."[30]

The nature of the power relations that determine the introduction, implementation, and enforcement of democratic institutions themselves may vary over time. The useful simplification of analyzing a system with only two groups, elites and citizens, leaves some complications unexplained. For some models they introduce a third group, the middle class, but this raises problems of its own.[31] Another important problem is to determine how the initial set of rules came about and what power relations influenced them, as the authors give only limited attention to Hobbes and Locke.[32] The types of political organizations and their characteristics could include dictatorship of a powerful ruler or rulers; or democracy of varying forms with, at times, constraints set by a constitution or with an implicit weighting system to allow privileges for an elite. There can also be continuous bargaining and negotiations among equal or unequal groups regarding voting and expenditures. And even with democracy, institutional rules are not always followed by members of society or enforced, providing a form of individual veto to those who wish to disregard the rules, although possibly at some risk or cost to the violator.

Acemoglu and Robinson examine a type of government that provides laws and public goods, influences the efficiency of the society's output, and affects the distribution of resources among members of society. The governments they consider vary from dictatorship to democracy. There may be restrictions on voting that limit the extent of democratic legal provisions, with the ruling elite influencing the political and economic terms. Restrictions on state confiscation of the resources of individuals are of critical importance, defining the key relations between government and individuals.

Although provisions of government goods tend to reflect the existing nature of power, there are circumstances under which provisions may occur for groups with little or no political power, whether as a one-shot experience or as something more permanent. To provide voting power might mean a long-term granting of an ability to influence resource distribution, whereas a system of temporary provision at the will of the

---

[30] They argue that in the case of nineteenth-century Europe, "the driving force behind political liberalization and the introduction of democratic measures is the threat of social disorder and, ultimately, revolution." See Acemoglu and Robinson, *Economic Origins*, 222, 67–75.

[31] Ibid., 38–40, 273–78.

[32] Ibid., 21, 120.

elite, without a change in voting arrangements, may achieve some desired results at lower long-term costs. Elites may provide goods and services to nonelites (a) because of the perceived effects on the health and productivity of the nonelite population, (b) because of a desire to limit emigration or to encourage immigration of nonelites, (c) as a response to the threat of revolution, or (d) as a bribe to attract votes or to get support for extended military activity or other government actions. An alternative to the provision of goods and services (in cash or kind) is the granting of some franchise rights, although presumably the nonelite would have opinions as to which alternative they prefer. Acemoglu and Robinson argue that the granting of franchise rights helps to resolve the commitment problem because it is presumably less reversible than expenditure decisions.[33]

IX

An important, if debatable, argument made for democracy is that it can generate rapid economic growth due to the links between the political and the economic spheres.[34] One standard definition of democracy is that there are contested elections between two and more parties, some alternation of office, and relatively stable transitions from one office-holder to the next.[35] In the economic sphere, this leads to individuals being able to capture much of what they produce, which in turn leads to more incentives to labor and invest and thus to higher per capita income. This, of course, presumes that people with higher potential income will demand more goods for themselves or their family members, rather than

[33] Ibid., 133–36.

[34] See Torsten Persson and Guido Tabellini, "Is Inequality Harmful for Growth? Theory and Evidence," *American Economic Review* 84 (June 1994): 600–21. Torsten Persson and Guido Tabellini, *The Economic Effect of Constitutions* (Cambridge, MA: MIT Press, 2003); Torsten Persson and Guido Tabellini, "The Growth Effect of Democracy: Is It Heterogeneous and How Can It Be Estimated," *Institutions and Economic Performance*. ed. E. Helpman, 544–84 (Cambridge, MA: Harvard University Press 2008): 544–84. J. Aron, "Growth and Institutions: A Review of the Evidence," *World Bank Research Observer* 15 (2000): 99–135; A. M. Przeworski, M. E. Alvarez, J. A. Cheibub, and F. Limongi, *Democracy and Development: Political Institutions and Well-Being in the World, 1950–1990* (Cambridge: Cambridge University Press, 2000); C. Boix, *Democracy and Redistribution* (Cambridge: Cambridge University Press, 2003); Acemoglu and Robinson, *Economic Origins*, 48–64; W. Easterly, "Inequality Does Cause Underdevelopment: Insights From a New Instrument," *Journal of Development Economics* 84 (November 2007): 755–76.

[35] Przeworski, et al., *Democracy and Development*, 20–30; see also Acemoglu and Robinson, *Economic Origins*, 15–30.

opt for increased leisure or other nonpecuniary benefits, including children. These would increase welfare but not measured per capita income. The broader the political participation, the more individuals can benefit from positive incentives, and the greater the number whose behavior permits benefits from market opportunities. This basic argument linking democracy and economic growth does, however, have some counterexamples. One, related to earlier debates on generating investment in less developed nations, concerns the impact of inequality on savings rates. If higher relative income leads to more savings, inequality presumably can lead to higher rates of savings and investment than would equality, so inequality could be expected to generate more savings and spur growth.[36] Similarly, majority rule in making policy decisions could lead to a set of policies less favorable to growth than policies that provide opportunities to only a limited part of the population. This argument has a long history and has posed numerous problems for political scientists. Writing in the late nineteenth century, the English jurist Henry Sumner Maine noted some of the problems of democracy. Among these are the prospects of a lower rate of innovation if workers could make decisions about the introduction of new machinery or new sources of labor, and the contention that majority rule could mean reduced rights for many minorities.[37]

To understand the impact of institutions as the outcome of individual decisions, and to see what individuals wish to accomplish, it is important to look at their motivations. At one level, the major motivations are the love of reward in contrast with the fear of punishment (and negative sanctions). Rewards can be financial improvement or social approval, or else present or future benefits promised by the current religious or ideological system. Individuals may pursue self-interest (financial or otherwise) or seek broader social goals such as efficiency, power, altruism, or an equal distribution of rewards. How individuals decide what goals to seek and whether they will be influenced to change motivations by present or expected future outcomes remains a major puzzle, as is understanding the role of changing motivations in exploring past as well as present growth.

Results of empirical work on the relation of democracy to equality are not clear-cut, since much depends on the years and countries studied as well as the details of model specification and variables included. Przeworski's detailed surveys of the relation of democracy to levels of income and the related question of the relation of growth to democracy find that "economic development does not tend to generate democracies, but

[36] Przeworski et al. *Democracy and Development*, 1–7, 142–46.
[37] H. S. Maine, *Popular Government* (London: S. Murray, 1885): 86–87, 112, 147–49.

democracies are more likely to survive in wealthy societies." In general, however, "the type of political regime has no impact on the growth of total national income," although "per capita incomes rise more rapidly in democracies because populations increase faster under dictatorships."[38] An analysis by Acemoglu and Robinson, however, concludes that during the time period they analyzed, although richer countries tend to be more democratic, there is no relation between changes in democracy and rates of economic growth.[39]

X

For reasons of complexity and the number of variables to be considered, any predictive value regarding the origin and impact of institutions can be rather uncertain.[40] It is difficult to predict what institutions society will choose, or even to anticipate whether similar environments and conditions will lead to the same institutions. Similarly, variations over time and place, with or without changes in circumstances, are not always predictable. The role of past institutions in influencing current institutions can serve as a constraint on what will happen, but it need not determine exactly what institutions will emerge. Transitions are not always easy to anticipate or understand.

There are further complications in trying to analyze the choices made regarding the desired institutions. There can be several alternative solutions to some particular set of economic problems, with different benefits and costs for each of the different possibilities. Even if there is only one optimal policy, a number of others may provide benefits, though not all possible benefits.[41] Is there only one specific type of rule or institution that can promote economic growth, or are there several possibilities to choose from, and how sensitive are these choices to what might seem to be minor changes in circumstances?

There is also the issue of the time-path of benefits from the choice of institutions, based on the rate of time preference of the decision makers. If policies provide large gains in the short run but smaller gains (or losses) in the long run, are they to be preferred to policies that may achieve little

---

[38] Przeworski, et al. *Democracy and Development*, front matter.

[39] Acemoglu and Robinson, *Economic Origins*, 51–58; see also Persson and Tabellini, "Is Inequality Harmful for Growth?" and "The Growth Effect."

[40] A related point is discussed by Greif, *Institutions*, 10–11, 209–11, 352–57.

[41] For example, the United States had a number of different financial and banking systems, with apparently somewhat limited impacts on differences in growth rates. Perhaps these reflected changes in conditions that made adaptations desirable.

in the immediate future but more in the distant future?[42] At times, this pattern of variation over time may not be known to decisionmakers but it is generally agreed that electoral politics makes desirable actions that yield benefits quickly, even if these are not the best for long-run purposes.

Another issue requiring attention is that of the optimal size of the decision-making and policy-implementing unit. This concerns differences between federal and unitary forms of government, and the degree of decentralization in setting taxes, expenditures, and regulatory mechanisms. The possibilities of such varying political forms will constrain the choices of institutions.

The range of important choices goes beyond choosing one specific appropriate institution as the basis for implementing policies. If, for example, it is desired that the government utilize resources obtained from the private sector, there are alternative means of acquiring resources. Resources can be acquired by purchase, tax and transfer policy, confiscation, borrowing, use of law and legal interpretations to seize assets, or the sale of rights to purchase assets. Clearly these different means of acquiring resources have quite different implications for members of society, and these can influence the rate of economic growth and the distribution of income.

Given the large number of institutional choices that must be made by a society, some combination of institutions may be necessary to provide the basis for economic growth. We have distinguished several key institutions to evaluate: suffrage, education, land policy, banking, industrial policy, market controls, patent policy, tax and expenditure policy, and monetary policy, but a choice that is appropriate in regard to one policy area may, however, be offset by negative effects in others.

XI

The recent study of institutions by economists and political scientists has had a large and beneficial impact on these disciplines. These studies have provided a greater understanding of the interactions among individuals

---

[42] Much of the revisionism concerning New Deal economic policies relates to what some see as its successes at the time that had negative impacts on the economy in subsequent years. See M. D. Bordo, C. Goldin, and E. N. White, eds., *The Defining Moment: The Great Depression and the American Economy of the Twentieth Century* (Chicago: University of Chicago Press, 1998). Also important is the expected time horizon over which a decision will have an impact. The shorter the expected horizon, the less likely the policy chosen is to be concerned with the benefits to other members of society.

and of the consequences of various economic and political systems. The gains may come more from the framing of questions and the enhanced awareness of the forces involved than from a precise forecast of future developments, or a guaranteed prediction of the link between political and economic systems and of the outcome of power relations. Nevertheless, a concern with the impact of institutions should be seen as an important step forward for both economists and political scientists.

Bibliography

Abrams, Burton A. and Russell F. Settle. 1993. "Pressure-group Influence and Institutional Change: Branch-banking Legislation During the Great Depression." *Public Choice* 77 (December): 687–705.

Acemoglu, Daron, and James A. Robinson. 2000a. "Political Losers as a Barrier to Economic Development." *American Economic Review* 90 (May): 126–30.

————. 2000b. "Why Did the West Extend the Franchise? Democracy, Inequality and Growth in Historical Perspective." *Quarterly Journal of Economics* 115 (November): 1167–99.

————. 2005. "Institutions as a Fundamental Cause of Long-run Growth." In *Handbook of Economic Growth*, eds. Philippe Aghion, and Steven N. Durlauf. 2 vol. 1A: 385–472. Amsterdam: Elsevier.

————. 2006a. *Economic Origins of Dictatorship and Democracy*. Cambridge: Cambridge University Press.

————. 2006b. "Economic Backwardness in Political Perspective." *American Political Science Review* 100 (February): 115–31.

Acemoglu, Daron, Simon Johnson, and James A. Robinson. 2001. "The Colonial Origins of Comparative Development: An Empirical Investigation." *American Economic Review* 91 (December): 1369–1401.

————. 2002. "Reversal of Fortune: Geography and Institutions in the Making of the Modern World Income Distribution." *Quarterly Journal of Economics* 117 (November): 1231–94.

Ackerman, Robert K. 1977. *South Carolina Colonial Land Policies*. Columbia: University of South Carolina Press.

Adelman, Jeremy. 1994. *Frontier Development: Land, Labor, and Capital on the Wheatlands of Argentina and Canada, 1890–1914*. New York: Oxford University Press.

————. 1999. *Republic of Capital: Buenos Aires and the Legal Transformation of the Atlantic World*. Stanford: Stanford University Press.

————. 2006. *Sovereignty and Revolution in the Iberian Atlantic*. Princeton: Princeton University Press.

Aguilar, Gustavo. 2003. "El sistema bancario en Sinaloa (1889–1926): Su influencia en el crecimento económico." In *La Banca Regional en Mexico, 1879–1930*, eds. Mario Cerutti and Carlos Marichal, 47–100. Mexico: Fondo de Cultura Económica.

Aidt, T. S., Jaysari Dutta, and Elena Loukoianova. 2006. "Democracy Comes to Europe: Franchise Extension, and Fiscal Outcomes, 1830–1938." *European Economic Review*, 50 (February): 249–83.

Alboites, Luis. 1994 *Breve Historia de Chihuahua*. Mexico: Fondo de Cultura Económica.

Albright, Spencer D. 1942. *The American Ballot*. Washington, D.C.: American Council on Public Affairs.

Alesina, Alberto F., and Dani Rodrik. 1994. "Distributive Politics and Economic Growth." *Quarterly Journal of Economics* 109 (May): 465–90.

Alesina, Alberto, Reza Baqir, and William Easterly. 1999. "Public Goods and Ethnic Divisions." *Quarterly Journal of Economics* 114 (November): 1243–84.

Allen, Robert C. 1992. *Enclosure and the Yeoman*. Oxford: Clarendon Press.

Alonso, Paula. 1993. "Politics and Elections in Buenos Aires, 1890–1898: The Performance of the Radical Party." *Journal of Latin American Studies* 25 (October): 465–487.

———. 1996. "Voting in Buenos Aires Before 1912." In *Elections Before Democracy: The History of Elections in Europe and Latin America*, ed. Eduardo Posada-Carbó. 181–200. New York: St. Martin's Press.

Alston, Lee J., Gary D. Libecap, and Bernardo Mueller. 1999. *Titles, Conflict, and Land Use: The Development of Property Rights and Land Reform on the Brazilian Amazon Frontier*. Ann Arbor: University of Michigan Press.

Altman, Ida. 1989. *Emigrants and Society: Extremadura and America in the Sixteenth Century*. Berkeley: University of California Press.

Altman, Ida, and James Horn, eds. 1991. *"To Make America:" European Emigration in the Early Modern Period*. Berkeley: University of California Press.

Amaral, Samuel. 1998. *The Rise of Capitalism on the Pampas: The Estancias of Buenos Aires, 1785–1870*. Cambridge: Cambridge University Press.

Anderson, Ralph V. and Gallman, Robert E. 1977. "Slaves as Fixed Capital: Slave Labor and Southern Economic Development." *Journal of American History* 64 (June): 24–46.

Annino, Antonio. 1996. "The Ballot, Land and Sovereignty: Cadiz and the Origins of Mexican Local Government, 1812–1820." In *Elections Before Democracy: The History of Elections in Europe and Latin America*, ed. Eduardo Posada-Carbó. 61–86. New York: St. Martin's Press.

Appleby, John C. 1996. "English Settlement in The Lesser Antilles during War and Peace, 1603–1660." In *The Lesser Antilles in the Age of European Expansion*, eds. Robert L Paquette and Stanley L. Engerman, 86–104. Gainesville: University Press of Florida.

Arce Gurza, Francisco. 1981. "En Busca de una Educación Revolucionaria: 1924–1934." In *Ensayos Sobre Historia de la Educación en México*, eds. Josefina Zoraida Vázquez, et al. Mexico, D.F.: Colegio de Mexico.

Arndt, H. W. 1978. *The Rise and Fall of Economic Growth: A Study in Contemporary Thought*. Chicago: University of Chicago Press.

———. 1987. *Economic Development: The History of an Idea*. Chicago: University of Chicago Press.

Aron, Janine. 2000. "Growth and Institutions: A Review of the Evidence." *World Bank Research Observer* 15 (February): 99–135.

Atack, Jeremy, and Fred Bateman. 1987. *To Their Own Soil: Agriculture in the Antebellum North*. Ames: Iowa State University Press.

Atack, Jeremy, Fred Bateman, and William N. Parker. 2000. "Northern Agriculture and the Westward Movement." In *The Cambridge Economic History of the United States* 3 vols., vol. 2, *The Long Nineteenth Century*, eds. Stanley L. Engerman and Robert E. Gallman, 285–328. Cambridge: Cambridge University Press.

Baldwin, Robert E. 1956. "Patterns of Development in Newly Settled Regions." *Manchester School of Economic and Social Studies* 24 (May): 161–79.

Barbosa, Francisco de Assis, ed., 1966. *João Pinheiro, Documentário sôbre a sua Vida*. Belo Horizonte: Publições do Arguiro Público Mineiro.

Barickman, B. J. 1998. *A Bahian Counterpoint: Sugar, Tobacco, Casava, and Slavery in the Recôncava, 1780–1860*. Stanford: Stanford University Press.

Barnes, Viola Florence. 1931. "Land Tenure in English Colonial Charters of the Seventeenth Century." In *Essays in Colonial History Presented to Charles McLean Andrews by his Students*, 4–40. New Haven: Yale University Press.

Barquin, Manuel. 1986. "La Reforma Electoral de 1986–87 en México: Retrospectiva y Analysis." In *Sistemas Electorales y Representación Política en Latinoamérica*, ed. Fundación Friedrich Ebert. Madrid: Instituto de Cooperación Iberoamericana.

Barro, Robert J. 1997. *Determinants of Economic Growth: A Cross-Country Empirical Study*. Cambridge, MA: MIT Press.

Barth, James R., Gerard Caprio Jr., and Ross Levine. 2006. *Rethinking Bank Regulation: Till Angels Govern*. Cambridge: Cambridge University Press.

Bartlett, Roger P. 1979. *Human Capital: The Settlement of Foreigners in Russia, 1762–1804*. Cambridge: Cambridge University Press.

Bartlett, Robert. 1993. *The Making of Europe: Conquest, Colonization and Cultural Change, 950–1300*. Princeton: Princeton University Press.

Basadre, Jorge. 1968–1970. *Historia de la República del Perú, 1822–1933*. 6th ed. 17 vols. Lima: Editorial Universitaria.

Baseler, Marilyn C. 1998. *"Asylum for Mankind": America 1607–1800*. Ithaca: Cornell University Press.

Bateman, Fred, and Thomas Weiss. 1981. *A Deplorable Scarcity: The Failure of Industrialization in the Slave Economy*. Chapel Hill: University of North Carolina Press.

Bayle, Constantino. 1952. *Los Cabildos Seculares en la América Española*. Madrid: Sapientia.

Bazant, Milada. 1982. "La Republica Restaurada y el Profiriato." In *Historia de las Profesiones en México*, eds. Francisco Arce Gurza, et al. Mexico, D.F.: Colegio de Mexico.

Beatty, Edward. 2001. *Institutions and Investment: The Political Basis of Industrialization in Mexico Before 1911*. Stanford: Stanford University Press.

———. 2002. "Patents and Technological Change in Latin American Industrialization: The Case of Nineteenth Century Mexico in Comparative Perspectives" *History of Technology* 24, 121–50.

Beck, J. Murray. 1968. *Pendulum of Power: Canada's Federal Elections*. Scarborough: Prentice-Hall of Canada.

Beck, Thorsten and Ross Levine. 2001, "Industry Growth and Capital Allocation: Does Having a Market-or-Bank-Based System Matter," *Journal of Financial Economics* 64 (May): 147–80.

Beck, Thorsten, Juan Miguel Crivelli and William Summerhill. 2005. "State Bank Transformation in Brazil – Choices and Consequences." *Journal of Banking & Finance* 29 (August–September): 2223–57.

Beck, Thorsten, Ross Levine and Norman Loayza. 2000. "Finance and the Sources of Growth." *Journal of Financial Economics*, 58 (Issues 1–2): 261–300.

Beck, Thorsten, Asli Demirgöc-Kunt, and Ross Levine. 2001. "Legal Theories of Financial Development." *Oxford Review of Economic Policy* 17 (Winter): 483–501.

Bénabou, Roland. 2000. "Unequal Societies: Income Distribution and the Social Contract." *American Economic Review* 90 (March): 96–129.

Benmelech, Efrain and Tobias J. Moskowitz. 2010. "The Political Economy of Financial Regulation: Evidence from U.S. State Usury Laws in the 19th Century." *Journal of Finance* 65 (June): 1029–1073.

Benton, Lauren A. 2002. *Law and Colonial Cultures: Legal Regimes in World History, 1400–1900*. Cambridge: Cambridge University Press.

Berg, Aaron and Stephen Haber. 2009. "Always Turkeys: Brazil's State-Owned Banks in Historical Perspective." Mimeo, Stanford University.

Berg, Maxine. 1994. *The Age of Manufactures, 1700–1820: Industry, Innovation, and Work in Britain*. 2nd ed., London: Routledge.

Bergquist, Charles W. 1978. *Coffee and Conflict in Columbia, 1886–1910*. Durham: Duke University Press.

Berman, Harold J. 1983. *Law and Revolution: The Formation of the Western Legal Tradition*. Cambridge, MA: Harvard University Press.

Bernecker, Walther L., and Hans Werner Tobler, eds. 1993. *Development and Underdevelopment in America: Contrasts of Economic Growth in North and Latin America in Historical Perspective*. Berlin: Walter de Gruyter.

Best, Michael H. 1976. "Political Power and Tax Revenues in Central America." *Journal of Development Economics* 3 (March): 49–82.

Bethell, Leslie, ed. 1984–2008. *The Cambridge History of Latin America*. 11 vols. Cambridge: Cambridge University Press.

———. 1986. *The Cambridge History of Latin America*. vols. IV–V, c. 1870 to 1930. Cambridge: Cambridge University Press.

Bidwell, Percy Wells and John I. Falconer. 1925. *History of Agriculture in the Northern United States, 1620–1860*. Washington, D.C.: Carnegie Institution.

Billington, Ray Allen. 1960. *Westward Expansion: A History of the American Frontier.* 2nd ed. New York: Macmillan.

Bird, Richard M. 1992. "Tax Reform in Latin America: A Review of Some Recent Experiences." *Latin American Research Review*, 27 (No. 1): 7–36.

———. 2003. "Taxation in Latin America: Reflections on Sustainability and the Balance Between Equity and Efficiency." Unpublished Working Paper. University of Toronto.

Black, Sandra E. and Philip E. Strahan. 2001. "The Division of Spoils: Rent-Sharing and Discrimination in a Regulated Industry." *American Economic Review* 91 (September): 814–31.

———. 2002. "Entrepreneurship and Bank Credit Availability." *Journal of Finance* 57 (December): 2807–33.

Bodenhorn, Howard. 1990. "Entry, Rivalry, and Free Banking in Antebellum America." *Review of Economics and Statistics* 72 (November): 682–86.

———. 1993. "The Business Cycle and Entry into Early American Banking." *Review of Economics and Statistics* 75 (August): 531–35.

———. 2000. *A History of Banking in Antebellum America: Financial Markets and Economic Development in an Era of Nation-Building.* Cambridge: Cambridge University Press.

———. 2003. *State Banking in Early America: A New Economic History.* New York: Oxford University Press.

———. 2006. "Bank Chartering and Political Corruption in Antebellum New York: Free Banking as Reform." In *Corruption and Reform: Lessons from America's Economic History*, eds. Edward Glaeser and Claudia Goldin, 231–57. Chicago: University of Chicago Press.

Boix, Carles. 2003. *Democracy and Redistribution.* Cambridge: Cambridge University Press.

Bond, Beverley W. 1919. *The Quit-Rent System in the American Colonies.* New Haven: Yale University Press.

Booth, John A. 1988. "Costa Rica: The Roots of Democratic Stability." In *Democracy in Developing Countries*, (4 vols.) vol. 4. *Latin America.* eds. Larry Diamond, Juan J. Linz, and Seymour Martin Lipset. Boulder, CO: L. Rienner.

Bordo, M. D., C. Goldin, and E. N. White, eds. 1998. *The Defining Moment: The Great Depression and the American Economy in the Twentieth Century.* Chicago: University of Chicago Press.

Bordo, Michael D., Hugh Rockoff, and Angela Redish. 1994. "The U.S. Banking System from a Northern Exposure: Stability Versus Efficiency." *Journal of Economic History* 54 (June): 325–341.

Bordo, Michael D. and Peter Rousseau. 2006. "Legal-Political Factors and the Historical Evolution of the Finance-Growth Link." *European Review of Economic History* 10 (December): 421–444.

Bornstein, Morris. 1954. "Banking Policy and Economic Development: A Brazilian Case Study." *Journal of Finance* 9 (September): 312–13.

Boucher, Philip P. 2008. *France and the American Tropics to 1700: Tropics of Discontent?* Baltimore: Johns Hopkins University Press.

Bourne, Edward Gaylord. 1904. *Spain in America, 1450–1580.* New York: Harper Brothers.

Brahm, Luis A., Patricio Cariola, and Juan José Silva. 1971. *Educación Particular en Chile: Antecedents y Dilemas*. Santiago de Chile: Centro de Investigación y Desarollo de la Educación.

Brenner, Robert. 1985. "Agrarian Class Structure and Economic Development in Pre-Industrial Europe." In *The Brenner Debate: Agrarian Class Structure and Economic Development in Pre-Industrial Europe*, eds. T. H. Aston, and C. H. E. Philpin. 10–63. Cambridge: Cambridge University Press.

Brewer, John. 1990. *The Sinews of Power: War, Money, and the English State, 1688–1783*. Cambridge, MA: Harvard University Press.

Britton, John A., ed. 1994. *Molding the Hearts and Minds: Education, Communications, and Social Change in Latin America*. Wilmington: Scholarly Resources.

Brownlee, W. Elliot. 1996. *Federal Taxation in America: A Short History*. Washington, D.C.: Woodrow Wilson Center Press.

Brunori, David. 2003. *Local Tax Policy: A Federalist Perspective*. Washington, D.C.: Urban Institute Press.

Bullock, Charles J. 1907. "Historical Sketch of the Finances and Financial Policy of Massachusetts from 1780 to 1905." *Publications of the American Economic Association*, 3rd series 8 (May): 1–144.

Bulmer-Thomas, Victor. 2003. *The Economic History of Latin America Since Independence*, 2nd ed. Cambridge: Cambridge University Press.

Bulmer-Thomas, Victor, John H. Coatsworth, and Roberto Cortés Conde (eds.). 2006a. *The Cambridge Economic History of Latin America*. Vol. I. *The Colonial Era and the Short Nineteenth Century*. Cambridge: Cambridge University Press.

———. 2006b. *The Cambridge Economic History of Latin America*. Vol. II. *The Long Twentieth Century*. Cambridge: Cambridge University Press.

Burgess, Robin, and Nicholas Stern. 1993. "Taxation and Development." *Journal of Economic Literature* 31 (June): 762–830.

Burkholder, Mark A., and Lyman L. Johnson. 1998. *Colonial Latin America*. 3rd ed. New York: Oxford University Press.

Burnard, T. G. 2001. "'Prodigious Riches': The Wealth of Jamaica before the American Revolution." *Economic History Review* 54 (August): 506–24.

Burroughs, Peter. 1965. "Wakefield and the Ripon Land Regulations of 1831." *Historical Studies* 11 (April): 452–66.

Bushnell, David. 1993. *The Making of Modern Colombia: A Nation in Spite of Itself*. Berkeley: University of California Press.

Butlin, N. G. 1983. *Our Original Aggression: Aboriginal Populations of Southeastern Australia, 1788–1850*. Sydney: G. Allen and Urwin.

Campos Harriet, Fernando. 1960. *Desarrollo Educacional 1810–1960*. Santiago de Chile: Editorial A. Bello.

Canada Bureau of Statistics. 1912–1915. *Census of Canada, 1911*. Ottawa: C. H. Parmelee.

Calomiris, Charles W. 1990. "Is Deposit Insurance Necessary? A Historical Perspective." *The Journal of Economic History* 50 (June): 283–95.

———. 2010. "The Political Lessons of Depression-Era Banking Reform." *Oxford Review of Economic Policy* 26 (Autumn): 540–560.

Calomiris, Charles W. and Eugene N. White. 1994. "The Origins of Federal Deposit Insurance." In *The Regulated Economy: A Historical Approach to Political Economy*, eds. Claudia Goldin and Gary D. Libecap, 145–188. Chicago: University of Chicago Press.

Canny, Nicholas, ed. 1994. *Europeans on the Move: Studies on European Migration, 1500–1800*. Oxford: Clarendon Press.

Canton, Darío. 1973. *Elecciones y Partidos Politicos en la Argentina: Historia, Interpretación y Balance: 1910–1966*. Buenos Aires: Siglo Veintiuno Argentina Editores.

Carcano, Miguel Angel. 1925. *Evolución Historica del Régimen de la Tierra Pública: 1810–1916*. 2nd edition. Buenos Aires: J. Roldán.

Cárdenas, Enrique. 2000. "The Process of Accelerated Industrialization in Mexico, 1929–82." In Enrique Cárdenas, José Antonio Ocampo, and Rosemary Thorp, eds., Industrialization and the State in Latin America: The Postwar Years, vol. 3 of An Economic History of Twentieth-Century Latin America (London: Palgrave, 2000): 176–204.

Carey, Henry Charles. 1837–1840. *Principles of Political Economy*. 4 pts. in vols, Philadelphia: Carey, Lea and Blanchard.

Carmagnani, Marcello, et al. eds. 1993. *Federalismos Latinamercanos: México, Brasil, Argentina*. México: Fondo de Cultura Ecónómica.

Carreira, Liberato de Castro. 1889. *Historia Financiera e Orçamentaria do Imperio do Brazil Desde a sua Fundação*. Rio de Janeiro: Imprensa Nacional.

Carter, Susan B., et al. (eds.) 2006. *Historical Statistics of the United States: Earliest Times to the Present, Millennial Edition*. 5 vols. Cambridge: Cambridge University Press.

Castro, Donald S. 1991. *The Development and Politics of Argentine Immigration Policy, 1852–1914: To Govern is to Populate*. San Francisco: Mellen Research University Press.

Central Intelligence Agency. 1992. *The World Factbook*. Washington, D.C.: Central Intelligence Agency.

Cerutti, Mario. 2003. "Empresariado y banca en el norte de Mexico, 1870–1910: La fundación del Banco Refaccionario de la Laguna." In *La Banca Regional en Mexico, 1870–1930*, eds. Mario Cerutti and Carlos Marichal, 168–215. Mexico: Fondo de Cultura Económica.

Cetorelli, Nicola and Philip Strahan. 2006. "Finance as a Barrier to Entry: Bank Competition and Industry Structure in U.S. Local Markets." *Journal of Finance* 61 (February): 437–61.

Channing, Edward. 1926. *A History of the United States* (6 Volumes) vol. 1. New York: Macmillan.

Chaudhary, Latika. 2009. "Determinants of Primary Schooling in British India." *Journal of Economic History* 69 (March): 269–302.

Checkland, S. G. 1983. *British Public Policy, 1776–1939: An Economic, Social, and Political Perspective*. Cambridge: Cambridge University Press.

Chevalier, François. 1963. *Land and Society in Colonial Mexico: The Great Hacienda*. Berkeley: University of California Press.

Chiappelli, Fredi, ed. 1976. *First Images of America: The Impact of the New World on the Old*. Berkeley: University of California Press.

Chihuaha, n.d. *Memoria de la Administración Pública del Estado de Chihuahua.* Chihuahua.

Chile, Central Bureau of Statistics. 1921. *Sinópsis Estadistica de la República de Chile.*

Chute, Marchette. 1969. *The First Liberty: A History of the Right to Vote in America, 1619–1850.* New York: Dutton.

Clark, Grover. 1938. *The Balance Sheets of Imperialism: Facts and Figures on Colonies.* New York: Columbia University Press.

Clarke, Peter, and Clive Trebilcock, eds. 1997. *Understanding Decline: Perceptions and Realities of British Economic Performance.* Cambridge: Cambridge University Press.

Clodfelter, Michael. 1992. *Warfare and Armed Conflicts: A Statistical Reference to Casualty and Other Figures, 1618–1991.* 2 vols. Jefferson, N.C.: McFarland.

Coates, Timothy J. 2001. *Convicts and Orphans: Forced and State-Sponsored Colonizers in the Portuguese Empire, 1550–1755.* Stanford: Stanford University Press.

Coatsworth, John H. 1993. "Notes on the Comparative Economic History of Latin America and the United States." In *Development and Underdevelopment in America: Contrasts of Economic Growth in North and Latin America in Historical Perspective*, eds. Walther L. Bernecker and Hans Werner Tobler, 10–30. Berlin: Walter de Gruyter.

———. 1998. "Economic and Institutional Trajectories in Nineteenth-Century Latin America." In *Latin America and the World Economy Since 1800*, eds., John H. Coatsworth and Alan M. Taylor. 33–54. Cambridge, MA: Harvard University/David Rockefeller Center for Latin American Studies.

Cobbett, W. 1816–1820. *Parliamentary History of England, From the Norman conquest to the Year 1803.* (23 volumes) London: T. C. Hansard.

Coghlan, T.A. 1918. *Labour and Industry in Australia: From the First Settlement in 1788 to the Establishment of the Commonwealth in 1901.* 4 vols. London: Oxford University Press.

Cohn, Raymond L. 2009. *Mass Migration under Sail: European Immigration to the Antebellum United States.* Cambridge: Cambridge University Press.

Cole, Jeffrey A. 1985. *The Potosí Mita, 1573–1700: Compulsory Indian Labor in the Andes.* Stanford: Stanford University Press.

Comisión Directiva del Censo de la República Argentina, 1898. *Segundo Censo de la República Argentina, Mayo 10 de 1895.* 3 vols. Buenos Aires: Taller Tip de la Pentenciara Nacional.

Condliffe, J.B. 1930. *New Zealand in the Making: A Survey of Economic and Social Development.* London: G. Allen and Unwin.

Copeland, Morris A. 1961. *Trends in Government Financing.* Princeton: Princeton University Press.

Costa, Emilia Viotti da. 1985. *The Brazilian Empire: Myths and Histories.* Chicago: University of Chicago Press.

Costeloe, Michael P. 2002. *The Central Republic in Mexico, 1835–1846: Hombres de Bien in the Age of Santa Anna.* Cambridge: Cambridge University Press.

Cottrol, Robert J. 2001. "The Long Lingering Shadow: Law, Liberalism, and Cultures of Racial Hierarchy and Identity in the Americas." *Tulane Law Review* 76 (November): 11–79.

Craig, John E. 1981. "The Expansion of Education." *Review of Research in Education* 9: 151–213.

Craven, Wesley Frank. 1968. *The Colonies in Transition, 1660–1713.* New York: Harper & Row.

———. 1970. *The Southern Colonies in the Seventeenth Century, 1607–1689.* Baton Rouge: Louisiana State University Press.

Cuban Economic Research Project. 1965. *A Study on Cuba: The Colonial and Republican Periods.* Coral Gables: University of Miami Press.

Cubberley, Ellwood P. 1920. *History of Education: Educational Practice and Progress Considered as a Phase of the Development and Spread of Western Civilization.* Boston: Houghton Mifflin.

Cunningham, William. 1890–1892. *The Growth of English Industry and Commerce.* 2nd ed., 2 vols. Cambridge: Cambridge University Press.

Curtin, Philip D. 1969. *The Atlantic Slave Trade: A Census.* Madison: University of Wisconsin Press.

Danhof, Clarence H. 1969. *Change in Agriculture: The Northern United States, 1820–1870.* Cambridge, MA: Harvard University Press.

Daunton, Martin. 2001. *Trusting Leviathan: The Politics of Taxation in Britain, 1799–1914.* Cambridge: Cambridge University Press.

Davie, Maurice R. 1936. *World Immigration: With Special Reference to the United States.* New York: Macmillan.

Davies, Keith A. 1984. *Landowners in Colonial Peru.* Austin: University of Texas Press.

Davis, Joseph Stancliffe. 1917. *Essays in the Earlier History of American Corporations.* 2 vols. Cambridge, MA: Harvard University Press.

Davis, Lance E., and Robert E. Gallman. 1978. "Capital Formation in the United States During the Nineteenth Century." In *The Cambridge Economic History of Europe. vol. 7, part 2. The Industrial Economies: Capital, Labour and Enterprise: the United States, Japan and Russia*, eds. Peter Mathias and M. M. Postan, 1–69. Cambridge: Cambridge University Press.

———. 1994. "Savings, Investment, and Economic Growth: The United States in the Nineteenth Century." In *Capitalism in Context: Essays on Economic Development and Cultural Change in Honor of R. M. Hartwell*, eds. John A. James and Mark Thomas, 202–29. Chicago: University of Chicago Press.

———. 2001. *Evolving Financial Markets and International Capital Flows: Britain, the Americas, and Australia, 1865–1914.* Cambridge: Cambridge University Press.

Davis, Lance E. and Robert A. Huttenback. 1986. *Mammon and the Pursuit of Empire: The Political Economy of British Imperialism, 1860–1912.* Cambridge: Cambridge University Press.

Davis, Lance E., and John Legler. 1966. "The Government and the American Economy: A Quantitative Study." *Journal of Economic History* 26 (March): 514–52.

Davis, Lance E., and Douglass C. North. 1971. *Institutional Change and American Economic Growth.* Cambridge: Cambridge University Press.

Davis, Ralph. 1973. *The Rise of the Atlantic Economies.* Ithaca: Cornell University Press.

De Ferranti, David, Guillermo Perry, Francisco Ferreira, and Michael Walton. 2004. *Inequality in Latin America: Breaking with History?* Washington, D.C.: World Bank.

Del Ángel-Mobarak, Gustavo. 2005. "La banca mexicana antes de 1892." In *Cuando el Estado se Hizo Banquero: Consecuencias de la Nacionalización Bancaria en México*, eds. Gustavo del Ángel-Mobarak, Carlos Bazdresch Parada, and Francisco Suárez Dávila. Mexico City: Fondo de Cultura Económica.

de Tocqueville, Alexis. 1969 [1835]. J. P. Mayer, ed. *Democracy in America.* Garden City: Doubleday.

De Vries, Jan. 1974. *The Dutch Rural Economy in the Golden Age, 1500–1700.* New Haven: Yale University Press.

———. 1976. *Economy of Europe in an Age of Crisis, 1600–1750.* Cambridge: Cambridge University Press.

———. 1994. "The Industrial Revolution and the Industrious Revolution." *Journal of Economic History* 54 (June): 249–270.

———. 2008. *The Industrious Revolution: Consumer Behavior and the Household Economy, 1650 to the Present.* Cambridge: Cambridge University Press.

Dean, Warren. 1971. "Latifundia and Land Policy in Nineteenth-Century Brazil." *Hispanic American Historical Review* 51 (November): 606–25.

DeBow, J. D. B. 1854. *Statistical View of the United States.* Washington, D.C.: A. O. P. Nicholson.

Deerr, Noël. 1949–1950. *The History of Sugar*, 2 vols. London: Chapman and Hall.

Deininger, Klaus and Lyn Squire. 1996. "A New Data Set Measuring Income Inequality." *World Bank Economic Review.* 10 (September): 565–91.

della Paolera, Gerardo and Taylor, Alan M. eds. 2003. *A New Economic History of Argentina.* Cambridge: Cambridge University Press.

Denevan, William M., ed. 1976. *The Native Population of the Americas in 1492.* Madison: University of Wisconsin Press.

Denoon, Donald. 1983. *Settler Capitalism: The Dynamics of Dependent Development in the Southern Hemisphere.* New York: Oxford University Press.

Departmento Administrativo Nacional de Estadística. 1981. *Panorama Estadístico de Antioquia, Siglos XIX y XX.* Bogotá D.E., República de Colombia, Departmento Administrativo Nacional de Estadística.

Diamond, Jared. 1997. *Guns, Germs, and Steel: The Fate of Human Societies.* New York: Norton.

Diaz Alejandro, Carlos F. 1970. *Essays on the Economic History of the Argentine Republic.* New Haven: Yale University Press.

Diaz, Alida. 1974. *El Censo General de 1876 en el Perú.* Lima: Seminario de Historia Rural Andina.

Domar, Evsey D. 1970. "The Causes of Slavery or Serfdom: A Hypothesis." *Journal of Economic History*, 30 (March): 18–32.

Dominion Bureau of Statistics. 1926. *Illiteracy and School Attendance in Canada: A Study of the Census of 1921 with Supplementary Data*. Ottawa: F. A. Acland.

Dorfman, Joseph. 1946–1959. *The Economic Mind in American Civilization, 1606–1933*, 5 vols. New York: Viking Press.

Drake, Paul W. 2009. *Between Tyranny and Anarchy: A History of Democracy in Latin America, 1800–2006*. Stanford: Stanford University Press.

Drazen, Allan, William Easterly, Enrico Spolaore, and Edward Glaeser. 2007. Four reviews of "Economic Origins of Dictatorship and Democracy." *Economic Journal*, 117 (February): 162–83.

Dubois, Laurent. 2004. *Avengers of the New World: The Story of the Haitian Revolution*. Cambridge, MA: Harvard University Press.

Duly, Leslie Clement. 1968. *British Land Policy at the Cape 1785–1844: A Study of Administrative Procedures in the Empire*. Durham: Duke University Press.

Dunn, Richard S. 1972. *Sugar and Slaves: The Rise of the Planter Class in the English West Indies, 1624–1713*. Chapel Hill: University of North Carolina Press.

Dutton, H. I. 1984. *The Patent System and Inventive Activity During the Industrial Revolution, 1750–1852*. Manchester: Manchester University Press.

Easterlin, Richard A. 1981. "Why Isn't the Whole World Developed?" *Journal of Economic History*. 41 (March): 1–19.

Easterly, William. 2007. "Inequality Does Cause Underdevelopment: Insights From a New Instrument." *Journal of Development Economics* 84 (November): 755–76.

Easterly, William, and Ross Levine. 2003. "Tropics, Germs, and Crops: How Endowments Influence Economic Development." *Journal of Monetary Economics* 50 (January): 3–39.

Ebrill, Liam, Michael Keen, Jean-Paul Bodin, and Victoria Summers. 2001. *The Modern VAT*. Washington, D.C.: International Monetary Fund.

Eccles, W. J. 1972. *France in America*. New York: Harper & Row.

Economides, Nicholas, R. Glenn Hubbard, and Darius Palia. 1996. "The Political Economy of Branching Restrictions and Deposit Insurance: A Model of Monopolistic Competition among Small and Large Banks." *Journal of Law and Economics* 39 (October): 667–704.

Economopoulos, Andrew and Heather O'Neill. 1995. "Bank Entry During the Antebellum Period." *Journal of Money, Credit, and Banking* 27 (November): 1071–85.

Egnal, Marc. 1996. *Divergent Paths: How Culture and Institutions Have Shaped North American Growth*. New York: Oxford University Press.

Einhorn, Robin. 2006. *American Taxation, American Slavery*. Chicago: University of Chicago Press.

Eisenberg, Peter L. 1974. *The Sugar Industry in Pernambuco: Modernization Without Change, 1840–1910*. Berkeley: University of California Press.

Eisner, Gisela. 1961. *Jamaica, 1830–1930: A Study in Economic Growth*. Manchester: Manchester University Press.

Ekirch, A. Roger. 1987. *Bound for America: The Transportation of British Convicts to the Colonies, 1718–1775*. New York: Oxford University Press.

Elbaum, Bernard and William Lazonick, eds. 1986. *The Decline of the British Economy.* New York: Oxford University Press.

Elliott, J. H. 2006. *Empires of the Atlantic World: Britain and Spain in America: 1492–1830.* New Haven: Yale University Press.

Elphick, Richard, and Hermann Giliomee. 1989. *The Shaping of South African Society, 1652–1840.* 2nd ed. Middletown: Wesleyan University Press.

Eltis, David. 1983. "Free and Coerced Transatlantic Migrations: Some Comparisons." *American Historical Review* 88 (April): 251–280.

———. 1987. *Economic Growth and the Ending of the Transatlantic Slave Trade.* New York: Oxford University Press.

———. 1995. "The Total Product of Barbados, 1664–1701." *Journal of Economic History* 55 (June): 321–38.

———. 1997a. "The Slave Economies of the Caribbean: Structure, Performance, Evolution and Significance." In *General History of the Caribbean. Vol. 3. The Plantation Economies,* ed. Franklin W. Knight. 105–137. Paris: UNESCO.

———. 1997b. "Seventeenth Century Migration and the Slave Trade: The English Case in Comparative Perspective." In *Migration, Migration History, History: Old Paradigms and New Perspectives,* eds. Jan Lucassen and Leo Lucassen. 87–110. Bern: P. Lang.

———. 1999. "Slavery and Freedom in the Early Modern World." In *Terms of Labor: Slavery, Serfdom and Free Labor,* ed. Stanley L. Engerman. 25–49. Stanford: Stanford University Press.

———. 2000. *The Rise of African Slavery in the Americas.* Cambridge: Cambridge University Press.

———. 2002. "Free and Coerced Migrations from the Old World to the New." In *Coerced and Free Migration: Global Perspectives,* ed. David Eltis, 33–74. Stanford: Stanford University Press.

Ely, Richard T. 1888. *Taxation in American States and Cities.* New York: Thomas Y. Crowell.

Emmer, P.C., ed. 1986. *Colonialism and Migration: Indentured Labour Before and After Slavery.* Dordrecht: Martinus Nijhoff.

Emmer, P. C., and M. Mörner, eds. 1991. *European Expansion and Migration: Essays on the Intercontinental Migration from Africa, Asia, and Europe.* New York: Berg.

Engerman, Stanley L. 1970. "A Note on the Economic Consequences of the Second Bank of the United States." *Journal of Political Economy,* 78 (July/August): 725–728.

———. 1982. "Economic Adjustments to Emancipation in the United States and British West Indies." *Journal of Interdisciplinary History* 12 (Autumn): 191–220.

———. 1983. "Contract Labor, Sugar and Technology in the Nineteenth Century." *Journal of Economic History* 43 (September): 635–59.

———. 1986. "Servants to Slaves to Servants: Contract Labour and European Expansion." In *Colonialism and Migration: Indentured Labour Before and After Slavery,* ed. P.C. Emmer, 263–94. Dordrecht: Martinus Nijhoff.

————. 1996. "The Land and Labour Problem at the Time of the Legal Emancipation of the West Indian Slaves." In *West Indies Accounts: Essays on the History of the British Caribbean and the Atlantic Economy in Honour of Richard Sheridan*, ed. Roderick A. McDonald. 297–318. Barbados: The Press of the University of West Indies.

————. 2002. "Changing Laws and Regulations and their Impact on Migration." In *Coerced and Free Migration: Global Perspectives*, ed. David Eltis, 75–93. Stanford: Stanford University Press.

————. 2003. "The History and Political Economy of International Labor Standards." In *International Labor Standards: History, Theory and Policy Options*, eds. Kaushik Basu, Henrik Horn, Lisa Román, and Judith Shapiro, 9–83. Malden: Blackwell.

————. 2007. *Slavery, Emancipation and Freedom: Comparative Perspectives*. Baton Rouge: Louisiana State University Press.

Engerman, Stanley L., and Kenneth L. Sokoloff. 2012. "Factor Endowments, Institutions, and Differential Paths of Growth Among New World Economies: A View from Economic Historians of the United States." In *How Latin America Fell Behind: Essays on the Economic Histories of Brazil and Mexico, 1800–1914*, ed. Stephen Haber, 260–304. Stanford: Stanford University Press.

————. 2002. "Factor Endowments, Inequality, and Paths of Development Among New World Economies." *Economía* 2 (Fall): 41–88.

————. 2005a. "Institutional and Non-Institutional Explanations of Economic Differences." In *Handbook of New Institutional Economics*, eds. Claude Ménard and Mary M. Shirley, 639–65. Dordrecht: Springer.

————. 2005b. The Evolution of Suffrage Institutions in the New World." *Journal of Economic History*, 65 (December): 891–921.

————. 2006. "Colonialism, Inequality, and Long- Run Paths of Development." In *Understanding Poverty*, eds. Abhijit Vinayak Banerjee, Roland Bénabou, and Dilip Mookherjee, 37–61. Oxford: Oxford University Press.

————. 2008. "Debating the Role of Institutions in Political and Economic Development: Theory, History, and Findings." *Annual Review of Political Science* 11: 119–135.

————. 2012. "Five Hundred Years of European Colonization: Inequality and Paths of Development," in Christopher Lloyd, et al., eds. *Settler Economics in World History*, Leiden: Brill.

Engerman, Stanley L., and Robert E. Gallman, eds. 1986. *Long-Term Factors in American Economic Growth*. Chicago: University of Chicago Press.

Engerman, Stanley L., and B. W. Higman. 1997. "The Demographic Structure of the Caribbean Slave Societies in the Eighteenth and Nineteenth Centuries." In *General History of the Caribbean*, vol. 3 *The Plantation Economy* ed. Franklin W. Knight, 45–104. Paris: UNESCO.

Engerman, Stanley L., Stephen Haber, and Kenneth L. Sokoloff. 2000. "Inequality, Institutions, and Differential Paths of Growth Among New World Economies." In *Institutions, Contracts, and Organizations: Perspectives from New Institutional Economics*, ed. Claude Ménard. 108–134. Cheltenham: Edward Elgar.

Engerman, Stanley L., Elisa V. Mariscal, and Kenneth L. Sokoloff. 2009. "The Evolution of Schooling Institutions in the Americas, 1800–1945." In *Human Capital and Institutions: A Long-Run View* eds. David Eltis, Frank D. Lewis, and Kenneth L. Sokoloff 93–142. Cambridge: Cambridge University Press.

Escobar Alvarez, Miguel Angel. 1987. *La Instrucción pública en México desde 1910 hasta 1917 los adminstrativos de Porfirio Díaz, León de la Barra, Francisco J. Madero, Victoriano Huerta y del gobierno pre constitucionalista.* Madrid: OEA.

Evans, George Heberton, Jr. 1948. *Business Incorporations in the United States, 1800–1943.* New York: National Bureau of Economic Research.

Evaristo, Molina A. 1898. *Bosquejo de la Hacienda Pública de Chile, Desde la Independencia Hasta la Fecha.* Santiago: Imprenta Nacional.

Farnam, Henry W. 1938. *Chapters in the History of Social Legislation in the United States to 1860.* Washington, D.C.: Carnegie Institution.

Feinstein, Charles H. 2005. *An Economic History of South Africa: Conquest, Discrimination and Development.* Cambridge: Cambridge University Press.

Feller, Daniel. 1984. *The Public Lands in Jacksonian Politics.* Madison: University of Wisconsin Press.

Ferguson, Niall. 2003. *Empire: The Rise and the Demise of the British World Order and the Lessons for Global Power.* New York: Basic Books.

Fernández, Hernan, and Jorge Rosales. 1990. *Educación, una Mirada Hacia Dentro: Analfabetismo, Repitencia y Deserción.* Lima: Instituto de Pedagogía Popular.

Fernández Rojas, José. 1933. *El Proceso de la Educación Pública en México.* Saltillo: Impresora de Coahuila.

Fetter, F. W. 1980. *The Economist in Parliament, 1780–1868.* Durham: Duke University Press.

Findlay, Ronald and O'Rourke, Kevin H. 2007. *Power and Plenty: Trade, War, and the World Economy in the Second Millennium.* Princeton: Princeton University Press.

Fischel, Astrid. 1987. *Consenso y Represión: Una Interpretación Socio-politica de la Educación Costarricense.* San José: Editorial Costa Rica.

———. 1992. *El uso Ingenioso de la Ideología en Costa Rica.* San José: Editorial Universidad Estatal a Distancia.

Fischer, David Hackett. 1989. *Albion's Seed: Four British Folkways in America.* New York: Oxford University Press.

Fishlow, Albert. 1965. *American Railroads and the Transformation of the Antebellum Economy.* Cambridge, MA: Harvard University Press.

———. 1966. "The Common School Revival: Fact or Fancy?" In *Industrialization in Two Systems: Essays in Honor of Alexander Gerschenkron by a Group of his Students,* ed. Henry Rosovsky, 40–67. New York: Wiley.

Fisman, Raymond and Inessa Love. 2004. "Financial Development and Growth in the Short- and Long-Run." NBER Working Paper 10236.

Fitzgerald, Ross. 1986. *A History of Queensland From the Dreaming to 1915.* St. Lucia: University of Queensland Press.

Fitzgibbon, Russell H. 1948. *The Constitutions of the Americas, as of January 1, 1948*. Chicago: University of Chicago Press.

Flora, Peter and Jens Alber, et al. 1983. *State, Economy, and Society in Western Europe, 1815–1975*. 2 volumes, vol. 1. The Growth of Mass Democracies and Welfare States. Chicago: St. James Press.

Fogel, Robert William. 1964. *Railroads and American Economic Growth: Essays in Econometric History*. Baltimore: Johns Hopkins University Press.

———. 1989. *Without Consent or Contract: The Rise and Fall of American Slavery*. New York: Norton.

———. 2000. *The Fourth Great Awakening & The Future of Egalitarianism*. Chicago: University of Chicago Press.

Fogel, Robert William, and Engerman, Stanley L. 1974. *Time on the Cross: The Economics of American Negro Slavery*. Boston: Little, Brown.

Ford, Amelia Clewley. 1910. *Colonial Precedents of Our National Land System as it Existed in 1800*. Madison: University of Wisconsin Press.

Ford, Thomas R. 1955. *Man and Land in Peru*. Gainesville: University of Florida Press.

Fox, William F., and Tami Gurley. 2005. "An Exploration of Tax Patterns Around the World." *Tax Notes International* 37 (February): 794–95.

Franco, Rolando. 1985. *Democracia "a la uruguaya": Análisis Electoral, 1925–1985*. 2nd ed. Montevideo: El Libro Libre.

Frankema, Ewout. 2009. "The Expansion of Mass Education in Twentieth Century Latin America: A Global Comparative Perspective," *Journal of Iberian and Latin American Economic History* 27 (Winter): 359–96.

Galenson, David W. 1981. *White Servitude in Colonial America: An Economic Analysis*. Cambridge: Cambridge University Press.

———. 1991. "Economic Opportunity on the Urban Frontier: Nativity, Work, and Health in Early Chicago." *Journal of Economic History* 51 (September): 581–603.

———. 1996. "The Settlement and Growth of the Colonies: Population, Labor, and Economic Development." In *The Cambridge Economic History of the United States*, 3 vols., vol. 1, *The Colonial Period*, eds Stanley L. Engerman and Robert E. Gallman, 135–207. Cambridge: Cambridge University Press.

Galenson, David W., and Clayne L. Pope. 1989. "Economic and Geographical Mobility on the Farming Frontier: Evidence from Appanoose County, Iowa, 1850–1870." *Journal of Economic History* 49 (September): 635–55.

Gallman, Robert E. 2000. "Economic Growth and Structural Change." In *The Cambridge Economic History of the United States*. 3 vols, vol. 2, *The Long Nineteenth Century*, eds. Stanley L. Engerman and Robert E. Gallman. 1–55 Cambridge: Cambridge University Press.

Gallo, Ezequiel. 1986. "Argentina: Society and Politics 1880–1916." In *The Cambridge Economic History of Latin America: 1870–1930*. vol. 5, ed. Leslie Bethell, 359–91. Cambridge: Cambridge University Press.

Galloway, J.H. 1989. *The Sugar Cane Industry: An Historical Geography from its Origins to 1914*. Cambridge: Cambridge University Press.

Gallup, John Luke and Jeffrey D. Sachs, with Andrew Mellinger. 1999. "Geography and Economic Development." In Boris Pleskovic and Joseph E. Stiglitz, eds. *Annual World Bank Conference on Development Economies.* 127–78. Washington, D.C.: World Bank.

Gamboa Ojeda, Leticia. 2003. "El Banco Oriental de Mexico y la formación de un sistema de banca, 1900–1911." In *La Banca Regional en Mexico, 1870–1930,* eds. Mario Cerutti and Carlos Marichal, 101–133. Mexico: Fondo de Cultura Económica.

Gatell, Frank Otto. 1966. "Sober Second Thoughts on Van Buren, the Albany Regency, and the Wall Street Conspiracy." *Journal of American History* 53 (June): 19–40.

Gates, Paul W. 1968. *History of Public Land Law Development.* Washington, D.C.: Government Printing Office.

Genovese, Eugene D. 1965. *The Political Economy of Slavery: Studies in the Economy and Society of the Slave South.* New York: Pantheon.

Gerschenkron, Alexander. 1962. *Economic Backwardness in Historical Perspective: A Book of Essays.* Cambridge, MA: Harvard University Press.

Gibbins, H. de. 1891. *History of Commerce in Europe.* New York: Macmillan.

Gibson, Charles. 1966. *Spain in America.* New York: Harper & Row.

Gilboy, Elizabeth. 1932. "Demand as a Factor in the Industrial Revolution." In *Facts and Factors in Economic History: Articles by Former Students of Edwin Francis Gay.* 620–639. Cambridge, MA: Harvard University Press.

Gipson, Lawrence Henry. 1936. *The British Empire Before the American Revolution.* Caldwell: Caxton Printers.

Glade, William P. 1969. *The Latin American Economies: A Study of Their Institutional Evolution.* New York: American Book.

Glaeser, Edward L., and Andrei Shleifer. 2002. "Legal Origins." *Quarterly Journal of Economics,* 117 (November): 1193–229.

Go, Sun and Peter Lindert. 2010. "The Uneven Rise of American Public Schools to 1850." *Journal of Economic History* 70 (March): 1–26.

Goldin, Claudia. 1999. "Egalitarianism and the Returns to Education During the Great Transformation of American Education. *Journal of Political Economy* 107 (December): 565–94.

Goldin, Claudia, and Lawrence F. Katz. 1999b. "Human Capital and Social Capital: The Rise of Secondary Schooling in America, 1910–1940." *Journal of Interdisciplinary History,* 29 (Spring): 683–723.

_____. 2008. *The Race Between Education and Technology.* Cambridge, MA: Harvard University Press.

_____. 2009. "Why the United States Led in Education: Lessons From Secondary School Expansion, 1910 to 1940." In *Human Capital and Institutions: A Long-Run View,* eds. David Eltis, Frank D. Lewis, and Kenneth L. Sokoloff. 143–178. Cambridge: Cambridge University Press.

Goldsmith, Raymond W. 1969. *Financial Structure and Development.* New Haven: Yale University Press.

González Casanova, Pablo. 1965. *La Democracia en México.* Mexico: Ediciones ERA.

Goode, Richard. 1984. *Government Finance in Developing Countries.* Washington, D.C.: Brookings Institution.

Goodrich, Carter. 1960. *Government Promotion of American Canals and Railroads, 1800–1890*. New York: Columbia University Press.

Gordon, Barry. 1979. *Economic Doctrine and Tory Liberalism, 1824–1830*. London: Macmillan.

Graham, Richard. 1990. *Patronage and Politics in Nineteenth-Century Brazil*. Stanford: Stanford University Press.

Graves, Adrian. 1993. *Cane and Labour: The Political Economy of the Queensland Sugar Industry, 1862–1906*. Edinburgh: Edinburgh University Press.

Gray, Lewis Cecil. 1933. *History of Agriculture in the Southern United States to 1860*. 2 vols. Washington, D.C.: Carnegie Institution.

Greene, Jack P. 1988. *Pursuits of Happiness: The Social Development of Early Modern British Colonies and the Formation of American Culture*. Chapel Hill: University of North Carolina Press.

———. 1993. *The Intellectual Construction of America: Exceptionalism and Identity from 1492 to 1800*. Chapel Hill: University of North Carolina Press.

———. 2002. "Transatlantic Colonization and the Redefinition of Empire in the Early Modern Era: The British-America Experience." In *Negotiated Empires: Centers and Peripheries in the Americas, 1500–1820*, eds. Christine Daniels and Michael V. Kennedy. 267–282. New York: Routledge.

Greif, Avner. 2006. *Institutions and the Path to the Modern Economy: Lessons from Medieval Trade*. Cambridge: Cambridge University Press.

Grinath, Arthur III, John Joseph Wallis, and Richard E. Sylla. 1997. "Debt, Default, and Revenue Structure: The American State Debt Crisis in the Early 1840s." *National Bureau of Economic Research*. Historical Working Paper, h0097.

Grubb, Farley. 1985. "The Incidence of Servitude in Trans-Atlantic Migration, 1771–1804." *Explorations in Economic History* 22 (July), 316–39.

Gudmundson, Lowell. 1986. *Costa Rica Before Coffee: Society and Economy on the Eve of the Export Boom*. Baton Rouge: Louisiana State University Press.

Guell, Tomás Soley. 1975. *Compendio de Historia Económica y Hacendaria de Costa Rica*. 2nd ed. San José: Editorial Costa Rica.

Guiso Luigi, Paola Sapienza, and Luigi Zingales. 2004. "Does Local Financial Development Matter?" *Quarterly Journal of Economics* 119 (August): 929–969.

Gunther, Jeffrey W., Robert S. Moore, and Genie D. Short. 1996. "Mexican Banks and the 1994 Peso Crisis: The Importance of Initial Conditions," *North American Journal of Economics and Finance* 7(ISSUE 2): 125–33.

Guy, Donna J. 1980. *Argentine Sugar Politics: Tucumán and the Generation of Eighty*. Tempe: Center for Latin American Studies, Arizona State University.

Haber, Stephen H. 1989. *Industry and Underdevelopment: The Industrialization of Mexico, 1890–1940*. Stanford: Stanford University Press.

———. 1991. "Industrial Concentration and the Capital Markets: A Comparative Study of Brazil, Mexico, and the United States, 1830–1930." *Journal of Economic History* 51 (September): 559–80.

———. 1997. "Financial Markets and Industrial Development: A Comparative Study of Governmental Regulation, Financial Innovation, and Industrial Structure in Brazil and Mexico, 1840–1930." In *How Latin America Fell Behind: Essays on the Economic Histories of Brazil and Mexico, 1800–1914*, ed. Stephen Haber, 146–78. Stanford: Stanford University Press.

———. 2000. *Political Institutions and Economic Growth in Latin America: Essays in Policy, History, and Political Economy.* Stanford: Hoover Institution Press.

———. 2005. "Mexico's Experiments with Bank Privatization and Liberalization, 1991–2003." *Journal of Banking and Finance* 29 (August–September): 2325–53.

———. 2006. "Development Strategy or Endogenous Process: The Industrialization of Latin America." Stanford: Center for International Development, Working Paper.

———. 2009. "Why Banks Don't Lend: The Mexican Financial System." In *No Growth without Equity? Inequality, Interests, and Competition in Mexico*, eds. Santiago Levy and Michael Walton, 283–320. Washington, D.C.: World Bank.

Haber, Stephen, Herbert S. Klein, Noel Maurer, and Kevin Middlebrook. 2008. *Mexico Since 1980.* Cambridge: Cambridge University Press.

Haber, Stephen H., Noel Maurer, and Armando Razo. 2003. *The Politics of Property Rights: Political Instability, Credible Commitments and Economic Growth in Mexico, 1876–1929.* Cambridge: Cambridge University Press.

Hall, Robert E., and Charles I. Jones. 1999. "Why Do Some Countries Produce So Much More Output Per Worker Than Others?" *Quarterly Journal of Economics* 114 (February): 83–116.

Halperín Donghi, Tulio. 1993. *The Contemporary History of Latin America.* Durham: Duke University Press.

Hammond, Bray. 1947. "Jackson, Biddle, and the Bank of the United States." *Journal of Economic History* 7 (March): 1–23.

———. 1957. *Banks and Politics in America, from the Revolution to the Civil War.* Princeton: Princeton University Press.

Hanham, H. J. 1968. *The Reformed Electoral System in Great Britain, 1832–1914.* London: Historical Association.

Hanke, Lewis, ed. 1964. *Do the Americans Have a Common History?: A Critique of the Bolton Theory.* New York: Knopf.

Hanley, Anne G. 2005. *Native Capital: Financial Institutions and Economic Development in São Paulo, Brazil, 1850–1920.* Stanford: Stanford University Press.

Haring, C. H. 1947. *The Spanish Empire in America.* New York: Oxford University Press.

Harris, Marshall Dees. 1953. *Origin of the Land Tenure System in the United States.* Ames: Iowa State College Press.

Hartwell, R. M. 1971. *The Industrial Revolution and Economic Growth.* London: Methuen.

Hawke, G. R. 1985. *The Making of New Zealand: An Economic History*. Cambridge: Cambridge University Press.

Heckscher, Eli F. 1935. *Mercantilism*. 2 vols. London: G. Allen and Unwin.

Helg, Aline. 1987. *La Educación en Colombia, 1918–1957: Una Historia Social, Económica y Política*. Bogatá: Fondo Editorial CEREC.

Hellmann, Ellen, ed. 1949. *Handbook on Race Relations in South Africa*. Cape Town: Oxford University Press.

Hernández Chavez, Alicia. 1996. "Las Tensiones Internas del Federalismo, Mexicanol" In *Hacia un Nuevo Federalismo?*, ed. Alicia Hernández Chávez. Mexico, D.F.: Fondo de Cultura Económica.

Herskovits, Melville J. 1948. *Man and His Works: The Science of Cultural Anthropology*. New York: Knopf.

Heywood, Colin. 1981. "The Role of the Peasantry in French Industrialization, 1815–1880." *Economic History Review*, 34 (August): 359–76.

Hibbard, Benjamin Horace. 1924. *A History of the Public Land Policies*. New York: Macmillan.

Higgs, Robert. 1977. *Competition and Coercion: Blacks in the American Economy, 1865–1914*. Cambridge: Cambridge University Press.

Himmerich, Robert. 1991. *The Encomenderos of New Spain, 1521–1555*. Austin: University of Texas Press.

Hirschman, Albert O. 1970. *Exit, Voice, and Loyalty: Response to Decline in Firms, Organizations, and States*. Cambridge, MA: Harvard University Press.

Hobson, John A. 1965[1902]. *Imperialism: A Study*. Ann Arbor: University of Michigan Press.

Hochschild, Adam. 1998. *King Leopold's Ghost: A Story of Greed, Terror, and Heroism in Colonial Africa*. Boston: Houghton Mifflin.

Holden, Robert H. 1994. *Mexico and the Survey of Public Lands. The Management of Modernization, 1876–1911*. DeKalb: Northern Illinois University Press.

Horwitz, Morton J. 1977. *The Transformation of American Law, 1780–1860*. Cambridge, MA: Harvard University Press.

Hoselitz, Bert F., J. J. Spengler, J. M. Letiche, E. McKinley, J. Buttrick, and H. J. Bruton. 1960. *Theories of Economic Growth*. Glencoe: Free Press.

Hurst, James Willard. 1956. *Law and the Conditions of Freedom in the Nineteenth-Century United States*. Madison: University of Wisconsin Press.

Hutchinson, E. P. 1981. *Legislative History of American Immigration Policy, 1798–1965*. Philadelphia: University of Pennsylvania Press.

Instituto Nacional de Estadística, Geografía e Informática. 1994. *Estadísticas Históricas de México*. 2 Vols. Aguascalientes: Instituto Nacional de Estadística, Geografía e Informática.

Inter-American Development Bank. 1997. *Latin America After a Decade of Reforms, Economic and Social Progress in Latin America: 1997 Report*. Washington D.C.: Inter-America Development Bank.

International Monetary Fund. Various years. *Government Finance Statistics Yearbook*. Washington, D.C.: International Monetary Fund, 2004 and 2006.

Irwin, James R. 1988. "Exploring the Affinity of Wheat and Slavery in the Virginia Piedmont." *Explorations in Economic History* 25 (July): 295–332.

Jacob, Margaret C. 1997. *Scientific Culture and the Making of the Industrial West*. New York: Oxford University Press.

Jacobsen, Nils. 1993. *Mirages of Transition: The Peruvian Altiplano, 1780–1930*. Berkeley: University of California Press.

Jamaica, Department of Statistics. 1950. *West Indian Census, 1946*. 2 vols. Kingston: Central Bureau of Statistics.

Jones, Alice Hanson. 1980. *Wealth of a Nation to Be: The American Colonies on the Eve of the Revolution*. New York: Columbia University Press.

Jones, E. L. 1981. *The European Miracle: Environments, Economies, and Geopolitics in the History of Europe and Asia*. Cambridge: Cambridge University Press.

———. 1988. *Growth Recurring: Economic Change in World History*. New York: Oxford University Press.

Jourdain, W. R. 1925. *Land Legislation and Settlement in New Zealand*. Wellington: W.A.G. Skinner.

Justman, Moshe, and Mark Gradstein. 1999. "The Industrial Revolution, Political Transtion, and the Subsequent Decline in Inequality in 19th Century Britain." *Explorations in Economic History*, 36 (April): 109–27.

Kaestle, Carl F. 1983. *Pillars of the Republic: Common Schools and American Society, 1780–1860*. New York: Hill and Wang.

Kamphoefner, Walter D., Wolfgang Helbich, and Ulrike Sommer, eds. 1991. *News From the Land of Freedom: German Immigrants Write Home*. Ithaca: Cornell University Press.

Katz, Friedrich. 1998. *The Life and Times of Pancho Villa*. Stanford: Stanford University Press.

Kearl, J. R., and Clayne Pope. 1986. "Choices, Rents, and Luck: Economic Mobility of Nineteenth-Century Utah Households." In *Long-Term Factors in American Economic Growth*, eds. Stanley L. Engerman and Robert E. Gallman. 215–60. Chicago: University of Chicago Press.

Kearl, J. R., Clayne L. Pope, and Larry T. Wimmer. 1980. "Household Wealth in a Settlement Economy, Utah 1850–1870." *Journal of Economic History* 40 (September): 477–96.

Keen, Michael, and Johanna Elizabeth Lighart eds. 1999. "Coordinating Tariff Reduction and Domestic Tax Reform." IMF Working Paper no. 9993. Washington, D.C.: International Monetary Fund.

Keyssar, Alexander. 2000. *The Right to Vote: The Contested History of Democracy in the United States*. New York: Basic Books.

Khan, B. Zorina. 1995. "Property Rights and Patent Litigation in Early Nineteenth-Century America." *Journal of Economic History* 55 (March): 58–97.

———. 1996. "Married Women's Property Laws and Female Commercial Activity." *Journal of Economic History* 56 (June): 356–88.

———. 2005. *The Democratization of Invention: Patents and Copyrights in American Economic Development, 1790–1920*. Cambridge: Cambridge University Press.

Khan, B. Zorina, and Kenneth L. Sokoloff. 1993. "'Schemes of Practical Utility': Entrepreneurship and Innovation Among 'Great Inventors' in the United States, 1790–1865." *Journal of Economic History* 53 (June): 289–307.

———. 1998. "Two Paths to Industrial Development and Technological Change." In *Technological Revolutions in Europe, Historical Perspectives*, eds. Maxine Berg and Kristine Bruland, 292–314. Cheltenham: Edward Elgar.

———. 2001. "History Lessons: The Early Development of Intellectual Property Institutions in the United States. *Journal of Economic Perspectives* 15 (Summer): 233–46.

Kindleberger, Charles P. 1961. "International Trade and Investment and Resource Use in Economic Growth" and William N. Parker, "Comment." In *National Resources and Economic Growth*, ed. Joseph J. Spengler, 151–187 and 187–190. Washington, D.C.: Resources for the Future.

King, Robert G. and Ross Levine. 1993a. "Finance and Growth: Schumpeter Might Be Right." *Quarterly Journal of Economics* 108 (August): 717–37.

———. 1993b. "Finance, Entrepreneurship, and Growth." *Journal of Monetary Economics*, 32 (December): 513–42.

Klein, Herbert S. 1983. "The Integration of Italian Immigrants into the United States and Argentina: A Comparative Analysis." *American Historical Review* 88 (April): 306–29.

———. 1986. *African Slavery in Latin America and the Caribbean*. New York: Oxford University Press.

———. 1993. *Haciendas and Ayllus: Rural Society in the Bolivian Andes in the Eighteenth and Nineteenth Centuries*. Stanford: Stanford University Press.

———. 1998. *The American Finances of the Spanish Empire: Royal Income and Expenditures in Colonial Mexico, Peru, and Bolivia, 1680–1809*. Albuquerque: University of New Mexico Press.

Kleppner, Paul. 1982. *Who Voted? The Dynamics of Electoral Turnout, 1870–1980*. New York: Praeger.

Knack, Stephen and Philip Keefer. 1997. "Does Social Capital Have an Economic Payoff: A Cross-Country Investigation." *Quarterly Journal of Economics* 112 (November): 1251–88.

Knight, Franklin W. 1990. *The Caribbean: The Genesis of a Fragmented Nationalism*. 2nd ed. New York: Oxford University Press.

Kornbluh, Mark Lawrence. 2000. *Why America Stopped Voting: The Decline of Participatory Democracy and the Emergence of Modern American Politics*. New York: New York University Press.

Kousser, J. Morgan. 1974. *The Shaping of Southern Politics: Suffrage Restriction and the Establishment of the One-Party South, 1880–1910*. New Haven: Yale University Press.

Kritz, Mary M. 1992. "The British and Spanish Migration Systems in the Colonial Era: A Policy Framework." In *The Peopling of the Americas, Proceedings*. vol. I, ed. Mary M. Kritz. 263–281. Leige: International Union for the Scientific Study of Population.

Kroszner, Randall S. and Philip E. Strahan. 1999. "What Drives Deregulation? Economics and Politics of the Relaxation of Bank Branching Restrictions." *Quarterly Journal of Economics* 114 (November): 1437–67.

Kuczynski, Robert R. 1936. *Population Movements*. Oxford: Clarendon Press.

Kupperman, Karen Ordahl. 1993. *Providence Island, 1630–1641: The Other Puritan Colony*. Cambridge: Cambridge University Press.

Kussmaul, Ann. 1981. *Servants in Husbandry in Early Modern England*. Cambridge: Cambridge University Press.

Labarca, Amanda. 1939. *Historia de la Enseñanza en Chile*. Santiago: Imprenta Universitaria.

La Porta, Rafael, Florencio Lopez-de-Silanes and Guillermo Zamarripa. 2003. "Related Lending," *Quarterly Journal of Economics* 18 (February): 231–68.

Lal, Deepak. 2004. *In Praise of Empires: Globalization and Order*. New York: Palgrave Macmillan.

Lamoreaux, Naomi. 1994. *Insider Lending: Banks, Personal Connections, and Economic Development in Industrial New England*. Cambridge: Cambridge University Press.

Lamoreaux, Naomi R., and Jean-Laurent Rosenthal. 2005. "Legal Regime and Contractual Flexibility: A Comparison of Business's Organizational Choices in France and the United States During the Era of Industrialization." *American Law and Economics Review*, 7 (Spring): 28–61.

Landes, David S. 1969. *The Unbound Prometheus: Technological Change and Industrial Development in Western Europe from 1750 to the Present*. London: Cambridge University Press.

———. 1998. *The Wealth and Poverty of Nations: Why Some are So Rich and Some So Poor*. New York: Norton.

Lane, Carl. 1997. "For a 'Positive Profit': The Federal Investment in the First Bank of the United States, 1792–1802." *William and Mary Quarterly* 54 (July): 601–12.

Leacy, F. H., ed. 1983. *Historical Statistics of Canada*: 2nd ed. Ottawa: Statistics Canada.

Leff, Nathaniel. 1978. "Industrial Organization and Entrepreneurship in the Developing Countries: The Economic Groups." *Economic Development and Cultural Change* 26 (July): 661–75.

LeGrand, Catherine. 1986. *Frontier Expansion and Peasant Protest in Colombia, 1850–1936*. Albuquerque: University of New Mexico Press.

Levine, Ross and Sarah Zervos. 1998. "Stock Markets, Banks, and Economic Growth." *American Economic Review* 88 (June): 537–58.

Levy, Juliette. 2003. "Yucatan's Arrested Development: Social Networks and Credit Markets in Merida, 1850–1899." unpublished Ph.D. dissertation, University of California, Los Angeles.

Lewis, Frank D., and M. C. Urquhart. 1999. "Growth and the Standard of Living in a Pioneer Economy: Upper Canada, 1826 to 1851." *William and Mary Quarterly*, 56 (January): 151–81.

Lewis, W. Arthur. 1955. "Economic Development with Unlimited Supplies of Labour." *Manchester School of Economic and Social Studies* 23 (May): 139–91.

Lindert, Peter H. 1994. "The Rise of Social Spending, 1880–1930." *Explorations in Economic History* 31 (January): 1–37.

Lindo-Fuentes, Héctor. 1990. *Weak Foundations: The Economy of El Salvador in the Nineteenth Century.* Berkeley: University of California Press.

Livermore, Shaw. 1935. "Unlimited Liability in Early American Corporations." *Journal of Political Economy* 43 (October): 674–87.

Lizzeri, Alessandro, and Nicola Persico. 2004. "Why Did the Elites Extend the Suffrage? Democracy and the Scope of Government,with an Application to Britain's 'Age of Reform.'" *Quarterly Journal of Economics*, 119 (May): 707–65.

Lockhart, James. 1994. *Spanish Peru: 1532–1560. A Social History.* 2nd ed. Madison: University of Wisconsin Press.

Lockhart, James and Stuart B. Schwartz. 1983. *Early Latin America: A History of Colonial Spanish America and Brazil.* Cambridge: Cambridge University Press.

Lockridge, Kenneth. 1974. *Literacy in Colonial New England: An Enquiry into the Social Context of Literacy in the Early Modern West.* New York: Norton.

Lokke, Carl Ludwig. 1932. *France and the Colonial Question: A Study of Contemporary French Opinion, 1763–1801.* New York: Columbia University Press.

López Garavito, Luis Fernando. 1992. *Historia de la Hacienda y el Tesoro en Colombia, 1821–1900.* Bogotá: Banco de la República.

López Murphy, Ricardo ed. 1995. *Fiscal Decentralization in Latin America.* Washington, D.C.: Inter-American Development Bank.

Lott, John R. Jr., and Lawrence W. Kenny. 1999. "Did Women's Suffrage Change the Size and Scope of Government?" *Journal of Political Economy* 107 (December): 1163–98.

Love, Joseph L. 1970. "Political Participation in Brazil, 1881–1969." *Luso-Brazilian Review*, 7 (December): 3–24.

Ludlow, Leonor. 2003. "El Banco Mercantil de Veracruz, 1898–1906." In *La Banca Regional en Mexico, 1870–1930*, eds. Mario Cerutti and Carlos Marichal, 134–167. Mexico: Fondo de Cultura Económica.

Lynch, John. 1986. *The Spanish American Revolutions, 1808–1826*, 2nd ed. New York: Norton.

Machlup, Fritz. 1958. *An Economic Review of the Patent System.* The Committee on the Judiciary, United States Senate. Washington, D.C.: Government Printing Office.

Macintyre, Stuart. 1999. *A Concise History of Australia.* Cambridge: Cambridge University Press.

Mackey, Michael W. 1999. "Report of Michael W. Mackey on the Comprehensive Evaluation of the Operations and Functions of the Fund for the Protection of Bank Savings 'FOBAPROA' and the Quality of Supervision of the FOBAPROA Program, 1995–1998."

Maddison, Angus. 1991. *Dynamic Forces in Capitalist Development: A Long-run Comparative View.* Oxford: Oxford University Press.

———. 1994. "Explaining the Economic Performance of Nations, 1820–1989." In *Convergence of Productivity, Cross-National Studies and Historical Evidence*, eds. William J. Baumol, Richard R. Nelson, and Edward N. Wolff, 20–61. New York: Oxford University Press.

———. 1995. *Monitoring the World Economy, 1820–1992*. Paris: OECD.

———. 2001. *The World Economy: A Millennial Perspective*. Paris: OECD.

———. 2003. *The World Economy: Historical Statistics*. Paris: OECD.

Magaloni, Beatriz. 2006. *Voting for Autocracy: Hegemonic Party Survival and its Demise in Mexico*. New York: Cambridge University Press.

Maine, Sir Henry Sumner. 1885. *Popular Government: Four Essays*. London: Murray.

Majewski, John. 2000. *A House Dividing: Economic Development in Pennsylvania and Virginia Before the Civil War*. Cambridge: Cambridge University Press.

———. 2004. "Jeffersonian Political Economy and Pennsylvania's Financial Revolution from Below, 1800–1820." Mimeo, UCSB.

Majewski, John, Christopher Baer, and Daniel B. Klein. 1993. "Responding to Relative Decline: The Plank Road Boom of Antebellum New York." *Journal of Economic History* 53 (March): 106–22.

Maltoni, Marta. 1988. *Educación y Reformas Constitucionales: 1819–1987*. Buenos Aires: Libería "El Ateneo" Editorial.

Mamalakis, Markos J. 1978–1989. *Historical Statistics of Chile*, 6 vols., vol. 2 *Demography and Labor Force*. Westport: Greenwood Press.

Margo, Robert A. 1990. *Race and Schooling in the South, 1880–1950: An Economic History*. Chicago: University of Chicago Press.

Marichal, Carlos. 1989. *A Century of Debt Crises in Latin America: From Independence to the Great Depression, 1820–1930*. Princeton: Princeton University Press.

———. 2002. "The Construction of Credibility: Financial Market Reform and the Renegotiation of Mexico's External Debt in the 1880's." In *The Mexican Economy, 1870–1930. Essays on the Economic History of Institutions, Revolution, and Growth*, eds. Jeffrey L. Bortz and Stephen H. Haber. 93–119. Stanford: Stanford University Press.

Marichal, Carlos, Manuel Miño Grijalva, and Paolo Riguzzi. 1994. *Historia de la Hacienda Pública del Estado de México, 1824–1990*. Mexico, D.F.: El Colegio Mexiquense.

Mariscal, Elisa V., and Kenneth L. Sokoloff. 2000. "The Persistence of Inequality in the Americas: Schooling and Suffrage, 1800–1945." In *Political Institutions and Economic Growth in Latin America: Essays in Policy, History, and Political Economy*, ed. Stephen Haber. 159–217. Stanford: Hoover Institution Press.

Markiewicz, Dana. 1993. *The Mexican Revolution and the Limits of Agrarian Reform, 1915–1946*. Boulder: Lynne Rienner.

Marshall, Alfred. 1919. *Industry and Trade: A Study of Industrial Technique and Business Organization and of their Influences on the Conditions of Various Classes and Nations*. London: Macmillan.

Martin, Chester. 1973. *Dominion Lands Policy*. Toronto: McClelland and Stewart (1st pub. 1938).

Martin, Robert Montgomery. 1967 [1843]. *History of the Colonies of the British Empire. From the Official Records of the Colonial Office*. London: Dawsons.

Martínez, Alberto B. 1910. *República Argentina. Censo General de Educación Levantado el 23 de Mayo de 1909.* 3 vols. Buenos Aires: Oficina Meteorológica Argentina.

Martinez Peria, Maria Soledad and Sergio J. Schmukler. 2001. "Do Depositors Punish Banks for Bad Behavior? Market Discipline, Deposit Insurance, and Banking Crisis," *Journal of Finance* 56 (June): 1029–51.

Martinez Fitscher, André C. and Aldo Musacchio. 2010. "Endowments, Fiscal Federalism, and the Cost of Capital for States: Evidence from Brazil, 1891–1930." *Financial History Review* 17 (April): 13–50.

Martinez Jimenez, Alejandro. 1973. "La Educación Elemental en el Profiriato." *Historia Mexicana* 22 (January-March): 514–52.

Matthew, W. M. 1977. "A Primitive Export Sector: Guano Production in Mid-Nineteenth-Century Peru." *Journal of Latin American Studies* 9 (May): 35–57.

Maurer, Noel. 2002. *The Power and the Money: The Mexican Financial System, 1876–1932.* Stanford: Stanford University Press.

Mauer, Noel and Andrei Gomberg. 2004. "When the State is Untrustworthy: Public Finance and Private Banking in Porfirian Mexico." *Journal of Economic History* 64 (December): 1087–1107.

Mauer, Noel and Stephen Haber. 2007. "Related Lending and Economic Performance: Evidence from Mexico." *Journal of Economic History* 67 (September): 551–581.

McAlister, Lyle N. 1984. *Spain and Portugal in the New World, 1492–1700.* Minneapolis: University of Minnesota Press.

McBride, George McCutchen. 1923. *The Land Systems of Mexico.* New York: American Geographic Society.

McClelland, David C. 1961. *The Achieving Society.* Princeton: Van Nostrand.

McCormick, Richard P. 1960. "New Perspectives on Jacksonian Politics." *American Historical Review* 65 (January): 288–301.

———. 1966. *The Second American Party System: Party Formation in the Jacksonian Era.* Chapel Hill: University of North Carolina Press.

McCreery, David. 1994. *Rural Guatemala, 1760–1940.* Stanford: Stanford University Press.

McCusker, John J., and Russell R. Menard. 1985. *The Economy of British America, 1607–1789.* Chapel Hill: University of North Carolina Press.

McDonald, J. D. N. 1952. "New Zealand Land Legislation." *Australian Historical Studies* 5 (November): 195–211.

McEvedy, Colin, and Richard Jones. 1978. *Atlas of World Population History.* Harmondsworth: Penguin.

McGovney, Dudley O. 1949. *The American Suffrage Medley: The Need for a National Uniform Suffrage.* Chicago: University of Chicago Press.

McGreevey, William Paul. 1971. *An Economic History of Colombia, 1845–1930.* Cambridge: Cambridge University Press.

McLauchlan, Gordon, ed. 1984. *Bateman New Zealand Encyclopedia.* Auckland: David Bateman.

McManus, Edgar J. 1973. *Black Bondage in the North.* Syracuse: Syracuse University Press.

McNaughtan, I. D. 1955. "Colonial Liberalism, 1851–91." In *Australia: A Social and Political History*, ed. Gordon Greenwood, 98–144. New York: Praeger.

Mein Smith, Philippa. 2005. *A Concise History of New Zealand*. Cambridge: Cambridge University Press.

Melo-Gonzalez, Jorge Orlando. 1989–1998. "La Evolucion Economica de Colombia, 1830–1900." In *Nueva Historia de Colombia*, 11 vols., ed. Jaime Jaramillo Uribe, vol. 2. Bogotá: Planeta. Colombiana Editorial.

Ménard, C., ed. 2000. *Institutions, Contracts, and Organizations: Perspectives from New Institutional Economics*. Cheltenham: Edward Elgar.

———. 2004. *The Foundations of the New Institutional Economics*. Cheltenham: Edward Elgar.

Ménard, C., and Mary M. Shirley, eds. 2008. *Handbook of New Institutional Economics*. Berlin: Springer.

Merrick, Thomas W., and Douglas H. Graham. 1979. *Population and Economic Development in Brazil: 1800 to the Present*. Baltimore: Johns Hopkins University Press.

Merton, Robert K. 1970[1938]. *Science, Technology and Society in Seventeenth Century England*. New York: H. Fertig.

Miller, Frank Hayden. 1900. "Legal Qualifications for Office in America, 1619–1899." In *Annual Report of the American Historical Association, 1899* (Washington, D.C.: Government Printing Office): 87–153.

Misuriello, Vincenzo. 1993. *Política de la Inmigración en la Argentina: 1853–1970*. Buenos Aires: Universidad National de Tucumán.

Mitchell, B. R. 1992 *International Historical Statistics: Europe 1750–1988*. 3rd edition New York: Stockton Press.

———. 1993. *International Historical Statistics: The Americas:1750–1988*. 2nd edition New York: Stockton Press.

Moch, Leslie Page. 1992. *Moving Europeans: Migration in Western Europe Since 1650*. Bloomington: Indiana University Press.

Mokyr, Joel. 2002. *The Gifts of Athena: Historical Origins of the Knowledge Economy*. Princeton: Princeton University Press.

Montesquieu Charles, de Secondat, Baron de. 1949 [1748]. *The Spirit of the Laws*. New York: Hafner.

Moohr, Michael. 1972. "The Economic Impact of Slave Emancipation in British Guiana, 1832–1852." *Economic History Review* 25 (November): 588–607.

Moreno Fraginals, Manuel. 1976. *The Sugarmill: The Socioeconomic Complex of Sugar in Cuba, 1760–1860*. New York: Monthly Review Press.

Morgan, Donald P., Bertrand Rime, and Philip E. Strahan. 2004. "Bank Integration and State Business Cycles." *Quarterly Journal of Economics* 119 (November): 1555–84.

Mörner, Magnus. 1985. *Adventurers and Proletarians: The Story of Migrants in Latin America*. Pittsburgh: University of Pittsburgh Press.

Morris, Henry C. 1900. *The History of Colonization from the Earliest Times to the Present Day*, 2 vols. London: Macmillan.

Moses, Bernard. 1898. *The Establishment of Spanish Rule in America. An introduction to the history and politics of Spanish American*. New York: G. P. Putnam.

Mosk, Sanford A. 1951. "Latin America Versus the United States." *American Economic Review* 41 (May): 367–83.

Moss, David and Sarah Brennan. 2004. "Regulation and Reaction: The Other Side of Free Banking in Antebellum New York." Harvard Business School Working Paper 04–038.

Moya Pons, Frank. 1995. *The Dominican Republic: A National History*. New Rochelle: Hispaniola Books.

Mulhall, M. G., and E. T. Mulhall. 1885. *Handbook of the River Plate: Comprising the Argentine Republic, Uruguay, and Paraguay*. 5th ed. London: Trübner and Co.

Musacchio, Aldo. 2009. *Experiments in Financial Democracy: Corporate Governance and Financial Development in Brazil, 1882–1950*. Cambridge: Cambridge University Press.

Musgrave, Richard A. 1969. *Fiscal Systems*. New Haven: Yale University Press.

Musgrave, Richard A., and Malcolm Gillis. 1971. *Fiscal Reform for Colombia, Final Report and Staff Papers of the Colombian Commission on Tax Reform*. Cambridge, MA: Law School of Harvard University.

Musgrave, Richard A., and Peggy B. Musgrave. 1984. *Public Finance in Theory and Practice*. 4th ed. New York: McGraw-Hill.

Nash, Gary B. 1993. *Quakers and Politics: Pennsylvania, 1681–1726*. new ed. Boston: Northeastern University Press.

Nef, John U. 1958. *Cultural Foundations of Industrial Civilization*. Cambridge: Cambridge University Press.

Nettels, Curtis P. 1963. *The Roots of American Civilization: A History of American Colonial Life*. 2nd ed. New York: Appleton-Century-Crofts.

Newell, William H. 1986. "Inheritance on the Maturing Frontier. Butler County, Ohio, 1803–1865." In *Long-Term Factors in American Economic Growth*, eds. Stanley L. Engerman and Robert E. Gallman, 261–303. Chicago: University of Chicago Press.

Newland, Carlos. 1991. "La Educación Elemental en Hispanoamérica: Desde la Independencia Hasta la Centralización de los Sistemas Educativos Nacionales." *Hispanic American Historical Review*, 71 (May): 335–64.

———. 1994. "The Estado Docente and its Expansion: Spanish America Elementary Education, 1900–1950." *Journal of Latin American Studies* 26 (May): 449–67.

Ng, Kenneth. 1988. "Free Banking Laws and Barriers to Entry in Banking, 1838–1860." *Journal of Economic History* 48 (December): 877–89.

Nohlen, Dieter, ed. 1993. *Enciclopédia Electoral Latinoamericana y del Caribe*. San José, Costa Rica: Instituto Interamericano de Derechos Humanos.

North, Douglass C. 1981. *Structure and Change in Economic History*. New York: Norton.

———. 1988. "Institutions, Economic Growth and Freedom: An Historical Introduction." In *Freedom, Democracy and Economic Welfare: Proceedings of an International Symposium*, ed. Michael A. Walker, 3–25. Vancouver: Fraser Institute.

———. 1990. *Institutions, Institutional Change and Economic Performance*. Cambridge: Cambridge University Press.

North, Douglass C., and Robert Paul Thomas. 1973. *The Rise of the Western World: A New Economic History.* Cambridge: Cambridge University Press.

North, Douglass C., and Barry R. Weingast. 1989. "Constitutions and Commitment: The Evolution of Institutions Governing Public Choice in Seventeenth-Century England." *Journal of Economic History* 49 (December): 803–32.

North, Douglass C., William Summerhill, and Barry R. Weingast. 2000. "Order, Disorder, and Economic Change: Latin America Versus North America." In *Governing for Prosperity*, eds. Bruce Bueno de Mesquita and Hilton L. Root. 17–58. New Haven: Yale University Press.

North, Douglass C., John Joseph Wallis, and Barry R. Weingast. 2009. *Violence and Social Orders: A Conceptual Framework for Interpreting Recorded Human History.* Cambridge: Cambridge University Press.

Nugent, Jeffrey B. and James A. Robinson. 2010. "Are Factor Endowments Fate?" *Journal of Iberian and Latin American Economic History* 28 (January), 45–82.

O'Brien, Patrick K. 1988. "The Political Economy of British Taxation, 1660–1815." *Economic History Review* 41 (February): 1–32.

Ochieng', William R. 1985. *A History of Kenya.* Nairobi: Macmillan Kenya.

Oficina de Estadística Nacional. 1875. *Relistro Estadístico de la República Argentina. Tomo Setimo Ano de 1872 y 1873.* Buenos Aires: Sociedad Anonima.

Oficina Nacional de Estadística. 1912. *Resúmenes Estadísticos: Años 1883–1910: Demografía.* San José: Impr Nacional.

Oliver, Roland and others, eds. 1963–1976. *History of East Africa.* 3 vols., vol. 2. Oxford: Clarendon Press.

Olmstead, Alan L., and Paul W. Rhode. 1995. "Beyond the Threshold: An Analysis of the Characteristics and Behavior of Early Reaper Adopters." *Journal of Economic History* 55 (March): 27–57.

Olson, Mancur. 1982. *The Rise and Decline of Nations: Economic Growth, Stagflation, and Social Rigidities.* New Haven: Yale University Press.

Olveda, Jaime. 2003. "Bancas y Banqueros de Guadalajara." In *La Banca Regional en Mexico, 1870–1930*, eds. Mario Cerutti and Carlos Marichal. Mexico: Fondo de Cultura Económica.

Ortuste, Gonzalo Rojas, and Moira Zuazo Oblitas. 1997. "Análisis Del Sistema Electoral y sus Consecuencias Politicas en el Marco de la Reforma Estatal: el Caso de Bolivia." In *Sistemas Electorales y sus Consecuencias Polítcas*, ed. Carlota Jakisch. Buenos Aires: Centro Interdisciplinario de Estudios Sobre el Desarollo Latinamericano.

Palacios, Marco. 1980. *Coffee in Colombia, 1850–1970: An Economic, Social, and Political History.* Cambridge: Cambridge University Press.

Pani, Alberto J. et al. 1918. *Una Encuesta Sobre Educacíon Popular.* Mexico: Departmento de Aprovisionamientos Generales.

Park, James William. 1985. *Rafael Núñez and the Politics of Colombian Regionalism 1863–1886.* Baton Rouge: Louisiana State University Press.

Parker, William N. 1970. "Slavery and Southern Economic Development: An Hypothesis and Some Evidence." *Agricultural History* 44 (January): 115–25.

Parry, J. H. 1966. *The Spanish Seaborne Empire.* London: Hutchinson.

Paulston, Rolland G. 1971. *Society, Schools and Progress in Peru*. Oxford: Pergamon.

Peláez, Carlos Manuel. 1975. "The Establishment of Banking Institutions in a Backward Economy: Brazil, 1800–1851." *Business History Review* 49 (Winter): 446–472.

Peláez, Carlos Manuel and Wilson Suzigan. 1981. *História Monetária do Brasil*. 2nd ed., Brasilia: Editora Universidade de Brasilia.

Peña, Moises T. de la. 1948, et al. *Chihuahua Económico*. 3 vols. México: Tall, Gráf de A. Morales S.

Pérez-Brignoli, Héctor. 1989. *A Brief History of Central America*. Berkeley: University of California Press.

Perkins, Edwin J. 1980. *The Economy of Colonial America*. New York: Columbia University Press.

———. 1994. *American Public Finance and Financial Services, 1700–1815*. Columbus: Ohio State University Press.

Perotti, Roberto. 1996. "Growth, Income Distribution, and Democracy: What the Data Say." *Journal of Economic Growth*, 1 (June): 149–87.

Perry, J. Harvey. 1955. *Taxes, Tariffs, & Subsidies: A History of Canadian Fiscal Development*. Toronto: University of Toronto Press.

Perry, James R. 1990. *The Formation of a Society on Virginia's Eastern Shore, 1615–1655*. Chapel Hill: University of North Carolina Press.

Perry, Laurens Ballard. 1978. *Juárez and Díaz: Machine Politics in Mexico*. DeKalb: Northern Illinois University Press.

Persson, Torsten, and Guido Tabellini. 1994. "Is Inequality Harmful for Growth? Theory and Evidence" *American Economic Review* 84 (June): 600–21.

———. 2003. *The Economic Effects of Constitutions*. Cambridge, MA: MIT Press.

———. 2008. "The Growth Effect of Democracy: Is It Heterogeneous and How Can It Be Estimated?" ed. E. Helpman. *Institutions and Economic Performance*, 544–584. Cambridge, MA.: Harvard University Press.

Peru, Dirección de Esadistíca. 1928, 1940: *Extracto Esadística del Peru*. Lima: Imprenta Americana.

Petersen, Mitchell A. and Raghuram G. Rajan. 2002. "Does Distance Still Matter? The Information Revolution in Small Business Lending." *Journal of Finance* 57 (December): 2533–70.

Phillips, Charles Edward. 1957. *The Development of Education in Canada*. Toronto: W. J. Gage.

Pietschmann, Horst. 1996. *Las Reformas Borbónicas y el Sistema de Intendencias en Nueva España: Un Estudio Politico Administrativo*. Mexico: Fondo de Cultura Económica.

Pineo, Ronn F. 1996. *Social and Economic Reform in Ecuador. Life and Work in Guayaquil*. Gainesville: University Press of Florida.

Plato. 1970. *The Laws*. Harmondsworth: Penguin.

Platt, D. C. M., and Guido di Tella, eds. 1985. *Argentina, Australia, and Canada: Studies in Comparative Development, 1870–1965*. London: Macmillan.

Pomeranz, Kenneth. 2000. *The Great Divergence: China, Europe, and the Making of the Modern World Economy*. Princeton: Princeton University Press.

Pomfret, Richard W.T. 1981. *The Economic Development of Canada*. Toronto: Methuen.

Porter, Dale H. 1970. *The Abolition of the Slave Trade in England, 1784–1807*. Hamden: Archon.

Porter, Kirk H. 1918. *A History of Suffrage in the United States*. Chicago: University of Chicago Press.

Postan, M. M. 1935. "Recent Trends in the Accumulation of Capital." *Economic History Review* 6 (October): 1–12.

Potash, Robert. 1983. *The Mexican Government and Industrial Development in the Early Republic: The Banco de Avio*. Amherst: University of Massachusetts Press.

Powell, J. M. 1970. *The Public Lands of Australia Felix: Settlement and Land Appraisal in Victoria 1834–91 with Special Reference to the Western Plains*. Melbourne: Oxford University Press.

Powell, J.M. and M, Williams., eds. 1975. *Australian Space, Australian Time: Geographic Perspectives*. Melbourne: Oxford University Press.

Pritchard, James. 2004. *In Search of Empire: The French in the Americas, 1670–1730*. Cambridge: Cambridge University Press.

Przeworski, Adam et al. 2000. *Democracy and Development: Political Institutions and Well-Being in the World, 1950–1990*. Cambridge: Cambridge University Press.

Putnam, Robert D., ed. 2002. *Democracies in Flux: The Evolution of Social Capital in Contemporary Society*. Oxford: Oxford University Press.

Qualter, Terence H. 1970. *The Election Process in Canada*. Toronto: McGraw-Hill.

Quintyn, Marc and Geneviéve Verdier. 2010. "Mother Can I Trust the Government? Sustained Financial Deepening – A Political Institutions View." IMF Working Paper.

Rabushka, Alvin. 2008. *Taxation in Colonial America*. Princeton: Princeton University Press.

Rajan, Raghuram and Luigi Zingales. 1998. "Financial Dependence and Growth." *American Economic Review* 88 (June): 559–86.

Ramírez, María Teresa, and Irene Salazar. 2010. "El Surgimento de la Educación en Columbia: En Qué Fallamos," In Adolfa Meisel Roca and María Teresa Ramírez eds. 419–48. *Economiá Columbiana del Siglo XIX*, Bogotá: Fondo de Culture Económia.

Ramirez, María Teresa, and Irene Salazar. 2008. "The Emergence of Education in the Republic of Colombia in the 19th Century: Where Did We Go Wrong?" Unpublished (English version).

Ransom, Roger L., and Richard Sutch. 1977. *One Kind of Freedom: The Economic Consequences of Emancipation*. Cambridge: Cambridge University Press.

Ratner, Sidney. 1980[1967]. *Taxation and Democracy in America*. New York: Octagon Books.

Razaghian, Rose. 2005. "Financing the Civil War: The Confederacy's Financial Strategy.: Yale ICF Working Paper no. 04-45. New Haven: Yale University.

Razo, Armando. 2008. *Social Foundations of Limited Dictatorship: Networks and Private Protection During Mexico's Early Industrialization.* Stanford: Stanford University Press.

Recchini de Lattes, Zulma L., and Alfredo E. Lattes. 1969. *Migraciones en la Argentina. Estudio de la Migraciones Internas e Internacionales Basado en Datos Censales, 1869–1960.* Buenos Aires: Instituto Torcuato di Tella.

Reese, Thomas J. 1980. *The Politics of Taxation.* Westport: Quorom.

República de Colombia, 1919. *Boletín de Estadística de Cundinamarca.* Bogotá: Imprent del Departmento.

República de Colombia, Registraduría Nacional del Estado Civil. 1988. *Historia Electoral Colombiana. 1810–1988.* Bogotá: La Registraduría.

República de Colombia, Registraduría Nacional del Estado Civil. *Resumen del Comercio Exteria de la República Argentina.* (n.d.) Buenos Aires: Argentina, Dirección General de Estadistica.

Reynolds, Robert L. 1965. "The Mediterranean Frontier, 1000–1400." In *The Frontier in Perspective*, eds. Walker D. Wyman and Clifton B. Kroeber, 21–34. Madison: University of Wisconsin Press.

Rife, Clarence White. 1931. "Land Tenure in New Netherlands." In *Essays in Colonial History Presented to Charles McLean Andrews by his Students*, 41–73. New Haven: Yale University Press.

Risch, Erna. 1937. "Encouragement of Immigration: Revealed in Colonial Legislation." *Virginia Magazine of History and Biography* 45 (January): 1–10.

Rivera Borbon, Carlos. 1970. *El Gasto del Gobierno Federal Mexicano a Través de la Secretaria de Educación Pública.* Mexico: S.E.P.

Robbins, Roy M. 1942. *Our Landed Heritage: The Public Domain, 1776–1936.* Princeton: Princeton University Press.

Roberts, G. W. 1957. *The Population of Jamaica.* Cambridge: Cambridge University Press.

Roberts, Stephen H. 1968 [1924]. *History of Australian Land Settlement (1788–1920).* Melbourne: Macmillan.

Rockoff, Hugh. 1974. "The Free Banking Era: A Reexamination." *Journal of Money, Credit, and Banking*, 6 (May): 141–67.

———. 1985. "New Evidence on Free Banking in the United States." *American Economic Review*, 75 (September): 886–889.

———. 2000. "Banking and Finance, 1789–1914." In *The Cambridge Economic History of the United States*, 3 vols., vol. 2. *The Long Nineteenth Centrury*, eds. Stanley L. Engerman and Robert E. Gallman. 643–684. Cambridge: Cambridge University Press.

Rodríguez López, María Guadalupe. 1995. "La Banca Porfiriana en Durango." In *Durango (1840–1915): Banca, Transportes, Tierra e Industria*, ed. Maria Guadaloupe, Rodriguez et al., 7–34. Durango Universidad Juárez del Estado de Durango.

———. 2003. "Paz y Bancos en Durango Durante el Porfiriato." In *La Banca Regional en Mexico, 1870–1930*, eds. Mario Cerutti and Carlos Marichal. 254–290. Mexico: Fondo de Cultura Económica.

Rodriguez, Victoria Elizabeth. 1987. "The Politics of Decentralization in Mexico: Divergent Outcomes of Policy Implementation." unpublished Ph.D. dissertation, University of California, Berkeley.

Román Trigo, Ana Cecilia. 1995. *Las Finanzas Públicas de Costa Rica: Metodología y Fuentes (1870–1948)*. San José: Universidad de Costa Rica.

Romero Ibarra, Maria Eugenia. 2003. "El Banco del Estado de Mexico 1897–1914." In *La Banca Regional en Mexico, 1870–1930*, eds. Mario Cerutti and Carlos Marichal. 216–251. Mexico: Fondo de Cultura Económica.

Roseberry, William, Lowell Gudmundson, and Mario Samper Kutschbach, eds. 1995. *Coffee, Society, and Power in Latin America*. Baltimore: Johns Hopkins University Press.

Rosenberg, Nathan and L. E. Birdzell, Jr. 1986. *How the West Grew Rich: The Economic Transformation of the Industrial World*. New York: Basic Books.

Rosenblat, Angel. 1954. *La Población Indígena y el Mestizaje en América*. 2 vols. vol. 1: *La Población Indígena, 1492–1950*. Buenos Aires: Editorial Nova.

Ross. Robert. 1993. *Beyond the Pale: Essays on the History of Colonial South Africa*. Middletown: Wesleyan University Press.

Rostow, W. W. 1960. *The Stages of Economic Growth: A Non-Communist Manifesto*. Cambridge: Cambridge University Press.

Rothenberg, Winifred Barr. 1992a. "The Productivity Consequences of Market Integration: Agriculture in Massachusetts, 1771–1801." In *American Economic Growth and Standards of Living Before the Civil War*, eds. Robert E. Gallman and John Joseph Wallis, 311–40. Chicago: University of Chicago Press.

———. 1992b. *From Market-Place to a Market Economy: The Transformation of Rural Massachusetts, 1750–1850*. Chicago: University of Chicago Press.

Rout, Leslie B., Jr. 1976. *African Experience in Spanish America: 1502 to the Present Day*. Cambridge: Cambridge University Press.

Ruiz Esquide, Andrea. 2000. "Migration, Colonization, and Land Policy in the Former Mapuche Frontier: Malleco, 1850–1900." unpublished Ph.D. dissertation, Columbia University.

Rusk, Jerrold G. 2001. *A Statistical History of the American Electorate*. Washington, D.C.: CQ Press.

Saint-Paul, Gilles, and Thierry Verdier. 1993. "Education, Democracy, and Growth." *Journal of Development Economics* 42 (December): 399–407.

Samuels, W. 1987. "Institutional Economics." In *The New Palgrave: A Dictionary of Economics*, eds. John Eatwell, Murray Milgate and Peter Newman, 864–66 4 vols., vol. 2. London: Macmillan.

Sánchez-Albornoz, Nicholas. 1974. *The Population of Latin America: A History*. Berkeley: University of California Press.

Schultz, Theodore W. 1963. *The Economic Value of Education*. New York: Columbia University Press.

———. 1964. *Transforming Traditional Agriculture*. New Haven: Yale University Press.

Schumpeter, J. A. 1950. *Capitalism, Socialism, and Democracy*. (3rd Edition) New York: Harper.

————. 1991. *The Economics and Sociology of Capitalism* ed. Richard Swedberg. Princeton: Princeton University Press.

Schwartz, Stuart B. 1982. "Patterns of Slaveholding in the Americas: New Evidence from Brazil." *American Historical Review* 87 (February): 55–86.

————. 1985. *Sugar Plantations in the Formation of Brazilian Society: Bahia, 1550–1835.* Cambridge: Cambridge University Press.

Scobie, James R. 1971. *Argentina: A City and A Nation.* 2nd ed. New York: Oxford University Press.

Seligman, Edwin R. A. 1895. *Essays in Taxation.* New York: Macmillan.

Shah, Anwar. 1991. "The New Fiscal Federalism in Brazil." World Bank Working Paper no. 124. Washington, D.C.: World Bank.

Shaw, A. G. L. 1966. *Convicts and the Colonies A Study of Penal Transportation From Great Britain and Ireland to Australia and Other Parts of the British Empire.* London: Faber.

Sheridan, Richard B. 1974. *Sugar and Slavery: An Economic History of the British West Indies. 1623–1775.* Baltimore: Johns Hopkins University Press.

Shlomowitz, Ralph. 1979. "Transition from Slave to Freedom: Labor Arrangements in Southern Agriculture, 1865–1870." unpublished Ph.D. dissertation, University of Chicago.

————— with Lance Brennan and John McDonald. 1996. *Mortality and Migration in the Modern World.* Aldershot: Variorum.

Shome, Parthasrathi. 1999. "Taxation in Latin America-Structural Trends and Impact of Administration." IMF Working Paper no. 99–19. Washington, D.C.: International Monetary Fund.

Sibaja Chasón, Luis Fernando. 1995. "Ayuntamientos y Estado en los Primero Años de Vida Independinete de Costa Rica (1821–1835)." In *Actas del III Congreso de Academias Iberoamericanas de la Historia: El Municipio en Iberoamérica (Cabildos e Instituciones Locales).* Montevideo: Instituto Histórico y Geográfico del Uruguay.

Simpson, Lesley Byrd. 1982 [1950]. *The Encomienda in New Spain: The Beginning of Spanish Mexico.* (revised edition) Berkeley: University of California Press.

Sinclair, Keith. 1959. *A History of New Zealand.* Harmondsworth: Penguin.

Sinclair, W. A. 1976. *The Process of Economic Development in Australia.* Melbourne: Cheshire.

Sitterson, J. Carlyle. 1953. *Sugar Country: The Cane Sugar Industry in the South, 1753–1950.* Lexington: University of Kentucky Press.

Skaggs, Jimmy M. 1994. *The Great Guano Rush: Entrepreneurs and American Overseas Expansion.* New York: St. Martin's Press.

Slemrod, Joel, and Jon Bakija. 1996. *Taxing Ourselves: A Citizen's Guide to the Great Debate over Tax Reform.* Cambridge, MA: MIT Press.

————. 2001. "Growing Inequality and Decreased Tax Progressivity." In *Inequality and Tax Policy,* eds. Kevin A. Hassett and R. Glenn Hubbard. 192–226, Washington, D.C.: AEI Press.

Smith, Abbot Emerson. 1947. *Colonists in Bondage: White Servitude of Convict Labor in America, 1607–1776.* Chapel Hill: University of North Carolina Press.

Smith, Adam. 1976 [1776]. *Inquiry into the Nature and Causes of the Wealth of Nations*. Oxford: Clarendon Press.

Sociedad y Educación; Ensayos Sobre Historia de la Educación en América Latina. 1995. Bogotá: Universidad Pedagógica Nacional, Colciencias.

Sokoloff, Kenneth L. 1984. "Was the Transition from the Artisimal Shop to the Nonmechanized Factory Associated with Gains in Efficiency? Evidence from the U.S. Manufacturing Censuses of 1820 and 1850." *Explorations in Economic History* 21 (October): 351–82.

———. 1986. "Productivity Growth in Manufacturing During Early Industrialization: Evidence from the American Northeast, 1820 to 1860." In *Long-Term Factors in American Economic Growth*, eds. Stanley L. Engerman and Robert E. Gallman, 639–736. Chicago: University of Chicago Press.

———. 1988. "Inventive Activity in Early Industrial America: Evidence From Patent Records, 1790–1846." *Journal of Economic History* 48 (December): 813–50.

———. 1992. "Invention, Innovation, and Manufacturing Productivity Growth in the Antebellum Northeast." In *American Economic Growth and Standards of Living Before the Civil War*, eds. Robert E. Gallman and John Joseph Wallis, 345–84. Chicago: University of Chicago Press.

———. 1995. "The Heights of Americans in Three Centuries: Some Economic and Demographic Implications," *The Biological Standard of Living on Three Continents*. ed. John Komlos, 135–151. Boulder: Westview Press.

Sokoloff, Kenneth L., and Stanley L. Engerman. 2000. "History Lessons: Institutions, Factor Endowments, and Paths of Development in the New World." *Journal of Economic Perspectives* 14 (Spring): 217–32.

Sokoloff, Kenneth L., and B. Zorina Khan, 1990. "The Democratization of Invention During Early Industrialization: Evidence from the United States, 1790–1846." *Journal of Economic History* 50 (June): 363–78.

Sokoloff, Kenneth L. and George C. Villaflor. 1982. "The Early Achievement of Modern Stature in America." *Social Science History* 6 (Summer): 453–81.

Sokoloff, Kenneth L., and Eric M. Zolt. 2007. "Inequality and the Evolution of Institutions of Taxation in the Americas." In *The Decline of Latin American Economies: Growth, Institutions, and Crises*, eds. Sebastian Edwards, Gerardo Esquivel, and Graciela Marquez. 83–136. Chicago: University of Chicago Press.

Solana, Fernando, Raúl Cardiel Reyes, and Raúl Bolaños eds. 1982. *Historia de la Educación Pública en México*. Mexico: Fondo de Cultura Económica.

Solberg, Carl E. 1969. "A Discriminatory Frontier Land Policy: Chile, 1870–1914." *The Americas* 26 (October): 115–133.

———. 1970. *Immigration and Nationalism: Argentina and Chile, 1890–1914*. Austin: University of Texas Press.

———. 1985. "Land Tenure and Land Settlement: Policy and Patterns in the Canadian Prairies and the Argentine Pampas, 1880–1930." In *Argentina, Australia and Canada: Studies in Comparative Development, 1870–1965*, 53–75, eds. D. C. M. Platt and Guido di Tella. London: Macmillan.

———. 1987. *The Prairies and the Pampas: Agrarian Policy in Canada and Argentina 1880–1930*. Stanford: Stanford University Press.

Soltow, Lee. 1975. *Men and Wealth in the United States, 1850–1870*. New Haven: Yale University Press.

———. 1992. "Inequalities in the Standards of Living in the United States." In *American Economic Growth and Standards of Living Before the Civil War*, eds. Robert E. Gallman and John Joseph Wallis, 121–72. Chicago: University of Chicago Press.

Soltow, Lee, and Stevens, Edward. 1981. *The Rise of Literacy and the Common School in the United States: A Socioeconomic Analysis to 1870*. Chicago: University of Chicago Press.

Sombart, Werner. 1969 [1913]. *The Jews and Modern Capitalism*. New York: B. Franklin.

Sommerfeld, Raynard M. 1966. *Tax Reform and the Alliance for Progress*. Austin: University of Texas Press.

Southworth, Constant. 1931. *The French Colonial Venture*. London: P. S. King.

Stampp, Kenneth M. 1990. *America in 1857: A Nation on the Brink*. New York: Oxford University Press.

Statesman's Yearbook (1864–). New York: Macmillan.

Statistics Canada 1972: Ottawa.

Stein, Stanley J., and Barbara H. 1970. *The Colonial Heritage of Latin America: Essays on Economic Dependence in Perspective*. Oxford: Oxford University Press.

Stephenson, George M. 1917. *The Political History of the Public Lands, from 1840 to 1862: From Pre-emption to Homestead*. Boston: R. G. Badger.

Steuart, Sir James. 1767. *An Inquiry Into the Principles of Political Economy*. 2 vols. London: A. Millar and T. Cadell.

Steuerle, C. Eugene. 2004. *Contemporary U.S. Tax Policy*. Washington, D.C.: Urban Institute Press.

Stone, Lawrence. 1969. "Literacy and Education in England, 1640–1900," *Past and Present* 42 (February): 69–139.

Stotsky, Janet Gale and Asegedech WoldeMariam. 2002. "Central American Tax Reform: Trends and Possibilities." IMF Working Paper No. 02227. Washington, D.C.: International Monetary Fund.

Strassman, W. Paul. 1956. "Economic Growth and Income Distribution." *Quarterly Journal of Economics* 70 (August): 425–440.

Summerhill, William R. 2003. *Order Against Progress: Government, Foreign Investment, and Railroads in Brazil, 1854–1913*. Stanford: Stanford University Press.

———. Forthcoming. *Inglorious Revolution: Political Institutions, Sovereign Debt, and Financial Underdevelopment in Imperial Brazil*. New Haven: Yale University Press.

Summers, Robert, and Alan Heston. 1991. "The Penn World Table (Mark 5): An Expanded Set of International Comparisons, 1950–1988." *Quarterly Journal of Economics*, 106 (May): 327–68.

Sydnor, Charles S. 1952. *Gentlemen Freeholders: Political Practices in Washington's Virginia*. Chapel Hill: University of North Carolina Press.

Sylla, Richard. 1969. "Federal Policy, Banking Market Structure, and Capital Mobilization in the United States, 1863–1913." *Journal of Economic History* 29 (December): 657–86.

———. 1975. *The American Capital Market, 1846–1914: A Study of the Effects of Public Policy on Economic Development.* New York: Arno Press.

———. 2000. "Experimental Federalism: The Economics of American Government, 1789–1914." In *The Cambridge Economic History of the United States* 3 vols., vol. 2, *The Long Nineteenth Century* eds. Stanley L. Engerman and Robert E., Gallman, 483–542. Cambridge: Cambridge University Press.

———. 2007. "The Political Economy of Early U.S. Financial Development." In *Political Institutions and Financial Development*, eds. Stephen Haber, Douglass C. North, and Barry R. Weingast, 60–91. Stanford: Stanford University Press.

Sylla, Richard, John B. Legler, and John J. Wallis. 1987. "Banks and State Public Finance in the New Republic: The United States, 1790–1860." *Journal of Economic History* 47 (June): 391–403.

Tait, Alan A., Wilfrid L. M. Grtz, and Barry J. Eichengreen. 1979. "International Comparisons of Taxation for Selected Developing Countries, 1972–76. *IMF Staff Papers* 26 (March): 123–56.

Tanck de Estrada, Dorothy. 1979. "Las Cortes de Cádiz y el Desarrollo de la Educación en México." *Historia Mexicana* 29 (July–September) 3–34.

Tannenbaum, Frank. 1929. *The Mexican Agrarian Revolution.* New York: Macmillan.

Tantalean Arbulú, Javier. 1983. *Política Economómico-Financiera y la Formación del Estado Siglo XIX.* Lima, Peru: CEDEP.

Tanzi, Vito. 1987. "Quantitative Characteristics of the Tax Systems in Developing Countries." In *The Theory of Taxation for Developing Countries*, eds.David Newberry and Nicholas Stern. 205–241. New York: Oxford University Press.

Tanzi, Vito and Ludger Schuknecht. 2000. *Public Spending in the 20th Century: A Global Perspective.* Cambridge: Cambridge University Press.

Tanzi, Vito, and Howell Zee. 2000. "Tax Policy for Emerging Markets-Developing Countries." IMF Working Paper no. 00–35. Washington, D.C.: International Monetary Fund.

Tawney, R. H. 1926. *Religion and the Rise of Capitalism: A Historical Study.* New York: Harcourt Brace.

Taylor, George Rogers. 1951. *The Transportation Revolution, 1815–1860.* New York: Rinehart.

Tchakerian, Viken. 1994. "Productivity, Extent of Markets, and Manufacturing in the Late Antebellum South and Midwest." *Journal of Economic History* 54 (September): 497–525.

Temin, Peter. 1968. "The Economic Consequences of the Bank War." *Journal of Political Economy* 76 (March-April): 257–274.

Tenenbaum, Barbara A. 1986. *The Politics of Penury: Debt and Taxes in Mexico, 1821–1856.* Albuquerque: University of New Mexico Press.

TePaske, John Jay. 2002. "Integral to Empire: The Vital Peripheries of Colonial South America." In *Negotiated Empires: Centers and Peripheries in the*

Americas, 1500–1820, eds. Christine Daniels and Michael V. Kennedy. 29–42, New York: Routledge.

Thelen, Kathleen. 1999. "Historical Institutionalism in Comparative Politics." *Annual Review of Political Science*, 2: 369–404.

Thirsk, Wayne, ed. 1997. *Tax Reform in Developing Countries*. Washington, D.C.: World Bank.

Thorp, Rosemary. 1998. *Progress, Poverty and Exclusion: An Economic History of Latin America in the 20th Century*. Baltimore: Johns Hopkins University Press.

Topik, Steven. 1980. "State Enterprise in a Liberal Regime: The Banco do Brasil, 1905–1930." *Journal of Interamerican Studies and World Affairs* 22 (November): 401–422.

_____. 1987. *The Political Economy of the Brazilian State, 1889–1930*. Austin: University of Texas Press.

Tornquist & Co., Ernesto. 1919. *The Economic Development of the Argentine Republic in the Last Fifty Years*. Buenos Aires: Ernesto Tornquist & Co.

Tôrres, João Camilo de Oliveira. 1961. *A Formação do Federalismo no Brasil*. São Paulo: Companhia Editora Nacional.

Townsend, Mary Evelyn. 1930. *The Rise and Fall of Germany's Colonial Empire, 1884–1918*. New York: Macmillan.

Toynbee, A. J. 1945–1957. *A Study of History*. 12 vols, vol. 1. New York: Oxford University Press.

Treff, Karin, and David B. Perry. 2004. *Finances of the Nation, 2003*. Toronto: Canadian Tax Foundation.

Triner, Gail D. 2000. *Banking and Economic Development: Brazil, 1889–1930*. New York: Palgrave.

Trudel, Marcel. 1971. *The Seigneural Regime*. Ottawa: Canadian Historical Association.

Turner, Frederick Jackson. 1906. *Rise of the New West, 1819–1829*. New York: Harper & Brothers.

_____. 1920. *The Frontier in American History*. New York: H. Holt.

Unal, Haluk and Miguel Navarro. 1999. "The Technical Process of Bank Privatization in Mexico," *Journal of Financial Services Research* 16 (September): 61–83.

United Nations Online Network in Public Administration and Finance 2006. (UNPAN)

U.S. Bureau of the Census. 1853. *Seventh Census of the United States: 1850*. Washington, D.C.: Robert Armstrong.

_____. 1864. *Population of the United States in 1860*. Washington, D.C.: Government Printing Office.

_____. 1902. *Twelfth Census of the United States, Taken in the Year 1900: Agriculture*. Washington, D.C.: U.S. Census Office.

_____. 1967. *Education of the American Population*. By John K. Folger and Charles B. Nam. Washington, D.C.: Government Printing Office.

_____. 1975. *Historical Statistics of the United States: Colonial Times to 1970*. Washington, D.C.: Government Printing Office.

———. 2001. *State and Local Revenue*. Washington, D.C.: Government Printing Office.

U.S. Department of the Interior. 1898. *Report of the Commissioner of Education, Made to the Secretary of the Interior*. Washington, D.C.: Government Printing Office.

Urquhart, M. C., and K. A. H. Buckley, eds. 1965. *Historical Statistics of Canada*. Cambridge: Cambridge University Press.

Valenzuela, J. Samuel. 1996. "Building Aspects of Democracy Before Democracy: Electoral Practices in Nineteenth Century Chile." In *Elections Before Democracy: The History of Elections in Europe and Latin America*, ed. Eduardo Posada-Carbó. 223–258. New York: St. Martin's Press.

Vamplew, Wray, ed. 1987. *Australians; Historical Statistics*. Broadway: Fairfax, Syme & Weldon.

Van Young, Eric. 1983. "Mexican Rural History Since Chevalier: The Historiography of the Colonial Hacienda." *Latin American Research Review* 18 (No. 3): 5–61.

van Zwanberg, R. M. A. and King, Anne. 1975. *An Economic History of Kenya and Uganda, 1800–1970*. London. Macmillan.

Vaughan, Mary Kay. 1982. *The State, Education, and Social Class in Mexico, 1880–1928*. DeKalb: Northern Illinois University Press.

———. 1990. "Primary Education and Literacy in the Nineteenth-Century: Research Trends, 1968–1988." *Latin American Research Review*, 25 (1): 31–66.

Vedoya, Juan Carlos. 1973. *Cómo fue la enseñanza popular en la Argentina*. Buenos Aires: Plus Ultra.

Virts, Nancy Lynn. 1985. "Plantations, Land Tenure and Efficiency in the Postbellum South: The Effects of Emancipation on Southern Agriculture." unpublished Ph.D. disssertation, University of California, Los Angeles.

Wadham, Sir Samuel, R. Kent Wilson, and Joyce Wood. 1964. *Land Utilization in Australia*. 4th ed. Melbourne: Melbourne University Press.

Wa-Githumo, Mwangi. 1981. *Land and Nationalism: The Impact of Land Expropriation and Land Grievances Upon the Rise and Development of Nationalist Movements in Kenya, 1885–1939*. Washington, D.C.: University Press of America.

Wakefield, Edward Gibbon. 1829. *Letter from Sydney: The Principal Town of Australasia, Together with the Outline of a System of Colonization*. London: J. Cross.

———. 1849. *A View of the Art of Colonization with Present Reference to the British Empire: in Letters Between a Statesman and a Colonist*. London: J. W. Parker.

Walker, David W. 1986. *Kinship, Business, and Politics: The Martínez del Rio Family in Mexico, 1824–1867*. Austin: University of Texas Press.

Walker, Geoffrey J. 1979. *Spanish Politics and Imperial Trade, 1700–1789*. Bloomington: Indiana University Press.

Wallis, John Joseph. 2001. "A History of the Property Tax in America." In *Property Taxation and Local Government Finance: Essays in Honor of C. Lowell*

Harriss, ed. Wallace E. Oates. 123–147. Cambridge, MA: Lincoln Institute of Land Policy.

Wallis, John, Richard Sylla, and John B. Legler. 1994. "The Interaction of Taxation and Regulation in Nineteenth Century U.S. Banking." In *The Regulated Economy: A Historical Approach to Political Economy*, eds. Claudia Goldin and Gary D. Libecap, 122–144. Chicago: University of Chicago Press.

Wang, Ta-Chen. 2006. "Courts, Banks, and Credit Market in Early American Development." unpublished Ph.D. dissertation, Stanford University.

Ward, Norman. 1950. *The Canadian House of Commons: Representation.* Toronto: University of Toronto Press.

Washburn, Wilcomb E. 1975. *The Indian in America*. New York: Harper & Row.

Wasserman, Mark. 1984. *Capitalists, Caciques, and Revolution: Elite and Foreign Enterprise in Chihuahua, Mexico, 1854–1911.* Chapel Hill: University of North Carolina Press.

Watts, David. 1987. *The West Indies: Patterns of Development, Culture, and Environmental Change Since 1492.* Cambridge: Cambridge University Press.

Weber, Max. 1958 [1904–1905]. *The Protestant Ethic and the Spirit of Capitalism*. New York: Scribner.

———. 1966 [1927]. *General Economic History*. New York: Collier Books.

Weisman, Steven R. 2002. *The Great Tax Wars: Lincoln to Wilson: The Fierce Battles over Money and Power that Transformed the Nation.* New York: Simon & Schuster.

Wellington, Raynor G. 1914. *The Political and Sectional Influence of the Public Lands, 1828–1842.* Cambridge, MA: Riverside Press.

Wettereau, James. 1942. "The Branches of the First Bank of the United States." *Journal of Economic History* 2 (December): 66–100.

Wiesner, Eduardo. 2003. *Fiscal Federalism in Latin America: From Entitlements to Markets.* Washington, D.C.: Inter-American Development Bank.

Wilcox, Marrion and George Edwin Rines. 1917. *Encyclopedia of Latin America.* New York: Encyclopedia Americana.

Willcox, Walter, with Imre Ferenci. 1929, 1931. *International Migrations.* 2 vols. New York: National Bureau of Economic Research.

Williamson, Chilton. 1965. *American Suffrage: From Property to Democracy 1760–1860.* Princeton: Princeton University Press.

Williamson, Jeffrey G., and Peter H. Lindert. 1980. *American Inequality: A Macroeconomic History.* New York: Academic Press.

Wills, Eliza, Christopher da C. B. Garman, and Stephen Haggard. 1999. "The Politics of Decentralization in Latin America." *Latin American Research Review* 34 (No. 1): 7–56.

Wilson, J. Donald, Robert M. Stamp, and Louis-Philippe Audet eds. 1970. *Canadian Education: A History.* Scarborough: Prentice-Hall of Canada.

Wilson, Monica and Leonard, Thompson, eds. 1969–1971. *The Oxford History of South Africa* 2 vols. New York: Oxford University Press.

Wittke, Carl. 1939. *We Who Built America: The Saga of the Immigrant.* New York: Prentice-Hall.

Womack, John. 1969. *Zapata and the Mexican Revolution.* New York: Knopf.

Wood, Betty. 1984. *Slavery in Colonial Georgia, 1730–1775.* Athens: University of Georgia Press.

Woodward, Ralph Lee, Jr. 1976. *Central America: A Nation Divided.* New York: Oxford University Press.

Woodward, C. Vann. 1951. *Origins of the New South, 1877–1913.* Baton Rouge: Louisiana State University Press.

World Bank. 1991. *World Development Report.* New York: Oxford University Press.

_____. 1992. *World Development Report.* New York: Oxford University Press.

_____. 1999. *World Development Report.* New York: Oxford University Press.

Wrigley, E. A. 1988. *Continuity, Chance, and Change: The Character of the Industrial Revolution in England.* Cambridge: Cambridge University Press.

Wurgler, Jeffrey. 2000. "Financial Markets and the Allocation of Capital." *Journal of Financial Economics* 58 (June): 187–214.

Yarrington, Doug. 1997. *A Coffee Frontier: Land, Society, and Politics in Duaca, Venezuela, 1830–1936.* Pittsburgh: University of Pittsburgh Press.

Yeager, Gertrude M. 1991. "Elite Education in Nineteenth-Century Chile." *Hispanic American Historical Review* 71 (February): 73–105.

Prior Publications

This volume is based on the revisions and editing of our publications over the past decade or so. These publications include:

Engerman, Stanley L., and Kenneth L. Sokoloff. "Factor Endowments, Institutions, and Differential Paths of Growth Among New World Economies: A View from Economic Historians of the United States." In *How Latin America Fell Behind*, ed. S. Haber, 260–304. Stanford: Stanford University Press, 1997.

————. "Factor Endowments, Inequality, and Paths of Development Among New World Economies." *Economía* (Fall 2002): 41–88.

————. "Inequality Before and Under the Law: Paths of Long-Run Development in the Americas." In *Toward Pro-Poor Policies: Aid, Institutions, and Globalization*, eds. B. Tungodden, N. Stern, and I. Kolstad, 213–230. New York: World Bank, 2004.

————. "Institutional and Non-Institutional Explanations of Economic Differences." In *Handbook of New Institutional Economics*, eds. C. Ménard and M. Shirley, 639–665. Amsterdam: Elsevier, 2005.

————. "The Evolution of Suffrage Institutions in the New World." *Journal of Economic History* 65 (December 2005), 891–921.

————. "The Persistence of Poverty in the Americas: The Role of Institutions." In *Poverty Traps*, eds., S. Bowles, S. Durlauf, and K. Hoff, 43–78. Princeton: Princeton University Press, 2006.

————. "Colonialism, Inequality, and Long-Run Paths of Development." In *Understanding Poverty*, eds. A. Banerjee, R. Benábou, and D. Mookherjee, 37–61. New York: Oxford University Press, 2006.

————. "Debating the Role of Institutions in Political and Economic Development: Theory, History, and Findings." *Annual Review of Political Science.* 2008, 119–135.

————. "Once Upon a Time in the Americas: Land and Immigration Policies in the Americas." In *Understanding Long-Run Economic Growth: Geography, Institutions and the Knowledge Economy*, eds. Dora L. Costa and Naomi R. Lamoreaux. Chicago: Chicago University Press, 2011.

————. "Five Hundred Years of European Colonization: Inequality and Paths of Development." In *Settler Economies in World History*, eds. Christopher Lloyd, et al., Leiden: Brill, 2012.

Engerman, Stanley L., Stephen Haber, and Kenneth L. Sokoloff. "Inequality, Institutions, and Differential Paths of Growth Among New World Economies." In *Institutions, Contracts, and Organizations*, ed. C. Ménard. 108–134. Cheltenham, Edward Elgar, 2000.

Engerman, Stanley L., Elisa V. Mariscal, and Kenneth L. Sokoloff. "The Evolution of Schooling Institutions in the Americas, 1800–1925." In *Human Capital and Institutions: A Long-Run View*, eds. David Eltis, Frank Lewis, and Kenneth L. Sokoloff, 93–142. New York: Cambridge University Press, 2009.

Mariscal, Elisa, and Kenneth L. Sokoloff. "The Persistence of Inequality in the Americas, Schooling and Suffrage 1800–1945." In *Political Institutions and Economic Growth in Latin America*, ed. S. Haber, 159–217. Stanford: Hoover Institution Press, 2000.

Robinson, James A., and Kenneth L. Sokoloff. "Historical Roots of Latin American Inequality." In *Inequality in Latin America: Breaking With History?* eds. De Ferranti et al., 109–122. Washington, D.C.: World Bank, 2004.

Sokoloff, Kenneth L. "The Evolution of Suffrage Institutions in the New World. A Preliminary View." In *Crony Capitalism and Economic Growth in Latin America: Theory and Evidence*, ed. S. Haber, 75–107, Stanford: Hoover Institution Press, 2002.

Sokoloff, Kenneth L. and Stanley L. Engerman, "History Lessons: Institutions, Factor Endowments, and Paths of Development in the New World. *Journal of Economic Perspectives*, 14 (Summer 2000): 217–232.

Sokoloff, Kenneth L., and Eric M. Zolt. "Inequality and the Evolution of Institutions of Taxation." In *The Decline of Latin American Economies: Growth, Institutions and Crises*, eds. Sebastian Edwards, Gerado Esquivel, and Graciela Márquez, 83–136. Chicago: University of Chicago Press, 2007.

Index